# Exercise and Sport Sciences Reviews

Volume 13, 1985

# EXERCISE AND SPORT SCIENCES REVIEWS

Volume 13, 1985

Edited by RONALD L. TERJUNG, Ph.D.

*State University of New York*
*Upstate Medical Center*
*Syracuse, New York*

American College of Sports Medicine Series

MACMILLAN PUBLISHING COMPANY
NEW YORK
COLLIER MACMILLAN CANADA, INC.
TORONTO
COLLIER MACMILLAN PUBLISHERS
LONDON

Copyright © 1985, American College of Sports Medicine

Printed in the United States of America

Macmillan Publishing Company
866 Third Avenue, New York, New York 10022

Collier Macmillan Canada, Inc.

Collier Macmillan Publishers · London

International Standard Book Number: 0–02–419890–0

Library of Congress Catalog Card Number: 72–12187

Printing: 1 2 3 4 5 6 7 8    Year: 5 6 7 8 9 0 1 2 3

# Contents

*Exercise and Sport Sciences Reviews* is an American College of Sports Medicine journal, published once per annum, in which reviews of research concerning clinical, physiological, biochemical, biomechanical, and behavioral aspects of exercise science appear. Beginning with Volume 10 an expanded editorial board was formed. Ten recognized authorities have each assumed primary responsibility for one of the following general areas of inquiry: Biochemistry, Exercise Physiology, Psychology, Motor Control, Athletic Medicine, Rehabilitation, Sociology of Sport, Environmental Physiology, Biomechanics, and Growth and Development. This organization of the editorial board will help realize the commitment of the American College of Sports Medicine to maintaining and extending the breadth and continuity of timely reviews in the broad areas of interest to practitioners, exercise scientists, and students. The editorial board members will endeavor to provide at least one review for each of their ten areas in each annual issue of *Exercise and Sport Sciences Reviews*. In addition, topics of specific interest that are not embraced by these areas of inquiry are occasionally reviewed, but only reviews on those topics deemed amenable to intellectual analysis and/or scientific investigation are considered for publication.

Contributors for all volumes are selected by the editor and the editorial board. Topics for review are determined on the basis of professional and scientific relevance, need, and the extent of information already available in the existing literature. Although the majority of reviews appearing per volume are invited, unsolicited manuscripts will be received by the editor and reviewed by section editors for possible inclusion in future volumes. The editorial board is receptive to suggestions concerning selections of potential contributors and topics worthy of review. Correspondence should be directed to Kent Pandolf, Ph.D., U.S. Army Research Institute for Environmental Medicine, Natick, Massachusetts, 01760, who will take over as *Exercise and Sport Sciences Reviews* series editor beginning with Volume 14 (1986).

*Ronald L. Terjung, Ph.D.*
*Editor*

# Contributors

R.B. Armstrong, Ph.D.
Department of Physiology
Oral Roberts University
School of Medicine
Tulsa, Oklahoma

Oded Bar-Or, M.D., F.A.C.S.M.
Children's Therapeutic Exercise and Health Centre
Department of Pediatrics
McMaster University and Chedoke McMaster Hospitals
Hamilton, Ontario, Canada

Arthur E. Chapman, Ph.D.
Department of Kinesiology
Simon Fraser University
Burnaby, British Columbia, Canada

Peter Donnelly, Ph.D.
School of Physical Education and Athletics
McMaster University
Hamilton, Ontario, Canada

Patricia M. Dubbert, R.N., Ph.D.
Veterans Administration Medical Center and
University of Mississippi Medical Center
Jackson, Mississippi

Roger M. Enoka, Ph.D.
Department of Physical Education
University of Arizona
Tucson, Arizona

Roger M. Glaser, Ph.D., F.A.S.C.M.
Professor of Physiology
Wright State University
School of Medicine
Dayton, Ohio

N. Gledhill, Ph.D.
York University and
Hospital for Sick Children
Toronto, Ontario, Canada

Ziaul Hasan, Ph.D.
Department of Physiology
University of Arizona
Tucson, Arizona

Wendy M. Kohrt, M.S.
Exercise and Sport Research Institute
Department of Health and Physical Education
Arizona State University
Tempe, Arizona

Gary S. Krahenbuhl, Ed.D., F.A.S.C.M.
Exercise and Sport Research Institute
Department of Health and Physical Education
Arizona State University
Tempe, Arizona

M.H. Laughlin, Ph.D.
Department of Physiology
Oral Roberts University
School of Medicine
Tulsa, Oklahoma

John E. Martin, Ph.D.
Veterans Administration Medical Center and
University of Mississippi Medical Center
Jackson, Mississippi

L.R. Morris, M.S.
Institute for Child Behavior and Development
University of Illinois
Champaign, Illinois

K.M. Newell, Ph.D.
Institute for Child Behavior and Development
University of Illinois
Champaign, Illinois

James M. Pivarnik, Ph.D.
Department of Physiology
St. Louis University School of Medicine
St. Louis, Missouri

Jack A. Rall, Ph.D.
Department of Physiology
Ohio State University
Columbus, Ohio

Deirdre M. Scully, M.S.
Institute for Child Behavior and Development
University of Illinois
Champaign, Illinois

Leo C. Senay, Jr., Ph.D.
Department of Physiology
St. Louis University School of Medicine
St. Louis, Missouri

James S. Skinner, Ph.D., F.A.S.C.M.
Exercise and Sport Research Institute
Department of Health and Physical Education
Arizona State University
Tempe, Arizona

Douglas G. Stuart, Ph.D.
Department of Physiology
University of Arizona
Tucson, Arizona

Keith R. Williams, Ph.D.
Department of Physical Education
University of California
Davis, California

W.W. Winder, Ph.D.
Division of Physiology and Anatomy
Department of Zoology
Brigham Young University
Provo, Utah

*Exercise and Sport Sciences Reviews*

*Volume 13, 1985*

# Regulation of Hepatic Glucose Production During Exercise

W.W. WINDER, Ph.D.

The liver is a remarkable organ with many diverse homeostatic functions. It is involved in glycogen storage, glycogenolysis, gluconeogenesis, ketogenesis, synthesis of lipoproteins, cholesterol synthesis, bile acid synthesis, ureogenesis, plasma protein synthesis, somatomedin production, detoxification and hormone inactivation, and fatty acid synthesis. During exercise, all other homeostatic functions of the liver are overshadowed by the necessity to maintain plasma glucose at reasonable levels despite markedly increased utilization of glucose by working muscles. The increased rate of glucose production can be by hepatic glycogenolysis and gluconeogenesis as long as liver glycogen is available. After liver glycogen is depleted all glucose must be produced by glucogenogenesis from lactate, alanine, glycerol, and other precursors. This review considers the control mechanisms that determine the metabolic set of the liver during exercise.

## LIVER GLYCOGENOLYSIS

### Liver Glycogen Use During Exercise
The liver plays a major role in glucose homeostasis at rest and during exercise. In times of glucose abundance (i.e., following ingestion of a carbohydrate meal) the liver is set for glycogen synthesis. Glucose absorbed from the intestine is incorporated into liver glycogen. In the fasting periods between meals the metabolic set of the liver is changed to a glucose production mode. Glycogen is converted to glucose to maintain a relatively constant blood glucose concentration during these short-term fasting periods. During exercise glucose is utilized at increased rates by working muscles so that liver glycogenolysis must be greatly accelerated in order to keep pace with the increased glucose utilization rate, thereby avoiding hypoglycemia. In rats, liver glycogen may be depleted in 90 to 120 minutes of moderately intense treadmill running or swimming [3, 4, 41, 51, 99].

Several studies have shown that the rate of decrease in liver glycogen content in exercising rats is approximately linear as a function of time when rats run continuously at a fixed treadmill speed [41, 97, 99]. The liver glycogenolytic rate is also dependent on work rate [96]. As indicated in Figure 1, this is not a linear relationship. Rats

1

FIGURE 1

*Effect of running at different treadmill speeds on the liver glycogenolytic rate of rats.*

SOURCE: Winder, W.W., M.A. Beattie, and E.O. Fuller. Glycogenolytic rates and cAMP in livers of rats running at different treadmill speeds. *Am. J. Physiol.* 245:R353–R356, 1983.

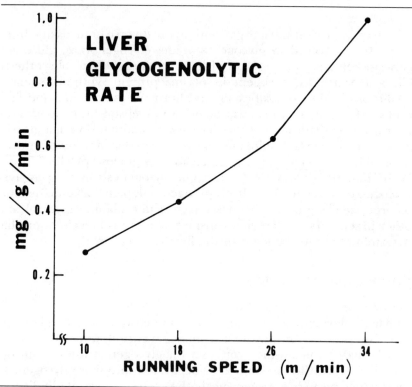

were run on a treadmill up a 15 percent grade at 10, 18, 26, or 34 m/min for 30 or 60 minutes. The liver glycogenolytic rate was obtained for each running speed by subtracting the mean end-exercise liver glycogen concentration from the mean preexercise value and dividing by elapsed time. The apparent curvilinear relationship between the rate of liver glycogenolysis and running speed is consistent with the relationship between stress hormone responses and relative work intensity. It is well established that as human subjects proceed from low to high work rates there is a disproportionately large increase in the sympathoadrenal response as maximal oxygen consumption is approached and surpassed [39, 45, 46]. It seems logical that the liver glycogenolytic rate, which is governed by the stress hormones, should follow the same pattern.

Little information is available on liver glycogen changes in human subjects during exercise. Hultman and Nilsson [54] obtained liver samples from human subjects by a needle biopsy technique before and after one hour of heavy bicycle exercise. They noted a marked decrease in liver glycogen during exercise. With the assumption of linearity they calculated the liver glycogenolytic rate to be 0.37 mg/g liver/min. At rest in the postabsorptive state the rate was 0.049 mg/g liver/min in the same subjects. Thus, a 7.6-fold increase occurred in the rate of liver glycogenolysis in response to the exercise. At that rate, assuming a concentration of 60 mg/g, glycogen would have been depleted after 2 to 3 hours of exercise at that work load.

*Mechanisms of Hormonal and Neuroendocrine*
*Control of Liver Glycogenolysis*
Several potential mechanisms exist for activation of glycogenolysis in the liver.

*Glucagon and beta-adrenergic receptor-mediated mechanisms requiring cAMP as the intracellular messenger.* The most familiar mechanism is the classical series of enzyme phosphorylations which are initiated by an increase in cytoplasmic cyclic adenosine 3,5 monophosphate (cAMP) [28, 29, 49]. The sequence is as follows:
1. Glucagon or catecholamines interact with specific receptors on the exterior surface of the hepatocyte plasma membrane.
2. This interaction activates the enzyme adenylate cyclase which in turn catalyzes formation of cAMP from adenosine triphosphate (ATP).
3. The cAMP binds to regulator subunits of protein kinase which results in dissociation of catalytic subunits of protein kinase.
4. The active protein kinase catalytic subunits then catalyze incorporation of phosphate from ATP into serine amino acid residues of phosphorylase kinase, resulting in activation of this enzyme.
5. The active phosphorylase kinase stimulates phosphorylation of phosphorylase b to form phosphorylase a, the active glycogenolytic enzyme.

Catecholamine-initiated increases in cAMP are apparently mediated by the beta-adrenergic receptor, although in the adult rat the alpha-receptor may also be coupled to adenylate cyclase [65].

*Alpha-adrenergic receptor-mediated mechanisms requiring calcium as the intracellular mediator.* Humoral catecholamines may also stimulate glycogenolysis in liver by cAMP-independent mechanisms. Exton et al. [27, 28] have described experiments showing that catecholamine activation of phosphorylase in isolated hepatocytes from adult rats can occur independently from any change in cAMP.

Phenoxybenzamine, an alpha-adrenergic blocking agent, was found to inhibit activation of phosphorylase by catecholamines but did not markedly inhibit the increase in cAMP that occurred when epinephrine was added to the incubation medium. Addition of propranolol, a beta-adrenergic antagonist, to the medium prevented the increase in cAMP but did not inhibit the increase in phosphorylase a. Thus, a second system was identified for activation of phosphorylase which did not involve activation of adenylate cyclase. This system includes the following features:

1. Catecholamines interact with alpha-adrenergic receptors on the hepatocyte membrane.
2. This interaction triggers a release of calcium from binding sites on the mitochondria, endoplasmic reticulum, and plasma membrane into the cytoplasm of the cell [7, 8, 13, 26, 28, 66, 90].
3. Both the dephosphorylated and phosphorylated forms of phosphorylase kinase are allosterically activated by an increase in free calcium [14, 49, 83, 93]. Preliminary evidence has been reported indicating that calmodulin is a subunit of liver phosphorylase kinase, similar to the muscle phosphorylase kinase [14].
4. Phosphorylase kinase then catalyzes phosphorylation of phosphorylase b to phosphorylase a and glycogenolysis proceeds.
5. This alpha-adrenergic receptor system predominates in adult male rats. Immature rats of both sexes and mature female rats exhibit a dominance of the beta-adrenergic receptor cAMP-mediated system [9, 65, 88]. In humans, the beta-adrenergic system seems to be operative [5]. Alpha-adrenergic receptor-mediated stimulation of glucose production in human subjects by epinephrine has also been described [81].

*Control by the direct sympathetic innervation of the liver.* A third potential means of stimulation of glycogenolysis is by activation of the sympathetic nerves of the liver [62]. Edwards and Silver [24] reported that direct electrical stimulation of the splanchnic nerves of adrenalectomized pancreatectomized calves resulted in increased glucose output by the liver accompanied by a reduction in liver glycogen. Histochemical and electron micrographic studies have identified the presence of neuron terminals closely associated with hepatocytes as well as with the liver vasculature [35, 64, 68, 69, 84, 105]. Human liver is richly supplied with sympathetic terminals containing norepinephrine [68, 69]. Direct stimulation of the liver sympathetic nerves in patients undergoing abdominal surgery results in hyperglycemia during and following the stimulation [69]. Shimazu and Amakawa [83] demonstrated in rabbits that splanchnic nerve stimulation results in activation of phosphorylase a with no concurrent change in hepatic cAMP. More recently, evidence has been presented showing that sympathetic nerve activation of liver glycogenolysis is mediated by alpha-adrenergic receptors in adult male rats and rabbits [48, 74].

The sequence of events in activation of liver glycogenolysis by the sympathetic innervation is postulated to be as follows:
1. Action potentials trigger release of norepinephrine from the sympathetic terminals in the liver.
2. Norepinephrine binds to alpha-adrenergic receptors on the hepatocyte membranes.
3. This interaction stimulates release of calcium ions from intracellular binding sites.
4. The increase in free calcium activates phosphorylase kinase allosterically.
5. Phosphorylase kinase catalyzes phosphorylation of phosphorylase b to phosphorylase a.

*Other possible hormonal mechanisms.* Other hormones have also been shown to stimulate liver glycogenolysis. Vasopressin and angiotensin II activate glycogenolysis by a calcium-dependent mechanism [28, 43, 49]. A single injection of growth hormone, designed to mimic the episodic surges of growth hormone release, has also been observed to enhance hepatic glucose output in dogs [92]. The importance of these hormones in normal regulation of blood glucose during exercise is not well understood.

### Regulation of Liver Glycogenolysis during Exercise

*Role of the adrenal medulla.* Despite the large amount of in vitro data available on the mechanisms of catecholamine activation of liver glycogenolysis, the role of adrenal medullary hormones in controlling hepatic glycogenolysis during exercise is not clearly defined. There is no question that high concentrations of catecholamines will stimulate glycogenolysis in isolated hepatocytes [27, 29], in perfused liver [29], and in the liver in vivo [33]. It is likewise well established that the concentration of plasma catecholamines increases during exercise [15, 36, 45, 46, 99, 101]. In human subjects the plasma concentration of epinephrine varies between 0.4 nM at rest and 7 nM during exercise at approximately 100 percent of $\dot{V}O_2$max [101]. When rats are accustomed to running on rodent treadmills and are quickly anesthesized by intravenous injection of pentobarbital immediately prior to blood collection, plasma epinephrine may increase to approximately 6 nM during short-term high-intensity bouts of exercise and to 10 nM during long-term bouts when liver glycogen is depleted and blood glucose is low [99]. Plasma epinephrine values as high as 50 nM have been reported for rats forced to swim 90 minutes with a weight equivalent to 4 percent of body weight attached to their tail [41]. Ether anesthesia used in this study may have accentuated the increase in epinephrine caused by the exercise [100]. Values for plasma epinephrine higher than 6 nM would be unusual when rats are running at submaximal exercise intensities after having been subjected to short daily exercise bouts for 2 to 3 weeks to allow them to become familiar with the procedure. In studies using isolated rat hepatocytes or perfused liver, little if any effect of epinephrine can be seen on phosphorylase a activity, calcium efflux, or cAMP at epinephrine concentrations of 1 to 10 nM [29, 87]. These observations leave some question as to the effectiveness of physiologic concentrations of epinephrine in stimulating liver glycogenolysis during exercise. The possibility of combined effects of subthreshold concentrations of the counterregulatory hormones (glucagon and catecholamines) in stimulating glycogenolysis must also be considered [31].

Clutter et al. [16] attempted to determine threshold plasma epinephrine concentration required to produce increases in glucose production in normal human subjects. They infused epinephrine at five different rates to produce plasma concentrations ranging from 0.3 nM to 4 nM. Significant increases in glucose production were observed when plasma epinephrine increased above approximately 1 nM. It is not possible from these data to determine if the increase in glucose production was due to a direct effect of epinephrine on liver glycogenolytic enzymes or to indirect effects such as inhibition of insulin secretion or to a stimulation of lactate production [16]. Rizza et al. [80] reported that infusion of epinephrine into human subjects at a rate which produced plasma concentrations of 4 nM stimulates glucose production even when insulin, glucose, and glucagon levels are maintained constant. This implies that in humans a physiologic concentration of epinephrine, such as would be observed during high-intensity exercise, does have a direct stimulatory effect on glucose production by the liver. The consequence of elevated blood lactate resulting from epinephrine-induced muscle glycogenolysis on hepatic glucose production was not considered, however.

In initial work on the role of hormones in regulation of metabolism during exercise, Gollnick and co-workers [44] found that adrenodemedullated and sham-operated rats running in motor-driven running wheels utilized liver glycogen at similar rates. They concluded that catecholamines from the adrenal medulla are not essential for controlling liver glycogenolysis during exercise [44]. Galbo et al. [40] reexamined the role of the adrenal medulla during exercise. They found that adrenodemedullation, combined with chemical sympathectomy of rats, markedly diminished the rate of glycogenolysis during swimming [40]. In a second experiment rats that were both demedullated and chemically sympathectomized exhibited liver glycogenolytic rates during 100 minutes of swimming 32 percent lower than rats which were only chemically sympathectomized [79]. These investigators concluded that during prolonged exercise adrenal medullary hormones enhance liver glycogenolysis, but that this effect may be secondary to epinephrine inhibition of insulin release from the pancreatic beta cells and not to a direct effect of epinephrine on the liver [79]. Plasma insulin was elevated threefold in the demedullated rats compared to sham-operated controls [79]. In a third study on the effect of demedullation alone on liver and muscle glycogenolysis, Richter et al. [77] saw an impairment in liver glycogenolysis in adrenodemedullated rats during the first 75 minutes of swimming. From 75 minutes until exhaustion at 191 minutes, the demedullated rats showed a liver glycogenolytic rate which apparently exceeded that of the controls [77]. In our laboratory we failed to note any difference in liver glycogenolytic rate during 60 minutes of treadmill exercise (21 m/min, 15 percent grade) in adrenodemedullated rats compared to sham-operated rats [13a].

It should be pointed out that although these studies appear to have produced conflicting results, close attention must be paid to the differences in modes and intensities of exercise, anesthetization procedures, extent of familiarization of rats with the exercise procedure, training status of the rats, and age and sex of the rats. The control of liver glycogenolysis in swimming rats may be different from that of rats running on the treadmill. In the swimming experiments, for example, massive adrenal medullary release of epinephrine due to combined stress of exercise and fear of drowning may have produced plasma concentrations of epinephrine sufficient to have an effect on the liver glycogenolytic rate. Values as high as 50 nM have been reported for plasma epinephrine under these conditions [41]. This concentration of epinephrine has been reported to have significant effects on activation of phosphorylase in isolated hepatocytes [29, 87]. Removal of the source of epinephrine by adrenodemedullation would, therefore, be expected to impair the liver glycogenolytic rate in these animals. Concentrations of plasma epinephrine seen during treadmill exercise are considerably lower and may not detectably influence the liver glycogenolytic rate, thus explaining the absence of an effect off demedullation on the glycogenolytic rate in rats run on the treadmill.

Adrenergic receptor blockade with drugs has also been utilized as a means of determination of the role of epinephrine in stimulation of muscle and liver glycogenolysis during exercise. Juhlin-Dannfelt et al. [58] found that propranolol, a beta-adrenergic receptor antagonist, did not inhibit liver glycogenolysis in rats running on the treadmill at 22–27 m/min up a 15 percent grade. This observation is consistent with in vitro studies on rat hepatocytes which have demonstrated that the alpha-adrenergic receptor, calcium-mediated system predominates over the beta receptor, cAMP-mediated system in the adult male rate [26, 65]. In our laboratory we have attempted to determine the effect of injection of the alpha-adrenergic antagonist, phenoxybenzamine, on liver glycogen mobilizaton during exercise. Rats treated with this blocking agent (200 ug/100 g body weight) had difficulty running even 30 minutes on the treadmill at the moderate pace of 21 m/min. The phenoxybenzamine-treated rats were hyperglycemic (9.1 ± 0.7 nM vs. 7.8 ± 0.4 mM for saline-injected running rats) after 30 minutes of running. We assume, therefore, that liver glycogen mobilization was not impaired. It is likely that inappropriate vasodilatation was the reason for the poor exercise tolerance. Human subjects treated with the alpha-adrenergic receptor blocker phentolamine also exhibit increased blood glucose during exercise [37, 47]. It is difficult to come to any certain conclusions from these in vivo experiments with adrenergic blocking agents due to the cardiovascular effects which may secondarily influence metabolic effects.

*Role of liver sympathetic nerves.* Electron microscopic and histochemical studies have shown that both the liver vasculature and liver parenchymal cells are innervated by autonomic nerve terminals [35, 62, 64, 68, 84, 105]. As indicated previously, electrical stimulation of the hepatic sympathetic nerves stimulates glycogenolysis [48]. Although the existence of this sympathetic innervation of the liver has been known for some time, the physiologic role is not well understood.

We have recently presented evidence for activation of the sympathetic nerves of the liver during exercise [99]. Norepinephrine can be measured in neutralized perchloric acid extracts of liver tissue [98]. The norepinephrine of liver is contained in storage vesicles in sympathetic nerve terminals. When sympathetic neurons are activated, storage vesicles fuse with the membrane of the terminals and the vesicle contents are released adjacent to parenchymal cells or the vasculature. Once released from the terminals, norepinephrine may be taken up again into terminals, it may diffuse into the blood, or it may be inactivated by monoamine oxidase or by catechol-O-methyltransferase in liver cells. We reasoned that conditions resulting in rapid firing of the liver sympathetic nerves may cause release of norepinephrine at a rate in excess of the rate of norepinephrine synthesis in the terminals. An acute decrease in total norepinephrine content of the liver would therefore provide evidence of activation of sympathetic neurons. A 72 percent decrease in liver norepinephrine content occurred in response to 60 minutes of swimming of nontrained rats. In rats accustomed to treadmill running a 52 percent decrease in liver norepinephrine was noted during 150 minutes of running at 21 m/min. Liver glycogenolysis occurs concurrently with the apparent activation of the liver sympathetics. This does not, however, establish a cause-effect relationship between liver sympathetic activation and activation of the glycogenolytic enzymes.

Attempts have been made to determine the effect of abolition of the sympathetic innervation on liver glycogenolysis during exercise. 6-Hydroxydopamine injected intravenously destroys sympathetic nerve terminals [91]. The extent of chemical sympathectomy is assessed by quantitation of norepinephrine content of the tissues involved. The intravenous injection of 6-hydroxydopamine induces a generalized sympathectomy, including heart, adipose tissue, liver, pancreas, and other organs. The interpretation of such experiments using generalized chemical sympathectomy becomes very complex, considering the multiple roles of the sympathetic innervation in controlling heart rate, blood flow to specific organs, lipolysis, and insulin and glucagon secretion.

Sembrowich et al. [82] reported chemical sympathectomy to have no effect on the amount of liver glycogen utilized in rats during a 90-minute bout of exercise in motor-driven running wheels. Norepinephrine content was not measured in liver of these rats, but heart norepinephrine was decreased from 1.25 to 0.12 $\mu g/g$ as a result of drug treatment, thus indicating the virtual completeness of the sympathectomy. Galbo et al. [40] later reported that chemical sympathectomy (combined with adrenal demedullation) completely inhibited glycogen breakdown in liver of rats subjected to 75 minutes of swimming with a tail weight of 2 percent body weight. In an experiment to delineate the separate influences of the direct sympathetic innervation, Richter et al. [77] attributed the inhibitory effects of combined adrenodemedullation and chemical sympathectomy on liver glycogenolysis during exercise to the adrenal demedullation.

To avoid the multiple uncontrolled factors accompanying generalized sympathectomy, Sonne et al. [85] used an isotopic dilution technique to study the effects of autonomic hepatic denervation on decrease in liver glycogen and glucose production and disappearance during exercise. No difference in glucose production or in magnitude of decline in liver glycogen was detected between the liver-denervated and control rats during 35 minutes of running at 21 m/min in a metabolism chamber. Liver norepinephrine was reduced to 15 percent of controls as a result of the denervation technique. Pancreatic norepinephrine content was not affected by the denervation procedure. It was concluded that the hepatic innervation is unimportant in the rat for stimulating glucose production during exercise [85].

The general approach in elucidating the roles of the various hormonal and neural factors in stimulating liver glycogenolysis has been to attempt to eliminate one or more of these systems and to determine whether the absence of the system has an effect on the rate of liver glycogenolysis during exercise. Care must be taken to avoid unwarranted extrapolation from these studies to the normal control during exercise for the following reasons: (1) When hepatic nerves are eliminated, the other systems may compensate for their absence. (2) It is difficult to obtain a complete liver sympathectomy. It is uncertain at this time whether or not functional sympathetic endings are present in liver tissue of these denervated rats. (3) As alluded to previously, control of liver glycogenolysis may not be the same at different work rates and in response to different types of exercise. It seems clear that the liver sympathetics are more active in naive swimming rats than in rats running on a treadmill for prolonged periods [98]. Care must be taken as attempts are made to elucidate the roles of the liver sympathetic nerves to avoid application of data obtained from rats working at one work rate to all forms and intensities of exercise.

*Role of glucagon.* It is well documented that plasma glucagon increases during exercise in experimental animals and in humans [36, 96, 99, 102]. It is also clear that glucagon stimulates glycogenolysis in isolated hepatocytes and perfused liver by cAMP-dependent activation of phosphorylase [28]. Demonstration of an essential role of glucagon in regulation of glycogenolysis in the exercising animal or in humans is much more difficult.

Two approaches have been used to assess the role of glucagon in stimulation of liver glycogenolysis during exercise. The first involves the use of somatostatin, the natural inhibitor of glucagon secretion by alpha cells of the pancreatic islets. In general, somatostatin is infused prior to and during exercise to inhibit the rise in plasma glucagon. Splanchnic glucose production is estimated from arteriovenous differences or total glucose production and disappearance rates are measured by isotopic dilution techniques. Bjorkman et al. [6] reported that somatostatin-induced hypoglucagonemia in human subjects failed to prevent the increase in hepatic glucose output which is normally induced by exercise at 49–56 percent of $\dot{V}O_2$max. A transient decrease in glucose output was observed in sheep early in the course of exercise bouts at moderate and heavy work rates when the rise in glucagon was prevented by somatostatin infusion [11]. Infusion of somatostatin into exercising dogs has been reported to decrease glucose production when plasma glucagon decreased below resting levels [57]. Restoration of plasma glucagon to normal levels seen during exercise also restored the glucose production rate. Since liver glycogen was not measured in these studies it is difficult to ascertain whether the glucose production represented glycogenolysis or gluconeogenesis. Somatostatin inhibits the release of not only glucagon, but also insulin, growth hormone, and gastrointestinal hormones. It has direct effects on the liver at high concentrations [36, 57]. Investigators using this technique also have difficulty in finding a somatostatin infusion rate which will not impair the basal glucagon secretion rate, but which prevents the increase during exercise [36].

The second approach in elucidation of the role of glucagon in stimulating glucose production involves the intravenous injection of glucagon antiserum into rats to neutralize the effects of the increased glucagon secretion during exercise. Initial studies using this approach failed to show any effect of the glucagon antiserum on hepatic glycogenolysis in swimming rats [36, 40] except when rats were severely stressed [38]. The glucagon antiserum preparation would, however, be expected to contain large amounts of glucagon bound to the antibodies. It was postulated that failure to observe an inhibitory effect of the glucagon antisera on liver glycogenolysis was due to the presence of bound glucagon in the preparation [36]. When the antiserum was stripped of bound glucagon prior to injection, the presence of the antiserum in blood of the rats caused a 37 percent reduction in the amount of glycogen utilized during a 100-minute bout of swimming [78]. Substantial amounts of glycogen can be converted to glucose during exercise after injection of glucagon-stripped high-affinity glucagon antiserum [78], thus implying that glucagon is not entirely responsible for regulation of glucose production during exercise. Since the amount of free glucagon in plasma is difficult to quantitate after injection of antiserum, certain conclusions regarding the role of glucagon in comparison to other systems cannot be made.

Increases in hepatic glycogenolysis have previously been noted in endurance-trained rats and in human subjects during exercise without a concurrent increase in peripheral plasma glucagon [32, 36, 103]. It is unclear at this time if glucagon levels in peripheral blood during exercise reflect portal blood glucagon levels.

As with the sympathoadrenal system, failure to detect an impairment of hepatic glycogenolysis due to elimination of the effects of glucagon with somatostatin or glucagon antiserum cannot be taken as conclusive evidence that glucagon plays no part in controlling glycogenolysis during exercise. The likely compensation by the other systems in the absence of the glucagon effect must be considered.

*Role of Insulin.* The actions of catecholamines and of glucagon on liver glycogenolysis are antagonized by insulin. Insulin inhibits the glucagon-induced increases in cAMP and phosphorylase in isolated rat hepatocytes [28]. It also inhibits the alpha-adrenergic responses to catecholamines [28]. Thus, even in the absence of an increase in glucagon, a decline in insulin might be expected to permit an increase in liver glycogenolysis. Insulin secretion declines during exercise due to effects of catecholamines on alpha-adrenergic receptors on the beta cells of the pancreatic islets [36]. Issekutz [56] reported a twofold increase in glucose production in exercising dogs when plasma insulin decreased from 8 to 3 $\mu$U/ml as a result of mannoheptulose infusion. Infusion of insulin reversed these changes. Elevation of plasma insulin to 12–15 $\mu$U/ml resulted in a marked decline in blood glucose. This decline in blood glucose was found to be due to a 38 percent reduction in glucose production and a 37 percent rise in glucose clearance. It was concluded that the exercise-induced decline in plasma insulin was essential for allowing adequate hepatic glucose production.

Infusion of glucose and consequent increase in plasma insulin in human subjects results in a marked diminution in splanchnic glucose output during exercise [32]. Infusion of insulin concurrently with glucose also prevented the increase in splanchnic glucose output during exercise [32]. It seems clear from these and other studies [36] that the decline in insulin is an important factor in allowing adequate liver glycogenolysis during exercise.

*Role of cAMP.* As indicated previously, both cAMP-dependent and cAMP-independent mechanisms exist for activation of liver glycogenolysis. We were interested, therefore, in documenting a change in hepatic cAMP in response to exercise. When rats were run on a rodent treadmill at 21 m/min up a 15 percent grade, little increase in hepatic cAMP occurred until liver glycogen was depleted. Small increases observed did not reach statistical significance until 60 minutes into the running bout [99]. If rats were run at speeds varying between 31 and 42 m/min up a 15 percent grade, a 30 percent increase in hepatic cAMP could be detected after 5 minutes of running [99].

More recently the relationship between hepatic cAMP concentration and the liver glycogenolytic rate has been determined [96]. Rats were run at treadmill speeds ranging from 10 to 34 m/min. Liver glycogen and cAMP were determined in resting rats and in rats run for 30 or 60 minutes (Fig. 2). The glycogenolytic rate was estimated by subtracting the mean end-exercise liver glycogen from the preexercise value and dividing by elapsed time. As noted in Figure 3 a high degree of correlation exists between the hepatic cAMP and the glycogenolytic rate. This data is consistent with the idea that liver glycogenolysis during exercise is controlled by cAMP-mediated mechanisms. This relationship is valid only within limits. When rats run at 10 m/min, liver glycogenolysis proceeds at a rate of 0.27 mg/g/min with no detectable change in cAMP relative to resting values. When hepatic cAMP is increased fourfold by injection of glucagon in rats running 26 m/min, the liver glycogenolytic rate does not exceed that observed in rats running at 34 m/min in which hepatic cAMP is

FIGURE 2

*Effect of running at different treadmill speeds on liver glycogen and cAMP of rats.*

SOURCE: Winder, W.W., M.A. Beattie, and E.O. Fuller. Glycogenolytic rates and cAMP in livers of rats running at different treadmill speeds. *Am. J. Physiol.* 245:R353–R356, 1983.

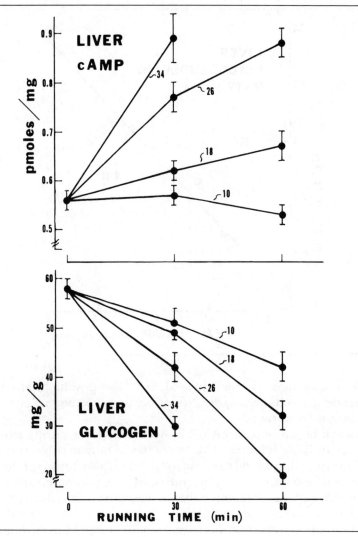

increased only 62 percent above resting values. It is conceivable that glucagon-induced activation of adenylate cyclase at low work rates does not result in detectable changes in tissue cAMP even though

FIGURE 3

*Correlation between liver glycogenolytic rate and liver cAMP in rats run at different treadmill speeds.*
SOURCE: Winder, W.W., M.A. Beattie, and E.O. Fuller. Glycogenolytic rates and cAMP in livers of rats running at different treadmill speeds. *Am. J. Physiol.* 245:R353–R356, 1983.

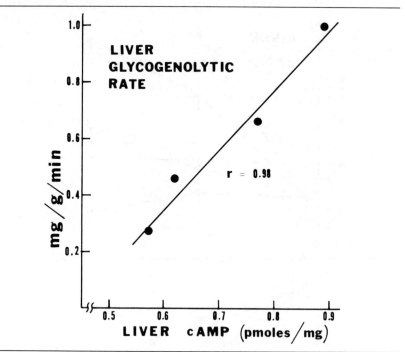

protein kinase may still be activated. It is also possible that cAMP-independent mechanisms are responsible for activation of glycogenolysis at low work rates.

Information on hepatic cAMP in human subjects during exercise is not yet available. Plasma cAMP increases in human subjects during high-intensity, short-term exercise [63, 67] and also during prolonged submaximal exercise [89]. The source of this plasma cAMP is unknown although authors imply that at least part of it is derived from adenylate cyclase activation in liver.

In summary, several systems have been identified by in vitro studies for regulation of glycogenolysis in the liver:
1. Glucagon-induced activation of adenylate cyclase.
2. Epinephrine- (from adrenal medulla) induced activation of adenylate cyclase via beta-adrenergic receptors.
3. Epinephrine- (from adrenal medulla) induced increase in cyto-

plasmic free calcium via alpha-adrenergic receptors with consequent allosteric activation of phosphorylase kinase.

4. Norepinephrine- (from sympathetic nerve terminals in the liver) induced increase in cytoplasmic free calcium via alpha-adrenergic receptors with consequent allosteric activation of phosphorylase kinase.

5. Vasopressin or angiotensin II activation by a calcium-dependent mechanism.

6. Insulin inhibition of the action of catecholamines and glucagon on hepatic glycogenolysis.

Glucagon and catecholamines increase in plasma during exercise and insulin decreases. Recent evidence indicates that the liver sympathetic nerves are activated during exercise. There is some question whether epinephrine at plasma concentrations seen during exercise has a direct effect on the liver. Liver cAMP increases during exercise. Within limits, the increase in cAMP correlates closely with the glycogenolytic rate. Glycogenolysis may also occur with no detectable concurrent increase in liver cAMP. It seems reasonable to suggest that since all these mechanisms exist all must operate in regulating glycogenolysis at one time or another in the live animal, but with data now available it is impossible to state with confidence which, if any, is the predominant system in controlling glycogenolysis during exercise.

## GLUCONEOGENESIS

*Gluconeogenesis During Exercise*
After liver glycogen is depleted by fasting or by prolonged exercise, gluconeogenesis becomes the only source of blood glucose. The gluconeogenic precursors, amino acids, lactate, pyruvate, and glycerol, are utilized as carbon sources for synthesizing glucose in the liver. The relative contribution of gluconeogenesis to total glucose output varies with intensity and duration of exercise and previous food intake. During prolonged mild exercise (30 percent of $\dot{V}O_2$max) an approximate threefold increase occurs in the rate of gluconeogenesis over a 4-hour period [2, 94, 95]. As estimated from splanchnic uptake of pyruvate, glycerol, amino acids, and lactate, gluconeogenesis was responsible for 25 percent of total glucose output at rest (subjects fasted over night) and 45 percent after 4 hours of mild cycle ergometer exercise. During short-term, heavy exercise (1200 kpm/min) gluconeogenesis can account for only 10 percent of total hepatic glucose output [2]. When subjects work at 58 percent of $\dot{V}O_2$max, splanchnic uptake of gluconeogenic precursors could account for approximately 60 percent of total splanchnic glucose output after 3 hours of exercise [1]. Theoretically, gluconeogenesis must be re-

sponsible for 100 percent of glucose production by the liver after glycogen is depleted. It should be clear that these estimations of the rate of gluconeogenesis (determined from splanchnic uptake) do not include possible contribution of precursors derived from liver tissue. Data in rats showing a decrease in total liver protein during prolonged exercise imply that gluconeogenic substrate may be derived in part from liver protein [22, 59].

### Control of Gluconeogenesis

*Enzyme properties.* Gluconeogenesis is a reversal of glycolysis with the exception of the glucokinase, phosphofructokinase-1 (PFK-1), and pyruvate kinase reactions (Fig. 4). Pyruvate carboxylase and phos-

FIGURE 4
*Abbreviated pathway for gluconeogenesis and glycogenolysis.*

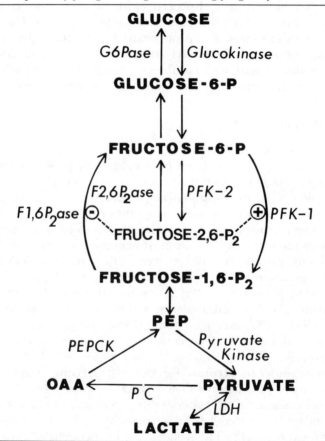

phoenolpyruvate carboxykinase (PEPCK) are required to convert pyruvate to PEP. Fructose-1, 6-bisphosphatase converts fructose-1, 6-bisphosphate to fructose-6-phosphate. Glucose-6-phosphatase removes a phosphate to form free glucose, which may then diffuse into the blood.

Net flux can occur in either the glycolytic direction or the gluconeogenic direction. Direction of flux is regulated primarily at two steps: pyruvate to PEP and fructose-1, 6-bisphosphate to fructose-6-phosphate [50]. Pyruvate kinase is allosterically activated by fructose-1, 6-bisphosphate, and PEP and inhibited by ATP and alanine [50]. Liver pyruvate kinase can also be phosphorylated by cAMP-dependent protein kinase and dephosphorylated by a phosphatase. Phosphorylation causes a decrease in affinity for activators and an increase in affinity for inhibitors. Under physiologic conditions this results in a great reduction in pyruvate kinase activity [50]. Pyruvate kinase is also subject to long-term regulation. The amount of pyruvate kinase is elevated up to fivefold by a high carbohydrate diet and is decreased to one-third normal values by prolonged fasting [50].

The short-term regulation of pyruvate carboxylase and PEPCK is less well defined. Pyruvate carboxylase is stimulated by acetyl coenzyme A (CoA) and inhibited by glutamate [50]. It is not clear whether mitochondrial fluctuations in acetyl CoA concentration are in the range which would influence the activity of this enzyme [50]. Glucagon may stimulate mitochondrial pyruvate carboxylation, but the mechanism is not clear. Liver PEPCK, but not pyruvate carboxylase, is increased by starvation and decreased by carbohydrate feeding [50].

The activities of phosphofructokinase and fructose-1, 6-bisphosphatase are controlled primarily by the liver concentration of AMP and of a newly discovered regulator, fructose-2, 6-bisphosphate [50]. This compound is a potent activator of phosphofructokinase and a potent inhibitor of fructose-1, 6-bisphosphatase (Fig. 4). The activities of two newly discovered enzymes control the concentration of fructose-2, 6-bisphosphate: phosphofructokinase-2 (PFK-2) catalyzes its formation from fructose-6-phosphate and fructose-2, 6-bisphosphatase removes the phosphate, forming fructose-6-phosphate. The activity of PFK-2 is inhibited by phosphorylation; that of fructose-2, 6-bisphosphatase is stimulated by phosphorylation. Both enzymes are substrates for cAMP-dependent protein kinase [50].

Glucose-6-phosphatase and glucokinase activities are regulated primarily by concentrations of their substrates. Fasting increases the amount of glucose-6-phosphatase and decreases glucokinase in liver [50].

*Hormonal regulation.* Glucagon stimulates gluconeogenesis from lactate, pyruvate, and from amino acids which enter the pathway at the level of pyruvate or oxaloacetate in perfused livers and in isolated hepatocytes [25, 50]. Glycerol incorporation into glucose is not stimulated by glucagon [25, 50]. These effects of glucagon are due to cAMP-dependent phosphorylation of pyruvate kinase, PFK-2, and fructose-2, 6-bisphosphatase [50]. The consequent decrease in hepatic fructose-2, 6-bisphosphate results in an increase in activity of fructose-1, 6-bisphosphatase and decrease in activity of PFK-1. This change, coupled with phosphorylation inactivation of pyruvate kinase, channels metabolic flux in the gluconeogenic direction.

High concentrations of catecholamines stimulate incorporation of gluconeogenic precursors into glucose as well as stimulating increased net glucose production by hepatocytes obtained from fasted rats [25, 50]. This effect is apparently mediated by the alpha-adrenergic receptor and is not dependent on cAMP [25]. There is some question whether physiologic levels of plasma catecholamines have a significant direct effect on hepatic gluconeogenesis in vivo [25, 50]. It is conceivable that high concentrations of norepinephrine adjacent to liver cells caused by release from sympathetic terminals could stimulate gluconeogenesis. Direct stimulation of hepatic nerves of rat liver perfused in situ has recently been reported to enhance lactate production rather than lactate uptake by the liver [48]. The authors urge caution in ruling out this mechanism for stimulation of gluconeogenesis on the basis of their data since glucagon, insulin, and other hormones were not included in the perfusion medium.

Insulin antagonizes the effects of glucagon and catecholamines on stimulation of gluconeogenesis in liver cells [25]. Pilkis et al. [72] recently reported that insulin antagonized the effects of glucagon, epinephrine, and cAMP on activation of fructose-2, 6-bisphosphatase in isolated rat hepatocytes. Both glucagon and epinephrine cause a marked decrease in fructose-2, 6-bisphosphatase in these cells. Simultaneous inclusion of insulin in the incubation medium with either of these hormones antagonizes their effects on fructose-2, 6-bisphosphate. The inhibitory effects of glucagon and catecholamines on pyruvate kinase activity are also antagonized by insulin [25, 72].

Glucocorticoids are important in maintaining adequate quantities of hepatic gluconeogenic enzymes, particularly PEPCK [25]. Perfused livers from fasted adrenalectomized rats fail to respond to glucagon or catecholamines with an increase in gluconeogenesis [25]. The increase in cAMP caused by glucagon is no different than in normal control animals, indicating that a step beyond the receptor and adenylate cyclase is impaired. Inclusion of cortisol in the perfusion medium repairs this defect within an hour. Protein synthesis is required.

The rate of hepatic gluconeogenesis is dependent not only on regulation of gluconeogenic enzymes in the liver, but also on the substrate supply from peripheral tissues. Catecholamines stimulate glycerol and lactate output by beta-adrenergic mechanisms in adipose tissue and muscle [25]. Glucocorticoids stimulate release of amino acids from skeletal muscle and are necessary for normal stimulation of lipolysis and glycerol production by adipose tissue [25]. Insulin inhibits net amino acid release from skeletal muscle [25].

*Regulation of Hepatic Gluconeogenesis During Exercise*
Much less attention has been devoted to study of the control of gluconeogenesis than to control of glycogenolysis during exercise. When rats are exercised for prolonged periods at 21 m/min up a 15 percent grade, liver glycogen is depleted between 90 and 120 minutes of exercise. At this time blood glucose declines to approximately 3 mM. When liver glycogen is depleted the rat must rely on gluconeogenesis to maintain blood glucose. Glucose utilization apparently exceeds glucose production, resulting in a decline in blood glucose concentration [99]. As liver glycogen is depleted a marked increase occurs in plasma glucagon and epinephrine. These changes are accomplished by an abrupt rise in hepatic cAMP [99]. Glucocorticoid concentration increases in plasma early in exercise and remains elevated throughout the exercise bout. Insulin declines to very low levels by the end of the exercise [99]. When rats are fasted prior to exercise, the rise in plasma glucagon and epinephrine and in hepatic cAMP occur much earlier in the course of exercise than when rats are not fasted [99]. In human subjects, also, a marked increase in plasma glucagon occurs after 3–4 hours of mild exercise on cycle ergometers [1, 95]. Insulin declined throughout the exercise bout. The rise in glucagon corresponds with an increase in the gluconeogenic rate estimated from uptake of gluconeogenic precursors [1, 95]. These hormonal changes would be expected to have a stimulatory effect on the rate of gluconeogenesis in the liver.

Dohm and Newsholme [20] presented evidence that fructose-2, 6-bisphosphate is decreased in livers of rats run at 28 m/min on a treadmill for 80 minutes. Liver extracts of the nonexercised rats stimulated the activity of purified muscle phosphofructokinase 4.5-fold. This stimulation was attributed to the presence of fructose-2, 6-bisphosphate in the extract. Liver extracts from exercised rats stimulated the phosphofructokinase only 2.8-fold, thus implying that the fructose-2, 6-bisphosphate concentration of liver is reduced in response to exercise. This change is consistent with changes in glucagon, insulin, and hepatic cAMP which have been reported previously for rats subjected to similar exercise bouts [99]. The decrease in fructose-2, 6-bisphosphate would be expected to result in inactivation of phosphofructokinase-1 and of activation of fructose-1, 6-bisphos-phatase [50], thus shifting from a glycolytic to a gluconeogenic mode during the exercise and allowing increased gluconeogenesis from lactate and other precursors.

The adrenal medullary hormones are essential for allowing adequate rates of gluconeogenesis in fasted rats during exercise. Born and Spratts [10] found that adrenodemedullated fasted rats running in a revolving exercise wheel at 12.7 m/min had lower plasma glucose (3.5 mM) at the end of 30 minutes than sham-operated controls (4.8 mM). As a crude indicator of gluconeogenesis, incorporation of intraperitoneally injected $^{14}$C-lactate into plasma glucose was quantitated. Demedullated rats had significantly lower (by 24%) radioactivity in plasma glucose than sham-operated controls at the end of 30 minutes of mild exercise. Subcutaneous injection of a large dose of epinephrine corrected the hypoglycemia and restored the gluconeogenic rate to normal.

We investigated the role of the adrenal medulla in the fasted rat and found that adrenodemedullated rats show a marked reduction in endurance run time (32 minutes) compared to sham-operated controls (92 minutes) [104]. After 30 minutes of running (21 m/min, 10% grade) adrenodemedullated rats blood glucose was $2.9 \pm 0.2$ mM compared to $4.5 \pm 0.3$ mM in controls. Blood lactate was three-fold higher in sham-operated controls than in demedullated rats after 30 minutes of exercise. Glycogenolysis in the white vastus lateralis and the soleus was impaired in the adrenodemedullated rats during exercise. Infusion of epinephrine into the demedullated rats at a rate which produced epinephrine concentrations similar to controls during exercise stimulated muscle glycogenolysis, increased blood lactate, and corrected the hypoglycemia. These data imply that epinephrine plays an important role in stimulating production of gluconeogenic substrate for the liver during exercise. At least part of the lactate appears to be derived from fast-twitch white, noncontracting muscle. This suggestion agrees with a recent report by Ahlborg and Felig [1], who found a net production of lactate by the forearm of subjects during prolonged leg exercise at 58 percent of $\dot{V}O_2$max. Plasma epinephrine was elevated 13.7-fold over resting values at the end of 3 hours of exercise in that study.

It is unclear whether epinephrine has a regulatory effect on the liver gluconeogenic enzymes. In our rat adrenodemedullation study, hepatic cAMP was $1.4 \pm 0.1$ p moles/mg in shams compared to $1.7 \pm 0.3$ p moles/mg in demedullated rats at the end of 30 minutes of exercise [104]. There was no impairment of the cAMP response to the exercise as a result of the demedullation.

Evidence has been obtained that indicates the liver sympathetic nerves are activated in fasted rats during exercise [98]. A 50 percent decrease in liver norepinephrine occurred in nontrained rats in response to running 60 minutes at 21 m/min up a 15 percent grade. Although data is lacking which would establish a regulatory role in gluconeogenesis for the liver sympathetics, this possible mechanism would allow concentrations of norepinephrine in the vicinity of the liver cells in the range of those reported to stimulate gluconeogenesis in vitro [25].

Changes in activities of the gluconeogenic enzymes have been reported to occur during prolonged exercise bouts. Phosphoenolpyruvate carboxykinase activity increased approximately threefold in trained rats run to exhaustion at 43 m/min for 206 ± 17 minutes [55]. A recent preliminary report on the time course of these changes indicates that this enzyme progressively increases in liver of untrained rats during the course of a prolonged bout of exercise (28 m/min) to a maximum of twofold above controls at exhaustion [19]. By 6 hours postexercise the activity had returned to control values. The increase in enzyme activity was postulated to be due to increased synthesis of the enzyme. Relatively small changes in activities of several glycolytic and gluconeogenic enzymes have been reported to occur in rats during 80 minutes of treadmill running. Rats were not exhausted at the end of the exercise bout [20].

In summary, hormone changes which are observed late in an exercise bout after liver glycogen is depleted or in fasted exercising rats are compatible with those expected to stimulate the gluconeogenic enzymes and inhibit the glycolytic pathway in the liver. Plasma glucagon and catecholamines are elevated and insulin is depressed. The liver sympathetics are activated. Liver cAMP is elevated approximately twofold above resting values. Evidence has been presented for an exercise-induced reduction in hepatic fructose-2, 6-bisphosphate. This change would tend to inhibit hepatic glycolysis and stimulate gluconeogenesis. The adrenal medulla is essential for allowing adequate rates of gluconeogenesis during exercise when liver glycogen is depleted. Epinephrine may be important for stimulating muscle glycogenolysis, thereby regulating the supply of gluconeogenic substrate. A direct effect of physiologic concentrations of epinephrine on liver gluconeogenic enzymes has not been demonstrated. Activity of phosphoenolpyruvate carboxykinase may increase acutely during prolonged exhaustive exercise bouts.

## EFFECTS OF ENDURANCE TRAINING ON LIVER GLYCOGENOLYSIS AND GLUCONEOGENESIS

### Liver Enzyme Adaptations to Training

When an animal or human subject exercises vigorously for 1 to 2 hours per day over a period of several weeks, distinct adaptive changes occur in skeletal muscle enzymes which are responsible in part for an increase in endurance [52, 53]. Particularly important are the increases in mitochondrial fatty acid oxidizing enzymes which enable the muscle to obtain a greater proportion of its ATP from fat oxidation, thereby reducing the rate of utilization of muscle glycogen and blood glucose [52, 53].

Several investigators have examined the effect of endurance training on liver enzymes. Although the liver is not directly involved in locomotion during training, it is without question an active organ during each training session. Liver glycogen is utilized to provide glucose for the working muscle. Lactate produced by the muscles is converted to glucose in the liver. Glycerol and amino acids must also be processed. During each postexercise period glycogen must be synthesized in preparation for the next bout of training. It is reasonable, therefore, to postulate that liver enzymes involved in these processes may adapt also in response to endurance training.

In a recent study to examine the effect of training on the liver, rats were run 2 hours per day in two 1-hour sessions for six weeks, beginning at 16 m/min and working up to 26 m/min. This training program increased citrate synthase activity of the deep red region of the vastus lateralis from $41 \pm 3$ to $70 \pm 3$ $\mu$ moles/g/min. Rats were killed 24 hours after the last training bout and were allowed to feed ad libitim during the postexercise period. Activities of four enzymes are shown in Table 1. No increase was seen in any of these enzymes. In fact, small decreases in the activity of citrate synthase, lactate dehydrogenase, and PEPCK were observed in this experiment. Huston et al. [55] previously reported that training rats 2 hours per day at 29.5 m/min for 12 weeks had no significant effect on PEPCK or pyruvate carboxylase of liver when rats were killed 48 hours following the last exercise bout.

Seven weeks of treadmill running 60 minutes per day at speeds up

TABLE 1

*Effect of Six Weeks Endurance Training (2 hours per day) on Hepatic Enzymes*

| Enzyme | Enzyme Activity ($\mu$ moles/g/min) | |
| --- | --- | --- |
| | Nontrained | Trained |
| Citrate synthase [86] | $12.1 \pm 0.6$ | $10.0 \pm 0.2$* |
| Lactate dehydrogenase [71] | $425 \pm 23$ | $327 \pm 30$* |
| Phosphoenolpyruvate carboxykinase [70] | $1.71 \pm 0.15$ | $1.28 \pm 0.11$* |
| Fructose-1, 6-bisphosphatase [70] | $8.6 \pm 0.4$ | $8.6 \pm 0.5$ |

*Significantly different from nontrained, $p < 0.05$. Enzyme activities were determined at 30°C by methods indicated in the references.

to 35 m/min does not cause any change in liver adenylate cyclase but produces a 29 percent reduction in liver phosphodiesterase in rats [21]. The activity of total phosphorylase was slightly decreased and that of total glycogen synthase was increased by 47 percent in rats which swam up to 6 hours per day for 12 weeks [42]. These swim-trained rats were killed 66 hours following the last swimming session. Activity of liver glucokinase has been reported to decrease by 40 percent in rats which ran 4–6 miles per day in voluntary running wheels for 36 days [106]. Contrary to expectations, endurance train-ing appears to have no remarkable effect on liver content of enzymes of gluconeogenesis or glycogenolysis.

*Effect of Endurance Training on Liver Glycogenolysis*
Hepatic glycogen metabolism is modified by endurance exercise training. Trained rats accumulate supernormal amounts of liver gly-cogen following each training session so that at the beginning of exercise on subsequent days they have higher concentrations of liver glycogen than do sedentary rats at the same time of day [32, 34, 41, 103]. This supercompensation effect appears to require the presence of glucocorticoids [61]. It is likely that an increase in plasma gluco-corticoids occurs during the course of each training session [17, 73, 99, 103]. The increase in corticosterone is similar in both trained and nontrained rats subjected to a long bout of treadmill exercise [99, 103]. The exact role of glucocorticoid surges in determining the extent of liver glycogen accumulation in the postexercise period, however, is not known.

In addition to having higher liver glycogen at the beginning of an exercise bout, endurance-trained rats also utilize liver glycogen at a slower rate during exercise than do nontrained rats when both are working at the same intensity [31, 34, 41, 103]. Endurance exercise training has been shown to induce major adaptations in the endocrine responses to exercise [36]. Plasma glucagon and catecholamine re-sponses to a prolonged bout of submaximal exercise are markedly lower after a period of several weeks of training [36, 46, 60, 102, 103]. Trained rats also have lower hepatic cAMP during prolonged exercise than do nontrained rats [103]. All these changes would be expected to result in a slower rate of glycogenolysis during exercise. The reason for the training-induced attenuation of stress hormone responses late in the course of a prolonged exercise bout is likely the difference in blood glucose concentration between trained and non-trained rats. Trained rats deplete their liver glycogen later in the course of the exercise than do nontrained rats. The consequent lower blood glucose in the nontrained rats would be expected to result in a higher rate of glucagon and catecholamine release [103]. Felig et al. [30] reported that infusion of glucose into human subjects exercising for prolonged periods prevents the marked rise in epinephrine seen after 90 minutes of exercise. The reason for the difference in hormone response early in the course of exercise is not clear, since blood glucose is similar in both trained and nontrained rats [103].

The primary adaptation which results in a slower rate of glycogen depletion in endurance trained rats is likely the increase in the capacity of the working muscle to oxidize fatty acids. Recent evidence has been presented indicating that after a 12-week training program human subjects obtained a greater proportion of their energy during exercise from fatty acid oxidation (53% vs. 40%) and that the source of the increased fatty acids for oxidation was muscle triglycerides [18]. Increased rates of fatty acid oxidation in muscle inhibit uptake and oxidation of glucose by the muscle [75, 76]. This hypothesis explains why less total carbohydrate is utilized by the trained animal or human subject during exercise, but it does not explain how the sympathoadrenal system and the alpha-cells of the pancreas get the message. Blood glucose is not detectably different in nonfasted trained than in nontrained rats or human subjects early in the course of exercise. It is unclear at this time exactly what the signal is or where it is detected for setting sympathetic tone early in the course of a submaximal exercise bout.

*Effect of Endurance Training on Gluconeogenesis*
Trained animals and human subjects have the capacity to maintain higher levels of blood glucose during prolonged bouts of exercise [60, 103]. Even when rats are fasted to deplete liver glycogen, trained rats are capable of maintaining blood glucose levels higher than nontrained controls during exercise [97]. Glucose is produced only by gluconeogenesis under these conditions. The increase in the ability of trained rats to maintain normoglycemia during exercise in the fasted state could be a consequence of an enhancement of glucose production by gluconeogenesis or to a reduction in glucose utilization by muscle or to a combination of these two adaptations [12]. The gluconeogenic rate from lactate (estimated from glucose specific activity during $^{14}$C-lactate infusion) has been reported to be similar in trained and nontrained rats at rest and during treadmill exercise at low work rates (14.3 m/min, 1% grade) [23]. In this study as the treadmill speed was increased from 14.3 m/min to 28.7 m/min the apparent gluconeogenic rate in trained rats was slightly increased, but in untrained rats a marked decrease was observed. As a result of this decrease, the calculated gluconeogenic rate at the higher work rate was 105 percent greater in trained rats than in nontrained rats. The decrease in calculated gluconeogenic rate in nontrained rats was

postulated to be due to a diversion of blood flow away from gluconeogenic organs at the high work rates [23]. This hypothesis has yet to be tested. Considering factors which are thought to influence the gluconeogenic rate, trained rats appear to have no advantage. There is apparently no lasting effect of endurance training on hepatic gluconeogenic enzymes. Gluconeogenic substrate concentrations, which markedly affect the gluconeogenic rate in isolated perfused livers, are similar or lower in trained rats during exercise [97]. Cyclic AMP is very similar in trained and nontrained liver during exercise in the fasted condition [97].

In summary, endurance-trained rats utilize liver glycogen at a slower rate during exercise than do nontrained rats. They also have higher resting hepatic glycogen. During prolonged exercise bouts nontrained rats deplete liver glycogen and exhibit hypoglycemia much sooner than do trained rats. The slower rate of glycogen depletion in trained rats during exercise is likely due to attenuation of the sympathoadrenal response, to lower plasma glucagon, and to consequent lower hepatic cAMP. The reason for the attenuation of stress hormone responses early in exercise is not known. Fasted endurance-trained rats and human subjects (glucose produced by gluconeogenesis) are capable of maintaining higher concentrations of blood glucose during prolonged exercise than are fasted nontrained controls. This is most likely due to a reduction in glucose uptake by trained muscle compared to controls, but may also be partially due to increased gluconeogenesis by the liver. Plasma concentrations of gluconeogenic substrates are similar or lower and hepatic cAMP is similar in trained and nontrained rats during exercise in the fasted state.

## REFERENCES

1. Ahlborg, G., and P. Felig. Lactate and glucose exchange across the forearm, legs, and splanchnic bed during and after prolonged leg exercise. *J. Clin. Invest.* 69:45–54, 1982.
2. Ahlborg, G., P. Felig, L. Hagenfeldt, R. Hendler, and J. Wahren. Substrate turnover during prolonged exercise in man. *J. Clin. Invest.* 53:1080–1090, 1974.
3. Baldwin, K.M., R.H. Fitts, F.W. Booth, W.W. Winder, and J.O. Holloszy. Depletion of muscle and liver glycogen during exercise—protective effect of training. *Pfluegers Arch.* 354:203–212, 1975.
4. Baldwin, K.M., J.S. Reitman, R.L. Terjung, W.W. Winder, and J.O. Holloszy. Substrate depletion in different types of muscle and in liver during prolonged running. *Am. J. Physiol.* 225:1045–1050, 1973.
5. Best, J.D., W.K. Ward, M.A. Pfeifer, and J.B. Halter. Lack of a direct α-adrenergic effect of epinephrine on glucose production in human subjects. *Am. J. Physiol.* 246:E271–E276, 1984.
6. Bjorkman, O., P. Felig, L. Hagenfeldt, and J. Wahren. Influence of hypoglucagonemia on splanchnic glucose output during leg exercise in man. *Clin. Physiol.* 1:43–57, 1981.
7. Blackmore, P.F., B.P. Hughes, R. Charest, E.A. Shuman, and J.H. Exton. Time

course of α-adrenergic and vasopressin actions on phosphorylase activation, calcium efflux, pyridine nucleotide reduction, and repiration in hepatocytes. *J. Biol. Chem.* 258:10488–10494, 1983.

8. Blackmore, P.F., B.P. Hughes, E.A. Shuman, and J.H. Exton. α-Adrenergic activation of phosphorylase in liver cells involves mobilization of intracellular calcium without influx of extracellular calcium. *J. Biol. Chem.* 257:190–197, 1982.

9. Blair, J.B., M.E. James, and J.L. Foster. Adrenergic control of glucose output and adenosine-3',5'-monophosphate levels in hepatocytes from juvenile and adult rats. *J. Biol. Chem.* 254:7579–7584, 1979.

10. Born, C.K., and G.R. Spratto. The role of the adrenal medulla in the control of gluconeogenesis in the rat. *Res. Comm. Chem. Path. Pharmacol.* 12:481–498, 1975.

11. Brockman, R.P. Effect of somatostatin on plasma glucagon and insulin, and glucose turnover in exercising sheep. *J. Appl. Physiol.* 47:273–278, 1979.

12. Brooks, G.A., and C.M. Donovan. Effect of endurance training on glucose kinetics during exercise. *Am. J. Physiol.* 244:E505–E512, 1983.

13. Charest, R., P.F. Blackmore, B. Berthon, and J.H. Exton. Changes in free cytosolic Ca$^{++}$ in hepatocytes following α$_1$-adrenergic stimulation. *J. Biol. Chem.* 258:8769–8773, 1983.

13a. Carlson, K.I., J.C. Marker, D.A. Arnall, M.L. Terry, H.T. Yang, L.G. Lindsay, M.E. Bracken, and W.W. Winder. Epinephrine is unessential for stimulation of liver glycogenolysis during exercise. *J. Appl. Physiol.* 58 (in press).

14. Chrisman, T.D., J.E. Jordan, and J.H. Exton. Purification of rat liver phosphorylase kinase. *J. Biol. Chem.* 257:10798–10804, 1982.

15. Christensen, N.J., and H. Galbo. Sympathetic nervous activity during exercise. *Ann. Rev. Physiol.* 45:139–153, 1983.

16. Clutter, W.E., D.M. Bier, S.D. Shah, and P.E. Cryer. Epinephrine plasma metabolic clearance rates and physiologic thresholds for metabolic and hemodynamic actions in man. *J. Clin. Invest.* 66:94–101, 1980.

17. Conlee, R.K., R.C. Hickson, W.W. Winder, J.M. Hagberg, and J.O. Holloszy. Regulation of glycogen resynthesis in muscles of rats following exercise. *Am. J. Physiol.* 235:R145–R150, 1978.

18. Dalsky, G., W. Martin, B. Hurley, D. Matthews, D. Bier, J. Hagberg, and J.O. Holloszy. Oxidation of plasma FFA during endurance exercise. *Med. Sci. Sport* 16:202, 1984.

19. Dohm, G.L., G.J. Kasperek, and H.A. Barakat. Time course of changes in gluconeogenic enzyme activities during exercise and recovery. *Med. Sci. Sports* 16:163, 1984.

20. Dohm, G.L., and E.A. Newsholme. Metabolic control of hepatic gluconeogenesis during exercise. *Biochem. J.* 212:633–639, 1983.

21. Dohm, G.L., S.S. Pennington, and H. Barakat. Effect of exercise training on adenyl cyclase and phosphodiesterase in skeletal muscle, heart, and liver. *Biochem. Med.* 16:138–142, 1976.

22. Dohm, G.L., F.R. Puente, C.P. Smith, and A. Edge. Changes in tissue protein levels as a result of endurance exercise. *Life Sci.* 23:845–850, 1978.

23. Donovan, C.M. and G. Brooks. Endurance training affects lactate clearance, not lactate production. *Am. J. Physiol.* 244:E83–E92, 1983.

24. Edwards, A.V., and M. Silver. The glycogenolytic response to stimulation of the splanchnic nerves in adrenalectomized calves. *J. Physiol.* 211:109–124, 1970.

25. Exton, J.H. Hormonal control of gluconeogenesis. *Adv. Exp. Med. Biol.* 111:125–167, 1979.

26. Exton, J.H. Mechanisms involved in adrenergic phenomena: Role of calcium ions in actions of catecholamines in liver and other tissues. *Am. J. Physiol.* 238:E3–E12, 1980.

27. Exton, J.H., F.D. Assimacopoulos-Jeannet, P.F. Blackmore, A.D. Cherrington, and T.M. Chan. Mechanisms of catecholamine actions on liver carbohydrate metabolism. *Adv. Cyc. Nuc. Res.* 9:441–452, 1978.

28. Exton, J.H., P.F. Blackmore, M.F. El-Refae, J.P. Dehaye, W.G. Strickland, A.D. Cherrington, T.M. Chan, F.D. Assimacopoulos-Jeannet, and T.D. Chrisman. Mechanisms of hormonal regulation of liver metabolism. *Adv. Cyc. Nuc. Res.* 14:491–505, 1981.

29. Exton, J.H., and S.C. Harper. Role of cAMP in the actions of catecholamines on hepatic carbohydrate metabolism. *Adv. Cyc. Nucleotide Res.* 5:519–532, 1975.

30. Felig, P., A. Cherif, A. Minagawa, and J. Wahren. Hypoglycemia during prolonged exercise in normal men. *N. Engl. J. Med.* 306:895–900, 1982.

31. Felig, P., R.S. Sherwin, V. Soman, J. Wahren, R. Hendler, L. Sacca, N. Eigler, D. Goldberg, and M. Walesky. Hormonal interactions in regulation of blood glucose. *Rec. Prog. Horm. Res.* 35:501–532, 1979.

32. Felig, P., and J. Wahren. Role of insulin and glucagon in the regulation of hepatic glucose production during exercise. *Diabetes* 28 (Suppl. 1):71–75, 1979.

33. Fell, R.D., S.E. Terblanche, W.W. Winder, and J.O. Holloszy. Adaptive responses of rats to prolonged treatment with epinephrine. *Am. J. Physiol.* 241:C55–C58, 1981.

34. Fitts, R.H., F.W. Booth, W.W. Winder, and J.O. Holloszy. Skeletal muscle respiratory capacity, endurance, and glycogen utilization. *Am. J. Physiol.* 228:1029–1033, 1975.

35. Forssmann, W.G., and S. Ito. Hepatocyte innervation in primates. *J. Cell Biol.* 74:299–313, 1977.

36. Galbo, H. *Hormonal and Metabolic Adaptation to Exercise.* New York, Thieme-Stratton, Inc., 1983.

37. Galbo, H., N.J. Christensen, and J.J. Host. Catecholamines and pancreatic hormones during autonomic blockade in exercising man. *Acta Physiol. Scand.* 101:428–437, 1977.

38. Galbo, H., and J.J. Holst. The influence of glucagon on hepatic glycogen mobilization in exercising rats. *Pflügers Arch.* 363:49–53, 1976.

39. Galbo, H., J.J. Holst, and N.J. Christensen. Glucagon and plasma catecholamine responses to graded and prolonged exercise in man. *J. Appl. Physiol.* 38:70–76, 1975.

40. Galbo, H., E.A. Richter, N.J. Christensen, and J.J. Holst. Sympathetic control of metabolic and hormonal responses to exercise in rats. *Acta Physiol. Scand.* 102:441–449, 1978.

41. Galbo, H., E.A. Richter, J.J. Holst, and N.J. Christensen. Diminished hormonal responses to exercise in trained rats. *J. Appl. Physiol.* 43:953–958, 1977.

42. Galbo, H., P. Saugmann, and E.A. Richter. Increased hepatic glycogen synthetase and decreased phosphorylase in trained rats. *Acta Physiol. Scand.* 107:269–272, 1979.

43. Garrison, J.C., and J.D. Wagner. Glucagon and the $Ca^{+2}$-linked hormones, angiotensin II, norepinephrine, and vasopressin stimulate the phosphorylation of distinct substrates in intact hepatocytes. *J. Biol. Chem.* 257:13135–13143, 1982.

44. Gollnick, P.D., R.G. Soule, A.W. Taylor, C. Williams, and C.D. Ianuzzo. Exercise-induced glycogenolysis and lipolysis in the rat: Hormonal influence. *Am. J. Physiol.* 219:729–733, 1970.

45. Haggendahl, H., L.H. Hartley, and B. Saltin. Arterial noradrenaline concentration during exercise in relation to the relative work levels. *Scand. J. Clin. Lab. Invest.* 26:337–342, 1970.

46. Hartley, L.H., J.W. Mason, R.O. Hogan, L.G. Jones, T.A. Kotchen, E.H. Mougey, F.E. Wherry, L.L. Pennington, and P.T. Ricketts. Multiple hormonal responses to graded exercise in relation to physical training. *J. Appl. Physiol.* 33:602–606, 1972.

47. Hartling, O.J., and J. Trap-Jensen. Haemodynamic and metabolic effects of α-adrenoceptor blockade with phentolamine at rest and during forearm exercise. *Clin. Sci.* 65:247–253, 1983.

48. Hartman, H., K. Beckh, and K. Jungermann. Direct control of glycogen metabolism in the perfused liver by the sympathetic innervation. *Eur. J. Biochem.* 123:521–526, 1982.

49. Hems, D.A., and P.D. Whitten. Control of hepatic glycogenolysis. *Physiol. Rev.* 60:1–50, 1980.

50. Hers. H.G., and L. Hue. Gluconeogenesis and related aspects of glycolysis. *Ann. Rev. Biochem.* 62:617–653, 1983.

51. Hickson, R.C, M.J. Rennie, R.K. Conlee, W.W. Winder, and J.O. Holloszy. Effects of increased plasma fatty acids on glycogen utilization and endurance. *J. Appl. Physiol.* 43:829–833, 1977.

52. Holloszy, J.O., and F.W. Booth. Biochemical adaptations to endurance exercise in muscle. *Ann. Rev. Physiol.* 38:273–291, 1976.

53. Holloszy, J.O., and E.F. Coyle. Adaptations of skeletal muscle to endurance exercise and their metabolic consequences. *J. Appl. Physiol.* 56:831–838, 1984.

54. Hultman, E., and L. Nilsson. Liver glycogen as a glucose-supplying source during exercise. In *Limiting Factors of Physical Performance*, J. Keul (Ed.). Stuttgart: Georg Thieme Publishers, 1973, pp. 179–189.

55. Huston, R.L., P.C. Weiser, G.L. Dohm, E.W. Askew, and J.B. Boyd. Effects of training, exercise and diet on muscle glycolysis and liver gluconeogenesis. *Life Sci.* 17:369–376, 1975.

56. Issekutz, B. The role of hypoinsulinemia in exercise metabolism. *Diabetes* 29:629–635, 1980.

57. Issekutz, B., and M. Vranic. Role of glucagon in regulation of glucose production in exercising dogs. *Am. J. Physiol.* 238:E13–E20, 1980.

58. Juhlin-Dannfelt, A.C., S.E. Terblanche, R.D. Fell, J.C. Young, and J.O. Holloszy. Effects of β-adrenergic receptor blockade on glycogenolysis during exercise. *J. Appl. Physiol.* 53:549–554, 1982.

59. Kasperek, G.J., G.L. Dohm, H.A. Barakat, P.H. Strausbauch, D.W. Barnes, and R.D. Snider. The role of lysosomes in exercise-induced hepatic protein loss. *Biochem. J.* 202:281–288, 1982.

60. Koivisto, V., R. Hendler, E. Nadel, and P. Felig. Influence of physical training on the fuel-hormone response to prolonged low-intensity exercise. *Metabolism* 31:192–197, 1982.

61. Kyrge, P.K., A.K. Eller, S.K. Timpmann, and E.K. Seppet. Role of glucocorticoids in the regulation of post-exercise glycogen replenishment and the mechanism of their action. *Fiziol. Zh. (USSR)* 68:1431–1437, 1982.

62. Lautt, W.W. Hepatic nerves: A review of their functions and effects. *Can. J. Physiol. Pharmacol.* 58:105–123, 1980.

63. Lin, T. Effects of treadmill exercise on plasma and urinary cyclic adenosine 3',5'-monophosphate. *Horm. Metab. Res.* 10:50–51, 1978.

64. Mikhail, Y., and A.L. Salek. Intrinsic nerve fibers in the liver parenchyma. *Anat. Rec.* 141:317–323, 1961.

65. Morgan, N.G., P.F. Blackmore, and J.H. Exton. Age related changes in the control of hepatic cyclic AMP levels by $\alpha_1$- and $\beta_2$-adrenergic receptors in male rats. *J. Biol. Chem.* 258:5103–5109, 1983.

66. Murphy, E., K. Coll, T.O. Rich, and J.R. Williamson. Hormal effects on calcium homeostasis in isolated hepatocytes. *J. Biol. Chem.* 255:6600–6608, 1980.

67. Naveri, H., S. Rehunen, K. Kuoppasalmi, T. Tulikoura, and M. Harkonen. Muscle metabolism during and after strenuous intermittant running. *Scand. J. Clin. Lab. Invest.* 38:329–336, 1978.

68. Nobin, A., H.G. Baumgarten, B. Falck, S. Ingemansson, E. Moghimzadeh, and E. Rosengren. Organization of the sympathetic innervation in liver tissue from monkey and man. *Cell Tissue Res.* 195:371–380, 1978.

69. Nobin, A., B. Falck, S. Ingemansson, J. Jarhult, and E. Rosengren. Organization and function of the sympathetic innervation of human liver. *Acta Physiol. Scand. (Suppl.)* 425:103–106, 1977.

70. Opie, L.H., and E.A. Newsholme. The activities of fructose 1,6-disphosphatase, phosphofructokinase and phosphoenolpyruvate carboxykinase in white muscle and red muscle. *Biochem J.* 103:391–399, 1967.

71. Pesce, A., R.H. McKay, F. Stolzenbach, R.D. Cahn, and N.O. Kaplan. Comparative enzymology of LDH. *J. Biol. Chem.* 239:1753–1761, 1964.

72. Pilkis, S.J., T.D. Chrisman, M. Raafat El-Maghrabi, A. Colosia, E. Fox, J. Pilkis, and T.H. Claus. The action of insulin on hepatic fructose 2, 6-bisphosphate metabolism. *J. Biol. Chem.* 258:1495–1503, 1983.

73. Poland, J.L., T.D. Myers, R.J. Witorsch, and R.B. Brandt. Plasma corticosterone and cardiac glycogen levels in rats after exercise. *Proc. Soc. Exp. Biol. Med.* 150:148–150, 1975.

74. Proost, C., H. Carton, and H. DeWulf. The $\alpha$-adrenergic control of rabbit liver glycogenolysis. *Biochem. Pharmacol.* 28:2187–2191, 1979.

75. Rennie, M.J., and J.O. Holloszy. Inhibition of glucose uptake and glycogenolysis by availability of oleate in a well-oxygenated perfused skeletal muscle. *Biochem. J.* 168:161–170, 1977.

76. Rennie, M.J., W.W. Winder, and J.O. Holloszy. A sparing effect of increased plasma fatty acids on muscle and liver glycogen content in the exercising rat. *Biochem J.* 156:647–655, 1976.

77. Richter, E.A., H. Galbo, and N.J. Christensen. Control of exercise-induced muscular glycogenolysis by adrenal medullary hormones in rats. *J. Appl. Physiol.* 50:21–26, 1981.

78. Richter, E.A., H. Galbo, J.J. Holst, and B. Sonne. Significance of glucagon for insulin secretion and hepatic glycogenolysis during exercise in rats. *Horm. Metab. Res.* 13:323–326, 1981.

79. Richter, E.A., H. Galbo, B. Sonne, J.J. Holst, and N.J. Christensen. Adrenal medullary control of muscular and hepatic glycogenolysis and of pancreatic hormonal secretion in exercising rats. *Acta Physiol. Scand.* 108:235–242, 1980.

80. Rizza, R.A., P.E. Cryer, M.W. Haymond, and J.E. Gerich. Adrenergic mechanisms for the effects of epinephrine on glucose production and clearance in man. *J. Clin. Invest.* 65:682–689, 1980.

81. Rosen, S.G., W.E. Clutter, S.D. Shah, J.P. Miller, D.B. Bier, and P.E. Cryer. Direct alpha-adrenergic stimulation of hepatic glucose production in human subjects. *Am. J. Physiol.* 245:E616–E626, 1983.

82. Sembrowich, W.L., C.D. Ianuzzo, C.W. Saubert, IV, R.E. Shepherd, and P.D. Gollnick. Substrate mobilization during prolonged exercise in 6-hydroxydopamine treated rats. *Pflügers Arch.* 349:57–62, 1974.

83. Shimazu, T., and A. Amakawa. Regulation of glycogen metabolism in liver by the autonomic nervous system. *Biochem. Biophys. Acta* 385:242–256, 1975.

84. Skaaring, P., and F. Bierring. On the intrinsic innervation of normal rat liver. *Cell Tissue Res.* 171:141–155, 1976.

85. Sonne, B., K.J. Mikines, and H. Galbo. Role of autonomic hepatic innervation for glucose turnover during running in rats. *Acta Physiol. Scand.* (in press).

86. Srere, P.A., Citrate synthase. *Methods Enzymol.* 13:3–5, 1969.

87. Studer, R.K., and A.B. Borle. Difference between male and female rats in the regulation of hepatic glycogenolysis. *J. Biol. Chem.* 257:7987–7993, 1982.

88. Studer, R.K., K.W. Snowdowne, and A.B. Borle. Regulation of hepatic glyco-genolysis by glucagon in male and female rats. *J. Biol. Chem.* 259:3596–3604, 1984.

89. Tanaka, H., and M. Shindo. Plasma cyclic adenosine-3',5'-monophosphate level during exercise in man. *Med. Sci. Sports* 11:89, 1979.

90. Thomas, A.P., J.S. Marks, K.E. Coll, and J.R. Williamson. Quantitation and early kinetics of inositol lipid changes induced by vasopressin in isolated and cultured hepatocytes. *J. Biol. Chem.* 258:5716–5725, 1983.

91. Tranzer, J.P., and H. Thoenen. An electron microscopic study of selective, acute degeneration of sympathetic nerve terminals after administration of 6-hydroxy-dopamine. *Experientia* 24:144–156, 1967.

92. Vaitkus, P., A. Sirek, K.H. Norwich, O.V. Sirek, R.H. Unger, and V. Harris. Rapid changes in hepatic glucose output after a pulse of growth hormone in dogs. *Am. J. Physiol.* 246:E14–E20, 1984.

93. Van de Werve, G., L. Hue, and H.G. Hers. Hormonal and ionic control of the glycogenolytic cascade in rat liver. *Biochem. J.* 162:135–142, 1977.

94. Wahren, J. Glucose turnover during exercise in healthy men and in patients with diabetes mellitus. *Diabetes* 28:82–88, 1979.

95. Wahren, J., P. Felig, and L. Hagenfeldt. Physical exercise and fuel homeostasis in diabetes mellitus. *Diabetologia* 14:213–222, 1978.

96. Winder, W.W., M.A. Beattie, and E.O. Fuller. Glycogenolytic rates and cAMP in livers of rats running at different treadmill speeds. *Am. J. Physiol.* 245:R353–R356, 1983.

97. Winder, W.W., M.A. Beattie, and R.T. Holman. Endurance training attenuates stress hormone responses to exercise in fasted rats. *Am. J. Physiol.* 243:R179–R184, 1982.

98. Winder, W.W., M.A. Beattie, C. Piquette, and R.T. Holman. Decrease in liver norepinephrine in response to exercise and hypoglycemia. *Am. J. Physiol.* 244:R845–R849, 1983.

99. Winder, W.W., J. Boullier, and R.D. Fell. Liver glycogenolysis during exercise without a significant increase in cAMP. *Am. J. Physiol.* 237:R147–R152, 1979.

100. Winder, W.W., E.O. Fuller, and R.K. Conlee. Adrenal hormones and liver cAMP in exercising rats—different modes of anesthesia. *J. Appl. Physiol.* 55:1634–1636, 1983.

101. Winder, W.W., J.M. Hagberg, R.C. Hickson, A.A. Ehsani, and J.A. McLane. Time course of sympathoadrenal adaptation to endurance exercise training in man. *J. Appl. Physiol.* 45:370–374, 1978.

102. Winder, W.W., R.C. Hickson, J.M. Hagberg, A.A. Ehsani, and J.A. McLane. Training-induced changes in hormonal and metabolic responses to submaximal exercise. *J. Appl. Physiol.* 46:766–771, 1979.

103. Winder, W.W., R.T. Holman, and S.J. Garhart. Effect of endurance training on liver cAMP response to prolonged submaximal exercise. *Am. J. Physiol.* 240:R330–R334, 1981.

104. Winder, W.W., V.M. Mitchell, and M.L. Terry. Sites of action of adrenal medullary hormones in fasted exercising rats. *7th International Congress of Endocrinology Abstracts*. New York: Elsevier, 1984, p. 1504.
105. Yamada, E. Some observations on the nerve terminal on the liver parenchymal cell of the mouse as revealed by electron microscopy. *Okajimas Folia Anat. Jpn.* 40:663–677, 1965.
106. Zawalich, W., S. Maturao, and P. Felig. Influence of physical training on insulin release and glucose utilization by islet cells and liver glucokinase activity in the rat. *Am. J. Physiol.* 243:464–469, 1982.

# Energetic Aspects of Skeletal Muscle Contraction: Implications of Fiber Types

JACK A. RALL, Ph.D.

Muscle is a machine that converts chemical free energy into mechanical force and work. Energy for muscular contraction is derived ultimately from metabolic oxidation of foodstuffs ingested from the environment. Skeletal muscles are composed of cells or fibers that are known to exhibit diverse functional, biochemical, and structural features. This diversification of fiber types is reflected in chemical energy utilization during and chemical energy replenishment resulting from muscular contraction.

Recently, a number of comprehensive reviews have appeared on the topic of muscle energetics [29, 68, 77]. In this review, basic concepts of muscle energetics are considered, predominantly from the viewpoint of energy output during muscular contraction in isolated skeletal muscle. The energetic implications of mammalian fiber types are evaluated. Finally, some consequences of basic muscle energetics in understanding locomotion are considered.

## EXPERIMENTAL APPROACHES TO THE STUDY OF MUSCLE ENERGETICS

The energetics of muscular contraction can be considered conceptually from two points of view. The first approach deals with the utilization of chemical energy by the contractile machinery during muscular contraction and relaxation. The second approach considers the aerobic and anaerobic metabolic processes replenishing utilized chemical energy. In the steady state, the rate of chemical energy utilization by the contractile machinery is equal to the rate of chemical energy replenishment by the metabolic machinery. Among the conventional chemical methods, those techniques that can be employed on living muscle involve measurement of substances that the muscle exchanges with the environment. Some examples include oxygen, carbon dioxide, lactate, glycogen, and fatty acids. Although these

The work conducted in my laboratory and cited in this chapter was supported in part by Public Health Service Grant AM-20792 and Research Career Development Award NS-00324.

techniques are nondestructive, they provide only indirect information about chemical reactions occurring within the muscle. More direct information can be derived from chemical analysis of the muscle itself. This approach involves rapid freezing of the muscle and subsequent fragmentation. Analysis can be made of the levels of high-energy phosphate (~P) compounds and various other chemical intermediates of metabolism. This technique provides direct information, but it is cumbersome and does not provide continuous temporal information.

An exciting new approach to the study of muscle chemistry in a nondestructive and direct manner involves the utilization of 31 phosphorous nuclear magnetic resonance spectroscopy ($^{31}P$ NMR) [71, 48]. With $^{31}P$ NMR it is possible to monitor the levels of ~P compounds in living, intact muscle during rest and contraction. However, the technique is quite insensitive and requires multiple collection periods and signal averaging. $^{31}P$ NMR has been successfully employed in the study of energetics in isolated amphibian [33] and mammalian [90] skeletal muscle, mammalian heart [47], and intact human skeletal muscle [24]. One unique application of $^{31}P$ NMR in muscle energetics relates to the direct measurement of reaction rates [49, 90].

Because chemical techniques of muscle energetics are either cumbersome or unable to follow adequately the time course of processes occurring during contraction, physical techniques have been developed that monitor changes in the muscle that can be correlated with chemical measurements. Some examples include measurement of pH, absorbance of cytochromes [74], fluorescence of mitochondrial nicotinamide adenine dinucleotide (NADH) [74], and heat production, the best developed. These techniques lack the specificity of the chemical techniques but have advantages in terms of temporal resolution. Measurement of muscle heat production allows the greatest temporal resolution but also possesses the least specificity.

In recent years, there has been an increasing interest in the application of a combination of techniques to the study of muscle energetics. Thus experiments have been performed comparing destructive measurements of ~P hydrolysis during contraction to heat production during contraction [29, 68] or to oxygen consumption and lactate production after contraction [77]. Despite the multitude of techniques employed for the study of muscle energetics, there is no technique currently available that can provide a continuous, direct measure of the time course of ~P hydrolysis during a single contraction. This deficiency has been a major impediment to understanding chemomechanical transduction during muscular contraction.

A fascinating variety of experimental preparations has been employed for the study of muscle energetics. The following enumeration is not meant to be exhaustive but rather to provide some impression of the scope of approaches to the study of muscle energetics. Starting from the most complex and integrative approach, experimental preparations include (1) whole body, (2) intact muscle, (3) muscle with isolated circulation (in situ), (4) isolated whole muscle, (5) isolated single muscle cell, (6) mechanically or chemically skinned muscle cell, (7) glycerinated muscle cell, and (8) isolated cellular components such as myofibrils, actomyosin, mitochondria, metabolic enzymes. All these preparations have contributed to our understanding of muscle energetics. Preparations 1–5 allow exploration of muscle energetics from the viewpoint of chemical energy utilization during contraction and chemical energy replenishment resulting from contraction. In preparation 6, the contractile machinery is intact and if substrate is supplied, ~P hydrolysis can be measured. But soluble enzymes and their substrates are lost from the cell after removal of the sarcolemma and thus the pathways for chemical energy provision are no longer intact. A choice of techniques and preparations depends upon one's point of view and the experimental problem to be addressed. This review concentrates on chemical energy utilization and the chemical energy requiring processes occurring during muscular contraction and relaxation. The preponderance of evidence is derived from chemical and physical approaches applied to isolated skeletal muscle.

## TIME COURSE AND AMOUNT OF CHEMICAL ENERGY UTILIZATION AND CHEMICAL ENERGY REPLENISHMENT IN ISOLATED SKELETAL MUSCLE

Isolated frog skeletal muscle provides the basis for understanding the fundamental aspects of the energetics of contraction. Why have frog skeletal muscles, especially the sartorius muscle, been so extensively studied? Because frog sartorius muscles are thin, they are able to remain viable outside the animal supported only by diffusion of oxygen from the incubation medium. Furthermore, the muscles function normally at 0°C. This point is important for two reasons. First, the muscle contracts 8 to 10 times more slowly at 0°C than at 20°C and thus the temporal resolution of the mechanical and energetic measurements is greatly enhanced at the lower temperature. But most important, at 0°C in frog skeletal muscle there is a complete separation of chemical energy utilization during contraction (due to so-called initial processes) from chemical energy replenishment which occurs after contraction (due to so-called recovery processes). It is therefore possible to study either initial or recovery processes in isolation. This is generally not possible in mammalian skeletal muscle and impossible in heart muscle. Nonetheless, it has become apparent that frog skeletal muscles have certain disadvantages. They seem to vary in performance with time of year, and different batches of frogs can exhibit somewhat different metabolic properties. These facts can be galling and increase experimental variability. Mammalian (mouse) skeletal muscles provide more reproducible results [25] but, unfortunately, do not exhibit a complete separation of initial and recovery processes.

The first technique to be extensively developed for the study of skeletal muscle energetics was the measurement of muscle heat production, i.e., the myothermic technique. This approach was champoined by A.V. Hill over a period of more than 50 years. Hill's viewpoint was predominantly physical and phenomenological rather than chemical and mechanistic. The myothermic technique is nondestructive and allows continuous measurement of the time course of energy liberation (as heat plus work, H + W) during and after contraction with a resolution in the 10 to 20 msec range. Furthermore, because of its nonspecificity, it provides a thermodynamic framework into which all models of muscle contraction must ultimately fit. But it is this nonspecificity that is also the major disadvantage of this approach for certain applications. Thus any reaction that produces heat, that is, exothermic, or absorbs heat, that is, endothermic, will contribute to the heat record. Thermoneutral reactions will go undetected. Despite the limitation, the results of myothermic investigations provide an insightful starting point for the understanding of skeletal muscle energetics.

Energetics of isolated frog skeletal muscle are considered when the muscle is at rest, during contraction, and after contraction. In resting skeletal muscle, as in other tissues, there is a continuous expenditure of metabolic energy to maintain cellular functions. Of the resting energy liberation a significant fraction can be attributed to (1) maintenance of ion gradients across membranes (sarcolemma and sarcoplasmic reticulum, SR) [75], and (2) residual actomyosin interaction [84]. In frog skeletal muscle at 20°C, the resting rate of heat production is $11 \text{ mJ·g}^{-1}\text{·min}^{-1}$ [22]. Also resting oxygen consumption is $22 \text{ nmol O}_2\text{·g}^{-1}\text{·min}^{-1}$ ([84] value corrected from 22.8 to 20°C using a $Q_{10}$ of 2.01). The ratio of heat production to oxygen consumption is consistent with the interpretation that resting frog sartorius muscle at 20°C is metabolizing carbohydrate. Resting oxygen consumption at 0°C is reported to be $2.7 \text{ nmol O}_2\text{·g}^{-1}\text{·min}^{-1}$ [84]. This would be equivalent to a resting heat production of $1.35 \text{ mJ·g}^{-1}\text{·min}^{-1}$ at 0°C. The resting heat production can be increased substantially by various experimental manipulations including increasing extracellular $K^+$

concentration (the Solandt effect [111]) and passive stretch (the Feng effect [42]). Curiously, not all skeletal muscles exhibit increased resting metabolism with passive stretch [22]. It has been proposed that the increase in resting metabolism is due to an increase in intracellular free $Ca^{2+}$ which then stimulates the SR $Ca^{2+}$ adenosine triphosphatase (ATPase) [22]. This interpretation is supported by direct measurements of intracellular free $Ca^{2+}$ activity in isolated single cells that have been stretched or exposed to increased $K^+$ concentration [110].

If an isolated frog sartorius muscle at a sarcomere length of 2.2 μm is stimulated at 0°C to produce a fused isometric tetanus, a record similar to that shown in Figure 1 would be observed. In this figure

FIGURE 1

*Semischematic representations of isometric tetanus force and energy liberation versus time during and after a 10-s tetanus at 0°C in isolated frog skeletal muscle. Results during contraction from D. Burchfield and J. Rall, unpublished observations. Results during recovery plotted as a single exponential with time constant of 13 min [80] and with an amplitude approximately equal to initial liberation of energy. Note difference in time bases for initial and recovery processes.*

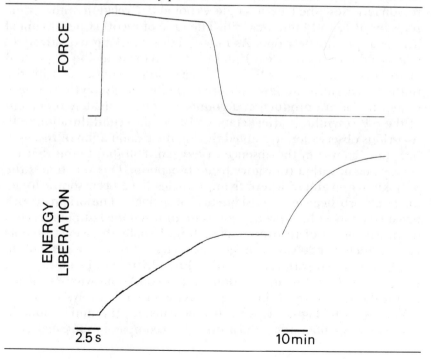

2.5 s          10 min

tetanus force and amount of energy (H + W) are both plotted versus time after the beginning of stimulation. Stimulus duration is 10 seconds. In this contraction, external work production is by definition zero, and the myothermal record represents essentially the time course of muscle heat production with a small correction applied for internal work production during force development. Experiments of this type were first done many years ago by Hill [58]. There are a number of important points to be gleaned from Figure 1. First, the energy liberation occurs in two distinct, nonoverlapping phases. The first phase occurs during contraction and relaxation and has been termed the initial heat. The second phase, occurring after contraction and on a much slower time scale is called recovery heat. Weizsacker [120], in Hill's laboratory, demonstrated that recovery heat but not initial heat was dependent on the presence of oxygen. Thus removal of oxygen from the system did not alter force production or the initial heat, indicating that these processes are not oxidative. On the contrary, recovery heat was greatly diminished in the absence of oxygen, i.e., in $N_2$, but not entirely eliminated. It is now known that recovery heat parallels oxygen consumption [65, 66] and the time course of resynthesis of ~P used during contraction [35]. More than 30 minutes is required in frog skeletal muscle at 0°C after a tetanus for recovery to be completed. The time course of recovery metabolism can be reasonably described by a single exponential relation with a time constant of 12 to 14 minutes [80]. The ratio of recovery heat to initial heat is approximately one. As noted above, blocking oxidative metabolism depresses recovery heat production to about 5 to 20 percent of the original values [20]. This observation is consistent with the finding that substrate level phosphorylation in glycolysis as represented by lactate production accounts for approximately 6 percent of the ~P resynthesis after tetani of 10- to 40-second duration [80]. A curious observation was noted during the examination of recovery heat time course in the absence of oxygen. Hill [63] found that recovery began with a transitory heat absorption. This situation is the only known example where living muscles have been shown to actually absorb heat as a consequence of activity. The origin of this negative delayed heat production is unknown. One last point relates to measurement of recovery metabolism. Usually these experiments are conducted at 20°C where the time course of recovery metabolism can be measured with less technical difficulty due to its more rapid time course. Experiments are done under conditions where contraction is thought to result in a step increase in ~P hydrolysis [85].

Returning to Figure 1, we can now consider the initial, nonoxidative, energy liberation which directly accompanies muscular contraction and relaxation. Note that the rate of energy liberation (slope of energy liberation versus time relation) reaches its maximum value early in the tetanus. In fact the maximum value actually occurs before force development begins [61]. After approximately 5 seconds of stimulation, the rate of energy liberation levels off to a steady rate known as stable maintenance heat rate. This steady rate of energy liberation in frog sartorius muscle at 0°C is about 10 to 15 $mJ \cdot g^{-1} \cdot s^{-1}$ depending on species of frog [68]. Comparing these numbers to the resting heat rate ($1.35 \, mJ \cdot g^{-1} \cdot min^{-1}$), one can conclude that stimulation results in an approximate 400- to 700-fold increase in the steady rate of energy liberation by the muscle. Stated in another way, maintenance of maximum steady force requires an expenditure of energy per unit time that is 400 to 700 times the energy expenditure to maintain the resting state. If the temperature of the muscle is increased from 0 to 10°C, both the resting heat rate and the steady rate of energy liberation during an isometric tetanus increase by greater than fourfold [84, 14]. Maximum tetanus force increases by 45 percent under these conditions. The temperature sensitivity of the steady rate of energy liberation appears to be twice as great in the 0–10°C range as in the 10–20°C range. The steady rate of energy liberation is fundamental in the energetic characterization of different muscles. Besides being sensitive to temperature, the steady rate of energy liberation is sensitive to changes in muscle length and to the amount of force developed during a tetanus.

How does energy liberation during contraction relate to ~P hydrolysis? This is an important topic that has attracted considerable interest and effort during the past 15 years. By way of introduction, consider the observed chemical changes due to repeated twitches in isolated frog sartorius muscle at 0°C with aerobic and anaerobic metabolism blocked [18]. Phosphocreatine (PC) content decreases in a linear fashion with respect to the number of twitches. The decrease represents approximately 0.9 percent of the PC content hydrolyzed per twitch, or $0.009 \, \mu mol \, C_T^{-1}$ (total creatine, $C_T$, is often employed as a measure of muscle mass) which, in this case, converts to $0.3 \, \mu mol \cdot g^{-1}$ (wet weight). Thus frog sartorius muscle contains enough PC for about 100 twitches. But the remarkable observation in this experiment is that the adenosine triphosphate (ATP) content of the muscle is unaltered with contraction. This fact caused great consternation for those scientists during the 1950s who were attempting to prove directly that ATP was the primary fuel for muscular contraction. We now know that the ATP content of the muscle is exceedingly well buffered at the expense of PC. PC is almost completely expended with no significant depletion of ATP content. ATP, of course, is the primary fuel for biological processses. The hydrolysis of ATP can be written:

$$ATP + H_2O \rightarrow ADP + Pi \tag{1}$$

Pi is inorganic phosphate; ADP, adenosine diphosphate. The decrease in ATP is buffered by a near equilibrium reaction catalyzed by creatine phosphokinase (CPK):

$$ADP + PC \rightleftharpoons ATP + C \tag{2}$$

Thus the net reaction is:

$$PC \rightleftharpoons C + Pi \tag{3}$$

The fact that the CPK catalyzed reaction is reversible indicates that during recovery resynthesized ATP can replenish the depleted PC pool. Since the content of ATP in a resting frog sartorius muscle at 0°C is approximately 4 $\mu$mol·g$^{-1}$ (wet weight) [77], there is enough ATP in a muscle to support approximately 13 twitches.

The basic relation between energy liberation and chemical change during contraction is dictated by the first law of thermodynamics. This law of energy conservation states that the energy output as heat plus work (H + W) is equal to the summation of the extents ($\xi$, in moles) of all reactions occurring during contraction times the heat of each reaction (the molar enthalpy change, $\Delta H_i$) or:

$$\text{energy liberation} = H + W = \sum_i \Delta H_i \xi_i \tag{4}$$

(Parenthetically, since muscular contraction occurs at essentially constant volume and constant atmospheric pressure, energy liberation equals enthalpy liberation.) This equation forms the basis for the energy balance experiment. In this type of experiment, energy liberation during contraction is measured as H + W produced, the extents of expected chemical reactions are also measured and molar enthalpy changes are determined from direct calorimetry of reaction components under conditions thought to exist in the cell. Wilkie [127] performed energy balance experiments on frog sartorius muscles at 0°C. Aerobic and anaerobic recovery metabolism was blocked. Under these conditions, the net chemical reaction should be PC hydrolysis. Inhibiting recovery metabolism allowed the amount of energy liberation and chemical change due to contraction to be measured on the same muscles. The unstimulated sartorius muscle from the other leg of the frog was employed as the control for chemical analyzes. Isometric and isotonic twitches and isometric tetani were examined. Within the accuracy of the experiments, energy liberation was found to be directly proportional to the extent of PC hydrolysis. If PC hydrolysis was the only net reaction occurring, then equation 4 predicts that the proportionality constant relating H + W to PC should represent the molar enthalpy change for PC hydrolysis ($\Delta H_{PC}$) under the conditions existing in the cell. $\Delta H_{PC}$ was 46.4 kJ·mol$^{-1}$. This value is significantly greater than the value of kJ·mol$^{-1}$ recently determined by calorimetry for the hydrolysis of PC under cellular conditions [29]. Thus more energy is liberated as a result of muscular contraction than can be attributed to PC hydrolysis alone.

The question of energy balance during the time course of a single contraction of unpoisoned frog sartorius muscle at 0°C has been carefully studied [30, 69]. Energy liberation is measured in a single isometric tetanus, and in parallel experiments chemical changes are measured in muscles frozen at various times during the tetanus. Figure 2 displays an example of such an experiment where energy (en-

FIGURE 2

*Plot of energy (enthalpy) production and chemical change versus isometric tetanus duration in frog sartorius muscle at 0°C. The solid curve shows observed energy (enthalpy, H + W) produced plotted as mJ·μmol$^{-1}$ of total creatine. The broken curve shows net chemical change (PC split). The broken curve has been multiplied by the molar enthalpy change ($-34$ kJ·mol$^{-1}$) for PC dephosphorylation. Error bars represent 1 SEM.*
SOURCE: Reprinted with permission from Homsher, E., et al. The time course of energy balance in an isometric tetanus. *J. Gen. Physiol.* 73:553–567, 1979.

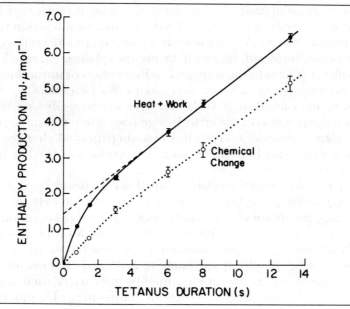

thalpy) liberation as H + W and chemical change ($\Delta\sim P$) are plotted versus tetanus duration (up to 13 seconds). It is important to note that no significant recovery metabolism occurs during contractions of up to 20 seconds duration in frog skeletal muscle at 0°C [80]. In Figure 2, $\Delta\sim P$ is converted to units of energy liberation using known values for the molar enthalpy changes. It is obvious that more energy is liberated than can be explained by $\Delta\sim P$. Within this context, two further points are apparent. First, the extra or unexplained energy is nearly completely evolved during the first 5 seconds of contraction at 0°C. After 5 seconds of stimulation, the energy output is completely explained by $\Delta\sim P$ (H + W parallels $\Delta\sim P$). Thus the steady rate of energy liberation during a tetanus is a faithful measure of the rate of $\sim P$ hydrolysis by the muscle. Second, when a muscle is allowed to shorten during stimulation, the unexplained energy increases above that observed in the isometric state [101]. Thus the amount and time course of unexplained energy is dependent on the conditions of the contraction.

What is (are) the source(s) of the unexplained energy? Potential sources have been discussed by others [29, 68], and only three hypotheses are briefly noted here. One hypothesis that has been eliminated is that there is an unknown $\sim P$ compound whose hydrolysis is contributing to the observed energy output. This theory is wrong because the measured increase in Pi is equal to the measured decrease in PC [29]. Thus all $\sim P$ compounds contributing to energy output are accounted for. The two currently pursued hypotheses have the same conceptual basis: during the time frame of the energy balance experiment, only one portion of a cyclic, unknown reaction has been completed [29, 68, 77]. In the steady state, or after all cyclic reactions have been completed, there will be no unexplained energy. The first hypothesis relates to the transient redistribution of intracellular $Ca^{2+}$ and accompanying exothermic reactions (for example, $Ca^{2+}$ binding to proteins) caused by stimulation. The second deals with the transient redistribution of the cross-bridge population throughout a multiple step cross-bridge cycle and resulting thermal changes during contraction. Both hypotheses seem promising, but further tests are necessary.

When considering the relationship of energy liberation during contraction to chemical changes in frog sartorius muscle at 0°C, the following points should be emphasized: (1) energy liberation after a single contraction-relaxation cycle or many cycles is proportional to $\Delta\sim P$, (2) during a single contraction the steady rate of energy liberation can be completely attributed to $\Delta\sim P$, and (3) transient changes in the rate of energy liberation cannot be interpreted unambiguously in terms of known chemical reactions. Thus energy liberation can be interpreted in terms of $\Delta\sim P$ after a complete contraction-relaxation cycle or during a maintained isometric contraction. Within these limits, the myothermic technique provides important information about $\sim P$ hydrolysis occurring during muscular contraction in a way that is nondestructive. This feature allows a wide variety of contractions to be studied in the same muscle.

## SYSTEMS UTILIZING HIGH-ENERGY PHOSPHATE DURING SKELETAL MUSCLE CONTRACTION AND RELAXATION

Since the steady rate of energy liberation is due completely to $\Delta\sim P$, this means that the rate of $\sim P$ hydrolysis, along with the rate of energy liberation, increases 400- to 700-fold during a steady isometric tetanus. What ATP-utilizing reactions can explain this dramatic increase in energy liberation and $\sim P$ hydrolysis during muscular contraction? During a contraction-relaxation cycle, three major ATP-utilizing systems are active: (1) actomyosin ATPase, (2) $Ca^{2+}$ transport ATPase of the SR, and (3) $Na^+$ - $K^+$ - ATPase of the sarcolemma. The $Na^+$ - $K^+$ - ATPase is not likely to make a significant contribution to energy liberation during contraction because muscles soaked in strongly hypertonic solutions (4 times normal tonicity) still generate and propagate action potentials but do not produce force or liberate energy [109].

To quantitate the contribution of actomyosin ATPase and $Ca^{2+}$ ATPase to the chemical energy utilization, the two processes must be separated. A convenient approach to this problem can be derived from consideration of the sliding-filament model of muscle contraction and the length-tension diagram as elucidated by A.F. Huxley and colleagues [53]. Maximum isometric force development occurs at sarcomere lengths of 2.0–2.25 $\mu$m where overlap of filaments is maximum. If a resting muscle is stretched to sarcomere lengths greater than 3.65 $\mu$mm and then stimulated, force generation is greatly depressed since myofilament overlap is near zero. Thus actomyosin ATPase is inhibited by physically preventing actin interaction with myosin. Nonetheless, $\sim P$ hydrolysis and energy liberation are not zero in muscles stimulated at a sarcomere length of approximately 3.6 $\mu$m [70, 73, 106, 109]. Furthermore, the amount of $\sim P$ hydrolyzed and energy liberated in isometric twitches and tetani decreases in a linear fashion as the muscle is stretched by increments from 2.2 $\mu$m to 3.7 $\mu$m [70]. This decrease in chemical energy utilization is due to a decrease in myofilament overlap and thus to suppression of the actomyosin ATPase. Figure 3 shows an example of an experiment done on frog semitendinosus muscle at 0°C. Energy liberation in an isometric twitch is plotted versus peak force development. Peak force

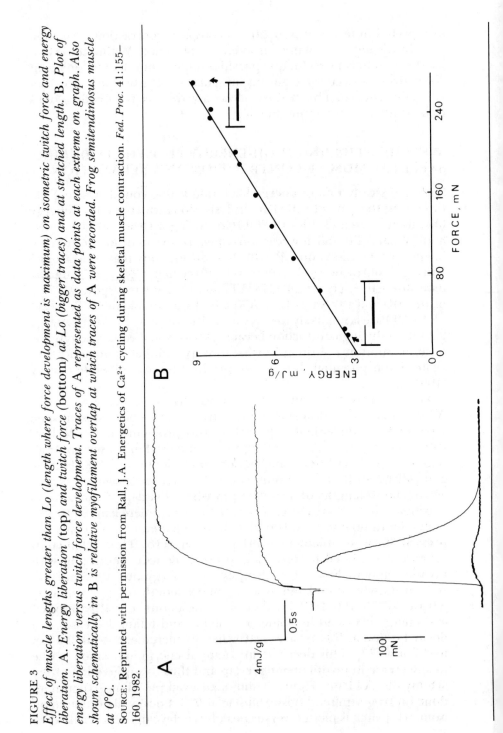

FIGURE 3

*Effect of muscle lengths greater than Lo (length where force development is maximum) on isometric twitch force and energy liberation. A. Energy liberation (top) and twitch force (bottom) at Lo (bigger traces) and at stretched length. B. Plot of energy liberation versus twitch force development. Traces of A represented as data points at each extreme on graph. Also shown schematically in B is relative myofilament overlap at which traces of A were recorded. Frog semitendinosus muscle at 0°C.*

SOURCE: Reprinted with permission from Rall, J.A. Energetics of $Ca^{2+}$ cycling during skeletal muscle contraction. *Fed. Proc.* 41:155–160, 1982.

development was manipulated by stretching the muscle by increments from a sarcomere length of 2.2 μm to one of 3.8 μm. Frog semitendinosus muscle is an especially convenient preparation for this type of experiment since it can be stretched to long sarcomere lengths without damage. In isometric twitches and tetanic contractions, the energy liberation and ~P hydrolysis at minimum myofilament overlap ranges from about 30 to 40 percent of the respective values at maximum filament overlap where force is also maximum [70, 73, 106, 109].

How are these results to be interpreted? Since the action potential is not inhibited when a muscle is stretched [106], since $Ca^{2+}$ is released into the sarcoplasm in stretched muscles [12], and since actomyosin ATPase is greatly inhibited, the chemical energy utilization at minimum myofilament overlap probably represents the activity of the $Ca^{2+}$ ATPase of the SR. Further evidence supporting this hypothesis has been reviewed [100]. An important point is that the fraction of chemical energy expenditure at minimum myofilament overlap is similar in a twitch and in tetani of varying duration [70, 109]. This result implies that during maintained muscle stimulation, $Ca^{2+}$ continually cycles from and eventually back to the SR at the expense of ~P. In a maintained isometric tetanus, the SR $Ca^{2+}$ ATPase represents approximately 30 percent of the steady rate of energy liberation at 2.2 μm [70]. This approximation depends on the assumption that the amount of $Ca^{2+}$ released and cycled during a contraction is not a function of sarcomere length in the range of 2.2 to 3.8 μm. Though indirect evidence supports this contention [100], other evidence suggests that $Ca^{2+}$ release may be decreased when muscles are activated at long sarcomere lengths [12]. The important result from an energetic point of view is that at least 30 percent of the ~P used during contraction developing maximum force is probably related to $Ca^{2+}$ movements and not to actomyosin interaction. Thus, approximately 70 percent of the chemical energy utilization during contraction can be attributed to actomyosin ATPase and thus to cross-bridge cycling.

## ENERGETICS OF MUSCLES THAT SHORTEN OR ARE STRETCHED DURING CONTRACTION

In the 1920s Fenn [43, 44] conducted what are considered to be among the most important experiments in the history of muscle energetics. To appreciate their significance, it is helpful to understand the prevailing view of muscular contraction in the 1920s. The viscoelastic theory held that after a stimulus a muscle acted like a stretched spring in a viscous medium. The stimulated muscle released an amount of chemical energy in an all-or-none fashion that could appear either as heat or as work. Because the amount of this energy that could be converted into work depended on the loading conditions, the work should bear no relation to the total energy liberated. Most important, this theory predicted that the amount of energy liberated by an isotonic contraction would be independent of work or load and be equivalent to the energy liberated in an isometric contraction. Fenn's results were inconsistent with this theory and proved unequivocally that the viscoelastic theory of muscle contraction was invalid. Using frog sartorius muscles at low temperatures, Fenn found that whenever a muscle shortened after stimulation and did work, extra energy was mobilized that did not appear in the isometric contraction. Thus a muscle shortening and doing work utilizes more energy than an isometric contraction of equivalent duration. This phenomenon is known as the Fenn effect. Similar results were found by measuring ~P hydrolysis and energy liberation in frog skeletal muscles at 0°C [17]. Interestingly, the rate of ~P hydrolysis in a maximally working contraction of frog sartorius muscle can be up to 4 times greater than the steady rate of ~P hydrolysis in an isometric tetanus [78, 79]. Thus chemical energy utilization during a maximally working contraction is more than 1,000 times greater than the value observed for an equivalent period of time at rest.

Results from other experiments under other conditions are considerably more variable than expected from Fenn's results [99]. Some of the reasons for this variability and a unifying approach to consideration of the Fenn effect are considered elsewhere [99]. But the quantitative details are not the most important aspect of the experiments. The most important aspect of Fenn's experiments and the reason that these results are still of significance today is that Fenn's experiments proved that there is some internal feedback in active muscles whereby chemical energy utilization is regulated by the mechanical conditions during the contractile process. Thus these results must be explained in molecular terms by any credible model of muscular contraction.

It is well known that the metabolic cost of performing negative work is less than that for positive work. Less oxygen is consumed descending stairs (negative work) than ascending stairs (positive work). In the latter case, muscles do work but in the former case work is done on the muscles. Energetic aspects of negative work have been investigated in isolated frog sartorius muscles at 0°C by stretching the muscle during contraction [1, 44]. The muscle responds by resisting the stretch with a force that is greater than the maximum isometric force development. This resistance to stretch is dependent on the velocity of stretch and is shown in Figure 4 by the characteristic force-velocity relation for muscle extended to the range of negative

FIGURE 4
*Mechanical and energetic properties of frog skeletal muscles that have shortened or are stretched. a. Plot of relative shortening velocity versus relative load. b. Force developed during shortening plotted versus power output [62] and versus mechanical efficiency [62]. c. Force developed versus velocity of shortening or lengthening in the region of maximum isometric force development [5].*
SOURCE: Reprinted with permission from White, D.C.S. Muscle mechanics. In *Mechanics and Energetics of Animal Locomotion,* edited by R. Alexander and G. Goldspink. London: Chapman and Hall, 1977, pp. 23–56.

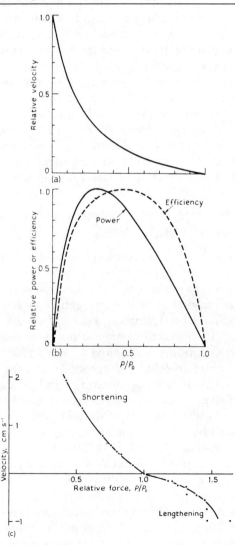

velocities. When muscle is stretched during contraction both energy liberation and ~P hydrolysis are substantially decreased compared to an isometric contraction [1, 28, 44]. In fact, the rate of ~P hydrolysis can be reduced to 25 percent of the rate during an isometric contraction. These results have been interpreted as demonstrating that the rate of ~P hydrolysis is inhibited by stretch during contraction. The alternative hypothesis is that stretch causes a reversal of the reactions utilizing ATP [64]. Evidence is lacking to support this hypothesis.

Thus stretch of a muscle during contraction apparently is resisted by attached cross-bridges and the extra force suppresses the normal cross-bridge cycle leading to diminished ~P hydrolysis and energy output. A noteworthy feature of the stretch results is that if the rate of ~P hydrolysis during stretch can be suppressed by 75 percent of the isometric rate and if actomyosin ATPase represents 70 percent of the isometric ~P hydrolysis rate stretch can cause complete suppression of actomyosin ATPase. From the viewpoint of whole body locomotion, muscular contractions with lengthening represent a normal physiologic response during limb movements. This mode of contraction leads to large force development and requires considerably less ATP than isometric or isotonic contractions.

## ECONOMY OF ISOMETRIC CONTRACTION: IMPLICATIONS OF FIBER TYPES

The generation of force in an isometric contraction results in a dramatic increase in energy expenditure by the muscle compared to the resting state. The relationship of force generation to metabolic cost of contraction is important in the energetic characterization of different muscles. Since, by definition, no external work is performed during an isometric contraction, one cannot determine its efficiency. Instead, the term economy is employed to describe the relationship between the isometric mechanical response and the energetic cost. Operationally, economy can be measured in different ways. For a tetanus where force is maintained, economy can be determined as the ratio of maximum force development per cross-sectional area divided by the steady rate of chemical energy expenditure per gram of muscle ($kN \cdot m^{-2} \div mJ \cdot g^{-1} \cdot s^{-1}$) [13]. Thus for a given tetanus force, economy is inversely proportional to the steady rate of energy expenditure. Rate of energy expenditure might be measured as rate of heat production or rate of ~P hydrolysis. Application of this definition becomes difficult when (1) tetanus force is not maintained at a constant level, (2) tetanus duration is not long enough to reach a steady state of energy expenditure, or (3) recovery processes are used as the determinant of energetic cost of contraction. Thus a second way to measure economy is as the ratio of the time integral of force production (area enclosed by the mechanical response trace) per cross-sectional area to the amount of chemical energy used during contraction or replenished during recovery per gram of muscle ($kN \cdot s \cdot m^{-2} \div mJ \cdot g^{-1}$) [79]. This measurement accounts for maximum force development, contraction duration, and force maintenance (degree of fatigue).

The economy of muscle contraction varies remarkably across the animal kingdom. Using the frog sartorius muscle as a reference, economy of contraction is 40 times greater in tortoise skeletal muscle [129] and 100 times greater in mammalian smooth muscle [108]. An especially noteworthy example is the anterior byssus retractor muscle (ABRM) of bivalve molluscs. Depending on the mode of stimulation, the ABRM can maintain isometric force with two distinctly different economies. During phasic contraction, economy is 250 times greater than for frog sartorius muscle [7]; and during tonic, or catch, contraction, economy is 2,750 times greater than for frog muscle [8]. Thus for maintenance of comparable force, the frog sartorius would utilize as much energy in 1 second as the ABRM would utilize in 46 minutes in catch. The other intriguing aspect of the ABRM is that the economy is variable and under neural control. Finally, there is, in general, an inverse correlation observed between the rate of force development or velocity of shortening and the economy of force maintenance. Muscles possessing a high economy contract slowly [105].

What are the factors that determine the economy of contraction? Ruegg [105] has written an insightful review concerning this topic. Since one measure of economy is the ratio of force production per cross-sectional area to the steady rate of energy utilization per gram of muscle, it is logical to consider factors that determine these parameters. The steady rate of energy liberation, as previously discussed, is determined by the sum of the cellular actomyosin ATPase (70%) and the SR $Ca^{2+}$ ATPase (30%) rates. The cellular actomyosin ATPase rate depends on the actomyosin content of the cells. The actomyosin content is porportional to the number of filaments per cross-sectional area. Barany [10] has shown that the rate of hydrolysis of ATP per gram of isolated actomyosin (specific actomyosin ATPase rate) derived from different muscles varies by over 200-fold. Furthermore, there is a direct correlation between the specific actomyosin ATPase rate and the maximum velocity of muscle shortening. Thus slower contracting muscles have lower specific actomyosin ATPase rates. This variation in ATPase rate was further shown to be a property of the myosin molecule and not the actin molecule. There has been much interest in the molecular causes of polymorphism among myosin molecules and the relationship of myosin polymorphism to muscle function [97].

Approximately one-third of the steady rate of energy liberation during muscular contraction can be attributed to the SR $Ca^{2+}$ ATPase. It seems intuitively reasonable to assume that there will be a matching of actomyosin ATPase rate with $Ca^{2+}$ ATPase rate. Thus it would be pointless to have a fast contracting muscle with a high actomyosin ATPase rate that relaxed slowly. This muscle would not be able to contract rapidly a second time until it relaxed slowly from the first contraction. Thus much of the advantage of the increased speed of response would be lost. In general, the ratio of time to peak force development to relaxation time is fairly constant for different muscles [105]. The SR $Ca^{2+}$ ATPase rate depends upon (1) the surface area of the SR, (2) the denisty of $Ca^{2+}$ transport sites in the SR, and (3) the specific activity of the $Ca^{2+}$ ATPase of the SR. The $Ca^{2+}$ ATPase activity of isolated SR vesicles is greater in mammalian fast-twitch than slow-twitch skeletal muscle [56]. Part of this difference is due to the lower concentration of $Ca^{2+}$ transport sites in the SR of slow muscles [32]. Nonetheless, there do appear to be distinct isoenzymes of the $Ca^{2+}$ ATPase, with the fast-twitch muscle possessing a faster $Ca^{2+}$ ATPase [32]. Also, the surface area of the terminal cisternae of the SR is greater in fast contracting than in slow contracting skeletal muscle [38]. Curiously, the total SR surface area is not dependent on fiber type [38]. Thus a high specific actomyosin ATPase activity could be matched by an increase in the quantity and quality of $Ca^{2+}$ transporting sites in the SR. The steady rate of energy liberation per gram of muscle ($\dot{E}$) during an isometric tetanus therefore is proportional to the specific actomyosin ATPase activity (AM ATPase), the actomyosin content (AM content), the specific SR $Ca^{2+}$ ATPase ($Ca^{2+}$ ATPase) and the number of $Ca^{2+}$ transporting sites in the SR ($Ca^{2+}$ sites):

$$\dot{E} \propto (AM \text{ content, } AM \text{ ATPase, } Ca^{2+} \text{ ATPase, } Ca^{2+} \text{ sites}) \qquad (5)$$

Although maximum force development per cross-sectional area ($F_{max}$) is similar in vertebrate skeletal muscle, that is, about 200 to 350 $kN \cdot m^{-2}$, it can vary considerably across the animal kingdom. For example, 800 $kN \cdot m^{-2}$ has been reported for crayfish muscle [130]. What factors determine the maximum force generating capacity of a muscle? The first factor is the actomyosin content per cross-sectional area, that is, the number of cross-bridges or force generating sites per cross-sectional area. The second factor is the length of the myofilaments. For the same number of myosin molecules, longer filaments have more cross-bridges in parallel and allow more force to be generated per cross-sectional area [72, 105]. Crayfish muscle has sarcomeres that are 4 times longer than in vertebrate skeletal muscle [130]. This discussion assumes that the force generated per cross-bridge is invariant across the animal kingdom, an assumption that has yet to be tested. Therefore, maximum force development (Fmax) is proportional to actomyosin content and myofilament length:

$$\text{Fmax} \propto (\text{AM content, myofilament length}) \qquad (6)$$

Since the economy of an isometric tetanus is the ratio of Fmax to $\dot{\text{E}}$:

$$\text{Economy} \propto (\text{myofilament length, AM ATPase}^{-1},$$
$$\text{Ca}^{2+} \text{ ATPase}^{-1}, \text{Ca}^{2+} \text{ sites}^{-1}) \qquad (7)$$

In vertebrate skeletal muscle where myofilament length is essentially invariant, economy is inversely proportional to specific actomyosin and $\text{Ca}^{2+}$ SR ATPase activity.

Economy is related to power output of the muscle. Power is the rate of doing work and is equal to force times velocity of shortening. The maximum velocity of shortening per muscle length (Vmax) is proportional to the specific actomyosin ATPase activity or cross-bridge cycling rate [10] and inversely proportional to myofilament length [105], i.e., Vmax $\propto$ (AM ATPase, myofilament length $^{-1}$). Consider two muscles of equal length. For the same rate of relative sliding of myofilaments, the muscle with shorter myofilaments, i.e., more sarcomeres in series, will shorten farther per unit time. Therefore maximum power output per gram of muscle ($\cong$ 0.1 Fmax·Vmax, see next section) is proportional to actomyosin content and specific actomyosin ATPase rate:

$$\text{Maximum power output} \propto (\text{AM content, AM ATPase}) \qquad (8)$$

The higher the actomyosin content or specific actomyosin ATPase activity, the higher the maximum power output. Comparing equation 8 for power output to 7 for economy, it is clear that there must be a compromise between economy and power output per gram of muscle. It is not possible to have a high economy of force maintenance and also a high rate of work production in a muscle of homogeneous cell type. The ABRM has found one solution to this problem by neurally modulating economy and thus power output.

It is now well established that mammalian skeletal muscle is composed of three more or less distinct fiber types [96]. These fiber types have been conveniently designated as slow twitch, oxidative (SO), fast twitch, oxidative, glycolytic (FOG), and fast twitch, glycolytic (FG). It was once thought that each fiber type was composed of a homogeneous population of cells, but recent studies of the metabolic properties of single cells has shown this to be incorrect [37, 41, 61, 112].

There is a wide range of enzyme activities within each class of cells. The current belief is that among muscle fibers there exists a spectrum of coordinated enzyme activities. Mammalian skeletal muscles are composed almost entirely of twitch type cells, that is, cells that respond to a single stimulus with a propagated action potential and twitch mechanical response. Even so, some tonic cells, that is, cells that do not respond mechanically to a single stimulus, also exist in certain mammalian skeletal muscles [87].

Mammalian skeletal muscle has not been studied as extensively as amphibian skeletal muscle from an energetic point of view. The in situ skeletal muscle and hindlimb preparations have been developed to study contractile, biochemical and histochemical properties in force-generating and/or working contractions [9, 45, 88, 113]. Isolated mammalian skeletal muscle preparations also have been developed to study energetic processes during contraction (energy liberation [51, 54, 122], ~P hydrolysis [6, 11, 25, 54] ) and processes occurring during recovery (heat production [114, 121], oxygen uptake [25], ~P replenishment [25], and mitochondrial NADH fluorescence [114, 121]). There are certain precautions that must be considered with isolated mammalian skeletal muscle preparations. These muscles are typically studied in the 20–30°C temperature range where resting and activity metabolism is high. Thus there is a potential for a hypoxic core to be formed in the muscle if it is too thick. In fact, it has been suggested that isolated rat skeletal muscles are hypoxic [77]. The isolated skeletal muscle should be parallel fibered, or nearly so, allowing mechanical responses to be more easily related to energetic responses during contraction. Also, the isolated muscle should be composed entirely, or at least predominantly, of cells of one fiber type. (Though not as well studied, it should be noted that amphibian skeletal muscle is also composed of multiple fiber types [81] ). Another potential problem is that measurements of heat production or rate of ~P hydrolysis during contraction are contaminated by recovery processes even for relatively brief tetanic contractions. This situation is worse for the more aerobic soleus (SOL) whose rate of recovery metabolism is 4 times greater than for the extensor digitorum longus (EDL) [77]. Of course total (initial plus recovery) heat production or oxygen uptake plus lactate production can be measured to determine the chemical energy utilization during contraction. Some isolated muscles studied to date include the rat SOL [51, 54, 123] and EDL [11, 122], hamster biceps brachii and SOL [6], and mouse SOL and EDL [16, 25, 114].

It appears that the mouse preparations are superior to those from the rat and have recently been well characterized from a mechanical and energetic point of view [16, 25, 26, 27, 114]. Both muscles are nearly parallel fibered [25]. The SOL contains 75 percent SO and 25 percent FOG fibers whereas the EDL contains 1 percent SO, 63 percent FOG, and 36 percent FG fibers [25]. At 20°C, the rate of oxygen consumption of unstimulated SOL and EDL is the same (Table 1). The respiratory quotient is near unity for both muscles, suggesting that the substrate supporting recovery oxidation is glycogen. The resting oxygen consumption of the EDL and SOL is approximately 7 times greater than for the frog sartorius at the same temperature [84]. This difference further emphasizes the potential for hypoxia to occur in isolated mammalian skeletal muscles. Maximum tetanus force per cross-sectional area is similar in EDL and SOL (Table 1) as are the percentages of cell volume containing myofibrils (75% for EDL; 81% for SOL [82] ). Tetanus force in the frog sartorius at 20°C is approximately 40 to 80 percent greater than for the SOL and EDL [68]. This difference in force, if real, cannot be attributed to differences in the percentage of cell volume containing myofibrils (83% for the frog sartorius [91] ). During the initial part of force maintenance in an isometric tetanus, the SOL is 3.4 times more economical than the EDL (calculated from Table 1). The economy of the EDL is similar to that for the frog sartorius at 20°C [68]. Economy depends on specific actomyosin ATPase rate and SR $Ca^{2+}$ ATPase rate, as already discussed. From Table 1 it is apparent that the ATPase rate attributed to $Ca^{2+}$ cycling (measured as ATPase rate during contraction at a sarcomere length of 3.9 μm) is 3 times greater for the EDL than SOL. Thus, by inference, the specific actomyosin ATPase rate is also approximately 3 times greater in the EDL than in the SOL. These data are in agreement with values for isolated actomyosin ATPase [10] and for the differences in the $Ca^{2+}$ ATPase in isolated

TABLE 1

*Mechanical and Energetic Parameters of Isolated Mouse Muscle at 20°C [25,27,77]*

| Parameter | Extensor Digitorum Longus | Soleus |
|---|---|---|
| Metabolic rate of resting muscle, nmol·g⁻¹·min⁻¹ | | |
| O₂ consumption rate | 150 | 150 |
| Aerobic lactate production rate | 9 | 5 |
| Tetanic rate of ~P | | |
| Consumption at rest length μmol·g⁻¹·s⁻¹ | 4 | 1.3 |
| Consumption at 3.9 μm, μmol·g⁻¹·s⁻¹ | 1.2 | 0.4 |
| Maximum velocity of muscle shortening: | | |
| Fiber length·s⁻¹ [77] | 5.9 | 2 |
| Tetanus force per cross-sectional area: | | |
| kN/m⁻² [27] | 190 | 210 |

SR vesicles [119]. The maximum velocity of muscle shortening (Vmax) is 3 times less in the SOL than EDL (Table 1). This difference is expected based upon the previous discussion. Thus the calculated maximum power output during an isotonic contraction is approximately threefold less in the SOL than EDL. A similar compromise is observed for chick skeletal muscles [102]. Compared to the tonic anterior latissimus dorsi muscle (ALD), the phasic posterior latissimus dorsi muscle (PLD) is 6 times less economical during an isometric tetanus but exhibits a fivefold greater Vmax. Also tortoise skeletal muscle is 40 times more economical in an isometric tetanus than frog sartorius muscle but tortoise muscle displays a Vmax that is 6 times less [129].

One of the most striking results that has emerged from the study of isolated mouse skeletal muscles is that the economy of isometric contraction and Vmax are not invariant but rather are modulated during maintained contraction. Figure 5 [25] is a plot of $\sim$P utilization (as measured from recovery reactions) versus isometric tetanus duration (expressed as the time integral of force) for the EDL and SOL. The initial rate of $\sim$P hydrolysis is threefold greater in the EDL but as tetanus duration increases (beyond 3s at 20°C), the $\sim$P hydrolysis rate decreases in the EDL so that it very nearly approaches the value observed for the SOL. Thus a fast contracting muscle has been converted to a slow contracting muscle by prolonged stimulation. When Vmax is measured by rapidly releasing the muscles during the tetanus [27], it is found that Vmax decreases in the EDL when the rate of $\sim$P hydrolysis decreases. The rate of $\sim$P hydrolysis and Vmax are not influenced by tetanus duration in the SOL. The $Ca^{2+}$ cycling energy utilization, based on chemical energy utilization at a sarcomere length of 3.9 $\mu$m, is not altered by tetanus duration in either the EDL or SOL [27]. The increase in economy and decrease in Vmax in the EDL are apparently due to a decrease in cross-bridge cycling rate during a prolonged tetanus.

What is the mechanism of this intracellular modulation of cross-bridge cycling rate? Phosphorylation is known to play an important role in the control of the activity of various proteins. For example, smooth muscle is thought to be activated via an obligatory phosphorylation of the myosin molecule [15]. Crow and Kushmerick [26, 27] found that phosphorylation of a subunit, light chain LC2f, of the myosin molecule correlated in time with the decrease in $\sim$P hydrolysis rate and Vmax in the EDL during an isometric tetanus. No changes in myosin phosphorylation were observed in the SOL during a tetanus. Thus, unlike smooth muscle, myosin phosphorylation in mouse EDL was proposed to lead to a down-regulation of actomyosin ATPase and consequently to a decrease in corss-bridge cycling rate. Unfor-

FIGURE 5

*The relationship between total recovery chemical input and the tension-time integral. The recovery chemical input ($\Delta \sim P_{rec}$) is expressed in $\mu mol \sim P \cdot g^{-1}$ and obtained from the following equation: $\Delta \sim P_{rec} = \kappa \xi\ O_2 + \lambda \xi\ lac$, where $\kappa$ and $\lambda$ are stoichiometric factors equal to 6.3 and 1.5, respectively. Open symbols represent the contribution to total recovery chemical input from oxygen consumption alone ($\kappa \xi O_2$) in the soleus (○) and EDL (□). Closed symbols represent the total recovery chemical input after the contribution of glycolytic ATP production ($\lambda \xi\ lac$) was added to the aerobic contribution in soleus (●) and EDL (■). Data from 13 soleus and EDL muscles each. Multiple determinations were performed on each muscle. Muscles were stimulated and allowed to recover for 30 min before stimulating again. Temperature 20°C.*

SOURCE: Reprinted with permission from Crow, M.T., and M.J. Kushmerick. Chemical energetics of slow- and fast-twitch muscles of the mouse. *J. Gen. Physiol.* 79:147–166, 1982.

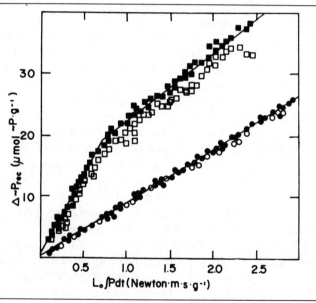

tunately, this exciting hypothesis seems to be incorrect [16]. Myosin dephosphorylation is known to occur slowly. Thus the mouse EDL can be stimulated for 2 seconds to increase myosin light chain phosphorylation, allowed to rest for 8 seconds, and then stimulated again when the level of myosin phosphorylation is still known to be maximum. According to the above hypothesis, velocity of shortening should be less than if the muscle was not previously stimulated. The velocity of shortening was not depressed in the previously stimulated muscle. Thus high levels of myosin phosphorylation do not necessarily result in depressed velocity of shortening. Further experiments have demonstrated that there is no alteration in economy in the rat EDL as a function of tetanus duration even though myosin becomes phosphoyrlated during the tetanus [11]. This not only provides further evidence against the myosin phosphorylation hypothesis of economy modulation but also brings into question the generality of the economy modulation result. Thus it appears that myosin phosphorylation in mammalian skeletal muscle continues to be a mechanism searching for a function. Alternative hypotheses to explain the intriguing and potentially important modulation of cross-bridge cycling rate are eagerly awaited. Also, other mammalian skeletal muscles need to be investigated in this regard.

One of the difficulties in interpreting the results of the mammalian skeletal muscle experiments is that the muscles are not homogeneous in fiber type. Furthermore, even within a single fiber type there are wide variations in metabolic enzyme activities [37, 41, 67, 112]. It seems likely that there is also variation in mechanical and energetic properties within a single class of fibers. Therefore it would be highly desirable to study functional, biochemical, and structural properties of single skeletal muscle cells. For example, it would be informative to be able to measure the following values in a single muscle cell: force production, energy liberation, Vmax, metabolic enzyme activities, oxygen consumption, actomyosin ATPase rate, structural parameters. These measurements are all feasible at the single-cell level. Recently, the first simultaneous measurements of isometric force production and energy liberation have been made on single frog skeletal muscle cells [31]. Also oxygen uptake can be measured in single frog skeletal muscle cells [40]. Nonetheless, all these measurements have yet to be made on the same cell. A first logical approach might be to study cells of differing characteristics in amphibian skeletal muscle. This is true because study of an intact single cell in an uninjured state currently is more feasible in amphibian skeletal muscle than in mammalian skeletal muscles. The difficulties in isolating viable mammalian cells include their small size and extensive connective tissues surrounding each cell, making dissection difficult. No preparation of an isolated, intact mammalian skeletal muscle cell suitable for mechanical and energetic experimentation has yet been reported. Many experiments have been done on mammalian fast-twitch and slow-twitch single cells where the membrane has been removed by mechanical or chemical techniques [92]. In these preparations, soluble cellular components diffuse from the cell unless specifically returned to the cell in the bathing medium. Thus the contractile machinery is intact but the metabolic machinery is probably incomplete. Nonetheless, force, Vmax, and steady state rate of ~P hydrolysis by the cross-bridges can be measured [76]. This preparation should be useful for studying the modulation of economy in mammalian skeletal muscle since only one cell is involved and the environment can be controlled or manipulated as necessary. It seems likely that in the future there will be an increasing utilization of single skeletal muscle cells in the investigation of muscle mechanics and energetics. A potential complication is that there appears to be more than one myosin isoenzyme in a single cell [83]. Much still needs to be learned about the subtle intracellular mechanisms modulating economy and power output during muscular contraction.

## EFFICIENCY OF ISOTONIC CONTRACTION: IMPLICATIONS OF FIBER TYPES

It is natural when studying chemomechanical energy transduction to consider the energetic cost for a mechanical response. The energetic cost of an isometric tetanus is evaluated by measurement of economy of contraction. Economy can vary across the animal kingdom by three orders of magnitude and in mammalian skeletal muscle by greater than threefold. One can also consider the energetic cost of work production or the efficiency of contraction. Intuitively, efficiency can be thought of as the work (W) actually obtained from a process divided by the maximum work (Wmax) obtainable. The Wmax obtainable from a reaction is equal to the free energy change ($\Delta G$) for that reaction and is related to the heat or enthalpy of the reaction ($\Delta H$) by:

$$\text{Wmax} = \Delta G = \Delta H - T\Delta S \tag{9}$$

Where T is temperature and $\Delta S$ the entropy change associated with the reaction. Thus Wmax is, in general, not equivalent to the heat of the reaction. The difference may be positive or negative. Therefore efficiency can be written as:

$$\epsilon_{therm} = W/\text{Wmax} = W/\Delta G \tag{10}$$

This expression of efficiency is called the thermodynamic efficiency ($\epsilon_{therm}$). The experimental difficulty with $\epsilon_{therm}$ is the difficulty in measurement of the $\Delta G$s for the reactions occurring in muscle. $\Delta G$ for a given reaction depends upon the cellular environment, including concentrations of reactants and products, and in general can only be estimated from known reactions occurring during muscular contraction. An experimentally measurable expression for efficiency is called the mechanical or enthalpy efficiency and is written as:

$$\epsilon_{mech} = W/W + H \tag{11}$$

Mechanical efficiency can be measured by determining during contraction external work produced and the energy liberated or the $\sim$P hydrolyzed. In the latter case, $\sim$P hydrolysis ($\mu$mol) can be converted to energy liberation (mJ) by considering the appropriate heats of reactions ($\Delta$Hs). Another approach is to express efficiency simply as:

$$\epsilon_{chem} = W/\Delta \sim P \tag{12}$$

This measurement, called chemical efficiency, has the advantage of specificity and avoids any uncertainty associated with unexplained energy production during shortening. Most of the measurements of efficiency have been derived from myothermic techniques. Wilkie [126, 128] and Carlson and Wilkie [19] have discussed in further detail thermodynamic principles as applied to biology and in particular to muscular contraction.

Efficiency of muscular contraction can be considered for (1) the complete contraction-relaxation-recovery cycle (initial plus recovery processes), (2) the recovery cycle, (3) the contraction cycle, and (4) the cross-bridge cycle. The simplest situation is probably the complete contraction-relaxation-recovery cycle. Under these circumstances, if carbohydrate (CHO) is the energy source, $\epsilon_{therm} \cong \epsilon_{mech}$ because $\Delta H_{CHO} \cong \Delta G_{CHO}$, i.e., $T\Delta S_{CHO} \cong 0$ [126]. Probably most thoroughly studied from an efficiency point of view is frog [59, 62] and tortoise [129] skeletal muscle. Reported values for maximum $\epsilon_{mech}$ of initial plus recovery processes in isolated skeletal muscles are 0.2 for frog [59] and 0.35 for tortoise [129]. The maximum $\epsilon_{mech}$ for the initial processes of muscular contraction are 0.45 for frog [62] and 0.77 for tortoise [129]. Thus efficiency of recovery processes in these muscles must be approximately 0.5, i.e., 50 percent of the heat of reaction of carbohydrate is converted to ATP during recovery and 50 percent is lost to the environment as heat. Determination of the chemomechanical energy conversion by the cross-bridges themselves is a matter of greater speculation. Assuming that approximately 30 percent of the energy liberation and $\sim$P hydrolysis during contraction in frog skeletal muscle is due to $Ca^{2+}$ cycling, this value would need to be subtracted from the measured values of H + W or $\sim$P to determine the efficiency of cross-bridge cycling. The corrected value of $\epsilon_{mech}$ for frog skeletal muscle becomes 0.64. (The energetic consequences of $Ca^{2+}$ cycling have not been measured in tortoise muscle.) The most serious attempt at estimating the maximum efficiency of chemomechanical transduction by the cross-bridges during work production was done in frog sartorius poisoned with fluorodinitrobenzene in order to block CPK (reaction 2) and to measure ATP hydrolysis directly [78]. The maximum $\epsilon_{chem}$ was 24 kJ·mol$^{-1}$ which was estimated to be equivalent to an $\epsilon_{therm}$ of 0.6. After making an estimate of non cross-bridge cycling ATP utilization, the $\epsilon_{therm}$ became greater than 0.9. The conclusion from these studies is that 90 to 100 percent of the chemical free energy of ATP hydrolysis can be converted to external work.

The efficiency during shortening is a function of the load or force against which the muscle shortens and consequently a function of the velocity of shortening. This relationship is shown in Figure 4b where $\epsilon_{mech}$ is plotted against relative load (relative to maximum isometric tetanus force). Obviously, when force is zero or maximum, efficiency is zero. For intermediate loads, $\epsilon_{mech}$ exhibits a maximum at a relative load of 0.45 and $\epsilon_{mech}$ varies little in the range of 0.35 to 0.60 [62]. Power output versus relative load peaks at 0.3 [62]. Even so, $\epsilon_{mech}$ at peak power output is only 3–5 percent less than maximum $\epsilon_{mech}$. A relative load of 0.3 is equivalent to a relative velocity (V/Vmax) of 0.3. This means that peak power output occurs when velocity of shortening is 30 percent of that with zero load and when force development is 30 percent of the isometric tetanus value.

Economy of contraction, maximum power output, and Vmax vary greatly among different muscles. Does the maximum efficiency of work production also vary widely? This point has not been thoroughly studied. Plus there is difficulty in comparing the different measures of efficiency, $\epsilon_{mech}$ and $\epsilon_{chem}$. Finally, it is not always clear that the experiments have been designed to extract the maximum efficiency from the muscle. Within these limitations, some comparisons can be made. The maximum value of $\epsilon_{chem}$ for frog skeletal muscle is 24 kJ·mol$^{-1}$ [78] and the value for ABRM during phasic contraction is remarkably similar (23 kJ·mol$^{-1}$ [93]). This is true despite the fact that the economy of contraction in the ABRM is 250 times greater than in frog skeletal muscle [7]. In chick skeletal muscles, maximum $\epsilon_{mech}$ is 0.6 for the slow contracting ALD and 0.5 for the fast contracting PLD [102]. Economy is 5 times greater in the ALD and Vmax is 6 times less. As mentioned above, maximum $\epsilon_{mech}$ is 0.77 for the slow tortoise skeletal muscle [129] and 0.45 for frog skeletal muscle [59]. The tortoise muscle is 40 times more economical in an isometric tetanus [129]. Thus efficiency of contraction does not vary nearly as widely as does economy of contraction. Furthermore, there appears to be no clear relationship between economy and efficiency of contraction.

An alternative hypothesis has been advanced that states that there is an inverse relationship between maximum efficiency of an isotonic contraction and Vmax and thus a direct connection between $\epsilon_{chem}$ and economy of contraction [52, 94]. Seven different skeletal muscles were studied at 30°C after blockade of anaerobic and aerobic recovery metabolism with iodoacetic acid, cyanide, and nitrogen [94]. Work and PC hydrolysis were measured in a series of contraction-relaxation cycles under optimum loading conditions. Vmax was determined for each muscle in separate experiments. The muscles studied (from slowest to fastest) included: tortoise rectus femoris, hamster soleus, mouse soleus, frog sartorius, hamster biceps brachii, mouse biceps brachii, and PLD. A strong inverse correlation was observed between Vmax and $\epsilon_{chem}$. Vmax ranged from 1 muscle length·s$^{-1}$ to 17.5 muscle lengths·s$^{-1}$ and $\epsilon_{chem}$ from 43 kJ·mol$^{-1}$ (tortoise) to 12 kJ·mol$^{-1}$ (PLD). There are several uncertainties associated with these results. Evidence of effective poisoning of recovery reactions without alteration of initial processes and mechanical performance was not presented. Since the estimated theoretical maximum work obtainable from 1 mol of ATP is 40 kJ ($\Delta G_{ATP}$ [78]), the $\epsilon_{therm}$ for the tortoise is 108 percent. This value does not include a correction for PC hydrolysis associated with Ca$^{2+}$ cycling and is thus a minimum value. Clearly, this number is greater than the theoretical maximum efficiency. The $\epsilon_{chem}$ for the PLD was one-half that for the frog sartorius muscle although the $\epsilon_{mech}$ is greater in the PLD [102]. Thus there appears to be a number of points regarding these efficiency measurements that require further explanation and experimentation. Nonetheless, from the point of view of mammalian skeletal muscle, the $\epsilon_{chem}$ of slow-twitch muscle (mouse or hamster) is reported to be 75 percent greater than the $\epsilon_{chem}$ for fast-twitch muscle [94].

In summary, maximum efficiency is experimentally difficult to obtain, and it is difficult to compare quantitatively efficiencies determined by different techniques. There does not appear to be compelling evidence in support of the hypothesis that, in general, slow-contracting muscles are inherently more efficient than fast-contracting muscles. Regarding mammalian fiber types, the issue has not been thoroughly examined. Furthermore, efficiency of muscular contraction does not vary as widely as does economy. Clearly, more careful experiments are needed before this issue can be completely resolved.

## IMPLICATIONS OF MUSCLE ENERGETICS IN LOCOMOTION

Mechanics and energetics of skeletal muscle contraction has been considered, thus far, from a somewhat limited perspective. Essentially all the results previously described were derived from isolated parallel-fibered skeletal muscles (or cells) under conditions of maximum synchronous activation of all cells in the muscle. Furthermore, the nature of the contractions was limited to constant length (isometric), constant force (isotonic), or constant velocity (isovelocity). These experimental conditions were considered because they provided the simplest approach for consideration of fundamental questions in skeletal muscle mechanics and energetics. They also allow for the greatest control of experimental parameters and for the best accuracy in measurement of pertinent variables. Properties such as force development per cross-sectional area, Vmax, and economy can be thought of as intrinsic to the cells and not dependent on the amount of or arrangement of cells in the muscle. A description of skeletal muscle mechanics and energetics would be incomplete without consideration of the action of skeletal muscles in the body and the implications of mechanics and energetics, as gleaned from isolated muscles, in locomotion.

As a preliminary step to the study of the action of skeletal muscles in the body, one must consider skeletal muscle architecture, attachment to the skeleton, and neural innervation. The influence of skeletal muscle architecture on function has been reviewed in detail in a previous volume of this series [50]. As an illustration of basic principles, consider an idealized muscle containing 100 sarcomeres. Each sarcomere is the same length and contains the same type of myosin, the same number and length of myofilaments. Thus each sarcomere can generate the same maximum isometric force, e.g., 0.5 $\mu$N, and can shorten at the same maximum velocity, e.g., 20 $\mu$m·s$^{-1}$. Nonetheless, these sarcomere building blocks can be arranged to produce muscles of widely varying properties. Consider the muscle with 100 sarcomeres in series. The maximum velocity of shortening of this muscle would be 2,000 $\mu$m·s$^{-1}$ and the maximum isometric force would be 0.5 $\mu$N. This series arrangement of sarcomeres does not produce more force than a single sarcomere but allows shortening to occur 100 times faster. Now consider the 100 sarcomeres arranged in parallel, i.e., side-by-side. This parallel arrangement of sarcomeres has a maximum shortening velocity of 20 $\mu$m·s$^{-1}$ but can generate 50 $\mu$N of isometric force. The series arrangement is 100 times longer than the parallel arrangement and the parallel arrangement has a cross-sectional area 100 times greater than the series arrangement. Expressed per length and cross-sectional area, Vmax and maximum force are the same in each sarcomere arrangement, but clearly absolute values are different. Thus with identical sarcomeres, muscles can be stronger or faster depending upon muscle length and cross-sectional area. In this situation there is a compromise between speed and strength. Of course not all muscles have fibers oriented parallel to the longitudinal axis of the muscle. In some muscles, fibers display a significant angle to the longitudinal axis of the muscle. These muscles are said to exhibit a pennate fiber arrangement [118]. Because more fibers can be accommodated in the same volume when the arrangement is pennate, muscles with this arrangement exert greater force per gram of muscle than do muscles with parallel fibers. However since the direction of shortening of individual fibers is different from that of the whole muscle, the distance shortened by pennate muscles is less than that for muscles of the parallel fiber arrangement. The speed and strength of a muscle is further determined by the nature of the attachment of muscle to the skeleton, that is, the mechanical advantage [3, 118, 124]. Therefore the speed of muscle shortening is dependent on the cross-bridge cycling rate (actomyosin ATPase rate), the number of sarcomeres in series, the arrangement of the fibers in the muscle, and the nature of the attachment to the skeleton.

What are the energetic implications of the various arrangements of muscle fibers in a skeletal muscle and of the attachment of the muscle to the skeleton? Consider once again the idealized 100 sarcomere muscles during a maintained isometric tetanus. The cross-bridge and $Ca^{2+}$ cycles occur at the same rate and therefore the rate of energy liberation will be the same in each sarcomere arrangement described above. But this consumption of ATP leads to widely varying force production (0.5 to 50 $\mu N$). Thus 100 times more ATP is utilized to maintain maximum force for the same duration in the series arrangement of sarcomeres. The economy of contraction, as defined above, is the same in the series and parallel arrangement of sarcomeres. This is true because economy was defined as force per cross-sectional area divided by rate of energy liberation per gram of muscle. Therefore differences in economy are normalized for differences in cross-sectional area and muscle mass. The measure of economy reflects intrinsic differences in the ATPase rates during contraction but does not reflect differences in the arrangement of the sarcomeres or fibers within the muscle. Nonetheless like force and shortening, the energetic cost of contraction is dependent on the arrangement of fibers in the muscle and the attachment of the muscle to the skeleton.

Also neural innervation of skeletal muscles has important consequences when considering the action of muscles in the body. Each axon in the nerve innervating a skeletal muscle branches to innervate a variable number of widely scattered muscle cells. The axon plus innervated muscle cells constitutes a motor unit. Consider a muscle with cells of identical properties (identical fiber types) which is subdivided into 10 equal sized motor units. Obviously by varying the number of motor units that are synchronously activated, this muscle can become stronger, and faster (when shortening against a finite load) and can hydrolyze more ATP and have a greater power output. The economy of contraction in this muscle is not dependent on the fraction of the motor units simultaneously activated. If the muscles possess different fiber types and if there is a fixed order of activation of fiber types [57], then further complexity and flexibility is obtained. Assuming that slow-twitch fiber types are activated first and then fast-twitch fiber types as more motor units are recruited, the muscle would become stronger and faster, hydrolize more ATP, have a greater power output, and become less economical as the fraction of activated motor units increased. Further flexibility is obtained by asynchronous activation of motor units and by variable neuronal stimulus rates. Thus variation in the arrangement of fibers in skeletal muscle, attachment of muscles to the skeleton, fiber types (actomyosin and $Ca^{2+}$ ATPase rates), and neural innervation lead to enormous complexity and flexibility in the action of muscles in the body. A general theme is one of compromise. For isolated muscles, compromises exist between economy of contraction and maximum power output. For muscles in the body, there are further compromises among force development, energetic cost, and speed of shortening. From the viewpoint of the mechanics and energetics of locomotion, the intrinsic properties of cells and the consequences of the architecture and location and innervation of the muscles in the body must be considered.

The study of locomotion includes motility of single cells, animal flight, swimming, and terrestial locomotion. Some of these topics have been reviewed in detail elsewhere [2, 4, 39, 89, 95, 107]. Only terrestial locomotion is considered here. An attempt has been made to apply knowledge gained from the study of the energetics of isolated skeletal muscle to the investigation of locomotion in an intact animal [103]. It is known that the economy of muscular contraction decreases as the muscle temperature increases. The change in economy depends on the temperature range, but the economy is expected to decrease by twofold to threefold for a 10°C increase in temperature [14, 104]. Rome [103] investigated the energetic cost of running at a given speed in monitor lizards at 28.5°C and 38°C. Oxygen consumption was measured. It was determined that the average force exerted per stride and the stride frequency were the same at the two temperatures studied. Results from isolated muscles would predict that the rate of oxygen consumption should increase by twofold to threefold. Instead the rate of oxygen consumption was constant within 2 percent. Clearly in vitro results cannot simply be extrapolated to the in vivo situation. Three hypotheses were considered. First, isolated lizard muscle does not exhibit the decrease in economy with increase in temperature shown by other muscles. Though this point has not been studied explicitedly in lizard muscle, the fact that the intrinsic velocity of shortening in lizard muscle increases by twofold in this temperature range renders this hypothesis unlikely. A second hypothesis is that the number of fibers activated at the two temperatures changes in such a way as to maintain force, shortening velocity and energetic cost of contraction constant. How could this happen? If the contractions during locomotion are primarily shortening contractions, then it is appropriate to consider the force-velocity relation (Fig. 4a) at each temperature. The force-velocity relations for the muscles at 38°C would be shifted to the right of those for the same muscles at 28.5°C, i.e., maximum isometric force would be slightly greater and Vmax about twofold greater. Thus a maximally activated muscle shortening at a constant velocity would generate more force at 38°C than at 28.5°C. Consequently the same force and velocity of shortening can be achieved at 38°C by activating fewer muscle cells than at 28.5°C. This would lead to concomitant decrease in the rate of energy liberation of the muscle during shortening, compensating for the increase in intrinsic rate of energy liberation due to the increased temperature. In principle the energetic cost of contraction could be independent of body temperature. A third hypothesis is that different fiber types are utilized at each temperature. If the contractions are primarily isometric during locomotion, then approximately the same cross-sections of the muscles are used at each temperature (since approximately the same force is generated). In this case energetic cost of locomotion could be temperature independent if different fiber types were recruited at each temperature. Fast-twitch fiber types would be utilized predominantly at low temperatures and slow-twitch fiber types at high temperatures. After considering the effects of temperature on velocity of shortening and economy, the energetic cost of locomotion could be independent of temperature. The second and third hypotheses remain to be tested. These experiments clearly show that extrapolation of results from isolated muscles to intact animals during locomotion must be done with caution. Also, these experiments emphasize the flexibility possible in muscles of different fiber types containing discrete motor units. Finally the interpretation of these experiments raises fundamental questions about the energetic nature of muscular contraction during locomotion.

From the perspective of energy utilization, are muscular contractions during locomotion primarily isometric or primarily shortening contractions? At first this seems like an odd question. After all, animals move during locomotion and thus muscular contraction muscle involves shortening. But are the shortening contractions quantitatively the most important component of locomotion from an energetic point of view? During locomotion energy is utilized to (1) overcome frictional drag of the air, (2) rhythmically accelerate and decelerate the limbs, and (3) rhythmically lift and lower the center of mass. Energy used to overcome the frictional resistance of air is small [98]. Also the energy utilized to accelerate and decelerate limbs is a small fraction of the energetic cost of locomotion [116]. Therefore the major energetic cost of locomotion is incurred in lifting and lowering the center of mass.

An important mechanism in minimizing the energetic cost of locomotion is the transient storage of elastic energy in and subsequent recovery of elastic energy from the muscles and tendons [34, 86]. The consequences of this mechanism have been most clearly described in the kangaroo [34]. The rate of oxygen consumption by the kangroo increases as a steep linear function of velocity of locomotion until the kangaroo starts to hop. Once hopping ensues at greater velocities of movement, the rate of oxygen consumption actually decreases slightly [34]. The interpretation of this result is that elastic energy is stored in the muscles and tendons as the kangaroo hits the ground and then is subsequently released to contribute to the work of lifting the animal forward into the air, thus decreasing necessary energy consumption. The importance of elastic energy storage in human locomotion has been verified by measurement of apparent efficiency of locomotion of about 40 percent [86]. This value is higher than the expected maximum value of about 0.2 for muscular contraction based on work on isolated frog skeletal muscle [59]. Such a result can be explained if elastic energy stored in muscles and tendons contributes to subsequent work production. In fact about half the positive work performed during running can be attributed to elasticity of muscles and tendons [86]. Running has been viewed as analogous to an elastic bouncing ball. In this case, the push is provided by the elastic recoil of the ball, which has been deformed by its impact with the ground. This force, as in running, is directly upward and forward [86]. In the elastic ball model of locomotion, energy is gradually lost due to friction, but a small input of energy can keep the ball bouncing indefinitely. This mechanism of work enhancement has been demonstrated by stretching isolated whole muscles [21] and single muscle cells [36] during contraction. In fact there is evidence that suggests that stretching a muscle during contraction actually enhances the subsequent intrinsic mechanical performance of the muscle during shortening [21, 36]. Further advantage is gained since there is a depression of ATP hydrolysis as a skeletal muscle is stretched [28]. The elastic energy of the stretch could be stored not only in the elastic tendons but also in the attached cross-bridges of the muscle since they too are known to possess elastic properties [46].

For elastic storage of energy to make a significant contribution to energy saving during locomotion, the skeletal muscles must generate isometric force during locomotion. It has been proposed that the major energetic cost of locomotion is the cost of development of isometric force as opposed to performance of mechanical work [55, 115, 117]. This hypothesis is based on the observation that the energetic cost ($\dot{E}_{metab}$) of running at a constant speed per gram of animal increases linearly with speed and varies inversely with body weight. Furthermore, total rate of mechanical work ($\dot{E}_{tot}$) performed by each gram of muscle per stride increases curvilinearly with speed and is independent of body weight. As a result, the apparent muscular efficiency ($\dot{E}_{tot}$ divided by $\dot{E}_{metab}$) increases with body size. An example will help emphasize the consequences of these observations [55]. Consider the chipmunk (30 g body weight) and a human (100 kg) running at the same speed ($3 m \cdot s^{-1}$). The chipmunk consumes 15 times more metabolic energy per gram of tissue while performing work at the same rate. Assuming that efficiency of muscular contraction is independent of fiber type and is relatively insensitive to velocity of shortening, if working contractions were the main source of energy utilization during locomotion, efficiency would have been approximately independent of animal size and speed. This prediction is clearly not supported by the experimental results. But it should be noted that the first assumption requires further verification and the second assumption is only approximately true. Nonetheless the energetic cost of locomotion is probably not due to working contractions. On the contrary the observed results could be explained if the energetic cost of locomotion was dominated by the energy of force development during an isometric contraction. The increase in $\dot{E}_{metab}$ with increasing speed could be due to recruiting muscle cells with faster ATPase and cross-bridge cycling rates (fast-twitch fiber types). The economy of contraction would decrease, which would be reflected in a decrease in the ratio of $\dot{E}_{tot}$ to $\dot{E}_{metab}$ or apparent efficiency of locomotion. According to this interpretation economy of contraction of equivalent muscles is inversely related to animal size. There is some evidence in support of this prediction [23]. The specific actomyosin ATPase and $Ca^{2+}$ ATPase rates would be predicted to be greater in equivalent muscles from smaller animals. This adaptation is reasonable since the smaller animal, to travel at the same speed, takes more strides per unit time and thus requires faster contracting and relaxing muscles [60]. It also follows that intrinsic Vmax would be greater for equivalent muscles in smaller animals. Only a relatively limited number of equivalent muscles isolated from animals of widely varying sizes have been characterized for differences in economy and Vmax. Clearly more work in this area would be fruitful. The simplest measurement might be that of Vmax in various skinned muscle cells. This intriguing hypothesis remains to be more extensively tested.

There are a number of interesting implications of this analysis of locomotion. First, if locomotion is primarily an isometric phenomenon from an energetic perspective, then the efficiency, as measured in isolated muscles, is not particularly revelant to the understanding of locomotion in animals of different sizes. Nonetheless the efficiency measurements from isolated muscles determine the upper limit for the extraction of work from metabolism and they provide a reference point for analyzing systems where stored elastic energy is thought to contribute to work production. Second, the concepts of economy of contraction and Vmax are crucial to the understanding of the energetics of locomotion. In equivalent muscles these intrinsic muscle properties should depend on animal size. Third, the efficiency of locomotion is considerably enhanced by the nearly reversible conversion of elastic energy into external work. Fourth, knowing only the speed of locomotion andd animal weight, the rate of oxygen consumption can be predicted [55].

## SUMMARY AND CONCLUSIONS

In this chapter fundamental energetic properties of skeletal muscles as elucidated from isolated muscle preparations are described. Implications of these intrinsic properties for the energetic characterization of different fiber types and for the understanding of locomotion have been considered. Emphasis was placed on the myriad of physical and chemical techniques that can be employed to understand muscle energetics and on the interrelationship of results from different techniques. The anaerobic initial processes which liberate energy during contraction and relaxation are discussed in detail. The high-energy phosphate ($\sim$P) utilized during contraction and relaxation can be distributed between actomyosin ATPase or cross-bridge cycling (70%) and the $Ca^{2+}$ ATPase of the sacroplasmic reticulum (30%). Muscle shortening increases the rate of $\sim$P hydrolysis, and stretching a muscle during contraction suppresses the rate of $\sim$P hydrolysis. The economy of an isometric contraction is defined as the ratio of isometric mechanical response to energetic cost and is shown to be a fundamental intrinsic parameter describing muscle energetics. Economy of contraction varies across the animal kingdom by over three orders of magnitude and is different in different mammalian fiber types. In mammalian skeletal muscles differences in economy of contraction can be attributed mainly to differences in the specific actomyosin and $Ca^{2+}$ ATPase of muscles. Furthermore, there is an inverse relationship between economy of contraction and maximum velocity of muscle shortening (Vmax) and maximum power output. This is a fundamental relationship. Muscles cannot be economical at developing and maintaining force and also exhibit rapid shortening. Interestingly, there appears to be a subtle system of unknown nature that modulates the Vmax and economy of contraction. Efficiency of a work-producing contraction is defined and contrasted to the economy of contraction. Unlike economy, maximum efficiency of work production varies little across the animal kingdom. There are difficulties associated with the measurement of maximum efficiency of contraction, and it has yet to be determined unequivocally if the maximum efficiency of contraction varies in different fiber types.

The intrinsic properties of force per cross-sectional area, economy, and Vmax determine the basic energetic properties of skeletal muscles. Nonetheless, the mechanics and energetics of skeletal muscles in the body are profoundly influenced by muscle architecture, attachment of muscles to the skeleton, and motor unit organization. Caution must be used in extrapolating results from isolated muscle preparations to in vivo situations. Despite this warning, insight into the energetic nature of locomotion in vivo can be gained by considering basic energetic properties of the skeletal muscles involved. The hypothesis that the energetic cost of locomotion primarily depends on the economy of isometric muscle contractions and not on the efficiency of working contractions is reviewed. This hypothesis is consistent with many observations but requires further testing. Also the importance of the transient storage of elastic energy in the muscle and tendons during locomotion is described.

In general, much more fundamental information about the energetics of mammalian fiber types is needed. Muscles need to be studied from mammals of widely varying sizes to determine further the effects of scaling and fiber types on Vmax, economy, and maximum efficiency. Single muscle cell preparations, though technically difficult, promise to provide the greatest potential for gaining accurate information regarding many of these energetic parameters. The study of fundamental problems in energetics is progressing through a transition period. In the past much emphasis was placed on understanding the mechanics and energetics of amphibian skeletal muscle contraction because of the experimental advantages associated with these muscles. In the future greater emphasis will undoubtedly be placed on the understanding of the fundamental energetic properties of mammalian skeletal muscle at the molecular level and on understanding the implications of these properties in locomotion. The future appears bright and promises to be a time for synthesis in the area of muscle energetics.

REFERENCES

1. Abbott, B.C., X.M. Aubert, and A.V. Hill. The absorption of work by a muscle stretched during a single twitch or a short tetanus. *Proc. R. Soc. Lond. Ser. B.* 139:86–104, 1951.
2. Alexander, R.M. *The Locomotion of Animals.* Glasgow: Blakie and Son, 1982.
3. Alexander, R.M. *Animal Mechanics.* 2nd ed. London: Blackwell, 1983.
4. Alexander, R.M., and G. Goldspink. *Mechanics and Energetics of Locomotion.* London: Chapman and Hall, 1977.
5. Aubert, X. *Le Couplage Energetique de la Contraction Musculaire.* Brussels: Arscia, 1956.
6. Awan, M.Z., and G. Goldspink. Energetics of the development and maintenance of isometric tension by mammalian fast and slow muscle. *J. Mechanochem. Cell Motil.* 1:97–108, 1972.
7. Baguet, F., and J.M. Gillis. The respiration of the anterior byssus retractor muscle of mytilus edulis (ABRM) after a phasic contraction. *J. Physiol. Lond.* 188:67–82, 1967.
8. Baguet, F., and J.M. Gillis. Energy cost of tonic contraction in a lamellibranch catch muscle. *J. Physiol. Lond.* 198:127–143, 1968.
9. Baldwin, K.M., and C.M. Tipton. Work and metabolic patterns of fast and slow twitch skeletal muscle contracting in situ. *Pflugers Arch.* 334:345–356, 1972.
10. Barany, M. ATPase activity of myosin correlated with of muscle shortening. *J. Gen. Physiol.* 50:197–218, 1967.
11. Barsotti, R.J., and T.M. Butler. Chemical energy usage and myosin light chain phosphorylation in mammalian skeletal muscle. *J. Muscle Res. Cell Mot.* 5:45–64, 1984.
12. Blinks, J.R., R. Rudel, and S.R. Taylor. Calcium transients in isolated amphibian skeletal muscle fibres: detection with aequorin. *J. Physiol. Lond.* 277:291–323, 1978.
13. Bozler, E. The heat production of smooth muscle. *J. Physiol. Lond.* 69:443–462, 1930.
14. Burchfield, D.M., and J.A. Rall. Effects of temperature on Vo, force, stiffness and energy liberation in frog skeletal muscle. *Abstr. Biophys. J.* 45:342a, 1984.
15. Butler, T.M., and M.J. Siegman. Chemical energy usage and myosin light chain phosphorylation in mammalian smooth muscle. *Fed. Proc.* 42:57–61, 1983.
16. Butler, T.M., M.J. Siegman, S.U. Mooers, and R.J. Barsotti. Myosin light chain phosphorylation does not modulate cross-bridge cycling rate in mouse skeletal muscle. *Science* 220:1167–1169, 1983.
17. Carlson, F.D., D.J. Hardy, and D.R. Wilkie. Total energy production and phosphocreatine hydrolysis in the isotonic twitch. *J. Gen. Physiol.* 46:851–882, 1963.
18. Carlson, F.D., and A. Siger. The mechanochemistry of muscular contraction. I. The isometric twitch. *J. Gen. Physiol.* 44:33–60, 1960.
19. Carlson, F.D., and D.R. Wilkie. *Muscle Physiology.* Englewood Cliffs, N.J.: Prentice-Hall, 1974.
20. Cattell, M., and W. Hartree. The delayed anaerobic heat production of stimulated muscle. *J. Physiol. Lond.* 74:221–230, 1932.
21. Cavagna, G.A., and G. Citterio. Effect of stretching on the elastic characteristics and the contractile component of frog striated muscle. *J. Physiol. Lond.* 239:1–14, 1974.
22. Clinch, N.F. On the increase of rate of heat production caused by stretch in frog's skeletal muscle. *J. Physiol. Lond.* 196:397–414, 1968.
23. Close, R.I. Dynamic properties of mammalian skeletal muscles. *Physiol. Rev.* 52:129–197, 1972.

24. Creshull, I., M.J. Dawson, R.H.T. Edwards, R.E. Gordon, G.K. Radda, D. Shaw, and D.R. Wilkie. Human muscle analyzed by [31]P nuclear magnetic resonance in intact subjects. *Abstr. J. Physiol. Lond.* 317:18P, 1981.

25. Crow, M.T., and M.J. Kushmerick. Chemical energetics of slow- and fast-twitch muscles of the mouse. *J. Gen. Physiol.* 79:147–166, 1982.

26. Crow, M.T., and M.J. Kushmerick. Myosin light chain phosphorylation is associated with a decrease in the energy cost of contraction in fast twitch mouse muscle. *J. Biol. Chem.* 257:2121–2124, 1982.

27. Crow, M.T., and M.J. Kushmerick. Correlated reduction of velocity of shortening and the rate of energy utilization in mouse fast-twitch muscle during a continuous tetanus. *J. Gen. Physiol.* 82:703–720, 1983.

28. Curtin, N.A., and R.E. Davies. Very high tension with very little ATP breakdown by active skeletal muscle. *J. Mechanochem. Cell Motil.* 3:147–154, 1975.

29. Curtin, N.A., and R.C. Woledge. Energy changes and muscular contraction. *Physiol. Rev.* 58:690–761, 1978.

30. Curtin, N.A., and R.C. Woledge. Chemical change and energy production during contraction of frog muscle: How are their time courses related? *J. Physiol. Lond.* 288:353–366, 1979.

31. Curtin, N.A., J.V. Howarth, J.A. Rall, M.G.A. Wilson, and R.C. Woledge. Simultaneous heat and tension measurements from single muscle cells. In *Contractile Mechanisms in Muscle Contraction*, edited by G.H. Pollack and H. Sugi. New York: Plenum Press, 1984, pp. 887–899.

32. Damiani, E., R. Betto, S. Salvatori, R. Volpe, G. Salviati, and A. Margreth. Polymorphism of sarcoplasmic-reticulum adenosine triphosphate of rabbit skeletal muscle. *Biochem. J.* 197:245–248, 1981.

33. Dawson, M.J., D.G. Gadian, and D.R. Wilkie. Contraction and recovery of living muscles studies by [31]P nuclear magnetic resonance. *J. Physiol. Lond.* 267:703–735, 1977.

34. Dawson, T.J., and C.R. Taylor. Energetic cost of locomotion in kangaroos. *Nature* 246:313–314, 1973.

35. Dydynska, M., and D.R. Wilkie. The chemical and energetic properties of muscles poisoned with fluorodinitrobenzene. *J. Physiol. Lond.* 184:751–796, 1966.

36. Edman, K.A.P., G. Elzinga, and M.J.M. Noble. Enhancement of mechanical performance by stretch during tetanic contractions of vertebrate skeletal muscle fibres. *J. Physiol. Lond.* 281:139–155, 1978.

37. Eisenberg, B.R. Quantitative ultrastructure of mammalian skeletal muscle. In *Handbook of Physiology. Section 10: Skeletal Muscle*, edited by L.D. Peachey, R.H. Adrian, and S.R. Geiger. Bethesda: American Physiological Society, 1983, pp. 73–112.

38. Eisenberg, B.R., and A.M. Kuda. Discrimination between fiber populations in mammalian skeletal muscle by using ultrastructure parameters. *J. Ultrastruct. Res.* 54:76–88, 1976.

39. Elder, H.Y., and E.R. Trueman. *Aspects of Animal Movement*. Cambridge: Cambridge University Press, 1980.

40. Elzinga, G., G.J. Langewouters, N. Westerhof, and A.H.C.A. Wiechmann. Oxygen uptake of frog skeletal muscle fibres following tetanic contractions at 18°C. *J. Physiol. Lond.* 346:365–377, 1984.

41. Essen, B., E. Fansson, J. Henriksson, A.W. Taylor, and B. Saltin. Metabolic characteristics of fiber types in human skeletal muscle. *Acta Physiol. Scand.* 95:153–165, 1975.

42. Feng, T.P. The effect of length on the resting metabolism of muscle. *J. Physiol. Lond.* 74:441–454, 1932.

43. Fenn, W.O. A quantitative comparison between the energy liberated and the work performed by the isolated sartorius muscle of the frog. *J. Physiol. Lond.* 58:175–203, 1923.

44. Fenn, W.O. The relation between the work performed and the energy liberated in muscular contraction. *J. Physiol. Lond.* 58:373–395, 1924.

45. Fitts, R.H., W.W. Winder, M.H. Brooke, K.K. Kaiser, and J.O. Holloszy. Contractile, biochemical, and histochemical properties of thyrotoxic rat soleus muscle. *Am. J. Physiol.* 238:C15–C20, 1980.

46. Ford, L.E., A.F. Huxley, and R.M. Simmons. The relation between stiffness and filament overlap in stimulated frog muscle fibres. *J. Physiol. Lond.* 311:219–249, 1981.

47. Fossel, E.T., H.E. Morgan, and J.S. Ingwall. Measurement of changes in high-energy phosphates in the cardiac cycle by using gated $^{31}P$ nuclear magnetic resonance. *Proc. Natl. Acad. Sci.* 77:3654–3658, 1980.

48. Gadian, D.G. *Nuclear Magnetic Resonance and Its Applications to Living Systems.* Oxford: Clarendon Press, 1982.

49. Gadian, D.G., G.K. Radda, T.R. Brown, E.M. Chance, M.J. Dawson, and D.R. Wilkie. The activity of creatine kinase in frog skeletal muscle studied by saturation-transfer nuclear magnetic resonance. *Biochem. J.* 145:1–14, 1981.

50. Gans, C. Fiber architecture and muscle function. *Exercise Sport Sci. Rev.* 10:160–207, 1982.

51. Gibbs, C.L., and W.R. Gibson. Energy production of rat soleus muscle. *Am. J. Physiol.* 223:864–871, 1972.

52. Goldspink, G. Muscle energetics and animal locomotion. In *Mechanics and Energetics of Animal Locomotion,* edited by R. Alexander and G. Goldspink. London: Chapman and Hall, 1977, pp. 57–81.

53. Gordon, A.M., A.F. Huxley, and F.J. Julian. The variation in isometric tension with sarcomere length in vertebrate muscle fibres. *J. Physiol. Lond.* 184:170–192, 1966.

54. Gower, D. and K.M. Kretzschmar. Heat production and chemical change during isometric contraction of rat soleus muscle. *J. Physiol. Lond.* 258:659–671, 1976.

55. Heglund, N.C., M.A. Fedak, C.R. Taylor, and G.A. Cavagna. Energetics and mechanics of terrestial locomotion. IV: Total mechanical energy changes as a function of speed and body size in birds and mammals. *J. Exp. Biol.* 97:57–66, 1982.

56. Heilmann, C., D. Brdiczka, E. Nickel, and D. Pette. ATPase activities, $Ca^{2+}$ transport and phosphoprotein formation in sarcoplasmic reticulum of fast and slow rabbit muscles. *Eur. J. Biochem.* 81:211–222, 1977.

57. Henneman, E., G. Somjen, and D.O. Carpenter. Functional significance of cell size in spinal motor neurons. *J. Neurophysiol.* 28:560–580, 1965.

58. Hill, A.V. The energy degraded in the recovery processes of stimulated muscle. *J. Physiol. Lond.* 46:28–80, 1913.

59. Hill, A.V. The mechanical efficiency of frog's muscle. *Proc. R. Soc. Lond. Ser. B.* 127:434–451, 1939.

60. Hill, A.V. The dimensions of animals and their muscular dynamics. *Sci. Prog. Lond.* 38:209–230, 1950.

61. Hill, A.V. Chemical change and mechanical response in stimulated muscle. *Proc. R. Soc. Lond. Ser. B.* 41:314–320, 1953.

62. Hill, A.V. The ratio of mechanical power developed to total power expended during muscular shortening. *Proc. R. Soc. Lond. Ser. B.* 159:319–324, 1964.

63. Hill, A.V. *Trails and Trials in Physiology.* London: Arnold, 1965.

72 | *Rall*

64. Hill, A.V., and J.V. Howarth. The reversal of chemical reactions in contracting muscle during an applied stretch. *Proc. R. Soc. Lond. Ser. B.* 151:169–193, 1959.
65. Hill, D.K. The time-course of the oxygen consumption of stimulated frog's muscle. *J. Physiol. Lond.* 98:207–227, 1940.
66. Hill, D.K. The time-course of evolution of oxidative recovery heat of frog's muscle. *J. Physiol. Lond.* 98:459–478, 1940.
67. Hintz, C.S., C.V. Lowry, K.K. Kaiser, D. McKee, and O. Lowry. Enzyme levels in individual rat muscle fibers. *Am. J. Physiol.* 239:C58–C65, 1980.
68. Homsher, E., and C.J. Kean. Skeletal muscle energetics and metabolism. *Annu. Rev. Physiol.* 40:93–131, 1978.
69. Homsher, E., C.J. Kean, A. Wallner, and V. Garibian-Sarian. The time-course of energy balance in an isometric tetanus. *J. Gen. Physiol.* 73:553–567, 1979.
70. Homsher, E., W.F.H.M. Mommaerts, N.V. Ricchiuti, and A. Wallner. Activation heat, activation metabolism and tension-related heat in frog semitendinosus muscles. *J. Physiol. Lond.* 220:601–625, 1972.
71. Hoult, D.I., S.J.W. Busby, D.G. Gadian, G.K. Radda, R.E. Richards, and P.J. Seeley. Observation of tissue metabolites using $^{31}P$ nuclear magnetic resonance. *Nature* 252:285–287, 1974.
72. Huxley, A.F. *Reflections on Muscle.* Liverpool: Liverpool University Press, 1980.
73. Infante, A.A., D. Klaupiks, and R.E. Davies. Length, tension and metabolism during short isometric contractions of frog sartorius muscles. *Biochem. Biophys. Acta* 88:215–217, 1964.
74. Jobsis, F.F. Energy utilization and oxidative recovery metabolism in skeletal muscle. In *Current Topics in Bioenergetics,* Vol. 3, edited by D.R. Sanadi. New York: Academic Press, 1969, pp. 279–349.
75. Keynes, R.D. The energy cost of active transport. In *Comparative Physiology: Functional Aspects of Structural Materials,* edited by L. Bolis, H.P. Maddrell, and K. Schmidt-Nielsen. Amsterdam: North-Holland, 1975, pp. 155–159.
76. Krasner, B.H., and M.J. Kushmerick. Tension and ATPase in steady-state contractions of rabbit soleus fiber segments. *Am. J. Physiol.* 14:C405–C414, 1983.
77. Kushmerick, M.J. Energetics of muscle contraction. In *Handbook of Physiology. Section 10: Skeletal Muscle,* edited by L.D. Peachey, R.H. Adrian, and S.R. Geiger. Bethesda: American Physiological Society, 1983, pp. 189–236.
78. Kushmerick, M.J., and R.E. Davies. The chemical energetics of muscle contraction. II. The chemistry, efficiency and power of maximally working sartorius muscles. *Proc. R. Soc. Lond. Sec. B.* 174:315–353, 1969.
79. Kushmerick, M.J., and R.J. Paul. Relationship between initial chemical reactions and oxidative recovery metabolism for single isometric contractions of frog sartorius at 0°C. *J. Physiol. Lond.* 254:711–727, 1976.
80. Kushmerick, M.J., and R.J. Paul. Aerobic recovery metabolism following a single isometric tetanus in frog sartorius muscle at 0°C. *J. Physiol. Lond.* 254:693–709, 1976.
81. Lannergren, J., and R.S. Smith. Types of muscle fibres in toad skeletal muscle. *Acta Physiol. Scand.* 68:263–274, 1966.
82. Luff, A.R., and H.L. Atwood. Changes in the sarcoplasmic reticulum and transverse tubular system of fast and slow skeletal muscles of the mouse during postnatal development. *J. Cell Biol.* 51:369–383, 1971.
83. Lutz, H., H. Weber, R. Billeter, and E. Jenny. Fast and slow myosin within single skeletal muscle fibres of adult rabbits. *Nature* 281:142–144, 1979.
84. Mahler, M. Diffusion and consumption of oxygen in resting frog sartorius muscle. *J. Gen. Physiol.* 71:533–557, 1978.
85. Mahler, M. The relationship between initial creatine phosphate breakdown and recovery oxygen consumption for a single isometric tetanus of the frog sartorius muscle at 20°C. *J. Gen. Physiol.* 73:159–174, 1979.

86. Margaria, R. *Biomechanics and energetics of muscular exercise.* Oxford: Clarendon Press, 1976.
87. Matyushkin, D.P. Motor systems in the oculomotor apparatus of higher animals. *Fed. Proc.* 23:T1103–1106, 1964 (translated from Russian).
88. McLane, J.A., R.D. Fell, R.H. McKay, W.W. Winder, E.B. Brown, and J.O. Holloszy. Physiological and biochemical effects of iron deficiency on rat skeletal muscle. *Am. J. Physiol.* 241:C47–C54, 1981.
89. McMahon, T.A. *Muscles, Reflexes, and Locomotion.* Princeton: Princeton University Press, 1984.
90. Meyer, R.A., M.J. Kushmerick, and T.R. Brown. Application of $^{31}$P-NMR spectroscopy to the study of striated muscle metabolism. *Am. J. Physiol.* 242:C1–C11, 1982.
91. Mobley, B.A., and B.R. Eisenberg. Sizes of components in frog skeletal muscle measured by methods of stereology. *J. Gen. Physiol.* 66:31–45, 1975.
92. Moss, R.L. The effect of calcium on the maximum velocity of shortening in skinned skeletal muscle fibres of the rabbit. *J. Musc. Res. Cell Mot.* 3:295–311, 1982.
93. Nauss, K.M., and R.E. Davies. Changes in inorganic phosphate and arginine during the development, maintenance and loss of tension in the anterior byssus retractor muscle of mytilus edulis. *Biochem. Z.* 345:173–187, 1966.
94. Nwoye, L.O., and G. Goldspink. Biochemical efficiency and intrinsic shortening speed in selected vertebrate fast and slow muscles. *Experientia* 37:856–857, 1981.
95. Pedley, T.J. *Scale Effects in Animal Locomotion.* London: Academic Press, 1977.
96. Peter, J.B., R.J. Barnard, V.R. Edgerton, C.A. Gillespie, and K.E. Stempel. Metabolic profiles of three fiber types of skeletal muscle in guinea pigs and rabbits. *Biochemistry* 11:2627–2633, 1972.
97. Pette, D. *Plasticity of Muscle.* Berlin: deGruyter, 1980.
98. Pugh, L.G.C.E. The influence of wind resistance in running and walking and the efficiency of work against horizontal or vertical forces. *J. Physiol. Lond.* 213:255–276, 1971.
99. Rall, J.A. Sense and nonsense about the Fenn effect. *Am. J. Physiol.* 242:H1–H6, 1982.
100. Rall, J.A. Energetics of $Ca^{2+}$ cycling during skeletal muscle contraction. *Fed. Proc.* 41:155–160, 1982.
101. Rall, J.A., E. Homsher, A. Wallner, and W.F.H.M. Mommaerts. A temporal dissociation of energy liberation and high energy phosphate splitting during shortening in frog skeletal muscles. *J. Gen. Physiol.* 68:13–27, 1976.
102. Rall, J.A., and B.A. Schottelius. Energetics of contraction in phasic and tonic skeletal muscles of the chicken. *J. Gen. Physiol.* 62:303–323, 1973.
103. Rome, L. Energetic cost of running with different muscle temperatures in Savannah monitor lizards. *J. Exp. Biol.* 99:269–277, 1982.
104. Rome, L.C., and M.J. Kushmerick. Energetics of isometric contractions as a function of muscle temperature. *Am. J. Physiol.* 244:C100–C104, 1983.
105. Ruegg, J.C. Smooth muscle tone. *Physiol. Rev.* 51:201–248 , 1971.
106. Sandberg, J.A., and F.D. Carlson. The length dependence of phosphorylcreatine hydrolysis during an isometric tetanus. *Biochem. Z.* 345:212–231, 1966.
107. Schmidt-Neilsen, K., L. Bolis, and C.R. Taylor. *Comparative Physiology: Primitive Mammals.* Cambridge: Cambridge University Press, 1980.
108. Siegman, M.J., T.M. Butler, S.U. Mooers, and R.E. Davies. Chemical energetics of force development, force maintenance, and relaxation in mammalian smooth muscle. *J. Gen. Physiol.* 76:609–629, 1980.
109. Smith, I.C.H. Energetics of activation in frog and toad muscle. *J. Physiol. Lond.* 220:583–599, 1972.
110. Snowdowne, K., and N.K.M. Lee. Subcontracture concentrations of potassium

and stretch cause an increase in activity if intracellular calcium in frog skeletal muscle. *Abstr. Fed. Proc.* 34:1733, 1980.

111. Solandt, D.Y. The effect of potassium on the excitability and resting metabolism of frog's muscle. *J. Physiol. Lond.* 86:162–170, 1936.

112. Spamer, C., and D. Pette. Activity patterns of phosphofructokinase, glyeraldehydephosphate dehydrogenase, lactate dehydrogenase and malate dehydrogenase in microdissected fast and slow fibers from rabbit psoas and soleus muscle. *Histochemistry* 52:201–216, 1977.

113. Stainsby, W.N., and C.R. Lambert. Determinants of oxygen uptake in skeletal muscle. *Exercise Sport Sci. Rev.* 7:125–151, 1979.

114. Stewart, A. Simultaneous heat and fluorescence measurements on mammalian fast- and slow-twitch skeletal muscle. Ph.D. thesis, Monash University, 1984.

115. Taylor, C.R. Mechanical efficiency of terrestrial locomotion: a useful concept? In *Aspects of Animal Movement,* edited by H.Y. Elder and E.R. Trueman. Cambridge: Cambridge University Press, 1980, pp. 235–244.

116. Taylor, C.R., A. Shkolnik, R. Dmiel, D. Baharav, and A. Borut, Running in cheetahs, gazelles, and goats: Energy cost and limb configuration. *Am. J. Physiol.* 227:848–850, 1974.

117. Taylor, C.R., N.C. Heglund, T.A. McMahon, and T.R. Looney. Energetic cost of generating muscular force during running: A comparison of large and small animals. *J. Exp. Biol.* 86:9–18, 1980.

118. Tricker, R.A.R., and B.J.K. Tricker. *The Science of Movement.* London: Mills and Boon, 1967.

119. Wang, T., A.O. Grassi de Gende, and A. Schwartz. Kinetic properties of calcium adenosine triphosphatase of sarcoplasmic reticulum from cat muscles. A comparison of caudofemoralis (fast), tibialis (mixed), and soleus (slow). *J. Biol. Chem.* 254:10675–10678, 1979.

120. Weizsacker, V. Myothermic experiments in salt solutions in relation to the various stages of muscular contraction. *J. Physiol. Lond.* 48:396–427, 1914.

121. Wendt, I.R., and J.B. Chapman. Fluorometric studies of recovery metabolism of rat fast- and slow-twitch muscles. *Am. J. Physiol.* 230:1644–1649, 1976.

122. Wendt, I.R., and C.L. Gibbs. Energy liberation of rat extensor digitorum longus muscle. *Am. J. Physiol.* 224:1081–1086, 1973.

123. Wendt, I.R., and C.L. Gibbs. Recovery heat production of mammalian fast- and slow-twitch muscles. *Am. J. Physiol.* 230:1637–1643, 1976.

124. White, D.S.C. *Biological Physics.* London: Chapman and Hall, 1974.

125. White, D.C.S. Muscle mechanics. In *Mechanics and Energetics of Animal Locomotion,* edited by R. Alexander and G. Goldpspink. London: Chapman and Hall, 1977, pp. 23–56.

126. Wilkie, D.R. Thermodynamics and the interpretation of biological heat measurements. *Prog. Biophys. Chem.* 10:260–298, 1961.

127. Wilkie, D.R. Heat, work, and phosphorylcreatine breakdown in muscle. *J. Physiol. Lond.* 195:157–183, 1968.

128. Wilkie, D.R. The efficiency of muscular contraction. *J. Mechanochem. Cell Motil.* 2:257–267, 1974.

129. Woledge, R.C. The energetics of tortoise muscle. *J. Physiol. Lond.* 197:685–707, 1968.

130. Zachar, J., and D. Zacharova. Potassium contractures in single muscle fibres of the crayfish. *J. Physiol. Lond.* 186:596–618, 1966.

# The Influence of Altered Blood Volume and Oxygen Transport Capacity on Aerobic Performance

N. GLEDHILL, Ph.D.

Although the interrelationships among blood volume (BV), hemo-globin concentration ([Hb]), and aerobic performance have received considerable attention in both scientific and lay publications, many questions persist. The interest of researchers is due both to the pur-ported ergogenic effect of alterations in BV and [Hb] on aerobic performance and to the insight that may be provided by these alter-ations concerning the physiologic mechanisms and limiting factor(s) in aerobic power ($\dot{V}O_2$max). The interest of the general public stems from a recently heightened awareness to the prominence of ergogenic aids in athletic competitions. Alterations in BV could affect $\dot{V}O_2$max via changes in cardiac output ($\dot{Q}$), and alterations in [Hb] could exert their effect through changes in arterial $O_2$ content ($CaO_2$). Hence, either manipulation could alter systemic $O_2$ transport ($\dot{Q} \times CaO_2$). If $O_2$ transport were increased, additional $O_2$ would be available to the working muscles, and the possible outcome would be an increase in both $\dot{V}O_2$max and aerobic performance.

This chapter focuses on the effects of alterations in BV and [Hb] on aerobic power and physical performance rather than on the re-lated changes in cardiovascular dynamics.

## BLOOD AND OXYGEN TRANSPORT

Approximately 45 percent of the volume of normal blood is red blood cells (RBCs) and this percentage is called the hematocrit (Hct). The RBCs contain Hb, and each gram of Hb can carry 1.34 ml $O_2$ (also reported as 1.39 ml/g). Therefore, the higher the [Hb], the greater the capacity of blood to carry $O_2$, and at any constant level of Q, an increase in [Hb] would result in an increase in $O_2$ transport. Muscle requires a great deal of $O_2$ during heavy exercise and any change in the $O_2$ carrying capacity of blood affects the amount of $O_2$ presented to the working muscles. Although factors such as an increased effi-ciency of work output at the same $\dot{V}O_2$ are also important, the amount

Supported by the Canadian Red Cross Blood Transfusion Service and NSERC Can-ada #A8203.

of $O_2$ presented to the muscles has a major influence on how much work the muscles can perform in a given period of time.

## SPORTS ANEMIA

The average [Hb] for men is 15.8 g/100 ml, and for women it is 13.9 g/100 ml. The range of normal values is 14.0–18.0 g/100 ml for men and 11.5–16.0 g/100 ml for women. Anemia is diagnosed when the [Hb] falls below this normal range. A number of clinical conditions can cause anemia, but sports anemia is a below normal [Hb] in an athlete in the absence of any clinical rationale. However, the term "sports anemia" is frequently applied to athletes when their [Hb] is merely below the average value, rather than below the lower limit of the normal range.

Given the $O_2$ transport implications of a low [Hb], sports anemia is of considerable significance to athletes, and they have been advised to take extensive precautions to avoid this condition [11]. Nevertheless, although the etiology is unclear, it is not uncommon for the [Hb] of an athlete to be below average [10]. That there is increased destruction of erythrocytes during strenuous muscular exercise has been known since the beginning of the century, and studies to determine the mechanism(s) that accounts for this observation were first made in 1922 [6]. Broun postulated that resistance in the membrane of the RBC was reduced by the wear and tear of increased circulation. It was later concluded that this decreased resistance is caused by the high body temperature during heavy exercise [16]. However, a subsequent study of the osmotic resistance of erythrocytes in athletes who were initiating training indicated that although erythrocyte fragility was initially increased, after two weeks it was restored to normal [63]. Other possible explanations for sports anemia include a dietary intake of iron below the recommended daily amount leading to a gradual depletion of bone marrow iron stores, or an inadequate rate of iron absorption, especially when coupled with increased iron depletion from erythrocyte destruction or increased loss of iron through sweating [11].

### Anemia and Performance

The importance of [Hb] in physical performance has been reviewed previously [1, 11, 38]. Patients with pronounced anemia demonstrate a substantially reduced $\dot{V}O_2$max compared with normal healthy individuals [13, 29, 36, 51]. However, the $\dot{Q}$max of anemic patients appears unaffected [36]. Early investigations of athletes as blood donors indicated a decreased performance after a blood loss of 500 ml [2, 35]. However, the authors pointed out that the effects were quite probably psychological, and although Balke et al. [2] observed a reduction in performance one hour after blood donation, $\dot{V}O_2$max had returned to normal two to three days later. It is possible, therefore, that the initial reduction was due to a change in BV. Alternatively, it could have been a psychological effect, since the identical trends reported by Balke et al. were also observed by Howell and Coupe [32], both in experimental subjects who lost 500 ml of blood and in control subjects who underwent a sham blood removal.

Ekblom et al. [18] observed decreases of 10.5 percent and 15.8 percent in $\dot{V}O_2$max (4.57 to 4.09 L/min and 4.49 to 3.78 L/min) when the [Hb] in two groups of healthy male physical education students was reduced by 13 percent and 18 percent, respectively. The corresponding treadmill endurance performance times of both groups decreased by approximately 30 percent. In a subsequent study from the same laboratory, $\dot{V}O_2$max decreased by 5.6 percent (4.27 to 4.03 L/min) and $\dot{Q}$max was unchanged when phlebotomy reduced [Hb] by 8 percent [19]. Horstman et al. [30] reported that a 25 percent reduction in [Hb] (14.3 to 10.7 g/100 ml) caused no change in $\dot{V}O_2$max in exercising dogs. However, $O_2$ transport was maintained by a 26 percent increase in $\dot{Q}$max, due to an increased stroke volume.

Woodson et al. [62] observed that in healthy male subjects, $\dot{V}O_2$max and endurance performance decreased by 16 percent, and $\dot{Q}$max increased by 13 percent following RBC removal which reduced [Hb] by 34 percent (15.3 to 10.0 g/100 ml) at a constant BV. However, when anemia was prolonged for two weeks by continued RBC removal, $\dot{V}O_2$max decreased even further to 29 percent below control, and $\dot{Q}$max fell from its initially elevated level to 7 percent below the control value [62]. The authors suggested that this fall was related to a concurrent reduction in renal blood flow and the redistribution of this blood. In recent studies, Freedson [21] reported a 6.2 percent decrease in $\dot{V}O_2$max four days after blood donation had reduced [Hb] by 18.6 percent (14.7 to 12.0 g/100 ml), and Kanstrup and Ekblom [33] observed that when blood donation caused a 10.1 percent decrease in [Hb], there was a corresponding 7.3 percent reduction in $\dot{V}O_2$max and a 34 percent decrease in treadmill running time to exhaustion. However, these authors also reported that increasing BV via a plasma expander so that [Hb] decreased by 11.1 percent, produced no significant changes in $\dot{V}O_2$max or $\dot{Q}$max.

In summary, the majority of reports on acute and chronic isovolemic anemia in humans indicate a reduction in $\dot{V}O_2$max consequent to a reduction in [Hb]. The decreased aerobic power is accompanied by a decrease in aerobic performance, but whether or not the corresponding $\dot{Q}$max is affected remains unclear.

*Monitoring and Treating Sports Anemia*

Since the presence of sports anemia in athletes is not uncommon [10], regular monitoring of the athlete is important. Hb is made up of iron and protein, and the synthesis of Hb is dependent upon adequate stores of iron in the bone marrow. Serum ferritin levels correlate well with iron stores in bone marrow, and iron deficiency is diagnosed when serum ferritin levels fall below 12 ng/ml of serum [42]. Therefore, it has been recommended that the [Hb] and serum ferritin levels of elite athletes be evaluated at least every 6 to 12 months [11].

Men and women normally lose approximately 1 mg of iron each day in sweat and stool, and women lose additional iron during menstruation. This loss must be balanced by the dietary intake of iron, and the recommended daily intake is 10 mg for men and 14 mg for women. Since only 10 percent of the ingested iron is absorbed, daily intake matches daily loss. Computer-processed nutritional intake analyses can be employed to monitor the adequacy of dietary iron intake, and deficiencies can be corrected by a variety of tablet or liquid supplements [11].

## INDUCED ERYTHROCYTHEMIA: BLOOD DOPING

Blood doping, blood boosting, and blood packing are terms used to describe a medical intervention that produces an abnormally high [Hb]. It is generally accomplished by removing a volume of blood from an individual, separating and storing the RBCs for a prescribed period of time, then reinfusing the cells back into the donor. While the RBCs are being stored, the body produces new RBCs at an accelerated rate and returns the blood to a normal [Hb], so that when the stored RBCs are reinfused, the [Hb] is elevated above normal. Early studies on this topic were contradictory and inconclusive, and reviewers generally concluded that research did not support a beneficial effect of blood doping on aerobic performance [44, 61]. However, recent studies in which a major flaw in early investigations was avoided have shown conclusively that blood doping increases $\dot{V}O_2$max and improves endurance performance at submaximal and maximal intensities [8, 25, 46, 50, 52, 53, 60].

*Methodology of Blood Doping*

It is possible to induce erythrocythemia by means of transfusions of fresh blood from a matched donor (homologous transfusions), and this procedure was utilized in one early study of blood doping [41]. Homologous transfusions are employed routinely when blood is transfused for medical and therapeutic purposes. There is a risk-benefit ratio associated with this procedure that is acceptable in life-threatening situations. However, when using homologous transfusions, even with the most stringent safeguards, there exists a possibility of hepatitis or bacterial communication and blood type incompatibility [40]. Homologous transfusions have even been described as liquid organ transplants with the same possible complications. Therefore, research involving healthy human subjects should not be conducted using blood from matched donors. For this reason, studies of blood doping generally involve the removal, storage, and subsequent reinfusion of a subject's own blood (autologous transfusions).

The majority of stored blood is preserved by refrigeration at 4°C. Since the average life span of RBCs is 120 days [39], each day approximately 1 percent of any RBC population is lost. In the body, the destruction of RBCs is matched by RBC synthesis through erythropoiesis. However, when blood is refrigerated, there is a progressive loss of erythrocytes. This results in a constant buildup of cellular aggregates in refrigerated blood, and health authorities in North America have imposed a maximum refrigeration storage time of three weeks. (In some countries this time is extended to four or five weeks.) At the termination of the storage period, the number of RBCs has declined by approximately 15–20 percent [54]. Additional erythrocytes are irretrievable because they adhere to the storage containers and transfer tubing. Also, some erythrocytes become so fragile during storage that they break up shortly after they are reinfused [54]. The net result is that when blood is refrigerated for the maximum allowable three-week period, only 60 percent (approximately) of the RBCs that were removed are viable after reinfusion.

The freeze-preservation technique of blood storage is utilized by transfusion services to maintain a readily available supply of rare blood types [38]. Unlike the refrigeration technique, when blood is stored as frozen cells the aging process of the RBCs is interrupted, and after reinfusion, the fragility of the stored cells is normal [54]. Loss due to cell handling is similar to that in the refrigeration process and amounts to approximately 15 percent whether the storage time is two days or two years. However, a major difference in the two storage techniques is that frozen cells can be safely stored for an indefinite period of time [54]. Therefore, by employing freeze preservation, it is not only possible to maximize the recovery of RBCs (approximately 85 percent), but it is also possible for the investigator to delay reinfusion as long as necessary to ensure that the normal erythrocyte level has been reestablished in the donor.

Before blood is freeze-preserved, it is centrifuged, and the separated RBCs are combined with glycerol at a Hct of approximately 90 percent. At the conclusion of storage, the RBCs are thawed, washed, and reconstituted with physiologic saline to a Hct of approximately 50 percent. Since the reconstituted "blood" has essentially the same Hct as normal blood, the BV of the recipient is increased, but there is no immediate increase in Hct. The acute hypervolemia disappears over the next 24 hours as the excess fluid is lost, and this process of hemoconcentration produces an elevated Hct and [Hb].

*Hematologic Changes Following Phlebotomy and Reinfusion*
The maximum storage duration for refrigerated blood is restricted by health regulations to three weeks. Therefore, the time course of hematologic changes following blood removal (phlebotomy) is an important consideration in achieving an erythrocythemic condition. Similarly, a knowledge of the time course of postreinfusion hematologic changes is necessary for applications of blood doping.

When healthy males underwent 400-ml phlebotomies, the [Hb] remained low for one to two weeks, then increased rapidly, reaching control levels in three to four weeks [57]. It was also illustrated that the iron stores of the blood donor play an important role in the time course of erythropoiesis [12, 28]. In a recent study that was designed to delineate the time course of hematologic changes following phlebotomy and reinfusion, Gledhill et al. [23] removed 900 ml of blood from normal healthy males and stored the RBCs via the high-glycerol freezing technique. Following blood removal, the [Hb] and Hct of the donors decreased by 11 percent. These hematologic values remained low for one to two weeks, then began increasing rapidly, and it took five to six weeks for them to return to control values. In a subsequent study from the same laboratory involving trained runners, it took up to 10 weeks for the hematologic values to return to control levels [8]. This time course discrepancy could be due to differences in the iron stores of the two groups of subjects [28] or differences in their training regimens.

Following reestablishment of control hematology levels in the donors, the cells were reinfused. Twenty-four hours after reinfusion, [Hb] and Hct were elevated 8 percent, and seven days after reinfusion they were elevated 11 percent [23]. The increase from the first to the seventh day was attributed to a continuing hemoconcentration. Over the next 15 weeks, hematology values returned gradually, in a linear fashion, from the erythrocythemic level to the control level.

The time course of hematologic changes discloses some important implications for blood doping. Most importantly, three weeks after a 900 ml phlebotomy, hematologic values in normal subjects had only partially returned to control values. Therefore, given that health regulations in North America restrict the storage duration for refrigerated blood to a maximum of three weeks, and that only 60 percent of the originally removed RBCs are viable following rein-fusion, it is highly improbable that an erythrocythemic condition could be induced using refrigeration-stored blood. It should also be noted, however, that in a study conducted under health regulations which permit longer periods of refrigeration storage, the reinfusion of 800 to 1,200 ml equivalent whole blood following four weeks of refrigeration storage did not produce a significant increase in [Hb] [18]. The second important implication for blood doping from the time course of hematologic changes is that a gradually decreasing condition of erythrocythemia was maintained for 120 days after rein-fusion. Thus, the increased $O_2$ carrying capacity is of value not just for a brief period following the blood infusion, but for several weeks thereafter.

*Oxygen Affinity in Stored Cells*
The $O_2$ affinity of [Hb] is related to the concentration of erythrocyte 2,3-diphosphoglycerate (2,3-DPG). When blood is stored by either refrigeration or freeze preservation, there is a reduction in the 2,3-DPG of the stored RBCs. This results in an increased $O_2$ affinity and a leftward shift of the oxyhemoglobin dissociation curve with a con-sequent reduction in $O_2$ unloading at the tissues. It has been argued, therefore, that the reinfusion of stored blood cannot bring about an increase in $O_2$ delivery and $\dot{V}O_2$max [47]. However, it was illustrated clearly that when RBCs with decreased 2,3-DPG were transfused, the 2,3-DPG level in the mixed RBC population of the recipient was restored to normal within 24 hours [5]. Since the postreinfusion erythrocythemic condition is maintained for an extended period of time, a reduced $O_2$ offloading in the initial 24 hours is inconsequential [23]. Moreover, in studies of blood doping in which 2,3-DPG levels were measured, no significant differences were reported between control and 24-hour postreinfusion values, both at rest and during exercise [8, 19, 60]. Furthermore, if the first 24 hours following blood reinfusion were critical for a particular application, the 2,3-DPG of the stored RBCs could be increased to 200 percent of the normal in vivo level by incubating the cells prior to reinfusion with a rejuven-ation mixture of pyruvate, inosine, glucose, phosphate, and adenine [54]. The result of this treatment is a temporary rightward shift of the dissociation curve so that $O_2$ offloading is transiently above the control level.

*Early Attempts at Blood Doping*
Since decreases in [Hb] and the resultant decrease in $O_2$ transport cause reductions in $\dot{V}O_2$max and aerobic performance, it seems rea-sonable that increases in [Hb] could augment $\dot{V}O_2$max and aerobic performance. This relationship assumes, however, that (1) $\dot{Q}$max is

not decreased by the corresponding increase in blood viscosity, (2) the distribution of blood to the working muscle is unaltered, and (3) there is adequate reserve oxidative capacity in the muscles to utilize the additional $O_2$. An increase in $\dot{V}O_2$max consequent to an increase in [Hb] with no concurrent change or an increase in $\dot{Q}$ would support the third of these assumptions and the hypothesis that the oxidative capacity of muscle exceeds the amount of $O_2$ delivered during maximal aerobic exercise; therefore, $O_2$ transport could be the limiting factor.

The earliest reported investigation of induced erythrocythemia and physical performance was a study of the hypoxic exercise tolerance of naval volunteers in 1946 [41]. Pace et al. transfused 2,000 ml of fresh blood from matched donors into five normal healthy males. Their mean Hct increased from 46.2 to 58.3 percent then returned to control values linearly over the following 50 days. The authors observed a 34.7 percent improvement in hypoxic exercise tolerance so that exercise at a simulated altitude of 15,500 feet was tolerated as well by the transfused group as was exercise at an altitude of 10,500 feet by the control group [41].

In two subsequent investigations of blood doping [27, 45], there were no significant differences in physical work capacity (+3%) [27] and $\dot{V}O_2$max (+1.4%) [45] following reinfusion of 610 ml and 1,000 ml of blood, respectively. However, in both studies, the increase in [Hb] was not significant (+0.7% and +4.9%) since the blood was stored via refrigeration and reinfused 7 and 14 days postphlebotomy.

Ekblom et al. [18] studied the effect of blood removal and reinfusion on healthy male physical education students. The blood was refrigerated for approximately 28 days after phlebotomy. Three subjects received 800 ml and four subjects received 1,200 ml. Treadmill running performance and $\dot{V}O_2$max increased overnight by 23 percent and 9 percent due to an increase in [Hb] of 13 percent above the preinfusion condition (no statistical analysis reported). However, at the time of the reinfusion the subjects were still somewhat anemic from the phlebotomy, and the actual increase in [Hb] above their prephlebotomy control values was only 2.1 percent (0.3 g/100 ml). The corresponding increases from the prephlebotomy condition in physical performance and $\dot{V}O_2$max were 15.6 percent and 5.5 percent. It should also be pointed out that the accuracy of the data in this study has been disputed due to the lack of a control group and blind design.

Van Rost et al. [56] reported that $\dot{V}O_2$max increased by 9 percent, and treadmill running time to exhaustion was prolonged by 37 percent in male physical education students when [Hb] increased 2.7

percent following 900 ml reinfusions, but no statistical analysis was reported. Their blood had been stored at 4°C for three weeks after phlebotomy. However, in both this investigation and the study of Ekblom et al. [18], it is difficult to account for the substantial increases in performance and $\dot{V}O_2$max by the relatively small increases in [Hb] and $O_2$ transport.

In a follow-up study, Ekblom et al. [19] reinfused five well-trained physical education students with autologous blood which had been refrigerated for 30 to 35 days. $\dot{V}O_2$max increased significantly (8.0%) consequent to a 4.5 percent increase in [Hb]. However, the corresponding increase in $O_2$ transport calculated from their data (176 ml/min) can only partially account for the observed 340 ml/min increase in $\dot{V}O_2$max.

Significant postreinfusion increases in $\dot{V}O_2$max and aerobic performance were observed in only two of the preceding studies. Furthermore, no significant improvement in $\dot{V}O_2$max or endurance performance was reported in an additional four concurrent investigations of blood doping in which the refrigeration storage technique was employed [4, 36, 43, 58]. Some reasons for the lack of agreement among these pre-1978 studies include the following: improper experimental designs, such as the absence of placebos and controls; the designation of prereinfusion (anemic) values rather than prephlebotomy (normocythemic) values as control values; protocols that could have produced a training effect in the experimental subjects; and most importantly, failure to achieve a significant increase in [Hb] due to inadequate transfusion volumes or the use of an inappropriate storage technique. Consequently, reviewers of these studies generally concluded that blood doping does not alter $\dot{V}O_2$max or endurance performance [44, 61].

*Recent Studies of Blood Doping and Performance*
The first investigation of blood doping and aerobic performance in which red cells were freeze-preserved to successfully induce erythrocythemia was reported in 1980 [7, 8]. Control studies were conducted on 11 elite endurance runners, both prior to and 10 weeks after a 900-ml phlebotomy. This protocol enabled the investigators to confirm that the athletes were at their control levels at the time the blood was reinfused. The study was conducted using a double-blind crossover design. Six of the athletes initially received a sham reinfusion of saline, then their blood reinfusion, and the remaining five athletes received their blood reinfusion initially, then a sham reinfusion. During both the blood and sham reinfusions, the athletes wore blacked-out goggles and listened to music via headphones to keep them un-

aware of the order of treatment. The effectiveness of this blind was confirmed by a questionnaire that was administered subsequent to each blood and sham reinfusion.

The runners were retested 24 hours and seven days following the reinfusions. Following the blood reinfusions there were significant increases in [Hb], $\dot{V}O_2$max and treadmill running time to exhaustion. Accompanying a 9.3 percent increase in [Hb] (15.1 to 16.5 g/100 ml) was a 5.1 percent increase in $\dot{V}O_2$max (5.11 to 5.37 L/min) and a 34 percent increase in treadmill running time to exhaustion (7.20 to 9.65 minutes). The authors attributed the disproportionate increase in treadmill running time to the fact that after reinfusion, the identical treadmill settings corresponded to a markedly lower percentage of the athletes' new $\dot{V}O_2$max. BV determinations also confirmed that the subjects were normovolemic. These results established conclusively the physiologic and aerobic performance advantages of blood doping.

In a subsequent study from the same laboratory [50], the effect of reinfusing both 900 and 1,350 ml of freeze-preserved blood on four elite endurance runners was investigated. A primary aim of this study was to examine whether there was any evidence of a compromise in the cardiovascular system consequent to the inducement of normovolemic erythrocythemia. Catheters were placed in a radial artery and the superior vena cava for determination of arterial blood pressure, arterial oxygenation, and $\dot{Q}$ via dye dilution. An electrocardiogram was recorded continuously while the runners exercised on a motor-driven treadmill. Throughout light to maximal exercise, no evidence of cardiovascular compromise was observed. Following the 900-ml reinfusion, Hct and $\dot{V}O_2$max increased by 7.9 percent and 3.9 percent, respectively, and after 1,350 ml had been reinfused, Hct and $\dot{V}O_2$max were elevated by 10.8 percent and 6.6 percent, respectively. These results confirmed the improvements reported in the previous study and indicated that the effect is even greater when the volume of reinfused blood is increased from 900 to 1,350 ml. However, during exercise at the highest reinfusion volume, the customary hemoconcentration resulted in a Hct which approached the clinical diagnostic value of erythrocythemia, and therefore, the use of even greater reinfusion volumes should be avoided.

Williams et al. [59] reported no significant change ($+4.1\%$) in the treadmill running time to exhaustion of distance runners when their [Hb] was increased by 3.3 percent following reinfusion of 460 ml of freeze-preserved autologous blood. Also, Cottrell [14] observed no significant change ($+2\%$) in $\dot{V}O_2$max after reinfusion of 405 ml of freeze-preserved blood. Therefore, it appears that regardless of the blood storage technique, the reinfusion of a single unit of blood (approximately 450 ml) is not sufficient to induce a significant increase in [Hb]. Nevertheless, it should be noted that there was an improvement in endurance performance in both studies.

In a subsequent investigation, Williams et al. [60] induced a significant increase in [Hb] (7%) with the reinfusion of 920 ml of freeze-preserved blood. Following reinfusion, long distance runners improved their five-mile treadmill running time by an average of 49 seconds. Similarly, Goforth et al. [25] reported that when Hct was elevated 10 percent by reinfusing freeze-preserved blood, $\dot{V}O_2$max increased 11 percent and three-mile run time was 23.7 seconds faster.

The ergogenic benefit of blood doping has also been confirmed in two recent reports by Thompson et al. [52, 53] who observed that a Hct increase of 9.3 percent following reinfusion of 1,000 ml of freeze-preserved blood increased $\dot{V}O_2$max (12.5%) and prolonged submaximal exercise performance. Also, Robertson et al. [46] demonstrated the value of blood doping (1,800 ml of autologous freeze-preserved blood) in preacclimatizing for performance at altitude. In normoxia, an increase in Hct of 26.6 percent was accompanied by a 12.8 percent increase in $\dot{V}O_2$max and a 15.8 percent increase in treadmill performance time. In addition, the decreases in $\dot{V}O_2$max and endurance performance that were observed between normoxia and hypoxia were diminished by 10.3 percent and 7.7 percent, respectively, following blood doping.

In summary, owing to a variety of methodological problems (most notably, the inability to achieve a significant increase in [Hb]), early attempts to investigate induced erythrocythemia must be largely discounted in evaluating the affect of blood doping. Nevertheless, it is important to note that when a tabulated summary of these studies is examined [22], it is striking that in every study the postreinfusion $\dot{V}O_2$max and aerobic performance values are above the control values. Although few of the individual increases are statistically significant, with this number of studies, if blood doping had no affect on $\dot{V}O_2$max and aerobic performance, it is highly improbable that the trend in every investigation would be in the same direction. After 1978, studies of blood doping were conceived with the advantage of learning from the shortcomings in previous investigations, and in these studies, the reinfusion of 900 ml or more of autologous freeze-preserved blood produced a normovolemic erythrocythemia which led to significant increases in aerobic power and endurance performance. When smaller volumes of freeze-preserved blood were reinfused, improvements were observed, but the increases were not statistically significant.

*Physiologic Alterations Accompanying Blood Doping*
This brief discussion of the hemodynamic and related effects of blood doping is limited to those studies in which a significant increase in [Hb] was achieved. During submaximal exercise in the erythrocythemic condition, both heart rate [8, 19, 46, 52] and $\dot{Q}$ were decreased [19] or unchanged [52], while stroke volume remained unchanged [19]. Maximal heart rate was unchanged or decreased slightly [8, 19, 50, 52] and both $\dot{Q}max$ and maximal stroke volume were reported to be either unchanged [19, 46] or increased [50, 52, 56]. Also, in the erythrocythemic condition, the plasma lactate concentration ([La]) following submaximal exercise was reported to be unchanged [46] or decreased [8, 19, 24] from normocythemia, and following maximal exercise in the erythrocythemic condition the [La] was unchanged [8, 19, 46, 60].

The available evidence regarding the effect of blood doping on $\dot{Q}$ is limited, and additional studies are definitely required to clarify this issue. However, the evidence to date supports the hypothesis that $O_2$ transport is the limiting factor in maximal aerobic exercise. However, it is also possible that the improvement in aerobic performance can be attributed either in part or in whole to physiologic alterations that are related to the increase in [Hb], such as in augmented buffering [24].

*Alterations in Blood Volume*
Changes in BV could influence $O_2$ transport by altering stroke volume and $\dot{Q}$, and alterations in $\dot{Q}max$ would affect $O_2$ transport capacity. It follows, therefore, that changes in BV could influence physical performance. Since alterations in BV and [Hb] are interdependent, it is helpful to specify whether a given [Hb] occurs in normovolemia, hypovolemia, or hypervolemia. By examining this information, it is possible to estimate the relative importance of [Hb] and BV as limiting factors in $\dot{V}O_2max$ and performance.

The reinfusion of either whole blood or packed RBCs (diluted with saline) is generally conducted at a Hct of 50 percent. Thus, immediately after reinfusion there exists a transient normocythemic hypervolemia. The excess fluid is removed from the circulatory system during the ensuing several hours, producing a normovolemic erythrocythemia [26]. Similarly, acute decreases in BV are compensated for in a matter of hours by an expansion of the plasma volume back to normovolemia [26].

By employing the appropriate manipulations, it is possible to achieve alterations in BV either with or without accompanying changes in [Hb]. Danzinger and Cumming [15] observed a decrease in $\dot{V}O_2max$ consequent to a chlorothiazide-induced erythrocythemic hypovolemia. They also reported that this condition was reversed by the infusion of dextran. On the other hand, Saltin [47] observed no changes in $\dot{V}O_2$max or $\dot{Q}$max when BV was reduced by thermal dehydration. However, he noted that the corresponding exercise time to exhaustion was markedly reduced.

Robinson et al. [45] reported that an acute (mildly erythrocythemic) hypervolemia, which was produced by infusing 1,000 to 1,200 ml of autologous blood, had no effect on $\dot{V}O_2$max or $\dot{Q}$max. Kanstrup and Ekblom [33] reported that following infusion of a plasma expander which created a hypervolemic anemia (reduction in [Hb] of 11.1%), $\dot{V}O_2$max was unchanged and $\dot{Q}$max was increased nonsignificantly (27.4 to 29.5 L/min) consequent to an increase in stroke volume. In the same study, they employed blood withdrawal to create an equivalent degree of anemia along with a mild hypovolemia, and observed significant reductions in $\dot{V}O_2$max (6.7%) and time to exhaustion on the treadmill (34%). They concluded that changes in BV can compensate for alterations in [Hb] and maintain $O_2$ transport capacity by affecting ventricular preload.

Kanstrup and Ekblom [34] recently examined the interrelationships among BV, [Hb], $\dot{V}O_2$max, and physical performance. Infusion of a plasma expander caused a 16 percent increase in BV and a 15 percent reduction in [Hb], and although $\dot{V}O_2$max was unchanged, treadmill running time to exhaustion decreased by 20 percent. Following blood withdrawal which caused a decrease in [Hb] of 15 percent and a decrease in BV of 6.9 percent, $\dot{V}O_2$max decreased 9 percent and performance time decreased 40 percent. Subsequent infusion of a plasma expander (6% dextran) produced an increase in BV to 10 percent above control and a further decrease in [Hb] to 27 percent below control, which caused decreases in $\dot{V}O_2$max and performance of 11 percent and 41 percent below control, respectively. Blood reinfusion which increased total body Hb by 6 percent, [Hb] by 2 percent, and BV by 4 percent, produced a 6 percent increase in $\dot{V}O_2$max and a 30 percent increase in performance. Infusion of a plasma expander while the subjects were erythrocythemic increased BV to 13.6 percent above control and reduced [Hb] to 7 percent below control. These changes produced increases in $\dot{V}O_2$max and performance of 4 percent and 13 percent above control, respectively.

Although the influence of [Hb] and BV on $\dot{V}O_2$max and physical performance has not been fully investigated, the information in Table 1 is an attempt to summarize (or predict) their interrelationships.

In summary, at a constant [Hb], a reduction in BV may cause decreases in $\dot{V}O_2$max and performance, but an increase in BV has no affect on $\dot{V}O_2$max and performance. However, at a constant BV, a decrease in [Hb] will cause decreases in $\dot{V}O_2$max and performance,

TABLE 1

*The Interrelationships among Total Body Hb (TBHb), Hemoglobin Concentration ([Hb]), Blood Volume (BV), $\dot{V}O_2$max, and Physical Performance (Perf)*

| Blood Volume | TBHb | [Hb] | BV | $\dot{V}O_2$max | Perf |
|---|---|---|---|---|---|
| Hypervolemic anemia | 0 or − | − | + | 0 or − | − |
| Normovolemic anemia | − | − | 0 | − | − |
| Hypovolemic anemia | − | − | − | − | − |
| Hypervolemic normocythemia | + | 0 | + | 0 | 0 |
| Normovolemic normocythemia | 0 | 0 | 0 | 0 | 0 |
| Hypovolemic normocythemia | − | 0 | − | 0 or − | 0 or − |
| Hypervolemic erythrocythemia | + | + | + | + | + |
| Normovolemic erythrocythemia | + | + | 0 | + | + |
| Hypovolemic erythrocythemia | 0 | + | − | 0 or − | 0 or − |

0 = no change; − = decreased; and + = increased.

and an increase in [Hb] will produce increases in $\dot{V}O_2$max and performance. It would appear, therefore, that [Hb] (through alterations in total body Hb) plays the dominant role in the influence of BV and [Hb] on $\dot{V}O_2$max and physical performance.

*Doping Controls and Altitude Acclimatization*

The use of physiologic substances in abnormal amounts, with abnormal methods, and with the exclusive aim of obtaining an artificial or unfair increase in performance in competition is prohibited by doping control regulations [17]. Since an increase in BV does not improve performance, its use is not banned. However, the above definition of doping undoubtedly applies to induced erythrocythemia, and the use of blood doping is banned.

When doping controls are conducted at a competition, selected athletes must pass a urine sample in the presence of a doping control official. They could also be required to give a blood sample from which the laboratory determination of [Hb] is a simple task. In typical studies of blood doping the [Hb] increased from 15 g/100 ml, to between 16 and 17 g/100 ml. The average [Hb] in normal and athletic populations varies from 14 to 18 g/100 ml. Thus, the problem facing doping control officials is that although a high [Hb] is relatively simple to detect, at present it is not possible to determine why it is high. For example, it may appear to be elevated due to either altitude acclimatization or genetic endowment [9, 10]. In fact, some endurance athletes (who were not suspected of blood doping) competed in the 1976 Olympiad with a [Hb] as high as 18 g/100 ml [10].

A consideration of the similarity between the effects of blood doping and altitude acclimatization further complicates the issue of doping controls. It is well known that due to a lower atmospheric pressure, athletes who normally reside at sea level are at a disadvantage when competing in endurance events at altitude [3, 20]. However, the body acclimatizes to hypoxic environments by creating a higher-than-normal level of RBCs, and therefore, altitude residents are not at an equal disadvantage. That is, the body adapts to altitude hypoxia by creating a condition identical to that produced by blood doping [37]. For this reason, many athletes were staged at altitude training camps in the weeks prior to the Mexico Olympiad to gain the benefit of altitude acclimatization. Some athletes even resided at altitudes higher than that of Mexico City to increase their [Hb] even further and gain a greater advantage. This practice was not banned by the International Olympic Committee (IOC).

A problem with altitude training, however, is that during the period that athletes are acclimatizing to altitude, their maximum exercise capacity is somewhat reduced, and since the intensity at which they can train is therefore slightly below normal, some detraining occurs [3]. The effect of the detraining partially negates the benefits of acclimatization and the net result is that only a small advantage is gained over nonacclimatized athletes. However, it has been shown that it is possible to avoid this problem by simply transporting the athletes to a lower altitude for daily training or having them train in an oxygen-enriched environment while residing at altitude [3].

Consequently, it was reasoned that if no concurrent detraining took place during altitude acclimatization, the adaptations should be even more beneficial to maximal performance upon returning to compete in normoxia. Using an experimental design that ruled out the potential interference from detraining, Horstman et al. [31] reported that a 10 percent increase in [Hb] due to altitude acclimatization resulted in increases of 6 percent in $\dot{V}O_2max$ and 25 percent in endurance performance upon returning to sea level. The magnitude of the observed changes in [Hb], $\dot{V}O_2max$, and endurance capacity are virtually identical to the findings in subjects who engaged in blood doping [8]. Thus, it is possible to gain all the benefits of blood doping through the manipulation of altitude acclimatization, a procedure that the IOC has permitted. The expense involved in this protocol is considerably greater than simply removing, storing, and reinfusing blood, and could only be afforded by a few countries.

In summary, although blood doping contravenes both the spirit and the law of doping in athletic competitions, practically speaking its use is not at present controlled. Moreover, it is possible to produce the same physiologic condition in the athlete by exploiting altitude acclimatization. A possible approach that the IOC could take in order to control the use of blood doping would be to establish an allowable upper limit for [Hb], for example 16 g/100 ml. It would be a routine task to identify competitors whose [Hb] was above the specified limit. Those individuals who, by virtue of altitude acclimatization or genetic endowment, had a [Hb] above the allowed limit could easily meet the standards by blood removal. However, realistically speaking, the only deterrents at the present time to the use of blood doping in competitions are accessibility to the appropriate blood storage technique and the integrity of the athletes and coaches involved.

OVERVIEW

Alterations in [Hb] affect $\dot{V}O_2$max via changes in arterial $O_2$ content, and alterations in BV influence $\dot{V}O_2$max through changes in $\dot{Q}$max. Therefore, changes in either [Hb] or BV could influence aerobic performance. Sports anemia refers to the presence of a low [Hb] in an athlete, and reductions in [Hb] are accompanied by decreases in $\dot{V}O_2$max and physical performance. Therefore, it is important to monitor the [Hb] and serum ferritin levels of athletes on a regular basis and to correct any deficiencies. Blood doping is the removal, storage, and subsequent return to the donor of a volume of blood. Early studies of blood doping were unsuccessful, primarily because they failed to achieve a significant increase in [Hb]. If 900 ml or more of blood is withdrawn and the RBCs are freeze-preserved for six weeks or longer, then after reinfusion of the stored RBCs to the donor there is a significant increase in [Hb] accompanied by increases in $\dot{V}O_2$max and aerobic performance. Although blood doping is banned from use in athletic competitions, it cannot at present be detected. At a constant [Hb], a decrease in BV may cause reductions in $\dot{V}O_2$max and physical performance, but an increase in BV above normovolemia has no effect on aerobic power and performance. However, an increased BV can compensate for the effect of moderate reductions in [Hb] by maintaining $O_2$ transport capacity through an increase in $\dot{Q}$max.

REFERENCES

1. Ästrand, P.-O. Experimental Studies of Physical Working Capacity in Relation to Sex and Age. Monograph, Enjnar Munksgaard: Copenhagen, 1952.
2. Balke, B., G.P. Grillo, E.B. Konecci, and U.C. Luft. Work capacity after blood donation. J. Appl. Physiol. 7:231–238, 1954.
3. Balke, B., J.T. Daniels, and J.A. Faulkner. Training for maximum performance at altitude. In Exercise at Altitude, R. Margaria (ed.). Milan: Exerpta Medica Foundation, 1976, pp. 179–186.
4. Bell, R.D., R.T. Card, M.A. Johnson, T.A. Cunningham, and F. Baker. Blood doping and athletic performance. Aust. J. Sports Med. 8:133–139, 1976.

5. Beutler, E., and L. Wood. The in vivo regeneration of red cell 2,3-Diphosphogly-ceric acid (DPG) after transfusion of stored blood. *J. Lab. Clin. Med.* 74:300–304, 1969.
6. Broun, G.O. Blood destruction during exercise I. Blood changes occurring in the course of a single day of exercise. *J. Exp. Med.* 36:481–500, 1922.
7. Buick, F.J., N. Gledhill, A.B. Froese, L. Spriet, and E.C. Meyers. Double blind study of blood boosting in highly trained runners. *Med. Sci. Sports* 10:49, 1978 (abstr.).
8. Buick, F.J., N. Gledhill, A.B. Froese, L. Spriet, and E.C. Meyers. Effect of induced erythrocythemia on aerobic work capacity. *J. Appl. Physiol.* 48:636–642, 1980.
9. Buskirk, E.R., J. Kollias, E. Piconreatique, R. Akers, E. Prokop, and P. Baker. Physiology and performance of track athletes at various altitudes in the United States and Peru. In *The Effects of Altitude on Physical Performance.* Albuquerque: The Athletic Institute, 1967, pp. 65–72.
10. Clement, D.B., R.C. Asmundson, and C.W. Medhurst. Hemoglobin values: Comparative survey of the 1976 Canadian Olympic team. *J. Can. Med. Assoc.* 117:614–616, 1977.
11. Clement, D.B., and L.L. Sawchuk. Iron status and sports performance. *Sports Med.* 1:65–74, 1984.
12. Coleman, D.H., A.R. Stevens, H.T. Dodge, and C.A. Finch. Rate of blood regeneration after blood loss. *Arch. Int. Med.* 92:341–349, 1953.
13. Cotes, J.E., J.M. Dobbs, P.C. Elwood, A.M. Hall, A. McDonald, and M.J. Saunders. The response to submaximal exercise in adult females: Relation to hemoglobin concentration. *J. Physiol. (Lond.)* 203:79–80, 1969.
14. Cottrell, R. British army tests blood boosting. *Phys. Sportsmed.* 7:14–16, 1979.
15. Danzinger, R.G., and G.R. Cumming. Effects of chlorothiazide on working capacity of normal subjects. *J. Appl. Physiol.* 19:636–638, 1964.
16. Davis, J.E., and Brewer, N. Effect of physical training on blood volume, hemoglobin alkalai reserve and osmotic resistance of erythrocytes. *Am. J. Physiol.* 113:586–591, 1935.
17. Dugal, R., and M. Bertrand. Doping. In *IOC Medical Commission Handbook.* Montreal: Comité Orginisateur des Jeux Olympiques, 1976, pp. 1–31.
18. Ekblom, B., A.N. Goldbarg, and B. Gullbring. Response to exercise after blood loss and reinfusion. *J. Appl. Physiol.* 33:175–180, 1972.
19. Ekblom, B., G. Wilson, and P.-O. Åstrand. Central circulation during exercise after venesection and reinfusion of red blood cells. *J. Appl. Physiol.* 40:379–383, 1976.
20. Faulkner, J.A., J. Kollias, C.B. Favour, E. Buskirk, and B. Balke. Maximum aerobic capacity and running performance at altitude. *J. Appl. Physiol.* 24:685–691, 1968.
21. Freedson, P.S. The influence of hemoglobin concentration on exercise cardiac output. *Int. J. Sports Med.* 2:81–86, 1981.
22. Gledhill, N. Blood doping and related issues: A brief review. *Med. Sci. Sports Exercise* 14:183–189, 1982.
23. Gledhill, N., F.J. Buick, A.B. Froese, L. Spriet, and E.C. Meyers. An optimal method of storing blood for blood boosting. *Med. Sci. Sports* 10:40, 1978 (abstr.).
24. Gledhill, N., L.L. Spriet, A.B. Froese, D.L. Wilkes, and E.C. Meyers. Acid-base status with induced erythrocythemia and its influence on arterial oxygenation during heavy exercise. *Med. Sci. Sports Exercise* 12:122, 1980 (abstr.).
25. Goforth, H.W., N.L. Campbell, J.A. Hodgson, and A.A. Sucec. Hematological parameters of trained distance runners following induced erythrocythemia. *Med. Sci. Sports Exercise* 14:174, 1982 (abstr.).
26. Gregersen, M.I., and R.A. Dawson. Blood volume. *Physiol. Rev.* 39:307–342, 1959.

27. Gullbring, B., A. Holgren, T. Sjostrand, and T. Strandell. The effect of blood volume variations on the pulse ratio in supine and upright positions during exercise. *Acta Physiol. Scand.* 50:62–71, 1960.
28. Hillman, R.S., and P.A. Henderson. Control of marrow production by level of iron supply. *J. Clin. Invest.* 48:454–460, 1969.
29. Holgren, A., and P.-O. Ästrand. $D_L$ and the dimensions and functional capacities of the $O_2$ transport system in humans. *J. Appl. Physiol.* 2:1463–1470, 1966.
30. Horstman, D.H., M. Gleser, D. Wolfe, T. Tryon, and J. Delehunt. Effects of hemoglobin reduction on $\dot{V}O_2$max and related hemodynamics in exercising dogs. *J. Appl. Physiol.* 37:97–102, 1974.
31. Horstman, D., R. Weiskopft, R. Jackson, and J. Severinghaus. The influence of polycythemia induced by four weeks sojourn at 4300 meters on sea level work capacity. In *Exercise Physiology,* F. Landry and W.A.R. Orban (eds.). Miami: Symposia Specialists, 1978, pp. 533–539.
32. Howell, M.L., and K. Coupe. Effect of blood loss upon performance in the Balke-Ware treadmill test. *Res. Q.* 35:156–165, 1964.
33. Kanstrup, I.-L., and B. Ekblom. Acute hypervolemia, cardiac performance and aerobic power during exercise. *J. Appl. Physiol.* 52:1186–1191, 1982.
34. Kanstrup, I.-L., and B. Ekblom. Blood volume and hemoglobin concentration as determinants of maximal aerobic power. *Med. Sci. Sports Exercise* 16:256–262, 1984.
35. Karpovich, P.V., and N. Millman. Athletes as blood donors. *Res. Q.* 13:166–168, 1942.
36. Kots, Y.M., M.M. Shcherba, Y.S. Kolner, V.D. Gorodetskii, and L.D. Sin. Experimental study of the relationship between the blood hemoglobin and physical aerobic working capacity. *Fiziol. Cheloveka* 4(1):53–60, 1978.
37. Lenfant, C., and K. Sullivan. Adaptation to altitude. *New Eng. J. Med.* 284:1298–1309, 1971.
38. Meryman, H.T., and M. Hornblower. A method for freezing and washing red blood cells using a high glycerol concentration. *Transfusion* 12:145–156, 1972.
39. Mollison, P.L. *Blood Transfusion in Clinical Medicine.* Philadelphia: Blackwell Scientific Publications, 1961, pp. 1–72.
40. Newman, M.N., R. Hamstra, and M. Block. Use of banked autologous blood in elective surgery. *JAMA* 218:861–863, 1971.
41. Pace, N., E.L. Lozner, W.V. Consolazio, G.C. Pitts, and L.J. Pecora. The increase in hypoxia tolerance of normal men accompanying the polycythemia induced by transfusion of erythrocytes. *Am. J. Physiol.* 148:152–163, 1947.
42. Pakarinen, A. Ferritin in sport medicine. *Nordiclab-Newslett.* 4:20–28, 1980.
43. Pate, R., J. McFarland, J. Van Wyck, and A. Okocha. Effects of blood reinfusion on endurance performance in female distance runners. *Med. Sci. Sports* 11:97, 1979 (abstr.).
44. Pate, R. Does the sport need new blood? *Runner's World Magazine* Nov.:25–27, 1976.
45. Robinson, B.F., S.E. Epstein, R.L. Kahler, and E. Braunwald. Circulatory effects of acute expansion of blood volume: Studies during maximal exercise and at rest. *Circ. Res.* 19:26–32, 1966.
46. Robertson, R.J., R. Gilcher, K.R. Metz, G.S. Skrinar, T.G. Allison, H.T. Bahnson, R.A. Abbott, R. Becker, and J. Falkel. Effect of induced erythrocythemia on hypoxia tolerance during physical exercise. *J. Appl. Physiol.* 53:490–492, 1982.
47. Saltin, B. Circulatory response to submaximal and maximal exercise after thermal dehydration. *J. Appl. Physiol.* 19:1125–1132, 1964.
48. Sjostrand, T. Volume and distribution of blood and their significance in regulating the circulation. *Physiol. Rev.* 33:202–228, 1953.
49. Smyth, S. Blood doping recap. *Track Field News* 32(May):58, 1979.

50. Spriet, L.L., N. Gledhill, A.B. Froese, D.L. Wilkes, and E.C. Meyers. The effect of induced erythrocythemia on central circulation and oxygen transport during maximal exercise. *Med. Sci. Sports Exercise* 12:122, 1980 (abstr.).
51. Sproule, B.J., J.H. Mitchell, and W.F. Miller. Cardiopulmonary physiological responses to heavy exercise in patients with anemia. *J. Clin. Invest.* 39:378–388, 1960.
52. Thompson, J.M., J.A. Stone, A.D. Ginsburg, and P. Hamilton. $O_2$ transport during exercise following blood reinfusion. *J. Appl. Physiol.* 53:1213–1219, 1982.
53. Thomson, J.M., J.A. Stone, A.D. Ginsburg, and P. Hamilton. The effects of blood reinfusion during prolonged heavy exercise. *Can. J. Appl. Sport Sci.* 8:72–78, 1983.
54. Valeri, C.R. *Blood Banking and the Use of Frozen Blood Products.* Cleveland: CRC Press, 1976, pp. 9–174.
55. Videma, T., and T. Rytomaa. Effect of blood removal and autotransfusion on heart rate response to a submaximal workload. *J. Sports Med. Phys. Fitness* 17:387–390, 1977.
56. Von Rost, R., W. Hollmann, H. Liesen, and D. Schulten. Uber den einfluss einer erythrozyten-retransfusion auf die kardio-pulmonale leistungsfahigkeit. *Sportarzt Sportmed.* 26:137–144, 1975.
57. Wadsworth, G.R. Recovery from acute hemorrhage in normal men and women. *J. Physiol.* 129:583–593, 1955.
58. Williams, M.H., A.R. Goodwin, R. Perkins, and J. Bocrie. Effect of blood reinjection upon endurance capacity and heart rate. *Med. Sci. Sports* 5:181–186, 1973.
59. Williams, M.H., M. Lindhejm, and R. Schuster. The effect of blood infusion upon endurance capacity and ratings of perceived exertion. *Med. Sci. Sports* 10:113–118, 1978.
60. Williams, M.H., S. Wesseldine, T. Somma, and R. Schuster. The effect of induced erythrocythemia upon 5-mile treadmill run time. *Med. Sci. Sports Exercise* 13:169–175, 1981.
61. Williams, M.H. Blood doping in sports. *J. Drug Issues* 3:331–340, 1980.
62. Woodson, R.D., R.E. Willis, and C. Lenfant. Effect of acute and established anemia on $O_2$ transport at rest, submaximal and maximal work. *J. Appl. Physiol.* 44:36–43, 1978.
63. Yamada, T. Hematological adaptations with training. *Jpn. J. Phys. Fitness* 7:231–242, 1958.

# Muscle Blood Flow During Locomotory Exercise

M. HAROLD LAUGHLIN, Ph.D.
R.B. ARMSTRONG, Ph.D.

It is generally agreed that Gaskell was the first to study the physiology of circulation in skeletal muscle in detail. He worked in Carl Ludwig's laboratory in the Institute of Physiology at Leipzig in the 1870s. Since that time there have been numerous studies performed on skeletal muscle circulation that have investigated central and local control mechanisms, autoregulation of blood flow, the response of the circulation to occlusion (i.e., reactive hyperemic responses), and the effects of contraction and exercise. Many reviews have been published on the general physiology of the circulation in skeletal muscle [18, 50, 70, 71, 79, 81, 92, 136–138, 141, 143, 146, 152]. The purpose of this article is to review available information concerning the blood flow responses of skeletal muscles during exercise. Since previous reviews have covered this topic in relation to studies conducted on isolated muscle preparations, we will focus on muscle blood flow responses in conscious animals during locomotory exercise.

The cardiovascular responses to rhythmic exercise are dramatic. Marked increases occur in oxygen consumption, ventilation, and cardiac output, and the distribution of cardiac output throughout the body is altered [24, 38, 40, 128, 133, 135, 157]. The basic reason for these changes is to support the increased muscle metabolism that accompanies exercise. If the exercise is to be maintained, it is necessary that the muscle contractions be fueled by aerobic metabolism, which is dependent upon muscle circulation. Thus, muscle blood flow must be sufficient to provide adequate oxygen and substrate (e.g., free fatty acids and glucose) for oxidative metabolism, to remove metabolites, and to maintain temperature homeostasis. When one considers the biological economy that is observed in organisms under most physiologic conditions and the magnitude of the total muscle mass of mammals (40–50% of body mass), it would be expected that blood flow during exercise would be directed primarily to the active fibers in the muscles that are designed for aerobic metabolism. All

The authors' work is supported by the National Institutes of Health Grants HL-29428, HL-26963, AM-25472, the Tulsa Chapter of the American Heart Association, and Oral Roberts University Research Funds.

95

available information indicates that this is true [8, 21, 22, 84, 88, 99, 100, 103, 147]. During normal muscular activities such as postural maintenance (standing), walking, running, or swimming, muscle blood flow is directed to the active oxidative fibers in the muscles.

## BLOOD FLOW IN RESTING MUSCLE

*Muscle Fiber Type Properties and Distributions*
Since there is evidence of a relationship between muscle fiber type and blood flow in resting and exercising muscle [8, 18, 25, 26, 28, 29, 56, 74, 79, 80, 81, 94, 102, 107, 111, 121, 125], we first briefly describe the types of skeletal muscle fibers and their distribution within and among muscles. Mammalian skeletal muscles are composed of fibers with different physiologic, morphologic, and biochemical characteristics. The properties of the fibers have been thoroughly reviewed by others [26, 32, 33, 133].

A number of different classification systems for the fibers based on histochemistry have been proposed [33, 41, 133]. One approach has been to indicate twitch speed from myofibrillar adenosine triphosphatase (ATPase) activity, and oxidative potential from the activity of a mitochondrial enzyme. In this review we refer to three different fiber types using the classification system suggested by Peter and co-workers [119] in which the fibers are identified as fast-twitch oxidative glycolitic (FOG), fast-twitch glycolitic (FG), and slow-twitch oxidative (SO). The advantage of this system is that the metabolic and physiologic properties of the muscle fibers are included in the terminology. This classification system is similar to that of Burke and co-workers [34] in which the fibers are referred to as fast fatigue resistant, fast fatigable, and slow, respectively. The system, based on ATPase and a mitochondrial enzyme, has also been considered transposable with that in which the fibers are treated with acid preincubation for myosin ATPase and identified as types IIa (FOG), IIb (FG), and I (SO) [145]. However, others have shown that the two methods of classification are not completely analogous [60, 116].

It is convenient to use histochemistry to classify the fibers in muscles into discrete types, but there is a continuum among the fibers for any given functional property [32]. For example, motor units in cat gastrocnemius muscle identified as slow-twitch from histochemistry have twitch contraction times that vary from 58 to 110 msec; twitch contraction times for fast motor units in the same muscle are 20 to 55 msec [34]. Also, not all mammals have these three distinct fiber types. For example, most dogs do not have the FG fiber type in their locomotory muscles [14, 69, 110], although white (FG) fibers have been observed in the muscles of some dogs [151]. Similarly, the FOG fiber type is not as obvious in human locomotory muscles as in most other mammalian muscles [133], but the FOG/FG/SO method of classification has been used for classifying human muscle fibers [51].

The three fiber types are distributed in typical patterns within and among the muscles in synergistic groups in most mammalian species [5, 6, 8, 13, 14, 16, 42, 99]. These distribution patterns are illustrated in Figure 1. In extensor, antigravity muscle groups (e.g., the ankle extensor group) the deepest muscle or muscles in the group (e.g., soleus in Fig. 1) usually have a high proportion of SO fibers. In the more peripheral muscles (e.g., gastrocnemius in Fig. 1) in the antigravity muscle groups the FOG and SO fibers are primarily situated in the deeper portions of the muscles and the FG fibers in the more superficial parts. Although this distribution pattern of fiber types within and among muscles is not as extreme in the leg and thigh muscle of human subjects, it nonetheless appears to exist [51, 61, 87, 106]. In flexor muscles the distribution of fiber types within the muscles is similar to that described for the extensor muscles, i.e., the SO and FOG fibers are primarily situated in the deeper parts of the muscles, and the FG fibers are primarily situated in the superficial parts of the muscles (e.g., tibialias anterior) [6, 13, 100]. However, the flexor muscle groups do not have a deeply situated muscle that is primarily composed of SO fibers [5, 13, 100]. The spatial distribution of the fiber types in locomotory muscles has made it convenient to study relationships between blood flow and fiber types in conscious animals [102].

*Blood Flow in Resting Muscles*
Prior to 1967 conclusions from muscle blood flow studies were made with the assumption (either stated or not stated) that muscle tissue is homogeneous [79]. Starting with the work of Reis et al. [125], the results of several investigations [56, 74, 80] indicated that blood flow in resting muscle is related to the predominant fiber type of the muscle with fast white muscles (primarily FOG and FG fibers) having lower blood flows than slow red (SO) muscles (Table 1). More recent studies [28, 29, 99, 107], starting with that of Bockman et al. [28], have shown no differences between blood flows to inactive fast and slow muscles in anesthetized animals (Table 1). The differences between these studies and the earlier work may be partially related to technical difficulties [29, 74, 75, 77, 78], particularly the surgical procedures used in isolating the muscles, which can cause changes in resting blood flow [25, 118]. This is illustrated by the experiments of Mackie and Terjung [107], in which there were no differences in resting blood flow among the red and white portions of the gastrocnemius muscle and the soleus muscle in anesthetized rats prior to

FIGURE 1

*Cross-section of rat leg (right) showing the distribution of high-oxidative (FOG plus SO) fibers within and among the muscles. Intensity of shading is proportional to the population of high-oxidative fibers. Muscles are: tibialis anterior (TA), red (R) and white (W) parts; tibialis posterior (TP); flexor hallicus longus (FHL); flexor digitorum longus (FDL); extensor digitorum longus (EDL); peroneals (PER); soleus (SO); plantaris (PL); and gastrocnemius (G), red (R), middle (M), and white (W) parts. Directions are anterior (A), lateral (L), posterior (P), and medial (M).*

SOURCE: Amrstrong, R.B., and Phelps, R.O. Muscle fiber type composition of the rat hindlimb. *Am. J. Anat.* 171:259–272, 1984. Reprinted with permission.

## RAT LEG MUSCLES : % SO + % FOG

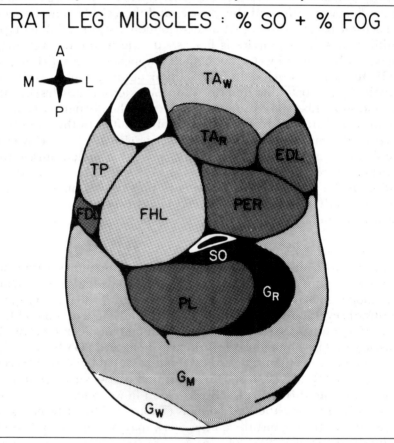

surgical isolation of the muscles (Table 1). However, after surgical preparation of the muscles for in situ studies the resting flow of the soleus muscle had doubled while no change occurred in the red and white parts of the gastrocnemius muscle. These findings demonstrate

TABLE 1
*Reported Resting Muscle Blood Flows as a Function of Fiber Type*

| Study | Muscle | Fiber Type (%) | | | Species | Blood Flow (ml/min/100 g) | Blood Flow Technique |
|---|---|---|---|---|---|---|---|
| | | SO | FOG | FG | | | |
| Reis et al., 1967 [125] | G | 22 | 15 | 63 | cat | 12 | Rb$^{86}$ K$^{42}$ |
| | S | 100 | 0 | 0 | | 31 | Rb$^{86}$ K$^{42}$ |
| Folkow and Halicka, 1968 [56] | G | 22 | 15 | 63 | cat | 9 | venous outflow |
| | S | 100 | 0 | 0 | | 20 | venous outflow |
| Hilton et al., 1970 [74] | EDL | 14 | 31 | 55 | cat | 14 | venous outflow |
| | S | 100 | 0 | 0 | | 52 | venous outflow |
| Hudlicka, 1975 [80] | G | 22 | 15 | 63 | cat | 7 | venous outflow |
| | S | 100 | 0 | 0 | | 40 | venous outflow |
| Bockman et al., 1980 [28] | Gra | 15 | 72 | 13 | cat | 4 | venous outflow |
| | S | 100 | 0 | 0 | | 7 | venous outflow |
| Bonde-Petersen and Robertson, 1981 [29] | G | 22 | 15 | 63 | cat | 7 | microspheres |
| | S | 100 | 0 | 0 | | 5 | microspheres |
| | P | 26 | 28 | 46 | | 7 | microspheres |
| Petrofsky et al., 1981 [121] | G | 22 | 15 | 63 | cat | 7 | venous outflow |
| | S | 100 | 0 | 0 | | 13 | venous outflow |
| Laughlin et al., 1982 [102] | G | 30 | 62 | 8 | rat | 8 | microspheres |
| | S | 80 | 20 | 0 | | 9 | microspheres |
| Mackie and Terjung, 1983 [107] | G$_R$ | 34 | 60 | 6 | rat (before surgery) | 10 | microspheres |
| | G$_W$ | 0 | 10 | 90 | | 6 | microspheres |
| | S | 80 | 20 | 0 | | 10 | microspheres |
| | G$_R$ | 34 | 60 | 6 | rat (after surgery) | 10 | microspheres |
| | G$_W$ | 0 | 10 | 90 | | 7 | microspheres |
| | S | 80 | 20 | 0 | | 20 | microspheres |

Fiber type data are means; blood flow data are means ± SEM.
Muscles are: gastrocnemius (G); soleus (S); extensor digitorum longus (EDL); gracilis (Gra); plantaris (P); red gastrocnemius (G$_R$); and white gastrocnemius (G$_W$). Cat fiber type data are from Ariano et al. [5], rat fiber type data are from Mackie and Terjung [107], and rat G fiber type data are from Armstrong and Phelps [13].

that in in situ muscle studies the surgical isolation procedure can alter resting blood flows, and available data suggest that these effects are more pronounced in muscles composed primarily of the SO fiber type [25, 78, 79, 107, 118].

The most important factor in producing differences in the resting muscle blood flow values in conscious animals is the level of contractile activity of the motor units in the muscles. Blood flows to intact soleus, plantaris, and gastrocnemius muscles in anesthetized rats are the same [102], but in conscious rats under various resting conditions there are large differences in blood flow among and within muscles [8, 99, 100, 102]. In these animals the blood flow in the deep slow antigravity muscles (e.g., soleus) is severalfold higher than in the synergistic fast muscles. Similarly, Reis et al. [125] reported that soleus muscle blood flow was about three times that in gastrocnemius muscle in conscious cats (Table 1).

During postural maintenance muscular force is provided by SO motor units [32, 140, 159]. Electromyographic (EMG) and tendon-force recordings in cats indicate the soleus muscle is nearly maximally active during quiet standing [140, 159]. The SO motor units in synergistic extensor muscles may also be recruited during postural maintenance, since these muscles produce some force in the postural mode [159]. This same pattern of recruitment probably occurs in all the major antigravity muscle groups since the extensor muscle groups of the forelimbs and hindlimbs of most mammals contain at least one deep slow-twitch muscle [5, 6, 42]. The blood flow distribution in rat muscles closely corresponds to these patterns of fiber recruitment [99]. Rats standing in the quadrupedal position have the highest blood flows in the regions of SO motor units and there is a close relationship ($r > 0.90$, $p < 0.05$) between the resting blood flows and SO fiber populations (% SO fibers) of the muscles [8, 99, 100].

The importance of fiber recruitment patterns on muscle blood flow is illustrated by comparing blood flows in rat soleus and plantaris muscles under various nonexercise (resting) conditions (Fig. 2). The variation in soleus muscle flows probably reflects to a large degree different levels of activity, since the animals were free to move about or groom under all conditions except when they were anesthetized (MOF anesthesia, Fig. 2). Thus, the fact that an animal is not exercising (i.e., the animal is resting) does not necessarily mean that its muscles are not active.

A second factor that appears to influence preexercise muscle blood flow values in conscious rats is the type, intensity, and duration of training of the rats prior to the experiments. The speed used in the training or treadmill familiarization protocol (1–2-week duration) is apparently anticipated by the rat before the treadmill is turned on,

FIGURE 2

*Resting muscle blood flows in rat soleus (S) and plantaris (P) muscles under various conditions.*

SOURCE: Data for the first two sets of bar graphs from [102]. The postswim and preswim data are from [103]. The postwalk data are from [100]. Preexercise (trained) data are from [10]. The preexercise (speed) data are from [99]. The preexercise (gallop) and postgallop (3-min) data are from [8].

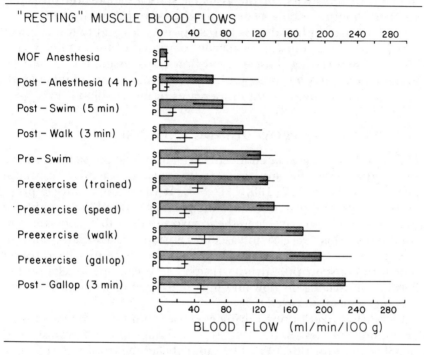

which in turn seems to influence the preexercise blood flow in the muscles (Fig. 2). Also, following prolonged treadmill training (13–17 weeks) rats have higher preexercise blood flows in deep red muscles and muscle parts [10]. The regulatory mechanisms involved in these adaptations in soleus muscle are not known. There is not as much variation in resting blood flows in the synergistic fast-twitch plantaris muscle as in the soleus muscle (Fig. 2). This may be because the plantaris muscle is minimally active during all preexercise conditions studied, since it contains less than 10 percent SO fibers [5, 99]. Bell et al. [19] studied muscle blood flow in the hindlimbs of standing oxen and found that flows ranged from 3 to 9 ml/min/100 g in semitendinosus and rectus femoris muscles, respectively. Blood flows in the same muscles of standing rats [99] and dogs [115] are severalfold higher. It is not known if ox blood flows are lower because of metabolic differences or because of possible differences in the mode of postural maintenance.

In conclusion, blood flows to intact muscles of various fiber types are quite similar if the muscles are completely inactive. There may be small differences in basal metabolic rates among the different types of fibers in inactive muscles, but these differences appear to be below the level of sensitivity for the available muscle blood flow measurement techniques. There is evidence that surgical manipulation can cause increases in blood flow to resting muscles and that this effect may be greater in muscles primarily composed of the SO fiber type. Finally, when resting muscle blood flow is discussed, it is important to define exactly what is meant by resting, since even minimal levels of motor unit activity result in increases in muscle blood flow.

## MUSCLE BLOOD FLOW DURING EXERCISE

Many studies using isolated in situ skeletal muscle preparations have shown that when the muscle starts to contract, vascular resistance decreases [17, 18, 137, 138, 141–143]. If the isolated muscle preparation is perfused under constant pressure (free-flow) conditions (which is more comparable to the in vivo situation than constant flow conditions), this decrease in vascular resistance is associated with increases in muscle blood flow [142]. Most investigators have found that with constant pressure perfusion there is a linear relationship between muscle blood flow and muscle oxygen consumption in contracting skeletal muscle [141].

Blood flow distribution during exercise is not homogeneous within or among muscles [8, 99, 100, 103], although many have assumed that it is [46, 118, 126, 144]. The radiolabeled microsphere technique has demonstrated a marked nonhomogeneity in blood flow in muscles of animals in which the fiber types are regionally concentrated within muscles [8, 99, 107]. Other techniques that have been used to study muscle blood flow have not permitted an appreciation for differences in flow within the muscles during contraction.

The incorrect assumption of homogeneity is also partially due to the fact that much of the information concerning the effects of muscle contraction on the muscle vascular bed has come from studies using in situ preparations. A typical in situ muscle blood flow experiment consists of electrical stimulation of a surgically isolated muscle in an anesthetized animal with the neural and vascular supply intact and the tendon of insertion connected to a force transducer. One of the major advantages of in situ experimentation is that it allows the investigator to control more variables than is possible with conscious animals. The stimulation characteristics are among the more important of these controlled variables. The muscles are usually electrically stimulated directly or through the motor nerve with supramaximal voltages so that all fibers in the muscle are simultaneously active [18, 79]. Muscle performance is typically varied by altering the stimulation frequency [79]. Attempts have been made to investigate the effects of varying fiber recruitment patterns in muscles on blood flow either by varying stimulation voltage so the more peripheral fibers are recruited first [91] or by the combination of stimulation and anodal block [121]. The latter technique is designed to produce a more physiologic order of recruitment of muscle fibers according to the size principle [72]. A second variable that is controlled in in situ studies is the type of contraction. Most investigators have used twitch or tetanic isometric contractions in studies of functional hyperemia, although some have employed isotonic contractions [79]. Although the stimulation and contraction characteristics can be controlled in in situ preparations, available techniques do not simulate the complex recruitment patterns and resulting mechanical changes that occur in muscles during locomotion in conscious animals [32, 33].

*Muscle Fiber Recruitment Patterns During Exercise*
Before discussing muscle blood flow during locomotory exercise, we consider the available information about spatial patterns of motor unit activation in normal locomotion. Information about fiber recruitment patterns within and among muscles during locomotion primarily comes from studies using EMG [52, 58, 140, 159], measures of muscle force on tendons [117, 159], and fiber glycogen loss [12, 15, 59, 148]. Recruitment patterns can also be inferred from spatial patterns of enzymatic adaptation among the muscles with training at different intensities [49, 149]. There are limitations to each of these techniques, but a general picture has emerged that is reasonably consistent. These recruitment patterns have been discussed in detail in recent reviews [32, 57, 133].

As described above, when an animal is standing prior to exercise, most of the force is supplied by SO fibers in the muscles [148, 159]. When the animal walks on the treadmill, FOG fibers are recruited to provide the increased forces [12], while SO fibers in the muscles continue to be active [12, 140, 159]. FG fibers are not active during slow locomotion. At slow trotting speeds, the force appears to be produced by SO and FOG fibers in most muscles [12, 148]; in some animals there is an additive recruitment of FG fibers in extensor muscles during high-speed trotting [12]. During galloping a progressive recruitment of FG muscle fibers occurs so that when the animal is obtaining maximal speeds FG fibers in the most superficial parts of the muscles are activated to produce force [12, 148]. There is probably a further peripheral recruitment of FG motor units when the animal jumps [140, 159]. Thus, during terrestrial locomotion there is an additive recruitment of SO to FOG to FG fibers as the animal increases running speed [32]. It is apparent from the metabolic characteristics of the fiber types that as long as the animal can perform the exercise with SO and FOG fibers, the exercise can be continued for relatively long periods of time [32]. However, once the exercise intensity is high enough to require recruitment of significant numbers of FG motor units, the duration of exercise is limited [49, 148]. The order of recruitment among the fiber types appears to be similar for most motor tasks [32], although there are exceptions [7, 139]. The spatial distribution patterns of the fiber types within and among human extensor muscles [51, 61, 87, 106] do not show the degree of stratification that is observed in most quadrupeds [5, 6], but it is probable that the patterns of recruitment in human locomotory muscles are generally similar to those described above [32, 133].

These general spatial patterns of fiber recruitment in the muscles during locomotory exercise can be described in simple terms as above, but the actual performance of the motor units in locomotion is exceedingly complex. Variations in muscular force are controlled by the central nervous system through a combination of recruitment of variable numbers of motor units and of frequency modulation or rate coding in the individual motor units [32]. Furthermore, in rhythmic terrestrial locomotion the muscles actively produce force while lengthening, shortening, and maintaining a constant length in each stride cycle, as well as passively changing length [63, 159]. It would be expected that the metabolic and mechanical effects associated with the muscular force and length changes in locomotion would influence the magnitude and patterns of circulation in the muscles [55, 99, 136].

It is clear that when muscles are stimulated to contract in in situ experiments the patterns of fiber activation and mechanical dynamics are not the same as the patterns that occur during locomotory exercise. With these considerations in mind it is misleading to refer to the muscle contractions in in situ experiments as "exercise." It is more accurate to describe these experiments simply as studies of contracting muscles.

*Muscle Blood Flow During Physiological Exercise*
Several studies performed in the late 1960s [4, 48, 153, 156] demonstrated that the elevations in blood flow to whole hindlimbs in conscious animals during exercise are rapid and dramatic. Until recently, techniques for measuring muscle blood flow during loco-

motory exercise did not permit study of flow distribution within and among muscles. In 1976, Fixler et al. [53] reported that blood flows (as determined with radio-labeled microspheres) to diaphragm, intercostal muscle, and gastrocnemius muscle increase from averages of 15 to 17 ml/min/100 g at rest up to 96, 43, and 55 ml/min/100 g, respectively, in conscious dogs performing moderate exercise on the treadmill. These findings demonstrated that there are differences in the magnitude of the elevations in blood flow to various skeletal muscles during locomotory exercise. Flaim et al. [54], who studied the response of rat skeletal muscle to aquatic and treadmill exercise with the microsphere technique, also found a diversity of responses of various skeletal muscles ranging from no change (when comparing rest to exercise) up to considerable increases in blood flow (100-fold). These authors [54] did not systematically sample muscles within groups or regions within muscles with widely divergent fiber populations, so it was not possible to determine relationships between blood flow and the fiber types or muscle fiber recruitment patterns.

Laughlin and Armstrong [8, 10, 99, 100, 102, 103] studied muscle blood flows in rats with the microsphere technique under various baseline conditions (as shown in Fig. 2) and during different levels, durations, and types of exercise. Since data are available concerning the fiber type populations of the muscles and the muscle fiber recruitment patterns of rats under similar conditions, the results of these blood flow studies have provided an understanding of relationships between the regional muscle blood flow patterns during locomotory exercise and the fiber types and fiber recruitment patterns. In rats standing on the treadmill anticipating exercise, muscle blood flow is proportional to the SO fiber population in the muscle [8, 99]. During treadmill locomotion blood flows increase as a function of speed in most muscles (Fig. 3). At each of the treadmill speeds studied in rats, from fast walking through high-speed galloping, the elevation in blood flow over preexercise is directly related to the FOG fiber percentage in the muscle [99]. These studies reveal that blood flow patterns in muscles consisting largely of FG fibers are different from those in muscles that are predominantly SO or FOG [99]. White muscles show initial decreases in blood flow below preexercise levels during walking (15 m/min, Fig. 3) indicating vasoconstriction of resistance vessels in the regions of inactive FG fibers [90]. At higher running speeds (75 m/min) when the fibers in the white portions of muscles are recruited [148], the blood flows are still only increased to 30–60 ml/min/100 g (GW, Fig. 3), while the deeper red portions of the same muscles (GR, Fig. 3) have blood flows of 250–300 ml/min/100 g [8, 99]. These data suggest that once fibers are active, the amount of blood flow received is proportional to the oxidative ca-

FIGURE 3

*Rat muscle blood flows as a function of treadmill running speed. GR, GM, and GW are red, middle, and white gastrocnemius muscle samples, respectively. P, S, and TA are plantaris, soleus, and tibialis anterior muscles, respectively.*

SOURCE: Data from [99]. Reprinted with permission.

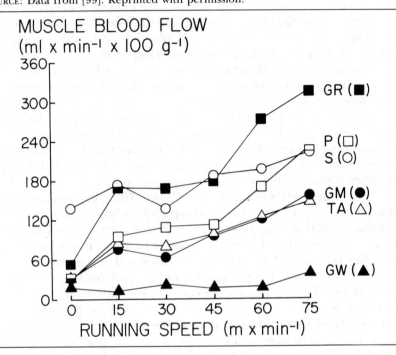

pacities of the fibers [99]. These studies on rats performing treadmill exercise were the first to demonstrate that muscle blood flow is preferentially distributed to the active oxidative fibers within muscles during in vivo exercise.

Blood flow continues to be directed to active FOG and SO fibers within extensor muscles in rats during prolonged, low-intensity treadmill exercise [100]. In addition, the blood flow response as a function of time during slow treadmill exercise is different within and among muscles [100]. Of particular interest is the fact that in rats red muscle blood flows progressively increase with time during low-intensity treadmill exercise so that by 1 hour flows are as high as those observed during high-speed running [100]. The reason for this elevation is not known. Muscle blood flow has also been investigated in rats as a function of time during high-speed running [8]. Blood flow increases rapidly in the deep red extensor muscles (red gastrocnemius in Fig.

4) at the start of high-speed running. Through 3 minutes of high-speed running (60 m/min), extensor muscle blood flow is a function of the FOG fiber population [8]. White muscle blood flow only increases to 70–80 ml/min/100 g through 3 minutes of high-speed exercise whereas red muscle flows increase to 350–400 ml/min/100 g [8] (Fig. 4). When the rats stop running, blood flow in the red muscles returns to preexercise levels (or below) within 30 seconds, whereas in the white muscles blood flow remains elevated for as long as 3 minutes after exercise (Fig. 4). Thus, FG fibers receive less blood flow per gram of tissue when they are active [8, 97, 100], and the temporal changes in blood flow to these fibers are different from those to the high-oxidative fibers [8, 99, 100].

Although the hypothesis that muscle blood flow is directed to active oxidative (SO and FOG) muscle fibers during normal exercise has consistently been supported by the data for rat extensor muscles during treadmill locomotion [8, 10, 99, 100], the relationships be-

FIGURE 4
*Muscle blood flow as a function of time in rats running at 60 m/min on a treadmill.*
SOURCE: Data are from Armstrong and Laughlin [8].

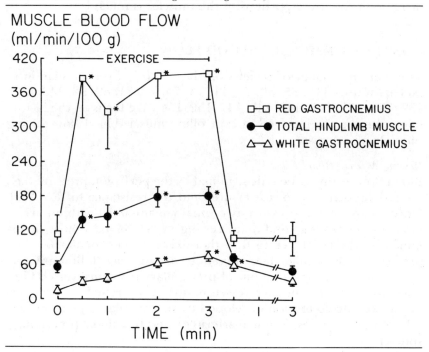

MUSCLE BLOOD FLOW
(ml/min/100 g)

tween blood flow and fiber type populations are less apparent in flexor muscles [8, 10, 100]. In swimming rats, the blood flows to the flexor muscles are relatively high compared to those in the extensor muscles, and the flexor muscle blood flows during swimming are a linear function of the populations of oxidative fiber types of the muscles [103]. Unlike terrestrial locomotion, during swimming the extensor muscle blood flows are not related to muscle fiber type. It is probable that these differences between the distribution patterns of muscle blood flow during swimming and treadmill exercise in rats are due to alterations in the relative activities of the respective muscle groups [103]. Whereas during terrestrial locomotion the extensor muscles are relatively more active than the flexors, during swimming the flexor muscles are as active or more so than the antagonistic extensors [67, 68].

In conclusion, blood flow within muscles is primarily directed to the active oxidative muscle fibers during all stages of locomotory exercise including standing, walking, running (at different speeds), and swimming. During postural maintenance, when the force is generated by SO fibers, blood flow is directed to the SO fibers in the extensor muscles. In locomotory exercise, elevations in flow are primarily directed to the recruited FOG fibers. At high running speeds, blood flow to FG fiber areas also increases, but the magnitude of the increase in the white portions of the muscles is much less.

## CONTROL OF MUSCLE BLOOD FLOW

There are a number of reviews on the control of the circulation in skeletal muscle [18, 35, 50, 70, 71, 73, 75, 79, 81, 89, 92, 113, 122, 129, 136–138, 141–143, 146, 147, 152, 154]. We focus on the factors that appear to be involved in controlling muscle blood flow during physiologic exercise.

### Resting Muscle Blood Flow
Blood flow to any tissue is determined by the perfusion pressure (i.e., arterial pressure–venous pressure) and the resistance to flow [79]. Since mean arterial pressure is normally maintained within narrow limits under resting conditions, resting muscle blood flow is determined by the resistance to flow that exists in the vascular bed. As predicted by Poiseuille's law, alterations in resistance to flow are normally due to changes in radius of precapillary resistance vessels [79]. The radius of the resistance vessels in turn is controlled by variations in the contractile tension developed by the vascular smooth muscle cells of the arterioles, terminal arterioles, and functional precapillary sphincters.

The level of contractile activity of the vascular smooth muscle is influenced by many factors. These can be divided into three general categories: myogenic, neurohumoral, and local metabolic. The myogenic factors include the inherent characteristics of the vascular smooth muscle (i.e., spontaneous activity, responses to stretch, responses to temperature change, etc.) [89, 154]. The influences of neurohumoral and tissue metabolic factors are then superimposed on the existing myogenic tone.

The neurohumoral control of muscle blood flow has been the subject of several recent reviews [35, 70, 71, 73, 79, 113, 136, 137, 147, 152, 156]. Sympathetic nervous system activity to intact resting skeletal muscle is generally believed to be high relative to other tissues, since there is a constant discharge of the sympathetic postganglionic neurons that terminate in the proximity of the vascular smooth muscle cells [136, 137]. These neurons release norepinephrine that binds to alpha receptors on the vascular smooth muscle cell membranes causing contraction. Interruption of sympathetic tone either with alpha adrenergic blocking drugs or with sympathetic denervation results in a 50–100 percent increase in resting muscle blood flow [56, 79, 130, 136, 137]. However, this increase is transient in that 12 to 24 hours following denervation resting blood flows return to normal levels [79]. The cause of this restoration of basal vascular tone in the sympathectomized muscles is unknown.

There are also several reviews on the local control of vascular tone [50, 70, 71, 89, 136, 143, 146, 148, 154]. As illustrated in Figure 5, several tissue metabolic factors have been proposed as mediators between muscle metabolism and blood flow. Local modulators that can cause vasodilation include low $PO_2$ in the blood or tissue, increased $H^+$ concentration, increased $CO_2$ concentration, changes in tissue osmolarity, and release of adenosine, adenine nucleotides, potassium ions, prostaglandins, histamine, kinins, and phosphates. It is not known which one or combination of these factors is primarily involved in regulation of resting blood flow.

*Muscle Blood Flow During Exercise*
Contraction of skeletal muscle, both in in situ and in vivo studies, is associated with a rapid and dramatic increase in blood flow. In 1961 Barcroft stated in the *Handbook of Physiology* that "the mechanism of the increase in blood flow associated with exercise is not yet understood" and that "it is the most important problem in the field of skeletal muscle circulation." More recently, Stainsby [146] observed that "rather little research into local control mechanisms has been very probing, and new ideas seem to be few relative to the amount of experimentation." Since these reviews were published, there have

FIGURE 5

*Metabolic factors proposed to be involved in the local control of muscle blood flow under resting conditions (left) and during exercise (right). The relative concentrations of metabolites in the interstitial fluid are illustrated by the size of the letters. When the skeletal muscle cells are inactive, the $O_2$ concentration is high, the metabolite concentrations are low, and the resistance vessels (arterioles) are constricted. During exercise, metabolites are released from the skeletal muscle cells causing the vascular smooth muscle cells to relax resulting in vasodilation. See the text for further details.*

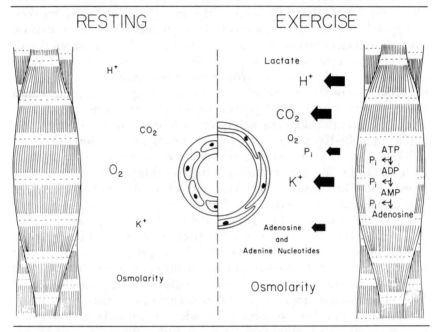

been a multitude of studies designed to determine the mechanisms responsible for the increase in blood flow associated with muscular activity [17, 25–28, 47, 50, 62, 64, 75, 77, 78, 92, 94, 112–114, 136, 141–143]. In spite of the effort devoted to solving this problem, the mechanism(s) is (are) still not fully understood [50, 79, 82, 89, 113, 136, 138, 141–143].

There are marked reductions in resistance in the vascular bed of muscle during contraction. This decrease in resistance may result from myogenic, neurohumoral, and local metabolic interactions as discussed above. Since evidence suggests that the factors responsible for the initial (0–1 min) and sustained (> 1 min) blood flow responses to exercise are different [71, 75, 77, 136], the two are considered separately.

*Initial phase.* During the first few seconds of low-intensity exercise, muscle blood flow increases rapidly in high-oxidative and mixed muscles and is transiently elevated above the exercise steady state levels for 30 to 60 seconds [100]. At the slower running speeds, this overshoot in initial hyperemia appears to be independent of exercise intensity, since the muscle flows at 1 min of exercise are similar from speeds of 15 m/min through 45 m/min for rats running on the treadmill (Fig. 3 [99]). By 5 min of exercise the blood flows decrease to steady state levels that are proportional to exercise intensity [10, 100]. At running speeds above 45 m/min, the 1-min blood flows are proportional to the exercise intensity (Fig. 3). These observations suggest that at the slower running speeds there is an "on" signal that activates hyperemia in the red muscle that is independent of the amount of contractile activity in the muscle, and that the flow is adjusted to the metabolic requirements of the active muscles as exercise continues.

The rapidity and the intensity-independent nature of the initial hyperemia at the slow speeds make it tempting to suggest some form of neural involvement, either through the sympathetic nervous system or a linkage to the motor system. However, the on signal could as well be provided by the release of a local vasodilator substance. Others have reported that the rapid increase in blood flow at the initiation of exercise may be partially related to the sympathetic nervous system through withdrawal of sympathetic adrenergic stimulation (or tone) or through sympathetic cholinergic stimulation [77, 86, 129, 136, 137, 141]. Also, rapid increases in muscle blood flow may be produced by the anticipation of exercise or other emotional stress [23, 73, 86, 152]. However, studies on animals with sympathectomized hindlimbs argue against a significant involvement of the sympathetic nervous system in the initial hyperemia. Donald et al. [48] reported that unilateral lumbar sympathectomy has no effect on the total hindlimb blood flow response recorded from iliac artery flow probes in dogs at the initiation of treadmill exercise. In studies of the distribution of flow within and among muscles in lumbar sympathectomized rats performing low-speed locomotory exercise on the treadmill, it was found that the sympathetic innervation is not required for the rapid increase in muscle blood flow observed at the start of exercise in the red oxidative muscles [120]. Therefore, the sympathetic nerve influences on the initial increases in muscle blood during exercise appear to be minimal. We also investigated the effects of circulating epinephrine released from the adrenal glands on the initial hyperemia of exercise (unpublished observations). Neither adrenalmedullectomy alone nor adrenalmedullectomy in combination with hindlimb sympathectomy significantly alters the initial blood flow response in rat muscles during exercise. Thus, the hyperemia in the active muscles at the initiation of locomotory exercise does not appear to be dependent upon the sympathetic nervous system, at least not in the species studied to date (dog and rat).

Although the sympathetic nervous system appears to have no net effect on the initial hyperemia in oxidative muscle during low-speed exercise, preferential beta blockade does alter the magnitude of the response. Use of the beta-adrenergic blocking drugs propranolol ($\beta_1$ and $\beta_2$) or butoxamine ($\beta_2$) decreases the initial elevation in blood flow by 20–30 percent during slow-speed treadmill exercise in rats [101].

A direct neural linkage between the motor units and their vascular supply is an attractive notion as a mechanism for rapidly matching blood flow to recruited muscle fibers [4], but there is little experimental evidence to support the idea. Honig et al. [77, 78] have suggested that the increase in blood flow during exercise is initiated by neuronal cell bodies located in the arteriolar walls that could be stimulated by collaterals from $\alpha$-motoneurons or muscle spindle afferents. According to this hypothetical scheme, motor unit recruitment and capillary recruitment with increased blood flow would occur together. In a recent study we [104] preferentially blocked recruitment of FOG and SO fibers in the deep extensor muscles during the initial stage of low-speed treadmill exercise with low doses of curare. The amount of glycogen lost in the deep red muscles was decreased during exercise, indicating that the fibers in these muscles were recruited less and/or were less metabolically active. However, the inital hyperemia (as indicated by the absolute blood flow) in the muscles was the same as in the control rats. Since curare blocks at the neuromuscular junction, and the $\alpha$-motoneurons to the SO and FOG fibers presumably continued to be activated [72], these findings are consistent with the notion that there is a direct link between the motoneurons and the vascular smooth muscle in adjacent resistance vessels.

The most popular concept for the control of muscle blood flow has been the metabolic control theory [7, 36, 50, 70, 71, 89, 136, 138, 143, 146, 154], described earlier. Denervated skeletal muscle that is directly stimulated to contract displays functional hyperemia [62], demonstrating that local factors unquestionably play a regulatory role in the initial hyperemia. There are many experiments suggesting that each of the various local metabolic factors (Fig. 5) may individually serve as a vasodilator. However, none acting alone can produce the degree of vasodilation that occurs with muscle contractions or in normal exercise [50, 70, 71, 79, 113, 136, 138, 141–143, 146]. It has therefore been proposed that no one factor controls blood flow to muscle, but rather that there is an orchestration of multiple factors, each of which may contribute at a different time from the initiation through the maintenance of the exercise hyperemia [70, 71, 79, 136, 142, 146]. The factors may also have different potencies for vasodilation depending on the changes in the microvascular environment produced by exercise.

As indicated above, the intensity-independence of the initial hyperemic response in red muscle is not observed at speeds above 45 m/min in rats. The slope of the relationship between initial blood flows and FOG percentages of the muscles increases with increasing running speed above 45 m/min [99]. This could either result from a progressive recruitment of FOG motor units within the muscles with concomitant elevations in flow to the newly recruited fibers as the running speed is increased, or from further increases in blood flow to the same fibers. The results of Sullivan and Armstrong [148] indicate that most of the fibers in deep red muscles and muscle parts of rats are active at 45 m/min. Therefore, the mechanism for the increase in blood flow in the red portion of the gastrocnemius muscle with increasing running speed above 45 m/min (Fig. 3) apparently is not related to progressive recruitment of new motor units. These observations suggest that as running speed is increased, the metabolic demands of the FOG fibers in the red muscles are progressively increased due to changes in force requirements related to gait, stride length, and stride frequency. Thus, elevated metabolic vasodilator release could cause progressive dilation of the resistance vessels.

It has been proposed that selective dilation of proximal or distal arterioles could change total muscle flow and capillary density independently [64, 78]. Honig et al. [78] have proposed that vasomotor control of capillary density is switched off by muscle contraction in an all-or-none fashion. From observations of the number of capillaries containing red blood cells (RBCs) in dog gracilis muscles frozen under various conditions in situ, these authors [78] concluded that the terminal arterioles controlled capillary perfusion in an ungraded fashion. According to this hypothesis, when a terminal arteriole dilates, all the capillaries downstream from this arteriole will be perfused. On the other hand, Gorczynski et al. [62], Klitzman et al. [98], and Damon and Duling [47] reported that perfused capillaries and nonperfused capillaries are often supplied by the same terminal arteriole in mammalian skeletal muscle tissue. Possible explanations for the differences reported in these studies include: (1) different muscles in different species were studied [78] (i.e., dog gracilis [78] vs. rodent cremaster muscle [62]); and (2) different methods were used to measure "perfused" capillaries [47]. The results obtained during treadmill exercise are consistent with either method of control of capillary perfusion [8, 10, 99, 100, 107].

Whatever the mechanisms are for the initial muscle hyperemia in exercise, there can be no question that the flow is specifically directed to the recruited fibers within and among the muscles [8, 10, 99, 100]. Perhaps the best demonstration of this fact is that flow in deep red parts of muscles may increase threefold to fourfold during the first seconds of low-intensity exercise in rats, while blood flows in the peripheral white parts of the same muscles actually decrease from preexercise levels [99, 100].

*Steady-state phase.* During the early stages of steady state submaximal exercise, it is probable that blood flow in muscles is reasonably well-matched to the oxidative metabolism of the muscle fibers [100]. One theory of the control of the distribution of cardiac output during exercise, that has been popular, proposed that sympathetc activity is increased to all tissues during exercise [147] so that blood flow to most nonmuscular tissues and to inactive skeletal muscle decreases (e.g., arm muscle blood flow during leg exercise [21, 22, 88] or white muscle flow during low speed locomotion [99]) at the same time that blood flow is elevated in the contracting muscles. Sympathetic vasoconstriction in the active muscles is presumably overridden by local metabolic factors that cause the vascular smooth muscle to be less sensitive to catecholamines or that act on the sympathetic adrenergic nerve endings in the blood vessel wall to inhibit the release of norepinephrine [136, 137]. This scheme is intuitively attractive, because it provides a relatively simple explanation for directing the increased cardiac output specifically to the active skeletal muscle. Evidence in support of this proposed balance between sympathetic vasoconstrictor and local metabolic dilator influences within the muscles during steady-state exercise comes from experiments we have done on rats with hindlimb sympathectomies [120]. Although, as discussed above, sympathectomy has no effect on the initial hyperemia during low-intensity exercise, from 5 to 15 minutes of exercise, blood flows in the high-oxidative muscles of the sympathectomized rats are elevated above those in normal animals. A similar apparent time dependency of the effects of the sympathetic nerves on blood flow in contracting muscle was previously observed by Rowland and Donald [130] in dog muscle in situ. On the other hand, Thompson and Mohrman [150] have reported that local metabolic mechanisms do not override sympathetic vasoconstriction in contracting skeletal muscle. These apparent discrepancies in the literature may result from the different approaches that have been used to express and analyze the data (percentage change in flow, absolute change in flow, percentage change in resistance, absolute change in resistance, etc.) [44, 48, 130,

137, 141, 147, 150]. Current information indicates that sympathetic stimulation causes muscle blood flow to decrease by a similar absolute amount, but the effect is relatively less during strenuous exercise because flows are higher [147, 150].

An appropriate question is whether control of blood flow differs in muscles composed of different fiber types. The search for a unifying hypothesis that explains blood flow control in all muscle tissue has caused many to attempt to combine all data from different types of muscle in different species into one control scheme. However, there is evidence that the mechanisms of control of muscle blood flow vary with the fiber type of the muscles. Reis et al. [124] reported that slow-oxidative muscles have a greater decrease in blood flow during rapid-eye-movement sleep than fast white muscle. More recently, Gorczynski et al. [62] found that electrical stimulation of single muscle fibers in hamster cremaster muscle results in arteriolar vasodilation that is localized to the regions close to the simulated muscle fibers. In approximately one-third of the fibers studied, single muscle fiber stimulation had no effect on the surrounding arterioles [62]. It seems possible that local vasodilators are released in proportion to the oxidative capacity of the active muscle fiber, and that the fibers that produced no vasodilation when stimulated were FG fibers. On the other hand, Mellander [112] has suggested that blood flow to muscles composed primarily of the FG fiber type may be influenced more by tissue osmolarity than FOG and SO muscles, and Hilton et al. [75] proposed that $K^+$ may be an important factor in blood flow control in FG but not in SO muscle.

There also is evidence indicating that neurohumoral control of muscle blood flow differs in muscles of varying fiber types: (1) the effects of sympathetic nerve stimulation are less pronounced in the vasculature of slow-oxidative muscles than in fast muscles [56, 65, 74]; (2) fast muscles are more sensitive to topically applied norepinephrine [65]; and (3) fast muscles show greater vasodilation with intraarterial infusion of epinephrine [74].

Finally, there may also be differences among muscles of different fiber types in blood flow control in treadmill exercise [8]. FG muscle blood flow does not show the initial overshoot response to low-intensity exercise [100]. With high-intensity exercise, FG muscle blood flow does not increase as rapidly as does blood flow to FOG and SO muscle; also, blood flow to FG muscle does not return to preexercise levels for several minutes after exercise, whereas FOG and SO muscle tissue have blood flows equal to preexercise values within 30 seconds of exercise termination [8]. These various findings demonstrate that future studies of the control of muscle blood flow should include consideration of the possible effects of muscle fiber type [8, 62, 99].

While it seems unlikely that the control mechanisms are totally different in qualitative terms, these observations suggest that the relative importance of each control mechanism may differ among muscles of different fiber types. Similarly, it is possible that the mechanisms responsible for the hyperemia of exercise observed in muscles during locomotory exercise are different from those involved in the hyperemia observed in in situ studies, just as exercise and reactive hyperemias in skeletal muscle appear to be due to different mechanisms [136].

## MAXIMAL BLOOD FLOW CAPACITIES

Most medical physiology textbooks and most reviews of skeletal muscle blood flow indicate that maximal blood flow in mammalian skeletal muscle is 50–120 ml/min/100 g muscle [38, 128]. These values can be quite misleading, however, unless the concept of "maximal blood flow" is used only in a very restricted sense. If maximal blood flow is considered in terms of the distribution of cardiac output to the total muscle mass on a per unit mass basis during exercise, the textbook values are reasonable. For example, an athlete who weighs 70 kg and has a maximal cardiac output of 25 L/min would have a maximal muscle blood flow of 76 ml/min/100 g if it is assumed that 85 percent of cardiac output goes to skeletal muscle [128] and 40 percent of body mass is muscle. On the other hand, if maximal muscle blood flow refers to the highest exercise blood flow that can be attained by a given muscle or muscle part, the textbook values represent underestimates of maximal flow. To illustrate this point, consider further the athlete with an average flow of 76 ml/min/100 g to his total skeletal musculature during exercise. If it is assumed that 80 percent of the increase in muscle blood flow during bicycle exercise is specifically directed to the active extensor muscles of the hindlimbs, and that the active hip, knee, and ankle extensor muscles make up 25 percent of the total skeletal muscle mass, bicycle exercise would produce blood flows of about 243 ml/min/100 g in the active extensor muscles. This estimate actually agrees quite well with recent work by Andersen [1], who reported blood flows of 220 ml/min/100 g in human quadriceps muscles during intense bicycle exercise. The values of Andersen [1] represent average blood flows in a muscle group and do not account for the potential differences in flow among the various parts within the extensor muscles or among muscles in the active group. Thus, the normal textbook values for maximal muscle blood flow markedly underestimate the capacity for flow in a given skeletal muscle.

There are several reasons for this underestimation. One important explanation stems from the fact that the bulk of our information about muscle blood flow comes from in situ electrical stimulation experiments. There is evidence that flows are not as high in muscles during electrical stimulation as during in vivo locomotion. For example, the highest blood flow obtained by Mackie and Terjung [107] in rat red gastrocnemius muscle under a variety of in situ stimulation conditions was 240 ml/min/100 g. However, this same muscle part had an average blood flow surpassing 400 ml/min/100 g during high-speed treadmill galloping at 105 m/min [9]. Musch et al. [115] studied untrained foxhounds and reported that blood flows in active muscles varied between 134 and 340 ml/min/100 g (average of 239 ml/min/ 100 g) at a $\dot{V}O_2$max of 114 ml/min/kg and $O_2$ extraction of 14.1 vol % (Table 2), whereas blood flows in dog muscles stimulated to contract in situ do not exceed about 140 ml/min/100 g [17, 18, 110, 114, 150]. The differences in rat muscle blood flows obtained with in situ versus in vivo exeriments with the same species, same muscles, and same measurement technique (microspheres) are illustrated in Figure 6. Peak muscle blood flows during treadmill exercise clearly exceed the maximal values obtainable with twitch or tetanic type contractions in rat soleus and red gastrocnemius muscles.

The observations that the increases in mucle blood flow during physiological exercise are larger than those seen in in situ preparations probably result from higher arterial and lower venous pressures in in vivo exercise. Exercise is usually accompanied by increases in mean arterial pressure [8, 38, 99, 128] and may result in decreases in venous pressure in vascular beds of active skeletal muscles [55, 136]. As reported by Folkow et al. [55], this latter phenomenon may be due to the venous valves and the so-called muscle pump. Thus, pressure reduction may occur in the small veins upstream from the venous valves between contractions that causes a gain in effective perfusion pressure, resulting in an increase in blood flow through the muscles.

We believe the "muscle pump" effect in locomotory exercise is more efficient in increasing blood flow than in the in situ type of contractions since the rhythmic contractions in locomotory exercise are dynamic and include active lengthening and shortening as well as passive lengthening movements [63, 159]. During the push-off phase of the stride cycle the extensor muscles actively shorten, which may serve to squeeze blood out of the capillaries and small veins toward the heart. On the other hand, during passive lengthening in the swing phase when the limb is being returned to position for the next step phase of the stride cycle, dramatic increases in pressure in the small veins may occur. The result would be an elevation in perfusion pressure ($\Delta P$) across the muscle vascular bed that would produce an

TABLE 2
*Reported Maximal Muscle Blood Flows*

| Study | Muscle | Fiber Type (%) | | | Species | Method of Vasodilation | Maximal Blood Flow (ml/min/100g) | Method of Measurement | Perfusion Pressure (torr) |
|---|---|---|---|---|---|---|---|---|---|
| | | SO | FOG | FG | | | | | |
| Kramer, 1939 (quoted by Barcroft [18]) | G | 51 | 49 | 0 | dog | tetanic (trains) | 140 | venous outflow | — |
| Folkow and Halicka, 1968 [56] | S | 100 | 0 | 0 | cat | twitch (8 Hz) | 50 | venous outflow | 100 |
| | S | 100 | 0 | 0 | cat | posttetanus | 118 | venous outflow | |
| | G | 22 | 15 | 63 | cat | twitch (4 Hz) | 46 | venous outflow | |
| | G | 22 | 15 | 63 | cat | posttetanus | 46 | venous outflow | |
| Hilton et al., 1970 [64] | S | 100 | 0 | 0 | cat | sustained tetanus | 76 | venous outflow | — |
| | S | 100 | 0 | 0 | cat | ACh | 262 | venous outflow | |
| | G + TA + EDL | 14–22 | 15–31 | 55–63 | cat | sustained tetanus | 62 | venous outflow | |
| | G + TA + EDL | 14–22 | 15–31 | 55–63 | cat | ACh | 67 | venous outflow | |
| Maxwell et al., 1977 [111] | G | 51 | 49 | 0 | dog | twitch (? Hz) | 92 | venous outflow | — |
| | ST | 27 | 73 | 0 | dog | twitch | 75 | venous outflow | |
| | EDL | 29 | 71 | 0 | dog | twitch | 130 | venous outflow | |
| | S | 100 | 0 | 0 | cat | twitch (? Hz) | 30 | venous outflow | |
| | G | 22 | 15 | 63 | cat | twitch | 24 | venous outflow | |
| Hudlicka, 1975 [80] | S | 100 | 0 | 0 | cat | isotonic twitches (1 Hz) | 48 | venous outflow | 120 |
| | G | 22 | 15 | 63 | cat | | 22 | | |
| Petrofsky et al., 1981 [121] | S | 100 | 0 | 0 | cat | sustained tetanus | 80 | venous outflow | — |
| | G | 22 | 15 | 63 | cat | sustained tetanus | 60 | venous outflow | |
| Thompson and Mohrman, 1983 [150] | EDL | 29 | 71 | 0 | dog | twitch (4 Hz) | 84 | electromagnetic flow probe | 125 |

| Study | Muscle | | | | Condition | Species | | Method | |
|---|---|---|---|---|---|---|---|---|---|
| Mohrman, 1982 [114] | G + P | 51–55 | 45–49 | 0 | twitch (6 Hz) | dog | 115 | electromagnetic flow probe | 125 |
| Barbee et al., 1983 [17] | G + P | 51–55 | 45–59 | 0 | twitch (4 Hz) | dog | 99 | electromagnetic flow probe | 100 |
| Honig et al., 1982 [78] | Gra | 34 | 66 | 0 | twitch (8 Hz) | dog | 120 | electromagnetic flow probe | — |
| Grimby et al., 1967 [66] | VL | 46 | 20 | 34 | exercise (bicycle) | human | 49 | $^{133}$Xe clearance | — |
| Andersen, 1982 [1] | Q | 46–52 | 15–20 | 33–34 | exercise (bicycle) | human | 220 | indicator dilution | — |
| Mackie and Terjung, 1983 [107] | $G_R$ | 34 | 60 | 6 | twitch (3 Hz) | rat | 159 | microspheres | 130 |
| | $G_W$ | 0 | 10 | 90 | twitch (3 Hz) | rat | 101 | microspheres | |
| | S | 80 | 20 | 0 | twitch (1 Hz) | rat | 118 | microspheres | |
| | $G_R$ | 34 | 60 | 6 | tetanic trains | rat | 302 | microspheres | |
| | $G_W$ | 0 | 10 | 90 | tetanic trains | rat | 80 | microspheres | |
| | S | 80 | 20 | 0 | tetanic trains | rat | 164 | microspheres | |
| Armstrong and Laughlin, 1983 [8] | S | 87 | 13 | 0 | exercise at 60 m/min on treadmill for 3 min | rat | 276 | microspheres | 130 |
| | $G_R$ | 30 | 62 | 8 | | rat | 395 | microspheres | |
| | $G_W$ | 0 | 16 | 84 | | rat | 76 | microspheres | |
| | $VL_R$ | 9 | 56 | 35 | | rat | 389 | microspheres | |
| | $VL_W$ | 0 | 3 | 97 | | rat | 86 | microspheres | |
| | Gra | 23 | 24 | 53 | | rat | 52 | microspheres | |
| Musch et al., 1984 [115] | ST | 27 | 73 | 0 | exercise on treadmill at $\dot{V}O_2$max | dog | 134 | microspheres | 142 |
| | SM | 28 | 72 | 0 | | dog | 289 | microspheres | |
| | BF | 32 | 68 | 0 | | dog | 340 | microspheres | |
| | G | 51 | 49 | 0 | | dog | 208 | microspheres | |

Fiber type and blood flow data are means. Muscles are: gastrocnemius (G); soleus (S); plantaris (P); gracilis (Gra); tibialis anterior (TA); whole quadriceps (Q); red gastrocnemius ($G_R$); white gastrocnemius ($G_W$); red vastus lateralis ($VL_R$); white vastus lateralis ($VL_W$); semitendinosus (ST); semimembranosus (SM); and biceps femoris (BF). Dog fiber type data are from Armstrong et al. [14]; ranges represent populations in the multiple muscles. Cat fiber type data are from Ariano et al. [5]. Human fiber type data are from Edgerton et al. [51]; ranges of fiber types for Q are for vastus lateralis and vastus intermedius only [51].

FIGURE 6

*Relative blood flow capacities in different rat skeletal muscles during various forms of contraction. Blood flows in the three sets of experiments were measured with the microsphere technique.*

SOURCE: Twitch and tetanic train data from in situ preparation are from Mackie and Terjung [107] and treadmill running (60 m/min) data from conscious rats are from Armstrong and Laughlin [8].

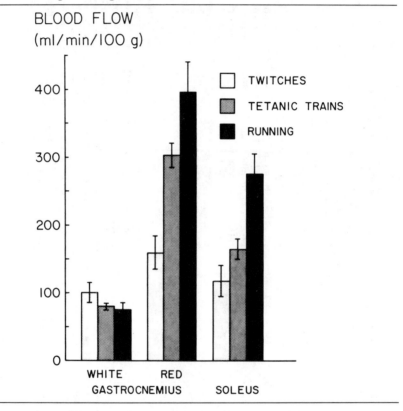

increase in perfusion. It is not technically possible at the present time to accurately measure the venous pressures in muscles during contraction. Until this can be accomplished, this explanation for the differences in in vivo and in situ muscle flows remains hypothetical.

Human muscle blood flow studies have used in vivo exercise, but the methods of measurement have not allowed an appreciation of the magnitude of flows within or among muscles. Dye or thermal dilution and phethysmographic techniques yield average flows for relatively large tissue masses, and the xenon clearance technique, which theoretically permits measurement of blood flow in a particular portion within a muscle, has not been used to study blood flow in deep extensor muscles. Also, the xenon clearance technique significantly underestimates blood flow as compared with other techniques when flows are relatively high [36, 93].

The in situ studies of Mackie and Terjung [107] and the in vivo studies of Laughlin and Armstrong [8, 99, 100, 102, 103] were the first to allow an appreciation of the blood flow capacities of all three of the skeletal muscle fiber types. The data from both laboratories indicate that the FOG muscle fiber type has the highest blood flow capacity in rats (Fig. 6). When peak blood flows in the hindlimb muscles of the rat during high intensity treadmill exercise are regressed on the percentage FOG fibers in the muscles, it may be estimated that peak blood flow in a pure FOG muscle would be about 600 ml/min/100 g [8]. This value for blood flow capacity is similar to that for canine respiratory muscle [123]. Peak flows in SO and FG muscle, using the same type of analysis, would be about 275 and 110 ml/min/100 g, respectively [8]. It is interesting that the peak soleus muscle blood flows observed during locomotory exercise in rats [8, 99] are similar to the values obtained by Hilton et al. [74] for soleus muscle in cats with acetylcholine (ACh) infusions. Peak blood flows in the muscles are directly related to the oxidative potentials of the muscles as indicated by their mitochondrial enzyme activities [10, 107, 110]. This relationship for rat muscles is presented in Figure 7.

Another problem is that many investigators have referred to the highest blood flows they measured under their particular experimental conditions as "maximal blood flows." The term "maximal blood flow" carries the implication that the flow is the highest attainable. As shown in Table 2, the large variation reported among different investigators for the same muscles in the same species illustrates this problem. If maximal vasodilation is produced, maximal blood flow becomes a linear function of blood pressure. Therefore, comparisons of data from various studies must include consideration of variable perfusion pressures. Also, the largest attainable degree of vasodilation produced by a given stimulus may or may not be "maximal" in comparison to other stimuli. Thus, comparisons of maximal blood flow measurements among studies from different laboratories under different conditions is tenuous. In fact, it appears that a truly maximal value cannot be obtained. Some have attempted to circumvent these problems by comparing maximal conductances and minimal resistances. However, during maximal vasodilation resistance will be influenced by distending pressures (i.e., resistance will decrease with increasing pressure). Also, during normal locomotory

FIGURE 7

*Peak blood flows during treadmill running at 60 m/min as a function of
succinate dehydrogenase (SDH) activity of rat extensor muscles. SDH
activity is indicative of oxidative capacity.*
SOURCE: Blood flow data are from [8] and SDH data from [10].

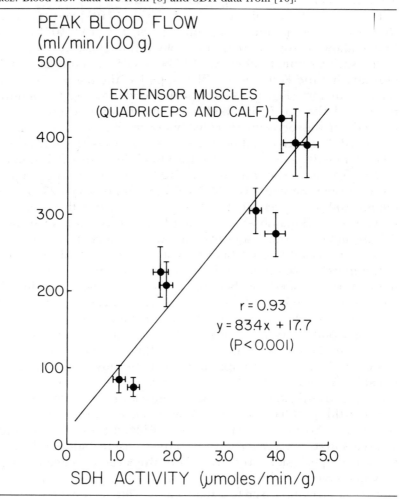

PEAK BLOOD FLOW
(ml/min/100 g)

EXTENSOR MUSCLES
(QUADRICEPS AND CALF)

r = 0.93
y = 83.4x + 17.7
(P < 0.001)

SDH ACTIVITY (µmoles/min/g)

exercise the true venous pressure within the skeletal muscle vasculature is unknown, making the calculations of the pressure difference
across the vascular bed impossible.

Hudlicka [79, 87] stated that muscle blood flow in in situ muscle
preparations is determined by the number of contracting muscle
fibers and frequency of stimulation. She concluded that repeated

rhythmic single-twitch stimuli produce larger increases in muscle blood flow than do repeated short lasting tetanic stimuli or sustained tetanic contractions, and that maximal flow is usually produced by stimulation frequencies of 4–6 Hz. The data in Table 2 and Figure 6 indicate that these conclusions are true for FG muscle. For example, Folkow and Halicka [56] found that as stimulation frequency was increased from 1–4 Hz in cat gastrocnemius muscle (63% FG fibers [5]), blood flow increased to 46 ml/min/100 g. As frequency was further increased, muscle blood flow was decreased during contraction, even during tetanic stimulation at 60 Hz. When tetanic stimulation was interrupted briefly, gastrocnemius muscle blood flow only increased to 46 ml/min/100 g. Under these conditions where blood flow appears to plateau as work rate is increased, one can refer to maximal "twitch" contraction values. In contrast to these findings in in situ studies, during locomotory exercise no plateau in blood flow as a function of exercise intensity is observed (Fig. 3) [99]. In fact, we have now measured blood flows in rat muscles during treadmill running at 90 and 105 m/min, and there is still no evidence of a plateau in red FOG muscles [9]. Although the maximal twitch blood flow was equal to or greater than the maximal tetanic exercise value in cat gastrocnemius muscle, Folkow and Halicka [56] found that the maximal twitch blood flow did not define maximal exercise blood flow in cat soleus muscle (100% SO). As soleus muscle stimulation frequency was increased, maximal twitch blood flow was observed at 4 Hz (39 ml/min/100 g). When stimulation frequency was further increased, summation and tetanic contractions were observed. Soleus muscle blood flow continued to increase during tetanic contractions to 47 ml/min/100 g and maximal flow (118 ml/min/100 g) was observed immediately after tetanic contractions produced by a stimulation frequency of 20 Hz (postcontraction hyperemia). Thus, slow-twitch and fast-twitch muscle of the cat appear to differ in these relationships [56]. Similar relationships have been reported for rat muscles by Mackie and Terjung [107]. Their data indicate maximal muscle blood flow does occur with twitch-type contractions in FG muscle whereas tetanic type contractions produce higher blood flow values in soleus muscle. The data of Mackie and Terjung [107] presented in Figure 6 and Table 2 were obtained after 10 minutes of stimulation. If the same data are compared after 4 minutes of twitch contractions, the maximal twitch blood flow is equal to the maximal tetanic blood flow for the soleus muscle. This may explain why some investigators have found that twitch type contractions produce maximal blood flows (i.e., they were studying muscles composed of a large percentage of FG or SO fibers) [79]. Hilton et al. [74] demonstrated that the peak blood flow following a 10-second tetanus was not the maximal flow in soleus muscle or in fast muscles in cats. In fact, maximal flow obtained with ACh infusions was 3 times the peak flow following tetanus in soleus muscle and 1.5 times the peak flow following tetanus in the fast muscles. Thus, a variety of factors influence the maximal blood flow values obtained during experimentation, which partially explains the wide divergence in reported values.

Finally, it seems important to discuss the determinants of maximal muscle blood flow. The data presented in Figure 7 clearly indicate that blood flow capacity is closely related to muscle oxidative capacity and therefore fiber type in the rat. Whether this is due in part to different sensitivities of the vascular smooth muscle to vasoconstrictor or vasodilator effectors within these types of skeletal muscle, to the amount of vasodilator substance released, or simply to the greater vascularity in oxidative muscles is not clear. However, if all vascular tone is abolished, then the determinants of maximal muscle blood flow must become $\Delta P$ and vascularity of the tissue. Although there are data that would indicate that this is not true under all circumstances [111], most investigators have concluded that a fairly close relationship exists between vascularity and maximum muscle flow.

## HETEROGENEITY OF SKELETAL MUSCLE BLOOD FLOW

At the present time, heterogeneity of blood flow is of considerable interest to those involved in studying the microcirculation in skeletal muscle. As in other sections of this review, it is helpful to consider resting (i.e., totally inactive) and active muscle separately. Some of the classical mathematical models describing vascular transport in skeletal muscle have assumed that blood flow is homogeneously distributed throughout the muscle [46, 126]. Subsequent experiments revealed that blood flow in resting skeletal muscle is not uniformly distributed, but distributed heterogeneously [118, 144]. It appears that most of the investigators interested in these phenomena have considered blood flow heterogeneity to be a random phenomenon, and have incorporated its potential influence in their theoretical analysis as such [93, 118, 144]. Observations at the microvascular level indicate that capillary blood flow distribution in resting muscle is also heterogeneous [47, 78, 83, 98]. The mechanisms responsible for the control of capillary perfusion and perfusion heterogenity have yet to be established [47, 50], but the control of capillary perfusion has been attributed to the terminal arterioles [47, 50, 62, 78, 98]. Microsphere and diffusable indicator techniques do not have sufficient resolution to provide information about the capillary perfusion heterogeneity observed in microvascular studies [50]. Therefore, comparisons among studies using these different techniques must be done with caution. In the light of currently available data it appears that blood flow heterogeneity exists in resting skeletal muscle, regardless of the fiber type composition, and that it can be described as a random phenomenon [47, 50, 78, 93, 118, 144]. However, resting blood flow heterogeneity has been shown to be affected by muscle activity [102, 107, 78], surgical isolation procedures [78, 107], and edema [118].

When the muscle begins to contract, the relationships described above for resting muscle are markedly altered. Blood flow heterogeneity in active muscles may be due to fiber type distribution patterns [107] and fiber recruitment patterns [8, 10, 99, 103]. Studies of blood flow patterns within muscles contracting in situ (homogeneous fiber activity) indicate that blood flow heterogeneity will exist due to the different blood flow capacities of the different fiber types (Fig. 6) and the distribution patterns of the fibers within the muscles (Fig. 1) [107]. As a result, even when all fibers within a mixed muscle are active the FOG fibers will have much higher blood flows than the FG fibers. Furthermore, in locomotory exercise, blood flow heterogeneity within muscles of homogeneous fiber types will also be determined by the muscle fiber recruitment patterns as discussed in detail earlier [8, 10, 99, 100, 103]. Thus, many factors can contribute to muscle blood flow heterogeneity. During exercise, random factors that produce heterogeneity (e.g., vasomotion) appear to be dominated by the blood flow heterogeneity that is the result of the spatial distribution of the muscle fiber types and recruitment patterns of the fibers within the muscles. In normally active muscle, blood flow heterogeneity appears to be largely of functional origin.

## MUSCLE BLOOD FLOW DURING
## EXERCISE AFTER TRAINING

A number of well-documented changes in the cardiovascular system occur as a result of exercise training [24, 38, 76, 128, 135, 157]. These changes are most apparent during maximal exercise. For example, following training there is an increase in maximal cardiac output that is proportional to the elevation in maximal oxygen consumption [24, 128, 135]. However, the significance of the various cardiovascular and muscular adaptations that occur with training is less clear when discussing improved performance during submaximal exercise. Although endurance time increases at a given submaximal exercise intensity following training, the total cardiac output and the oxygen consumption by the active muscles during the exercise do not change from the pretrained condition [133]. Also, a number of studies on muscle blood flow using radiotracer and dye dilution techniques have indicated that trained subjects have the same or lower blood flows during a given level of submaximal exercise than untrained subjects [20, 39, 66, 95, 134, 155]. One major drawback to these studies is the fact that the techniques used did not permit measurement of distribution of blood flow within or among the active muscles.

Although some controversy exists, morphological studies have shown that increases in capillarity occur with training [24, 30, 85, 96, 97, 109, 161], and that there is a direct proportionality between capillary to fiber ratio and both $\dot{V}O_2$max and mitochondrial density in the muscles [161]. Also, preferential increases in capillary density may occur with training in association with high oxidative muscle fibers in rodent muscles [109]. These findings suggest there may be a redistribution of blood flow within the muscles during submaximal exercise that would permit greater extraction of oxygen and blood-borne substrates by the active high oxidative muscle fibers. This suggestion is supported by the observations that after training the a-v $O_2$ difference increases across exercising muscles [97, 134, 160]. We have recently shown that blood flow distribution within and among muscles during exercise is different after training in rats [10]. During submaximal exercise in rats, there is a higher blood flow in muscular regions composed of FOG fibers in trained animals, whereas in the untrained animals there is a relatively higher blood flow in the regions composed of FG fibers. Total hindlimb muscle flow is the same in the untrained and trained animals. Thus, following training there is a closer matching of flow to the active high oxidative fibers during submaximal exercise. This redistribution may play a role in providing the active high oxidative muscle fibers with a greater availability of free fatty acids for metabolism, since elevated fat metabolism is one of the alterations that occurs in muscles during exercise after training [76, 133].

Similar to the literature on the effects of training on muscle blood flow during submaximal exercise, there is some confusion on the effects of training on maximal muscle blood flow. Some authors have shown that maximal blood flows increase following training [40, 97, 105, 108], whereas others have shown no change [66]. Studies in which subjects perform either one-legged or two-legged exercise training shed light on this problem [105, 134]. For example, Klausen and co-workers [134] compared changes in leg blood flow during maximal one-leg exercise and maximal two-leg exercise following training. The training sessions consisted of separately exercising the right leg and the left leg three times a week for eight weeks. These authors found that following training there was a 20 percent increase in capillarization of the muscles. During maximal one-leg exercise, the subjects showed an increase of 16 percent in maximal cardiac output, and this was accompanied by an increase of 16 percent in leg blood flow. However, when the subjects performed maximal two-leg exercise, there was no increase in leg blood flow even though the cardiac output increased by about 11 percent following training. These data suggest that the maximal blood flow capacity of the local muscles increases with training, and that during exercise of a limited muscle mass (one-leg exercise) there are increases in the maximal blood flow. On the other hand, when a larger muscle mass (two-leg exercise) is involved in the maximal exercise, the blood flow in individual muscles does not increase because of central cardiovascular system limitations (cardiac output). In the two-legged experiments, the increase in $\dot{V}O_2$max during maximal exercise occurred because of increased oxygen extraction from the blood. It seems quite possible that during maximal exercise there is a more precise matching of blood flow to active oxidative fibers, which would facilitate increased $O_2$ extraction.

Mackie and Terjung [108] recently showed with an in situ rodent preparation that previous long-term training caused increases in maximal blood flow in muscles primarily composed of FG fibers. Although these authors did not observe elevations in maximal steady state blood flow in FOG or SO muscles, the elevations in flow to white fibers in the muscles would indicate overall increases in maximal muscle blood flow capacity, since about 76 percent of the total rat hindlimb muscle mass is composed of FG fibers [13].

## SUMMARY

Mammalian skeletal muscles are composed of three primary muscle fiber types, FOG, FG, and SO. These fiber types are distributed within and among muscles in predictable patterns. Current data indicate that blood flows to inactive muscles composed of the various fiber types are approximately equal.

Total muscle blood flow increases when the animal stands up. When maintaining posture (standing), the muscular force is provided by the SO fibers. These fibers receive the highest blood flows under these conditions. When the animal walks the SO fibers remain active and the additional muscular force is provided by FOG fibers. The increased muscle blood flow during exercise is primarily directed to the active FOG fibers. At fast running speeds, FG fibers are additionally recruited and blood flow increases in muscle areas composed of FG fibers. However, the FG blood flows per gram of tissue are much less than in the oxidative muscles. Thus, muscle blood flow is primarily directed to the active high oxidative muscle fibers within and among the muscles during normal activities.

Much is known about factors believed to link blood flow to metabolism in skeletal muscle and about the reflex control of skeletal muscle vascular beds. However, the mechanisms responsible for blood flow control during locomotory exercise are yet to be established. It appears that the different muscle fiber types may have qualitatively similar blood flow control mechanisms with quantitative differences in relation to each fiber type.

The capacity for blood flow in skeletal muscle is related to the oxidative potential of the muscles. Blood flows in high-oxidative muscles may reach 400–600 ml/min/100 g, which is considerably higher than the commonly accepted values for maximal muscle blood flow. Also, muscle blood flows are higher during locomotory exercise in conscious animals than in in situ electrical stimulation experiments.

Chronic exercise training does not appear to change total muscle blood flow during locomotory exercise. However, the distribution of blood flow within and among muscles changes so that the deep red muscle fibers have higher flows during exercise. While data exist suggesting that blood flow capacity is increased with exercise training, this remains controversial.

## REFERENCES

1. Andersen, P. Maximal blood flow and oxygen uptake of an isolated exercising muscle group in man. *Acta Physiol. Scand.* 119:2:374, 1982.
2. Andersen, P. Capillary density in skeletal muscle of man. *Acta Physiol. Scand.* 95:203–205, 1975.
3. Andersen, P., and J. Henriksson. Capillary supply of the quadriceps femoris muscle of man: adaptive response to exercise. *J. Physiol.* 270:677–690, 1977.
4. Antal, J. Changes in blood flow during exercise in unanesthetized animals. In *Circulation in Skeletal Muscle.* O. Hudlicka, ed. New York: Pergamon Press, 1968, pp. 181–187.
5. Ariano, M.A., R.B. Armstrong, and V.R. Edgerton. Hindlimb muscle fiber populations of five mammals. *J. Histochem. Cytochem.* 21:51–55, 1973.
6. Armstrong, R.B. Properties and distributions of the fiber types in the locomotory muscles of mammals. In *Comparative Physiology: Primitive Mammals.* K. Schmidt-Neilsen and C.R. Taylor, eds. Cambridge: Cambridge University Press, 1980, pp. 243–254.
7. Armstrong, R.B., and M.H. Laughlin. Is rat soleus recruited during swimming? *Brain Res.* 258:173–176, 1983.
8. Armstrong, R.B., and M.H. Laughlin. Blood flows within and among rat muscles as a function of time during high speed treadmill exercise. *J. Physiol.* 344:189–208, 1983.
9. Armstrong, R.B., and M.H. Laughlin. Metabolic indicators of fiber recruitment in mammalian muscles during locomotion. *J. Exp. Biol.* in press, 1985.
10. Armstrong, R.B., and M.H. Laughlin. Exercise blood flow patterns within and among rat muscles after training. *Am. J. Physiol.* 246:H59–H68, 1984.
11. Armstrong, R.B., L. Rome, and C.R. Taylor. Metabolism of rats running up and down an incline. *J. Appl. Physiol.* 55:518–521, 1983.
12. Armstrong, R.B., P. Marum, C.W. Saubert IV, H.W. Seeherman, and C.R. Taylor. Muscle fiber activity as a function of speed and gait. *J. Appl. Physiol.* 43:672–677, 1977.

13. Armstrong, R.B., and R.O. Phelps. Muscle fiber type composition of the rat hindlimb. *Am. J. Anat.* 171:259–272, 1984.
14. Armstrong, R.B., C.W. Saubert IV, H.J. Seeherman, and C.R. Taylor. Distribution of fiber types in locomotory muscles of dogs. *Am. J. Anat.* 163:87–98, 1982.
15. Armstrong, R.B., C.W. Saubert, W.L. Sembrowich, R.E. Shepherd, and P.D. Gollnick. Glycogen depletion in rat skeletal muscle fibers at different intensities and durations of exercise. *Pfleugers Arch.* 352:243–256, 1974.
16. Baldwin, K.M., G.H. Klinkerfuss, R.L. Terjung, P.A. Mole, and J.O. Holloszy. Respiratory capacity of white, red, and intermediate muscle: Adaptive response to exercise. *Am. J. Physiol.* 222:373–378, 1972.
17. Barbee, R.W., W.N. Stainsby, and S.J. Chirtel. Dynamics of $O_2$, $CO_2$, lactate and acid exchange during contractions and recovery. *J. Appl. Physiol.* 54:1687–1692, 1983.
18. Barcroft, H. Circulation in skeletal muscle. In *Handbook of Physiology*, Sec. 2, Vol. II. Bethesda, Md.: American Physiology Society, 1963, pp. 1353–1385.
19. Bell, A.W., T.E. Hilditch, P.W. Horton, and G.E. Thompson. The distribution of blood flow between individual muscles and non-muscular tissues in the hind limb of the young ox (*Bos Taurus*): Values at thermoneutrality and during exposure to cold. *J. Physiol.* 257:229–243, 1976.
20. Bergman, H., P. Bjorntorp, T.B. Conradson, M. Fahlen, J. Stenberg, and E. Varnasukas. Enzymatic and circulatory adjustments to physical training in middle-aged men. *Eur. J. Clin. Invest.* 3:414–418, 1973.
21. Bevegard, B.J., and J.T. Shepherd. Reaction in man of resistance and capacity vessels in forearm and hand to leg exercise. *J. Appl. Physiol.* 21:123–132, 1966.
22. Blair, D.A., W.E. Gloves, and I.C. Roddie. Vasometer response in the human arm during leg exercise. *Cir. Res.* 9:264–274, 1961.
23. Blome, P., and J. Novotny. Conditional reflex activation of the sympathetic cholinergic vasodilator nerves in the dog. *Acta Physiol. Scand.* 77:58–67, 1969.
24. Blomqvist, C.G. Cardiovascular adaptations to physical training. *Ann. Rev. Physiol.* 45:169–189, 1983.
25. Bockman, E.L. Blood flow and oxygen consumption in active soleus and gracilis muscles in cats. *Am. J. Physiol.* 244:H546–H551, 1983.
26. Bockman, E.L., and J.E. McKenzie. Adenosine production in skeletal muscles of different fiber types. In *Physiological and Regulatory Functions of Adenosine and Adenosine Nucleotides.* H.P. Baer and G.I. Drummond, eds. New York: Raven Press, 1979, pp. 145–153.
27. Bockman, E.L., and J.E. McKenzie. Tissue adenosine content in active soleus and gracilis muscles of cats. *Am. J. Physiol.* 244:H552–H559, 1983.
28. Bockman, E.L., J.E. McKenzie, and J.L. Ferguson. Resting blood flow and oxygen consumption in soleus and gracilis muscles of cats. *Am. J. Physiol.* 239:H516–H524, 1980.
29. Bonde-Peterson, F., and C.H. Robertson. Blood flow in "red" and "white" calf muscles in cats during isometric and isotonic exercise. *Acta Physiol. Scand.* 112:243–251, 1981.
30. Brodal, P., F. Ingher, and L. Hermansen. Capillary supply of skeletal muscle fibers in untrained and endurance-trained men. *Am. J. Physiol.* 232:H705–H712, 1977.
31. Brooke, M.H., and K.K. Kaiser. Three "myosin adenosine triphosphatase" systems: The nature of their pH lability and sulfhydryl dependence. *J. Histochem. Cytochem.* 18:670–672, 1970.
32. Burke, R.E. Motor units: Anatomy, physiology, and functional organization. In *Handbook of Physiology. The Nervous System*, Sect. 1. Bethesda, Md.: American Physiological Society, 1981, pp. 345–422.

33. Burke, R.E., and V.R. Edgerton. Motor unit properties and selective involvement in movement. *Exercise Sport Sci. Rev.* 3:31–81, 1975.

34. Burke, R.E., D.N. Levine, F.E. Zajac III, P. Tsairis, and W.K. Engel. Mammalian motor units: Physiological-histochemical correlations in three types in cat gastrocnemius. *Science* 174:709–712, 1971.

35. Burnstock, G. Cholinergic and purinergic regulation of blood vessels. In *Handbook of Physiology, Sect. 2. The Cardiovascular System. Vol. II: Vascular Smooth Muscle.* Bethesda, Md.: American Physiological Society, 1980, pp. 567–612.

36. Cerretelli, P., C. Marconi, D. Pendergast, M. Meyer, N. Heisler, and J. Piiper. Blood flow measurement in exercising gastrocnemius by venous outflow, $^{133}$Xe and microspheres. *Fed. Proc.* 41:1680, 1982.

37. Clarke, J.H., and R.K. Conlee. Muscle and liver glycogen content: diurnal variation and endurance. *J. Appl. Physiol. Resp. Environ. Exercise Physiol.* 47:425–428, 1979.

38. Clausen, J.P. Circulatory adjustments to dynamic exercise and effect of physical training in normal subjects and in patients with coronary artery disease. *Prog. Cardiovas. Diseases* 18:459–495, 1976.

39. Clausen, J.P., O.A. Larsen, and J. Trap-Jensen. Physical training in the management of coronary artery disease. *Circulation* 40:143–154, 1969.

40. Clausen, J.P., and J. Trap-Jensen. Effects of training on the distribution of cardiac output in patients with coronary artery disease. *Circulation* 42:611–624, 1970.

41. Close, R.I. Dynamic properties of mammalian skeletal muscles. *Physiol. Rev.* 52:129–197, 1972.

42. Collatos, T.C., V.R. Edgerton, J.L. Smith, and B.R. Botterman. Contractile properties and fiber type compositions of flexors and extensors of elbow joint in cat: Implications for motor control. *J. Neurophysiol.* 40:1292–1300, 1977.

43. Corcondilas, A., G.T. Koroxenidis, and J.T. Shepherd. Effect of a brief contraction of forearm muscles on forearm blood flow. *J. Appl. Physiol.* 19:142–146, 1964.

44. Costin, J.C., and N.S. Skinner, Jr. Competition between vasoconstrictor and vasodilator mechanisms in skeletal muscle. *Am. J. Physiol.* 220:462–466, 1971.

45. Crayton, S.C., R. Aung-din, B.E. Fixler, and J.H. Mitchell. Distribution of cardiac output during induced isometric exercise in dogs. *Am. J. Physiol.* 236:4218–4224, 1979.

46. Crone, C. The permeability of capillaries in various organs as determined by use of the "indicator diffusion" method. *Acta Physiol. Scand.* 58:292–305, 1963.

47. Damon, D.H., and B.R. Duling. Distribution of capillary blood flow in the microcirculation of the hamster: An in vivo study using epifluorescent microscopy. *Microvas. Res.* 27:81–95, 1984.

48. Donald, D.E., D.J. Rowlands, and D.A. Ferguson. Similarity of blood flow in the normal and the sympathectomized dog hind limb during graded exercise. *Cir. Res.* 46:185–199, 1970.

49. Dudley, G.A., W.A. Abraham, and R.L. Terjung. Influence of exercise intensity duration on biochemical adaptations in skeletal muscle. *J. Appl. Physiol.* 53:844–850, 1982.

50. Duling, B.R., and B. Klitzman. Local control of microvascular function: Role in tissue oxygen supply. *Ann. Rev. Physiol.* 42:373–382, 1980.

51. Edgerton, V.R., J.L. Smith, and D.R. Simpson. Muscle fibre type populations of human leg muscles. *Histochem. J.* 7:259–266, 1975.

52. Engberg, I., and A. Lundberg. An electromyographic analysis of muscular activity in the hindlimb of the cat during unrestrained locomotion. *Acta Physiol. Scand.* 75:614–630, 1969.

53. Fixler, D.E., J.M. Atkins, J.H. Mitchell, and L.D. Horwitz. Blood flow to res-

piratory, cardiac and limb muscles in dogs during graded exercise. *Am. J. Physiol.* 231:1515–1519, 1976.

54. Flaim, S.F., W.J. Minteer, D.P. Clark, and R. Zelis. Cardiovascular response to acute aquatic and treadmill exercise in the untrained rat. *J. Appl. Physiol.* 46:302–308, 1979.

55. Folkow, B., P. Gaskell, and B.A. Waaler. Blood flow through limb muscles during heavy rhythmic exercise. *Acta Physiol. Scand.* 80:61–72, 1970.

56. Folkow, B., and H.D. Halicka. A comparison between red and white muscle with respect to blood supply, capillary surface area and oxygen uptake during rest and exercise. *Microvas. Res.* 1:1–14, 1968.

57. Freund, H.J. Motor unit and muscle activity in voluntary motor control. *Physiol. Rev.* 63:387–436, 1983.

58. Gardiner, K.R., P.F. Gardiner, and V.R. Edgerton. Guinea pig soleus and gastrocnemius electromyograms at varying speeds, grades and loads. *J. Appl. Physiol.* 52:451–457, 1982.

59. Gollnick, P., R.B. Armstrong, C.W. Saubert IV, W.L. Sembrowich, and R.E. Shepherd. Glycogen depletion patterns in human skeletal muscle fibers during prolonged work. *Pfleugers Arch.* 244:1–12, 1973.

60. Gollnick, P.D., D. Parsons, and C.R. Oakley. Differentiation of fiber types in skeletal muscle form the sequential inactivation of myofibrillar actomyosin ATPase during acid preincubation. *Histochemistry* 77:543–555, 1983.

61. Gollnick, P.D., B. Sjodin, J. Karlsson, E. Jansson, and B. Saltin. Human soleus muscle: A comparison of fiber composition and enzyme activities with other leg muscles. *Pfleugers Arch.* 348:247–255, 1974.

62. Gorczynski, R.J., B. Klitzman, and B.R. Duling. Interrelations between contracting striated muscle and precapillary microvessels. *Am. J. Physiol.* 235:H494–H504, 1978.

63. Goslow, G.E., H.J. Seeherman, C.R. Taylor, M.N. McCutchin, and N.C. Heglund. Electrical activity and relative length changes of dog limb muscles as a function of speed and gait. *J. Exp. Biol.* 94:15–42, 1981.

64. Granger, H.J., A.H. Goodman, and D.N. Granger. Role of resistance and exchange vessels in local microvascular control of skeletal muscle oxygenation in the dog. *Cir. Res.* 38:379–385, 1976.

65. Gray, S.D. Responsiveness of the terminal vascular bed in fast and slow skeletal muscle to adrenergic stimulation. *Angiologica* 8:285–296, 1971.

66. Grimby, G., E. Häggendal, and B. Saltin. Local xenon 133 clearance from the quadriceps muscle during exercise in man. *J. Appl. Physiol.* 22:305–310, 1967.

67. Gruner, J.A., and J. Altman. Swimming in the rat: Analysis of locomotor performance in comparison to stepping. *Exp. Brain Res.* 40:374–382, 1980.

68. Gruner, J.A., J. Altman, and N. Spivack. Effects of arrested cerebellar development on locomotion in the rat. *Exp. Brain Res.* 40:361–373, 1980.

69. Gunn, H.M. Differences in the histochemical properties of skeletal muscles of different breeds of horses and dogs. *J. Anat.* 127:615–634, 1978.

70. Haddy, F.J., and J.B. Scott. Metabolically linked vasoactive chemicals in local regulation of blood flow. *Physiol. Rev.* 48:688–707, 1968.

71. Haddy, F.J., and J.B. Scott. Metabolic factors in peripheral circulatory regulation. *Fed. Proc.* 34:2006–2011, 1975.

72. Henneman, E., and L.M. Mendell. Functional organization of motoneuron pool and its inputs. *Handbook of Physiology*, Sec. 1, Vol. II. Bethesda, Md.: American Physiological Society, 1981, pp. 423–507.

73. Hilton, S.M. Central command for cardiorespiratory regulation. *Proc. Int. Union Physiol. Sci.* 15:479, 1983.

74. Hilton, S.M., M.G. Jeffries, and G. Vrbová. Functional specializations of the vascular bed of soleus. *J. Physiol. Lond.* 206:543–562, 1970.

75. Hilton, S.M., O. Hudlicka and J.M. Marshall. Possible mediators of functional hyperemia in skeletal muscle. *J. Physiol. Lond.* 282:131–147, 1978.

76. Holloszy, J.O., and F.W. Booth. Biochemical adaptations to endurance exercise in muscle. *Ann. Rev. Physiol.* 38:273–291, 1976.

77. Honig, C.R. Contributions of nerves and metabolites to exercise vasodilation: A unifying hypothesis. *Am. J. Physiol.* 236:H705–H719, 1979.

78. Honig, C.R., C.L. Odoroff, and J.L. Frierson. Active and passive capillary control in red muscle at rest and in exercise. *Am. J. Physiol.* 243:H196–H206, 1982.

79. Hudlicka, O. *Muscle blood flow: Its relation to muscle metabolism and function.* Amsterdam: Swets and Zeitlinger, 1973.

80. Hudlicka, O. Uptake of substrates in slow and fast muscles in situ. *Microvas. Res.* 10:17–28, 1975.

81. Hudlicka, O. Effect of training on macro- and microcirculatory changes in exercise. *Exercise Sport Sci. Rev.* 5:181–230, 1977.

82. Hudlicka, O., D. Pette, and A. Staudte. The relation between blood flow and enzymatic activities in slow and fast muscles during development. *Pfleugers Arch.* 343:341–356, 1973.

83. Hudlicka, O., B.W. Zweifach, and R.R. Tyler. Capillary recruitment and flow velocity in skeletal muscle after contraction. *Microvas. Res.* 23:201–217, 1982.

84. Humphreys, P.W., and A.R. Lind. The blood flow through active and inactive muscles of the forearm during sustained hand-grip contractions. *J. Physiol. Lond.* 166:120–135, 1963.

85. Ingjer, F. Capillary supply and mitochondrial content of different skeletal muscle fiber types in untrained and endurance-trained men. A histochemical and ultrastructural study. *Eur. J. Appl. Physiol.* 40:197–209, 1979.

86. Iriuchijima, J., Y. Kawane, and Y. Teranishi. Blood flow distribution in the transposition response of the rat. *Jpn. J. Physiol.* 32:807–816, 1982.

87. Johnson, M.A., J. Polgar, D. Weightman, and D. Appleton. Data on the distribution of fiber types in thirty-six human muscles. *J. Neurol. Sci.* 18:111–129, 1973.

88. Johnson, J.M., and L.B. Rowell. Forearm skin and muscle vascular responses to prolonged leg exercise in man. *J. Appl. Physiol.* 39:920–924, 1975.

89. Johnson, P.C. The myogenic response. In *Handbook of Physiology. Sec. 2. The Cardiovascular System. Vol. II: Vascular Smooth Muscle.* Bethesda, Md.: American Physiological Society, 1980, pp. 409–442.

90. Jorfeldt, L., and J. Wahren. Leg blood flow during exercise in man. *Clin. Sci.* 41:459–473, 1971.

91. Khayutin, V.M. Determinants of working hyperaemia in skeletal muscle. In *Circulation in Skeletal Muscle.* O. Hudlicka, ed. New York: Permagon Press, 1968, pp. 145–157.

92. Kjellmer, I. Studies on exercise hyperemia. *Acta Physiol. Scan. Suppl.* 244:1–64, 1965.

93. Kjellmer, I., I. Lindbjerg, I. Prerovsky, and H. Tonnesen. The relation between blood flow in an isolated muscle measured with the $^{133}$Xe clearance and a direct recording technique. *Acta Physiol. Scand.* 69:69–78, 1967.

94. Klabunde, R.E., and S.E. Mayer. Effect of ischemia on tissue metabolites in red and white skeletal muscle of the chicken. *Cir. Res.* 45:366–373, 1979.

95. Klassen, G.A., G.M. Andres, and M.R. Becklake. Effect of training on total and regional blood flow and metabolism in paddlers. *J. Appl. Physiol.* 28:397–406, 1970.

96. Klausen, K., L.B. Andersen, and I. Pelle. Adaptive changes in work capacity, skeletal muscle capillarization and enzyme levels during training and detraining. *Acta Physiol. Scand.* 113:9–16, 1981.

97. Klausen, K., N.H. Secher, J.P. Clausen, O. Hartling, and J. Trap-Jensen. Central

and regional circulatory adaptations to one-leg training. *J. Appl. Physiol.* 52:976–983, 1982.

98. Klitzman, B., D.N. Damon, R.J. Gorczynski, and B.R. Duling. Augmented tissue oxygen supply during striated muscle contraction in the hamster: Relative contributions of capillary recruitment, functional dilation and reduced tissue $PO_2$. *Cir. Res.* 51:711–721, 1982.

99. Laughlin, M.H., and R.B. Armstrong. Muscular blood flow distribution patterns as a function of running speed in rats. *Am. J. Physiol.* 243:H296–H306, 1982.

100. Laughlin, M.H., and R.B. Armstrong. Rat muscles blood flows as a function of time during prolonged slow treadmill exercise. *Am. J. Physiol.* 244:H814–H824, 1983.

101. Laughlin, M.H., and R.B. Armstrong. Beta adrenergic influence on regional distribution of blood flow within and among muscles during low speed treadmill exercise. *Int. J. Microcir. Clin. Exp.* 3:370, 1984.

102. Laughlin, M.H., R.B. Armstrong, J. White, and K. Rouk. A method for using microspheres to measure muscle blood flow in exercising rats. *J. Appl. Physiol.* 52:1629–1635, 1982.

103. Laughlin, M.H., S.J. Mohrman, and R.B. Armstrong. Muscular blood flow distribution patterns in the hindlimb of swimming rats. *Am. J. Physiol.* 246:H398–H403, 1984.

104. Laughlin, M.H., C.B. Vandenakker, and R.B. Armstrong. Regional muscle blood flow at one minute of exercise in partially curarized rats. *Microvas. Res.* 27:251–252, 1984.

105. Leinonen, H., S. Salminen, and P. Peltokallio. Capillary permeability and maximal blood flow in skeletal muscle in athletes and non-athletes measured by local clearances of [123]Xe and [131]I. *Scand. J. Clin. Lab. Invest.* 38:223–227, 1978.

106. Lexell, J., K. Henriksson-Larsen, and J. Sjostrom. Distribution of different fibre types in human skeletal muscles. *Acta Physiol. Scand.* 117:115–122, 1983.

107. Mackie, B.G., and R.L. Terjung. Blood flow to different skeletal muscle fiber types during contraction. *Am. J. Physiol.* 245:H265–H275, 1983.

108. Mackie, B.G., and R.L. Terjung. Influence of training on blood flow to different skeletal muscle fiber types. *J. Appl. Physiol. Resp. Environ. Exercise Physiol.* 55:1072–1078, 1983.

109. Mai, J.V., V.R. Edgerton, and R.J. Barnard. Capillarity of red, white, and intermediate muscle fibers in trained and untrained guinea pigs. *Experientia* 26:1222–1223, 1970.

110. Maxwell, L.C., J.K. Barclay, D.E. Mohrman, and J.A. Faulkner. Physiological characteristics of skeletal muscles of dogs and cats. *Am. J. Physiol.* 233:C14–C18, 1977.

111. Maxwell, L.C., T.P. White, and J.A. Faulkner. Oxidative capacity, blood flow, and capillarity of skeletal muscles. *J. Appl. Physiol.* 49:627–633, 1980.

112. Mellander, S. Differentiation of fiber composition, circulation and metabolism in limb muscles of dog, cat, and man. In *Vasodilation.* P.M. Vanhoutte and I. Lensen, eds. New York: Raven Press, 1981, pp. 243–254.

113. Mellander, S., and B. Johansson. Control of resistance, exchange and capacitance functions in the peripheral circulation. *Pharmacol. Rev.* 20:117–196, 1968.

114. Mohrman, D.E. Lack of influence of potassium or osmolality on steady-state exercise hyperemim. *Am. J. Physiol.* 242:H949–H954, 1982.

115. Musch, T.I., G.C. Haidet, G.A. Ordway, J.C. Longhurst, and J.H. Mitchell. Dynamic exercise training in foxhounds: Distribution of regional blood flow during maximal exercise. *Cir. Res.* in press, 1985.

116. Nemeth, P., H.W. Hoffer, and D. Pette. Metabolic heterogeneity of muscle fibers classified by myosin ATPase. *Histochemistry* 63:191–210, 1979.

117. O'Donovan, M.J., M.J. Pinter, R.D. Dum, and R.E. Burke. Actions of FDL and

FHL muscles in intact cats: Functional dissociation between anatomical synergists. *J. Neurophysiol.* 48:1126–1143, 1982.

118. Paradise, N.F., C.R. Swayze, D.H. Shin, and I.J. Fox. Perfusion heterogeneity in skeletal muscle using tritiated water. *Am. J. Physiol.* 220:1107–1115, 1971.

119. Peter, J.B., R.J. Barnard, V.R. Edgerton, C.A. Gillespie, and K.E. Stemel. Metabolic profiles of three types of skeletal muscle in guinea pigs and rabbits. *Biochemistry* 11:2627–2633, 1972.

120. Peterson, D.F., R.B. Armstrong, M.H. Laughlin, J.J. Rivera, J.A. White, R.O. Phelps, R.C. Stroup, R. Rouk, and S. Mohrman. Post-sympathectomy changes in hindlimb blood flow in running rats: ten minutes vs 48 hours after nerve sections. *Fed Proc.* 43:699, 1983.

121. Petrofsky, J.S., C.A. Phillips, M.N. Sawka, D. Hanpeter, and D. Stafford. Blood flow and metabolism during isometric contractions in cat skeletal muscle. *J. Appl. Physiol.* 50:493–502, 1981.

122. Pittman, R.N. Influence of oxygen lack on vascular smooth muscle contraction. In *Vasodilation.* P.M. Vanhoutte and I. Lensen, eds. New York: Raven Press, 1981, pp. 181–191.

123. Reid, M.B., and R.L. Johnson. Efficiency, maximal blood flow and aerobic work capacity of canine diaphragm. *J. Appl. Physiol.* 54:763–772, 1983.

124. Reis, D.J., D. Moorehad, and G.F. Wooten. Differential regulation of blood flow to red and white muscle in sleep and defense behavior. *Am. J. Physiol.* 217:541–546, 1969.

125. Reis, D.J., G.F. Wooten, and M. Hollenberg. Differences in nutrient blood flow of red and white skeletal muscles in the cat. *Am. J. Physiol.* 213:592–596, 1967.

126. Renkin, E.M. Transport of potassium-42 from blood to tissue in isolated mammalian skeletal muscles. *Am. J. Physiol.* 197:1205–1210, 1959.

127. Richardson, D., and R. Shewchuk. Effects of contraction force and frequency on postexercise hyperemia in human calf muscles. *J. Appl. Physiol.* 49:649–654, 1980.

128. Rowell, L.B. Human cardiovascular adjustments to exercise and thermal stress. *Physiol. Rev.* 54:75–159, 1974.

129. Rowell, L.B. Active neurogenic vasodilation in man. In *Vasodilation.* P.M. Vanhoutte and I. Leusen, eds. New York: Raven Press, 1981, pp. 1–17.

130. Rowland, D.J., and D.E. Donald. Sympathetic vasoconstrictive responses during exercise- or drug-induced vasodilation: A time-dependent response. *Cir. Res.* 23:45–60, 1968.

131. Saito, M., H. Matsui, and M. Miyamura. Effects of physical training on the calf and thigh blood flows. *Jpn. J. Physiol.* 30:955–959, 1980.

132. Saltin, B. Muscle fibre recruitment and metabolism in prolonged exhaustive dynamic exercise. In *Human Muscle Fatigue: Physiological Mechanisms.* R. Potter and J. Whelan, eds. London: Pitman Press, 1981, pp. 41–52.

133. Saltin, B., and P.D. Gollnick. Skeletal muscle adaptability: significance for metabolism and performance. In *Handbook of Physiology. Skeletal Muscle.* Bethesda, Md.: Am. Physiological Society, 1983, pp. 555–631.

134. Saltin, B., K. Nazar, D.L. Costill, E. Stein, E. Jansson, B. Essen, and P.D. Gollnick. The nature of the training response; peripheral and central adaptations to one-legged exercise. *Acta Physiol. Scand.* 96:289–305, 1976.

135. Saltin, B., and L.B. Rowell. Functional adaptations to physical activity and inactivity. *Fed. Proc.* 39:1506–1513, 1980.

136. Shepherd, J.T. Circulation to skeletal muscle. In *Handbook of Physiology. The Cardiovascular System. Sec. 2, Vol. III: Peripheral Circulation.* Bethesda, Md.: American Physiological Society, 1983.

137. Shepherd, J.T., and P.M. Vanhoutte. Skeletal-muscle blood flow: neurogenic determinants. In *The Peripheral Circulations*. R. Zelis, ed. New York: Grune & Stratten, 1975, pp. 3–55.

138. Skinner, N.S. Skeletal-muscle blood flow: Metabolic determinants. In *The Peripheral Circulations*. R. Zelis, ed. New York: Grune & Stratten, 1975, pp. 57–78.

139. Smith, J.L., B. Betts, V.R. Edgerton, and R.F. Zernicke. Rapid ankle extension during paw shakes: Selective recruitment of fast ankle extensors. *J. Neurophysiol.* 43:612–620, 1980.

140. Smith, J.L., V.R. Edgerton, B. Betts, and T.C. Collatos. EMG of slow and fast ankle extensors of cat during posture, locomotion, and jumping. *J. Neurophysiol.* 40:503–513, 1977.

141. Sparks, H.V. Skin and muscle. In *Peripheral Circulation*. P.C. Johnson, ed. New York: John Wiley and Sons, 1978, pp. 193–230.

142. Sparks, H.V. Effect of local metabolic factors on vascular smooth muscle. In *Handbook of Physiology. Sec. 2. The Cardiovascular System. Vol. II: Vascular Smooth Muscle*. Bethesda, Md.: American Physiological Society, 1980.

143. Sparks, H.V., and F.L. Belloni. The peripheral circulation: Local regulation. *Ann. Rev. Physiol.* 40:67–92, 1978.

144. Sparks, H.V., and D.E. Mohrman. Heterogeneity of flow as an explanation for the multi-exponential washout of inert gas from skeletal muscle. *Microvas. Res.* 13:181–184, 1977.

145. Spurway, N.C. Interrelationship between myosin-based and metabolism-based classifications of skeletal muscle fiber. *J. Histochem. Cytochem.* 29:87–88, 1981.

146. Stainsby, W.N. Local control of regional blood flow. *Ann. Rev. Physiol.* 35:151–168, 1973.

147. Strandell, T., and J.T. Shepherd. The effect in humans of increased sympathetic activity on the blood flow to active muscles. *Acta Med. Scand. Suppl.* 472:146–167, 1967.

148. Sullivan, T.E., and R.B. Armstrong. Rat locomotory muscle fiber activity during trotting and galloping. *J. Appl. Physiol.* 44:358–363, 1978.

149. Terjung, R.L. Muscle fiber involvement during training of different intensities and durations. *Am. J. Physiol.* 230:946–950, 1976.

150. Thompson, L.P., and D.E. Mohrman. Blood flow and oxygen consumption in skeletal muscle during sympathetic stimulation. *Am. J. Physiol.* 245:H66–H71, 1983.

151. Trevino, G.S., R.S. Demaree, B.V. Saunders, and T.A. O'Donnel. Needle biopsy of skeletal muscle in dogs: Light and electron microscopy of resting muscle. *Am. J. Vet. Res.*, 34:507–515, 1973.

152. Uvnäs, B. Cholinergic vasodilator nerves. *Fed. Proc.* 25:1618–1622, 1966.

153. VanCitters, R.B., and D.L. Franklin. Cardiovascular performance of Alaska sled dogs during exercise. *Circ. Res.* 24:33–42, 1969.

154. Vanhoutte, P.M. Physical factors of regulation. In *Handbook of Physiology. Sec. 2. The Cardiovascular System. Vol. II: Vascular Smooth Muscle*. Bethesda, Md.: American Physiological Society, 1980, pp. 443–474.

155. Varnasukas, E., P. Bjorntorp, M. Fahlen, I. Prerovsky, and J. Stenberg. Effects of physical training on exercise blood flow and enzymatic activity in skeletal muscle. *Cardiovasc. Res.* 4:418–422, 1970.

156. Vatner, S.F., D. Franklin, R.L. VanCitters, and E. Braunwald. Effects of carotid sinus nerve stimulation on blood-flow distribution in conscious dogs at rest and during exercise. *Cir. Res.* 27:495–503, 1970.

157. Vatner, S.F., and M. Pagani. Cardiovascular adjustments to exercise: Hemo-dynamics and mechanisms. *Prog. Cardiovas. Dis.* 19:91–108, 1976.
158. Wahren, J., B. Saltin, L. Jorfeldt, and B. Pernow. Influence of age on the local circulatory adaptation to leg exercise. *Scand. J. Clin. Lab. Invest.* 33:79–86, 1974.
159. Walmsley, B., J.A. Hodgson, and R.E. Burke. Forces produced by medical gastrocnemius and soleus muscles during locomotion in freely moving cats. *J. Neurophysiol.* 41:1103–1216, 1978.
160. Zetterquist, S. The effect of active training on the nutritive blood flow in ex-ercising ischemic legs. *Scand. J. Clin. Lab. Invest.* 25:101–111, 1970.
161. Zumstein, A., O. Mathieu, H. Howald, and H. Hoppeler. Morphometric analysis of the capillary supply in skeletal muscles of trained and untrained subjects: Its limitations in muscle biopsies. *Pfleugers Arch.* 397:277–283, 1983.

# Adherence to Exercise

JOHN E. MARTIN, Ph.D.
PATRICIA M. DUBBERT, R.N., Ph.D.

Exercise appears to play an important role in the improvement of physical and mental health. Even relatively low levels of physical activity, when performed on a regular basis, are associated with reduced cardiovascular morbidity and mortality in the apparently healthy [35, 52, 54, 68, 76, 79] as well as in higher risk individuals and clinical populations [8, 9, 11, 17, 28, 33, 80, 93, 98]. Exercise has also been associated with psychological and quality-of-life improvements in both clinical and nonclinical populations [20, 21, 34, 64, 87, 97]. Yet, for many of these benefits to accrue, the exercise must be performed on a regular basis (i.e., three times a week) [2]. Furthermore, research indicates that aerobic/endurance type exercise that is regularly performed produces the optimal effects. For example, weight and blood pressure reduction or cardiovascular improvements are best produced by a systematic program of aerobic exercise; however, those benefits last only as long as the exercise is regularly maintained.

In spite of these potentially significant physical and mental health benefits connected with exercising, a significant number of people do not exercise regularly enough to experience any truly lasting improvements in health. A growing body of research suggests that the majority of people who begin an exercise program will stop, often within the first few months [25, 26, 36, 58, 59, 63, 71, 72, 75, 96]. Surveys have indicated that even in spite of the exercise and fitness boom, two-thirds of Americans still do not exercise on a regular basis, while between 28 percent and 45 percent do not exercise at all [16, 40, 41, 51]. Even among those who are enrolled in structured exercise programs for prevention/health enhancement and for rehabilitation following the appearance of coronary heart disease, adherence is disappointingly low: Approximately half the participants in primary prevention studies drop out within 3–6 months [14, 27, 43, 57, 61, 63, 71, 88], or, at most, 12 months in secondary prevention programs [16, 47, 70, 77, 85, 98]. This point is illustrated in a well-controlled study reported by Kentala [38] who found that only 77 out of 298 postmyocardial infarction patients entered a recommended exercise program. Furthermore, 71 percent of the exercisers dropped out

137

within 5 months, and only 13 percent continued to exercise through one year.

## EXERCISE: THE TARGET BEHAVIOR

As is well recognized, there are many types of exercise, depending on the goal of the exerciser. For the most part, this chapter deals with aerobic exercise, designed for improving endurance and cardiovascular fitness—the focus of most exercise programs and studies on exercise adherence.

By emphasizing the development of programmed (aerobic) exercise interventions in this chapter, we do not wish to deemphasize the potential importance of strategies designed to increase routine or "aerobic" activities (i.e. taking stairs instead of elevators, walking instead of driving short distances). These routine activities have significant health benefits according to Morris [68], may serve as an effective first step in shaping exercise in the extremely sedentary, and have the advantage of requiring no special equipment, places, or times. There also is evidence from studies with obese children to support the hypothesis [12] that long-term adherence to increased routine activity is superior to that for programmed exercise [31], and both can produce fitness changes [31, 68].

*Assessment of Exercise Adherence*
Before presenting and interpreting the results of the exercise adherence research, it should be noted that it is difficult to evaluate the present exercise adherence literature because definitions and actual measurement of adherence vary so widely from study to study. For example, many of the cardiac rehabilitation studies determined overall dropout rate [72, 75]; some studies employed a preset attendance criterion to identify adherers [70]; and others reported attendance to prescribed classes [54]. Unfortunately, most investigators reported only adherence or attendance to ongoing treatment programs, providing little information regarding maintenance of exercise subsequent to termination of treatment [58]. For instance, some of the dropouts may actually have been exercising on their own [98], but this would not have been reflected in the adherence data. Furthermore, in many cases only a single adherence measure is reported, such as treatment dropout, while ignoring the various other measures of adherence to an exercise regimen, particularly documentation that the exercise was performed to criterion/goal levels [30, 42, 58]. As a function of this practice, exercise might be inappropriately viewed as a dichotomy (exerciser/nonexerciser) as. opposed to a continuum

(intensity, frequency, duration, and mode of exercise participation) [26].

One of the more reliable measures of adherence is program attendance, as used by a number of investigators. Ideal adherence, a measure introduced by Martin and Dubbert [59] to assess the "ideal" combination of home and on-site sessions, is potentially more closely associated not only with the simplest effective aerobic regimen for producing health benefits (i.e., three times a week), but also with optimal conditions for generalization (i.e., exercising in both the treatment and home environment). Some cardiac rehabilitation programs promote maximal fitness changes with less regard for conditions conducive for maximal adherence and generalization (requiring more than three on-site sessions per week, and no home sessions or exercise generalization training). Unfortunately, this can lead to an overdependence on the program such that when patients are graduated to make room for new patients [72] they are unsuccessful in maintaining their exercise program in the home environment. On the other hand, if some of the exercise sessions are performed in the home environment, thus enhancing generalization, measurement of ideal adherence is dependent on the reliability of the component measures, program attendance, and self-reported home exercise.

It is important to note, however, that mere attendance at exercise sessions, or home participation, does not constitute adequate exercise adherence unless the exercise performance meets the specific exercise prescription. Conversely, program dropouts may actually be performing the exercise at home on their own [74, 98]. Thus, attendance and program dropout may be invalid measures of adherence to prescribed exercise [30, 42]. On the other hand, if the regularity of exercise is considered the key component of early exercise adherence, as we believe it is [57, 58, 60], then attendance and three-day-per-week adherence do hold validity as a measure of exercise adherence. That is, if the habit of regular exercising is not well established, then no lasting benefits can accrue. [60].

A further indirect indication of the regularity and quality of exercise participation is objective measurement of the physical performance changes desired or expected as a result of the exercise. Especially for briefer programs with older or less fit individuals or medicated cardiac patients, fitness assessment may not be the best measure for corroborating home exercise adherence since the testing may not be sensitive or reliable enough to detect small changes. In addition, fitness gains do not constitute the primary focus of all programs, particularly during maintenance. At best, documented changes in fitness are only indirectly related to adherence [30, 42].

*Exercise Adherence/Dropout Profile*

Despite the difficulties inherent in properly defining and measuring exercise adherence, it appears that many individuals who begin an exercise program relapse, often within the first three to six months. Regrettably, there are few experimental studies on the factors influencing exercise adherence; most of the data are derived from retrospective, correlational analyses of variables which characterize the dropouts, poor adherers, and good adherers in heart disease prevention and treatment trials [26, 56, 58, 59].

Variables that have been found to predict exercise participation and level of adherence at least to some extent may be loosely separated into subject factors, social/environmental factors, and exercise program factors [26, 56, 58, 59]. The following sections briefly elaborate on these correlates of adherence.

*Subject factors.* Subject factors consist of preexisting psychological/personality and behavior patterns, and biological characteristics found to correlate positively or negatively with the probability of remaining in or dropping out of an exercise program. One obvious *psychological* predictor, one's attitude toward physical activity, does not appear to offer any predictive value with respect to exercise participation or subsequent adherence [11, 63]. In fact, studies suggest that even sedentary individuals have favorable attitudes toward personal exercise [22, 63]. However, several investigators have shown significant associations between other psychological variables and exercise adherence. Low self-motivation, as measured by Dishman's self-motivation inventory (SMI) [23, 24], a measure of the person's tendency to persit regardless of extrinsic reinforcement, has predicted attrition from at least one large-scale exercise program [22–24]. This seems consistent with the findings of Oldridge and associates [77], who determined that psychosocial reasons, primarily lack of motivation, were frequently reported by cardiac patients as responsible for their exercise dropout. Blumenthal and associates [10] found significant differences between cardiac patients who continued in an exercise program for one year and dropouts on several Minnesota Multiphasic Personality Inventory (MMPI) scale scores obtained prior to entry into treatment. Dropouts from the program were significantly more depressed, anxious, and introverted and had lower ego-strength scores.

Some studies have documented the adverse effects of the perceived (health) benefit of the exercise [26, 85]. In cardiac patients, increased denial of the seriousness of the heart disease has been associated with poor exercise adherence [10, 86]. Conversely, increased compliance with prescribed exercise by chronic obstructive pulmonary disease (COPD) patients has been associated with increased (self-efficacy) expectations for being able to maintain exercise performance [45]. This suggests a link may also exist between the achievement of one's exercise goals and the maintenance of exercise-related self-motivation. For example, Danielson and Wanzel [19] found that those exercisers who failed to attain their own exercise goals dropped out roughly twice as fast as those who did attain them.

*Behavioral* factors associated with exercise dropout include smoking [4, 61, 70, 77], blue-collar vocational status [75, 77], inactive leisure-time pursuits [70, 89], type A behavior pattern [18, 77], and poor credit rating [43, 61]. When some of these factors are considered together, the prediction can be significantly enhanced. For example, Oldridge found that 80 percent of smokers who had inactive jobs and leisure-time pursuits and were blue-collar workers eventually dropped out of the Ontario Exercise-Heart Collaborative Study (OEHCS) [70, 75]. Smoking was the single best predictor in the Ontario study, associated with a 59 percent likelihood of drop out; similarly, smoking has also been found to predict poor exercise program enrollment [61].

While few *biological* factors appear to predict adherence [22, 25, 63], several studies have related overweight, especially high percentage body fat, with dropout and poor adherence [22, 61], although no relationship between level of obesity and exercise adherence was found for children who were already overweight [30]. According to Dishman [25], a combination of biological and psychological variables may prove much more powerful in predicting adherence. Dishman and Gettman [22] proposed a "psychobiologic" model based on self-motivation (SMI) and body composition measures, which they found correctly identified 80 percent of individuals as potential adherers or dropouts. Ward and Morgan [96] applied this model to a separate exercise program and found it effective in predicting adherence for 83 percent of the males and 91 percent of the females, but the model was not effective in predicting dropout for either sex. Although the psychobiological model has not been systematically replicated, it is understandable that overweight individuals with low self-motivation might seek to avoid or escape the embarrassment and pain of higher intensity, public exercising. In cardiac patients, overweight and angina (but not ST-segment depression or other physical findings) were associated with dropout in the OEHCS program [74]. Blumenthal and colleagues [10] also reported significant biological differences for cardiac rehabilitation dropouts, who were found to have had significantly reduced left ventricular ejection fractions at entry to the program, as compared with those who maintained their exercise.

*Social/Environmental factors.* A second category of factors known to influence degree of adherence to exercise programs derives from the exercisers' personal and social environment. Specifically, *social support* or reinforcement for exercise adherence from the home environment has consistently been related to increased exercise adherence [58]. For example, Heinzelmann and Bagley [43] found that subjects with spouses who actively supported their exercise habit were twice as likely to have good adherence than those whose spouses were either neutral or negative toward exercising. Significantly, neutral spouses had the same effect as those opposed to the exercise program. Similarly, Andrew et al. [5] found that their cardiac patients without spouse support were two to three times more likely to drop out of the Ontario exercise program. Unfortunately, the specific meaning of support and nonsupport were not always clear. Generally, the more active supporters reported that they encouraged and praised the exerciser for his attempts and were in agreement with the goals of the exercise. Also, it should be remembered that this support predictor for exercise adherence was gleaned from self-report data, not from actual observations or experimental evidence.

In the following section on the modification of exercise behavior, several studies provide experimental evidence suggesting the importance of applied social support, both within the exercise facility and in the home environment. Oldridge et al. [77] pointed out two additional important dropout variables that were cited frequently by former exercisers as responsible for their poor adherence or dropout from the Ontario exercise program: *family problems* and *change of job or residence.* Finally, a number of exercise dropouts have attributed their poor adherence or dropout to *job conflicts* (i.e., exercise/job interference) [14, 85].

*Program factors.* The final category of adherence variables relates to the characteristics of the exercise program or facility. Carrying on with the social support theme, one of the most critical factors in determining the level of exercise adherence relates to the type and degree of *social support during* the *exercise*. In one of the first demonstrations of the potency of this factor, Wilhelmsen and associates [98] found significantly poorer long-term adherence in those who exercised alone. Likewise, Massie and Shephard [6] found that while only 47 percent of participants in individual aerobic exercise programs were adherent, 82 percent participating in group exercise were adherent. Lastly, Heinzelmann and Bagley [43] reported that 90 percent of a sample of 195 cardiac rehabilitation patients stated that they either did prefer or would have preferred exercising with others; similarly although 63 percent of the participants in our community exercise program reported they had previously attempted to exercise alone, 83 percent said they would have preferred to exercise with others [57].

A second very important factor is the *convenience* of the exercise center. For example, inconvenient exercise program location has been found by many investigators to detract significantly from adherence to the program components and overall participation [5, 14, 47, 61, 63, 77, 85, 89].

Convenience of the exercise center, and even the parking facilities [4], has been noted as an important factor influencing both the initial decision to join an exercise program and its continuation. This suggests that more decentralized exercise programs might be superior to one-site, large-scale centers, as is typically the case. That is, smaller, self-contained neighborhood or work-site exercise facilities might promote fitness over the long run better because of their much greater convenience to exercisers.

An additional critical program-mediated predictor of adherence is the overall *intensity of exercise.* Pollock et al. [82] and others [30, 48, 54] found higher intensity exercise to be associated with lower exercise adherence. This relationship appears to hold for children [30] as well as adults [48, 54, 82]. Only in one study was this not found to be the case. In the Ontario Exercise Heart Collaborative Study (OEHCS) [71], higher vs. lower intensity exercise groups had similar adherence, probably because there was such good social support in both groups, and because the higher intensity exercise was only moderate compared to the other studies cited. Importantly, Pollock [82], Kilbom [48], and Mann [54] all reported that half the participants in their programs developed orthopedic injuries that necessitated discontinuation of exercise and that many of the injuries appeared due to excessive intensity. Finally, recent results from the OEHCS also implicate fatigue and perceived exertion as important factors in attrition, factors probably related to exercise intensity (either as prescribed or, quite possibly, as performed incorrectly by participants) [4].

In summary, the most critical factors characterizing the high-risk dropouts appear to be biological/psychological handicaps (such as overweight, low self-motivation, anxiety), no active spouse support, inconvenient exercise/facility, and exercise consisting of individual, high intensity activity with little or no social support/reinforcement during or after the exercise [25, 58, 72].

## MODIFYING EXERCISE PARTICIPATION AND ADHERENCE

These correlational data have prompted a number of suggestions as to how to retain more exercisers and enhance overall adherence levels [25, 36, 69]. Thus far, however, there have been few experimental studies in which investigators have evaluated the effects of adherence promotion strategies on exercise behavior in either healthy or coronary subjects [29, 56, 58]. Those studies which have been conducted with the express goal of manipulating exercise participation and adherence levels through the use of behavioral interventions show generally positive results of a variety of behavioral and cognitive-behavioral strategies. Published group studies evaluating interventions designed to improve short- and long-term adherence to physical activity have been compiled and are shown in Table 1. These studies are discussed along with some of the more important single-subject and smaller studies on shaping exercise in inactive individuals in the subsequent sections.

While important improvements in exercise of 50 percent to 100 percent or more have resulted from these interventions, these changes have typically been documented only over relatively short periods [26, 59]. It should also be noted that, in contrast to the correlational studies that have documented dropout and program adherence, the behavioral interventions have focused more on relatively convenient (and, perhaps, more highly motivated) populations such as students and healthy adult volunteers. It is only more recently that behavior modification techniques have been applied to the problem of exercise adherence with high-risk or chronically ill populations.

The existing exercise participation/adherence promotion studies have been categorized according to the primary controlling variables targeted [58]. Reinforcement or consequent control, stimulus or antecedent control, and cognitive/self-control procedures have been employed in an effort to modify exercise behavior. The emphasis here is on the presentation, interpretation, and critical analysis of these studies.

### Reinforcement Control

Consequent control procedures, or the provision of reinforcement contingent upon exercise program attendance/adherence, have frequently been manipulated in exercise modification studies [58, 60]. For example, as illustrated in Table 1, several studies have shown the relative effectiveness of contracting and lottery procedures in improving short-term exercise program attendance. Epstein and colleagues [32] compared weekly attendance contracts with an attendance lottery and control condition across a five-week jogging program. Subjects consisted of predominatly female college students.

TABLE 1
*Published Exercise Adherence Modification Group Studies*

| Author | Subjects | Program Requirements | Treatment Duration | Intervention Groups | Attendance | Dropout | Adherence | Follow-Up: Percentage still exercising at 2 mo. | 3 mo. | 6 mo. |
|---|---|---|---|---|---|---|---|---|---|---|
| | | | | | | **Results (%)** | | | | |
| Reid and Morgan [75] | N = 124 (firefighters) | aerobic exercise on own >2x/wk, for >15 min | 8 wks | control (M.D. consult) | | 19 | 29[a] | | | |
| | | | | education | | 4 | 56 | No differences at 6 mo. | | |
| | | | | education plus self-monitoring (pulse and aerobics pts) | | 4 | 55 | | | |
| Epstein, Wing, Thompson, Griffin [63] | N = 41 (F students) | attend jogging class 5 days/wk, and jog 1 or 2 miles | 5 wks | control | 46 | 0 | | | | |
| | | | | contract for attendance | 64 | 0 | | | | |
| | | | | attendance lottery | 64 | 0 | | | | |
| Wankel and Thompson [72] | N = 36 (Adult F) | exercise at health club 2x/wk following exercise prescription | 6 wks | perceived choice of exercise | ≈83[b] | | | | | |
| | | | | no perceived choice | ≈63 | | | | | |

TABLE 1
*(continued)*

| Author | Subjects | Program Requirements | Treatment Duration | Intervention Groups | Results (%) | | | Follow-Up: Percentage still exercising at | | |
|---|---|---|---|---|---|---|---|---|---|---|
| | | | | | Attendance | Dropout | Adherence | 2 mo. | 3 mo. | 6 mo. |
| Oldridge and Jones [44] | N = 120 (CHD, males) | 2x/wk attendance physician supervised rehab program, exercise at 65–85% max HR + exercise on own 3x/wk | 6 mo. | Control | | | 42ᶜ | | | |
| | | | | Asked to sign adherence agreement | | | 54 | | | |
| | | | | signed | | | 65 | | | |
| | | | | did not sign | | | 20 | | | |
| Gettman, Pollock, and Ward [76] | N = 47 (M police officers) | aerobic training: walk/jog 3 days/wk, 45 min/session | 20 wks | sedentary control | | 30ᵈ | | | | |
| | | | | supervised (all sessions at center) | | 45 | | | | |
| | | | | unsupervised (exercise on own after 4th wk) | | 35 | | | | |

| Study | Sample | Exercise prescription | Duration | Group | | | | |
|---|---|---|---|---|---|---|---|---|
| King and Frederiksen [80] | N = 58 (F students) | suggested frequency 4x/wk; jog on indoor track | 5 wk | control | 6.3[e] | | 35.7 | |
| | | | | relapse prevention training | 12.0 | | 83.3 | |
| | | | | group support | 12.3 | | 38.5 | |
| | | | | group support plus relapse training | 7.0 | | 38. | |
| Epstein et al. [86] | N = 19 (overweight girls) | 2 days/wk; morning day camp | 5 wk | control (baseline only) | | | | Activity scores for group 2 > group 1 on days when activity reinforced; differences decreased over time; energy expenditure (est. from HR) was sig. > for group 2 Ss. |
| | | | | experimental (alternated) | | | | |
| | | | | reinforcement for "activity" vs. "sharing" during free play | | | | |
| Martin et al. [37], study 1 | N = 33 (4 M, 29 F Adults) | attend jogging class 2x/wk; exercise on own 1x/wk | 10 wk | group feedback distance | 51.6[f] | 86 | 30.0[g] | ⎫ |
| | | | | group feedback plus time goals | 78.3 | 25 | 61.3 | ⎬ 17 |
| | | | | | | | | ⎭ |

TABLE 1
*(continued)*

| Author | Subjects | Program Requirements | Treatment Duration | Intervention Groups | Results (%) | | | Follow-Up: Percentage still exercising at | | |
|---|---|---|---|---|---|---|---|---|---|---|
| | | | | | Attendance | Dropout | Adherence | 2 mo. | 3 mo. | 6 mo. |
| | | | | personal feedback + distance goals | 74.9 | 10 | 53.1 | | 54 | |
| | | | | personal feedback + time goals | 74.9 | 11 | 41.9 | | | |
| Martin et al. [37], study 2 | N=34 (6 M, 28 F) | same as study 1 | 11 wk | fixed goals, no lottery | 69.3 | 29 | 45.6 | | | |
| | | | | attendance lottery + fixed goals | 66.7 | 33 | 42.2 | | 28 | |
| | | | | flexible goals, no lottery | 93.1 | 93.1 | 66 | | | |
| | | | | attendance lottery + flexible goals | 76.1 | 76.1 | 52.8 | | 47 | |
| Martin et al. [37], study 3 | N=15 (2 M, 13 F) | same as study 1 | 12 wk | fixed goals 1st 6 wk then flexible | 71.4 | | | | | |

| Study | N | Design | Duration | Condition | | | | | |
|---|---|---|---|---|---|---|---|---|---|
| Martin et al. [37], study 4 | N=24 (4 M, 20 F) | same as study 1 | 10 wk | flexible goals 1st, then fixed | 85.8 | | | | |
| | | | | proximal goals (new goal each week) | 71 | 17 | 35.6 | | 33 |
| | | | | distal goals (5 wk) | 83 | 17 | 36.3 | | 67 |
| Martin et al. [37], study 5 | N=17 (5 M, 12 F) | same as study 1 | 12 wk | cognitive associative strategies (internal focus) | 58.7 | 12 | 34.9 | | 43 |
| | | | | cognitive dissociation strategies (external focus) | 76.6 | 12 | 56.2 | | 67 |
| Martin et al. [37], study 6[h] | N=35 (5 M, 30 F) | same as study 1 | 12 wk | basic program | 79.8 | 50 | 74 | 100 | |
| | | | | relapse prevention | 78 | 25 | 57 | 88.9 | |
| | | | | relapse prevention trng + continued contact | 76.6 | 36 | 40 | 83.3 | |

TABLE 1
*(continued)*

| Author | Subjects | Program Requirements | Treatment Duration | Intervention Groups | Results (%) Attendance | Dropout | Adherence | Follow-Up: Percentage still exercising at 2 mo. | 3 mo. | 6 mo. |
|---|---|---|---|---|---|---|---|---|---|---|
| Atkins et al. [6] | N = 56 COPD patients | walking prescription; 7 treatment sessions | 9 wk | behavior modification<br><br>cognitive modification<br><br>cognitive-behavior modification<br><br>attention-social support<br><br>no treatment control | minutes walking: behavior modification = cognitive modification; combined cognitive behavior modification better than all other groups<br><br>Exercise tolerance: behavior modification, cognitive modification, and cognitive-behavior modification groups improved more than attention social support and no treatment control | | | | | |

[a]Adherence = % subjects still exercising twice per week at 3 months and also increased their predicted $\dot{V}_2$max 9.5% or more.

[b]Estimated from graph.

[c]Adherence = % subjects still attending regularly at 6 months.

[d]Dropout = % subjects who failed to complete the program.

[e]Adherence = number jogging episodes initiated by subjects

[f]Attendance = % days present at exercise class.

[g]Ideal adherence = % weeks with 2 class attendance plus 1 home exercise session (3 aerobic sessions/week).

[h]Note that adherence data for study 6 include only subjects who attended 75% of the treatment small group discussions, or 50% of the original subjects.

Each was trained to monitor performance and was provided daily feedback on resting and maximal heart rates. In spite of the small weekly deposit return ($1) in the contracting group, both the contracting and lottery interventions were associated with superior and essentially equal dropout and attendance. In another study testing the effects of an attendance lottery (for weekly prize drawings), shown in Table 1, Martin and colleagues (study 2) [57] found essentially equal program attendance, adherence to out-of-class exercise assignments, and exercise maintenance, when the lottery was added to a program emphasizing personalized feedback/praise administered by enthusiastic participant-therapists. It was hypothesized that the enhanced program of shaping, modeling, and personalized feedback and reinforcement during exercise, provided by running-enthusiast "therapists" was such a powerful intervention in and of itself that the tangible reinforcement represented by the lottery held little or no marginal utility for the beginning exercisers.

In a study by Wysocki and associates [99], a group multiple-baseline design [44] was employed in an attempt to study specific effects of contracting on adherence to a home-based exercise program. Undergraduate and graduate student volunteers met weekly with the experimenters and were given exercise choices and aerobic point goals and scheduled to exercise in small groups, where they were periodically observed. Interestingly, exercise adherence contracts were for return of personal valuables left on deposit by participants. All subjects kept their own exercise records, which they had corroborated by other exercisers and turned in at meetings. Seven of the 12 subjects at least doubled their aerobic points earned at 10 weeks; however, only 4 maintained or improved upon this level at one year. Unfortunately, fitness assessment was not performed, as it was in both the Epstein [32] and Martin and Dubbert [57] studies, to confirm that subjects showed an aerobic fitness change.

Three other studies successfully used reinforcement control to enhance exercise participation [62, 91, 92]; however, two of these studies were more self-control based and are discussed in that section. The third, by Mayer and Geller [62], employed newspaper announcements and a lottery to stimulate biking, walking, and running on a jogging/biking trail in which coupons were left by exercisers at a special "drop-box" on the trail. Use of the path increased during the brief intervention phase.

Finally, contingency management procedures and token reinforcement have been used to enhance adherence to physical activity programs [58, 60]. Allen and Iwata [1] successfully implemented an exercise program in 10 mentally retarded adults by making game-time contingent upon exercising (calesthenics) for a 15-minute period. No maintenance procedures or follow-up were conducted after the initial seven-week treatment period. Libb and Clements [53] found that exercising (stationary bicycling) could be increased in three of four institutionalized geriatric patients by providing tokens (exchangeable for candy, cigarettes, etc.) for exercising across a several week period. The latter two studies should be interpreted with some caution, however, due to their small N and special populations.

*Stimulus Control*

Antecedent or stimulus control over physical activity has been attempted in several studies [58]. Specifically, these procedures attempted to promote exercise/fitness program participation and adherence through the manipulation of antecedents, or cues and prompts, that stimulate or are reliably followed by exercise [60]. In one study, Brownell, Stunkard, and Albaum [12] increased stair climbing by posting a cartoon sign by an escalator/stairway showing a healthy heart coaxing people up the stairs rather than the escalator. This was a discrete attempt on a single stairway, however, and not an ongoing program with follow-up. In another study, Wankel and Thompson [75] found that telephone prompts to health club dropouts successfully increased attendance and maintenance if the nonattender could be persuaded to write down positive reasons for returning. In a follow-up study [90] female health club members who were led to believe that their activity preferences helped determine their prescribed exercise program showed superior attendance to those members who were told that their preferences were not considered. An additional series of 10-week interventions by Wankel [94] provided further support for these findings. Finally, Oldridge and Jones [76] found that cardiac rehabilitation patients who signed a written agreement to adhere to an exercise program in fact did so. Their adherence rate of 65 percent was superior to those who were asked, but refused to sign the document (20%), and to control subjects who were not asked to sign the agreement (42%).

*Cognitive/Self-Control Procedures*

The remaining exercise modification studies employed some form of self-management strategies, including self-reward, stimulus control, self-monitoring, self-contracting and goal setting, cognitive distraction, and relapse prevention strategies [58]. These programs generally were home-based or had some kind of generalization or maintenance programming, and stressed personal/internal rather than structured program/external control over exercise [60]. In an early $N = 1$ application of self-control procedures in this area, Turner, Polly, and Sherman [91] employed self-monitoring, self-reward/self-punishment, and self-contracting in a fitness improvement program for a young adult woman. Fitness improvements were documented through five months to validate self-reports of aerobic points earned. In a second preliminary study of this nature, Keefe and Blumenthal [46] evaluated the effects of a self-control-based exercise program on three overweight men. The training program involved a very gradual shaping procedure in which subjects set easily attainable goals, with self-reinforcement for meeting these goals. At the two-year follow-up, the three subjects reported they were still exercising, and all scored in the excellent fitness category. Importantly, each reported he no longer needed to rely on the self-control procedures because they found the exercise itself to be rewarding.

Both instructional control and self-monitoring of the target behavior (exercise duration, frequency, intensity, mode) have been considered as techniques designed to enhance self-control [60]. For example, in a study by Reid and Morgan [83], health education with and without exercise self-monitoring was compared with a physician instruction control group, in promoting home exercising in 124 firefighters. As shown in Table 1, at 8 weeks, the education and self-monitoring groups had essentially equal exercise participation rates (55%), that were roughly twice that of the physican instruction controls (29%). Differences in dropout rates showed even greater differences (4%, 4%, 19%, respectively). In a comparison of a self-contol-based exercise program and a supervised treatment program, Gettman, Pollock, and Ward [38] provided supervised or unsupervised aerobic training to 47 male police officers. At the end of 20 weeks, exercise adherence levels were 45 percent and 35 percent, respectively, as compared to a sedentary control level of 30 percent.

An additional important component of the self-control of exercise relates to the setting of individual goals. As noted earlier, the achievement of one's exercise goals appears to have an important bearing on the adherence to exercise [19]. Several studies conducted by Martin and Dubbert and associates [57] focused on goal setting, including manipulations of the type of goal (e.g., distance vs. time jogging), the person responsible for goal setting (e.g., therapist vs. exerciser), and the goal-setting topography (e.g., frequency and flexibility of goal setting).

In each of the studies the exercise program was offered as an adult education course at one of the colleges in the community. In the first of the studies examining goal-setting effects on the acquisition and maintenance of exercise, subjects were assigned progressive exercise goals by distance (e.g., jog one mile) or time (e.g., jog 15 minutes). The results of study 1, shown in Table 1, indicated that when personalized feedback and praise were provided during exercise it did not matter whether subjects were assigned distance or time-based goals; however, when provided with less individualized, group-oriented feedback following exercise, those assigned distance goals showed significantly poorer adherence than those assigned time goals. In the second study, subjects were either encouraged to set their own, flexible (distance) exercise goals or they were given fixed, progressive goals by the instructor. The group setting their own flexible goals showed better attendance ideal and adherence, and exercise maintenance than those receiving fixed exercise goals. The final goal-setting study (study 4) was an attempt to partially replicate Bandura and Simon's [7] work with obese subjects. This study evaluated the effects of proximal (weekly) exercise goal selection by participants vs. distal (every six weeks) exercise goal selection. Contrary to the results of Bandura and Simon, proximal (weekly) setting did not produce significantly better adherence, as measured by class attendance and self-monitoring records. In fact, the difference, although not significant, favored the distal goal-setting group. As suggested by Kirschenbaum and Tomarken [49] in their discussion of optimal goal-setting strategies, fewer goal dates may have allowed subjects to alter their goal or to progress slower than desired without frequent goal deadlines serving as reminders of failure (i.e., abstinence violation effect [55]). Also, distal goals may tend to encourage changes in lifestyle as opposed to transient behavioral changes.

A subsequent study by the same group (study 5) evaluated the effects of two cognitive interventions within the context of flexible goal setting by the individuals. Subjects were trained in this study to use either distraction/dissociation during running, i.e., think pleasant, coping thoughts, set small mental goals, and "go slowly and smell the flowers," or to associate by focusing on bodily sensations while challenging their bodies to push harder and further ("be your own coach"). The group employing distraction-dissociational strategies exhibited significantly better attendance and three-day-a-week exercise adherence than subjects trained to associate to their bodily sensations. It was hypothesized that, for beginning exercisers, excessive awareness of minor discomfort associated with exercise and inflexible high performance goals may be detrimental to enjoyment and subsequent exercise adherence.

Two experimental analog studies have been conducted that would appear to validate this hypothesis that dissociational strategies during exercise promote endurance through distraction from sensory discomfort. Pennebaker and Lightner [81] found that runners on a treadmill who were fed back their own breathing sounds reported more exertional symptoms than those who were given distracting sounds. In addition, these authors reported that joggers on a cross-country course were able to go significantly faster with the same number of exertional symptoms as those required to run on a track. Morgan and colleagues [67] found that subjects trained in dissociative/distraction strategies were able to run significantly longer on a treadmill at 80 percent of maximal aerobic power than subjects not trained in these strategies. While blood lactate and other physiologic indices were similar across groups, plasma catecholamine levels were higher in the dissociation group, suggesting that dissociation subjects were tolerating a greater degree of physiologic stress.

It should be noted, that the same dissociative strategies that proved beneficial during the early exercise training of apparently healthy subjects may be counterproductive or even potentially harmful in athletes and in high-risk (e.g., cardiac) subjects in whom dissociative strategies may lead to overexertion, injury, or impairment by shutting out or ignoring important biological danger signals. Morgan [65, 66] reports, for example, that world class/elite athletes employ associative strategies to elicit and monitor peak performance while avoiding overstress and breakdown. In higher risk/clinical populations, such as the cardiac patient, it may also be important to avoid distraction-based strategies, especially in the early stages of training and in the absence of careful physiologic monitoring. Nevertheless, dissociative cognitive strategies appear to hold promise for increasing endurance and possibly adherence in the apparently healthy, would-be regular exerciser.

Atkins et al. [6] have recently conducted an interesting evaluation of various cognitive and behavioral interventions to improve exercise compliance in chronic obstructive pulmonary disease. They found that a combination of behavioral (contracting, goal setting, relaxation training ) and cognitive (coping self-statments) training produced better adherence to daily walking than either treatment alone, and that patients who received either of the cognitive-behavioral treatments or a social support control treatment walked more than those who received no treatment.

A final variety of cognitive/self-control techniques is that of relapse prevention or inoculation. Since it is commonly accepted that many, if not most beginning exercisers will go through a period of inactivity, either due to injury, sickness, environment change, or motivational slip, some researchers have taken a cue from the field of addiction treatment and provided training in preparing for dealing with these high-risk relapse situations (i.e., it is not whether you will slip, but how you will cope with it). Addictive behavior research suggests that individuals may even set themselves up for relapse, or poor coping when it does occur, by how they think about it [55]. For example, the perfectionistic tendency of many to give up on their program completely after a minor or temporary slip ("I blew it, what's the use of even trying to get back on my program") has been termed the "abstinence violation effect" [55]. Special training, designed to provide individuals with cognitive coping strategies to prevent or abort relapse, have been successfully employed in the addictions, and more recently with exercise.

In one study, King and Frederiksen [50] evaluated single-session relapse prevention training and group social support for college women in a beginning jogging program. Self-reported exercise data showed that subjects given relapse prevention training or group social support exerciseed twice as often as the control group who received neither treatment (see Table 1). A noteworthy feature of this study was the unobtrusive observation of subjects who jogged in special numbered t-shirts within an indoor coliseum, which allowed validation of self-reported exercise. At a two-month follow-up, more than 80 percent of subjects who received relapse prevention training alone reported regular participation in exercise, as compared with fewer than 40 percent in each of the other groups.

In the final study of their series (study 6), Martin and Dubbert and colleagues [57] attempted to enhance exercise maintenance by adding relapse prevention training to the enhanced behavioral and cognitive training described earlier. The relapse training consisted of group discussions of the abstinence violation effect, how to substitute alternative positive thoughts ("I've only slipped from 100% to 95% adherence on my program after missing one in 20 weeks, I haven't dropped to 0% . . . no big deal . . . I can and will start back tomorrow"), and actions (calling exercise buddy and making plans to meet and exercise, wearing exercise clothes, visiting exercise facility,). In addition, individuals in the relapse training group were required to relapse and recover (no exercise for one week) during the treatment program, to troubleshoot for potential problems in reinstituting home exercise, and to implement coping strategies taught earlier in the course. Contrary to expectations, however, at three-month follow-up, the relapse training did not add to the effectiveness of the basic exercise adherence training program. Significantly, a powerful social support influence may have accounted for the equivalent performance of the subjects who had received everything but relapse prevention training: An overzealous program assistant had continued to arrange exercise meeting times even after the course ended, and a close-knit social network developed between the members of that group.

*Critical Analysis of Exercise Modification Research*
The studies to date on the correlates and modification of exercise adherence indicate that exercise is a behavior that occurs more or

less consistently in particular types of individuals (i.e., nonsmoking, nonobese white-collar workers with good self-motivation and active spouse support), who exercise in a particular place (convenient facility), and in a particular way (moderate aerobic exercise, with others). Furthermore, preliminary research that has been reviewed here (Table 1) indicates that exercise is a behavior, subject to the laws of learning, that can be modified using consequent/reinforcement control, stimulus control, and cognitive/self-control techniques derived from the field of behavior modification. With few exceptions, these strategies have not been attempted with the higher risk dropout individuals identified in the larger exercise/heart disease trials; however, the results of these studies using the apparently healthy have been quite encouraging. In particular, the use of reinforcement procedures such as contracting and lotteries, praise and social support during exercise, cognitive self-control procedures such as self-contracting and reinforcement, individualized, flexible goal setting, and cognitive distraction have been shown to be effective in select populations over relatively short training and maintenance periods. Yet, problems in defining and measuring adherence, experimental control, subject selection and sample size, and treatment and follow-up periods make overall interpretation of current results and recommendations for widespread clinical application premature at this point. Also, the potential danger of employing dissociative cognitive strategies with patients at risk must be considered.

The studies that were specifically designed to improve exercise adherence through some special intervention(s), while showing from 50 percent to 100 percent improvements over comparison, pretreatment, or control condition adherence (however defined), suffer from several important additional flaws. First, of the studies that included a home exercise component or obtained data on home/posttreatment exercise during the maintenance or follow-up period, many relied exclusively on self-report or self-monitoring records of home exercise adherence—measures which are highly susceptible to expectation and experimenter/subject bias, inaccuracy, and even deliberate falsification. In some cases, physiologic or exercise test measures of fitness change were attempted to confirm home adherence; however, a number of subjects failed to appear for testing [57] and some who showed no decrement in fitness may not have been more than partially adherent to their home program. In addition, in some who did not attend follow-up sessions or who did not show maintenance or improvement of physical condition, exercise adherence may still have been excellent.

Second, little systematic attention has been paid to generalization of the exercise habit to nontreatment settings, either through assessing longer term posttreatment follow-up, or through programming generalization to the home environment during treatment (e.g., maintenance training or booster sessions). Finally, the studies were generally solitary attempts to show an effect of reinforcement contingencies or self-control procedures without systematic replication or follow-up studies.

The exercise modification studies not only suffer from unclear and inconsistent definitions of adherence, potentially unreliable/invalid adherence measurement, and inadequate treatment and follow-up periods, but they also tend to be characterized by poor (or lack of) treatment control groups, generally inadequate numbers of subjects in treatment groups, limited representativeness of populations and types of exercise studied, and poor or no theoretical rationales for intervention strategies [25].

The potential for over or misinterpretation of results in these exercise modification studies is further complicated by the subject self-selection factor noted earlier [42]. Indeed, highly motivated clinical as well as apparently healthy individuals who want to exercise are different from the majority of lower motivated, clinical subjects for whom adherence is a far greater problem.

Table 1 illustrates the variety of populations, types of exercise, and exercise modification strategies studied. It is clear that jogging is the predominant exercise evaluated, even though it is less frequently prescribed than walking, swimming, cycling, and strength training [84]. The populations are generally healthy individuals who were most conveniently located by the experimenters and probably more highly motivated since most volunteered to exercise. No minority and relatively few clinical subjects were studied. The variety of definitions of exercise adherence is also quite apparent, making comparisons across studies difficult or impossible. Short treatment duration, averaging around nine weeks, and inadequate or no follow-up asessment is the rule for most of the studies. Few used treatment control groups, thus making it hard to know whether and how much these individuals would have exercised in the absence of the specific treatments or programs. Unfortunately, one of the most popular forms of exercise, aerobic dance, is not investigated at all, although it has been suggested that adherence to this type of exercise may be superior to other aerobic activities. Similarly, routine physical activities have not been properly investigated, with one notable exception [31]. Thus, the analysis and interpretation of results, much less generalization of results, becomes difficult given the problems of inadequate measures, measurement periods, sample sizes and makeup, poor or no experimental control groups, and limited exercise modes. Clearly, more and especially better studies are needed in this important area of investigation.

## CONCLUSIONS

The exercise literature emphasizes several primary factors that seem to reliably influence exercise adherence. First, social support factors have been implicated in the effective acquisition and maintenance of exercising. Previous surveys have indicated that most beginning exercisers prefer or would have preferred to exercise with others [4, 43, 57]; other studies indicate that those who did exercise in groups had roughly twice the adherence as those who attempted to exercise alone [38, 61, 98]. In addition, studies of exercise dropouts have indicated the importance of positive spouse support for the exercise habit [4, 43, 72, 77].

The studies on the modification of the exercise response also provide validation of this and other factors. Experimental evidence from King and Frederiksen [50], and Martin et al. [57], corroborate the importance of social support to exercise adherence and particularly maintenance. In the Martin and Dubbert study series [57], social reinforcement was just one of the several behavioral and cognitive-behavioral components that appeared to enhance adherence to program and home exercise. The results of these and other studies would suggest that, at least for earlier stages of exercise training, an effective treatment package for promoting the acquisition and maintenance of the exercise habit might include personalized feedback and praise during exercise [57, 79] special (tangible) reinforcement for class attendance or adherence [32], a group/social setting [38, 57], flexible exercise goals set by the individual [57] and finally training in cognitive dissociation in lower risk populations. When these strategies are implemented by enthusiastic participant therapists, average adherence (attendance) levels may approach 80–85 percent, with minimal dropout during the first three-month treatment period [57]. When these strategies are used together, as in the Martin studies [57], the resulting exercise adherence (attendance) compares quite favorably with the mean adherence of approximately 55 percent reported for other exercise studies using apparently healthy adults [27, 63, 88] as well as the 40–70 percent reported for cardiac populations [4, 47, 76, 77, 98] and the 60–65 percent adherence reported for other group behavioral studies [32, 38, 83].

It may be that 80–85 percent program attendance is maximal for a structured program, given the unavoidable difficulties such as job and family conflicts, illness, and so on, that are frequently reported as affecting adherence and dropout [72, 75]. Any improvements over this apparent asymptote might better come in ensuring maintenance of those participation and adherence levels over greater lengths of time. Although the exercise benefits continue only as long as the exercise is performed on a regular basis [2, 68, 80], a significant number of individuals drop out or exhibit poor exercise adherence up through 1–2 years [13, 72, 75].

As noted earlier, many of the exercise rehabilitation programs that abruptly discontinue their three to five on-site sessions per week, following graduation of the individual (patient), are very likely to experience significant exercise dropout at this point. The follow-up data of the various studies reviewed attest to the fact that it is insufficient to provide a treatment program alone, followed by abrupt cessation of formal training and with no maintenance programming. Features which may help to maximize long-term adherence might include early generalization training, creating or plugging individuals into home-based exercise (social) support networks for those wishing to continue programmed, group exercise; and shaping lower level, routine exercise in others [26, 31, 58].

## DISCUSSION

Our present body of knowledge regarding the questions of who does and does not participate in physical activity regimens, under what conditions, and for what duration, appears to be in the early stages of development and refinement. There is a considerable amount of correlational data, particularly with male coronary heart disease (CHD) and higher risk populations, designating the characteristics of the individuals most likely to drop out and, conversely, those most likely to adhere well to a prescribed exercise program. While these studies are certainly informative, it is interesting that no studies have used these findings to develop and test a model or theory of exercise adherence/fitness pursuit, nor have any targeted the specific high-risk dropouts for comprehensive adherence interventions. The most critical need at this point would appear to be the development and refinement of specific strategies and interventions that serve to significantly enhance the adopting and maintaining of physical fitness as a lifestyle. For this reason, and because of the relative wealth of published data and interpretations regarding the dropout and adherent personality, this chapter has focused more on the modification of exercise. The comments in this final section are therefore directed more toward assimilating the findings of these studies and examining some of the needed directions in this relatively newer area.

Unfortunately, the exercise modification studies were conducted

with generally small, specialized populations, limiting broad generalizations as to the needed components in an exercise promotion
package. They do, however, provide a useful beginning framework
and measurement system for future investigation and elaboration.
The primary focus of most studies has been on the early acquisition
of the exercise habit—a stage when most would-be exercisers fail to
maintain their initial, well-intentioned desire to make exercise a lifetime commitment. At this point, a more promising line of inquiry
might be toward the development and evaluation of methods for
retaining current exercisers who are likely to quit, the investigation
of the various forms of exercising and their adherence quotients (e.g.,
walking, aerobic dance, competitive games such as racquetball), and
the tailoring of exercise regimens to the individual. It is probable
that many of the factors which are important in the acquisition/adop-
tion phase of exercise and fitness become less important in the maintenance phase, when other factors such as opportunities to socialize,
awareness of the relationship between exercise and mood and energy
levels may be dominant. It may be that maintenance can best be
assured with specifically planned generalization training, for example, shaping a single exercise in a specific setting and then generalizing to new exercises (response generalization) and new environments
(stimulus generalization) [58].

Importantly, we know very little at this time about the many thousands of individuals who do initiate and successfully adhere to regular
exercise programs outside of hospital or other institutionally based
treatment. Perhaps these individuals have tapped into the reinforcers
available in the natural environment, learned to exercise in a way
that is more pleasurable (or less aversive) or perhaps they have come
to associate *not exercising* with unpleasant consequences. Learning
what is different about these successful adherers, or especially their
exercise environments, may provide new hypotheses for improving
training for those who have been less successful.

One potential difference is that those with the longest uninter-
rupted period of exercise may be the ones who engage in easier forms
of activity which require little or no preparation or strain. Thus, the
use of lower intensity, more routine forms of exercise may be an
appropriate goal for many individuals wishing or needing to exercise.
As pointed out by Morris [68], our epidemiological research suggests
that regular or routine physical activities such as walking are sufficient
for many improvments in health, including some protection from
coronary heart disease. In fact, a recent study by Epstein et al. [31]
indicates that the long-term health benefit of increases in routine
lifestyle activities may be superior to more intense, programmed exercise because of superior long-term adherence. Clearly, more re-

search is needed which evaluates the relative merits of routine lifestyle exercise and programmed (aerobic) exercise from a long-term adherence standpoint as well as in terms of overall health benefit (the two, of course, are linked to one another).

At this stage of inquiry, greater attention should also be paid to experimental analyses of interventions designed to improve short-term and especially long-term maintenance. As Dishman [25] and Folkins and Sime [34] have cogently pointed out, previous research on exercise adherence has suffered from lack of theoretical models of exercise behavior. Additional conceptual and theoretical groundwork could provide a stronger foundation for future exercise research. A stage-theory model, for example, could lead to investigation of specific factors and interventions important at different stages of exercise [25].

At the present time, the overall effectiveness of exercise as a preventive treatment modality for a variety of disorders can be questioned because of the problem of adherence [42]. Most of the data concerning adherence factors concerns what may be a rather unique population, i.e., males with diagnosed coronary disease, or at high risk, who have received exercise prescriptions as part of a structured treatment program. The available evidence suggests that adherence may not be much better among those who begin an exercise program to aid treatment of other health problems; however, it is difficult to compare the results of different types of programs or outcomes with particular types of populations because investigators have used different definitions of adherence and dropout. In future research, more consistently interpretable information about attendance and attrition is needed.

In summary, although optimal exercise training packages must still be developed, the research suggests that certain training components as well as program characteristics do promote adherence [58]. These include exercise (site and type) convenience, social support, individual goal setting, feedback, low to moderate intensity exercise, instruction in cognitive and self-control strategies, and various forms of consequation for exercise behavior (e.g., contracting). It also seems likely that many exercise participants will need assistance to make their natural environments more supportive of exercise, e.g., providing exercise cues, finding and shaping other people to exercise with them, or gaining the support of spouses or significant others.

Prior to the acquisition and maintenance phases, there is an additional need for information about what factors are important for successful marketing [37] of exercise programs, so that we can expose more sedentary individuals to the potential benefits of (and persuade them to adopt) more active lifestyles.

# REFERENCES

1. Allen, L.C., and B.A. Iwata. Reinforcing exercise maintenance using high-rate activities. *Behav. Mod.* 4:337–354, 1980.
2. American College of Sports Medicine (ACSM). Position statement on the recommended quantity and quality of exercise for developing and maintaining fitness in health adults. *Med. Sci. Sports Exercise* 10:7–10, 1978.
3. American College of Sports Medicine. In *Guidelines for Graded Exercise Testing and Exercise Prescription*. Philadelphia: Lea & Febiger, 1980.
4. Andrew G.M., et al. Reasons for dropout from exercise programs in postcoronary patients. *Med. Sci. Sports Exercise* 13:164–168, 1981.
5. Andrew, G.M., and J.O. Parker. Factors related to dropout of post myocardial infarction patients from exercise programs. *Med. Sci. Sports Exercise* 11:376–378, 1979.
6. Atkins, C.J., R.M. Kaplan, R.M. Timms, S. Reinsch, and K. Lofback. Behavioral exercise program in the management of chronic obstructive pulmonary disease. *J. Consult. Clin. Psychol.* 52:591–603, 1984.
7. Bandura, A., and K.M. Simon. The role of proximal intentions in self-regulation of refractory behavior. *Cog. Ther. Res.* 1:177–193, 1977.
8. Bjorntorp, P. Exercise and obesity. *Psychiatr. Clin. North Am.* 1:691–696, 1978.
9. Boyer, J.L., and F.W. Kasch. Exercise therapy in hypertensive men. *J. Am. Med. Assoc.* 211:1168–1671, 1970.
10. Blumenthal, J.A., S. Williams, A.G. Wallace, R.B. Williams, and T.L. Needles. Physiological and psychological variables predict compliance to prescribed exercise therapy in patients recovering from mycardial infarction. *Psychol. Med.* 44:519–527, 1982.
11. Brownell, K.D., P.S. Bachorik, and R.S. Ayerle. Changes in plasma liquid and lipoprotein levels in men and women after a program of moderate exercise. *Circulation* 65:477–484, 1982.
12. Brownell, K.D., and A.J. Stunkard. Physical activity in the development and control of obesity. In A.J. Stunkard (ed.). *Obesity*. Philadelphia: W.B. Saunders, 1980.
13. Brownell, K.D., A.J. Stunkard, and J. Albaum. Evaluation and modification of exercise patterns in the natural environment. *Am. J. Psychiatry* 137:1540–1545, 1980.
14. Bruce, E.H., R.A. Frederick, R.A. Bruce, L.D. Fisher. Comparison of active participants and dropouts in cardiopulmonary rehabilitation programs. *Am. J. Cardiol.* 37:53–60, 1976.
15. Bucher, C.A. National adult physical fitness survey: Some implications. *J. Health Ed. Recr.* 45:25–31, 1974.
16. Carmody, T.P., J.W. Senner, M.R. Malinow, and J.D. Matarazzo. Physical exercise rehabilitation: Long-term dropout rate in cardiac patients. *J. Behav. Med.* 3:163–168, 1980.
17. Clausen, J.P. Circulatory adjustments to dynamic exercise and effect of physical training in normal subjects and patients with coronary artery disease. *Prog. Cardiovasc. Dis.* 18:459–495, 1976.
18. Cox, M.H. Fitness and lifestyle programs for business and industry: Problems in recruitment and retention. *J. Cardiac Rehab.* 4:136–142, 1984.
19. Danielson, R.R., and R.S. Wanzel. Exercise objectives of fitness program dropouts. In *Psychology of Motor Behavior and Sports*, D.M. Landers, and R.W. Christina (eds.) pp. 310–320. Champaign, Ill.: Human Kinetics Publishers, 1977.
20. deVries, H.A. Tranquilizer effects of exercise: A critical review. *Physician Sports Med.* 9:46–53, 1981.

21. Dimsdale, J.E., and J. Moss. Plasma catecholamines in stress and exercise. *J. Am. Med. Assoc.* 243:340–342, 1980.
22. Dishman, R.K., and L.R. Gettman. Psychobiologic influences on exercise adherence. *J. Sport Psychol.* 2:295–310, 1980.
23. Dishman, R.K., and W. Ickes. Self-motivation and adherence to therapeutic exercise. *J. Behav. Med.* 4:421–438, 1981.
24. Dishman, R.K., W. Ickes, and W.P. Morgan. Self-motivation and adherence to habitual physical activity. *J. Appl. Soc. Psychol.* 2:115–132, 1980.
25. Dishman, R.K. Compliance/adherence in health-related exercise. *Health Psychol.* 1:237–267, 1982.
26. Dubbert, P.M., J.E. Martin, and L.H. Epstein. Self-Management of exercise. *Self Management Approaches to the Prevention and Treatment of Physical Illness.* New York: Academic Press (in press).
27. Durbeck, D.C., F. Heinzelman, J. Schacter, et al. The National Aeronautics and Space Administration—U.S. Public Health evaluation and enhancement program. *Am. J. Cardiol.* 30:784–790, 1972.
28. Ehsani, A.A., G.W. Heath, J.M. Hagberg, B.E. Sobel, and J.O. Holloszy. Effects of 12-months of intense exercise training on ischemic ST-segment depression in patients with coronary artery disease. *Circulation* 64:1116–1124, 1981.
29. Epstein, L.H., and R.R. Wing. Behavioral approaches to exercise habits and athletic performance. In *Advances in Behavioral Medicine,* vol. 1, J. Ferguson and C.B. Taylor, (eds.), pp. 125–137. N.Y.: Spectrum, 1980.
30. Epstein, L.H., R. Koeske, and R.R. Wing. Adherence to exercise in obese children. *J. Cardiac Rehab.* 4:185–195, 1984.
31. Epstein, L.H., R.R. Wing, R. Koeske, D. Ossip, and S. Beck. A comparison of life-style change and programmed aerobic exercise on weight and fitness changes in obese children, *Behav. Ther.* 13:651–665, 1982.
32. Epstein, L.H., R.R. Wing, J.K. Thompson, and W. Griffin. Attendance and fitness in aerobics exercise. *Behav. Mod.* 4:465–479, 1980.
33. Ferguson, R.J., P. Cote, P. Gauthier, and M.G. Bourassa. Changes in exercise coronary sinus blood flow with training in patients with angina pectoris. *Circulation* 58:41–47, 1978.
34. Folkins, C.H., and W.E. Sime. Physical fitness training and mental health. *Am. Psychol.* 36:373–389, 1981.
35. Fox, S.M., J.P. Naughton, and W.L. Haskell. Physical activity and prevention of coronary heart disease. *Ann. Clin. Res.* 3:404–432, 1971.
36. Franklin, B.A. Motivating and education adults to exercise. *J. Phys. Educ. Recr.* (June), 13–17, 1978.
37. Frederiksen, L.W., L.S. Solomon, and K.A. Brehony, (eds.). *Marketing Health Behavior.* New York: Plenum, 1984.
38. Gettman, L.R., M.L. Pollock, and A. Ward. Adherence to unsupervised exercise. *Physician Sportsmed.* 11(10):56–66, 1983.
39. Greist, J.H., M.H. Klein, J.F. Eischens, A.S. Gurman, and W.P. Morgan. Running as treatment for depression. *Compr. Psychiatry* 20:41–54, 1979.
40. Harris, L. (Poll). *Health Maintenance.* Pacific Mutual Life Insurance Company, 1978.
41. Harris, L. "Fitness in america" (Perrier study). Vital and Health Statistics of the National Center for Health Statistics, 1978.
42. Haynes, R.B. Compliance with health advice: An overview with special reference to exercise program. *J. Cardiac Rehab.* 4:120–123, 1984.
43. Heinzelmann, F., and R.W. Bagley. Response to physical activity programs and their effects on health behavior. *Public Health Rep.* 85:905–911, 1970.
44. Hersen, M., and D. Barlow. *Single Case Experimental Designs: Strategies for Studying Behavior Change,* 1st ed. New York: Pergamon Press, 1976.

45. Kaplan, R.M., C.J. Atkins, and S. Reinsch. Specific efficacy expectations mediate exercise compliance in patients with COPD. *Health Psychol.* 3(3):223–242, 1984.
46. Keefe, F.J., and J.A. Blumenthal. The life-fitness program: A behavioral approach to making exercise a habit. *J. Behav. Ther. Exp. Psychiatry* 11:31–34, 1980.
47. Kentala, E. Physical fitness and feasibility of physical rehabilitation after mycardial infarction in men of working age. *Ann. Clin. Res.* 4:1–84 (Suppl. 9), 1972.
48. Kilbom, A., L.H. Hartley, B. Saltin, I. Bjure, G. Grimby, and I. Astrand. Physical training in sedentary middle-aged and older men. I. Medical evaluation. *Scand. J. Clin. Lab. Invest.* 24:315–322.
49. Kirschenbaum, D.S., A.J. Tomarken, and A.M. Ordman. Specificity of planning and choice applied to self-control. *J. Pers. Soc. Psychol.* 42:576–585, 1982.
50. King, A.C., and L.W. Frederiksen. Low-cost strategies for increasing exercise behavior: Relapse preparation training social support. *Behav. Mod.* 8:3–21, 1984.
51. Lambert, C.A., D.R. Nethertor, L.J. Finison, et al. Risk factors and lifestyle: A statewide health interview survey. *New Engl. J. Med.* 306:1048–1051, 1984.
52. Leon, A.S., and H. Blackburn. The relationship of physical activity to coronary heart disease and life expectancy. *Ann. N.Y. Acad. Sci.* 301:561–578, 1977.
53. Libb, J.W., and C.B. Clements. Token reinforcement in an exercise program for hospitalized geriatric patients. *Percept. Mot. Skills* 28:957–958, 1969.
54. Mann, G.V., H.L. Garrett, A. Farhi, H. Murray, and F.T. Billings. Exercise to prevent coronary heart disease: An experimental study of the effects of training on risk factors for coronary disease in men. *Am. J. Med.* 46:12–27, 1969.
55. Marlatt, G.A., and J.R. Gordon. Determinants of relapse: implications for the maintenance of behavior change. In *Behavioral Medicine.* P.O. Davidson and S.M. Davidson (eds.). New York: Brunner/Mazel, 1980.
56. Martin, J.E. Exercise management: Shaping and maintaining physical fitness. *Behav. Med. Adv.* 4:3–5, 1981.
57. Martin, J.E., P.M. Dubbert, A.O. Katell, et al. Behavioral control of exercise in sedentary adults. Studies 1 through 6. *J. Consult. Clin. Psychol.* 52:795–811, 1984.
58. Martin, J.E., and P.M. Dubbert. Exercise applications and promotion in behavioral medicine: Current status and future directions. *J. Consult. Clin. Psychol.* 50:1004–1017, 1982a.
59. Martin, J.E., and P.M. Dubbert. Exercise and health: The adherence problem. *Behav. Med. Update.* 4:16–24, 1982.
60. Martin, J.E. and P.M. Dubbert. Behavioral Management Strategies for Improving Health and Fitness. *J. Cardiac Rehab.* 4(5):200–208, 1984.
61. Massie, J.F. and R.J. Shephard. Physiological and psychological effects of training—a comparison of individual and gymnasium programs with a characterization of the exercise "drop-out". *Med. Sci. Sports* 3:110–117, 1971.
62. Mayer, J., and E.S. Geller. Motivating energy efficient travel: A community-based intervention for encouraging biking. *J. Environ. Syst.* 12:99–112, 1982.
63. Morgan, W.P. Involvement in vigorous physical activity with special reference to adherence. In *National College of Physical Education Proceedings,* L.I. Gedvials and M.E. Kneer (eds.), pp. 235–246. Office of Public Service, University of Illinois at Chicago, 1977.
64. Morgan, W.P. Psychological benefits of physical activity. In *Exercise, Health and Disease,* F. Nagle and H. Montoye (eds.). Springfield, Ill.: Thomas, 1981.
65. Morgan, W.P. The mind of the marathoner. *Psychol. Today* April 1978.
66. Morgan, W.P. Mind over matter. In. W.F. Straub and J.M. Williams (eds.), *Cognitive Sports Psychology* Lansing, N.Y.: Sport Science Associates, 1984.
67. Morgan. W.P., D.H. Horstman, A. Cymerman, and J. Stokes. Facilitation of physical performance by means of a cognitive strategy. *Cogn. Ther. Res.* 7:251–264, 1983.
68. Morris, J.N., M.G. Everitt, R. Pollard, S.P.W. Chase, and A.M. Semmence. Vig-

orous exercise in leisure-time: Protection against coronary heart disease. *Lancet* 2:1207–1210, 1980.

69. Oldridge, N.B. What to look for in an exercise class leader. *Physician Sports Med.* 5:85–88, 1977.

70. Oldridge, N.B. Compliance of post myocardial infarction patients to exercise programs. *Med. Sci. Sports.* 11:373–375, 1979.

71. Oldridge, N.B. Compliance with exercise programs. In *Heart Disease and Rehabilitation*, M.L. Pollock and D.H. Schmidt, (eds.), pp. 619–629. Boston, Houghton Mifflin, 1979.

72. Oldridge, N.B. Compliance and exercise in primary or secondary prevention of coronary heart disease: A review. *Prev. Med.* 11:56–70, 1982.

73. Oldridge, N.B. Efficacy and effectiveness: Critical issues in exercise and compliance. *J. Cardiac Rehab.* 4:119, 1984.

74. Oldridge, N.B. Compliance and dropout in cardiac exercise rehabilitation. *J. Cardiac. Rehab.* 4:166–177, 1984.

75. Oldridge, N.B., A.P. Donner, C.W. Buck, et al. Predictors of dropout cardiac exercise rehabilitation. *Am. J. Cardiol.* 51:70–74, 1983.

76. Oldridge, N.B. and N.L. Jones. Improving patients compliance in cardiac exercise rehabilitation: Effects of written agreement and self-monitoring. *J. Cardiac Rehab.* 3:257–262, 1983.

77. Oldridge, N.B., J.R. Wicks, C. Hanley, J.R. Sutton, and N.L. Jones. Non-compliance in an exercise rehabilitation program or men who have suffered a myocardial infarction. *Can. Med. Assoc. J.* 118:361–364, 1978.

78. Paffenbarger, R.S., W. Hale, R. Brand, and R.J. Hyde. Work-energy level, personal characteristics and fatal heart attack: A birth-cohort effect. *Am. J. Epidemiol.* 105:200–213, 1977.

79. Paffenbarger, R.S., A.L. Wing, and R.T. Hyde. Physical activity as an index of heart risk in college alumni. *Am. J. Epidemiol.* 108:161–175, 1978.

80. Paffenbarger, R.S., A.L. Wing, R.T. Hyde, and D.L. Jung. Physical activity and incidence of hypertension in college alumni. *Am. J. Epidemiol.* 117:245–257, 1983.

81. Pennebaker, J.W., and J.A. Lightner. Competition of internal and external information in an exercise setting. *J. Pers. Soc. Psychol.* 39:165–174, 1982.

82. Pollock, M.L., L.R. Gettman, C.A. Milesis, M.D. Bah, L. Durstine, and R.B. Johnson. Effects of frequency and duration of training on attrition and incidence of injury. *Med. Sci. Sports.* 9:31–36, 1977.

83. Reid, E.L., and R.W. Morgan, Exercise prescription: A clinical trial. *Am. J. Pub. Health* 69:592–595, 1979.

84. Ryan, A.J. (ed.). Special survey on exercise prescription. *Physician Sportsmed.* 11:10, 1983.

85. Sanne, H., D. Elmfeldt, G. Grimby, Rydin, and L. Wilhelmsen. Exercise tolerance and physical training of non-selected patients after myocardial infarction. *Acta Med. Scand.* 551:1–124, (Supplement), 1973.

86. Soluff, P.H. Effects of denial on mood, compliance, and quality of functioning after cardiovascular rehabilitation. *Gen. Hosp. Psychiatry* 2:134–140, 1980.

87. Stern, M.J., and P. Cleary. National exercise and heart disease project: Psychosocial changes observed during a low-level exercise program. *Arch. Intern. Med.* 141:1463–1467, 1981.

88. Taylor, H.L., R.R. Buskirk, and R.D. Remington. Exercise in controlled trials of the prevention of coronary heart disease. *Fed. Proc.* 32:1623–1627, 1973.

89. Teraslinna, P., T. Partanen, A. Koskela, and P. Oja. Characteristics affecting willingness of executives to participate in an activity program aimed at coronary heart disease prevention. *J. Sports Med. Phys. Fitness* 9:224–229, 1969.

90. Thompson, C.E., and L.M. Wankel. The effects of perceived anxiety choice upon frequency of exercise behavior. *J. Appl. Soc. Psychol.* 10:436–443, 1980.

91. Turner, R.D., S. Polly, and A.R. Sherman. A behavioral approach to individualized exercise programming. In *Counseling Methods,* J.D. Krumboltz and C.E. Thoresen (eds.). New York: Holt, Rinehart and Winston, 1976.

92. Vance, B. Using contacts to control weight and to improve cardiovascular physical fitness. In *Counseling Methods,* J.D. Krumboltz and C.E. Thoresen (eds.), pp. 527–541. New York: Holt, Rinehart and Winston, 1976.

93. Vranic, M., and M. Berger. Exercise and diabetes. *Diabetes* 28:147–167, 1979.

94. Wankel, L.M. Decision-making and social support strategies for increasing exercise involvement. *J. Cardiac Rehab.* 4:124–135, 1984.

95. Wankel, L., and C. Thompson. Motivating people to be physically active: Self-persuasion versus balanced decision making. *J. Appl. Soc. Psychol.* 7:332–340, 1977.

96. Ward, A., and W.P. Morgan. Adherence patterns of healthy men and women enrolled in an adult exercise program. *J. Cardiac Rehab.* 4:143–152, 1984.

97. Wenger, N.K. Early ambulation after myocardial infarction: Early ambulation and patient education. In *Heart Disease and Rehabilitation,* M.L. Pollock and D.H. Schmidt, (eds.). Boston: Houghton Mifflin, 1978.

98. Wilhelmsen, L., H. Sanne, D. Elmfeldt, G. Grimby, G. Tibblin, and H. Wedel. A controlled trial of physical training after myocardial infarction. *Prev. Med.* 4:491–508, 1975.

99. Wysocki, T., G. Hall, B. Iwata, and M. Riordan. Behavioral management of exercise: Contracting for aerobic points. *J. Appl. Behav. Anal.* 12:55–64, 1979.

# The Interface Between Biomechanics and Neurophysiology In the Study of Movement: Some Recent Approaches

ZIAUL HASAN, Ph.D.
ROGER M. ENOKA, Ph.D.
DOUGLAS G. STUART, Ph.D.

Historically, the study of the control of movement and posture has been approached from two quite different perspectives. In one approach, emphasis is placed on the mechanics of movement and the constraints imposed by the musculoskeletal system. The other approach has concentrated on the neuronal interactions that form the basis of motor control. These two approaches, the biomechanical and the cellular, are now beginning to be integrated. It is the purpose of this review to provide students of motor control with the information necessary for the appreciation of these developments. As far as the level of presentation is concerned, we have endeavored to meet the needs of students, such as our own, in the fields of physical education, physiology, and related disciplines. To this end, a conceptual rather than historical framework of presentation has been adopted.

## RELEVANT BACKGROUND

Inasmuch as a reader may be more versed with either the *biomechanical* or the *neurophysiological* perspective on motor control, we attempt in this section to establish the requisite background for both perspectives. There are, however, certain global ideas that are common to both perspectives, and these are considered first.

*The Complexity of Movement*
The movements performed in the course of everyday life are often regarded as simple, owing to the feeling of ease with which they are

For their criticisms of a draft of this manuscript, we would like to thank Drs. A.G. Feldman, J.C. Houk, and F.E. Zajac and the following students. Graduate School: Jeannette Hoit-Dalgaard (Speech and Hearing Sciences); Brenda Plassman (Psychology); James Howard and Kathryn Volz (Physical Education); and, Debra Gordon, Lucinda Rankin, and Sharyn Vanden Noven (Physiology). Medical School: Michael Joyner. Undergraduate School: Pamela Pierce (Electrical Engineering). We also thank Dolores Sierra for her typing of the manuscript and Patricia Pierce for the illustrations. This work was supported by USPHS grants HL07249 (Department of Physiology), NS19407 (Z.H.), and NS07888 (D.G.S.), and NASA grant NAGW 338 (D.G.S. and R.M.E.)

carried out and the abundance of the individuals who are able to perform them. But if one examines such ordinary movements in detail, and tries to understand how they are controlled, the complexity appears daunting. Consider, for example, the movements of an upper extremity involved in opening a door. Excluding the joints of the hand, for the moment, these movements comprise separate but coordinated rotations about the shoulder, elbow, radioulnar, and wrist joints. The speed of each rotation, and in some cases the axis of rotation as well, changes with time. The result is that the door is first accelerated and then smoothly brought to rest in an open position. To achieve this performance, the nervous system must vary, during the course of the movement, the activity of muscles that act across the shoulder, elbow, radioulnar, and wrist joints in an appropriate fashion. There are 33 such muscles, and each of the muscles, when active, tends to rotate the limb in a specific direction; however, this task is made more difficult by the 16 muscles which operate across more than one joint simultaneously. The nervous system must select the appropriate set of muscles, and alter this set during the course of the movement if necessary.

The door-opening movement can be executed from a variety of different initial positions of the subject with respect to the doorknob. For each position, however, the details of the movement are different. The initial position, therefore, must play a role in determining the pattern of commands to the muscles from the nervous system. In addition, the resistance that the door offers is an important consideration, not only for the commands to the muscles of the moving arm, but also for the commands to the leg and trunk muscles, whose activity must be adjusted so as to maintain the individual's balance.

It has been conjectured that most movements are associated with a change in activity of practically all the muscles in the body, with the possible exception of some that are inactive in the initial postural state [103, 104]. For example, Belen'kii et al. [12] have demonstrated that even the execution of the fastest possible movements must begin by satisfying postural requirements. Broer and Houtz [21] have recorded the electrical signals picked up from 68 muscles in different parts of the body during the performance of several sports activities. The complexity of such records precludes a simple answer to the central question in motor control, namely, how does the nervous system decide the activity level of each muscle in the body in order for a movement to be executed or a posture to be stabilized? In the organization of the nervous system there is, of course, a comparable complexity to that encountered in the control of movement.

*The Hierarchy of Command*

The structure of the central nervous system, despite its complexity, exhibits an orderliness that allows us to delineate various parts of it, for example, the spinal cord, the brainstem, the sensorimotor cortex, the basal ganglia, and the cerebellum. The different parts play different roles in motor control, as revealed originally by the effects of damage (lesion) to them. It is not our purpose here to summarize the vast neurologic literature that exists on the subject [95], but a few examples may be useful. Spinal cord transection causes paralysis (flaccid, inactive muscles) below the lesion, but leads, eventually, to a state of spasticity, with preservation of certain coordinated, multijoint movements such as withdrawal from a noxious stimulus. Lesions of certain regions of the basal ganglia lead to involuntary, dance-like movements (chorea), whereas cerebellar lesions are associated with gross oscillations but only during attempted movement.

Although knowledge of the functional interrelations of the different parts of the nervous system is meager, the idea has become popular that the nervous system is organized for motor control in a hierarchical fashion [54]. It is postulated that higher centers command what may be called the bare outline of a movement, while the lower centers fill in the details. The lowest center (spinal cord) supplies the last details, and also directly commands the muscles.

A scheme of hierarchical command was in fact suggested in the 1920s by Bernstein on the basis of certain regularities of natural movements, rather than on the basis of brain structure [13, 177]. Most of the subsequent developers of this idea have continued to refrain from specifying precisely the correspondence between the functional levels of the hierarchy and the anatomical parts of the brain [67, 92]. This appears advisable since the possibility always exists that a function may be performed by a network of neurons that spans several parts of the nervous system. In the case of the movements generated by the isolated spinal cord, however, we are more secure in assigning function to structure since we know that the relevant networks must lie within the spinal cord. Spinally generated movements were studied at the turn of the century by Sherrington and his students [30], particularly Graham Brown [175], who discovered some of the "details" that the spinal cord is equipped to furnish.

To illustrate how the coordinating capability is manifested at a low level of the hierarchy, consider the spinally generated movement of withdrawal of a leg when it is pinched. The withdrawal could conceivably have taken the form of rotation about the hip joint alone, or uncoordinated, staccato rotations about several joints. The fact that it does not take such forms implies that the spinal cord contains the necessary circuitry for generating coordinated commands to the various muscles associated with different joints in response to a simple input from the pinched skin. If one examines the situation in more detail, it is obvious that the rotation about any one of the joints could have been carried out by commanding one or the other of the several muscles whose actions are similar. The particular combination of muscles chosen, therefore, reflects a decision-making capability inherent in the spinal cord. Sherrington [150] claimed that the combination of the muscles employed was the same in the case of bending of the leg during withdrawal as it was for bending the leg during normal walking, underscoring the idea that the combinations are activated in the spinal cord in a stereotyped fashion.

Since the spinal cord evidently contains the machinery for deciding which muscles to employ and what commands to send to them for the coordinated rotations of the joints that result in bending the leg, the higher levels of the nervous system need not specify the details but can simply issue the command, "Bend the leg." This is but one example of the utilization of the capabilities inherent in the spinal cord. In the metaphor used by Greene [67], the "brain is like a general, who commands 'Take Hill 7!' without having to specify as many individual movements as there are soldiers, because low-level organization can furnish the details."

Another way of stating the importance of hierarchical command is in terms of the reduction of the *degrees of freedom*. The degrees of freedom associated with a joint equals the number of coordinates necessary to specify the configuration of the articulating segments, that is, the number of axes about which the joint can rotate. For example, a hinge joint possesses only one degree of freedom, whereas a ball-and-socket joint has three. The upper extremity, as in the door-opening example, has seven degrees of freedom (shoulder = 3, elbow = 1, radioulnar = 1, wrist = 2). Given the many degrees of freedom of our limbs, there is an infinity of different paths that can be followed if, for instance, we wish to touch our nose with our finger. But in reality a given subject usually follows a particular, preferred path. The preferred path implies a certain relationship among the angles at the various joints. Due to this preference, the nervous system can be said to have reduced the exhibited degrees of freedom from those that were geometrically possible. Bernstein suggested that the concept of coordination can be made precise if one identifies it with the reduction in the apparent degrees of freedom brought about by the activity of the nervous system.

A more modern metaphor for the hierarchical levels of command could be phrased in terms of high- and low-level computer languages. A subroutine written in a low-level language is called by a simple statement in a high-level language, and results in the performance of a stereotyped operation. A sequence of such calls itself can comprise a subroutine at a still higher level. In this hierarchy the higher levels are less concerned with the complex details of the operation. Whatever the metaphor, a shortcoming of this perspective is that it does scant justice to the ability of humans and animals to perform atypical movements, an ability presumably involved in breaking the stranglehold of the stereotyped patterns in order to perform new movements.

Despite the allure of hierarchical organization, the concept has not been developed sufficiently to provide answers to many questions, such as the following three.

1. When one reaches with one's hand for an object, is the position of the object specified in terms of the final values of the joint angles necessary to reach it, or in terms of some other, more global coordinate system? The insight gained into "natural" coordinate systems by the results of psychophysical experiments [154] is difficult to relate to the concept of hierarchy, since the coordinate system could be different at different levels in the hierarchy [132].

2. What is the relative rank in the hierarchy of (a) the level at which the identity of the active muscles is decided, and (b) the level at which the timing of the muscle activity is decided? It would appear that timing takes precedence over the identity of muscles, since the handwriting of a person is similar whether he uses the wrist and finger muscles (e.g., with pen and paper), or uses the elbow and shoulder muscles (e.g., on a chalkboard), or with the pen gripped by the teeth, or with the pen taped to the foot [142]. On the other hand, in the case of spinal generation of locomotion on a treadmill, the timing is readily altered by changing the speed of the treadmill, but the identity of the muscles involved in each of the different phases is not altered [68, 69].

3. For movements performed against different external resistances, which of the hierarchical levels is (are) involved in adjusting the activity of the muscles to the resistance encountered? Experimental investigation of this question seems to indicate that anatomically and functionally high as well as low levels are involved [16, 29, 59], which is not what one would have expected of the hierarchical scheme.

In summary, while the control of movements appears to be hierarchically organized, many of the details of the hierarchical scheme remain undefined.

*Programs for Movement*
Since movement involves a sequence of positions in time, it is tempting to postulate that the nervous system, at some level of its orga-

nization, prescribes the positions of the moving parts as a sequence in time. However, the simplicity of this postulate is deceptive.

The idea that movement is prescribed at some level of the nervous system as a position-time sequence leads to the question of how the sequence of muscle activations at the various joints may be computed so as to achieve the requisite movement. This is the so-called inverse dynamics problem. Theoretical investigations of the problem have led to a number of possible mathematical techniques for its solution [78, 128, 143]. For the purposes of these investigations, groups of muscles are modeled as idealized motors. However, when implemented on a high-speed digital computer (which essentially handles one computation at a time), the techniques that allow the determination of the sequence of muscle activations require an inordinate amount of time (or memory), making it difficult to imagine that the nervous system could be employing such techniques [24, 79, 99].

This impasse can be traced to the arbitrary prescription of the detailed and precise movement sequence. No allowance has been made in the computations for the fact that most actual movements of humans and animals are far from arbitrary, but are quite constrained, i.e., the degrees of freedom are less than are geometrically available. Another consideration, emphasized by Loeb [99], is that living organisms, unlike present-day robots, develop the precision of their movements through the process of learning, not a priori. This important point can be summarized in Loeb's words: "Ask not what your subjects can do, but how they learn to do it." The "it," however, implies knowledge of the subjects' capabilities.

It is not necessary to assume that movement is represented at some level of the nervous system as a position-time sequence. The possibility must be considered that when the spinal cord receives the command to bend the leg, it may simply send out a stereotyped sequence of commands to the muscles (the *motor program*), and let the amount of actual bending depend upon whether the leg is free to move or not. In fact, the motor-program commands are sent out even when the muscles are rendered unable to respond (i.e., by an experimentally produced paralysis), and therefore there is no movement [32, 68, 69, 156].

Along these lines, we can schematize the motor control system in a simplified form in terms of two levels. A signal from the higher level is communicated to the lower level, which responds by playing out the appropriate motor program from its repertoire, a program that requires no translation since it is already in the form of muscle-activity patterns. To this scheme, however, must be added a third component which represents the information about the moving body part that is conveyed to the central nervous sytem (Fig. 1). The ne-

FIGURE 1

*A tripartite model for the neural control of movement. The central program located in the Low-level Controller (spinal cord or brainstem) is conceptualized to elaborate the motor program for the neuromuscular apparatus and in turn (1) is activated and sustained by descending signals from the High-level Controller (supraspinal centers) and (2) interacts with the afferent feedback from peripheral receptors.*

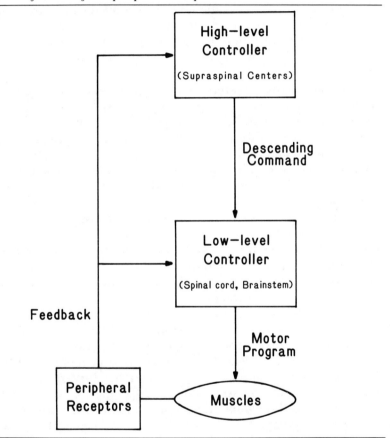

cessity of the feedback of information may be illustrated by the following two examples. (1) If the moving part encounters resistance, feedback is needed for the nervous system to be cognizant of this fact. Furthermore, if the decision is made to overcome the resistance, feedback information is required to adjust the motor program accordingly. (2) If the initial position of the joints is changed, the appropriate tailoring of the motor program cannot be done without information concerning the position. For these and other reasons [53, 56], the tripartite scheme shown in Figure 1 includes feedback in addition to the two hierarchical command levels. (For further details see [68–70, 151, 175, 176].)

*Biomechanical Considerations*

The discussion so far has been concerned with both the controller (the central nervous system) and the controlled (the musculoskeletal apparatus), taken as whole. We turn now to a closer examination of the controlled system, and the concepts developed for its study. These concepts, which lie in the domain of engineering and physics, are important in the study of motor control.

*Feedback.* Feedback refers to the signals emanating from various peripheral transducers (receptors or sensors), which serve to report to the nervous system the mechanical events in muscles, joints, and associated tissues. Although we do not use this term to prejudge how the nervous system utilizes this information, we consider the advantages of feedback information for man-made "servomechanisms." This focus may serve as a guide in understanding the role of feedback in the nervous system.

As an example of the utility of feedback, consider the problem of maintaining the temperature in an oven. A heater of suitably chosen power, operated continuously or according to a fixed regimen, can maintain the oven's temperature at some value; therefore, a temperature sensor is not required. The oven temperature, however, will change significantly if the outside, ambient temperature changes, or if there is a change in the voltage supplied to the heater. In the face of these changes, the oven temperature will be maintained better if use is made of the feedback signal from a temperature sensor located in the oven. Specifically, in the scheme of *servoregulation* of temperature, the power supplied to the heater is adjusted in accordance with the *error* in temperature, i.e., the difference between the desired temperature and the temperature reported by the sensor. The larger the error, the greater the power supplied to the heater. In this scheme, if the ambient temperature falls, or if the voltage of the power supply decreases, there will be only a slight decrease in oven temperature, which will cause an increase in the power supplied to the heater so as to prevent further decrease in oven temperature. Thus, the oven temperature (the *regulated variable*) will stay close to the desired temperature (the *set point*), despite variations in ambient temperature that change the rate of heat loss (the *load*), or variations in the characteristics of the heater itself (the *controlled system* or the *plant*).

This example of servoregulation of oven temperature can be used to illustrate the semantic confusion that often arises in connection with the word "control." The word is used with different meanings from one context to another, e.g., the control of the heater and the control of temperature. Clearly, in the example of the servoregulation of temperature, the oven must contain the machinery that compares the set point with the actual temperature, and on the basis of this comparison *controls* the heater. What, then, controls the temperature? The answer, in the context of this example, is that the temperature is not controlled, it is *regulated.* This answer may appear unduly pedantic, but the necessity of precise terminology becomes apparent when we consider a situation in which the temperature is indeed controlled. Suppose we want the oven temperature to change in a prescribed way. In other words, we want to *control* the temperature. There are various ways of achieving this, but the one that is commonly used in engineering practice is to change the set point in the prescribed way. This method of controlling the temperature will be referred to as *servocontrol* of temperature. Another method of achieving control of temperature is to dispense with the feedback altogether, and simply vary the heater power in an appropriate fashion. The latter method is prone to the imprecision that results from change in ambient temperature; nevertheless, it is important to point out that control need not always be servocontrol, even though in engineering parlance the two are often equated.

In summary, the regulation of a variable means the attempt to keep it constant. Regulation can be realized by a system that uses the signal from a sensor (the feedback signal), compares it with the desired constant value (the set point), and makes the appropriate correction. This scheme is known as *servoregulation,* and the system is called a *servomechanism.* The word "control" is used with two different meanings: the control of a thing and the control of a variable. To control a thing is to have an effect on it, whereas to control a variable is to change its value according to a specified function of time. One method of controlling a variable, although not the only one, is to make use of a servomechanism, but instead of keeping the set point constant, to vary it as a function of time in the desired manner. This scheme is known as *servocontrol.*

To return to the motor system, there are, embedded in muscles, certain sensors whose responses are related to the parameters of the movement, and other sensors that respond to the muscular force [74, 108]. The nervous system controls the muscles, in the same sense in which the heater was controlled in the previous example. But these facts do not tell us whether there is servocontrol, or even a servoregulation, of any of the mechanical variables such as position, velocity, or force. Based on additional facts, certain hypotheses have been advanced for servocontrol of position, force, or other variables, but the status of these hypotheses remains unsettled (for review see [158, 159]). There is good evidence, however, for the servoregulation of position during maintained posture [120]. This regulation implies that muscle activity is automatically altered (analogous to the change in heater power) to counter the effects of an external disturbance that may otherwise result in a change in position (analogous to a change in temperature). It is an interesting possibility, not usually envisaged in the engineering literature, that the control of movement may not be servocontrol, and yet there may be servoregulation of the initial and final positions [65].

There is one aspect of servomechanisms (whether for control or regulation) that is of great interest in motor control; namely, a servomechanism can promote or inhibit *stability*. Stability refers to the tendency for a small error not to become larger with time. In an unstable system, the attempt to correct a small error may result in a greater error, possibly in the opposite direction. The engineering design of servomechanisms is concerned with how to keep the system stable while making it precise. Precision requires efficient correction of errors, but overcorrection can lead to instability which may be manifested as oscillations.

An appropriately designed servomechanism is theoretically capable of promoting stability in an otherwise unstable situation. Consider a skeleton that is made to stand up, with its joints prevented from rotating or slipping so that it does not collapse under its own weight. The structure is unstable because a slight push will topple it. That the skeletons within us are able to stand up in a stable manner is indicative of stabilization due to servoregulation of position. In fact, patients who have lost the pathways of information from the legs to the spinal cord are unable, with their eyes closed, to remain in a standing position.

While there is no doubt that feedback is important for motor control, the question of whether the motor system employs feedback in the same way as servomechanisms cannot be answered unequivocally.

*Rotations about joints.* The program for a movement is manifested in the form of rotations about joints. In this section we consider how the *forces* acting on a limb segment affect the joint rotations, which is an issue of Newtonian mechanics and has nothing to do with properties of muscle. In the following section, muscle properties will be discussed in the context of how joint rotation affects muscle force. Before pursuing these matters, it is convenient to define the term *kinematics*, which is the detailed description of the positions of each component of a mechanical assembly as functions of time, without regard to the agency (such as muscle activity or gravity) that impels the movement of the components. Implicit in the kinematics is a description of the velocities, accelerations, and other derivatives of position.

Force, whether it be due to muscular, gravitational, magnetic, or any other agency, is a measure of the effect of that agency on the kinematics of an object. As a general rule, the net force (i.e., the vector sum of the forces) acting on an object results in a proportionate acceleration of the object. At the same time, however, movement of the object may alter the forces acting on it. This alteration is in accordance with rules that depend upon the specific type of force. For instance, the force due to a spring is proportional to the elongation of the spring, whereas the force due to a dashpot (a shock absorber-type element) is proportional to the velocity of movement. The force, obviously, is not proportional to the acceleration associated with the spring or dashpot. In the traditional problems of mechanics, the kinematics are predicted by solving two sets of simultaneous equations. One set describes how the forces are altered due to movement (e.g., muscle mechanics), a dependence that is specific to the problem. The other set describes, for each object, the effect of the forces on its movement (e.g., skeletal mechanics), in accordance with the general rule of equating the acceleration of the object to the net force on the object divided by its mass. Predictions made along these lines have been verified experimentally in a vast variety of situations.

In regard to the rotary motion of a joint, the two segments (bones) that meet and articulate at the joint can be considered as two separate objects, each influenced by the various forces that act on it. The net force on a segment is the result of: (1) the forces exerted by muscles that have a tendon of attachment on that segment, (2) the weight of the segment and any additional external forces, (3) the forces due to ligamentous and other "passive" tissues, and (4) the force exerted by the adjoining segment. We know, however, that the segment is not in reality a free body, and therefore the result of all the forces must be such that the segment displays no other motion but rotations about the joint. In other words, we normally confine attention to the situations when the joint is not dislocated. The last mentioned category of force (that exerted by the adjoining segment) does not contribute to the kinematics of rotation. A rigorous analysis reveals that acceleration of *angular* motion is proportional not to the net force on the segment, but rather to the net *torque*. Torque (also called *moment of force*) is defined, for each force, as the product of the force and the length of the perpendicular distance between the axis of rotation and the line of action of the force. This distance is known as the *moment arm*. Thus, the same force at a greater distance from the axis of rotation will produce a greater torque since the moment arm is longer. In analogy with the equation

acceleration = (net force)/(mass),

we can write

angular acceleration = (net torque)/(moment of inertia).

As long as the force exerted by the adjoining segment acts along a line that passes through the axis of rotation, and thus contributes zero torque, such forces can be left out of consideration as far as the kinematics of rotation are concerned.

Figure 2A shows an idealized hinge joint between two segments, and one flexor muscle that acts across the joint. The proximal segment is presumed to be fixed, and a weight is attached to the distal segment. If the segment is not rotating, the net torque about the joint must be zero (Figure 2B). This is the condition of *equilibrium*. For equilibrium, the torques due to the muscle and the external forces must be equal and opposite in direction. Note that, when we consider the torques at a different joint anglè, as shown in Figure 2C, each of the moment arms is different in length. As the torque due to the weight is now different, so too must the muscle torque be different, if equilibrium is to be achieved.

If the segment can rotate about a joint in more than one direction, i.e., there is more than one degree of freedom or axis of rotation (for example, the shoulder joint), the condition for equilibrium is that the net torques for each degree of freedom must be zero. Similarly, the equilibrium of multijoint structures is equivalent to the equilibrium of each joint. In the case of multijoint structures, however, the forces in the various muscles must be chosen in accordance with the fact that many muscles span more than one joint.

The problem of controlling the muscles for a multijoint movement brings to the fore certain mechanical considerations that are not relevant in the case of single-joint movement [14]. In multijoint movements, rotation about one of the joints can cause a neighboring joint to experience a torque in the absence of any muscular or external forces acting directly on it. For instance, if a subject performs a rotation about the elbow joint with the wrist relaxed, the hand tends to flail. In addition, simultaneous rotations of two joints give rise to an interaction described in the field of mechanics as the Coriolis effect. It is these complexities of interaction among the segments that make it difficult to compute the muscular torques necessary for prescribed kinematics [80].

These complexities of interaction among the different moving seg-

FIGURE 2

*A model of the forces acting on a simple articulating system. A. An idealized hinge joint (a) between two body segments with a flexor muscle acting across the joint. A weight is attached to the distal segment. B. A free body diagram of the distal segment in which the forces acting on the segment include: the force exerted by the muscle (M), the weight attached to the segment (W), the weight of the segment (S), and the force exerted by the proximal segment (J). The moment arms for the three forces which exert a torque about the joint (a) are indicated with dashed lines. When the net torque about the joint is zero, the segment will remain stationary and hence is described as being in equilibrium. C. The segment has been rotated to a new position. Since the moment arms for the two weight forces have changed, the torque due to these two forces is now different. Accordingly, the torque exerted by the muscle activity will change to match the new conditions if the system is to remain in equilibrium.*

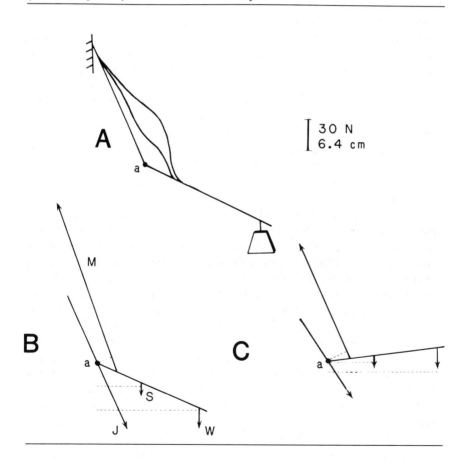

ments of a limb can be viewed, from another perspective, to be of advantage. At least for the swing phase of walking it has been shown [116] that the mechanical interactions among the segments are sufficient to account for many of the observed features, without any necessity for the activation of the muscles! While this seems contrary to common sense, the situation may be clarified by considering the much simpler case of the movements of a swing. The movement can be maintained, at least for some time, without the necessity of precisely timed pushes applied to the swing. Similarly, the movements of locomotion, once started, can be carried out, as it were, on their own momentum. Muscle activity is necessary, however, not only for starting the movement and for the replenishing of energy losses, but also for preventing collapse if the foot happens to step on a stone or if the terrain is uneven. In addition, faster speeds of locomotion necessitate muscle activity for braking the movement at appropriate times [135].

Muscle activity during locomotion on an even surface is not confined to occasional bursts of energy replenishment, but exhibits a timed sequence throughout each cycle [68, 69]. Furthermore, the generation of the locomotor activity pattern by the nervous system is not contingent on the actual movement since it can be elicited when the muscles are unable to respond [68, 69]. Thus, both the nervous system and the mechanical assemblage of joints have rhythm-generating properties that come together during locomotion, in a manner whose details are only beginning to be understood. It is possible that the motor output is "tuned" to the utilization of mechanical interactions among joints, perhaps even in the case of nonrhythmic movements.

*Muscles as motors.* The mechanical effects of the nerve signals that are sent to the muscles are the subject of this section. The effects have been studied thoroughly in situations where the mechanical variables have stabilized, but only scantily when they are changing. Although emphasis here is placed on the mechanical variables of muscle length and force, it should be kept in mind that for a given muscle length, one can determine the joint angle and also the moment arm, which allows muscle force to be converted to torque.

The simplest situation for the study of the mechanical properties of muscle is when the muscle is prevented from changing its length. In this *isometric* condition, a certain nerve signal gives rise to a certain muscle force which varies with muscle length [141]. A sudden change (milliseconds) in the nerve signal causes only a gradual change (hundreds of milliseconds) in the isometric muscle force [129]. A sudden change in the length of the active muscle, on the other hand, causes an immediate change in muscle force, followed by a complex series of changes over time [86, 141]. The initial, immediate change in force is reminiscent of the behavior of a spring, which, when pulled, exhibits an immediate change in force. The subsequent changes in muscle force, however, are quite unlike those expected of a spring.

If the active muscle is allowed to shorten against a constant, externally applied force, the speed of shortening rapidly settles to a more or less constant value. This value is greater for smaller external forces, and the relationship has been characterized thoroughly [76, 133]. If, on the other hand, the active muscle is elongated, the relationship between stretch velocity and force is more complicated [141] and has not been as well characterized.

Muscles are used in everyday life not only to cause movements but also to brake or damp them [58, 96]. For any of these purposes, the final output of the nervous system can directly affect only the activity of the muscles. The muscular activity, in turn, establishes relationships among the mechanical variables about joints (torque, angle, and their derivatives) without specifying the value of any single variable.

*Neurophysiologic Considerations*
Communication to, from, and within the central nervous system takes the form of electrochemical disturbances that travel along the nerve fibers *(axons)*. The disturbance is of a discrete (all-or-none) character, and its electrical manifestation is called the "discharge of an *action potential*." The axons responsible for communicating the motor output to the muscles are the *motor axons*. Each motor axon is a slender tube that emanates, at its central end, from the body of a cell called the *motoneuron*. At the other, peripheral end, the motor axon splits into many branches, each of which terminates in a specialized structure *(endplate)* in close juxtaposition with a muscle fiber. Thus, a single motor axon *innervates* a group of muscle fibers. The groups innervated by different motor axons usually have no common members.

The muscle fibers innervated by a single motor axon, together with the motor axon and its parent cell body, are referred to as a *motor unit*. A motor unit comprises an irreducible functional component of the motor system, since it can only be activated as a whole, or not at all. When the action potential travels down a motor axon and reaches the endplates, a sequence of processes occur [90], the result of which is the activation of the innervated muscle fibers.

In conjunction with the activation of the muscle fibers of a motor unit there are ionic currents that flow through the muscle fiber membranes, which can be detected by monitoring the voltage of a wire inserted into the muscle. If the area of exposure of the wire electrode is sufficiently small, it is possible to detect the activations of individual motor units, though only a few of the active motor units can be so monitored. On the other hand, a large electrode, whether inserted into the muscle or simply placed on or close to its surface, detects the activity of many, or perhaps all, of the motor units at the same time. Such gross recordings provide an indication of the activity of the whole muscle. The electrode voltage, when suitably "smoothed," is commonly used as a measure of the CNS motor output directed to a muscle. The record of voltage is called an *electromyogram*, or EMG. It should be emphasized that a particular amplitude of the EMG, since it is a measure of muscle activity, does not correspond to a particular muscle force, or length, or velocity of movement, but rather to a complicated combination of these variables and their derivatives, which depend also on the external condition.

*Orderly recruitment of motoneurons.* A muscle responds to the action potentials sent from its motoneurons. This group of nerve cells is of special significance since they represent the only pathway for commanding the muscle. The number of motoneurons is quite limited in comparison with the total number of neurons in the nervous system (perhaps a trillion). There are, typically, only a few hundred motoneurons for each limb muscle. From another point of view, however, this number is large enough to present serious difficulty since the motor units are not identical to each other. The difficulty arises because an intended level of activation of the muscle can, conceivably, be produced by many different combinations of motor units, and the number of such combinations is astronomical. How does the nervous system decide from among the many possible combinations of motor units that it can employ?

A large body of evidence supports the idea that the nervous system follows a rather simple rule for deciding which motor units to employ [23, 75]. For a given muscle, there is a rank ordering of motor units, as number 1, number 2, and so on. Motor unit number 15, for example, is not activated unless motor units number 1 through 14 have already been activated. In other words, the only combinations employed are those for which the motor units are recruited in a certain fixed order. One does not, for example, observe the use of motor units number 5 and 68, with the rest of the motor units inactive.

This principle of orderly recruitment [34, 41, 163] implies the following. (1) A certain degree of whole-muscle activation is achieved by one, and only one, combination of motor units. Certainly, this simplifies the problem of choosing the appropriate combination. (2) The available number of levels of muscle activation is limited to the number of motor units, with no "vernier" gradations between them. These inferences are somewhat mitigated by the fact that the nervous system has, at its disposal, a means of altering the activation of an individual motor unit. Namely, the *rate* at which the action potentials are sent along the motor axon can be varied and this will alter the level of activation. Available evidence, however, indicates that this rate, too, is not chosen arbitrarily [3, 27].

The lack of arbitrariness in the choice of motor units and their activity is a simplifying feature of motor output. However, if a certain muscle is involved (along with other muscles) for movements in more than one direction, it may be that the rank ordering of the motor units of that muscle may depend upon the direction of movement [33, 36], but little is known about this fundamental issue.

*Muscle afferent discharge during movement.* Embedded in a muscle are a number of sensory receptors for reporting the mechanical events in the muscle to the central nervous system. (For a review see [74].) The nerve fibers along which the communication from the periphery to the central nervous system takes place are referred to as *afferents*. (The term "sensory fibers," often employed as an equivalent, is used on other occasions to imply a resultant conscious sensation, whereas the term "afferent" is noncommittal in this regard.) The number of afferents from a muscle usually exceeds the number of motor axons to the muscle [108]; however, many of the afferents respond only to noxious stimuli or respond belatedly to tension in the muscle [93]. Only two classes of afferents report the mechanical events on a moment-to-moment basis and with high sensitivity; presumably, therefore, these afferents are important in the operation of the motor system. They arise from two highly specialized types of receptors in the muscle, the *Golgi tendon organ* (named after its discoverer), and the *muscle spindle* (named for its appearance).

Golgi tendon organs are found, most commonly, at the junction of the muscle fibers and the tendon (or, to be more accurate, at the junction of the fibers and the aponeurosis, which is a tendinous sheath often extending into the muscle). Each tendon organ is connected ("in-series") to a few muscle fibers, and therefore responds to the forces exerted by these muscle fibers. Hence, the rate of discharge of action potentials along a Golgi tendon-organ afferent is related to the force exerted by a small number of muscle fibers representing a subset of motor units. The receptor is so sensitive that the force of a single muscle fiber has a demonstrable effect on the rate of discharge of the afferent [52]. Although the number of muscle fibers or motor units "sampled" by all the Golgi tendon organs in a muscle is only a small fraction of the total number of fibers in the muscle, the sampling appears to be essentially random [23]; therefore, the central nervous sytem can obtain a good estimate of total muscle force based on the discharge rates of all the tendon-organ afferents [82, 160].

It has become possible in recent years to monitor the discharge of action potentials in single afferent axons during movement, both in humans [22, 166] and in animals [100, 137]. The information available concerning the discharge of Golgi tendon-organ afferents during natural movements [139, 166] supports the notion that these afferents respond to force on a moment-to-moment basis [82]. The view, held earlier, that these afferents respond only in nonphysiologic conditions (such as overstretch of the muscle) is no longer held to be valid.

Muscle spindles are structurally complex receptor organs embedded in muscle, but unlike the Golgi tendon organs, they are arranged in parallel with the muscle fibers [74, 108, 109]. The mechanical arrangement constrains the muscle spindle to monitor the length of the muscle fibers (and quantities such as velocity of movement related to the length), but does not allow it to distinguish between a change in length caused by muscle activity and a change in length caused by external forces. Furthermore, unlike the Golgi tendon organs, muscle spindles are found scattered throughout the muscle, and each spindle gives rise to several afferent axons. The afferent axons (but not the spindles) fall into two categories called *primary* and *secondary*. This classification is based on anatomical differences between the respective nerve endings, and these differences are reflected in the responsiveness of the afferents [100, 108].

A primary spindle afferent responds with the highest sensitivity to very small stretches of the muscle (e.g., 0.01 mm). If, on the other hand, the muscle is stretched by a large amount (e.g., 5 mm), the discharge rate increases enormously initially but then decreases. At the new length, once again, a high sensitivity to small stretch can be demonstrated. The secondary spindle afferent, on the other hand, is not as sensitive to small changes in length. The discharge rate of this type of afferent, therefore, provides a better indication of absolute muscle length. However, the velocity of movement also has some effect on the secondary afferent response, as it does, indeed, for the primary afferent [72, 74, 84].

The muscle spindle, though a receptor, is innervated by motor *(fusimotor)* axons which modulate its responsiveness. This feature of the muscle spindle makes it quite unlike all other peripheral receptors, with the exception of the eye and ear. Some of the fusimotor axons are specific to spindles, whereas others are branches of ordinary motor axons that innervate the muscle. The discharges of fusimotor axons have the following effects on spindle afferents: (1) The afferent discharge rate is increased, either significantly or only marginally, when the muscle length is held constant. (2) The sensitivity of the afferent discharge rate to change in muscle length may be increased or decreased, depending upon the type of afferent, the type of fusimotor axon, and the amount of change in length. Without going into the intricacies of these phenomena [74, 100, 109], it is clear that the knowledge of spindle-afferent discharge alone does not allow one to extricate the effects of muscle length and movement (i.e., kinematics), on the one hand, and fusimotor discharge, on the other.

It is often conjectured that the central nervous system can deduce the kinematics from knowledge of the spindle-afferent discharge, since it has the information concerning fusimotor discharge, which, after all, is generated in the central nervous system. This possibility seems unlikely in view of the complicated changes in afferent sensitivity to muscle stretch that occur even in the absence of fusimotor discharge, not to speak of the profound effects of the latter. Besides, it makes little evolutionary sense to "corrupt" the afferent signal by means of a fusimotor system, only to have to neutralize the fusimotor effects by elaborate processing of the signals within the central nervous system. Nevertheless, the fact remains that our psychological "sense of position," which is quite accurate even with the eyes closed, is largely contingent, in this circumstance, on spindle-afferent discharge [110–112].

Recording of spindle-afferent discharge in humans and in animals during natural or quasi-natural movements has not provided a clear description of what it is that the afferent signals report to the central nervous system during movement. At the onset of a movement, the central nervous system seems to bring into play not only the motor axons that innervate the muscle, but also, at about the same time, the fusimotor axons that innervate the spindles [22, 166]. As a result of the fusimotor discharges, the spindle-afferent discharge rate may increase despite muscle shortening; but there are exceptions, especially when the muscle shortening is particularly fast [138]. It seems that, at least for some natural movements, the primary spindle afferents remain quite sensitive to small irregularities of movement, though they can hardly be said to signal muscle length [165].

The information content of spindle-afferent discharge during natural movements is obscured by the complexities discussed before. Loeb [100] has recently suggested that the information conveyed by the afferent should be viewed in the context of what the afferent discharge is expected to be if no external perturbations disrupt the planned movement. Specifically, according to Loeb, the fusimotor discharge is chosen so as to keep spindle-afferent discharge in the midrange of its possible extremes when the movement proceeds as planned. Any external circumstances that promote or impede the movement, then, would be reported by the spindle afferent since its discharge rate would veer away from the expected midrange rate. From this perspective, the fusimotor system is employed to enable the spindle to report, not what is going on, but whether it is different from what is expected. This error detection by the spindle does not, however, imply servocontrol of movement, since movements can be performed after removal of all afferent channels of information, albeit with lessened ability to respond to external changes.

In summary, the Golgi tendon-organ afferents report muscle force, whereas the muscle-spindle afferents convey information concerning a complicated combination of the actual kinematics and the fusimotor output. This combination may be interpreted in terms of departures from the expected kinematics.

*Spinal reflex pathways.* The afferents from muscle receptors project to a variety of different levels of the central nervous system. The influences of muscle-afferent discharge exerted directly or indirectly on the motoneurons are responsible for the adjustment of the motor output to the external circumstances. Many of the neuronal pathways responsible for this adjustment lie entirely within the spinal cord, and considerable attention has been given to their study [11]. The effects of afferent discharge on motoneuronal discharge are often called *reflexes*, especially when they are demonstrable at the spinal level. The study of reflexes, and of the neurons that mediate them, has for many years been carried out under highly controlled experimental conditions in which the animal does not exhibit any movements. More recently, however, the study of reflexes during movement has begun to receive attention [5] as discussed in a later section.

A muscle-afferent axon, upon entering the spinal cord, splits into many branches, each of which ends in a *synapse* on a neuron. The synapse, like the endplate on a muscle fiber, is a specialized structure that allows the discharge of the axon to influence the electrochemical properties of the target neuron, thus changing the propensity of the target neuron to discharge an action potential. Each neuron receives a large number (hundreds of thousands) of synapses from various axons, most of which originate within the central nervous system. The likelihood of its discharge is increased by the action of certain synapses (*excitatory* synapses), and decreased by the action of others (*inhibitory* synapses). The target neuron discharges an action potential whenever the net balance of the concurrent influences of the excitatory and inhibitory synapses exceeds a certain threshold. The axon that originates from this neuron transmits the discharge, in turn, to the synapses it makes on other neurons. Such chains and networks of neurons are thought to be the basis of the operation of the nervous system. The identification of the chain of neurons from the afferent to the motoneuron is an important part of the study of reflexes.

Most neurons in the nervous system are neither motoneurons nor afferent neurons, and are known by the nonspecific term *interneurons.* The recording, in anesthetized animals, of the electrical potentials of spinal cord interneurons in their relation to afferent discharges has revealed complex patterns of synaptic influence [20] that are difficult to relate to the biomechanics of motor control. Nevertheless, there are certain features of the afferent influences that are relatively simple, some of which are outlined below.

1. Spindle afferents make excitatory synaptic contact with many of the motoneurons that innervate the muscle from which the afferent originates, as well as some motoneurons that supply other muscles of similar location. One component of the synaptic effect is direct, i.e., it does not involve any interneurons; its serviceability is tested by means of the familiar "knee tap" reflex. In addition to the direct (monosynaptic) effect there are other excitatory and inhibitory effects of spindle afferents mediated by interneurons [71, 87]. The significance of the excitatory influences of spindle-afferent discharge upon the motoneurons of the muscle of origin is believed to be the following. If the external conditions are such that the muscle is stretched, the increased discharge of spindle afferents promotes increased discharge (and recruitment) of the motoneurons. Consequently, the muscle activity increases, which tends to shorten the muscle, thus opposing the effect of the external conditions. This sequence of events, called the *stretch reflex,* is reminiscent of the operation of a servomechanism for the regulation of muscle length. Since spindle afferent discharge is more sensitive to the smaller stretches, one would expect the regulation to be better for smaller perturbations [42].

2. Primary spindle afferents excite a certain category of interneurons, which, in turn, inhibit motoneurons of those muscles whose action is opposed to the muscle of origin of the afferent. In this manner, the stretch of a muscle inhibits the activity of opposing muscles. This is an instance of *reciprocal inhibition,* seen in interactions between flexor and extensor muscles of the limb, but not other muscle control systems such as limb abductors and adductors or jaw openers and closers [89].

3. Golgi tendon-organ afferents, together with primary spindle afferents, make excitatory synapses on certain "shared" interneurons. These interneurons are inhibitory to the motoneurons of the muscle of origin. Thus, the effect of Golgi tendon-organ afferents on the muscle is largely inhibitory, although excitatory effects have also been observed [174].

4. Cutaneous (skin) afferents, projecting to many interneurons, tend to be excitatory to flexor motoneurons and inhibitory to extensor motoneurons [102]. Therefore cutaneous stimuli tend to promote flexion of the limb *(flexion reflex)*. However, the other, contralateral limb is affected in the opposite manner, a phenomenon known as the *crossed-extension reflex*. These reflexes are involved in the withdrawal of one limb and the shifting of the weight to the other limb upon skin stimulation. Alternative reflex patterns are also common. These involve afferent input from restricted skin areas and receptors leading to excitation of selected groups of motoneurons [11, 23, 55].
5. There is a strong possibility that there are alternative (excitatory and inhibitory) interneuronal pathways connecting each of the afferent systems to their target cells. This possibility is currently most certain for primary muscle spindle afferents [81].

Every interneuron in a spinal reflex pathway receives a large number of synapses from other sources, such as higher brain regions, and also other spinal interneurons. The variability of these influences (together with alternative pathway possibilities) makes a spinal reflex quite changeable. The efficacy of spinal reflexes can be altered, for instance, by the cerebellum [19] or by the spinal interneurons that are involved in generating the program for locomotion [5, 50].

Despite the changeability of the effectiveness of afferent discharge in eliciting muscle activity, it is important to keep in mind that the neural networks that underlie the reflex are permanently present. Other parts of the nervous system can utilize the same networks, quite irrespective of the afferents. For instance, since the stretch reflex and the concomitant reciprocal inhibition tend to activate groups of muscles of like action and to inhibit opposing muscles, it is possible that the networks underlying these phenomena may be utilized by a signal from the brain, with or without input from muscle spindles, for achieving the same pattern of muscle activity.

*Muscular synergy.* The preceding discussion introduced the idea that there is some correspondence between the "hardwired" synaptic connections among neurons and the physical arrangement of the muscles. This idea deserves further elaboration.

Rotation about a joint is typically controlled by many muscles, each of which, when active, tends to rotate the joint in a certain direction. For instance, the elbow joint is flexed by muscles such as biceps brachii, brachialis, and brachioradialis, and extended by triceps and anconeus. Whereas it is true that the biceps brachii is not only a flexor of the elbow but has other actions on the forearm and the shoulder as well, it can be classified, as far as elbow movements are concerned, among the flexors. In other words, it is an *anatomical synergist* of the pure elbow flexors, brachialis and brachioradialis. By the same token, triceps brachii is an *anatomical antagonist* of the elbow flexors. Similarly, groups of muscles about other joints can be classified, in the context of a particular degree of freedom of movement, as anatomical synergists and antagonists.

In large measure, the anatomical synergy of a group of muscles is reflected in their normal ("physiologic") use. The entire elbow flexor group, for example, is found to be activated when a subject flexes his elbow [18]. However, the relative activation of the different elbow flexors is altered [152] if the elbow flexion is performed with a different torsion of the forearm (pronated or supinated). This observation indicates that the neural networks responsible for the simultaneous activity of elbow flexors cannot be as simple as one might first have imagined. The necessity for a concept of *physiologic synergy* (i.e., simultaneous activity of muscles), as different from anatomical synergy (i.e., similar action of muscles), is brought out more clearly by the following example.

The muscles which flex the fingers cross the wrist and therefore also tend to flex the wrist. If one wishes to flex the fingers alone, it is necessary to activate simultaneously the wrist extensors to prevent wrist flexion. This simultaneous activation is extremely common in everyday movements, and constitutes a well-ingrained physiologic synergy, even though the simultaneously active muscles have opposite actions on the wrist. Some of the synergies of anatomically opposing muscles are disrupted when certain pathways from the brain to the spinal cord are severed [63], which suggests that there may be more than one level of the nervous system that determines which muscles are activated together.

It was mentioned earlier that almost any movement involves practically the whole musculature of the body. The concept of physiologic synergy represents an attempt to dissect this bewildering complexity into manageable portions, and to relate the regularities of muscle use to neuronal networks. From this perspective, muscles can by synergistic even when they operate on entirely different joints.

Two methods have been employed to search for synergies among muscles. One method is to perturb the limb in some way, and observe the changes in muscle activity that follow almost immediately. The perturbation may be a mechanical one [121], or may consist of electrical stimulation of afferents [134]. The pattern of the effects on a number of the muscles of the limb establishes the existence of a synergy. Another, different method is to observe which muscles are activated together during a natural movement. Of course, for a movement such as locomotion, different muscles are active in different phases. But within a certain phase, one can identify the active muscles and classify them as synergists. Sherrington [150] had thought that the two methods for delineating synergy were equivalent in their results. Although there are exceptions [32, 157], this has turned out to be largely true.

In short, the study of physiologic synergy among muscles allows us to identify the regularities concerning the use of muscles, and to try to relate these regularities to what is known about the neuronal networks. The alteration of the synergies as a result of various lesions of the nervous system can help in the localization of the responsible networks in the hierarchical scheme of command.


CURRENT CONCEPTS

In this section we discuss a number of current hypotheses concerning motor control. The hypotheses, which are by no means mutually exclusive, represent attempts to bring together certain aspects of the neurophysiology and the mechanics of movement. Each of the hypotheses has received experimental support, but the scope (including the limitations) of each remains to be determined. These developments, one hopes, are a prelude to the formulation of a more general theoretical framework.

A theme that is common to these ideas is that the nervous system must choose a *strategy* (i.e., a pattern of muscle activation) from among the many patterns that are theoretically capable of achieving the same end result. The question of whether the strategy is such as to simplify the generation of activity patterns, or to optimize some measure of the "cost" associated with the movement, is answered in different ways by the different hypotheses. It is possible, indeed likely, that the strategy is not the same in all situations. The hypotheses, therefore, should not be viewed as mutually contradictory. They simply represent different attempts to solve the problem of how the exhibited degrees of freedom might be reduced.

We have classified the current hypotheses into three categories. The categorization is along the lines of an old and persistent division between those who regard the control of movement and the regulation of posture as different expressions of the operation of the same mechanism, and those who regard movement and posture to be quite disparate as far as the underlying mechanisms are concerned [107]. Ideas concerning movement that seemed to us as conforming to one or the other of these viewpoints are presented under the rubrics of "postural emphasis" or "kinetic emphasis." A third category, "combined emphasis," is for ideas that combine facets of both.

*Concepts with a Postural Emphasis*

The ideas to be discussed, although they apparently evolved relatively independently, are related conceptually as well as in terms of their exploitation of the experimental technique of applying unexpected mechanical disturbances. To avoid confusion, we reserve the word "movements" for those actions that are generated by the subject, while changes in position that are the result of manipulations by the experimenter are referred to as "perturbations."

If a perturbation is applied to a limb in a postural state, i.e., while movement is not being attempted, the limb resists the perturbation to some extent. During movement, also, there is resistance to perturbation. According to the postural emphasis concepts, the mechanism underlying this resistance is the same during movement as it is in a postural state. To some degree this notion is necessarily correct, because part of the resistance to perturbation stems from the mechanical properties of the muscles, and is not contingent upon the CNS being informed of the perturbation. This mechanism of providing resistance would operate whether or not the CNS issues commands for movement. However, another part of the resistance to perturbation derives from change in muscle activity as a result of the CNS response to the perturbation, a response which could, conceivably, differ between posture and movement. While the hypotheses we are about to discuss are not unanimous in the importance they give to the CNS response, they agree nevertheless in making no fundamental distinction between states of posture and movement insofar as the mechanism of resistance to perturbation is concerned. Furthermore, they agree in modeling the resistance, at least to a first approximation, in the form of the resistance of a spring to changes in its length, i.e., the stiffness of the spring.

*Stiffness regulation.* The designer of a robot would prefer to employ a muscle instead of a conventional motor or engine because of the high efficiency of muscle in its utilization of energy, and its small size for the power it can produce. These advantages, however, would be offset by the complexity of the mechanical properties of muscle. The mechanical properties are so intricate that there does not yet exist an equation describing the interrelations between muscle activity, length, force, and their derivatives, which would remain valid when these quantities vary with time. Perhaps muscle has evolved for energy efficiency rather than for ease of controllability. The concept of *stiffness regulation* holds that, although the mechanical properties of a muscle are extremely complicated, there is no need for the higher levels of command to take these properties into account. From the vantage point of the higher levels, muscle properties can be assumed to be quite simple, since spinal reflexes vary the muscle activation in such a fashion that the muscle appears to have simple mechanical properties.

Data presented by Nichols and Houk [126] indicate that, as a result of the operation of the spinal reflexes, the mechanical response (force) of a muscle to imposed stretch is no more complicated than that of an ordinary spring, at least to a first approximation. This simplicity is to be contrasted with the mechanical properties of a muscle whose activation is kept constant, that is, in the absence of spinal reflexes. Namely, muscle stretch results in an initial increase in muscle force followed by a series of changes in force (including *decrease* of the force during stretch), a behavior quite unlike that of a spring (Fig. 3A). On the basis of this comparison, it is clear that spinal reflexes can act to vary the muscle activation in response to muscle stretch (Fig. 3B), in such a fashion that the combined effect of the stretch and the change in activation is an uncomplicated increase in muscle force. The reflexes, it should be emphasized, are not the sole determinants of muscle force for a given muscle length, as there are many nonreflex[1] influences on the motoneurons, which also affect muscle force. But when the muscle is stretched, the nonreflex influences are, by definition, unchanged, and only the reflexes modulate muscle activation, with the result that the muscle appears to the outside world as a simple spring (Fig. 3B and C).

Stiffness, for a spring or any other elastic material, is defined as the ratio of change in force to change in length; this ratio has the property of being independent of the time course of the changes [178]. In the case of a muscle whose activation is kept at a constant level, the ratio of change in force to change in length varies drastically with the time of measurement, and with the direction and speed of the change in length (e.g., Fig. 3A). As a consequence of this time dependency, areflexive muscle cannot be assigned a stiffness value. In contrast, a muscle with reflex modulation of its activation can be assigned a stiffness, as the ratio of the change in force to change in length is, to a first approximation, independent of the time at which the measurement is taken, as well as the direction and speed of length change [126]. It is this action of the reflexes—what may be called

---

1. By "nonreflex influences" we simply mean the synaptic effects, excitatory or inhibitory, that would be present in the absence of afferent input from the limb. In this category are the influences of the descending commands from higher brain regions, as well as the influence of "pattern generator" neurons in the spinal cord. We do not imply that two separate sets of pathways, one reflex and the other nonreflex, impinge on the motoneurons. In fact the reflex as well as the nonreflex influences are exerted largely via interneurons, many of which receive synaptic input from limb afferents as well as from other sources (e.g., Fig. 3B).

FIGURE 3
*The regulation of muscle stiffness by reflexes. A. The effect of stretch on the force exerted by muscle in the absence of afferent feedback (note the constant EMG). Symbols: n = nonreflex input, i = interneurons, α = motoneuron pool. In all three parts of the figure, the graphs against time in the right column are drawn on the assumption that the nonreflex input (n) is constant. B. The stretch-induced force exerted by muscle in the presence of afferent feedback (aff). The force more or less appears as a scaled version of the stretch. The EMG, however, does not appear scaled to force or length. (A similar parallel relationship exists between length and force when the muscle is shortened.) C. The stretch-induced force for a spring, hence the suggestion the reflexes confer spring-like properties to muscle. The spring is attached to a rack-and-pinion device which can affect the length-force relationship in a manner analogous to the nonreflex inputs to muscle.*
SOURCE: Adapted from [81, 126].

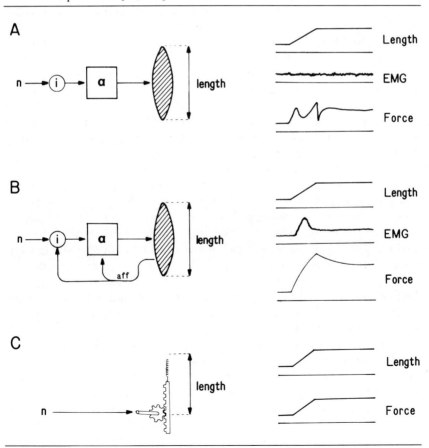

the "regularization" of muscle stiffness—that is referred to as stiffness regulation.

The actual magnitude of the stiffness, which is measured by applying a perturbation and determining the ratio of change in force to change in length, varies with the prestretch (or prerelease) state of the muscle. The preperturbation length and activation of the muscle uniquely determine the magnitude of the stiffness [81]. Acceptance of this contention implies that the CNS cannot independently control muscle stiffness. Since the stiffness is determined uniquely by the preperturbation conditions, it cannot be varied independently of these conditions. Indeed, Crago et al. [29] have demonstrated the inability of human subjects to control muscle stiffness, as long as the initial length and activity of the muscle were set by the experimental conditions [105]. Whether the subject was instructed to resist the perturbation, or to assist it, the response was the same, which is not what one might intuitively expect. It was only a considerable time (> 70 ms) after the onset of perturbation that the prior instruction had an effect, presumably via supraspinal processes.

It should be emphasized that the spring-like behavior of muscle under the influence of the spinal reflexes is evident only for imposed changes in muscle length and force. Unlike the case for a simple, fixed spring, the muscle force can vary over a wide range for the same absolute length of the muscle. This range is available due to the nonreflex influences on the motoneurons. Just as the muscle stiffness, as revealed by perturbation, can be represented by a spring, the effect of the nonreflex influences can be modeled by the effect of turning the crank of a rack-and-pinion arrangement (Fig. 3C) in series with the spring [81]. In this model the two elements (the spring and the rack and pinion) together represent the mechanical properties of the muscle whose reflex connections are intact. As long as the rack and pinion remains locked (i.e., the nonreflex influences do not change), the resistance to perturbation is provided by the spring. On the other hand, the turning of the crank (which corresponds to a change in the nonreflex influences) without change in length of the two-element assembly can elongate the spring and thus increase the force. In this manner the force can be altered for the same muscle length by the nonreflex inputs.

As for the identity of the neuronal pathways that are responsible for the appropriate change in muscle activity in response to a perturbation, two possibilities may be considered. (1) The excitatory synaptic influences of spindle afferents upon motoneurons of the muscle of origin may be sufficient to increase the muscle activation upon stretch in order for stiffness regulation to be exhibited. These influences may not be strong enough to prevent a change in muscle length, as would be expected of an ideal mechanism for the servoregulation of muscle length, but may nevertheless suffice to overcome the peculiarities of the mechanical properties exhibited by muscle in the absence of reflexes (Fig. 3A). (2) While the influences of spindle afferents may favor servoregulation of muscle length, the inhibitory effects of Golgi tendon organ afferents upon the same motoneurons would tend to favor servoregulation of muscle force. The simultaneous operation of these two servomechanisms would result in the servoregulation of a combination of muscle length and force, a combination that may be identified with muscle stiffness. In their original formulation, Nichols and Houk [126] argued for the simultaneous operation of the two servomechanisms (hence the term "stiffness regulation").

Subsequent experiments, however, have provided substantial evidence against the dual servomechanism hypothesis [77, 146]. Rather, the mechanism which relies on spindles alone is now favored. It is sometimes referred to as "predictive compensation" [83] because the spindle responds immediately to a change in muscle length, and therefore the correction for the impending "failure" of muscle stiffness (Fig. 3A) is initiated before the failure occurs. That is, muscle stiffness, which is maintained for a small amount of muscle stretch in any case, continues to be maintained because the response to the spindle occurs before the limit has been reached.

Although the force of a muscle can be converted to the torque about a joint if the joint angle is known, knowledge of the total torque about a joint does not allow the separation of the contribution from the various muscles. For example, the simultaneous activity of anatomically antagonistic muscles may contribute little net torque about the joint, since their contributions tend to cancel. In this situation, however, the stiffness about the joint is the sum of the stiffness contributions of the opposing muscles. As long as only one set of anatomically synergistic muscles is active, the stiffness about the joint is uniquely related to the initial angle and the torque, as expected on the basis of the hypothesis of stiffness regulation applied to each muscle. When opposing muscle groups are simultaneously active, the stiffness about the joint cannot be predicted from knowledge of the initial joint angle and net torque, even if it is true that the stiffness of each muscle can be predicted from the knowledge of its length and force. Thus, the simultaneous activity of antagonists provides the nervous system with the means of controlling the stiffness of the joint [47, 85], whereas the stiffness of individual muscles is not controlled.

Some of the limitations of the hypothesis of stiffness regulation are as follows. (1) Much of the detailed information regarding muscle mechanical properties with and without reflex modulation of activation has come from experiments on a rather atypical muscle (the homogeneously slow-twitch cat soleus [4]). Similar attempts to measure reflex effects in a heterogeneous human finger flexor muscle have revealed only a small difference between the reflexive and areflexive conditions [147]. (2) The delays involved in the conduction of action potentials along afferent and motor axons may not always be appropriate for the urgency of the need for stiffness regulation. The conduction delays do not depend upon the velocity of muscle stretch, whereas the latency of the "failure" of the stiffness of areflexive muscle would depend upon the velocity. (3) The central actions of spindles and Golgi tendon organs on motoneurons are far more complex [20, 71, 87] than was known when the concept of stiffness regulation was formulated [126]. In our opinion, the pattern of their synaptic connections currently appears too complex to be used in the elaboration of neuromechanical hypotheses on motor control. However, knowledge of connectivity is valuable for setting constraints on how afferentation might be used during movement. (4) In an actively shortening muscle, essentially elastic behavior is exhibited even without reflexes [126]. There is, therefore, little need for reflexly mediated stiffness regulation. (5) The hypothesis of stiffness regulation has not been tested for perturbations applied during movement. Recently recruited motor units, in response to stretch, seem not to exhibit the peculiarities of the mechanical properties of motor units recruited much before the stretch [28]. If the recruitment of new motor units is important for movement, there may be little need for reflex-mediated changes for the preservation of muscle stiffness.

Some of the strengths of the hypothesis of stiffness regulation are as follows. (1) It is based upon clear-cut experimental observations [126]. (2) It accounts for the inability to change muscle stiffness as long as the preperturbation conditions remain the same [29]. As a corollary, it sets new standards for demonstrating that any changes in reflex efficacy ("gain") are authentic, and not concomitant to changes in initial state [125]. (3) It accounts for the observed asymmetry of EMG responses for symmetrical changes in muscle force and length [29]. (4) It is consistent with the observation of a simple shift in the length-force relation of a muscle (whose reflex connections are intact) when various supraspinal regions are stimulated [48]. (5) It provides a view of spinal reflexes in their entirety as relieving higher command levels from attention to the mechanical properties of muscle, in place of the earlier views that regarded spinal reflexes as servocontrol mechanisms [114], only to find them severely deficient in correcting the errors [16].

In summary, the concept of stiffness regulation refers to the process of confering spring-like properties on muscle. However, evidence for this hypothesis comes from a rather restricted experimental paradigm. In addition, the most recent data on the complexity of the central connections of afferents argues against simple explanations of the mechanisms purportedly associated with stiffness regulation.

*Invariant characteristics.* This concept, based largely on the work of Feldman, stipulates that when the central nervous system sets a *postural state* it prescribes neither a particular joint angle nor a particular joint torque, but rather a relation between the two. The relation is called the invariant characteristic. Movement, from this point of view, is a transition from one prescribed postural state to another, rather than from one prescribed joint angle to another. Thus, when a subject performs a goal-directed movement, the final joint angle depends in a predictable manner upon the torque applied to the joint.

Before discussing the experiments on which the concept is based, it is important to point out that, in general, joint angle and torque are independent variables. A subject can, for a particular angle of the elbow, exert any desired isometric elbow torque against an infinite load, the limitation being the subject's strength. If certain experimental conditions reveal a relationship between angle and torque, this suggests a constraint that the motor system must follow in those particular experimental conditions.

Feldman [44, 46, 47] asked his subjects to maintain a steady elbow torque and angle, though the apparatus allowed movement. Unexpectedly for the subject, the external conditions were altered, so that equilibrium at the previously maintained angle and torque was no longer possible. The subject had been instructed "not to intervene voluntarily" to the disturbance. The old and new values were plotted as points on an angle-torque graph. In Fig. 4A, the old (initial) values are indicated by the asterisk, and the new values by one of the points. Different changes in external conditions were used on successive trials, keeping unaltered the initial angle and torque that the subject maintained. The result was an orderly arrangement of the points on the angle-torque graph, which could be joined by a smooth curve [168].

The interpretation of the orderliness is that when the subject maintains the initial angle and torque, the nervous system, at some "voluntary" level of command, prescribes a relation (the smooth curve) between angle and torque. The angle and torque are not prescribed separately. When external conditions are altered and the "voluntary" command remains unchanged, the relation between angle and torque remains unchanged. Equilibrium, then, occurs at an angle and torque that satisfy the unchanged relation, as well as the altered constraints of the external conditions. The latter determine the point on the

FIGURE 4

*The invariant relationship between joint angle and the torque about a joint for a given postural state. A. The subject exerted a torque against a load and attained an initial (\*) joint angle. The load was unexpectedly perturbed by varying amounts; each perturbation resulted in the joint moving to a new position of equilibrium. The resulting angle-torque relationship has been termed an invariant characteristic. B. A practiced movement against a spring load was executed from an initial (I) to a final (F) position. When the spring was unexpectedly detached, the limb moved to a new final position (D) which was located on a previously defined invariant characteristic depicted by the dashed line.*
SOURCE: Adapted from [45].

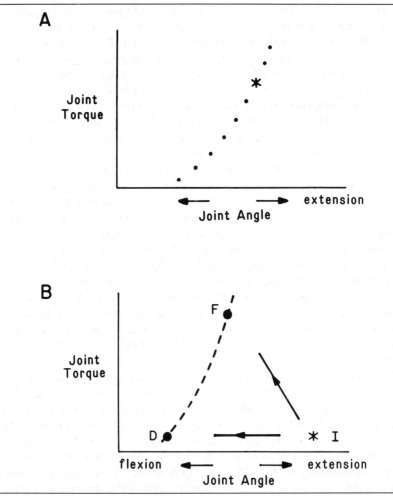

curve where equilibrium is possible, but the curve itself remains unchanged. The curve is an invariant characteristic of an unchanging "voluntary" command.

The instruction "do not intervene voluntarily" is obviously problematic. Without delving into the issue of whether a particular invariant characteristic is a true reflection of "involuntary" changes, it is sufficient to note that the instruction results in orderly data, which must represent the constraints at some level, possibly spinal, of the nervous system. The invariant characteristic, however, is not simply an expression of the mechanical properties of areflexive muscle, since EMG changes are evident in association with the perturbation [29, 168].

Different invariant characteristics are obtained for different initial points [47]. A noteworthy feature of this family of curves is that no two curves intersect. A point of intersection would have implied that, if the initial angle and torque happened to correspond to the intersection, a change in external conditions would have allowed two different points of equilibrium. The nonintersecting feature of the invariant characteristics implies that, given the initial angle and torque, a certain change in the external load results in an unambiguously predictable final angle and torque.

A remarkable example of the predictive power of the concept of invariant characteristics is provided by Feldman [45]. Although the observations are anecdotal, the experiment was a direct test of the idea that the goal of a movement is specified in the nervous system not in terms of the final joint angle, but rather by the selection of a particular torque-angle relation. The subject practiced, and repeatedly carried out, an elbow movement against a spring load. Fig. 4B illustrates the initial (I) and final (F) points. The spring was such that it offered little opposition at the initial position but a substantial one at the final, more flexed position. For some of the trials, the spring was unexpectedly detached. In such trials, the opposing torque was nearly zero, and the elbow angle seemed to settle at a different value, labeled D in Fig. 4B. It is not surprising that the extent of the movement was greater in the absence of the opposing torque, compared to the change in elbow angle when the movement was made against the spring. What is remarkable is that Feldman found that the invariant characteristic (the torque-angle curve) that passed through the final position when the movement was made against the load (the spring) was a curve that also passed through the final position associated with the no-load movement. The determination of this invariant characteristic, of course, involved only a perturbation, rather than movement by the subject. This demonstrates that the error, caused by unexpected change in load in the final position attained by means of movement, is predictable on the basis of observations made exclusively with postural perturbations.

The observations of Feldman may be interpreted in terms of the two-element model of Fig. 3C if muscle length and force are replaced by joint angle and torque, respectively. The invariant characteristic may be identified with the springlike behavior of the system when the rack and pinion is locked. Movement, in this model, is generated by the turning of the crank, but the actual angle and torque depend upon the external conditions.

The question of the mutability of the invariant characteristics has not received sufficient attention. Gielen and Houk [62] found that when identical perturbations of joint angle are repeated, some of the torque responses are quite different from others. However, they found at least 20 percent of the responses to be clustered together, the variation within the cluster being less than 5 percent. The clustering, no doubt, represents a certain degree of invariance, but the numbers do not allow one to be dogmatic about the invariance of the characteristics. The variability may be due to the indefinite nature of the instruction. Another type of "variance", found by G.L. Gottlieb and G.C. Agarwal (unpublished observations), is a hysteresis phenomenon, i.e., the torque-angle relation is different depending upon whether the torque is increasing or decreasing. Moreover, Vincken [167] has found a gradual change in the slope of the curve after the completion of a goal-directed movement.

The notion of an invariant characteristic and that of stiffness regulation have much in common. Both deal with the mechanical effects of perturbation, whether it be in terms of muscle force and length, or joint angle and torque. They give prominence to predictable features, and for this they require rigorous experimental control of the initial state. Both advance the notion that the nervous system, under certain conditions, specifies a relation between length (angle) and force (torque) variables, not the individual values of these variables. There are two differences in emphasis, however. Whereas stiffness regulation is concerned with dynamic changes in muscle length and force, the invariant characteristic represents a basically static phenomenon, in that the time course of the change in torque or angle is not usually investigated (see, however, [124]). Second, the invariant characteristic is based on evidence which covers most of the range of motion, while stiffness regulation is based on more-limited excursions from an initial position.

*Equilibrium-point hypothesis*[2]. In contrast to the invariant-characteristic and stiffness-regulation hypotheses, the notion of equilibrium-point control has evolved mostly from consideration of the mechanisms associated with the generation of movement rather than the mechanical effects of perturbation. The equilibrium-point hypothesis was originally proposed by Bizzi et al. [17] on the basis of experimental evidence obtained from examining mechanisms underlying the achievement of final head position in relation to a visual target (see [46] for precedents). The observations suggested that the motor program associated with the task specified the final equilibrium between any external forces and the length-dependent tensions of an agonist-antagonist muscle set. Recent efforts, however, have expanded this postulate to suggest that the CNS, in addition to specifying the final equilibrium point, also controls movement trajectories by varying the equilibrium point over time.

The basic concept of equilibrium-point control may be illustrated by means of the following analogy. Imagine a small sphere of iron on a flat, horizontal sheet of cardboard. Underneath the sheet, and close to it, there is a magnet whose position we can vary. If the magnet is held stationary, the iron ball comes to rest in a position right above the magnet. Wherever the magnet is located, the *equilibrium point* for the ball corresponds to the magnet's position. Thus, if we move the magnet, we can speak of a moving equilibrium point for the ball. Suppose the magnet is moved from one stationary position to another in a gradual fashion. The ball follows, but the time course of its movement (i.e., its kinematics) is, in general, different from the time course of movement of the magnet. (The two will coincide only in the case of extremely slow movements.) Nevertheless, the position of the ball eventually corresponds to the final position of the magnet. In other words, the equilibrium point moves at its own pace and the ball follows, but the position of the ball eventually coincides with the final equilibrium point. It is important to note that the force between the magnet and the ball varies throughout the movement, as does the distance between them. If the ball is prevented from moving, the magnet's movement would not be affected, and, when the ball is released, it would go to the correct final position, though the kinematics and the force would be very different in this case. If, instead,

---

2. The term "equilibrium-point hypothesis" is used here for the concepts formulated by Bizzi and his colleagues [14–17, 136]. However, there are two versions of the equilibrium-point hypothesis (A.G. Feldman, personal communication). The alternative version [44–46, 83] represents equilibrium as a postural state in which the stretch reflexes in a given musculature balance the forces due to the mechanical properties of a load.

the ball is made more massive, its kinematics, again, would be altered, and might even include a transient overshoot of the final position, but the final position would not be altered. The record of force, too, would be quite different for a more massive ball.

In this analogy, it is clear that the control of movement of the ball is carried out not by the prescription of its kinematics, nor of the force that acts on it, but rather by the prescription of the movement of the magnet, i.e., the equilibrium point. Bizzi and coworkers have proposed that the motor system, in an analogous fashion, sets the equilibrium point for a joint for each moment in time, and the joint gravitates toward it.

The equilibrium point for a joint is determined by the activity of the muscles that operate on it and any external forces that act on it. For the moment, we will confine attention to the final equilibrium point for a goal-directed movement and assume that there are no forces other than muscular forces when the joint is at the final position. Since the only torques then acting about the joint are muscular, equilibrium requires equal and opposite torques contributed by mutually antagonist muscles. The torque contributed by a muscle with a constant activation varies with joint angle; therefore it may be supposed that constant activation of antagonist sets of muscles prescribes a certain equilibrium point, i.e., a joint angle for which the muscular torques are equal and opposite. If the joint angle happens to be different from the prescribed equilibrium point, the joint experiences a net torque that tends to rotate it toward equilibrium without requiring any intervention by the nervous system.

When a subject has learned to perform a goal-directed movement, which includes holding a final, steady position, it is obvious that the motoneuronal output (and hence the muscle activity) at the final position must be such that the final position is one of equilibrium, i.e., the net torque is zero. The question arises as to whether the subject has learned to produce the requisite final levels of motoneuronal output, or has learned to produce the requisite input to the motoneurons, which, in conjunction with the afferent input to the motoneurons, results in the requisite motoneuronal output. To answer this question Polit and Bizzi [136] trained a monkey to point with its forearm toward a target light without being able to see the arm. After the training, the dorsal roots containing the afferent nerve fibers from the entire upper limb were cut (*deafferentation*), so that the nervous system had no afferent input from the limb. After recovery from the surgery, it was found that the animal could perform the pointing task just as well as before the surgery. Polit and Bizzi [136] concluded that, for a learned task, the final equilibrium point is prescribed in terms of motoneuronal output without need of afferent input.

While the question regarding afferent input posed above is answered in a clear-cut fashion by these experimental findings, there are several limitations on the applicability of the answer to other situations. (1) The goal-directed movement whose performance was not compromised by the deafferentation was an elbow movement, whereas the shoulder was stabilized by the apparatus. If, after deafferentation, the position of the shoulder was altered, the animal's performance of the elbow movement did not lead to the target [136]. This shows that an important role is normally played by the afferent input from the upper limb. (2) The muscle activities required for equilibrium at the final position are not unique. As long as the net torque is zero, a wide range of agonist and antagonist activities is possible for the maintenance of the same position [97]. It is conceivable that, in the deafferented situation, the animal may choose different levels of activation of the mutually antagonist muscles, compared to the intact situation. (3) Although the application of a transient external torque at the onset of movement did not affect the final position, with or without deafferentation [136], the issues concerning a maintained external load have not been elucidated. Having learned the movement without an external load, an intact subject would be expected to correct for the unexpected imposition of load by higher processes, if not by reflexes. A deafferented animal, on the other hand, cannot sense the load and therefore cannot correct the error. Furthermore, if the subject learns to perform the movement against an external load, the same final position of equilibrium would entail very different muscle activations compared to the case of no external torque. It is not clear how the same equilibrium point is set for different external conditions. (4) It is difficult to see the significance of equilibrium-point control if the goal of a movement is *not* a position of equilibrium, as, for instance, when one strikes a tennis ball with a racquet.

Nonetheless, when attention is confined to goal-directed movements for which there is no external torque at the final, steady position, and only one joint is involved in the movement, it is clear that the nervous system can set the final position of equilibrium (once learned) without benefit of afferent information from the moving limb. In this context the question arises whether the equilibrium point shifts suddenly or graudally from the inital to the final position. In terms of the analogy introduced previously, does the magnet move suddenly or gradually to the final position, given that the ball is observed to move only gradually? It is tempting to postulate a sudden shift in the equilibrium point since it is the simpler of the alternatives [91] but the evidence supports a gradual shift of the equilibrium point [15].

There are a number of experimental findings that support the idea of a gradual shift of the equilibrium point, for both intact and deafferented animals [15]. The following is perhaps the simplest. A deafferented animal was shown the target light to which it had been trained to point, but unbeknownst to the animal, the limb was already placed in the correct position by the application of an external torque. The torque was removed following the onset of EMG activity consequent to the presentation of the target light. If the equilibrium point had shifted suddenly to the final position, there would have been no movement of the limb since it was already in the correct final position. Instead, when the target light was turned on, the limb was observed to move away from the correct final position and then come back to it. The conclusion is that upon presentation of the light the equilibrium point moved gradually toward the final position. The movement of the limb, directed always toward the equilibrium point, was at first directed away from the final position because at that time the equilibrium point fell short of the final position.

The findings of Bizzi and co-workers underscore the notion that what is specified by the nervous system is the motion of the equilibrium point, or, in other words, "a reference trajectory which specifies a gradual shift in the equilibrium point" [14]. The choice of the "reference trajectory", however, may not be a simple interpolation between the initial and final positions. As Bizzi and Abend [14] have pointed out, it is possible that, for especially rapid movements, the equilibrium point may overshoot its final location and then come back to it, while the actual movement shows no such overshoot. Furthermore, recent experiments by two of the present authors indicate that when a constant external torque is present, the equilibrium point is not specified uniquely by muscle activations [73]. Consequently, the direction of change (increase or decrease) in muscle activation during movement is unrelated to the direction of change requisite for equilibrium at the final position.

The idea of a programmed change in the equilibrium point, though a concept with a postural emphasis, is a major advance over the earlier ideas, based on the servocontrol of position or force, that could not be supported experimentally. But there is little information as yet concerning how the motion of the equilibrium point is chosen in light of the external conditions.

The hypotheses discussed so far have a feature in common that we have called a postural emphasis. The essential idea shared among these hypotheses is that the nervous system turns a crank, as it were, and the motion of the crank is transmitted to the limb indirectly by a spring. When the crank is not being turned, we have a postural state in which the spring provides some resistance to perturbations, whereas a movement is the result of a turning of the crank. Higher level or "voluntary" interventions may affect the turning of the crank, but the immediate resistance to perturbation still comes from the spring.

*Concepts with a Kinetic Emphasis*
An object can be moved from one position to another by being dragged, i.e., pulled continuously, as is envisaged in the crank-and-spring model. Alternatively, the object could be propelled or thrown (i.e., impart momentum to it), allowed to coast free, and then caught at the appropriate position [161]. The latter method (throw-coast-catch) features what we are calling a kinetic emphasis. This approach to the control of movement is concerned primarily with the muscle activations required for the acceleration and deceleration of the inertia represented by the moving limb, and the effects of external loads during movement.

There is an extensive body of data concerning the EMGs associated with movements of different extents and durations, with and without various types of external loading, including the effects of unexpected loads. Certain regularities have been extracted from these data, but the regularities are often contingent upon the precise experimental conditions [25]. At the present time, the regularities do not have descriptive names, and the contingencies for which the regularities are observed are only beginning to be delineated. Hampered by the lack of a conceptual framework, we attempt only to sketch the ideas and experiments in broad outline.

*Pulse-step control.* To start with, we will confine attention to the problem of accelerating the moving segment of a one-joint system during the initial part of the movement. The muscles whose activity can provide the force necessary for the acceleration will be referred to as the *agonists,* as distinguished from their anatomical *antagonists.* Clearly, a "burst" of agonist EMG is required in order to rapidly accelerate the segment. (In actuality, what is required is a burst of motoneuron action potentials, but it is convenient to speak of its readily measurable manifestation, the EMG.) As depicted in Fig. 5 (left of the vertical broken line), there is indeed a burst of agonist EMG, followed by a "silent period" [96, 113]. However, there is also some antagonist activity during the acceleration phase [51, 113], whose possible significance will be discussed later.

The duration as well as the amplitude of the agonist EMG burst have a determining influence on the acceleration of the segment. If

FIGURE 5

*Movement-related records associated with the testing of kinetic-emphasis concepts.*

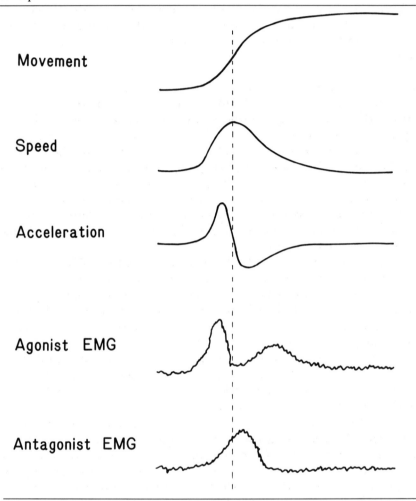

we consider movements of the same extent but performed at different speeds, it is evident that the faster movements not only require a greater initial acceleration, but also allow less time during which the acceleration must occur. Although greater acceleration can, in principle, be achieved by prolonging the duration of the agonist EMG burst, this mechanism cannot be availed for performing a movement at increased speed. Instead, higher speed can be achieved by reducing the duration of the burst, and increasing the EMG amplitude so as to more than make up for the reduced duration, and thus provide increased acceleration. Indeed, faster movements are associated with increased amplitude and reduced duration of the EMG burst; however, there is a certain minimum duration beyond which there is no reduction when there is further increase in speed [96].

The fastest movements, therefore, involve a constant-duration burst of agonist EMG. This irreducible duration is often considered to be an important feature of the operation of the motor control system for the following reasons: (1) The irreducible duration remains the same for different extents of movement [57, 96]. (2) The irreducible duration remains the same if the inertia of the moving segment is increased substantially, provided the subject is able to achieve a sufficiently fast speed of movement in the presence of the added inertia [96]. (3) If the subject exerts a force against an external object in *isometric* conditions, and does so as fast as he can, the duration of the agonist EMG is, again, independent of the actual force exerted [51, 60]. These findings support the idea that the nervous system emits a motor output of a certain minimum duration (see, however, [171]), irrespective of the actual movement (or lack of it). Within this irreducible period, however, gradation of the output can be accomplished by modulation of the recruitment and discharge rates of motor units [35].

When the experimental design requires the subject to vary the isometric force rapidly from one value to another, the *rate* of change of force is highly correlated with the change in the amplitude of force [60]. In other words, different excursions of force are achieved in approximately the same time. Since a sudden change in muscle activation results in a more gradual change in the isometric force, the observed constancy of the time for change in force has been interpreted (in conjunction with other correlations) to imply the following scheme. The muscle activation does not simply change in a steplike manner to the level necessary for the development of the desired force. An additional, pulse-like increase in the activation level is responsible for overcoming the "lag" of the muscle. This scheme is referred to as *pulse-step control,* a term that was originally introduced in connection with eye movements [144].

As mentioned earlier, the pulsatile EMG burst is readily apparent at the onset of movement. Similarly, the "step" part of the EMG change was discussed in connection with the equilibrium-point hypothesis. Consequently, it has been pointed out [14, 83] that the pulse-step command amounts to an abrupt shift of the equilibrium point to a position beyond the intended position, followed by a shift back to the intended position. However, the pulsatile EMG is commonly followed by a silent period, and, if there is a "step" increase in EMG, it may occur only after the silent period. The significance of the silent period remains unclear, as does its neurophysiologic origin, though there are suggestions that it is the result of reduction of spindle afferent discharge during shortening of the agonist muscle [10, 162].

What emerges from the foregoing discussion is that the onset of motor activity, at least in the case of a single joint, is marked by a burst of muscle activity whose duration is essentially constant when there is a sufficiently rapid attempt at either movement or force development, whereas the amplitude of the burst changes with the intent and with the load.

In an attempt to test the contingencies of this behavior, one of the present authors examined a skilled, multijoint movement, namely, the double-knee-bend "clean" in Olympic weightlifting [39]. With respect to displacement about the knee joint, this movement comprises two intervals of extension which are separated by an interval of flexion. Since the muscles about the knee joint cocontract throughout the movement, an assessment of the constant duration notion was based on calculated resultant muscle torque values. Essentially the movement was accomplished by an alternating sequence of net extensor-flexor torques. Variation of the weight lifted by the subjects was found not to be associated with a significant change in the duration of extensor torque about the knee joint, which supports the idea of constant duration. However, the duration of the following phase, one of flexor torque, not only changed with the weight, but also depended upon the subject's level of expertise. These results indicate that the strategy of keeping the duration of activity constant while changing its amplitude is followed in some but not all cases.

*Three-burst EMG pattern.* In the preceding section we considered the strategy employed for getting the limb started on the course of its movement. We now focus attention on the problem of stopping the movement at the targeted position. Although there are situations in which the impact of the limb with an external object can be relied upon to stop the movement, it is more common that the movement is slowed down so that the limb can stop gently at the targeted position by the deceleration that occurs as the result of antagonist activity. At slower speeds, the damping of movement may also be accomplished, at least in part, by passive tissues. The necessity for accurate deceleration, one might assume, is analogous to that for the safe landing of a rocket on the moon.

It may be imagined that antagonist muscle activity for deceleration would be prominent only when the limb comes close to the target position, i.e., toward the end of the movement. Surprisingly, this is not the case for well-practiced movements. Antagonist activity begins, in many instances, before the initial agonist burst has subsided, and reaches a peak sometime in the middle of the movement. Toward the end of the movement there is little if any activity of the antagonists; instead, there is often another burst of agonist activity. This commonly observed pattern of agonist-antagonist-agonist activity is the three-burst EMG pattern, first reported by Wachholder and Altenburger [169]. It is convenient to refer to the three components of this pattern as the AG1, ANT, and AG2 EMG bursts, but it should be emphasized that there is significant overlap of the three time periods; in particular, ANT EMG may commence before the AG1 burst ends (see Fig. 5). The three-burst EMG pattern appears restricted to the muscles contributing to the movement and not those involved in postural stabilization [170].

The time period from the onset of movement to the beginning of the ANT EMG depends upon the speed and extent of the movement. The beginning of the ANT EMG occurs earlier for faster or smaller movements [96, 106]. For particularly fast movements, not only does the ANT EMG commence during AG1, the peak of the ANT EMG may occur at a time when the speed of movement has not yet reached its maximum value.

The amplitude of the ANT EMG is greater for faster or smaller movements [96, 106]. For particularly slow movements, the ANT burst does not occur, as passive properties of the tissues of the limb appear to suffice for deceleration. The presence of an external, opposing torque also seems to abolish the ANT burst [73]. Inertial loading of the limb, on the other hand, results in an increase in the ANT EMG amplitude, without change in its time of onset, when movements of the same speed and extent are performed in the presence and in the absence of extra inertia [96]. This is consistent with the requirement for a greater antagonist force for deceleration when the inertia is greater.

One interpretation of these observations is that the ANT burst is carefully shaped to suit the deceleration requirements of the task, given the specific external conditions that prevail. On this basis, however, it is difficult to understand the significance of the period of simultaneous activity of the agonist and antagonist muscles. Ghez et al. [61] favor a different interpretation, namely, that "increasing demands for control of the terminal phase of movement are normally met by decreasing the initial phasic command [AG1] coupled with cocontraction [of antagonists], rather than by producing a precisely timed phasic burst in antagonist muscles [ANT] to decelerate the limb." This statement implies that the AG1-ANT overlap serves merely to stiffen the joint, which reduces the possibility of a significant overshoot of the final position; the stiffening is greater when external conditions are such as to increase the likelihood of an overshoot, as for instance in the case of increased inertia. In support of this point of view, Ghez et al. [61] cite the results of an experiment in which the extra inertia was present only during acceleration, but was made to vanish as soon as the limb began to decelerate. In this peculiar loading condition the movement record was similar to the record of the unloaded movement. This is presumably because there was no need for enhanced ANT EMG in the presence of the peculiar load, as the load did not increase the possibility of overshoot of the final position.

It is true that cocontraction of antagonists, wasteful though it seems, is an important part of the strategy of movement [85], presumably for stiffening the joint so that the effects of external loads become relatively less important. Such stiffening is commonly observed when the movement task is unfamiliar [153], and one is subjectively aware of this phenomenon. The fact remains, however, that the ANT burst outlasts the AG1 burst, and therefore must play a role not merely in the stiffening of the joint but also in the deceleration of the movement about the joint. This is especially pertinent in the case of moderately slow, well-practiced movements for which there is little overlap between AG1 and ANT EMGs.

If we focus attention on the period when the antagonist muscles alone are active, it is clear that the timing and amplitude of this activity depends upon the task and the external conditions. Since information about the external conditions is conveyed by the discharge of peripheral afferents, the question arises whether the timing and amplitude of antagonist activity are a function of the afferent discharge during the movement, or are learned on the basis of information from peripheral receptors gained during earlier attempts at movement in the same condition. There is no consensus on this issue, but some of the evidence that bears on it is outlined in what follows.

Terzuolo et al. [164] found that the normal three-burst EMG pattern was altered profoundly when the same movement task was attempted after deafferentation. (The subject, a monkey, had learned to perform a rather fast elbow movement against a varying load before deafferentation, and due to these speed-load requirements, the experiment was quite different from that of Polit and Bizzi [136] discussed earlier.) In the deafferented animal the termination of the AG1 burst occurred at different times in different trials, and was sometimes quite gradual. More importantly, activity of the antagonist appeared to be essentially random, exhibiting no structure in relation to the kinematic parameters, unlike the observations prior to deafferentation. These findings support a role for afferents in shaping the three-burst EMG pattern during movement.

Since in normal subjects the ANT EMG is more prominent for movements of smaller extent [106], one may expect that the disruption of ANT EMG as a result of deafferentation would reveal a greater deficit in performance for small as compared to large movements. Indeed, Sanes et al. [149] report that patients with sensory neuropathy exhibited a greater relative error for small compared to large movements, but the effects on the ANT EMG were not recorded in their study.

Ghez and Martin [58] trained cats in an isometric task in which the animal was required to alter the elbow torque. The difference between the desired and actual torques was displayed for the animal. The task was to minimize the difference between the desired and actual torques. There was no ANT EMG in this situation. On randomly interspersed trials, the limb was allowed to move, and the display in these trials indicated the difference between the desired and actual angles for the elbow joint. In these nonisometric trials an ANT EMG was present. The conclusion based on this and other observations was that the ANT burst is due to stretch of the antagonist muscle; in other words, it is dependent upon peripheral feedback, and is not a part of a central program [9, 106].

Despite the evidence outlined in the preceding paragraph, one cannot rule out the possibility of a central generation of the EMG pattern that includes the ANT burst. For example, the absence of the ANT burst noted by Ghez and Martin [58] occurred with an isometric torque that was a small fraction of the capability of the muscle group. In contrast, when large torques are involved (albeit in a different experimental situation), the ANT burst has been demonstrated under isometric conditions by Gordon and Ghez [64]. In addition, the fact that the subject learned an isometric task may, when movement is allowed, result in a strategy which is different from the strategy that is observed when the learning itself took place under nonisometric conditions [94]. The phasic or transient nature of the change in force also apparently plays a role in promoting the ANT burst under isometric conditions [148]. Also, the onset of the ANT burst bears no fixed relationship in timing to such kinematic events as the time at which peak velocity is reached. The sequence of ANT onset and peak velocity varied with the speed and extent of movement [96]. Furthermore, Sanes and Jennings [148] have demonstrated in human subjects that the three-burst pattern survived the "functional deafferentation" caused by prolonged occlusion of the blood supply of the limb, although this procedure did alter the amplitudes of the bursts.

As can be seen from the literature reviewed above, the origin of the three-burst EMG pattern remains controversial. However, at this time, we believe that the three-burst pattern is an expression of a central program, in which the timing and amplitudes of the EMG bursts depend upon prior experience, an experience that is necessarily contingent upon peripheral afferent input. The afferent input, however, plays the further role of moment-to-moment modification of the program when the program is played out.

The teleological significance of the three-burst pattern remains obscure, since other patterns can be imagined that can serve the purpose of movement or isometric force development. Of what possible use is the ANT burst in isometric conditions in which deceleration is not needed? Gordon and Ghez [64] have argued that, since the force development by a muscle outlasts the neural impulse (and therefore the nervous system cannot instantaneously turn off the force development), activity of the antagonist is employed to counteract the force due to the agonist when only a brief pulse of force is required. It is not clear how this role of ANT EMG relates to the role of deceleration when movement is allowed. One can also speculate about the role of the AG2 burst, which has been rarely studied; it has been associated with the correction for oscillations at the end of the movement [58, 179]. On the other hand, Angel [8] found the AG2 burst in the absence of terminal oscillations, and noted that this burst may not occur on the first few movements of a series performed under novel loading conditions.

The influence of practice on these phenomena is probably of paramount importance. Darling and Cooke [31], for example, observed systematic increases in the amplitudes of the AG1 and ANT bursts with practice, in addition to changes in timing. In spite of these variations, and the uncertainties concerning its teleological significance, there is no doubt that the nervous system has a propensity for generating a sequence of agonist-antagonist-agonist activations for carrying out a target-oriented [173] motor task at a single joint, and can finely tune the details of the pattern in the light of afferent information.

*Optimal strategies.* Any quantifiable feature of motor performance which is exhibited with some degree of regularity lends itself to two types of inquiry, the mechanistic and the teleological. As an example, the existence of the three-burst EMG pattern raises mechanistic questions concerning the neural circuitry that underlies its generation and the effects of afferent discharge on its elaboration, in addition to teleological questions concerning the possible advantage to the organism of employing a three-burst rather than, say, a four-burst pattern. The teleological type of inquiry is considered by some to be less than fully respectable, partly because a particular feature may represent merely an evolutionary happenstance rather than the optimal solution to a meaningful problem. As an example, it appears pointless to ask what advantage we gain by possessing five rather than six fingers in each hand. In certain cases, however, such questions can be the key to the understanding of function. For instance, the advantage of having two eyes with overlapping visual fields is clearly related to depth perception, and this knowledge is useful in understanding the neural processing in the visual system.

In the present section we introduce some recent attempts to describe selected features of motor performance as optimal solutions to certain problems, and we also touch upon attempts to extract from movement data features that may be amenable to such analysis. The theoretical technique of optimization proceeds as follows. A cost function is selected, perhaps arbitrarily, such that for every possible movement that satisfies certain constraints, a number can be assigned to the cost function. Subsequently, it is determined which among the possible movements minimizes the cost, i.e., which movement is optimal. Alternatively, the inverse of the cost may be maximized. In either case, we call the maximized or minimized variable the optimized variable, whereas the predicted movement itself is referred to as the optimal solution. The test of the theoretical analysis is based on comparing the predicted optimal solution with experimental results.

To begin with, we consider a movement for which there is no question as to the variable that should be optimized. This movement is the vertical jump, and the variable to be maximized is the height of the jump. Levine et al. [98] have investigated the question of which pattern of muscle activity would result in the maximal jump, confining attention to the ankle joint and presuming that the other joints are locked, for the sake of simplicity. This problem, however, is by no means simple to solve. Before discussing the solution obtained by these authors, and its experimental validity, a brief description of the mechanics of jumping is necessary [101, 115].

The reason one is able to jump at all is that by pushing with one's feet against the ground, an equal and opposite "reaction" force is elicited from the ground, which, if it is greater than the body weight, results in a net force acting on the body in the upward direction. Thus the center of mass of the body accelerates in the upward direction, but only as long as the feet remain in contact with the ground and push against it. Once the feet lose contact with the ground ("toe-off"), the body is in free flight, and the movement of its center of mass cannot be influenced by muscular activity. To maximize the height attained in a vertical jump, the center of mass of the body must acquire as much speed in the upward direction as possible before contact with the ground is lost.

Since it is the extensor muscles of the leg that need to be activated for the foot to push against the ground, one may expect intuitively that the highest vertical jump would be achieved with maximal activation of the extensor muscles. Maximal activation of the extensor muscles, however, would result in different heights of the jump depending upon the conditions that precede the maximal activation. In particular, the joint angles (and angular velocities and muscle forces) that are attained in the preparatory phase prior to maximal extensor activation would affect the muscle torque as well as the time available before toe-off, and thus influence the jump height.

Levine et al. [98] showed on the basis of a theoretical calculation that, prior to the period in which the extensors should be maximally active, a preparatory phase which involves setting the initial conditions (e.g., joint angle) is needed for optimum performance. At the end of the preparatory phase, according to their calculations for optimality, a certain limb configuration should be achieved, and the shank should be rotating about the ankle joint at a certain speed while the foot stays flat on the ground. Comparison with experimental observations revealed that the human subject did indeed exhibit very nearly the predicted optimal configuration of the leg just prior to the maximal extensor activation. But there was a discrepancy between the predicted and measured rotation speed at this time. This discrepancy, however, did not have a significant effect on the jump height. In other words, the performance, though theoretically suboptimal, was, for practical purposes, close to optimal.

An investigation of vertical jumps performed by cats also revealed that this animal achieved a stereotyped state (in terms of joint angles and velocities) before maximal extensor activation [181]. This is in line with the expectation that optimization of jump height requires a preparatory phase. During the ensuing phase of maximal extensor activity, however, the hip, knee, and ankle extensors began their activation in sequence rather than simultaneously. Two joint hip extensor-knee flexor muscles have recently been found to be activated only during the preparatory phase [180]. The significance of these timing patterns in the context of optimal strategies is unclear [140].

In summary, the optimal-strategy claim that the vertical jump should comprise two phases—the preparation and the launch—each displaying its characteristic strategy of control, has been supported experimentally, although questions remain concerning the details of these strategies.

Unlike jumping, it is often not possible to specify the variable to be optimized for most other activities. For instance, it is not at all clear which, if any, variable is maximized (or minimized) in stepping, or, to choose a simpler example, for a reaching movement of an arm. Among all the different kinematic possibilities in reaching for an object, a particular one is usually exhibited by a given subject. This raises the question of whether one can find a cost function whose optimization predicts the kinematics actually exhibited, from among all that are possible, as the optimal one. Indeed one can contrive a cost function such that the observed trajectory can be deemed optimal. This circular reasoning is avoided, however, if there are independent grounds for believing that the proposed cost function may be of significance to the organism (e.g., energy use), or the optimization leads to correct prediction of a variety of different trajectories in different conditions.

With target-directed one-joint movements, the velocity profile associated with the three-burst EMG pattern comprises a smooth increase followed by a decrease. Qualitatively speaking, the velocity profile is bell-shaped. Nelson [123] has investigated various cost functions (e.g., optimization of movement time, peak velocity, peak acceleration, and average rate of change in acceleration), and determined which ones were consistent with the observed, bell-shaped velocity profile. It was assumed that a mass was to be displaced from one position to another by the action of a force that varied with time, but the magnitude of the force was limited to a certain maximum value. With the condition that the cost function be minimized (i.e., each of the cost functions was examined one at a time) the initial velocity was taken to be zero and the force as a function of time was constrained to be such that the final velocity would be zero. A bell-shaped velocity profile, consistent with the observed one, was predicted to be the optimal solution if the cost was selected to be either the average force, or the average of the time-derivative of acceleration ("jerk"). In this context, "average" connotes the mean square value. Various other cost functions, when minimized, did not lead to the bell-shaped velocity profile. (Nelson noted, however, that the minimization of peak velocity led to a velocity profile which resembled that associated with the bow-arm movements of a skilled violinist.) In short, the techniques of optimization are capable of predicting certain observed kinematic features on the basis of cost functions that appear reasonable to assume.

The kinematics of multi-joint movements exhibit certain features over and above the bell-shaped velocity profile. Bizzi and Abend [14] consider it likely that these features indicate "the presence of specific trajectory strategies that are determined by a central [i.e., neural] reference signal which optimizes some variable such as the distance moved, the energy dissipated, or mechanical stress and wear." It is in the spirit of this statement that we touch upon these features in the present section, even though no specific cost function has been put forward. The description in the following paragraph is based upon the work of Abend et al. [2] and Morasso [117, 118].

Although rotation about a single joint necessarily results in a circular motion of the limb segment, when rotations are possible about two joints (the shoulder and the elbow) simultaneously, the rotations tend to be so coordinated that the motion of the distal part (the hand, with the wrist locked) closely follows a straight-line path (i.e., a path of zero curvature). This tendency in favor of small curvature of the path is associated with the occurrence of a peak in the velocity profile. When instructed to follow a curved path, subjects approximate it by following a sequence of nearly straight portions, with a peak in the velocity occurring during the traversing of each portion. Thus, the occurrences of peak velocities and peak curvatures alternate during the movement. This behavior is observed even in the case of freely executed, complicated movements in three-dimensional space. (The twist or torsion of the path, however, bears no relationship to the velocity.) The slowing of movement when curvature of the path is high cannot be attributed to mechanical constraints of the joints or the inertias involved, and therefore probably represents a neurally mediated strategy.

It remains to be seen how these features might be related to solving the problem of interjoint coordination in the face of the dynamic interaction effects described previously.

*Concepts with a Combined Emphasis*
The current concepts of motor control presented in the preceding sections were classified into those in which the control of movement was regarded as a progression of postural controls, and those in which it was viewed as the playing out of a program that does not rely on the neural circuitry involved in postural stabilization. Now we focus on certain ideas that are not amenable to such classification. Before beginning this discussion, however, it is well to clarify our use of the term "reflex."

Although the entire sequence of a movement performed on cue by a subject can be regarded as a reflex elicited by the cue, the word reflex is used in this chapter with a narrower meaning. Namely, reflex refers to the alteration in muscular activity that follows an unexpected perturbation, and does so within a short period of time. (This period is shorter than what psychologists call the "reaction time.") The imposed perturbation and the consequent reflex-mediated change in activity of the muscles, though they certainly affect the kinematics of the movement, are not considered part of the movement. This terminology is not fully rigorous, but we employ it nonetheless because it is commonly used by those who seek the role, during movement, of reflexes that were originally discovered and studied in postural conditions.

*Reflexes and motor programs.* The program for a movement can be elaborated, at least in broad outline, without benefit of afferent information. The program is modified (or "sculpted") by the afferent information so that it takes a form that is, in some sense, more appropriate for the external conditions. It might be added that for certain movements such as those involved in speech, the subject is often consciously unaware of perturbations, though the compensatory responses are exhibited [1].

Studies on the influence of afferent information on motor programs have been carried out extensively in insects and crustaceans [43, 130, 131, 156], and the results show that the afferent effects differ qualitatively in different phases of the motor program. For example, there are periods in which the afferent discharge has a strong influence on the sequential timing of muscle activations, whereas in certain periods the afferent discharge may alter the amplitude of muscle activity, in analogy with servomechanisms. One can expect that the elucidation of these rules will eventually rely more on studies of vertebrate motor behavior, including those of higher mammals [50, 145, 172].

In humans, the reflex effects of unexpected perturbations applied to a joint during the performance of simple movements have revealed that the effects depend upon what phase of the movement is perturbed. Gottlieb and Agarwal [65] found, in the case of perturbations to the ankle joint that caused a stretch of the soleus muscle, that a large reflex EMG in the soleus could be elicited if the perturbation was applied just prior to the involvement of the soleus in the movement. In comparison, the same perturbation had a smaller reflex effect when a movement was not going to be performed. Surprisingly, once the movement was underway and the soleus was active, the perturbation elicited a minimal reflex effect [40]. Similar results were obtained by Soechting et al. [155] in the context of rapid flexion movements of the elbow, although the depression of the reflex at movement onset was followed by later augmentaion. (These authors employed a random but continuous sequence of torque rather than angle perturbations to the elbow joint and noted the effects on both biceps and triceps brachii.) However, when the task involved tracking a slow moving target, the reflex was enhanced rather than depressed following the onset of movement. The conclusion is that the strength of the reflex for a muscle appears to follow a program which depends upon the task. For the same task, the variation in the reflex strength can be qualitatively different from the variation of muscle activity, such that the reflex may be depressed while the muscle activity increases.

As observed with invertebrates, the change in reflex strength probably represents different specific roles of afferent information at different phases of the movement. It is attractive, however, to imagine that a more general role can be formulated which arises from the specific, varying roles. The experiments of Andersson and Grillner [6, 7] address these issues in an animal preparation which exhibits the rhythmic, neurally generated motor program for locomotion, but in which the muscles have been paralyzed. Although there is no actual movement, perturbations applied to the limb result in afferent discharges, which modify the motoneuronal output. Two kinds of experiments have been performed in this preparation: (1) the effects of an occasional perturbation applied at various phases of the motor program are studied, and (2) the limb is moved rhythmically and continuously back and forth by the experimenter, independent of the natural rhythm of the motor program, and the effects on the motor program are noted.

The first kind of experiment [6] has revealed that the same perturbation can have opposite effects in different phases of the movement. When the effect of muscle stretch is an increase in motoneuronal activity for that muscle (i.e., stretch reflex), the analogy with servomechanisms may be appropriate, as in the case of maintenance of posture, but when the effect is a decrease in motoneuronal activity the analogy breaks down. Furthermore, the duration of the cycle of the motor output is also affected by the perturbation, again in a phase-dependent fashion. The significance of these complex effects for the performance of the animal is partially addressed by the second kind of experiment.

For the second type of experiment, Andersson and Grillner [7] perturbed the limb rhythmically. In this situation, they found that the neurally generated motor program was altered, insofar as the frequency of its rhythm was concerned, so that it became synchronized to the imposed rhythm communicated by afferents. This "entrainment" was "strict" (i.e., perfect) over a certain broad range of imposed frequencies, but was "relative" outside this range. Surprisingly the flexor motoneuron discharge occurred at the time that the imposed rhythmic motion was shortening the flexor muscles; similar effects were observed with the extensor muscles. These actions are the opposite of what one might have expected on the basis of the stretch reflex.

In an earlier section, it was noted that not only can the nervous system generate a rhythmic output without afferent input but also that the skeletal system is capable, within limits, of continuing a rhythm without signals from the nervous system, under appropriate conditions. The entrainment phenomenon may be interpreted as a means of synchronizing the two rhythm-generating machineries. It is conceivable that the phase dependence of the reflex is so organized that the synchronization can occur under a variety of external conditions. This speculation, however, in no way diminishes the role of the stretch reflex in postural stability.

*Task-dependent synergies.* Most studies in the field of motor control tend to concentrate, for reasons of practicality, on the involvement of, at most, a few muscles in restricted tasks. Although attempts have been made to study the reflexes in certain muscles while the subject activated a variety of other muscles [134], the complexity of the interactions thus revealed defies interpretation. This complexity is not surprising given such conditions as the door-opening example discussed earlier. The movements involved in opening a door necessitate quite different programs, as far as the specific muscles are concerned, for different initial positions of the subject with respect to the doorknob, especially the relative position of the hand. Since it is the afferents that communicate the initial configuration, the afferent discharges are clearly capable of modifying the program, even to the extent that a different set of muscles may be brought into play. This necessitates complicated rules for the modification of the activity of each of the muscles by afferent input. The rules, moreover, may pertain only to the specific task of opening a door.

The concept of synergy, namely, that certain muscles tend to be activated together, offers the possibility of considerable simplification of the rules of afferent influences on motor programs. Since the monosynaptic (direct) effects of primary spindle afferents from one muscle are "hardwired," i.e., fixed, these synaptic connections may be expected to compel certain unvarying patterns of coordination among the muscles. Indeed, a large amount of evidence has been forthcoming in favor of this Sherringtonian notion [37, 38]. Muscles that tend to be active more or less simultaneously in the course of locomotion tend to have relatively strong monosynaptic projections of primary afferents on the motoneurons of the other muscles of the group.

Recently, a striking exception to the above rules has been discovered. In the cat's hindlimb, there are two muscles that run in parallel and whose actions on the digits are very similar (the flexor digitorum longus and the flexor hallucis longus). Electrophysiologic investigation indicates that there are monosynaptic connections between primary spindle afferents and the motoneurons of these two muscles [49]. However, during locomotion, these muscles exhibit different patterns of activity [127], and therefore they cannot be considered physiologic synergists in the context of locomotion. Consistent with this lack of synergy is the observation that the synaptic influences of certain skin afferents on the motoneurons of these muscles are quite different [49]. The possibility remains, of course, that these muscles may be activated together in some other task, such as grooming [66].

It should be emphasized that while electrophysiologic techniques can reliably demonstrate the strengths of direct (mono-) synaptic connections on motoneurons, there are, in addition, a large number of indirect synaptic effects exerted via interneurons. Since the efficacy of these pathways can, in turn, be modulated by the discharge of other neurons, there are countless possibilities for synergistic organization. It has been proposed, however, that for a given task a particular synergistic organization prevails, which includes even the fusimotor neurons that innervate spindles in the particular "task group" of muscles [100].

The idea that reflex effects among muscles are organized according to the task finds its most remarkable instances in work on human subjects. An example is provided by the following experiments performed by Marsden et al. [104]. The subject pulls a load with his left hand while bracing with his right hand against a firm support. As the subject displaces the load toward himself, the backward movement of the body concomitant with the pull by the left hand results in the stretching of certain muscles of the right arm, and, not surprisingly, the activity of the stretched muscles increases. The situation is now altered so that the subject holds a teacup with his right hand (or his right hand touches some other object of low inertia) instead of the firm support. A backward movement of the body, in these circumstances, would lead to spilling of the tea if the muscle activity in the right arm was to remain unchanged or if the muscles stretched in the earlier experiment were to increase their activity, jerking the teacup closer to the body. Instead, it is observed that the position of the teacup is maintained by reduction in the activity of the muscles, which thus elongate, allowing a greater distance between the teacup and the body as the body moves backward. Muscle elongation is associated in this situation with decreased activity of the muscle, while the simultaneous action of the other arm remains unaltered.

On the basis of examples such as this, it is difficult to distinguish between the following two possibilities. (1) The mere presence of changed external conditions is sufficient to alter the reflexes and the synergistic patterns. (2) The subject learns to make the alterations on the basis of the experience of performing movements in the changed conditions. Both phenomena are indeed known to occur and, in what follows, an example is provided of each.

Nashner et al. [122] applied various perturbations to the surface on which a subject was standing. The subject had each foot on a separate platform, and the two platforms, together or separately, could be displaced by the experimenter in the vertical direction. The subject could anticipate neither the time of occurrence nor the type of perturbation, as simultaneous displacements of the two platforms were interspersed with reciprocal displacements in which the platform displacements would occur in opposite directions. When the displacements were simultaneous, the stretched muscles of the leg increased their activity. However, when the displacements of the two platforms were in opposite directions, the flexor muscles of the leg in which these muscles had been shortened by the perturbation were found to increase their activity. (This behavior could not be attributed to different vestibular inputs in the two situations, as the records of head movement did not support this possibility.) The conclusion is that reciprocal vertical displacement of the two legs elicits a locomotor-like synergy, whereas simultaneous displacements does not elicit such a synergy. This phenomenon may be an expression of the mechanism that underlies the synchronization effect that was described earlier [7]. Irrespective of the mechanism, these alterations of synergy and of reflex responsiveness are not contingent upon the subject's anticipation of a predictable perturbation.

There are, on the other hand, learned changes in the response when the same perturbation is repeated and the subject can anticipate the type of perturbation, though not its time of occurrence. For example, in one investigation [119] both feet of the subject were placed on a platform that, at unexpected times, shifted backward in the horizontal plane. This backward displacement provoked stretch, and therefore activation, of the gastrocnemius (an ankle extensor muscle), followed by activation of the hamstrings (knee flexor and hip extensor). These activations (constituting the "sway synergy") helped restore the body to an upright position. After a series of these perturbations, a different type of perturbation was introduced. Unexpectedly, the platform rotated so that the ankle joint rotated with the toes pointing up. In this situation, increased activation of the stretched gastrocnemius muscle would have acted to destabilize the body by contributing to a backward tilt of the body. On the first few such perturbations, the gastrocnemius activity was indeed increased, though later the backward fall was counteracted by the activity of other muscles. After a few such perturbations, however, the subject learned not to exhibit an increase in gastrocnemius activity upon stretch of this muscle.

Nashner [121] has distinguished two processes that underlie the ability to maintain the upright posture in the presence of perturbations that tend to destabilize it, whether as a result of external conditions or self-initiated actions such as pulling a load while standing. One process ("sensory organization") determines which combination of the different afferent inputs (e.g., from muscle receptors, vestibular organs, or the eyes) would be utilized to initiate corrective action. This determination is presumably based upon the preceding experience of the relative reliability of the different input channels. For instance, vestibular information may be more reliable than muscle stretch information in the case of rotations of the platform, but not in the case of horizontal displacement of the platform. The other process ("muscle coordination") determines the sequence of muscle activations needed to express the postural correction. This determination is presumably based upon information concerning the external conditions.

There is some evidence that the latter process, the prescription of muscular synergies, may rely on the identification of which part of the body is supported by the external world [121]. For example, the EMG responses to a backward, horizontal displacement of the platform are initiated in the gastrocnemius and spread to more proximal muscles. This progression of activity has been found to emanate from the base of support. When a freely standing subject pulls on a fixed handle on cue, the sequence of muscle activity again begins with the gastrocnemius and spreads upward; this happens before the body begins to move forward and the gastrocnemius is stretched [26]. In fact, activation of the biceps brachii and forward movement of the body are the last events in the sequence. The tendency for the muscles closer to the base of support to be activated earlier is, therefore, independent of whether there is a perturbation that stretches the muscle (as in the case of platform displacement) or the activity is self-initiated (as in the case of pulling on the handle). Furthermore, if the base of support is altered by having the subject lean with the chest on a rigid framework, the period of time from presentation of the cue for pulling the handle to the initiation of biceps brachii activity is substantially reduced. Also, if the experimenter pulls the subject's hand while the subject is leaning on the framework, there is a prominent, short-latency reflex activation of the biceps brachii, whereas for a freely standing subject the same perturbation results in a significant biceps brachii EMG only after a longer latency. These findings lend weight to the notion that muscles closer to the base of support respond more quickly to imposed stretch or to the cue for movement. However, when the movement involves a change in the base of support itself, the more proximal muscles may be activated earlier, as in the case of a jumping movement [181].

The process of determining muscular synergies appears to follow a simple rule related to the base of support as perceived by the subject. Future research may confirm the possibility that this determination does not require experience with attempted movements or with repetitive perturbations. If so, the learned changes, when they are observed (as for example in the case of the ankle rotation perturbation), can be attributed to the workings of the other process (sensory organization) that chooses the inputs which would elicit the corrective response. These ideas are promising, as they reveal unsuspected regularities in the operations of the motor control system.

## CONCLUDING REMARKS

In this chapter, we outline the current status of studies which have begun to integrate neurophysiologic and biomechanical approaches to the study of motor control. Sufficient experimental progress has been made to permit the generalization that the brain is able to exploit the biomechanical properties of the body. Nonetheless, feedback is required for moment-to-moment modifications during movement. Whether studied at the level of neuronal activity in the nervous system or the kinesiology of moving body parts, analysis of these modifications is a particular challenge because the expectations continually change during the movement. The concepts examined in this chapter represent mechanistic and teleological attempts to account for various facets of motor control. These concepts range from consideration of the probable role of spinal reflexes and their altered efficacy during movement to the notion that movements may be structured to optimize particular features of the movement. In general, however, the concepts have evolved from rather specific experimental paradigms, and as a consequence the major challenge to this field of inquiry is to extend the limits of these various concepts so that it becomes possible to develop a more general theoretical framework.

### REFERENCES

1. Abbs, J.H., and V.L. Gracco. Control of complex motor gestures: Orofacial muscle responses to load perturbations of lip during speech. *J. Neurophysiol.* 51:705–723, 1984.
2. Abend, W., E. Bizzi, and P. Morasso. Human arm trajectory formation. *Brain* 105:331–348, 1982.
3. Adrian, E.D., and D.W. Bronk. The discharge of impulses in motor nerve fibres. Part II. The frequency of discharge in reflex and voluntary contractions. *J. Physiol. (Lond.)* 67:119–151, 1929.

4. Al-Amood, W.S., and R. Pope. A comparison of the structural features of muscle fibres from a fast- and a slow-twitch muscle of the pelvic limb of the cat. *J. Anat.* 113:49–60, 1972.

5. Andersson, O., H. Forssberg, S. Grillner, and P. Wallén. Peripheral feedback mechanisms acting on the central pattern generators for locomotion in fish and cat. *Can. J. Physiol. Pharmacol.* 59:713–726, 1981.

6. Andersson, O., and S. Grillner. Peripheral control of the cat's step cycle. I. Phase dependent effects of ramp-movements of the hip during "fictive locomotion." *Acta Physiol. Scand.* 113:89–101, 1981.

7. Andersson, O., and S. Grillner. Peripheral control of the cat's step cycle. II. Entrainment of the central pattern generators for locomotion by sinusoidal hip movements during "fictive locomotion." *Acta Physiol. Scand.* 118:229–239, 1983.

8. Angel, R.W. Electromyography during voluntary movement: The two-burst pattern. *Electroenceph. Clin. Neurophysiol.* 36:493–498, 1974.

9. Angel, R.W. Antagonist muscle activity during rapid arm movements: central versus proprioceptive influences. *J. Neurol. Neurosurg. Psychiat.* 40:683–686, 1977.

10. Angel, R.W., W. Eppler, and A. Iannone. Silent period produced by unloading of muscle during voluntary contraction. *J. Physiol. (Lond.)* 180:864–870, 1965.

11. Baldissera, F., H. Hultborn, and M. Illert. Integration in spinal neuronal systems. In *Handbook of Physiology, sec. 1, vol. II, The Nervous System: Motor Control, Part I,* V.B. Brooks, ed. Bethesda: American Physiological Society, 1981, pp 509–595.

12. Belen'kii, V. Ye., V.S. Gurfinkel', and Ye. I. Pal'tsev. Elements of control of voluntary movements. *Biophysics* 12:135–141, 1967.

13. Bernstein, N. *The Co-ordination and Regulation of Movements.* New York: Pergamon, 1967.

14. Bizzi, E., and W. Abend. Posture control and trajectory formation in single- and multi-joint arm movements. In *Motor Control Mechanisms in Health and Disease,* J.E. Desmedt, ed. New York: Raven, 1983, pp. 31–45.

15. Bizzi, E., N. Accornero, W. Chapple, and N. Hogan. Arm trajectory formation in monkeys. *Exp. Brain Res.* 46:139–143, 1982.

16. Bizzi, E., P. Dev, P. Morasso, and A. Polit. Effect of load disturbances during centrally initiated movements. *J. Neurophysiol.* 41:542–556, 1978.

17. Bizzi, E., A. Polit, and P. Morasso. Mechanisms underlying achievement of final head position. *J. Neurophysiol.* 39:435–444, 1976.

18. Bouisset, S., F. Lestienne, and B. Maton. The stability of synergy in agonists during the execution of a simple voluntary movement. *Electroenceph. Clin. Neurophysiol.* 42:543–551, 1977.

19. Boylls, C.C. Prolonged alterations of muscle activity induced in locomoting premammillary cats by microstimulation of the inferior olive. *Brain Res.* 159:445–450, 1978.

20. Brink, E., E. Jankowska, D. McCrea, and B. Skoog. Inhibitory interactions between interneurones in reflex pathways from group Ia and group Ib afferents in the cat. *J. Physiol. (Lond.)* 343:361–373, 1983.

21. Broer, M.R., and S.J. Houtz. *Patterns of Muscular Activity in Selected Sport Skills: An electromyographic study.* Springfield: Charles C. Thomas, 1967.

22. Burke, D. Muscle spindle function during movement. *Trends Neurosci.* 3:251–253, 1980.

23. Burke, R.E. Motor units: anatomy, physiology, and functional organization. In *Handbook of Physiology, sec. 1, vol. II, The Nervous System: Motor Control, Part I.* V.B. Brooks, ed. Bethesda: American Physiological Society, 1981, pp. 345–422.

24. Chandler, C., J. Hewit, and S. Miller. Computers, brains and the control of movement. (Letter to the editor.) *Trends Neurosci.* 5:376, 1982.

25. Cooke, J.D. The organization of simple, skilled movements. In *Tutorials in Motor*

*Behavior.* G.E. Stelmach and J. Requin, eds. Amsterdam: North-Holland, 1980, pp. 199–212.

26. Cordo, P.J., and L.M. Nashner. Properties of postural adjustments associated with rapid arm movements. *J. Neurophysiol.* 47:287–302, 1982.

27. Cordo, P.J., and W.Z. Rymer. Motor-unit activation patterns in lengthening and isometric contractions of hindlimb extensor muscles in the decerebrate cat. *J. Neurophysiol.* 47:782–796, 1982.

28. Cordo, P.J., and W.Z. Rymer. Contributions of motor-unit recruitment and rate modulation to compensation for muscle yielding. *J. Neurophysiol.* 47:797–809, 1982.

29. Crago, P.E., J.C. Houk, and Z. Hasan. Regulatory actions of human stretch reflex. *J. Neurophysiol.* 39:925–935, 1976.

30. Creed, R.S., D. Denny-Brown, J.C. Eccles, E.G.T. Liddell, and C.S. Sherrington. *Reflex Activity of the Spinal Cord.* London: Oxford University Press, 1932.

31. Darling, W.G., and J.D. Cooke. The influence of practice on movement dynamics and muscle activity. *Soc. Neurosci. Abstr.* 9:1032, 1983.

32. Deliagina, T.G., G.N. Orlovsky, and C. Perret. Efferent activity during fictitious scratch reflex in the cat. *J. Neurophysiol.* 45:595–604, 1981.

33. Denny-Brown, D. Interpretation of the electromygram. *Arch. Neurol. Psychiat.* 61:99–128, 1949.

34. Denny-Brown, D., and J.B. Pennybacker. Fibrillation and fasciculation in voluntary muscle. *Brain* 61:311–333, 1938.

35. Desmedt, J.E., and E. Godaux. Ballistic contractions in fast or slow human muscles: discharge patterns of single motor units. *J. Physiol. (Lond.)* 285:185–196, 1978.

36. Desmedt. J.E., and E. Godaux. Spinal motoneuron recruitment in man: Rank deordering with direction but not with the speed of voluntary movement. *Science.* 214:933–936, 1981.

37. Eccles, R.M., and A. Lundberg. Integrative pattern of Ia synaptic actions on motoneurones of hip and knee muscles. *J. Physiol. (Lond.)* 144:271–298, 1958.

38. Engberg, I., and A. Lundberg. An electromyographic analysis of muscular activity in the hindlimb of the cat during unrestrained locomotion. *Acta Physiol. Scand.* 75:614–630, 1969.

39. Enoka, R.M. Muscular control of a learned movement: The speed control system hypothesis. *Exp. Brain Res.* 51:135–145, 1983.

40. Enoka, R.M., R.S. Hutton, and E. Eldred. Changes in excitability of tendon tap and Hoffmann reflexes following voluntary contractions. *Electroenceph. Clin. Neurophysiol.* 48:664–672, 1980.

41. Enoka, R.M., and D.G. Stuart. Henneman's "size principle": Current issues. *Trends Neurosci.* 7:226–228, 1984.

42. Evarts, E.V. Sherrington's concept of proprioception. *Trends Neurosci.* 4:44–46, 1981.

43. Evoy, W.H., and J. Ayers. Locomotion and control of limb movements. In *Biology of Crustacea*, vol. 4. New York: Academic Press, 1982, pp. 61–105.

44. Feldman, A.G. Functional tuning of the nervous system with control of movement or maintenance of a steady posture. II. Controllable parameters of the muscles. *Biophysics* 11:498–508, 1966.

45. Feldman, A.G. Functional tuning of the nervous system during control of movement or maintenance of a steady posture. III. Mechanographic analysis of the execution by man of the simplest motor tasks. *Biophysics* 11:667–675, 1966.

46. Feldman, A.G. Change in the length of the muscle as a consequence of a shift in the equilibrium in the muscle-load system. *Biophysics* 19:534–538, 1974.

47. Feldman, A.G. Superposition of motor programs. I. Rhythmic forearm movements in man. *Neuroscience* 5:81–90, 1980.

48. Feldman, A.G., and G.N. Orlovsky. The influence of different descending systems on the tonic stretch reflex in the cat. *Exp. Neurol.* 37:481–494, 1972.

49. Fleshman, J.W., A. Lev-Tov, and R.E. Burke. Synaptic organization in FDL and FHL motor nuclei: A search for mechanisms underlying the functional disparity in strict anatomical synergists. *Soc. Neurosci. Abstr.* 7:689, 1981.

50. Forssberg, H. Phasic gating of cutaneous reflexes during locomotion. In *Muscle Receptors and Movement.* A. Taylor and A. Prochazka, eds. London: MacMillan, 1981, pp. 403–412.

51. Freund, H.-J., and H.J. Büdingen. The relationship between speed and amplitude of the fastest voluntary contractions of human arm muscles. *Exp. Brain Res.* 33: 1–12, 1978.

52. Fukami, Y. Responses of isolated Golgi tendon organs of the cat to muscle contraction and electrical stimulation. *J. Physiol. (Lond.)* 318:429–443, 1981.

53. Fukson, O.I., M.B. Berkinblit, and A.G. Feldman. The spinal frog takes into account the scheme of its body during the wiping reflex. *Science* 209:1261–1263, 1980.

54. Gallistel, C.R. *The Organization of Action: A New Synthesis.* Hillsdale: L. Erlbaum, 1980.

55. Garnett, R., and J.A. Stephens. Changes in the recruitment threshold of motor units produced by cutaneous stimulation in man. *J. Physiol. (Lond.)* 311:463–473, 1981.

56. Georgopoulos, A.P., J.F. Kalaska, R. Caminiti, and J.T. Massey. Interruption of motor cortical discharge subserving aimed arm movements. *Exp. Brain Res.* 49:327–340, 1983.

57. Ghez, C. Contributions of central programs to rapid limb movement in the cat. In *Integration in the Nervous System.* H. Asanuma and V.J. Wilson, eds. Tokyo: Igaku-Shoin, 1979, pp. 305–320.

58. Ghez, C., and J.H. Martin. The control of rapid limb movement in the cat. III. Agonist-antagonist coupling. *Exp. Brain Res.* 45:115–125, 1982.

59. Ghez, C., and Y. Shinoda. Spinal mechanisms of the functional stretch reflex. *Exp. Brain Res.* 32:55–68, 1978.

60. Ghez, C., and D. Vicario. The control of rapid limb movement in the cat. II. Scaling of isometric force adjustments. *Exp. Brain Res.* 33:191–202, 1978.

61. Ghez, C., D. Vicario, J.H. Martin, and H. Yumiya. Sensory motor processing of target movements in motor cortex. In *Motor Control Mechanisms in Health and Disease.* J.E. Desmedt, ed. New York: Raven, 1983, pp. 61–92.

62. Gielen, C.C.A.M., and J.C. Houk. Nonlinear viscosity of human wrist, *J. Neurophysiol.* 52:553–569, 1984.

63. Goldberger, M.E. The extrapyramidal systems of the spinal cord. II. Results of combined pyramidal and extrapyramidal lesions in the macaque. *J. Comp. Neurol.* 135:1–26, 1969.

64. Gordon, J., and C. Ghez. EMG patterns in antagonist muscles during isometric contraction in man: Relations to response dynamics. *Exp. Brain Res.* 55:167–171, 1984.

65. Gottlieb, G.L., and G.C. Agarwal. Response to sudden torques about ankle in man. III. Suppression of stretch-evoked responses during phasic contraction. *J. Neurophysiol.* 44:233–246, 1980.

66. Goslow, G.E., E.K. Stauffer, W.C. Nemeth, and D.G. Stuart. Digit flexor muscles in the cat: Their action and motor units. *J. Morphol.* 137:335–352, 1972.

67. Greene, P.H. Problems of organization of motor systems. *Prog. Theor. Biol.* 2:303–338, 1972.

68. Grillner, S. Locomotion in vertebrates: Central mechanisms and reflex interaction. *Physiol. Rev.* 55:247–304, 1975.

69. Grillner, S. Control of locomotion in bipeds, tetrapods, and fish. In *Handbook*

*of Physiology, sec. 1, vol. II, The Nervous System: Motor Control, Part 2.* V.B. Brooks, ed. Bethesda: American Physiological Society, 1981, pp. 1179–1236.

70. Gurfinkel, V.S., and M.L. Shik. The control of posture and locomotion. In *Motor Control.* A.A. Gydikov, N.T. Tankov, and D.S. Kosarov, eds. New York: Plenum, 1973, pp. 217–234.

71. Harrison, P.J., E. Jankowska, and T. Johannisson. Shared reflex pathways of Group I afferents of different cat hind-limb muscles. *J. Physiol. (Lond.)* 338:113–127, 1983.

72. Hasan, Z. A model of spindle afferent response to muscle stretch. *J. Neurophysiol.* 49:989–1006, 1983.

73. Hasan, Z., and R.M. Enoka. Isometric torque-angle relationship and movement-related activity of human elbow flexors: Implications for the equilibrium-point hypothesis, *Exp. Brain Res.* (in press).

74. Hasan, Z., and D.G. Stuart. Mammalian muscle receptors. In *Handbook of the Spinal Cord, vol. 3.* R.A. Davidoff, ed. New York: Marcel Dekker, 1984, pp. 559–607.

75. Henneman, E., and L.M. Mendell. Functional organization of motoneuron pool and its inputs. In *Handbook of Physiology, sec. 1, vol. II, The Nervous System: Motor Control, Part 1.* V.B. Brooks, ed. Bethesda: American Physiological Society, 1981, pp. 423–507.

76. Hill, A.V. The heat of shortening and the dynamic constants of muscle. *Proc. R. Soc.* B126:136–195, 1938.

77. Hoffer, J.A., and S. Andreassen. Regulation of soleus muscle stiffness in pre-mammillary cats: intrinsic and reflex components. *J. Neurophysiol.* 45:267–285, 1981.

78. Hollerbach, J.M. A recursive Lagrangian formulation of manipulator dynamics and a comparative study of dynamics formulation complexity. *IEEE Trans. Sys. Man. Cyb.* 10:730–736, 1980.

79. Hollerbach, J.M. Computers, brains and the control of movement. *Trends Neurosci.* 5:189–192, 1982.

80. Hollerbach, J.M., and T. Flash. Dynamic interactions between limb segments during planar arm movement. *Biol. Cybern.* 44:67–77, 1982.

81. Houk, J.C. Regulation of stiffness by skeletomotor reflexes. *Ann. Rev. Physiol.* 41:99–114, 1979.

82. Houk, J., and E. Henneman. Responses of Golgi tendon organs to active contractions of the soleus muscle of the cat. *J. Neurophysiol.* 30:466–481, 1967.

83. Houk, J.C., and W.Z. Rymer. Neural control of muscle length and tension. In *Handbook of Physiology, sec. 1, vol. II, The Nervous System: Motor Control, Park 1.* V.B. Brooks, ed. Bethesda: American Physiological Society, 1981, pp. 257–323.

84. Houk, J.C., W.Z. Rymer, and P.E. Crago. Dependence of dynamic response of spindle receptors on muscle length and velocity. *J. Neurophysiol.* 46:143–166, 1981.

85. Humphrey, D.R., and D.J. Reed. Separate cortical systems for control of joint movement and joint stiffness: Reciprocal activation and coactivation of antagonist muscles. In *Motor Control Mechanisms in Health and Disease.* J.E. Desmedt, ed. New York: Raven, 1983, pp. 347–372.

86. Huxley, A.F. Muscular contraction. (Review Lecture.) *J. Physiol. (Lond.)* 243:1–43, 1974.

87. Jankowska, E., and D.A. McCrea. Shared reflex pathways from Ib tendon organ afferents and Ia muscle spindle afferents in the cat. *J. Physiol. (Lond.)* 338:99–111, 1983.

88. Jankowska, E., D. McCrea, and R. Mackel. Pattern of 'non-reciprocal' inhibition of motoneurones by impulses in group Ia muscle spindle afferents in the cat. *J. Physiol. (Lond.)* 316:393–409, 1981.

89. Jankowska, E., and A. Odutola. Crossed and uncrossed synaptic actions on motoneurones of back muscles in the cat. *Brain Res.* 194:65–78, 1980.
90. Kandel, E.R., and J.H. Schwartz. *Principles of Neural Science.* New York: Elsevier/North-Holland, 1981.
91. Kelso, J.A.S., and K.G. Holt. Exploring a vibratory systems analysis of human movement production. *J. Neurophysiol.* 43:1183–1196, 1980.
92. Kelso, J.A.S., and B. Tuller. A dynamical basis for action systems. In *Handbook of Cognitive Neuroscience.* M.S. Gazzaniga, ed. New York: Plenum, 1984, pp. 321–356.
93. Kniffki, K.-D., S. Mense, and R.F. Schmidt. Muscle receptors with fine afferent fibres which may evoke circulatory reflexes. *Circ. Res.* (Suppl. I) 48:25–31, 1981.
94. Lamarre, Y., G. Spidalieri, L. Busby, and J.P. Lund. Programming of initiation and execution of ballistic arm movements in the monkey. *Prog. Brain Res.* 54:157–169, 1980.
95. Lance, J.W., and J.G. McLeod. *A Physiological Approach to Clinical Neurology,* 3rd ed. London: Butterworths, 1981.
96. Lestienne, F. Effects of inertial load and velocity on the braking process of voluntary limb movements. *Exp. Brain Res.* 35:407–418, 1979.
97. Lestienne, F., A. Polit, and E. Bizzi. Functional organization of the motor process underlying the transition from movement to posture. *Brain Res.* 230:121–132, 1981.
98. Levine, W.S., F.E. Zajac, M.R. Belzer, and M.R. Zomlefer. Ankle controls that produce a maximum vertical jump when other joints are locked. *IEEE Trans. Automat. Control* AC-28:1008–1016, 1983.
99. Loeb, G.E. Finding common ground between robotics and physiology (Letter to the editor) *Trends Neurosci.* 6:203–204, 1983.
100. Loeb, G.E. The control and responses of mammalian muscle spindles during normally executed motor tasks. *Exercise and Sport Sci. Rev.* 12:157–204, 1984.
101. Luhtanen, P., and P.V. Komi. Segmental contribution to forces in vertical jump. *Eur. J. Appl. Physiol.* 38:181–188, 1978.
102. Lundberg, A. Multisensory control of spinal reflex pathways. *Prog. Brain Res.* 50:11–28, 1979.
103. Marsden, C.D., P.A. Merton, and H.B. Morton. Anticipatory postural responses in the human subject. *J. Physiol. (Lond.)* 275:47–48P, 1977.
104. Marsden, C.D., P.A. Merton, and H.B. Morton. Human postural responses. *Brain* 104:513–534, 1981.
105. Marsden, C.D., P.A. Merton, H.B. Morton, J.E.R. Adam, and M. Hallet. Automatic and voluntary responses to muscle stretch in man. In *Cerebral Motor Control in Man: Long Loop Mechanisms.* J.E. Desmedt, ed. Basel: Karger, 1978, pp. 167–177.
106. Marsden, C.D., J.A. Obeso, and J.C. Rothwell. The function of the antagonist muscle during fast limb movements in man. *J. Physiol. (Lond.)* 335:1–13, 1983.
107. Martin, J.P. A short essay on posture and movement. *J. Neurol. Neurosurg. Psychiat.* 40:25–29, 1977.
108. Matthews, P.B.C. *Mammalian Muscle Receptors and Their Central Actions.* London: Arnold, 1972.
109. Matthews, P.B.C. Muscle spindles: Their messages and their fusimotor supply. In *Handbook of Physiology,* sec. 1, vol. II, *The Nervous System: Motor Control, Part 1.* V.B. Brooks, ed. Bethesda: American Physiological Society, 1981, pp. 189–228.
110. Matthews, P.B.C. Where does Sherrington's "muscular sense" originate? Muscles, joints, corollary discharges? *Ann. Rev. Neurosci.* 5:189–218, 1982.

111. McCloskey, D.I. Kinesthetic sensibility. *Physiol. Rev.* 58:763–820, 1978.
112. McCloskey, D.I. Corollary discharges: motor commands and perception. In *Handbook of Physiology, sec. 1, vol. II, The Nervous System: Motor Control, Part 2.* V.B. Brooks, ed. Bethesda: American Physiological Society, 1981, pp. 1415–1447.
113. Merton, P.A. The silent period in a muscle of the human hand. *J. Physiol. (Lond.)* 114:183–198, 1951.
114. Merton, P.A. Speculations on the servo-control of movement. In *The Spinal Cord.* G.E. Wolstenholme, ed. London: Churchill, 1953, pp. 247–255.
115. Miller, D.I., and D.J. East. Kinematic and kinetic correlates of vertical jumping in women. In *Biomechanics V-B.* P.V. Komi, ed. Baltimore: University Park Press, 1976, pp. 65–72.
116. Mochon, S., and T.A. McMahon. Ballistic walking. *J. Biomech.* 13:49–57, 1980.
117. Morasso, P. Spatial control of arm movements. *Exp. Brain Res.* 42:223–227, 1981.
118. Morasso, P. Three dimensional arm trajectories. *Biol. Cybern.* 48:187–194, 1983.
119. Nashner, L.M. Adapting reflexes controlling the human posture. *Exp. Brain Res.* 26:59–72, 1976.
120. Nashner, L.M. Fixed patterns of rapid postural responses among leg muscles during stance. *Exp. Brain Res.* 30:13–24, 1977.
121. Nashner, L.M. Adaptations of human movement to altered environments. *Trends Neurosci.* 5:358–361, 1982.
122. Nashner, L.M., M. Woollacott, and G. Thuma. Organization of rapid responses to postural and locomotor-like perturbations of standing man. *Exp. Brain Res.* 36:463–476, 1979.
123. Nelson, W.L. Physical principles for economies of skilled movements. *Biol. Cybern.* 46:135–148, 1983.
124. Newell, K.M., and J.C. Houk. Speed and accuracy of compensatory responses to limb disturbances. *J. Exp. Psychol.* 9:58–74, 1983.
125. Nichols, T.R. Evidence for authentic changes in the gain of an autogenetic reflex in the soleus muscle of the decerebrate cat. *Soc. Neurosci. Abstr.* 7:688, 1981.
126. Nichols, T.R., and J.C. Houk. Improvement in linearity and regulation of stiffness that results from actions of stretch reflex. *J. Neurophysiol.* 39:119–142, 1976.
127. O'Donovan, M.J., M.J. Pinter, R.P. Dum, and R.E. Burke. Actions of FDL and FHL muscles in intact cats: Functional dissociation between anatomical synergists. *J. Neurophysiol.* 47:1126–1143, 1982.
128. Orin, D.E. R.B. McGhee, M. Vukobratović, and G. Hartoch. Kinematic and kinetic analysis of open-chain linkages utilizing Newton-Euler methods. *Math. Biosci.* 43:107–130, 1979.
129. Partridge, L.D. Modification of neural output signals by muscles: A frequency response study. *J. Appl. Physiol.* 20:150–156, 1965.
130. Pearson, K.G. Function of sensory input in insect motor systems. *Can. J. Physiol. Pharmacol.* 59:660–666, 1981.
131. Pearson, K.G., D.N. Reye, and R.M. Robertson. Phase-dependent influences of wing stretch receptors on flight rhythm in the locust. *J. Neurophysiol.* 49:1168–1181, 1983.
132. Pellionisz, A., and R. Llinás. Space-time representation in the brain. The cerebellum as a predictive space-time metric tensor. *Neuroscience* 7:2949–2970, 1982.
133. Petrofsky, J.S., and C.A. Phillips. The influence of temperature, initial length

and electrical activity on the force-velocity relationship of the medial gastrocnemius muscle of the cat. *J. Biomech.* 14:297–306, 1981.

134. Pierrot-Deseilligny, E. and P. Lacert. Amplitude and variability of monosynaptic reflexes prior to various voluntary movements in normal and spastic man. In *New Developments in Electromyography and Clinical Neurophysiology*, vol. 3. J.E. Desmedt, ed. Basel: Karger, 1973, pp. 538–549.

135. Phillips, S.J., E.M. Roberts, and T.C. Huang. Quantification of intersegmental reactions during rapid swing motion. *J. Biomech.* 16:411–417, 1983.

136. Polit, A., and E. Bizzi. Characteristics of motor programs underlying arm movements in monkeys. *J. Neurophysiol.* 42:183–194, 1979.

137. Prochazka, A., and M. Hulliger. Muscle afferent function and its significance for motor control mechanisms during voluntary movements in cat, monkey, and man. In *Motor Control Mechanisms in Health and Disease.* J.E. Desmedt, ed. New York: Raven, 1983, pp. 93–132.

138. Prochazka, A., J.A. Stephens, and P. Wand. Muscle spindle discharge in normal and obstructed movements. *J. Physiol. (Lond.)* 287:57–66, 1979.

139. Prochazka, A., and P. Wand. Tendon organ discharge during voluntary movements in cats. *J. Physiol. (Lond.)* 303:385–390, 1980.

140. Putnam, C.A. Interaction between segments during a kicking motion. In *Biomechanics VIII-B.* H. Matsui and K. Kobayashi, eds. Champaign, Ill.: Human Kinetics, 1983, pp. 688–694.

141. Rack, P.M.H., and D.R. Westbury. The effects of length and stimulus rate on tension in the isometric cat soleus muscle. *J. Physiol. (Lond.)* 204:443–460, 1969.

142. Raibert, M.H. *Motor Control and Learning by the State-Space Model.* Technical Report (AI-TR-439). Cambridge: Artificial Intelligence Laboratory, MIT, 1977.

143. Raibert, M.H. A model for sensorimotor control and learning. *Biol. Cybern.* 29:29–36, 1978.

144. Robinson, D.A. Oculomotor unit behavior in the monkey. *J. Neurophysiol.* 33:393–404, 1970.

145. Rossignol, S., C. Julien, L. Gauthier, and J.P. Lund. State-dependent responses during locomotion. In *Muscle Receptors and Movement.* A. Taylor and A. Prochazka, eds. London: MacMillan, 1981, pp. 389–402.

146. Rymer, W.Z., and Z. Hasan. Absence of force-feedback regulation in soleus muscle of the decerebrate cat. *Brain Res.* 184:203–209, 1980.

147. Rymer, W.Z., Z. Hasan, and B.C. Corser. Servo-regulation of muscle contraction in man: A reevaluation. *Soc. Neurosci. Abstr.* 4:304, 1978.

148. Sanes, J.N., and V.A. Jennings. Centrally programmed patterns of muscle activity in voluntary motor behavior of humans. *Exp. Brain Res.* 54:23–32, 1984.

149. Sanes, J.N., K.-H. Mauritz, E.V. Evarts, M.C. Dalakas, and A. Chu. Motor deficits in patients with large-fiber sensory neuropathy. *Proc. Natl. Acad. Sci.* 81:979–982, 1984.

150. Sherrington, C.S. Flexion-reflex of the limb, crossed extension-reflex, and reflex stepping and standing. *J. Physiol. (Lond.)* 40:28–121, 1910.

151. Shik, M.L., and G.N. Orlovsky. Neurophysiology of locomotor automatism. *Physiol. Rev.* 56:465–501, 1976.

152. Simons, D.G., and E.N. Zuniga. Effect of wrist rotation on the XY plot of averaged biceps EMG and isometric tension. *Am. J. Phys. Med.* 49:253–256, 1970.

153. Smith, A.M. The coactivation of antagonist muscles. *Can. J. Physiol. Pharmacol.* 59:733–747, 1981.

154. Soechting, J.F., and B. Ross. Psychophysical identification of coordinate representation of human arm. *Soc. Neurosci. Abstr.* 9:1033, 1983.

155. Soechting, J.F., J.R. Dufresne, and F. Lacquaniti. Time-varying properties of

myotatic response in man during some simple motor tasks. *J. Neurophysiol.* 46:1226–1243, 1981.

156. Stein, P.S.G. Motor systems, with specific reference to the control of locomotion. *Ann. Rev. Neurosci.* 1:61–81, 1978.

157. Stein, P.S.G., G.A. Robertson, and J. Keifer. Fictive scratch and fictive flexion reflexes display different motor neuron activity patterns in the turtle. *Soc. Neurosci. Abstr.* 7:139, 1981.

158. Stein, R.B. Peripheral control of movement. *Physiol. Rev.* 54:215–243, 1974.

159. Stein, R.B. What muscle variable(s) does the nervous system control in limb movements? *Behav. Brain Sci.* 5:535–577, 1982.

160. Stephens, J.A., R.M. Reinking, and D.G. Stuart. Tendon organs of cat medial gastrocnemius: Responses to active and passive forces as a function of muscle length. *J. Neurophysiol.* 38:1217–1231, 1975.

161. Stetson, R.H., and H.D. Bouman. The coordination of simple skilled movements. *Arch. Neerl. Physiol. Homme Anim.* 20:177–254, 1935.

162. Struppler, A., D. Burg, and F. Erbel. The unloading reflex under normal and pathological conditions in man. In *New Developments in Electromyography and Clinical Neurophysiology.* J.E. Desmedt, ed. Basel:Karger, 1973, pp. 603–617.

163. Stuart, D.G., and R.M. Enoka. Motoneurons, motor units, and the size principle. In *The Clinical Neurosciences, sec. 5, Neurobiology.* R.N. Rosenburg, ed. New York: Churchill Livingstone, 1983, pp. 471–517.

164. Terzuolo, C.A., J.F. Soechting, and N.A. Ranish. Studies on the control of some simple motor tasks. V. Changes in motor output following dorsal root section in squirrel monkey. *Brain Res.* 70:521–526, 1974.

165. Vallbo, A. Basic patterns of muscle spindle discharge in man. In *Muscle Receptors and Movement.* A. Taylor and A. Prochazka, eds. London: MacMillan, 1981, pp. 263–275.

166. Vallbo, A.B., K.-E. Hagbarth, H.E. Torebjork, and B.G. Wallin. Somatosensory, proprioceptive, and sympathetic activity in human peripheral nerves. *Physiol. Rev.* 59:919–957, 1979.

167. Vincken, M.H. Control of limb stiffness. Ph.D. Thesis, Rijksuniversiteit, Utrecht, 1983.

168. Vincken, M.H., C.C.A.M. Gielen, and J.J. Denier van der Gon. Intrinsic and afferent components in apparent muscle stiffness in man. *Neuroscience* 9:529–534, 1983.

169. Wachholder, K., and H. Altenburger. Beiträge zur Physiologie der willkurlichen Bewegung. X. Mitteilung, Einzelbewegungen. *Pflügers Arch. Physiol.* 214:642–661, 1926.

170. Wadman, W.J., J.J. Denier van der Gon, and R.J.A. Derksen. Muscle activation patterns for fast goal-directed arm movements. *J. Human Movt. Stud.* 6:19–37, 1980.

171. Wadman, W.J., J.J. Denier van der Gon, R.H. Geuze, and C.R. Mol. Control of fast goal-directed arm movements. *J. Human Movt. Stud.* 5:3–17, 1979.

172. Wand, P., A. Prochazka, and K.-H. Sontag. Neuromuscular responses to gait perturbations in freely moving cats. *Exp. Brain Res.* 38:109–114, 1980.

173. Waters, P., and P.L. Strick. Influence of 'strategy' on muscle activity during ballistic movements. *Brain Res.* 207:189–194, 1981.

174. Watt, D.G.D., E.K. Stauffer, A. Taylor, R.M. Reinking, and D.G. Stuart. Analysis of muscle receptor connections by spike-triggered averaging. I. Spindle primary and tendon organ afferents. *J. Neurophysiol.* 39:1375–1392, 1976.

175. Wetzel, M.C., and D.G. Stuart. Ensemble characteristics of cat locomotion and its neural control. *Prog. Neurobiol.* 7:1–98, 1976.

176. Wetzel, M.C., and D.G. Stuart. Activation and co-ordination of vertebrate lo-

comotion. In *Mechanics and Energetics of Animal Locomotion*. R. McN. Alexander and G. Goldspink, eds. London: Chapman Hall, 1977, pp. 115–152.

177. Whiting, H.T.A. *Human Motor Actions. Bernstein Reassessed*. Amsterdam: North-Holland, 1984.

178. Wilkie, D.R. General discussion. In *Cross-bridge Mechanism in Muscle Contraction*. H. Sugi and G.H. Pollack, eds. Baltimore: University Park Press, 1979, p. 634.

179. Woodworth, R.S. The accuracy of voluntary movement. *Psychol. Rev.* (Suppl.) III:1–114, 1899.

180. Zajac, F.E. Thigh muscle activity during maximum height jumps by cats. *J. Neurophysiol.* (in press).

181. Zajac, F.E., M.R. Zomlefer, and W.S. Levine. Hindlimb muscular activity, kinetics and kinematics of cats jumping to their maximum achievable heights. *J. Exp. Biol.* 91:73–86, 1981.

# Augmented Information and the Acquisition of Skill in Physical Activity

K.M. NEWELL, Ph.D.
L.R. MORRIS, M.S.
DEIRDRE M. SCULLY, M.S.

> Skill consists in the ability to bring about some end-results with maximum certainty and minimum outlay of energy, or time, or of time and energy.
>
> —E.R. Guthrie, *The Psychology of Learning*

Skilled performance in any physical activity is usually the reflection of many hours of practice by the performer in that action. Practice does not merely involve repeated engagements in an activity but often interactions between the performer and an advisor, such as a trainer or instructor and/or some apparatus not normally available within the task constraints of the given activity. The central thrust of these interactions, particularly those between the performer and advisor, is the conveyance of information. The flow of information is not unidirectional from advisor to performer although it is the information transmitted by the advisor that is usually the focus of the study of augmented information in the acquisition of skill in physical activity.

The term augmented information is often confined to the feedback of augmented information to the performer [31] which refers to information about previously completed elements of the action. It should be apparent, however, that a consideration of augmented information in motor skill learning does not have to be restricted to the feedback situation. Indeed, the conveyance to the performer of any information not naturally available within the task constraints can usefully be construed as augmented. This chapter focuses on this broader role of augmented information in the acquisition of skill in physical activity and, in particular, the issue of *what* information should be conveyed to the performer. The task focus is that of discrete and serial skills so that higher order strategy information necessary for

This work was supported in part by the National Science Foundation Awards DAR 80-16187 and BNS 83-17691 to K.M. Newell, Institute for Child Behavior and Development, University of Illinois, Champaign, Ill. 61810. We would like to thank Jack Adams, Ron Marteniuk, Dan Southard, Tony Sparrow, and Howard Zelaznik for helpful comments on an initial draft of this chapter.

235

the acquisition of continuous tasks such as car driving, video games, and team ball games is not discussed.

The study of augmented information in motor skills has a rich tradition in learning theory [48]. For example, the transmission of information through demonstrations has been linked with the principles of social learning theory [8] while the role of information feedback has been central to theories of motor learning [1]. A major limitation of the general learning theory approach to augmented information is that insufficient effort has been directed to the question of *what* information should be conveyed to the performer. In line with much of the work in perception [63] the focus of augmented information in skill learning has been more toward the *how* of information processing. And where efforts have been made to understand the nature of information to be conveyed [1, 46], they have been typically limited to what in essence are discrete single-degree-of-freedom movements, such as the linear positioning task.

The emphasis given to the study of single-degree-of-freedom tasks in motor learning has been restrictive because, by definition, it has eliminated the problem of coordination from the study of motor skill acquisition and the analysis of the effect of learning variables such as augmented information on the acquisition of coordination. A central focus here is the attempt to consider augmented information more directly with the problems of coordination, control, and skill in action. It is hoped that this orientation might contribute to the establishment of some common ground between the traditionally separate literatures of motor learning and motor control and, importantly, provide principles which have direct relevance to both the performer and advisor in the practical setting of physical activity.

## AUGMENTED KINEMATIC INFORMATION

Augmented information about action may be conveyed to the performer at many levels and in many categories of analysis. A behavioral level of analysis of augmented information may lead explicitly, although on most occasions implicitly, to an understanding of kinematics. Kinematic information relates to the space-time properties of movement and examples include the displacement, velocity, and acceleration of body and limb motion. Kinematics and the related measurement category of kinetics may be analyzed in terms of the environment and Euclidean three-dimensional space or a body-relative framework [43]. Augmented information could also be provided about other levels of analysis such as muscle activity (electromyogram, EMG), brain activity (electroencephalogram, EEG), respiratory activity, and heart rate (electrocardiogram, ECG). A discussion of the impact on skill acquisition of augmented information and biological parameters is given in the closing sections.

Kugler, Kelso, and Turvey [35] outlined the basis for an operationalization of skill acquisition that involves a hierarchical embedding of the coordination, control and skill concepts (see Newell [49] for an elaboration of this framework and its significance for motor learning in general). Descriptions of stages of learning have been advanced previously [19, 22], but the Kugler et al. formulation appears particularly useful because aside from its distinct theoretical orientation, it relates more directly to characteristics of the response dynamics than previous accounts of skill learning. In this view, the early stages of learning are characterized by the search for the appropriate coordination function with further practice leading to the optimal parameterization of this function and the expression by the performer of skill in the activity at hand.

The discussion of augmented kinematic information follows this formulation in postulating that the categories of augmented information should relate in the early stages of learning to the attainment of the appropriate topological characteristics of relative motions for the activity with subsequent emphasis on the refinement of the scaling of these relative motions. Traditionally, augmented information has not been analyzed in these terms but it is a framework that appears to hold much theoretical and practical utility. As a heuristic to facilitate synthesis and discussion, augmented information is classified here as prior to, during, and after action [51].

*Information: Prior to Action*
Prior to engaging in a motor task the performer establishes the goal or objective of the task. The performer may be aware of the task goal through previous observation of others performing the task, trial and error of actual performance, or written or verbal instructions. In addition, the performer usually attempts to produce the most appropriate pattern of coordination of body and limbs to successfully achieve the goal of the task. On occasions, these two categories of information are synonymous as, for example, in certain closed skills such as gymnastics and high-board diving, where the generation of a certain set of topological characteristics of relative motion is, in effect, the goal of the task.

A consideration of the role of augmented information prior to action traditionally pertains to the generation of the appropriate patterns of coordination rather than the goal of the task itself. This is not to imply that transmission and augmentation of goal-related information is not relevant. Rather, knowledge on the part of the performer of the goal of the task is usually taken as a given in the study of motor skill acquisition.

The two most common modes utilized by teachers and trainers to transmit information to the performer about the optimal coordination solution to the task at hand are verbal instructions and visual demonstrations, although auditory demonstrations can be very effective in certain tasks [47, 73]. The visual transmission of information may take place from either a live or filmed demonstration. As the optimal coordination function for most tasks has never been determined formally, it typically reflects the intuitions of the advisor about what pattern of coordination is optimal and/or it mimics the coordination pattern that other successful performers have utilized. To our knowledge, there is no research on augmented information prior to action which has been based upon a determination of the optimal coordination and control solution for a given performer. In effect, and at best, therefore, the teacher of motor skills is implying that the coordination solution communicated to the performer is on average optimal for a performer of a given somatotype and skill level in this task.

Before examining issues pertaining to the transmission of information to the performer prior to action, it is necessary to recognize some apriori biases by both teachers and researchers alike. First, there has been a tendency to confuse the *nature* of the information to be conveyed with the *mode* of information transmission. For example, verbal instructions from an advisor have often been interpreted as conveying different information to the performer than demonstrations. This could be the case but is not necessarily so, implying that the effectiveness of instructions versus demonstrations should be considered relative to the issues of both medium of presentation and information conveyed. Second, there has been a failure to distinguish on a consistent basis the issue of information conveyed with the frequency or scheduling with which this information should be transmitted. In an early categorization of factors influencing the effectiveness of demonstrations, Sheffield [64] distinguished between utilization and demonstration variables. Utilization variables are those which relate to the ways in which demonstrations and types of practice may be combined. In contrast, demonstration variables relate to the fidelity of the demonstration itself. In spite of this distinction, the information processing orientation to demonstrations has generally failed to determine what information about coordination and control should be conveyed to the performer prior to action.

There has been little systematic research on the effectiveness of verbal instructions. Holding [31], in his discussion of this problem, suggests that instructions about the action pattern should be unambiguous and simple. It appears to have been assumed by practitioners and researchers alike that demonstrations are a more effective medium than instructions for conveying relevant information prior to action, presumably because of the adage that "a picture is worth a thousand words." In particular, gross motor activities appear difficult to describe verbally because they involve the constraint of many biomechanical degrees of freedom (see [68] for an elaboration of the degrees-of-freedom problem). As a consequence of these trends the balance of examples in the following synthesis relates to demonstrations, although it should be borne in mind that the key general issue about augmented information prior to action is the nature of the information to be conveyed to the performer, irrespective of mode of presentation.

The two guiding theoretical orientations to research on demonstrations and skill acquisition are both consistent with what is now labeled a cognitive orientation [8, 64]. Sheffield [64] was one of the early theorists to depart from the traditional stimulus-response approach to motor skill acquisition in promoting a symbolic representational theory. In this view, observers symbolically code perceptual responses to sensory stimuli, and this perceptual code cues response production through the matching of overt behavior with the perceptual memory of the action. It is noteworthy that no indication was provided by Sheffield of the movement cues that are coded by the observer. This has implicitly conveyed the impression that every feature of response production is in some fashion transformed and coded. Bandura's [8] mediational contiguity theory holds some similar principles to Sheffield's formulation in that observers are presumed to code perceptual cues, thus allowing them covert rehearsal. In both these theoretical orientations to demonstrations, cognitive processes are postulated as central to skill acquisition. In general, these theoretical propositions have provided a convenient framework from which empirical work on demonstrations might be interpreted [24], although direct examination of the theoretical propositions advanced has been limited.

A key operational element mediating the impact of demonstrations is the relative novelty to the performer of the movement sequence to be learned [14]. Novelty of the movement sequence is a feature that is often invoked to account for the impact of learning variables; yet, a formal definition of novelty is rarely advanced. Although it generally refers to a task that the performer has never attempted previously, this is not a helpful definition since any new task constraint engenders this condition. A useful operational definition of a novel task is one in which the performer cannot generate the appropriate topological characteristics of relative motion.

It appears that demonstrations are effective in studies employing tasks which require a coordination pattern already learned by the performer, e.g., motor maze [69], motor sequence tasks [55, 67], multiple-choice mazes [29, 57, 58], and roll-up ball task [41]. "Effective" means that over the initial acquisition trials the group receiving a demonstration of the movement sequence prior to action performed at a higher level relative to the goal of the task than the relevant control groups receiving no demonstration or a demonstration of a neutral task. It is not clear whether this advantage is maintained over long-term practice because such practice conditions are rarely examined in skill learning studies. The implication is, however, that demonstrations initially facilitate performance in scaling an already established movement pattern, but this is only a temporary advantage as practice and knowledge of results (KR) soon became the primary variables in generating the appropriate level of scaling to the coordination function. Thus, demonstrations can improve the efficiency of modifying an already learned movement pattern. Where they do not, as in the pursuit rotor [14, 44], the subjects probably can adequately scale the coordination pattern from prior experience by either observation or participation.

The effect of demonstrations in tasks where subjects cannot generate the appropriate set of relative motions is also equivocal, although an explanatory principle may be discerned from the findings. Demonstration of the Bachman ladder task has been shown to facilitate early performance [14, 18] although McCullagh [42] failed to replicate these findings. Similarly, in a shoot-the-moon task, Martens et al. [41] showed that performance was not improved by a prior-to-action demonstration although the demonstration group exhibited a higher probability of employing the appropriate pattern of relative motion by the hands. In the shoot-the-moon task, a high scoring performance can only be achieved by a ballistic coordinated response of the two hands, a high risk technique that requires considerable practice. The consequence of poor execution of this ballistic technique is often a lower score than with a graded controlled two-handed technique. The demonstration group from Martens et al. [41] attempted to employ the technique (coordination function) transmitted by the demonstration, but poor execution led to a lower performance score than the control group on the initial trials. Unfortunately, the practice session was relatively short in this study, but presumably continued practice would eventually have led to an appropriate execution of the ballistic technique by the demonstration group and eventually higher performance scores than the control group who could only achieve a mediocre score with the continued use of the controlled technique. This study highlights the necessity of distinguishing between performance scores and the pattern of coordination in interpreting the effects of demonstrations.

Gould [23] has interpreted the effect of task specificity on demonstration effectiveness by invoking the informational load of the task as a mediating factor. Informational load is vaguely defined as the number of procedural steps or strategies involved in the task. Gould conducted demonstration experiments on three tasks, a ball roll-up (accuracy) task, a geometric-construction-assembly task and a ball-snatch (speed) task, which were estimated to be of moderate to high information loads. The findings from the three experiments were viewed as supportive of the notion that high information load tasks are more susceptible to modeling influences than low information load tasks. However, the determination of task information load had no rational basis, and the results also seem consistent with the a priori ability of the subjects to generate the appropriate action pattern.

The significance of response complexity in determining the role of demonstrations is another variable which has been investigated empirically [15] in the context of social learning theory [8]. The proposition is that the acquisition of novel action patterns is facilitated by demonstrations because they provide the information to develop an internal model for response production. This conceptual representation is generated by transforming the observed movement sequences into symbolic codes which may be cognitively rehearsed to strengthen their probability of retention. If the movement sequence of the demonstration is already in the repetoire of the performer, then an adequate conceptual representation exists to guide movement production without practice and accompanying feedback. In novel movement sequences, by contrast, actual performance is usually required to detect errors in response production, and the additional availability of information feedback may facilitate this process.

The sequence of the movement pattern modeled in the Carroll and Bandura [15] study is shown in Figure 1. The action required the attainment of eight separate postures with specific movement characteristics between postures. The initial position was held for 5 seconds with each of the eight subsequent positions and linking movements lasting 2 seconds. The design of the study generated four independent groups; a vision condition, a nonvision condition, a vision-nonvision condition and a nonvision-vision condition. The vision and nonvision groups attempted all the initial six trials under their respective feedback conditions whereas the other two groups either

FIGURE 1

*a. Examples of the movement sequences to be learned by subjects. b. Mean reproduction accuracy as a function of treatment conditions, component complexity, and trial block.*

SOURCE: Carroll and Bandura [15], Figures 1 and 3, respectively.

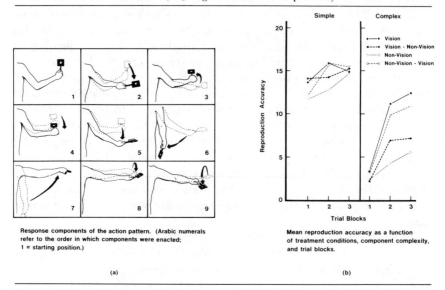

Response components of the action pattern. (Arabic numerals refer to the order in which components were enacted; 1 = starting position.)

Mean reproduction accuracy as a function of treatment conditions, component complexity, and trial blocks.

(a)                                                                 (b)

had visual feedback of their performance added or withdrawn after trial 3. All subjects observed the modeled sequence prior to each trial. In the visual feedback condition subjects viewed an online videotape of their ongoing performance. After trial 6, all four groups completed a further three trials without either visual feedback or the a priori model demonstration. Each response component and movement sequence could be judged a maximum of 2 points for a perfect match of the modeled performance, with appropriate reduction of points for deviations from the standard. The initial position was not scored in each movement sequence and, therefore, a maximum of 16 points could be attained on each trial.

As might be expected, the results revealed that simple sequences were modeled better than those designated as complex. Of more importance to the predictions of social learning theory [8] was the finding that visual feedback is not crucial in the early trials of learning the complex sequence (see Fig. 1). This supports the postulation that visual feedback is only useful if a conceptual model of the act exists and this requires a few performance trials to develop. Of further interest is the fact that performance did not deteriorate in block 3 when both the model and visual feedback were unavailable to all subjects. Thus, model effectiveness relates to the complexity of the movement sequence to be learned, and visual feedback can play a facilitory role in this process at key stages of learning.

A reasonably consistent pattern of results can be discerned from the above studies by utilizing the operational interpretation of coordination and control advanced earlier, together with findings in the literature on the visual perception of biological motion [16, 30, 33]. First, it needs to be recognized that all tests of the effectiveness of demonstrations have been based on subsequent response production by the observer. This approach negates examination of the realistic possibility that information can or is conveyed by the demonstration but that it is not realized, at least immediately, in response production. Hence, greater care is required to distinguish between the pickup of information regarding action and the effective utilization of this information in terms of response production. Second, and related to the preceding point, is the fact that the effectiveness of demonstrations on response production has primarily been ascertained through scores reflecting the goal of the task rather than a kinematic analysis of the coordination and control of the movement sequence. The Martens et al. [41] experiment with the shoot-the-moon task reflects the different interpretations that may be drawn of the effect of demonstrations on the basis of observing either the kinematics of response production or the goal-oriented product of the response itself. The Carroll and Bandura [15] study provided the rudiments of a kinematic analysis of demonstrations on response production.

Demonstrations provide information regarding the topological characteristics of the relative motion to the observer [16, 33], and this is the essential information in the search for the appropriate coordination function. The problem is that one cannot assume that the pickup of information regarding relative motion will lead instantaneously to the production of the appropriate relative motion [41]. Thus, separate tests are required of information pickup from demonstrations (perception) and the resulting execution of movement (action). In short, the failure of a demonstration group to produce superior performance scores on the appropriate relative motion is not sufficient to determine whether relative motion information was picked up by the observers or, in a more general sense, whether any information was conveyed by the demonstration.

If the performer already has knowledge of the appropriate relative motion the demonstrations serve to confirm this and provide some indication of the effort [60] or scaling of the relative motion required by the observer. It is important to note that the only invariant characteristic between the observer's perception of the demonstration and the observer's eventual performance is the topology of the relative motion. Of course, optimization procedures could dictate that the optimal pattern of coordination for the observer is different from that presented in the demonstration due to individual differences. However, implicit in a demonstration is the inference that the learner (observer) should match the relative motion of body and limbs exhibited in the demonstration. The absolute motion is bound to vary between the example of the demonstration and the observer's eventual performance due to individual differences and the uniqueness of the optimal coordination and control solution. Observers can discern some general perspective of effort from a demonstration [60], but it would seem that only practice can provide the essential information regarding the unique solution if optimization procedures have not been utilized in determining the coordination and control function in the demonstration.

The invariant information to be conveyed to the performer by prior-to-action variables such as demonstrations and instructions is the topology of the relative motion. The acquisition of new patterns of relative motion in the acquisition of both phylogenetic and ontogenetic skills is largely an unchartered course in motor learning. It would seem that the learning of a coordination pattern is a problem to which prior-to-action augmented information should be considered a primary learning variable, regardless of the mode by which this information is conveyed to the performer.

*Augmented Information: During Action*
There have been two approaches to the practical presentation and experimental investigation of augmented information during action. The first, which is categorized by the practical effects of the manipulation, has been called guided practice. The second approach, which is categorized by the nature of the information provided the performer, has been called action feedback or augmented concurrent feedback [31]. These two categories of augmented information during action, therefore, are not mutually exclusive because they have been defined on different bases. However, understanding the nature of the information provided the performer by the during-action training techniques allows a common basis for synthesis of the experimental findings.

The guided practice approach has two primary techniques: forced response and physical restriction. In forced response, the performer is passively moved by the instructor or machine through what is presumed to be the appropriate coordination and control for the task at hand. The implicit assumption with this technique is that it facilitates the acquisition of the appropriate coordination function. Thus, for example, the tennis coach holds the beginner's arm and wrist and moves the upper limbs in such a fashion that it approximates the kinematics that emerge from the appropriate coordination and control for hitting the ball. However, in actions requiring the constraint of a large number of degrees of freedom, the instructor, unlike the puppeteer, cannot adequately cope with the control problem. The outcome is that in the above example the instructor typically fixes a correct posture for the lower segments of the arm and moves the arm by motion at the shoulder joint. Hence, by freezing the degrees of freedom at the lower joints, the coordination problem for the tennis forehand has still not been approached.

The literature suggests that the forced response technique has not been operationally examined in relation to the development of the coordination function in the acquisition of skill. At best it provides some "feel" for the rudiments of the action pattern by virtue of the available proprioceptive and visual feedback, and this has been the working assumption underlying its pervasive use in rehabilitation. It has the major problem, however, that the performer is not active in generating the response [34], that is, determining the coordination function.

In the physical restriction mode, the performer actually generates the response but some constraint is provided by the instructor or a machine as to the range of motion allowed at a given body point. A reflection of this approach is the golf-o-tron technique which constrains the spatial pathway of the golf club on the down stroke. This technique, in effect, narrows or even specifies the kinematic scaling of the coordination function. However, this technique also has several limitations. First, the provision of an external physical constraint to human motion does not preclude the performer from exerting force on these physical constraints. As a consequence, the performer will not necessarily follow the designated trajectory in the absence of the physical constraint. Second, in spite of the assumptions of most practitioners, this technique seems to be limited to the development of the appropriate scaling of the coordination function rather than the determination of the fundamental relative motion. Third, there is the suggestion that practice without variability in the scaling of action (i.e., errorless learning [32]) is not an optimal approach to learning. This perspective is also consistent with the predictions of schema theory [62]. Finally, the physical restriction applied to the performer in practice is inevitably what is deemed appropriate or average for a performer rather than being based upon an individually tailored protocol.

Thus, the guided practice techniques of forced response and physical restriction have essentially provided augmented information regarding the scaling of a given coordination function. They do not seem to provide adequate information for the performer to determine the coordination function itself. There is a guided practice technique that contributes to this role, but it is rarely acknowledged in the skill learning literature. This is the situation where the advisor provides either verbally or via a mechanical gadget a discrete cue to the performer during the ongoing response. This cue is usually related to the timing of the onset of a given segment in an extended movement sequence to precipitate the correct relative motion. It informs the performer *when* to initiate a given movement segment. Sometimes the mechanical aid utilized, such as a support ring in gymnastics, allows the advisor to also provide an external force in the appropriate direction. Consequently, information can be provided to the performer about when and what to do next in a given movement sequence. Systematic research on this category of augmented concurrent information has yet to take place.

The role of augmented concurrent information feedback has probably received the most empirical attention of the categories of augmented information during action [6]. In some tasks the availability of relevant task information from the sensory systems is limited. For example, during action the performer may not be able to watch his own movements directly, or input from the proprioceptors may be minimal. Ongoing information pickup from the sensory systems can be augmented by either providing information not naturally available in performance of the task or through enriching the fidelity of the existing sensory feedback.

In both situations, augmented concurrent information has been shown to be effective in facilitating performance [2, 15, 65]. However, a common finding has been that once the augmented concurrent information feedback is withdrawn performance deteriorates immediately [3]. This effect is magnified progressively as the gain between the augmented information and the information from the natural movement situation departs increasingly from a one-to-one correspondence, as for example, in the presentation of visual displays [5, 21, 54]. These findings have led to the generalization that augmented concurrent information acts as a temporary crutch to performance rather than as a lasting aid to the acquisition of skill [6, 48]. The common interpretation of this performance deterioration on withdrawal of augmented feedback during action is that it occurs because attention is focused on the peripheral and irrelevant movement cues rather than the central and relevant cues [3].

The degree of performance decrement exhibited on withdrawal of augmented concurrent feedback seems to depend on the scheduling of the presentation of the augmented feedback. Lintern [37] has shown that reducing the frequency of the augmented concurrent information feedback prior to total withdrawal reduces and can even eliminate the performance decrement during the full withdrawal or no augmented information performance phase [38]. Augmented concurrent information feedback has also been successfully used for rehabilitation. Normal balanced weight bearing by the legs [71] and the control of normal head posture by cerebral palsy patients [36, 72] has been facilitated by augmented concurrent feedback techniques. In summary, the scheduling of augmented concurrent information seems to determine the level of performance exhibited under the no-feedback conditions.

Synthesis of the augmented concurrent feedback studies suggests that they have all provided information about the scaling of the coordination function. Only when concurrent visual videotape feedback of the limb motion is provided has information about the relative motion of the action also been conveyed. This concurrent absolute motion information is transmitted to the performer so that it might be utilized on that trial. Presumably, then, the augmented information is peculiar to the trial on which it is presented, and its availability generates a different strategy to response production from the natural situation. Only when the movement duration is short (less than the designated minimal error correction time) will augmented concurrent information hold the potential to act on the next trial [39, 47]. In this situation, withdrawal of augmented concurrent information feedback is not as deleterious as in slow movements, presumably because it is acting more for terminal KR than for on-line closed-loop correction purposes.

*Augmented Information: After Action*
Augmented information after action has traditionally been exclusively focused on information feedback about the product of the action in relation to the goal of the task, namely KR. There are, however, other types of information that can be presented to the performer on completion of the act. These include information about the movement sequence just executed by the performer and a yet to be developed category of augmented information, which refers directly to the change required in the action pattern on the next trial. Both goal KR and information about the movement sequence just performed are reflections of terminal information feedback.

*Information feedback.* If a performer is to change behavior in relation to some externally defined goal, it is clear that information feedback of performance in relation to that goal is necessary. This strong empirical principle is what has made KR such a potent learning variable [1, 4, 11, 46]. There have, however, been a number of claims recently that goal KR is insufficient to optimize performance in many tasks [20, 22, 51]. It seems that information feedback of the response dynamics in the form of kinematic and kinetic parameters is required to augment goal KR if skilled performance is to be attained [51]. This section focuses on the relative effectiveness of goal KR and kinematic information feedback through examining the information conveyed by these sources of feedback in relation to task criteria.

As the opening sections discussed, it is a knowledge of the movement parameter(s) to be optimized that determines the sufficiency of the type of information feedback provided the performer. The optimal configuration of coordination and control will be specified by an analysis of the organismic, environmental, and task constraints. A guiding principle advocated by Fowler and Turvey [20] in relation to the attainment of this pattern of coordination and control is "that for the degrees of freedom necessitating control there must be at least as many degrees of constraint in the information supporting that control" (p. 36). Based on our synthesis of the goal KR and kinematic information feedback literature, we suggest that the intuition of Fowler and Turvey is holding up empirically.

KR of a discrete position or time parameter provides all the necessary information in the single-degree-of-freedom positioning or timing tasks [1, 47] This is because the information provided the performer matches the task criterion of a single point on the spatial or temporal dimension. Thus, in retrospect, the search for a simple and so-called novel motor task to examine learning variables such as KR has produced a task that can be optimized by information of a single discrete parameter.

In discrete positioning and timing tasks constrained to one spatial dimension, subjects benefit from increasingly accurate information regarding the discrete outcome as long as the post-KR interval is of sufficient length to allow for the processing of the more precise information [56]. There is probably some limit to which increasingly precise outcome information of a discrete parameter can be effectively utilized in response production. In addition, this optimal precision of goal KR interacts with the chronological age level of the developing child [9, 50] and probably the skill level of the performer.

KR of a discrete outcome parameter begins to lose its sufficiency once the task criteria extend beyond a discrete point on a single spatial dimension. This is not to infer that learning in these task situations will not occur with traditional goal KR but rather that performance cannot be optimized because the information feedback does not match the task constraints. For example, when both space and time are outcome criteria of a given task, the subject tends to improve in relation to the dimension of the KR given or the instructional emphasis [40]. Furthermore, KR becomes insufficient even within a single-degree-of-freedom task if the task criterion demands, for example, the achievement of a set of points in position or force over time. That is, insufficient information is conveyed to the performer by a traditional discrete KR parameter once a continous kinematic or kinetic event enters into the criterion rather than just a discrete point on a single space or force dimension.

Some recent experiments in our laboratory have begun examining the proposition that the task criterion specifies the appropriate information feedback for skill learning in that the information feedback must match the constraint imposed upon response output. This requires an examination of the optimal trajectory specified by the task constraints and the presentation of information feedback that matches the constraints imposed. The use of control space representations from topological dynamics is helpful to both prescribe and describe the movement in the same terms of kinematics [43]. This approach may be used in tasks requiring either the control of a single degree of biomechanical freedom or multiple degrees of freedom. Our empirical approach has been to begin examination of kinematic and kinetic information feedback in single-degree-of-freedom responses before moving on to multiple-degree-of-freedom tasks. In the single-degree-of-freedom tasks, the information feedback is available to more appropriately scale the control of the action in a single plane of motion at a given anatomical joint.

An initial set of experiments focused on kinetic information feedback for the acquisition of isometric tasks where ostensibly no movement is required by the performer [53]. In experiment 1 the subject's task was to activate the flexors of the biceps and produce a criterion peak force (30 N). No constraint was imposed as to the rate of force production or the overall force-time history of the impulse to be produced. Thus, the task criterion reflected a discrete kinetic parameter. Two feedback groups were constrasted. One group received traditional goal KR of the peak force produced while the other group additionally observed on completion of the action a continuous force-time trace of the impulse just produced. Figure 2A shows that there was no difference between the two feedback groups over the initial acquisition feedback trials. There was a tendency for the continuous kinetic feedback group to maintain performance better over the no-KR trials but this advantage was not statistically significant.

In experiment 2 the criteria was changed to the production of an impulse that was similar to the shape of a gaussian curve with a peak force of 30 N and an impulse duration of 300 ms. Impulse error was determined by the absolute area differences between the criteria and

FIGURE 2

*Mean absolute peak force error (A) and mean absolute impulse error (B) as a function of feedback condition and trials.*

SOURCE: Newell, Sparrow, and Quinn [53], experiments 1 and 2, respectively.

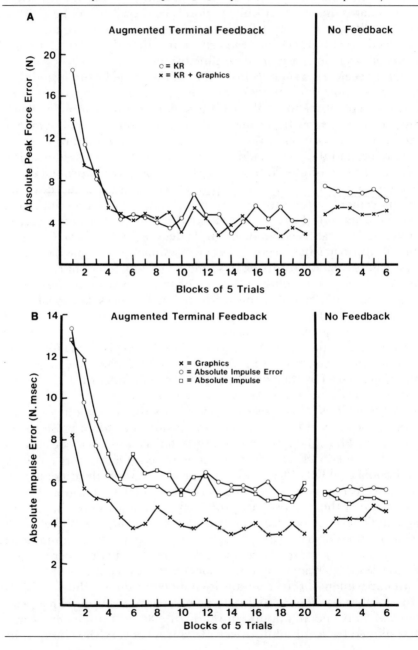

performance impulses after they had been aligned at their peaks. Three independent feedback groups were tested under the following conditions: one group received terminal goal KR reflecting the discrete value of the absolute area difference; a second group received terminal KR reflecting the actual size of the impulse produced; and a third group received on completion of the response a graphics force-time representation of the impulse produced superimposed on the criterion force-time curve. It was hypothesized that only the continuous presentation of the augmented information through the graphics force-time representation provided sufficient information to minimize error. The graphics condition reflected an application of the event control space framework [43] for the measurement category of kinetics by graphing continuous force-time information feedback to the subjects.

Figure 2B shows that the continuous force-time group reduced error considerably more than both the other discrete KR information feedback groups. This advantage dissipated to some degree over the no-KR trials, and feedback withdrawal of the continuous information feedback needs to be examined further. However, in taking the results of these experiments collectively, the findings are consistent with the proposition that the task criteria specify the appropriate information feedback for skill learning in that the information feedback must match the constraint imposed upon response output.

Another set of experiments contrasted the effect of traditional goal KR with various kinematic feedback parameters in the acquisition of single-degree-of-freedom response requiring the minimization of movement time over a given amplitude [52]. The findings of these two experiments, together with some earlier data from Walter [70], show that kinematic information feedback facilitates minimization of movement time performance, in contrast to traditional goal KR, as long as the representation of kinematic information feedback is continuous rather than discrete. Figure 3 shows the movement time data from the experiment with continuous velocity over time graphic terminal feedback contrasted against a KR movement time feedback group and a no-KR group. The introduction of the velocity-time information engendered an immediate facilitory effect on performance. Furthermore, it is interesting to note, in contrast to Hatze [27], that facilitation occurs even without knowledge of the kinematic trajectory for optimal performance. Presumably, knowledge of the trajectory with KR of the movement time allows subjects to understand features of trajectory-outcome relationship, although from this experiment it cannot be determined to what the degree subjects approached optimal performance.

The data from the above experiments are consistent with the idea

FIGURE 3

*Mean movement time (ms) as a function of feedback condition and practice over trial blocks and days.*

Source: experiment 2, Newell et al. [52].

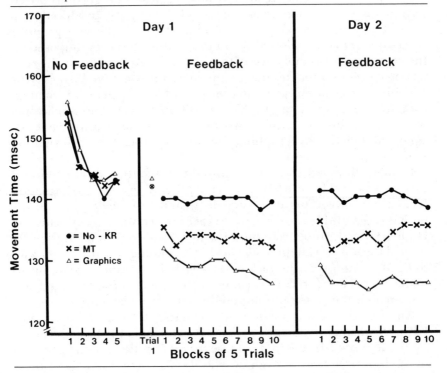

that, even in single-degree-of-freedom tasks, continuous kinematic or kinetic information feedback can facilitate performance. The practical problem is to understand the task constraints and then to provide information feedback which matches the constraints imposed on the optimal kinematic or kinetic trajectory. In theory, one needs to ascertain the control space that unambiguously allows prescription and description of the task constraints and actual performance, respectively.

In tasks requiring the control of more than a single biomechanical degree of freedom the initial problem for the learner, as outlined previously, is to determine the appropriate coordination function. Sometimes multiple-degree-of-freedom tasks require the use of an already learned coordination function and simply require the appropriate scaling of that function. The pursuit-rotor task reflects these latter demands. Thus, the provision of augmented information in multiple degrees of freedom tasks needs to be consistent with the stage of learning exhibited by the performer with respect to the development of the appropriate coordination and control.

Hatze [27] in the first direct demonstration of the effectiveness of kinematic information feedback required a subject to optimize a leg raise task by minimizing movement time to traverse a given angle of motion in the sagittal plane. A weight was attached to the foot of the leg to be raised which in effect forced the subject to bend the knee and coordinate and control two degrees of freedom, namely, the hip and knee joints. Hatze conducted optimization procedures for one subject prior to the learning trials to provide an estimate of the kinematic trajectories of both the lower and upper leg limb segments required to minimize movement time.

On the initial 120 acquisition trials, the subject received traditional goal KR of movement time after each trial. As Figure 4 depicts, the performance improved at a negatively accelerating rate to the point that an initial performance plateau was revealed by the end of this practice phase. After trial 120, the subject received information feed-

FIGURE 4
*Timing error from predicted optimum for leg raise as a function of*
*feedback condition over trials.*
SOURCE: Hatze [27]. Reproduced by permission of the author and the University Park Press, Baltimore, © 1976.

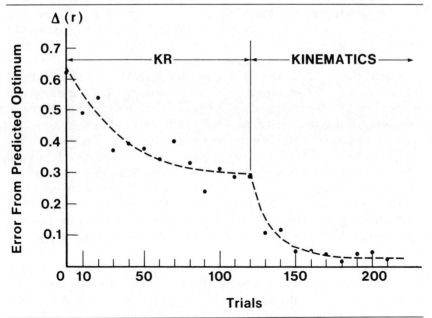

back of position-time plots of both the upper and lower leg segment movement in relation to the optimal kinematic trajectory. Performance improved immediately with the kinematic information feedback and even approached the optimum as determined by the optimization procedures. Hatze provided the kinematic information feedback of each limb segment individually to the subject. No analysis was reported of the actual change in the upper and lower leg kinematics over the acquisition trials. Thus it is not clear to what degree the kinematic information feedback helped establish the appropriate coordination function or merely scale the same topology of relative motion at the hip and knee.

Information feedback in relative motion terms has not been examined in skill acquisition, but in the early stages of learning multiple-degree-of-freedom tasks where the performer cannot generate the appropriate coordination function, this would appear the most crucial information. The graphic representation of the relative motion of two degrees of freedom is comparatively straightforward [25], but it becomes more difficult the greater the number of degrees of freedom. However, Hatze [28] has shown that a reasonable facsimile of a human being can be created with a 17-segment hominoid that has 42 degrees of freedom in three diminsions of motion. Furthermore, this hominoid has only 21 degrees of freedom when motion is confined to the sagittal plane. In addition, the various equations of constraint reduce the degrees of freedom that are effectively controlled [68]. In conclusion, the examination of augmented relative motion information feedback can relate to multiple-degree-of-freedom tasks although a determination will have to be made of the key relative motions for the task at hand.

In effect, videotape feedback captures both the relative and absolute motion information in gross motor activities but the empirical verification of the effectiveness of demonstrations is not clear cut [59]. It appears that videotape feedback is more effective when utilized in conjunction with demonstration of the criterion action. This suggests that the effectiveness of augmented information feedback can be facilitated by the presentation of information (e.g., demonstrations) regarding the optimal or desired configuration of coordination and control, and similarly the effectiveness of augmented information prior to action can be enhanced by presentation of the appropriate augmented information feedback [15]. It is also possible that videotape feedback diffuses the focus of the learner's attention because both structural and transformational information of the performance is available in the video display. Point-light displays minimize the structural information of the performer available to the observer, yet in spite of this, naive observers are remarkably adept at picking up a variety of movement cues [16].

Relative and common motion information about the optimal action pattern (prescription) and the attained action pattern (description) have been shown to facilitate the development of coordination and control in physical activity. Indeed, these have been the traditional categories of augmented information in both the theory and practice of motor skill learning. However, it would seem that augmented information directly related to how to change the action pattern on the next trial may also be useful to the performer. This represents a different category of augmented information from the traditional forms of prescription and description. This class of after-action augmented information we label here as transition information.

*Transition information.* Augmented information presented prior to action provides a prescription of the idealized coordination and control for the task at hand. Augmented information during and after action has primarily been feedback which is information or a description of elements of the action previously completed. Information feedback, in effect, informs the performer of what he has done and, thereby, only indirectly informs the performer of what to do next. Augmented information directly informing the subject of the change to make in the coordination and/or control on the next trial is a different and potentially valuable category of augmented information.

In practice the advisor typically provides both information feedback and transition information regarding the kinematics. Kinematic information is transmitted to the learner of the performance of the just completed trial and what kinematic changes need to be invoked on the next trial. The category of transition information has not been examined either conceptually or empirically in the scientific literature. Intuitively, it would seem to be a potent source of information for the performer that is particularly relevant to the determination of the coordination function in the acquisition of skill. Indeed, information about how to change the relative motion of the next trial may well prove to be more appropriate than information feedback in the acquisition of coordination.

An important point that needs to be emphasized by way of summary is that any augmented information feedback is typically withdrawn at some point in the practice session. This follows directly from the definition provided in the opening section of this chapter that augmented refers to that which is not naturally available in the task constraints. Withdrawal of augmented feedback can lead to a decrement in performance in contrast to the performance level exhibited under the augmented conditions. However, as outlined previously with augmented concurrent feedback, the rate and degree of performance decrement on withdrawal of augmented terminal feedback is directly related to the structure of the initial scheduling of the augmented information [12, 45].

A strong challenge to the traditional assumptions about the laws of KR has been advanced by Salmoni, Schmidt, and Walter [61] who propose that all the laws of KR are based on assessments of performance situations where the augmented information is available rather than a "true" test of learning with the augmented information withdrawn. This is a provocative challenge based in the main on isolated examples of performance reversals of various KR conditions under no-KR test conditions. The degree to which this challenge can be sustained in other terminal KR situations awaits experimentation. In the mean time, the practical inference from this challenge is that concern needs to be exhibited about the scheduling of terminal information feedback while theoretically a thorough reconsideration of what a test of learning should represent seems in order.

## AUGMENTED BIOLOGICAL INFORMATION

The thrust of this chapter on augmented information and motor skill acquisition has been augmented kinematic information. This is because augmented kinematic information represents the focus of both experimental investigation and practical application in motor learning. However, the role of augmented information of certain biological systems of the performer has taken on a new departure of late, in part because of its presumed significance for the top-class athlete [7]. In line with augmented kinematic information, the focus of augmented information of biological systems has been on the category of information feedback (biofeedback).

Biofeedback has been a popular technique to examine the limitations of controlling certain autonomic systems of the body and more voluntary aspects such as the degree of muscle activity exhibited in movement production. However, the potential significance of providing augmented information about biological parameters in addition to traditional performance measures in a given activity has only recently been recognized. Again, most effort has been directed to biofeedback of muscle activity but augmented biological information in other phases of action could also be relevant.

Indeed, an understanding of the optimal phase relationship between the cyclical behavior of different biological systems seems an essential prerequisite to utilizing augmented information of biological parameters. For example, Bramble and Carrier [13] have demonstrated the tight coupling of the phase relationships between the respiratory cycle and the gait pattern in efficient locomotion. Thus, the determination of the appropriate augmented biological information can only be based upon knowledge of how biological systems interact in supporting action.

An interesting example of the facilitation of performance through augmented information feedback has been provided in the task of rifle shooting by Daniels and Landers [17]. They experimentally showed that continuous augmented auditory information of the heart beat during the act of rifle shooting allowed the performer to time the squeeze of the rifle trigger between heart beats and, that the development of this phase relationship, led to improved scores in rifle shooting. Biofeedback facilitated the acqution of a more appropriate timing of the firing of the rifle in relation to the status of the biological system of performer. Therefore, as hinted at in Guthrie's quote opening the chapter, skill reflects the optimal coordination and control of body systems in relation to task demands, not merely the appropriate kinematics that emerge from the activity.

It would seem that for the development of skill in most activities, augmented information about biological parameters would only be required in the later stages of practice after the performer has established the appropriate coordination function for the task. The exception, of course, would be the case where the optimization of a given biological parameter is the goal of the task. The full significance of augmented biological information and its relation to augmented kinematic information for the acquisition of skill in physical activity has yet to be determined.

## CONCLUDING REMARKS

The guiding theoretical principle of this synthesis of augmented information has been that the nature of the information to be presented to the performer must be consonant with the stage of learning within the embedded hierarchy of coordination, control, and skill in physical activity. Acquisition of the basic coordination function can be facilitated with augmented information regarding the topology of relative motion and associated biological parameters while control may be refined through augmented information regarding the scaling of the topological characteristics. Knowledge of the optimal coordination of body systems is a fundamental prerequisite to the selection of the appropriate augmented information.

The functional framework for describing coordination, control, and skill [35] provides coherence to synthesizing augmented information whether it be presented prior to, during, or after action. The focus of augmented information to date has been the prescription and description of action, although it is proposed here that augmented transition information could prove very potent in the early stages of learning. It would seem that different prescriptive and descriptive modes naturally lend themselves to optimizing the pickup by the performer of either relative or absolute motion information and further work is clearly required if we are to understand how to optimize the mode of information transmission.

The linking of traditional augmented information parameters with a motor control framework seems to provide many interesting theoretical and practical avenues for future efforts in the motor learning domain. A central point to emphasize by way of closure is that consideration of motor learning variables such as augmented information must be made in relation to a concept of skilled performance [10, 66], rather than a framework of nonoptimal control that has been promoted implicitly by the traditional product-oriented approach to the positioning of single-degree-of-freedom limb movements.

## REFERENCES

1. Adams, J.A. A close-loop theory of motor learning. *J. Motor Behav.* 3:111–150, 1971.
2. Adams, J.A., E. Goetz, and P.H. Marshall. Response feedback and motor learning. *J. Exp. Psych.* 92:391–397, 1972.
3. Annett, J. Learning a pressure under conditions of immediate and delayed knowledge of results. *Q. J. Exp. Psych.* 11:3–15, 1959.
4. Annett, J. *Feedback and Human Behavior.* Baltimore, Md: Penguin, 1969.
5. Annett, J. The role of action feedback in the acquisition of simple motor responses. *J. Motor Behav.* 11:217–221, 1970.
6. Armstrong, T.R. *Feedback and Perceptual-Motor Skill Learning: A Review of Information Feedback and Manual Guidance Training Techniques.* Technical Report No. 25, Human Performance Center, University of Michigan, 1970.
7. Ash, M.J., and R.D. Zellner. Speculations on the use of biofeedback training in sport psychology. In *Psychology of Motor Behavior and Sport.* D.M. Landers and R.W. Christina, eds. Champaign, Ill.: Human Kinetics, 1978.
8. Bandura, A. *Social Learning Theory.* Englewood Cliffs, N.J.: Prentice Hall, 1977.
9. Barclay, C.R., and K.M. Newell. Children's processing of information in motor skill acquisition. *J. Exp. Child Psych.* 30:98–108, 1980.
10. Bernstein, N. *The Coordination and Regulation of Movement.* New York: Pergamon, 1967.
11. Bilodeau, I.M. Information feedback. In *Acquisition of Skill.* E.A. Bilodeau, ed. London: Academic Press, 1966.
12. Bilodeau, E.A., I.M. Bilodeau, and D.A. Schumsky. Some effects of introducing and withdrawing knowledge of results early and late in practice. *J. Exp. Psych.* 58:142–144, 1959.
13. Bramble, D.M., and D.R. Carrier. Running and breathing in mammals. *Science* 219:251–256, 1983.
14. Burwitz, L. *Observational Learning and Motor Performance.* Edinburgh: FEPSAC, Conference Proceedings, 1975.

15. Carroll, W.R., and A. Bandura. The role of visual monitoring in observational learning of action patterns: Making the unobservable observable. *J. Motor Behav.* 14:153–167, 1982.

16. Cutting, J.E., and D.R. Proffitt. The minimum principle and the perception of absolute, common and relative motions. *Cog. Psych.* 14:211–246, 1982.

17. Daniels, F.S., and D.M. Landers. Biofeedback and shooting performance: A test of disregulation and systems theory. *J. Sport Psych.* 4:271–282, 1981.

18. Feltz, D.L., and D.M. Landers. Enhancing self-efficacy in high avoidance motor tasks: A comparison of modeling techniques. *J. Sport Psych.* 1:112–122, 1979.

19. Fitts, P.M. Perceptual-motor skill learning. In *Categories of Human Learning*. A.W. Meton, ed. New York: Academic Press, 1964, pp. 243–285.

20. Fowler, C.A., and M.T. Turvey. Skill acquisition: An event approach with special reference to searching for the optimum of a function of several variables. In *Information Processing in Motor Control and Learning*. G.E. Stelmach, ed. New York: Academic Press, 1978, pp. 1–40.

21. Fox, P.W., and C.M. Levy. Acquisition of a simple motor response as influenced by the presence or absence of action visual feedback. *J. Motor Behav.* 1:169–180, 1969.

22. Gentile, A.M. A working model of skill acquisition with application to teaching. *Quest* 17:3–23, 1972.

23. Gould, D.R. *The influence of motor task types on model effectiveness.* Unpublished doctoral dissertation, University of Illinois, 1980.

24. Gould, D.R., and G.C. Roberts. Modeling and motor skill acquisition. *Quest* 33:214–230, 1981.

25. Grieve, D.W. The assessment of gait. *Physiotherapy* 55:452–460, 1969.

26. Guthrie, E.R. *The Psychology of Learning.* New York: Harper, 1935.

27. Hatze, H. Biomechanical aspects of a successful motion optimization. In *Biomechanics V-B*. P. Komi, ed. Baltimore: University Park Press, 1976, pp. 5–12.

28. Hatze, H. Computerized optimization of sports motions: an overview of possibilities, methods and recent developments. *J. Sports Sci.* 1:3–12, 1983.

29. Hillix, W.A., and M.H. Marx. Response strengthening by information and effect in human learning. *J. Exp. Psych.* 60:97–102, 1960.

30. Hoenkamp, E. Perceptual cues that determine the labeling of human gait. *J. Human Mov. Stud.* 4:59–69, 1978.

31. Holding, D.H. *Principles of Training.* Oxford: Pergamon Press, 1965.

32. Holding, D.H. Learning without errors. In *Psychology of Motor Learning*. L.E. Smith, ed. Chicago: Athletic Institute, 1970.

33. Johansson, G., C. von Hofsten, and G. Jansson. Event perception. *Annu. Rev. Psych.* 31:27–63, 1980.

34. Jones, B. The importance of memory traces of motor efferent discharges for learning skilled movements. *Dev. Med. Child Neurol.* 12:620–628, 1974.

35. Kugler, P.N., J.A.S. Kelso, and M.T. Turvey. On the concept of coordinative structures as dissipative structures: 1. Theoretical lines of convergence. In *Tutorials in Motor Behavior*. G.E. Stelmach and J. Requin, eds. Amsterdam: North-Holland, 1980, pp. 3–47.

36. Leiper, C.I., A. Miller, L. Lang, and R. Herman. Sensory feedback for head control in cerebral palsy. *Phys. Ther.* 61:512–518, 1981.

37. Lintern, G. Transfer of landing skill after training with supplementary visual cues. *Human Fac.* 22:81–88, 1980.

38. Lintern, G., and D. Gopher. Adaptive training of perceptual-motor skills: Issues, results, and future directions. *Int. J. Man Mach. St.* 10:521–551, 1978.

39. Lionvale, J.T. The effect of augmented auditory feedback and auditory modelling on learning a complex motor skill. Unpublished doctoral dissertation, University of Oregon, 1979.

40. Malina, R.M. Effects of varied information feedback practice conditions on throwing speed and accuracy. *Res. Q.* 40:134–145, 1969.
41. Martens, R., L. Burwitz, and J. Zuckerman. Modeling effects on motor performance. *Res. Q.* 47:277–291, 1976.
42. McCullagh, P.D. Model status and attention: A partial test of social learning theory. Unpublished doctoral dissertation, University of Wisconsin, 1976.
43. McGinnis, P.M., and K.M. Newell. Topological dynamics: A framework for describing movement and its constraints. *Human Mov. Sci.* 1:289–305, 1982.
44. McGuire, W.J. Some factors influencing the effectiveness of demonstration films: Repetition of motivations, slow motion, distribution of showings, and explanatory narrations. In *Student Responses in Programmed Instruction.* A.A. Lumsdaine, ed. Washington, D.C.: National Academy of Sciences, National Research Council, 1961.
45. Newell, K.M. Knowledge of results and motor learning. *J. Motor Behav.* 6:235–244, 1974.
46. Newell, K.M. Knowledge of results and motor learning. In *Exercise Sport Sci. Rev.* J. Keogh and R.S. Hutton, eds. Santa Barbara: Journal Publishing Affiliates, 1976.
47. Newell, K.M. Motor learning without knowledge of results through the development of a response recognitiion mechanism. *J. Mot. Behav.* 8:209–217, 1976.
48. Newell, K.M. Skill learning. In *Human Skills.* D.H. Holding, ed. New York: Wiley, 1981.
49. Newell, K.M. Coordination, control and skill. In *Differing Perspectives in Motor Control.* I. Franks, D. Goodman, and R. Wilberg, eds. Amsterdam: North-Holland, in press.
50. Newell, K.M., and J.A. Kennedy. Knowledge of results in children's motor learning. *Dev. Psych.* 14:531–536, 1978.
51. Newell, K.M., and C.B. Walter. Kinematic and kinetic parameters as information feedback in motor skill acquisition. *J. Human Mov. Stud.* 7:235–254, 1981.
52. Newell, K.M., J.T. Quinn, Jr., W.A. Sparrow, and C.B. Walter. Kinematic information feedback for learning a rapid arm response. *Human Mov. Sci.* 2:255–270, 1983.
53. Newell, K.M., W.A. Sparrow, and J.T. Quinn, Jr. Kinetic information feedback for learning isometric tasks. *J. Human Mov. Stud.* in press.
54. Patrick, J., and F. Mutlusoy. The relationship between types of feedback, gain of a display and feedback precision in acquisition of a simple motor task. *Q. J. Exp. Psych.* 34A:171–182, 1982.
55. Pomeroy, D.N. The effect of verbal pretraining, verbal modeling and modeling on learning a four-part motor sequence by educable mentally retarded children. Unpublished master's thesis, Pennsylvania State University, 1975.
56. Rogers, C.A. Feedback precision and postfeedback interval duration. *J. Exp. Psych.* 102:604–608, 1974.
57. Rosenbaum, M.E. The effect of verbalization of correct responses by performers and observers on retention. *Child Dev.* 38:615–622, 1967.
58. Rosenbaum, M.E., and L.J. Schultz. The effects of extraneous response requirements on learning by performers and observers. *Psych. Sci.* 8:51–52, 1967.
59. Rothstein, A.L., and R.K. Arnold. Bridging the gap: Application of research on videotape feedback and bowling. *Mot. Skills Theory Prac.* 1:35–62, 1976.
60. Runeson, S., and G. Frykholm. Visual perception of a lifted weight. *J. Exp. Psych. Human Percept. Perform.* 8:733–740, 1981.
61. Salmoni, A.W., R.A. Schmidt, and C.B. Walter. Knowledge of results and motor learning: A review and critical reappraisal. *Psych. Bull.* 95:355–386, 1984.
62. Schmidt, R.A. A schema theory of discrete motor skill learning. *Psych. Rev.* 82:225–260, 1975.

63. Shaw, R., and M. McIntyre. Algoristic foundations for cognitive psychology. In *Cognition and the Symbolic Processes*. W. Weimer and D. Palmero, eds. Hillsdale, N.J.: Erlbaum, 1974, pp. 305–362.

64. Sheffield, F.D. Theoretical considerations in the learning of complex sequential tasks from demonstration and practice. In *Student Response in Programmed Instruction*. A.A. Lumsdaine, ed. Washington, D.C.: National Academy of Science, National Research Council, 1961.

65. Smith, K.U. Cybernetic theory and analysis of learning. In *Acquisition of Skill*. E.A. Bilodeau, ed. New York: Academic Press, 1966.

66. Sparrow, W.A. The efficiency of skilled performance. *J. Motor. Behav.* 15:237–261, 1983.

67. Taffee, J. Observational learning and symbolic coding of a sequential motor task by educable mentally handicapped children. Unpublished master's thesis, University of Illinois, 1977.

68. Turvey, M.T., R.E. Shaw, and W. Mace. Issues in the theory of action: Degrees of freedom, coordinative structures and coalitions. In *Attention and Performance, VII*. J. Requin, ed. Hillsdale, N.J.: Erlbaum, 1978.

69. Twitmeyer, E.M. Visual guidance in motor learning. *Am. J. Psych.* 43:165–187, 1931.

70. Walter, C.B. Contrasting information feedback parameters for learning a simple rapid response. Unpublished master's thesis, University of Illinois at Urbana-Champaign, 1981.

71. Warren, C.G., and J.F. Lehman. Training procedures and biofeedback methods to achieve controlled partial weight bearing: An assessment. *Arch. Phys. Med. Rehab.* 56:449–455, 1975.

72. Wooldridge, C.P., and G. Russell. Head position training with the cerebral palsied child: An application of biofeedback techniques. *Arch. Phys. Med. Rehab.* 57:407–414, 1976.

73. Zelaznik, H.N., D.C. Shapiro, and K.M. Newell. On the structure of motor recognition memory. *J. Mot. Behav.* 10:313–323, 1978.

# Exercise and Locomotion for the Spinal Cord Injured

ROGER M. GLASER, Ph.D.

In recent years, there has been an increased awareness of the problems and needs of the physically disabled who suffer from neuromuscular dysfunction. Generally, these individuals exhibit substantial loss of voluntary muscle control because of paralysis, paresis, and spasticity. Common medical conditions which result in impaired neuromuscular function include stroke, multiple sclerosis, muscular dystrophy, cerebral palsy, and traumatic injury to the central nervous system (brain and spinal cord). Although this chapter focuses on the exercise and locomotive capabilities of spinal cord injured individuals, many of the principles and data presented could be applied to individuals with other neuromuscular disorders.

## SPINAL CORD INJURY

All instances of muscle paralysis are tragic to the victim, family, and friends. However, spinal cord injury (SCI) is particularly devastating because it most often results from accidents which, in retrospect, could have been avoided or prevented. Although motor vehicle accidents are the major cause of SCI (over 38%), many young SCI victims sustained their injuries while participating in sports or physical activities (e.g., gymnastics, football, wrestling, and diving) [25, 166].

Before World War II, 80 percent of SCI victims died within three years of the injury [86], largely because of kidney and pulmonary infections [141]. With the advent of antibiotic drugs and surgical advances, 80 percent of paraplegics now have a normal life expectancy [86], and quadriplegics have a life expectancy that is only 10 percent lower than able-bodied individuals [141]. It has been estimated that there are currently more than 200,000 spinal cord injured paraplegic and quadriplegic individuals in the United States [166]. Approximately 8,000 accident victims survive each year to join and expand this group.

Problems encountered by paraplegic and quadriplegic individuals are of an impact unequaled by most other medical conditions. Besides the inability to ambulate, many are unable to control bladder and bowel functions or even feed themselves. Thus, many have an utter

263

dependence on others for their daily subsistence. Compounding these primary problems are secondary complications, such as disuse atrophy of the paralyzed muscles, demineralization of bones (osteoporosis), impaired circulation in the sedentary lower extremities which may result in abnormal thrombus formation and decubitus ulcers, and a general loss of aerobic (cardiopulmonary) fitness. Changes in family life patterns and diminished self-image can have drastic psychological impact, and the opportunities for societal interactions (e.g., education, employment, and recreation) are usually diminished. The financial burden is also extreme [166].

## REHABILITATION AND EXERCISE

A primary aim of rehabilitation for those who are paralyzed because of SCI (or suffering from other neuromuscular dysfunction) is to increase their independence. This has been accomplished by appropriate medical treatment; physical, psychological, and occupational therapy; adaptive devices; environments which are free of architectural barriers; and, opportunities to interact in society.

Providing locomotive ability is of utmost importance. For those with paralyzed legs, this is usually accomplished by making compensatory use of muscles which are still functional and orthopedic devices. Thus, wheelchairs that are propelled by the arms are commonly prescribed. Some individuals with paralyzed legs (who have trunk control) use long leg braces and crutches to permit them to walk via "swing through gait." Use of the arms for locomotion, however, has been shown to be inefficient and stressful to the muscles involved, and to the cardiovascular and pulmonary systems [58, 65, 68, 71, 74, 75, 81].

To help improve and maintain physical fitness, many paraplegics and quadriplegics participate in training programs which utilize arm exercise. In addition, sporting events which are wheelchair adapted have become quite popular over the past 35 years [133]. Many beneficial physiologic and psychologic effects have been reported for wheelchair-dependent individuals who engage in habitual physical exercise [1, 28, 35, 76, 79, 86, 87, 112, 121, 141, 155]. Considering the success of many of these individuals in their independence and lifestyles, physical exercise appears to be quite important in the rehabilitation process.

The purpose of this chapter is to present information and research data related to exercise and locomotion performed by spinal cord injured individuals. Topics addressed include: pathophysiology; metabolic and cardiopulmonary responses to wheelchair locomotion; physical fitness assessment of wheelchair-dependent individuals (by exercise stress testing); physical fitness improvement for wheelchair-dependent individuals (by exercise training programs); functional electrical stimulation of paralyzed muscles; and, sports participation. It is hoped that this presentation will contribute to better understanding of the problems and needs of these individuals, and how their rehabilitation may be improved by appropriate orthopedic devices and exercise programs.

## PATHOPHYSIOLOGY

This section provides a brief overview of how skeletal muscles are controlled by the central nervous system (CNS) and how this control is impaired with spinal cord injury and other common neuromuscular disorders. A more complete description of muscle function and control can be obtained from medical physiology textbooks.

In order for skeletal muscles to contract, stimulation by electrical impulses (action potentials) is required. These motor (efferent) signals originate in the CNS and are transmitted to the muscle fibers by way of α-motoneurons. There are both voluntary and involuntary components of skeletal muscle control. Action potentials for voluntary control originate in the higher centers of the brain (i.e., motor cortex). These signals are propagated down the spinal cord along neurons that eventually synapse onto the α-motoneurons, which carry the information to skeletal muscles. In contrast, reflex contractions are involuntary (and unconscious) in nature. Action potentials for these contractions are regularly induced in neurons by sensory receptors which may be peripherally or centrally located. Neuronal pathways to the α-motoneurons may involve lower centers of the brain or be isolated to one or more segments of the spinal cord. Reflex contractions can be stimulated by various forms of sensory input, including rapid muscle stretch, pain, postural changes, and cold. Neurons which originate in the brain and extend into the spinal cord to provide motor signals to the α-motoneurons are termed *upper motoneurons*, whereas the α-motoneurons which leave the CNS to provide motor signals to the skeletal muscles are termed *lower motoneurons*.

The CNS not only stimulates the contraction of skeletal muscles, it also monitors performance of the muscles. Sensory receptors located in muscles, tendons, and joints, in conjunction with afferent neurons, provide the CNS with information concerning muscle length, limb position, rate of movement, and muscle tension. This feedback information enables stimulation to the muscles to be continuously and appropriately modified so that actual performance closely matches desired performance. Figure 1 diagrammatically illustrates efferent

FIGURE 1

*Diagrammatic illustration of the central nervous system (CNS) with efferent (motor) and afferent (sensory) pathways for precise control of skeletal muscle contractions. This feedback arrangement permits comparison by the CNS of the intended skeletal muscle performance with the actual performance and enables immediate modification of muscle stimulation when appropriate.*

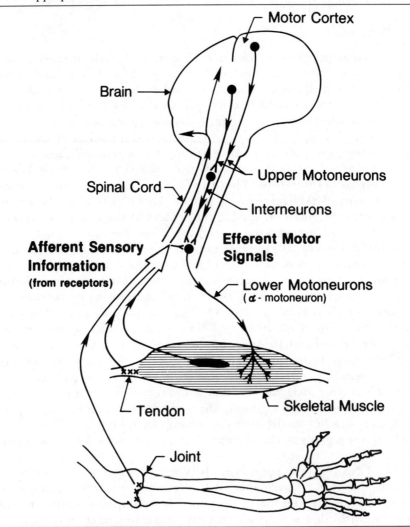

and afferent pathways which, under normal conditions, permit precise control of skeletal muscle contractions.

A primary reason that both contraction force and shortening velocity of skeletal muscles can be gradually graded (increased or decreased in small increments) is that the whole muscle functionally consists of numerous groups of fibers (cells). Each group is innervated by its own α-motoneuron so that it can be stimulated to contract individually. The α-motoneuron and all the muscle fibers that it innervates is termed the *motor unit*. Figure 2 diagrammatically illustrates two overlapping motor units. Since skeletal muscle fibers of motor units do not contract in the absence of action potentials in the α-motoneuron, or all the muscle fibers are stimulated to contract with the presence of action potentials in the α-motoneuron, motor units are said to operate in an all-or-none fashion. Thus, the contraction strength and velocity of shortening of the whole muscle is directly dependent upon the number of activated motor units (multiple motor unit summation). Muscle contraction force and shortening velocity are also influenced by the action potential frequency of motor units. Within limits, higher action potential frequency results in greater force generation and shortening velocity because of wave summation

FIGURE 2

*Diagrammatic illustration of two overlapping motor units. Presynaptic neurons which converge onto the bodies of the α-motoneurons are excitatory (+) or inhibitory (−). Action potential generation in an α-motoneuron causes all the skeletal muscle fibers which it innervates to contract in an all-or-none fashion.*

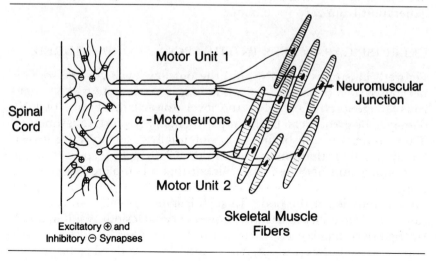

and tetanus (fusion of individual twitches together by subsequent muscle fiber stimulation prior to complete relaxation).

Figure 2 also shows that the axons of numerous neurons (typically thousands) converge onto the cell body of each α-motoneuron in the spinal cord and attach through synaptic connections. Synapses provide the functional contact between communicating neurons through neurotransmitter release. A synapse at a neuronal ending may be either excitatory (+) or inhibitory (−) depending upon the particular neurotransmitter-receptor site combination. Because both (+) and (−) presynaptic neurons terminate on an α-motoneuron body, the α-motoneuron is effectively an integrator of information received from various portions of the nervous system. It is the final common pathway to skeletal muscle control.

When muscle contraction is intended, the (+) drive to the motoneuron becomes greater than the (−) drive. At threshold level, action potentials are generated in the α-motoneuron. These action potentials are propagated along the α-motoneuron to the neuromuscular junctions of the innervated muscle fibers. The small quantity of chemical transmitter (acetylcholine), which is released with each action potential, diffuses across each neuromuscular junction to stimulate action potentials in each muscle fiber. All of the muscle fibers of the motor unit then begin to contract. With increased (+) drive, the action potential frequency to an extent increases, thus resulting in stronger, smoother contractions. Decreasing (+) and increasing (−) drive result in lower action potential frequency and weaker contractions. Complete relaxation occurs when (+) drive to the α-motoneuron falls below threshold level. Thus, combinations of (+) and (−) drive to α-motoneurons provide for a continuum of muscle force generation from zero to maximal.

## EXERCISE CAPABILITY IN THE SPINAL CORD INJURED

Figure 3 illustrates the CNS and the outflow levels for the somatic nervous system (SNS) and the autonomic nervous system (ANS) neurons. In general, the higher the level (toward the brain) of CNS damage, the greater can be the impairment of SNS and ANS function. Thus, injuries to the brain could potentially result in more loss of bodily functions than those lower in the CNS. With respect to spinal cord injury and SNS loss, it is evident that a complete lesion at the upper cervical level (above C3) would result in paralysis of most skeletal muscles of the body. In such instances, death can occur because of the inability to breathe. Lower cervical lesions result in quadriplegia (tetraplegia). Here, there can be considerable loss of upper body and complete loss of trunk and lower body skeletal muscle

FIGURE 3

*Diagrammatic illustration of the central nervous systems and the outflow*
*levels for the somatic and autonomic nervous system neurons. General*
*innervations from each spinal cord level are indicated.*

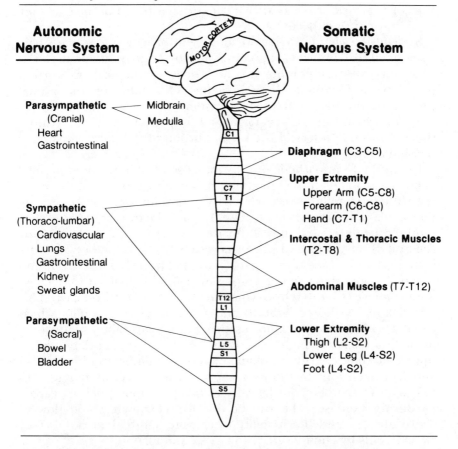

Autonomic Nervous System

Parasympathetic (Cranial)
Heart
Gastrointestinal

— Midbrain
— Medulla

Sympathetic (Thoraco-lumbar)
Cardiovascular
Lungs
Gastrointestinal
Kidney
Sweat glands

Parasympathetic (Sacral)
Bowel
Bladder

Somatic Nervous System

Diaphragm (C3-C5)

Upper Extremity
Upper Arm (C5-C8)
Forearm (C6-C8)
Hand (C7-T1)

Intercostal & Thoracic Muscles (T2-T8)

Abdominal Muscles (T7-T12)

Lower Extremity
Thigh (L2-S2)
Lower Leg (L4-S2)
Foot (L4-S2)

function. Lesions in the thoracic region result in paraplegia, with
various degrees of trunk involvement and complete loss of leg function. Lesions in the lumbar region also result in paraplegia; however,
some leg function may be spared.

Commonly accompanying SCI-caused skeletal muscle paralysis is
the loss of sensory information (e.g., touch, pressure, pain, temperature, proprioception) from the afflicted portion of the body. This
is because afferent signals from peripheral receptors are interrupted
at the same level in the spinal cord as motor signals from upper
motoneurons. Although spinal cord reflexes are usually intact, they
are exaggerated because of the loss of inhibitory efferent signals from

higher CNS levels. Furthermore, loss of this inhibition renders α-motoneurons more susceptible to stimulation from various portions of the CNS and peripheral nervous system. These excitatory signals result in uncontrolled and often prolonged or repetitive muscle contractions termed spasms. Muscle spasms can be a nuisance as they tend to occur unexpectedly.

Skeletal muscle paralysis and sensory information loss that occur with spinal cord injuries are accompanied by ANS dysfunction. Cervical lesions cause loss of the sympathetic division and the sacral portion of the parasympathetic division of the ANS; however, the cranial portion of the parasympathetic division remains intact. Lesions to the thoracic and lumbar regions result in partial loss of the sympathetic division and loss of the sacral portion of the parasympathetic division of the ANS.

Diminished sympathetic outflow because of SCI can limit aerobic exercise capability of the remaining functioning muscles. Adrenergic sympathetic stimulation is particularly important for appropriate cardiovascular adjustments to exercise. In part, the increased blood flow required by exercising muscle for delivery of $O_2$ and fuels, and for removal of metabolic end products results from sympathetically mediated vasoconstriction in inactive tissues. This reflex redistribution of blood is absent to varying degrees in SCI individuals. Additionally, lesions above T1 interrupt sympathetic outflow to the heart. This would limit cardioacceleration and myocardial contractility which could greatly reduce maximal cardiac output capability. Inadequate blood flow to exercising muscles could result in a greater dependence upon anaerobic energy supplementation, accumulation of lactic acid and hydrogen ions in the muscles, and early onset of fatigue. Diminished sympathetic outflow also reduces thermoregulatory capacity during exercise. This can be due to inadequate blood flow to active muscles and the inability to activate a sufficient number of sweat glands by cholinergic sympathetic stimulation.

Loss of the sacral portion of the parasympathetic division of the ANS results in the inability to voluntarily control bladder and bowel function. This occurs with most spinal cord injuries, and manual means of collecting and discarding urine and fecal material must be employed.

Whether congenital or acquired, most skeletal muscle dysfunction caused by CNS damage is usually considered to be permanent. This is because human CNS neurons are not known to regenerate (reconnect to appropriate synaptic sites once destroyed). With SCI, the exact extent of this dysfunction may not be known for several months postinjury, as dramatic returns of function have occurred with the diminution of spinal shock. Because of the long-term or permanent nature of most neuromuscular disorders, rehabilitation usually focuses upon making compensatory use of muscles which are functional and providing facilities and adaptive devices specially designed for the disabled. In cases of muscle paresis, exercise programs designed to strengthen the weakened muscles may result in their greater function.

To help control the muscle spasms which usually accompany SCI, pharmacotherapy is commonly employed. Treatment may involve oral antispasmatic and muscle relaxant drugs. However, CNS side effects of these drugs include dizziness, ataxia, and depression. In instances of severe spasticity, more radical surgical techniques might be employed. These include myotomy, tenotomy, tendon lengthening, and severing of α-motoneurons supplying the spastic muscles [141].

From the above discussion, it is evident that individuals suffering from nueromuscular dysfunctions such as SCI can have severely limited exercise capability. This may be due to the direct effects of skeletal muscle dysfunction, as well as the loss of sympathetic control to the cardiovascular and other organ systems essential to support the increased metabolic rate of the contracting muscles. Exercise capability can be further reduced by the CNS side effects of pharmacotherapy and diminished physical fitness due to inappropriate or insufficient exercise.

## METABOLIC AND CARDIOPULMONARY RESPONSES TO WHEELCHAIR LOCOMOTION

*Problems*
Disabled individuals who are dependent upon manual wheelchairs are required to use their relatively small upper body musculature for locomotion. This places them at an immediate disadvantage because of the limited maximal (peak) oxygen uptake ($\dot{V}O_2$) and power output (PO) capability for arm exercise (approximately two-thirds of leg exercise values for able-bodied individuals who are not arm-exercise trained) [7, 9, 11, 14, 98, 125, 142, 167]. Peak $\dot{V}O_2$ and max PO capability may be further reduced because of neuromuscular disorders (as indicated earlier), as well as diminished muscular and cardiopulmonary fitness resulting from wheelchair confinement and sedentary lifestyle [65, 67, 81, 91, 151]. Additionally, arm exercise appears to be inherently inefficient and stressful to the cardiovascular and pulmonary systems.

In comparing arm and leg exercise for able-bodied subjects at equivalent submaximal PO levels, greater metabolic demand for arm exercise was indicated by higher $\dot{V}O_2$ and blood lactate values. Heavier cardiac load was indicated by higher heart rate (HR), peripheral vascular resistance, intraarterial blood pressure, and stroke work. Greater demand on the pulmonary system was indicated by higher pulmonary ventilation. Arm exercise may also result in lower cardiac output and ventricular stroke volume [7, 8, 16, 18, 132, 142]. Decreased pumping capability may be due to a greater afterload on the heart because of the higher peripheral vascular resistance, and a decreased end diastolic volume because of a diminished venous return of blood to the heart. During wheelchair propulsion by SCI individuals, venous return of blood may be restricted by inactivity of the skeletal muscle pump because of leg muscle paralysis [65]. Also, increased intrathoracic pressure during strenuous handrim stroking could decrease the effectiveness of the thoracic pump [65]. These factors may result in an inadequate effective blood volume during wheelchair exercise which could contribute to limitations of peak $\dot{V}O_2$ and max PO. Therefore, wheelchair locomotion even at low PO levels could represent relatively high exercise loads that can have fatiguing effects. Excessive cardiovascular and pulmonary stresses which may occur could hinder rehabilitation efforts and impose potential risks upon certain patients—especially those with cardiovascular or pulmonary impairments, and the elderly [65].

Ideally, physiologic stresses for wheelchair locomotion should be minimized to provide optimal locomotive capability and rehabilitation. Factors which influence the magnitude of physiologic stresses to wheelchair locomotion are summarized in Figure 4. As indicated, characteristics of the user [61, 62, 67], wheelchair [13, 71, 81, 139], and locomotive environment [13, 22, 61, 70, 163, 164] must be taken into consideration to determine mechanisms which influence locomotive capability. To better understand the stressfulness of manual wheelchair locomotion, metabolic and cardiopulmonary responses for this form of exercise have been compared to those for familiar forms of leg exercise. Some studies exclusively used able-bodied subjects to perform both wheelchair and leg exercise, whereas other studies used SCI subjects for the wheelchair exercise.

*Wheelchair vs. Walking*
Wheelchair locomotion on a hard level surface has been reported to require less [81, 117], similar [65], and greater [149, 164] energy expenditures than walking. These discrepancies may be due to differences in the above-mentioned factors, as well as the method of study. Most of these investigations directly determined the energy cost of wheelchair locomotion, but then predicted the energy cost of walking from data in the literature. When directly comparing wheelchair locomotion for disabled and able-bodied subjects to walking for

FIGURE 4

*Flow diagram of energy transfer between the wheelchair user, the wheelchair, and the locomotive environment. Included are factors at each stage of transfer which may affect efficiency of locomotion. It is assumed that increased locomotive ability will increase rehabilitation of the wheelchair user.*

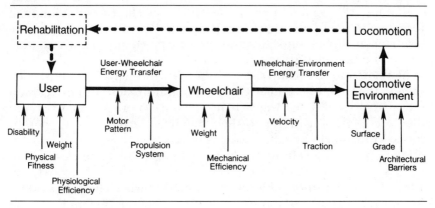

able-bodied subjects at the same velocities on a smooth level surface, energy expenditure for wheelchair locomotion tended to be lower at velocities lower than 3.5 km·h$^{-1}$, and greater at higher velocities [65, 165]. For wheelchair locomotion at velocities of 1, 2, and 3 km·h$^{-1}$, paraplegic and able-bodied subjects (mean weight = 63 kg) had similar gross energy costs of about 1.7, 2.0, and 2.5 kcal·min$^{-1}$ [165]. In another study, able-bodied individuals (mean weight = 74 kg) had a gross energy cost in excess of 5 kcal·min$^{-1}$ for wheelchair locomotion at 4.5 km·h$^{-1}$ [65]. In contrast, these values for wheelchair use were about 22 percent, 24 percent, and 16 percent lower, and 18 percent higher than for walking by the able-bodied subjects at velocities of 1, 2, 3, and 4.5 km·h$^{-1}$ [65, 165].

Despite this similarity on hard level surfaces, carpeted surfaces greatly elevate the energy expenditure for wheelchair locomotion because of marked increases in rolling resistance [22, 65, 70, 164]. It has been determined that the PO requirements for a 70-kg person operating a conventional wheelchair on a level tiled surface at 3 km·h$^{-1}$ is about 7 watts [26, 61, 151]. PO is increased about 2.5-fold for such locomotion on a low-piled carpeted surface [61]. At 3 km·h$^{-1}$, gross energy expenditure for wheelchair locomotion on a level low-pile carpeted surface was about 40 percent higher than for a tiled surface [70]. In contrast, energy expenditure for walking on a carpeted surface was found to be about the same as for a tiled surface

[70]. Thus, carpet can substantially increase the stressfulness of wheelchair locomotion and present an architectural barrier for disabled individuals which may not be recognized by those who walk. Of course, ramps greatly increase PO requirements and can represent substantial architectural barriers as it is necessary to propel one's own weight and the weight of the wheelchair against gravity [49, 61, 151].

$\dot{V}E$ and HR also tend to be higher for wheelchair locomotion than for walking at the same velocity [65, 70]. This observation is more dramatic at higher velocities and on a carpeted surface where metabolic rate becomes greater for wheelchair use. These variables tend to be related to the relative stressfulness of the activities. Thus, even though there may be similar energy expenditure levels under certain locomotive conditions, wheelchair users are more stressed because they are exercising closer to their maximal aerobic energy output (peak $\dot{V}O_2$) capability than those who walk.

One's preferred velocity for locomotion appears to be based upon factors of relative stress and locomotive efficiency [17, 39, 51, 72, 123]. In a recent study, older institutionalized wheelchair-dependent (mean age = 62 years) and ambulatory patients (mean age = 58 years) were observed to determine their self-selected velocities for locomotion [72]. Although the wheelchair users selected 2.0 km·h⁻¹ and walking patients selected 3.1 km·h⁻¹, the percentages of their predicted peak $\dot{V}O_2$ for these activities were quite similar (55% and 58%), as were heart rates (95 and 92 beats·min⁻¹). Similar to the reductions seen in able-bodied individuals (for leg exercise) with age [6], peak $\dot{V}O_2$ and max PO for wheelchair activity are lower in older wheelchair-dependent individuals than in their younger counterparts. Thus, older individuals must use a greater percentage of their maximal capability to perform commonly encountered locomotive tasks [72, 129]. Indeed, operating a wheelchair at a PO of just 7 watts elicits a $\dot{V}O_2$ of about 0.5 L·min⁻¹. This is estimated to represent 9 percent of max PO and 29 percent of peak $\dot{V}O_2$ for 20 to 30 year olds; 44 percent of max PO and 51 percent of peak $\dot{V}O_2$ for 50 to 60 year olds; and 100 percent of max PO and peak $\dot{V}O_2$ for 80 to 90 year olds [72, 129]. Therefore, in order to reduce the PO requirement and relative stresses for wheelchair locomotion, older individuals usually reduce their locomotive velocity or are pushed by attendants.

*Wheelchair vs. Bicycle*

To compare metabolic and cardiopulmonary responses for wheelchair vs. bicycle exercise, combination wheelchair-bicycle ergometers were constructed [58, 68]. Such devices enable both velocity and PO to be equated for these modes of propulsion, permitting well controlled experiments. When able-bodied subjects performed both forms of exercise, it was found that $\dot{V}O_2$, $\dot{V}E$, HR, respiratory exchange ratio, and ventilatory equivalent of $O_2$ were significantly higher for wheelchair ergometer propulsion at tested submaximal PO levels (5–25 watts) [65, 68]. In addition, blood lactate concentration was found to be significantly higher following this arm exercise, suggesting a greater component of anaerobic energy supplementation [68]. Although it would seem that able-bodied subjects would be unduly stressed during wheelchair activity because of their inexperience, it has been shown that many chronic wheelchair users exhibit greater stresses during a given task because of their disability and lack of fitness [81].

*Efficiency of Wheelchair Locomotion*
Handrim- (grab ring) propelled manual wheelchairs are generally considered to be inefficient [49, 71, 131, 151]. Mechanical or net efficiency (PO divided by net energy expenditure) has been reported to be about 7–10 percent for wheelchair ergometer exercise [21, 26, 36, 69, 81] and about 5 percent for actual wheelchair locomotion [65], compared to values in excess of 20 percent for walking [43] and leg cycling [14, 42, 54, 134]. Despite the calculated inefficiency for wheelchair locomotion, the lower or similar energy expenditure for this activity vs. walking at the same velocities may be due in part to the support given to body weight by the wheelchair, resulting in relatively low PO levels. Inefficiency for wheelchair vs. bicycle activity at equated PO levels suggests that the wheelchair propulsion system is energy wasteful and the physiologic efficiency is low because of the particular muscles used. Factors which may contribute to energy wasteful biomechanics of the handrim propulsion system include position of the arms, synchronicity of the arm movements, and a large component of static work [21, 49, 58, 66, 71, 81, 131, 139, 151]. Inefficiency may also be due to inherent histochemical characteristics of the upper body skeletal muscles [71, 89, 105, 145]. These muscles appear to have a greater concentration of fast twitch fibers [46, 89, 105, 145] which require a greater energy to perform a given task and are more fatiguable than lower body skeletal muscles [57, 84, 147, 156]. Thus, even if a more efficient drive system could be employed, locomotion with the arms will probably remain less efficient than locomotion with the legs.

The diameter of the handrim with respect to the diameter of the wheel can influence the efficiency of wheelchair locomotion because of alterations in muscle force-velocity relationships [13, 65, 71]. Large diameter handrims (up to the diameter of the wheel) provide for a low drive ratio because of the long lever length (the fulcrum being the wheel axle). Such high mechanical advantage handrims require less force to turn, but the stroking velocity must be higher for given wheelchair velocities [65, 71]. Conversely, smaller diameter handrims require more force to turn, but stroking velocity is lower for given wheelchair velocities. The higher drive ratio of small diameter handrims has been found to reduce metabolic and cardiopulmonary stresses for wheelchair exercise [65, 71]. Greater efficiency may be due to less frequent, more forceful arm strokes. Optimal force-velocity relationships have been suggested to be individual-specific, because of differences in strength, fiber composition, and fiber recruitment patterns of the skeletal muscles used [54, 71, 134]. Wheelchair track athletes typically use small-diameter handrims because of their great upper body strength, and their desire to propel their wheelchairs at high velocities. Most wheelchair-dependent individiuals, however, utilize larger diameter handrims. Although these handrims may be less efficient to operate, they are easier to turn and increase the ability of the users to overcome obstacles such as inclines [71]. It thus seems that wheelchair designs that incorporate selectable drive ratio transmissions (such as many bicycles) would be advantageous to increase efficiency and better match the locomotive task to the user's capability [65, 71, 139].

An arm crank propulsion system appears to have several advantages over the conventional handrim propulsion system of manual wheelchairs. When comparing submaximal effort arm cranking to handrim stroking on a combination ergometer, $\dot{V}O_2$, $\dot{V}E$, HR, cardiac output, and arterial blood pressure were significantly lower for arm cranking at given PO levels [131]. The mechanical efficiency for arm crank exercise has been reported to be as high as 18 percent [16, 21, 99]. In addition, max PO for arm cranking had been determined to be about 50 percent higher than for handrim stroking, although peak $\dot{V}O_2$ values were similar [66]. Improved performance for arm cranking may be due to greater continuity of movement of the arms and more muscle mass available for propulsion, and the asynchronous pattern of movement may take advantage of inherent neural pathways for reciprocal innervation of contralateral muscle groups [71, 139]. A study of young wheelchair-dependent individuals (mean age = 24 years) demonstrated that an arm-crank-propelled wheelchair elicited significantly lower average $\dot{V}O_2$ ($-33\%$), $\dot{V}E$ ($-32\%$), and HR ($-19\%$) in comparison to handrim propulsion over a given test course at the same velocity [139]. In another study, older wheelchair-dependent individuals (mean age = 61 years) operated a conventional handrim-propelled wheelchair and an arm-crank-propelled wheelchair at their self-selected velocities [140]. A higher velocity was selected for the arm-crank-propelled wheelchair (2.8 vs. 2.1 km·h$^{-1}$), whereas $\dot{V}O_2$, $\dot{V}E$, and HR values were quite similar. Data from these studies indicate that higher locomotive efficiency can be achieved with arm crank propulsion which may lead to less stressful locomotion and improved rehabilitation. However, wheelchairs which employ an arm crank system tend to lack portability and maneuverability, and it is difficult to transfer in and out of them. Lever-operated wheelchairs have also been found to be advantageous with respect to operating stress [13, 49]. This propulsion system seems to be better suited than the arm crank system for wheelchair designs which retain many of the desirable features of modern conventional wheelchairs.

*Swing Through Gait*
Many paraplegics who have trunk control can use long leg braces and crutches to enable "swing-through-gait" walking. Similar to wheelchair locomotion, this form of walking makes extensive use of the upper body musculature. However, much more strength, stamina, and skill are required. Studies have demonstrated that it takes several times the energy expenditure to perform swing-through-gait walking than to operate a manual wheelchair or walk at the same velocity [31, 74, 75]. There are also greater risks of injuries due to falls. These factors could be discouraging to all but the highly motivated to employ this form of locomotion.

## PHYSICAL FITNESS ASSESSMENT OF WHEELCHAIR-DEPENDENT INDIVIDUALS

*Need for Fitness Evaluation*
For the able-bodied, there are numerous well-established stress-testing protocols available for objective evaluation of physical exercise capability and cardiopulmonary (aerobic, endurance type) fitness. These protocols usually employ leg exercise modes such as treadmill walking or running, bicycle pedaling, and bench stepping. Leg exercise, rather than arm exercise, is preferred for such stress testing because the large muscle mass of the legs is more resistant to fatigue than the smaller muscle mass of the arms. It is thus likely that the limiting factor for maximum $\dot{V}O_2$ and PO is central circulatory (the inability to deliver sufficient blood and $O_2$ to the exercising muscles) rather than peripheral (local fatigue of the exercising muscles despite the delivery of sufficient blood and $O_2$) [3, 4, 12, 82, 98, 102, 125, 128].

There is, however, a conspicuous absence of analogous exercise stress-testing protocols which can be used by individuals with lower limb disabilities. Such tests would provide valuable information concerning physical capabilities and limitations which could aid health care professionals in prescribing wheelchairs, advising users as to their safe and effective operation, and evaluating fitness changes over a period of time [62]. To exercise stress test paraplegics and quadriplegics, arm exercise must be used. Arm exercise, however, may not provide the same information as leg exercise does for able-bodied individuals because of the small muscle mass utilized. The resulting localized fatigue with upper body exercise tends to limit aerobic performance—rather than the inability to deliver blood and $O_2$. This is evidenced by significantly higher peak $\dot{V}O_2$ being obtained from SCI subjects when their maximal effort arm crank exercise was supplemented by simultaneous exercise of paralyzed leg muscles (quadriceps) which was induced by electrical stimulation [144]. Therefore, arm exercise tests may be more valuable to determine muscle performance capability than cardiopulmonary fitness [12, 98, 125, 128]. Since $\dot{V}O_2$ values obtained during maximal effort arm exercise may be somewhat lower than the true physiologic maximum ($\dot{V}O_2$ during large muscle activity that is limited by the cardiovascular system), the term "peak $\dot{V}O_2$" rather than maximum $\dot{V}O_2$ is often used. However, individuals who are highly acclimated to arm exercise appear better able to utilize the capability of their $O_2$ delivery system and achieve a higher percentage of their $\dot{V}O_2$ max during arm exercise [167].

Physiologic monitoring to analyze metabolic and cardiopulmonary performance before, during, and after arm exercise typically includes ECG, HR, arterial blood pressure, $\dot{V}O_2$, respiratory exchange ratio, $\dot{V}E$, and blood lactate concentration. Additionally, cardiac output, ventricular stroke volume, and arteriovenous $O_2$ difference could be monitored by noninvasive techniques ($CO_2$ rebreathing and impedance cardiography) to evaluate myocardial performance and $O_2$ extraction by the tissues [82, 106, 107, 131, 161].

In addition to exercise performance during aerobic type stress testing, tests of muscle strength are valuable for the disabled, because strength is a primary factor in locomotive capability [40, 41, 112, 143]. Strength testing usually takes the form of momentary static (isometric) contractions or repetitive dynamic contractions. Since strength evaluation of the upper body musculature is commonly performed for able-bodied individuals, equipment and protocols which can be adapted for use by disabled individuals are readily available.

Anthropometrical measurements and determinations can also be helpful in constructing fitness profiles of disabled individuals [56, 96, 121, 167]. Data such as weight, stature, chest, waist, and limb circumference, body density, and percentage of body fat provide insight into the effects of the disability and wheelchair confinement, status of muscle and bones, dietary requirements, and benefits of exercise programs.

*Arm Exercise Modes*

*Actual wheelchair locomotion.* The most direct method of evaluating fitness of wheelchair-dependent individuals is to have them exercise by propelling their own wheelchairs. Physiologic variables such as $\dot{V}O_2$, $\dot{V}E$, and HR can be monitored as the wheelchair is operated over a predetermined test course at given velocities [29, 55, 65, 70, 72]. This provides information as to the energy cost of propulsion and cardiopulmonary stresses. By expressing energy cost of locomotion (net kcal) per unit of body weight (kg) per unit of distance traveled (km), the net locomotive energy cost (NLEC; net $kcal \cdot kg^{-1} \cdot km^{-1}$) can be determined [70, 72]. NLEC provides a relative index inversely related to the efficiency of locomotion: the lower the NLEC the higher the efficiency, and vice versa. NLEC values of 0.46 and 0.80 $kcal \cdot kg^{-1} \cdot km^{-1}$ have been reported for wheelchair locomotion on tile and carpet, respectively [70]. (Although NLEC provides information concerning the efficiency of locomotion, it should not be confused with the mechanical efficiency for operating the propulsion system.) High test-retest reliability for physiologic responses characterizes this method of fitness evaluation [72].

In general, the lower the physiologic stresses during locomotion, the greater the fitness of the wheelchair user [62, 65]. Besides fitness testing, the above stress-testing techniques could be used to aid wheelchair prescription. In this way, wheelchair selection could be individualized to each user on the basis of lower operating stresses and highest locomotive efficiency [50].

The PO requirement for actual wheelchair locomotion at given velocities has been estimated by the following techniques: measuring the force necessary to keep a weight-loaded wheelchair in a stationary position on a motor-driven treadmill [48, 56, 151]; measuring the distance and elapsed time a weight-loaded wheelchair coasts after the cessation of pushing force [22]; and measuring the average force (via a strain-gauge transducer) necessary to push a wheelchair and its occupant [61]. Data from the latter technique were used to calculate the linear regression equations provided in Figure 5. This composite summary of forces and velocities permits estimation of wheelchair PO requirements ($kpm \cdot min^{-1}$) on a tiled and a low-pile carpeted surface if body weight, the degree of incline, and propulsion velocity are known [61]. For example, a 70-kg person operating a wheelchair on a 2-degree tiled incline at 4 $km \cdot h^{-1}$ is estimated to have a PO of 262 $kpm \cdot min^{-1}$ (43 watts); for the same conditions, but on a low-pile carpeted surface, 346 $kpm \cdot min^{-1}$ (57 watts).

*Arm crank and wheelchair ergometers.* Arm crank and wheelchair ergometers have been used in the laboratory to determine physiologic

FIGURE 5

*Composite summary of linear regression equations used for the prediction of power output requirements (kpm·min⁻¹) for wheelchair locmotion over given terrains.*

SOURCE: Glaser, R.M., S.R. Collins, and S.W. Wilde. Power output requirements for manual wheelchair locomotion. *Proc. IEEE National Aerospace and Electronics Conference.* New York: Inst. Electr. Electron. Eng., 2:507, 1980.

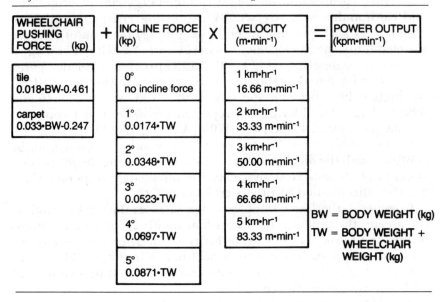

responses to these modes of exercise. Such devices allow for precise setting and maintenance of PO and can be used for progressive intensity exercise stress testing, exercise training programs, and comparative stress studies [73]. Arm crank exercise is typically accomplished by using commercial ergometers specifically designed for arm cranking, or by arm cranking of leg cycle ergometers. In contrast, most wheelchair ergometers have been specially constructed [21, 24, 26, 44, 58, 66, 68, 97, 138, 158].

Figure 6 illustrates a combination wheelchair–arm crank ergometer which has been constructed for use by disabled individuals [66]. This combination ergometer is basically an extension of the popular Monark bicycle ergometer. Wheelchair wheels are mounted on a solid steel axle supported by low friction ball bearings. A chain and sprockets couple this axle to the Monark flywheel. The arm crank unit is inserted into the seat support of the Monark by a solid steel bar secured by a bolt and clamp. A chain and sprockets also couple the arm crank to the flywheel. Standard gearing of the Monark is re-

FIGURE 6

*Combination wheelchair-arm crank ergometer: A. Electronic speedometer. B. Lengthened pendular arm. C. Expanded braking force scale.*
SOURCE: Glaser, R.M., M.N. Sawka, M.F. Brune, and S.W. Wilde. Physiological responses to maximal effort wheelchair and arm crank ergometry. *J. Appl. Physiol. Respirat. Environ. Exercise Physiol.* 48:1061, 1980.

tained, so that for each wheelchair wheel and arm crank revolution the flywheel travels 6 m. An electronic speedometer is observed by subjects to maintain the required velocity ($m \cdot min^{-1}$) of the Monark flywheel [61]. In addition, an electronic odometer (wheel revolution counter) allows calculation of the precise distance the flywheel travels over a period of time.

Because of the relatively low braking forces usually used for arm ergometry, the measuring scale is modified to increase its sensitivity. For this, the pendular arm was lightened by removing the weight, and lengthened with Plexiglas (the exact weight depends upon the braking force range desired). An expanded scale at the end of the pendular arm is calibrated by hanging known weights from the friction belt. A constant force of 0.035 kp is added to all braking force readings to account for the internal friction of the ergometer. PO for wheelchair or arm crank ergometry is calculated as follows:

PO ($kpm \cdot min^{-1}$) = braking force (kp)
$\times$ flywheel velocity ($m \cdot min^{-1}$)

PO in units of $kpm \cdot min^{-1}$ may be converted to units of watts by dividing by a factor of 6.12.

The wheelchair ergometer portion of this combination ergometer has been shown to have a high degree of validity (ability to simulate actual wheelchair locomotion) and reliability (test-retest repeatability) [59, 63]. More complex wheelchair ergometer designs may simulate actual wheelchair operation for various locomotive conditions to a higher degree [26, 44]. This would be desirable in wheelchair design studies. Treadmills which could accommodate wheelchairs have also been used for determining the stresses of this activity [13, 48, 81, 151]. For exercise stress testing, however, the ergometer illustrated in Figure 6 appears to be quite adequate.

With respect to wheelchair ergometry vs. arm crank ergometry for exercise stress testing and training of SCI individuals, the concept of specificity of exercise suggests that wheelchair ergometry would be the desired exercise mode [23, 52, 103, 104]. This should permit better evaluation of one's capability to operate a manual wheelchair, and be advantageous in training for improved wheelchair locomotive performance. It is interesting to note that both modes of ergometry have been reported to elicit similar peak $\dot{V}O_2$ values [66, 158, 159], and either mode of exercise may provide a valid estimation of an individual's aerobic energy potential for wheelchair-type exercise.

*Stress-Testing Protocols*
Stress testing with upper body exercise modes employs the same principles that have been established for lower body exercise modes. These tests are usually progressive with respect to exercise intensity (PO), and have well defined endpoints for termination. Stress testing protocols may be continuous or discontinuous and submaximal or maximal with respect to the stress at the termination of the test.

For SCI individuals, discontinuous tests of submaximal exercise intensities may be preferred [62, 65]. Such tests are relatively safe, and they provide information concerning physiologic responses to exercise levels which may actually be encountered during locomotive activity [62, 65]. For wheelchair ergometry, 5 watts appears to be a reasonable initial intensity, as this PO level is frequently encountered during actual locomotion [61]. Increments of 5–10 watts have been used for the PO progression, and maximal PO has been limited to 25–35 watts [62, 65, 69, 131]. This PO range may have to be modified for arm crank ergometry depending upon the purpose of the test and capability of the subjects since arm cranking tends to elicit lower physiologic responses than handrim stroking at given PO levels. Most protocols increase PO by keeping velocity constant and increasing the braking force of the ergometer. This is analogous to operating a wheelchair up inclines or on floor surfaces which offer high rolling resistance, such as carpets [61]. Other tests keep the braking force constant and increase the velocity of propulsion [158, 159]. Exercise bouts are usually 4–6 minutes in duration to permit steady state (or steady rate) conditions to be achieved, and rest periods between exercise bouts tend to be 5–10 minutes or more in duration [58, 62, 65, 68, 129, 131, 137, 161, 162]. Physiologic data are usually collected during the final minute of each exercise bout. Criteria for test termination are typically: (1) symptoms of cardiovascular or pulmonary abnormalities (e.g., chest discomfort, ECG changes, dyspnea); (2) physical exhaustion; (3) attainment of a predetermined heart rate (e.g., 80% of age adjusted max HR reserve); and (4) completion of the maximal PO level for the test [62]. For high-level SCI subjects, however, the HR criterion for test termination and fitness evaluation may not be usable because lack of intact sympathetic innervation to the heart would limit HR responses to exercise [53, 112].

For submaximal exercise testing, criteria for fitness have been based upon: (1) magnitude of physiologic responses at each PO level; and (2) maximal PO level achieved [62]. As stated previously, $\dot{V}O_2$ at given PO levels is indicative of aerobic energy expenditure and the efficiency for performing the task; $\dot{V}E$ and HR responses are indicative of the relative stress encountered. Thus, individuals exhibiting lower responses during exercise would be expected to be more fit and to possess greater metabolic and cardiopulmonary reserve (a given task is performed at a lower percentage of peak $\dot{V}O_2$ and max PO). When such data are collected from a large number of individuals, fitness norms for various populations can be established for comparison purposes [62]. Furthermore, if instrumentation for monitoring $\dot{V}O_2$ is unavailable, HR responses for given PO levels and the maximal PO level achieved can be used as indices of fitness [62]. It has been found that $\dot{V}O_2$ and HR are linear with respect to PO level for both wheelchair and arm crank ergometry [5, 62, 68, 82, 131, 152]. This is similar to leg ergometry findings. Also, $\dot{V}E$ tends to be linear at low PO levels, but becomes curvilinear at higher PO levels [62]. Because of the linear relationship of PO to HR and $\dot{V}O_2$ (in mid- to low-level SCI individuals), it is possible to predict peak $\dot{V}O_2$ and max PO from the submaximal data by extrapolating these variables to the point of maximal HR [130, 160]. For this, the maximal HR for the particular arm exercise may be 10–20 beats·min$^{-1}$ lower than for leg exercise, and maximal HR (as predicted by the formula 220 beats·min$^{-1}$ minus age in years) should be reduced by 10–20 beats·min$^{-1}$ for wheelchair and arm crank ergometry [130, 142, 160].

To determine actual, rather than predicted, peak $\dot{V}O_2$ and max PO during arm ergometry, the discontinuous submaximal exercise protocol (as described above) could be extended to a maximal exercise protocol by increasing the number of PO levels used. A drawback to such a maximal exercise testing protocol is the extensive time that may be required to complete the test. Also, the multiple exercise bouts could have fatiguing effects, and $\dot{V}O_2$ and PO values at maximal effort may be lower than for a shorter more direct testing protocol. Therefore, unless submaximal physiologic data are desired at several PO levels, continuous exercise protocols are desirable to obtain peak $\dot{V}O_2$ and max PO data. With continuous protocols for arm ergometry, the subject usually begins exercising at a relatively low PO level to serve as a warm-up. PO is then increased (by increasing braking force or velocity) by a certain increment every 1–2 minutes until maximal effort exercise is reached. By estimating fitness via submaximal pre-testing prior to maximal testing, the initial PO level and magnitude of PO increments can be adjusted for individual subjects so that the test could be completed in several minutes [12, 45, 47, 83, 91, 92, 112, 121, 157, 158].

## PHYSICAL FITNESS IMPROVEMENT FOR WHEELCHAIR-DEPENDENT INDIVIDUALS

### Need for Exercise Training
Elevated physiologic responses observed during wheelchair activity may be due in part to the users' lack of fitness for upper body exercise [48, 62, 65, 67, 167]. Upper body fatigue may discourage SCI individuals from wheelchair locomotion of sufficient intensity and duration to maintain muscular and cardiovascular fitness. This relative inactivity may subsequently lead to further decreases in exercise capability, compounding rehabilitation problems [67]. It has been stated that normal daily wheelchair activity may not be sufficient to train the cardiopulmonary system, and that supplemental arm exercise is necessary for fitness improvement [81, 91]. Therefore, it appears that wheelchair locomotion could become less stressful if one's fitness were increased through specific exercise programs [48, 67]. Indeed, well-trained wheelchair athletes (mean age = 25 years) are predicted to utilize less than 7 percent of their max PO and 18 percent of peak $\dot{V}O_2$ for wheelchair locomotion at 7 watts [108].

### Arm Exercise Modes
Both muscular strength and cardiopulmonary fitness development are desirable for wheelchair users. Strength training of the upper body musculature could be accomplished by high resistance, low-repetition exercise such as weight training [27, 40, 41, 112, 122]. Essentially the same equipment and protocols used for able-bodied individuals could be adapted for use by SCI individuals. For endurance training, arm crank ergometers have traditionally been used. Recently, wheelchair ergometers have also been used for this purpose. Since it has been found that both modes of ergometry elicit similar peak $\dot{V}O_2$ values [66, 158, 159], they may have similar effec-

tiveness in promoting cardiopulmonary fitness. However, as indicated in the previous section, the concept of exercise specificity suggests that an activity which more closely resembles wheelchair activity may be more advantageous to the wheelchair user [23, 52, 103, 104]. Therefore, wheelchair ergometer exercise training would probably be more effective in improving performance for actual wheelchair locomotion.

Whether training for strength or endurance gains, the principle of "overload" should be followed [8, 23, 52, 98, 103]. This is where exercise is carried out at an intensity (and/or duration) beyond that which is normally encountered during daily activities. As fitness increases, the exercise intensity (and duration) should be progressively increased until fitness goals are reached. Periodic exercise at the final level achieved should be used to maintain fitness or detraining will occur and fitness level will diminish [52, 103, 122, 146].

Although endurance type arm exercise has been reported to increase aerobic fitness because of higher posttraining peak $\dot{V}O_2$ values and improved cardiac performance [98, 108, 112, 121, 137], there are some doubts as to the effectiveness of arm exercise training in promoting high levels of aerobic fitness in comparison to leg exercise. This is because the relatively small muscle mass employed cannot increase the body's metabolic rate to sufficiently high levels for long enough durations for marked central training effects to take place [12, 14, 30, 48, 81, 91, 98, 135, 142, 148, 167]. Thus, most of the observed gains in performance for arm exercise may be due to peripheral adaptations (i.e., improved muscle blood flow and/or metabolic capability). This training is especially difficult for quadriplegic and other SCI individuals who lack upper body strength and have very low levels of physical fitness. For most SCI individuals, however, improvements in fitness as indicated by greater arm exercise performance and lower levels of physiologic responses for given exercise tasks can be expected with regular arm exercise [40, 41, 44]. Within limits, greater gains in fitness tend to be found for individuals who initiate training at relatively low fitness levels [67]. This may be due in part to habituation to the exercise mode, especially if it is unfamiliar to the individual [67].

There are certain precautions that should be taken with arm exercise training of SCI individuals to reduce risks that may be encountered. These risks include bladder distension reflexes (which could result in extreme hypertension), pressure sores, myocardial dysfunction, orthostatic reactions, and hypotension [32, 34, 91, 120]. Therefore, it is advisable to empty the bladder prior to exercise, and to relieve the pressure on body supporting skin areas at regular intervals [91]. It is also suggested that HR and blood pressure be monitored periodically [91]. If fainting occurs, the person should be quickly placed in a horizontal position [53, 91].

*Exercise Training Protocols*
Similar to exercise stress-testing protocols, arm exercise training protocols can be continuous or discontinuous. Since the primary purpose of most training on arm ergometers is to improve endurance type (aerobic) fitness, PO is adjusted to permit relatively long duration bouts of exercise without excessive fatigue. If anaerobic fitness training is desired, such as with wheelchair athletes who require sprinting ability, exercise bouts are shorter in duration but of higher intensity resulting in a marked accumulation of lactic acid in the blood [8, 23, 52, 103]. Most training protocols require exercise 2–5 times per week.

Exercise intensity is usually established by having participants exercise at a certain percentage of their maximal HR (aerobic training: 60–90% of max HR reserve, which usually corresponds to 50–85% of peak $VO_2$) as determined by stress testing [8, 52, 98, 103, 108, 121, 122]. In actuality, each individual usually requires several trials to achieve the appropriate intensity. As fitness improves with training, exercise intensity must be set higher to elicit the same target HR. Thus, changes in ergometer PO during the training program are almost automatic. The use of HR as the exercise intensity criterion enables participation by most individuals in training programs regardless of absolute fitness levels. As indicated previously, however, HR may not be a usable criterion for exercise stress in high-level SCI individuals.

Continuous training protocols usually consist of one exercise bout per session that is 15–60 minutes in duration [38, 44, 121, 137]. In contrast, discontinuous training protocols, which are commonly termed "interval training programs," consist of a series of relatively short duration exercise bouts separated by relief periods of similar duration. The intensity and duration of the exercise bouts, and the duration of the relief periods can be selected to train the desired energy source(s) (aerobic, anaerobic) for muscular activity [8, 52, 103]. Guidelines for construction of interval training programs for various modes of exercise have been thoroughly described [52]. For training of the aerobic system, exercise bouts and relief periods are typically 3–5 minutes in duration, with 3–4 repetitions per exercise session. For a greater anaerobic system training component, exercise bouts are shorter in durations (1–2 min) and more intense (HR may reach maximal). Relief periods are also shorter.

As a result of several weeks of arm exercise training by SCI and other lower limb disabled men, significantly higher peak $VO_2$ values have been reported [108, 112, 121]. Arm crank training for 20 weeks has resulted in a 19 percent increase in peak $\dot{V}O_2$ (1.88 to 2.23 L· min$^{-1}$) [121]; arm crank training in conjunction with weight training and medicine ball throwing for 7 weeks has resulted in an 11 percent increase in peak $\dot{V}O_2$ (1.88 to 2.09 L·min$^{-1}$) [112]; whereas wheelchair ergometer training of wheelchair basketball athletes for 10 weeks has resulted in a 26 percent increase in peak $\dot{V}O_2$ (2.19 to 2.76 L·min$^{-1}$) [108]. In addition, significant increases in max PO (as high as 31%) and max $\dot{V}E$ (as high as 32%) have been reported for arm exercise training programs for the disabled [91, 108, 112, 121]. The expected magnitude of fitness gain is influenced greatly by the particular disability and the initial fitness level of the participant. Following arm training, it has also been found that exercise at given submaximal PO levels elicits lower $\dot{V}O_2$, $\dot{V}E$, and HR values [65, 67, 98, 137]. This improved efficiency and lower cardiopulmonary stress could be due to cellular and circulatory adaptations of the upper body musculature which permit better blood perfusion; an increased extraction and utilization of $O_2$; improved cardiac function; or higher levels of skill for these forms of arm exercise [67, 98, 137].

More research is needed in this area to optimize arm exercise training protocols for wheelchair-dependent individuals and to determine physiologic mechanisms responsible for changes in performance.

## FUNCTIONAL ELECTRICAL STIMULATION OF PARALYZED MUSCLES

Recently, effort has been directed at restoring purposeful movement to paralyzed muscles via functional electrical stimulation (FES) [15, 110, 113]. As indicated earlier, with SCI, motor units of the paralyzed muscles are usually intact, but dormant, except for occasional spasms. Thus, if appropriate electrical signals are applied directly to the motoneurons with implanted electrodes or indirectly with skin-surface electrodes placed over motor points of the muscles, contractions can be stimulated. In effect, FES ignores the damaged CNS and controls paralyzed muscles by peripheral means. With damage to motor units ($\alpha$-motoneurons, neuromuscular junctions and skeletal muscle fibers), FES will not be effective. Three primary purposes of FES in rehabilitation are to permit (1) exercise training of paralyzed limbs, which may improve health and fitness; (2) accomplishment of skilled activities such as feeding and grooming oneself; and (3) improved locomotive capability through the use of paralyzed muscles.

*Exercise Training Via FES*
In the period following occurrence of muscle paralysis, disuse of the limb(s) usually results in muscle atrophy and bone demineralization.

Accompanying muscle atrophy are biochemical changes in slow twitch muscle fibers which shorten twitch duration and lower their resistance to fatigue when electrically stimulated to contract [111, 114, 115, 124, 126, 127]. Exercise training of paralyzed muscles using FES has been reported to increase their strength and endurance severalfold [78, 93, 114, 119]. Changes observed with FES exercise which may account for improved strength and endurance characteristics include muscle hypertrophy [111, 119, 124], conversion of fast to slow twitch muscle fibers [77, 111, 115, 127, 153], and increased levels of oxidative enzymes [77, 111, 115, 124, 126]. Other changes which may be beneficial to the health of SCI individuals include improved circulation [119], increased bone density [119], alleviation of muscle spasms [10, 94, 119], and improved cardiovascular stability [119]. Psychological benefits have also been suggested, including improved self-image [64, 78].

Although there may be health benefits for FES exercise of paralyzed muscles (which need to be substantiated by further research), the muscles remain paralyzed and no return of voluntary function has been reported. In contrast, however, FES exercise of incomplete SCI individuals, who are capable of weak voluntary movements, could possibly enable greater return of voluntary function by strengthening the afflicted muscles [78]. Thus, FES exercise training programs which induce strong contractions may promote training effects in muscles beyond those achieved with low levels of voluntary exercise. It is currently unknown whether FES exercise that is commenced shortly after SCI will alleviate much of the characteristic muscle atrophy and bone demineralization. If such exercise is effective, it potentially could result in greater return of skeletal muscle function in incomplete SCI individuals.

There is little information in the literature concerning protocols and procedures for safe and effective FES training of paralyzed muscles. Prior to the 1980s, most FES exercise studies simply involved application of stimulation to the muscles in periodic on-off patterns [37, 93, 114]. Either isometric contractions or dynamic contractions without external load resistance were employed [93, 114]. Although improvements in muscle performance of the hands and legs have been reported, recent studies which utilized well-known weight training principles in conjunction with FES techniques appear to provide more dramatic results [78, 119]. This has been demonstrated using FES-induced exercise of the quadriceps muscles with a closed loop (feedback) stimulator system [78, 119]. By adjusting the load imposed upon the muscles during knee extension and the number of repetitions, both strength and endurance can be gradually increased toward the desired endpoint goals [78, 119]. It is common for SCI individuals to lift loads in excess of 20 pounds for two sets of 20 repetitions each during FES exercise of the quadriceps muscles [78]. FES has also been used to permit paraplegics and quadriplegics to pedal a modified Monark bicycle ergometer [118, 119]. Prolonged exercise bouts on this device have been reported to markedly increase endurance capability of the paralyzed muscles. If FES exercise is discontinued for several weeks to months, however, most gains in muscle performance due to training are lost.

*Problems with FES exercise.* Although evidence is favorable that FES exercise can restore much strength and endurance to muscles which have been rendered useless by SCI, there are problems and potential hazards with this form of exercise. Some of these are quite basic to FES techniques, such as the type of electrodes and stimulation parameters to use [15, 19, 85, 110, 116]. Others, which are of more concern, relate to the physiologic adjustments of the body to this form of exercise [33, 60, 78, 136].

It would appear that direct stimulation of the motor nerves via implanted electrodes would be advantageous because of the low levels of stimulation required and the more precise control that can be achieved [37, 110]. However, such electrode placements require surgery or insertion by hypodermic needles. Unless the entire stimulator is implanted, electrode leads pass through the skin. This can result in greater risk of infection and eventual breakage of the leads. There is also the potential for damaging the nerves, and rejection of the foreign materials by body tissues [19, 37, 110].

Skin surface electrodes are easier and less traumatic to apply, but they cannot remain in place for prolonged periods of time as skin irritations can occur. Also, electrical conductivity between these electrodes and the skin tends to decrease with drying of the electrolyte. These electrodes are placed over motor points (in close proximity to where motor nerves enter the muscles), where the threshold for stimulation is lowest. However, high current levels of stimulation are required during strong contractions (because of the recruitment of many fibers) which may cause electrode burns to the skin [78, 110]. Also, this type of stimulation is not precise as both efferent and afferent neurons in the vicinity of the electrodes can respond. This can result in unwanted contractions, spinal cord reflex activity, and the perception of pain if sensory pathways in the spinal cord are functional.

When using FES exercise with the spinal cord injured, care must be taken not to damage weakened bones and joints. It appears possible to develop strength quite rapidly; therefore, muscle contractions can become stronger than the bones and joints can withstand [78]. Protocols which employ smooth dynamic contractions with gradual load weight progressions may be safer than forceful isometric contractions. Also, in comparison to isometric contractions, dynamic contractions may result in performance gains throughout the range of motion, enhanced circulation in active muscles, and lower arterial blood pressure responses [8, 102, 150].

Another concern with FES exercise is that organ system adjustments which normally accompany voluntary exercise may not occur to the same extent [33, 60, 78, 101, 136]. This is because of the peripheral nature of the stimulation and the loss of some or all of the ANS sympathetic division outflow in SCI [36, 53, 91]. Thus, maximal aerobic metabolism and performance may be limited by lack of sufficient blood and $O_2$ to the exercising muscles, and failure to adequately remove metabolic end products. This is evidenced by lack of HR and cardiac output responses with increases in $\dot{V}O_2$ as exercise load is increased [33, 60, 78, 101, 136, 144]. However, $\dot{V}E$ appears to be well regulated with respect to $\dot{V}O_2$ levels [33, 60, 78, 136, 144]. This suggests the predominance of humoral rather than neurogenic control of $\dot{V}E$ during this exercise. Thus, increases in $\dot{V}O_2$ appear to be supported mostly by increases in $O_2$ extraction from the blood rather than the delivery of additional blood to the exercising muscles [136]. Since voluntary arm exercise in most SCI individuals elicits cardiovascular response patterns similar to those seen for able-bodied individuals (increased HR and cardiac output with increased $\dot{V}O_2$), combinations of voluntary arm exercise and FES leg exercise may be advantageous. It has been shown that this hybrid exercise can improve performance of the FES stimulated paralyzed muscles which may be due to enhanced sympathetic stimulation and cardiovascular adjustments [144]. It seems feasible that such an exercise combination could also result in better aerobic conditioning than for FES leg or voluntary arm exercise alone because of the larger muscle mass involved and the greater peak $\dot{V}O_2$ achieved [144].

Additionally, a pilot study indicated that knee extension FES exercise performed by paralyzed individuals is inefficient when compared to able-bodied individuals performing the same exercise voluntarily [60]. Indeed, for similar $\dot{V}O_2$ levels, 40 pounds could be lifted for voluntary exercise compared to 20 pounds for FES exercise [60]. This inefficiency for FES exercise may be due to stimulation of inappropriate muscle fibers (recruitment order), inappropriate stimulation pattern, muscle biochemical changes with long-term paralysis, and reflex activity [60]. It should be realized that there is a potential danger of overheating the active muscles with FES exercise because normal thermoregulatory mechanisms (alterations in blood flow patterns and sweating) may not be operative [78]. Furthermore, in some high-level SCI subjects, blood pressure may become excessive (higher than 175 mmHg) because of dysreflexia after only a few FES-induced contractions of the quadriceps muscles [78]. Such occurrences put the subjects at risk, and exercise should be discontinued. Therefore, it is recommended that blood pressure be monitored periodically, at least during initial FES exercise sessions.

*Locomotion by FES.* FES has been used to perform rudimentary tasks to assist in ambulation [20, 88, 95, 100, 154]. Recent demonstrations of FES-assisted walking of SCI individuals (using the aid of parallel bars, walkers, counter weights, or technicians for support) have raised considerable hope that scientists are close to a solution that would permit free walking of SCI individuals by FES of paralyzed muscles. In actuality, there are numerous and enormous problems involved. Despite advances in computer technology, this is not likely to occur for some time. Some of the physiologic, medical, and engineering problems that need to be addressed are: (1) adequate fitness of muscles, bones, and joints, as well as the cardiopulmonary system; (2) fine control and coordination of multiple muscles; (3) obtaining necessary motor (efferent) and sensory (afferent) signals for regulating limb position and maintaining posture and equilibrium; (4) providing sensations of touch, pressure, and pain in the paralyzed limbs; (5) adjustments of organ systems to support metabolic demands; and (6) miniaturization and implantation of required electronic circuits [64, 110].

Because of these extensive problems in using paralyzed muscles for walking, an intermediate system has been developed to permit locomotion by electrically stimulated paralyzed muscles—in a sitting position [64]. For this purpose, a leg-propelled vehicle (LPV) has been developed. The LPV basically consists of a wheelchair that has been modified by the addition of movable footrests and a drive system that permits propulsion via back and forth movements of the electrically stimulated paralyzed legs. Thus, this device can potentially alleviate many of the problems associated with conventional arm-propelled wheelchairs, while helping to develop and maintain fitness of the paralyzed legs [64]. In some cases, the LPV may even serve as a substitute for motorized wheelchairs. Here, paralyzed muscles would take the place of the electric motor, and metabolism would provide the energy instead of a battery.

## SPORTS PARTICIPATION

Opportunities for the disabled to participate in sports are increasing rapidly. Many local, national, and international organizations for the disabled provide olympic-type games with sporting events that are adapted for the physical capabilities of participants. In attempts to allow evenly matched competition in sporting events for the spinal cord injured, several classification systems have arisen. The International System, which was originated for use in the International Stoke-Mandeville Games (currently named the Olympics for the Physically Disabled), and the system used by the National Wheelchair Athletic Association (NWAA) are frequently employed [1, 28, 35, 86, 159]. Both classification systems are quite similar in that they use six major classes, I–VI, which are divided by the level of SCI and remaining muscle function (IA being the highest level of injury with severe loss of muscle function, and VI being the lowest level of injury with minimal loss of muscle function). Figure 7 provides specific details of the NWAA medical classification system. Peak $\dot{V}O_2$ of wheelchair athletes during arm crank [159] and wheelchair ergometer [36, 159] exercise was shown to be directly related to the functional muscle mass available. Table 1 provides peak $\dot{V}O_2$ values obtained from wheelchair athletes with mid to lower level (below T5) SCI, who would be in classes III, IV, and V.

Depending on interest, motivation, and physical capability, simple or complex modifications of rules and equipment can enable SCI athletes to participate in almost all sports (e.g., basketball, marathon racing, track and field, and swimming) [1, 2, 35, 76, 79, 80, 86, 109, 133]. Thus, the popularity of sports participation by the physically disabled is increasing. For example, there are currently more than 130 teams in the National Wheelchair Basketball Association playing in 22 conferences [28]. Additionally, the United States Olympic Committee now has a subcommittee on the disabled (the Disabled in Sports Committee) which represents the National Wheelchair Athletic Association as well as other groups [2]. Improving media coverage of the achievements of SCI individuals has done much to bolster support and participation in athletic programs.

The Boston Marathon has done much to illustrate the achievements and contributions of SCI individuals to athletics [35]. In 1978, George Murray became the first wheelchair athlete to beat all runners with a time of 2:26:52. The current male and female records for wheelchair athletes were set in 1983 by Jim Knaub (1:47:10) and Candace Cable (2:12:43). Major international competition for SCI athletes in 1984 included the Seventh World Wheelchair Games which were held at the Stoke-Mandeville Sports Stadium in Aylesbury, England, and the Games of the XXIIIrd Olympiad which were held in Los Angeles.

The benefits of sports participation for SCI individuals are psychosocial, as well as physiological. The physical well-being and sense of accomplishment help alleviate the depression which commonly accompanies SCI [28, 76, 109, 112, 155]. Sports participation is a

**FIGURE 7**
*The National Wheelchair Athletic Association medical classification system for spinal cord injured athletes.*
SOURCE: National Wheelchair Athletic Association.

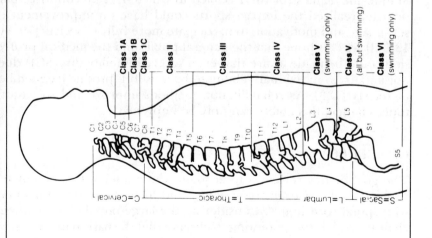

**Class 1A**

All cervical lesions with complete or incomplete quadriplegia who have involvement of both hands, weakness of triceps (up to and including grade 3 on testing scale) and with severe weakness of the trunk and lower extremities interfering significantly with trunk balance and the ability to walk

**Class 1B**

All cervical lesions with complete or incomplete quadriplegia who have involvement of upper extremities but less than 1A with preservation of normal or good triceps (4 or 5 on testing scale) and with a generalized weakness of the trunk and lower extremities interfering significantly with trunk balance and the ability to walk

**Class 1C**

All cervical lesions with complete or incomplete quadriplegia who have involvement of upper extremities but less than 1B with preservation of normal or good triceps (4 or 5 on testing scale) and normal or good finger flexion and extension (grasp and release) but without intrinsic hand function and with a generalized weakness of the trunk and lower extremities interfering significantly with trunk balance and the ability to walk

**Class II**

Complete or incomplete paraplegia below T1 down to and including T5 or comparable disability with total abdominal paralysis or poor abdominal muscle strength (0-2 on testing scale) and no useful trunk sitting balance

**Class III**

Complete or incomplete paraplegia or comparable disability below T5 down to and including T10 with upper abdominal and spinal extensor musculature sufficient to provide some element of trunk sitting balance but not normal

**Class IV**

Complete or incomplete paraplegia or comparable disability below T10 down to and including T12 without quadriceps or very weak quadriceps with a value up to and including 2 on the testing scale and gluteal paralysis

**Class V**

Complete or incomplete paraplegia or comparable disability below L2 with quadriceps in grades 3-5

**For Swimming Events Only**

**Class VI**

Complete or incomplete paraplegia or comparable disability below L2.

Class 1A
Class 1B
Class 1C

Class II

Class III

Class IV

Class V
(swimming only)

Class V
(all but swimming)

Class VI
(swimming only)

C1 C2 C3 C4 C5 C6 C7
T1 T2 T3 T4 T5 T6 T7 T8 T9 T10 T11 T12
L1 L2 L3 L4 L5
S1
S5

C=Cervical
T=Thoracic
L=Lumbar
S=Sacral

TABLE 1

*Peak $\dot{V}O_2$ data obtained from male wheelchair athletes during maximal effort arm exercise. Subjects were generally mid to lower level spinal cord injured paraplegics which would be in classes III, IV, or V of the International or National Wheelchair Athletic Association Classification systems. Where given, data from subjects in classes III, IV, and V were averaged because of similarities in peak $\dot{V}O_2$ values.*

| Reference | Exercise Mode | Peak $\dot{V}O_2$ (L· min$^{-1}$) | Peak $\dot{V}O_2$ (ml· kg$^{-1}$·min$^{-1}$) |
|---|---|---|---|
| Zwiren and Bar-Or [167] | arm crank ergometry | 2.07 | 35 |
| Wicks et al. [159] | arm crank ergometry | 2.04 | 32 |
| Wicks et al. [159] | wheelchair ergometry | 2.08 | 32 |
| Skrinar et al. [138] | wheelchair ergometry | 2.48 | 38 |
| Coutts et al. [36] | wheelchair ergometry | 2.10 | 31 |
| Miles et al. [108] | wheelchair ergometry | 2.19* | 31* |
| Miles et al. [108] | wheelchair ergometry | 2.76† | 39† |
| Gass and Camp [55] | wheelchair on treadmill | 2.04 | 34 |

*Pretrained.
†Posttrained.

great outlet for emotional stress, and offers relief from boredom, thus contributing to a fuller, more personally productive lifestyle. The late Sir Ludwig Guttmann, founder of the International Stoke-Mandeville Games for the Disabled in which over 20 countries participate, realized the impact sports could have on improvement of self-image and motivation to participate more fully in society [79, 80, 133]. It was his hope that the general public and the medical profession could be made aware that even severe disability (like SCI) does not impair an individual's ability to be a useful, productive member of society [133]. As rehabilitation methods improve and social attitudes change, this ability can only be improved.

## CONCLUSION

The goal of this review is to acquaint the reader with some of the problems related to exercise ability and locomotion for individuals with spinal cord injury. Considering the large population of wheelchair users, it is disappointing to observe that the basic handrim drive system of commonly prescribed wheelchairs has not been changed in over 100 years [90], despite the inefficiency and stressfulness of this form of locomotion. It is also of concern that the physical fitness of many wheelchair-dependent individuals is extremely low despite their apparent capacity to improve fitness through exercise. Although research in these areas has markedly increased over the past 15 years, much more work involving interactions among exercise scientists, health care professionals, and engineers needs to be accomplished. This would lead to innovative methods of rehabilitation which would improve the quality of life for SCI individuals.

## REFERENCES

1. Adams, R.C., A.N. Daniel, and L. Rullman. *Games, Sports and Exercises for the Physically Handicapped.* Philadelphia: Lea and Febiger, 1981.
2. American Academy of Orthopedic Surgeons. *Proceedings of the Winter Park Seminar.* Winter Park, Colorado, 1983.
3. American College of Sports Medicine. *Guidelines for Graded Exercise Testing and Exercise Prescription.* Philadelphia: Lea and Febiger, 1980.
4. American College of Sports Medicine. The recommended quantity and quality of exercise for developing and maintaining fitness in healthy adults. *Med. Sci. Sports* 10:VII–X, 1978.
5. Asmussen, E., and I. Hemmingsen. Determination of maximum working capacity at different ages in work with the legs or with the arms. *Scand. J. Clin. Lab. Invest.* 10:67–71, 1958.
6. Åstrand, I., P.-O. Åstrand, I. Hallbäck, and Å. Kilbom. Reduction in maximal oxygen uptake with age. *J. Appl. Physiol.* 35:649–654, 1973.
7. Åstrand, P.-O., B. Ekblom, R. Messin, B. Saltin, and J. Stenberg. Intra-arterial blood pressure during exercise with different muscle groups. *J. Appl. Physiol.* 20:253–256, 1965.
8. Åstrand, P.-O., and K. Rodahl. *Textbook of Work Physiology.* New York: McGraw-Hill, 1977.
9. Åstrand, P.-O., and B. Saltin. Maximal oxygen uptake and heart rate in various types of muscular activity. *J. Appl. Physiol.* 16:977–981, 1961.
10. Baker, L.L., C.Y. Ma, D. Wilson, and R.L. Waters. Electrical stimulation of wrist and fingers for hemiplegic patients. *Phys. Ther.* 59:1495–1499, 1979.
11. Bar-Or, O. Arm ergometry vs treadmill running and bicycle riding—submaximal and maximal exercise in men with different conditioning levels. *Proceedings: The 3rd International Ergometry Seminar:* Berlin: Springer, 1972, pp. 123–124.
12. Bar-Or, O., and L.D. Zwiren. Maximal oxygen consumption test during arm exercise—reliability and validity. *J. Appl. Physiol.* 38:424–426. 1975.
13. Bennedik, K., P. Engel, and G. Hildebrandt. *Der Rollstuhl: experimentelle Grundlagen zur technischen und ergometrischen Beuteilung handbetriebener Krankenfahrzeuge.* Rheinstetten: Schindele-Verlag, 1978.
14. Bergh, U., I.-L. Kanstrup, and B. Ekblom. Maximal oxygen uptake during exercise with various combinations of arm and leg work. *J. Appl. Physiol.* 41:191–196, 1976.
15. Benton, L.A., L.L. Baker, B.R. Bowman, and R.L. Waters. *Functional Electrical Stimulation: A Practical Clinical Guide.* Downey, Calif.: Professional Staff Association of the Rancho Los Amigos Hospital, 1981.
16. Bevegård, S., U. Freyschuss, and T. Strandell. Circulatory adaptation to arm and leg exercise in supine and sitting position. *J. Appl. Physiol.* 21:37–46, 1966.

17. Blessey, R.L., H.J. Hislop, R.L. Waters, and D. Antonelli. Metabolic energy cost of unrestrained walking. *Phys. Ther.* 56:1019–1024, 1976.

18. Bobbert, A.C. Physiological comparison of three types of ergometry. *J. Appl. Physiol.* 15:1007–1014, 1960.

19. Bowman, B.R. Acute and chronic implantation of coiled wire intraneural electrodes. *Proc. Sixth Annual Conference on Rehabilitation Engineering.* Bethesda: Rehabilitation Engineering Society of North America, 1983, pp. 69–71.

20. Brandell, B.R. Development of a universal control unit for functional electrical stimulation (FES). *Am J. Phys. Med.* 61:279–301, 1982.

21. Brattgård, S.-O., G. Grimby, and O. Höök. Energy expenditure and heart rate in driving a wheel-chair ergometer. *Scand. J. Rehabil. Med.* 2:143–148, 1970.

22. Brauer, R.L. An ergonomic analysis of wheelchair wheeling. Ph.D. dissertation, University of Illinois, 1972.

23. Brooks, G.A., and T.D. Fahey. *Exercise Physiology: Human Bioenergetics and Its Applications.* New York: John Wiley and Sons, 1984.

24. Brouha, L., and H. Krobath. Continuous recording of cardiac and respiratory functions in normal and handicapped people. *Hum. Factors* 9:567–572, 1967.

25. Bruce, D.A., L. Schut, and L.N. Sutton. Brain and cervical spine injuries occurring during organized sports activities in children and adolescents. *Primary Care* 11:175–194, 1984.

26. Brubaker, C., J. Wood, J. Gibson, and T. Soos. Wheelchair propulsion studies. In *Rehabilitation Engineering.* W.G. Stamp and C.A. McLaurin, eds. Charlottesville: University of Virginia, 1979, pp. 1–7.

27. Chawla, J.C., C. Bar, I. Creber, J. Price, and B. Andrews. Techniques for improving strength and fitness of spinal injured patients. *Paraplegia* 17:185–189, 1979–80.

28. Clark, M.W. Competitive sports for the disabled. *Am. J. Sports Med.* 8:366–369, 1980.

29. Clarke, K.S. Caloric costs of activity in paraplegic persons. *Arch. Phys. Med. Rehabil.* 47:427–435, 1966.

30. Clausen, J.P., K. Klausen, B. Rasmussen, and J. Trap-Jensen. Central and peripheral circulatory changes after training of the arms or legs. *Am. J. Physiol.* 225:675–682, 1973.

31. Clinkingbeard, J.R., J.W. Gersten, and D. Hoehn. Energy cost of ambulation in the traumatic paraplegic. *Am. J. Phys. Med.* 43:157–165, 1964.

32. Cole, T.M., F.J. Kottke, M. Olson, L. Stradal, and J. Niederloh. Alterations of cardiovascular control in high spinal myelomalacia. *Arch. Phys. Med. Rehabil.* 359–368, 1967.

33. Collins, S.R., R.M. Glaser, and S.D. Feinberg. Electrically induced exercise of paralyzed leg muscles: metabolic and cardiopulmonary responses (Abstract). *Physiologist* 26:1172, 1983.

34. Corbett, J.L., H.L. Frankel, and P.J. Harris. Cardiovascular reflexes in tetraplegia. *Paraplegia* 9:113–119, 1971.

35. Corcoran, P.J., R.F. Goldman, E.F. Hoerner, C. Kling, H.G. Knuttgen, B. Marquis, B.C. McCann, and A.B. Rossier. Sports medicine and the physiology of wheelchair marathon racing. *Orthop. Clin. North Am.* 11:697–716, 1980.

36. Coutts, K.D., E.C. Rhodes, and D.C. McKenzie. Maximal exercise responses of tetraplegics and paraplegics. *J. Appl. Physiol. Respirat. Environ. Exercise Physiol.* 55:479–482, 1983.

37. Crago, P.E., P.H. Peckham, J.T. Mortimer, and J.P. Van Der Meulen. The choice of pulse duration for chronic electrical stimulation via surface, nerve, and intramuscular electrodes. *Ann. Biomed. Eng.* 2:252–264, 1974.

38. Cross, D.L. The influence of physical fitness training as a rehabilitation tool. *Int. J. Rehabil. Res.* 3:163–175, 1980.

39. Cunningham, D.A., P.A. Rechnitzer, M.E. Pearce, and A.P. Donner. Determinants of self-selected walking pace across ages 19 to 66. *J. Gerontol.* 37:560–564, 1982.

40. Davis, G.M., P.R. Kofsky, J.C. Kelsey, and R.J. Shephard. Cardio-respiratory fitness and muscular strength of wheelchair users. *Can. Med. Assoc. J.* 125:1317–1323, 1981.

41. Davis, G.M., R.J. Shephard, and R.W. Jackson. Cardio-respiratory fitness and muscular strength in the lower limb disabled. *Can. J. Appl. Spt. Sci.* 6:159–165, 1981.

42. Dickinson, S. The efficiency of bicycle-pedalling, as affected by speed and load. *J. Physiol. (Lond.)* 67:242–255, 1929.

43. Donovan, C.M., and G.A. Brooks. Muscular efficiency during steady-rate exercise II. Effects of walking speed and work rate. *J. Appl. Physiol. Respirat. Environ. Exercise Physiol.* 43:431–439, 1977.

44. Dreisinger, T.E., and B.R. Londeree. Wheelchair exercise: A Review. *Paraplegia* 20:20–34, 1982.

45. Ekblom, B., and Å. Lundberg. Effect of physical training on adolescents with severe motor handicaps. *Acta Paediatr. Scand.* 57:17–23, 1968.

46. Elder, G.C.B., K. Bradbury, and R. Roberts. Variability of fiber type distributions within human muscles. *J. Appl. Physiol. Respirat. Environ. Exercise Physiol.* 53:1473–1480, 1982.

47. Emes, C. Physical work capacity of wheelchair athletes. *Res. Q. Am. Assoc. Health Phys. Educ. Recreat.* 48:209–212, 1977.

48. Engel, P., and G. Hildebrandt. Long-term spiroergometric studies of paraplegics during the clinical period of rehabilitation. *Paraplegia* 11:105–110, 1973.

49. Engel, P., and G. Hildebrandt. Wheelchair design—technological and physiological aspects. *Proc. R. Soc. Med.* 67:409–413, 1974.

50. Fichtenbaum, B.M., R.M. Glaser, J.S. Petrofsky, E. Peizer, and D.W. Wright. Physiological evaluation of a stand-up manual wheelchair. *Proc. IEEE National Aerospace and Electronics Conference.* New York: Inst. Electr. Electron. Eng. 1:186–193, 1982.

51. Fisher, S.V., and G. Gullickson, J. Energy cost of ambulation in health and disability: A literature review. *Arch. Phys. Med. Rehabil.* 59:124–133, 1978.

52. Fox, E.L., and D.K. Mathews. *Interval Training: Conditioning for Sports and General Fitness.* Philadephia: W.B. Saunders, 1974.

53. Freyschuss, U., and E. Knuttson. Cardiovascular control in man with transverse cervical cord lesions. *Life Sci.* 8:421–424, 1969.

54. Gaesser, G.A., and G.A. Brooks. Muscular efficiency during steady-rate exercise: Effects of speed and work rate. *J. Appl. Physiol.* 38:1132–1139, 1975.

55. Gass, G.C., and E.M. Camp. Physiological characteristics of trained Australian paraplegic and tetraplegic subjects. *Med. Sci. Sports* 11:256–259, 1979.

56. Gass, G.C., J. Watson, E.M. Camp, H.J. Court, L.M. McPherson, and P. Redhead. The effects of physical training on high level spinal lesion patients. *Scand. J. Rehabil. Med.* 12:61–65, 1980.

57. Gibbs, C.L., and W.R. Gibson. Energy production of rat soleus muscle. *Am. J. Physiol.* 223:864–871, 1972.

58. Glaser, R.M., S.A. Barr, L.L. Laubach, M.N. Sawka, and A.G. Suryaprasad. Relative stresses of wheelchair activity. *Hum. Factors* 22:177–181, 1980.

59. Glaser, R.M., and S.R. Collins. Validity of power output estimation for wheelchair locomotion. *Am. J. Phys. Med.* 60:180–189, 1981.

60. Glaser, R.M., S.R. Collins, and S.D. Feinberg. Electrically stimulated exercise of paralyzed muscles vs voluntary exercise: metabolic and cardiopulmonary responses (Abstract). *Proc. 9th International Congress of Physical Medicine & Rehabilitation,* 1984, p. 44.

61. Glaser, R.M., S.R. Collins, and S.W. Wilde. Power output requirements for manual wheelchair locomotion. *Proc. IEEE National Aerospace and Electronics Conference.* New York: Inst. Electr. Electron. Eng. 2:502–509, 1980.

62. Glaser, R.M., D.M. Foley, L.L. Laubach, M.N. Sawka, and A.G. Suryaprasad. An exercise test to evaluate fitness for wheelchair activity. *Paraplegia* 16:341–349, 1978–79.

63. Glaser, R.M., J.F. Ginger, and L.L. Laubach. Validity and reliability of wheelchair ergometry (Abstract). *Physiologist* 20:34, 1977.

64. Glaser, R.M., J.A. Gruner, S.D. Feinberg, and S.R. Collins. Locomotion via paralyzed leg muscles: Feasibility study for a leg-propelled vehicle. *J. Rehabil. R.D.* 20:87–92, 1983.

65. Glaser, R.M., L.L. Laubach, M.N. Sawka, and A.G. Suryaprasad. Exercise stress, fitness evaluation and training of wheelchair users. In *Proceedings—International Conference on Lifestyle and Health, 1978: Optimal Health and Fitness for People with Physical Disabilities.* A.S. Leon and G.J. Amundson, eds. Minneapolis: University of Minnesota Press, 1979, pp. 167–194.

66. Glaser, R.M., M.N. Sawka, M.F. Brune, and S.W. Wilde. Physiological responses to maximal effort wheelchair and arm crank ergometry. *J. Appl. Physiol. Respirat. Environ. Exercise Physiol.* 48:1060–1064, 1980.

67. Glaser, R.M., M.N. Sawka, R.J. Durbin, D.M. Foley, and A.G. Suryaprasad. Exercise program for wheelchair acticity. *Am. J. Phys. Med.* 60:67–75, 1981.

68. Glaser, R.M., M.N. Sawka, L.L. Laubach, and A.G. Suryaprasad. Metabolic and cardiopulmonary responses to wheelchair and bicycle ergometry. *J. Appl. Physiol. Respirat. Environ. Exercise Physiol.* 46:1066–1070, 1979.

69. Glaser, R.M., M.N. Sawka, and D.S. Miles. Efficiency of wheelchair and low power bicycle ergometry. *Proc. IEEE National Aerospace and Electronics Conference.* New York: Inst. Electr. Electron. Eng. 2:946–953, 1984.

70. Glaser, R.M., M.N. Sawka, S.W. Wilde, B.K. Woodrow, and A.G. Suryaprasad. Energy cost and cardiopulmonary responses for wheelchair locomotion and walking on tile and on carpet. *Paraplegia* 19:220–226, 1981.

71. Glaser, R.M., M.N. Sawka, R.E. Young, and A.G. Suryaprasad. Applied physiology for wheelchair design. *J. Appl. Physiol. Respirat. Environ. Exercise Physiol.* 48:41–44, 1980.

72. Glaser, R.M., C.A. Simsen-Harold, J.S. Petrofsky, S.E. Kahn, and A.G. Suryaprasad. Metabolic and cardiopulmonary responses of older wheelchair-dependent and ambulatory patients during locomotion. *Ergonomics* 26:687–697, 1983.

73. Glaser, R.M., A.G. Suryaprasad, M.N. Sawka, and B.M. Fichtenbaum. Methodology devised for a program to improve efficiency and reduce risks for wheelchair locomotion. *Bull. Prosth. Res.* 18:63–68, 1981.

74. Gordon, E.E. Physiological approach to ambulation in paraplegia. *JAMA* June 23, 1956. Pp. 686–688.

75. Gordon, E.E., and H. Vanderwalde. Energy requirements in paraplegic ambulation. *Arch. Phys. Med.* 37:276–285, 1956.

76. Grainger, D.H. Sport in the rehabilitation of the disabled. *Center Afr. J. Med.* 24:247–252, 1978.

77. Green, H.J., H. Reichmann, and D. Pette. Fiber type specific transformations in the enzyme activity pattern of rat vastus lateralis muscle by prolonged endurance training. *Pflügers Arch.* 399:216–222, 1983.

78. Gruner, J.A., R.M. Glaser, S.D. Feinberg, S.R. Collins, and N.S. Nussbaum. A system for evaluation and exercise-conditioning of paralyzed leg muscles. *J. Rehabil. R.D.* 20:21–30, 1983.

79. Guttmann, L. *Textbook of Sport for the Disabled.* Aylesbury, England: HM and M, 1976.

80. Guttmann, L. Reflection of the 1976 Toronto Olympiad for the physically disabled. *Paraplegia* 14:225–240, 1976.

81. Hildebrandt, G., E.-D. Voigt, D. Bahn, B. Berendes, and J. Kröger. Energy costs of propelling wheelchair at various speeds: Cardiac response and effect on steering accuracy. *Arch. Phys. Med. Rehabil.* 51:131–136, 1970.

82. Hjeltnes, N. Oxygen uptake and cardiac output in graded arm exercise in paraplegics with low level spinal lesions. *Scand. J. Rehabil. Med.* 9:107–113, 1977.

83. Huang, C.-T., A.B. McEachran, K.V. Kuhlemeier, M.J. DeVivo, and P.R. Fine. Prescriptive arm ergometry to optimize muscular endurance in acutely injured paraplegic patients. *Arch. Phys. Med. Rehabil.* 64:578–582, 1983.

84. Hultén, B., A. Thorstensson, B. Sjödin, and J. Karlsson. Relationship between isometric endurance and fibre types in human leg muscles. *Acta Physiol. Scand.* 93:135–138, 1975.

85. Hultman, E., H. Sjöholm, I. Jäderholm-Ek, and J. Krynicki. Evaluation of methods for electrical stimulation of human skeletal muscle in situ. *Pflügers Arch.* 398:139–141, 1983.

86. Jackson, R.W., and A. Fredrickson. Sports for the physically disabled: The 1976 Olympiad (Toronto). *Am. J. Sports Med.* 7:293–296, 1979.

87. Jackson, R.W., and G.M. Davis. The value of sports and recreation for the physically disabled. *Orthop. Clin. N.A.* 14:301–315, 1983.

88. Jaeger, R.J., and A. Kralj. Studies in functional electrical stimulation for standing and forward progression. *Proc. Sixth Annual Conference on Rehabilitation Engineering.* Bethesda: Rehabilitation Engineering Society of North America, 1983, pp. 75–77.

89. Johnson, M.A., J. Polgar, D. Weightman, and D. Appleton. Data on the distribution of fibre types in thirty-six human muscles: An autopsy study. *J. Neurol. Sci.* 18:111–129, 1973.

90. Kamenetz, H.L. *The Wheelchair Book.* Springfield, Ill.: Charles C Thomas, 1969.

91. Knutsson, E., E. Lewenhaupt-Olsson, and M. Thorsen. Physical work capacity and physical conditioning in paraplegic patients. *Paraplegia* 11:205–216, 1973.

92. Kofsky, P.R., G.M. Davis, R.J. Shephard, R.W. Jackson, and G.C.R. Keene. Field testing: Assessment of physical fitness of disabled adults. *Eur. J. Appl. Physiol.* 51:109–120, 1983.

93. Kralj, A., T. Bajd, and R. Turk. Electrical stimulation providing functional use of paraplegic patient muscles. *Med. Prog. Technol.* 7:3–9, 1980.

94. Kralj, A., T. Bajd, R. Turk, J. Krajnik, and H. Benko. Gait restoration in paraplegic patients: A feasibility study using multi-channel surface electrode FES. *J. Rehabil. R.D.* 20:3–20, 1983.

95. Kralj, A., and L. Vodovnik. Functional electrical stimulation of the extremities: Part 1. *J. Med. Eng. Technol.* 1:12–15, 1977.

96. Laubach, L.L., R.M. Glaser, and A.G. Suryaprasad. Anthropometry of aged male wheelchair-dependent patients. *Ann. Hum. Biol.* 8:25–29, 1981.

97. Lundberg, Å. Wheelchair driving: Evaluation of a new training outfit. *Scand. J. Rehab. Med.* 12:67–72, 1980.

98. Magel, J.R., W.D. McArdle, M. Toner, and D.J. Delio. Metabolic and cardiovascular adjustment to arm training. *J. Appl. Physiol. Respirat. Environ. Exercise Physiol.* 45:75–79, 1978.

99. Marinček, Č.R.T., and V. Valenčič. Arm cycloergometry and kinetics of oxygen consumption in paraplegics. *Paraplegia* 15:178–185, 1977–78.

100. Marsolais, E.B., R. Kobetic, G.F. Cochoff, and P.H. Peckham. Reciprocal walk-

ing in paraplegic patients using internal functional electrical stimulation. *Proc. Sixth Annual Conference on Rehabilitation Engineering*. Bethesda: Rehabilitation Engineering Society of North America, 1983, pp. 78–80.

101. May, K.P., R.M. Glaser, and J.R. Strayer. Central hemodynamic responses for electrically stimulated leg exercise of paralyzed individuals (Abstract). *Fed. Proc.* (In press), 1985.

102. McArdle, W.D., R.M. Glaser, and J.R. Magel. Metabolic and cardiorespiratory response during free swimming and treadmill walking. *J. Appl. Physiol.* 30:733–738, 1971.

103. McArdle, W., F. Katch, and V. Katch. *Exercise Physiology: Energy, Nutrition, and Human Performance*. Philadelphia: Lea and Febiger, 1981.

104. McCafferty, W.R., and S.M. Horvath. Specificity of exercise and specificity of training: a subcellular response. *Res. Q. Am. Assoc. Health Phys. Educ. Recreat.* 48:358–371, 1977.

105. McComas, A.J., and H.C. Thomas. Fast and slow twitch muscles in man. *J. Neurol. Sci.* 7:301–307, 1968.

106. Miles, D.S., M.N. Sawka, S.W. Wilde, B.M. Doerr, M.A.B. Frey, and R.M. Glaser. Estimation of cardiac output by electrical impedance during arm exercise in women. *J. Appl. Physiol. Respirat. Environ. Exercise Physiol.* 51:1488–1492, 1981.

107. Miles, D.S., M.N. Sawka, R.M. Glaser, S.W. Wilde, B.M. Doerr, and M.A.B. Frey. Assessment of central hemodynamics during arm-crank exercise. *Proc. IEEE National Electronics and Aerospace Conference*. New York: Inst. Electr. Electron. Eng., 3:442–448, 1982.

108. Miles, D.S., M.N. Sawka, S.W. Wilde, R.J. Durbin, R.W. Gotshall, and R.M. Glaser. Pulmonary function changes in wheelchair athletes subsequent to exercise training. *Ergonomics* 25:239–246, 1982.

109. Molnar, G. Rehabilitative benefits of sports for the handicapped. *Conn. Med.* 45:574–577, 1981.

110. Mortimer, J.T. Motor Prostheses. In *Handbook of Physiology: The Nervous System II*. J.M. Brookhart, V.B. Mountcastle, V.B. Brooks, and S.R. Geiger, eds. Bethesda, Md.: American Physiological Society, 155–187, 1981.

111. Munsat, T.L., D. McNeal, and R. Waters. Effects of nerve stimulation on human muscle. *Arch. Neurol.* 33:608–617, 1976.

112. Nilsson, S., P.H. Staff, and E.D.R. Pruett. Physical work capacity and the effect of training on subjects with long-standing paraplegia. *Scand. J. Rehabil. Med.* 7:51–56, 1975.

113. Peckham, P.H., E.B. Marsolais, and J.T. Mortimer. Restoration of key grip and release in the C6 tetraplegic patient through functional electrical stimulation. *J. Hand Surg.* 5:462–469, 1980.

114. Peckham, P.H., J.T. Mortimer, and E.B. Marsolais. Alteration in the force and fatigability of skeletal muscle in quadriplegic humans following exercise induced by chronic electrical stimulation. *Clin. Orthop. Rel. Res.* 114:326–334, 1976.

115. Peckham, P.H., J.T. Mortimer, and J.P. Van Der Meulen. Physiologic and metabolic changes in white muscle of cat following induced exercise. *Brain Res.* 50:424–429, 1973.

116. Peckham, P.H., J.P. Van Der Meulen, and J.B. Reswick. Electrical activation of skeletal muscle by sequential stimulation. In *The Nervous System and Electrical Currents*. N. Wulfson and A. Sances, Jr., eds. New York: Plenum, 1970, pp. 45–50.

117. Peizer, E., D. Wright, and H. Freiberger. Bioengineering methods of wheelchair evaluation. *Bull. Prosth. Res.* 1:77–100, 1964.

118. Petrofsky, J.S., R.M. Glaser, C.A. Phillips, and J.A. Gruner. The effect of electrically induced bicycle ergometer exercise on blood pressure and heart rate. *Physiologist* 25:253, 1982.

119. Petrofsky, J.S., and C.A. Phillips. Active physical therapy: A modern approach to rehabilitation therapy. *J. Neurol. Orthop. Surg.* 4:165–173, 1983.
120. Pierce, D.S., and V.H. Nickel. *The Total Care of Spinal Cord Injuries.* Boston: Little, Brown, 1977.
121. Pollock, M.L., H.S. Miller, A.C. Linnerud, E. Laughridge, E. Coleman, and E. Alexander. Arm pedaling as an endurance training regimen for the disabled. *Arch. Phys. Med. Rehabil.* 55:418–424, 1974.
122. Pollock, M.L., J.H. Wilmore, and S.M. Fox. *Exercise in Health and Disease: Evaluation and Prescription for Prevention and Rehabilitation.* Philadelphia: W.B. Saunders, 1984.
123. Ralston, H.J. Energy-speed relation and optimal speed during level walking. *Int. Z. Angew. Physiol.* 17:277–283, 1958.
124. Reddanna, P., C.V.N. Moorthy, and S. Govindappa. Pattern of skeletal muscle chemical composition during *in vivo* electrical stimulations. *Indian J. Physiol. Pharmacol.* 25:33–39, 1981.
125. Reybrouck, T., G.F. Heigenhauser, and J.A. Faulkner. Limitations to maximum oxygen uptake in arm, leg, and combined arm-leg ergometry. *J. Appl. Physiol.* 38:774–779, 1975.
126. Riley, D.A., and E.F. Allin. The effects of inactivity, programmed stimulation and denervation on the histochemistry of skeletal muscle fiber types. *Exp. Neurol.* 40:391–413, 1973.
127. Salmons, S., and G. Vrbova. The influence of activity on some contractile characteristics of mammalian fast and slow muscles. *J. Physiol.* 201:535–549, 1969.
128. Sawka, M.N., M.E. Foley, M.M. Pimental, N.A. Toner, and K.B. Pandolf. Determination of maximal aerobic power during upper body exercise. *J. Appl. Physiol. Respirat. Environ. Exercise Physiol.* 54:113–117, 1983.
129. Sawka, M.N., R.M. Glaser, L.L. Laubach, O. Al-Samkari, and A.G. Suryaprasad. Wheelchair exercise performance of the young, middle-aged, and elderly. *J. Appl. Physiol. Respirat. Environ. Exercise Physiol.* 50:824–828, 1981.
130. Sawka, M.N., R.M. Glaser, S.W. Wilde, D.S. Miles, and A.G. Suryaprasad. Submaximal test to predict peak oxygen uptake for wheelchair exercise (Abstract). *Fed. Proc.* 39:287, 1980.
131. Sawka, M.N., R.M. Glaser, S.W. Wilde, and T.C. von Luhrte. Metabolic and circulatory responses to wheelchair and arm crank exercise. *J. Appl. Physiol. Respirat. Environ. Exercise Physiol.* 49:784–788, 1980.
132. Schwade, J., C.G. Bolmqvist, and W. Shapiro. A comparison of the response to arm and leg work in patients with ischemic heart disease. *Am. Heart J.* 94:203–208, 1977.
133. Scruton, J. Sir Ludwig Guttmann: Creator of a world sports movement for the paralysed and other disabled. *Paraplegia* 17:52–55, 1979.
134. Seabury, J.J., W.C. Adams, and M.R. Ramey. Influence of pedalling rate and power output on energy expenditure during bicycle ergometry. *Ergonomics* 20:491–498, 1977.
135. Secher, N.H., N.R. Larsen, R.A. Binkhorst, and F. Bonde-Petersen. Maximal oxygen uptake during arm cranking and combined arm plus leg exercise. *J. Appl. Physiol.* 36:515–518, 1974.
136. Sheldon, W.S., and R.M. Glaser. Cardiovascular and metabolic responses to isometric leg exercise performed voluntarily and via electrical stimulation (Abstract). *Physiologist* 27:260, 1984.
137. Simmons, R., and R.J. Shephard. Effects of physical conditioning upon the central and peripheral circulatory responses to arm work. *Int. Z. Angew. Physiol.* 30:73–84, 1971.
138. Skrinar, G.S., W.J. Evans, L.J. Ornstein, and D.A. Brown. Glycogen utilization in wheelchair-dependent athletes. *Int. J. Sports Med.* 3:215–219, 1982.

139. Smith, P.A., R.M. Glaser, J.S. Petrofsky, P.D. Underwood, G.B. Smith, and J.J. Richards. Arm crank vs handrim wheelchair propulsion: metabolic and cardiopulmonary responses. *Arch. Phys. Med. Rehabil.* 64:249–254, 1983.

140. Stanley, D.E. Physiological responses of geriatric patients to conventional and arm crank wheelchair propulsion. M.S. thesis, Wright State University, 1982.

141. Stauffer, E.S. Long-term management of traumatic quadriplegia. *The Total Care of Spinal Cord Injuries.* D.S. Pierce and V.H. Nickel, eds. Boston: Little, Brown, 1978, pp. 81–102.

142. Stenberg, J., P.-O. Åstrand, B. Ekblom, J. Royce, and B. Saltin. Hemodynamic response to work with different muscle groups, sitting and supine. *J. Appl. Physiol.* 22:61–70, 1967.

143. Stoboy, H., and B. Wilson-Rich. Muscle strength and electrical activity, heart rate and energy cost during isometric contractions in disabled and non-disabled. *Paraplegia* 8:217–222, 1971.

144. J.R. Strayer, R.M. Glaser, and K.P. May. Metabolic responses to voluntary arm and electrically stimulated leg exercise in spinal cord injured individuals (Abstract). *Fed. Proc.* (In press), 1985.

145. Susheela, A.K., and J.N. Walton. Note on the distribution of histochemical fibre types in some normal human muscles: A study on autopsy material. *J. Neurol. Sci.* 8:201–207, 1969.

146. Thorstensson, A. Observations on strength training and detraining. *Acta Physiol. Scand.* 100:491–493, 1977.

147. Thorstensson, A., and J. Karlsson. Fatiguability and fibre composition of human skeletal muscle. *Acta Physiol. Scand.* 98:318–322, 1976.

148. Toner, M.M., M.N. Sawka, L. Levine, and K.B. Pandolf. Cardiorespiratory responses to exercise distributed between the upper and lower body. *J. Appl. Physiol. Respirat. Environ. Exercise Physiol.* 54:1403–1407, 1983.

149. Traugh, G.H., P.J. Corcoran, and R.L. Reyes. Energy expenditure of ambulation in patients with above-knee amputations. *Arch. Phys. Med. Rehabil.* 56:67–71, 1975.

150. Tuttle, W., and S.M. Horvath. Comparison of effects of static and dynamic work on blood pressure and heart rate. *J. Appl. Physiol.* 10:294–296, 1957.

151. Voigt, E.-D., and D. Bahn. Metabolism and pulse rate in physically handicapped when propelling a wheelchair up an incline. *Scand. J. Rehabil. Med.* 1:101–106, 1969.

152. Vokac, Z., H. Bell, E. Bautz-Holter, and K. Rodahl. Oxygen uptake/heart rate relationship in leg and arm exercise, sitting and standing. *J. Appl. Physiol.* 39:54–59, 1975.

153. Vrbova, G. Factors determining the speed of contraction of striated muscle. *J. Physiol.* 185:17–18, 1966.

154. Waters, R., D.R. McNeal, and J. Perry. Experimental correction of footdrop by electrical stimulation of the peroneal nerve. *J. Bone Joint Surg. (Am.)* 57:1047–1054, 1975.

155. Weiss, M., and J. Beck. Sport as part of therapy and rehabilitation of paraplegics. *Paraplegia* 11:166–172, 1973.

156. Wendt, I.R., and C.L. Gibbs. Energy production of rat extensor digitorum longus muscle. *Am. J. Physiol.* 224:1081–1086, 1973.

157. Whiting, R.B., T.E. Dreisinger, and C. Abbott. Clinical value of exercise testing in handicapped subjects. *South. Med. J.* 76:1225–1227, 1983.

158. Wicks, J.R., K. Lymburner, S.M. Dinsdale, and N.L. Jones. The use of multistage exercise testing with wheelchair ergometry and arm cranking in subjects with spinal cord lesions. *Paraplegia* 15:252–261, 1977–78.

159. Wicks, J.R., N.B. Oldridge, B.J. Cameron, and N.L. Jones. Arm cranking and wheelchair ergometry in elite spinal cord-injured athletes. *Med. Sci. Sports Exercise* 15:224–231, 1983.
160. Wilde, S.W., R.M. Glaser, M.N. Sawka, D.S. Miles, and E.L. Fox. Prediction of peak oxygen uptake from submaximal arm crank exercise (Abstract). *Fed. Proc.* 39:289, 1980.
161. Wilde, S.W., D.S. Miles, R.J. Durbin, M.N. Sawka, A.G. Suryaprasad, R.W. Gotshall, and R.M. Glaser. Evaluation of myocardial performance during wheelchair ergometer exercise. *Am. J. Phys. Med.* 60:277–291, 1981.
162. Wolf, E., and A. Magora. Orthostatic and ergometric evaluation of cord-injured patients. *Scand. J. Rehabil. Med.* 8:93–96, 1976.
163. Wolfe, G.A., R. Waters, and H.J. Hislop. Influence of floor surface on energy costs of propelling wheelchair at various speeds: Cardiac response and effect on steering accuracy. *Arch. Phys. Med. Rehabil.* 51:131–136, 1970.
164. Wolfe, G.A., R. Waters, and H.J. Hislop. Influence of floor surface on the energy cost of wheelchair propulsion. *Phys. Ther.* 57:1022–1027, 1977.
165. Woodrow, B.K. Cardiopulmonary and metabolic responses for walking and wheelchair locomotion on different floor surfaces. M.S. thesis, Wright State University, 1979.
166. Young, J.S., P.E. Burns, A.M. Bowen, and R. McCutcheon. *Spinal Cord Injury Statistics: Experience of the Regional Spinal Cord Injury Systems.* Phoenix: Good Samaritan Medical Center, 1982.
167. Zwiren, L.D., and O. Bar-Or. Responses to exercise of paraplegics who differ in conditioning level. *Med. Sci. Sports* 7:94–98, 1975.

# Physical Conditioning in Children with Cardiorespiratory Disease

ODED BAR-OR, M.D., F.A.C.S.M.

Recent years have seen a surge of interest in the relevance of physical exertion to children's health. To the clinician the following questions are of interest: What are the physiologic and behavioral factors that limit the child's capacity to exercise? Is the child sufficiently active? Is physical conditioning beneficial to his health? Is exertion detrimental to his health? Can exercise be used as a diagnostic tool in pediatrics?

The purpose of this chapter is to review available information on the effects of physical conditioning and training on children with cardiorespiratory disease. Specific issues to be discussed include: trainability of these children, beneficial effects of chronic exercise to their health, and detrimental effects of acute or of chronic exercise. The latter issue is of particular relevance to the planning of intervention programs. Often, the real or implied detrimental effects of exertion may render the child inactive and unwilling to exert. Even those who do join a program may be reluctant to exert intensely, so that a training threshold may not be reached and their maximal ability cannot be assessed.

While data are accumulating on the effects of conditioning in children with cardiovascular or respiratory disease, this area of research is bound to develop slowly. Both methodological and ethical constraints limit one's freedom in designing intervention studies with these pediatric groups. First are the confounding effects of growth, maturation, and development which are common to healthy and sick children alike: physiologic changes known to take place with conditioning also occur during growth. These include, for example, a reduction in submaximal heart rate, pulmonary ventilation, and $O_2$ cost of locomotion and an increase in maximal $O_2$ uptake, ventilation, blood lactate, and sweating rate, as well as in strength, speed, and other fitness components.

Additional issues relate to the sick child with a cardiorespiratory disease. One is the selection of control subjects in an intervention study. Should these be patients with the same disease, patients with noncardiac, nonrespiratory disease, or healthy age-matched children who also undergo training? Another, perhaps more important, issue is that regarding the continuation or cessation of drug therapy. If

305

medication is continued, one may not be able to isolate the effects of conditioning *per se*. Discontinuation of therapy, on the other hand, may not be permitted for clinical or ethical reasons.

The study of detrimental effects of exertion—acute or chronic—involves ethical constraints, particularly when working with children. One is the need to exercise special precaution when studying, for example, the relationship between the occurrence of syncope and the intensity of exercise in advanced aortic stenosis or when evaluating the effects of exercise-induced dehydration on the child with cystic fibrosis.

These and other constraints are manifested in the quality of many of the intervention studies hitherto performed. Very few of these have conformed to the strict requirements of a randomized controlled trial. Others have neglected to include a proper control group, to quantify the conditioning regimen, to establish a blinding approach to medication, or to define the clinical severity of the disease. Any conclusions from such studies are therefore limited.

## RESPIRATORY DISEASES

### Bronchial Asthma

The effect of exertion on the child with bronchial asthma is twofold: while an acute bout of exercise may trigger bronchoconstriction (exercise-induced bronchoconstriction, EIB) and an overt asthmatic attack, physical conditioning may be beneficial.

*Response to acute exercise.* It is beyond the scope of this review to discuss in detail the etiology, epidemiology, mechanisms, and management of EIB. These are adequately reviewed elsewhere [3, 12, 57, 118, 138]. It is, however, important to realize that, when exposed to exercise of a sufficient intensity and to certain climatic conditions, any asthmatic patient may experience EIB. This has obvious implications for the habitual activity of many asthmatics who select a sedentary lifestyle to avoid such attacks. The presence or absence of EIB may also determine the attitude and motivation of the asthmatic to participate in training programs. It is therefore useful to recognize means, as outlined below, for the prevention and treatment of EIB.

MODIFICATION OF EXERCISE. The type, intensity, and duration of exercise often determine its asthmogenicity: swimming is less asthmogenic than running, walking, or cycling [2, 25, 47, 78], even at equal levels of ventilation [12, 16]; reduction of the exercise intensity diminishes the risk of EIB [60, 141, 163]; short-term exertion (30–60 seconds) is less asthmogenic than prolonged exertion [133, 141], unless the former is highly intense [77]. Following an exercise bout, subsequent exertion may not provoke EIB. The patient is said to be in a "refractory period" which may last 45 to 120 minutes. [18, 43, 69]. While the mechanism of this phenomenon is still debatable [5, 43, 69], it has a practical implication: EIB can be minimized by warming-up prior to an intense activity or by repeated sprints [133].

MEDICATION. EIB in most patients can be virtually prevented, or aborted, by the use of drugs [7, 58, 126]. The drugs with the highest efficacy for both prevention and postexertional termination of EIB are the β2-sympathomimetics, such as salbutamol, fenoterol, or terbutaline [4, 8, 58, 142, 143]. Salbutamol, the often-prescribed β2-sympathomimetic is especially active, and with few systemic side effects, when taken as aerosol [8, 50]. Disodium cromoglycate is also useful in prevention, but it cannot abort an attack once bronchoconstriction has started. Other preparations such as methylxanthines [10, 22], anticholinergics [127, 166], or calcium antagonist [28, 124] are also effective in some patients.

WARMING AND HUMIDIFICATION OF INSPIRED AIR. The bronchoconstrictive effect of exercise is strongly related to the degree of airway cooling during the activity [6, 11, 14, 26, 31, 40, 100, 144, 160]. Respiratory heat loss results from convective and, particularly, evaporative cooling by the inspired air. It is also related to minute ventilation. The degree of EIB can be reduced when nasal inhalation is substituted for oral or oronasal inhalation [101, 140, 170]. It is yet to be ascertained, however, if children with asthma can adopt nasal breathing during play and sports. Conditioning of the inspired air can also be achieved by the use of a facemask with effective protection against EIB [130]. Although epidemiologic evidence is not yet available, the prevalence of EIB will most likely be curtailed if children with asthma reduce the intensity and duration of exercise in cold or dry weather.

*Physical conditioning in bronchial asthma.* Two issues have been studied on the effects of conditioning in asthma: the trainability of asthmatic children and the possible amelioration of EIB through conditioning.

TRAINABILITY OF THE CHILD WITH ASTHMA. *A priori*, there should be no reason why a child with bronchial asthma will not respond to conditioning in the same way as a healthy child. The one difference is that some asthmatics may not be willing, or able, to exert with sufficient intensity for fear of EIB.

Conditioning has been found in many studies to raise the maximal aerobic power of asthmatic children [1, 48, 64, 70, 73, 79, 95, 111, 119, 134] but not in others [52, 63, 155]. Other fitness components found to improve with training include muscle strength [119, 125] and speed [125]. Programs found to improve maximal aerobic power include swimming [48], long-distance running [111], a combination of land activities [64, 70, 95, 119, 134], or a combination of running and swimming [134, 145]. To study the relative merits of various activities one must equate their dosage. A study employing such a design has yet to be carried out. Although controlled data are lacking, repeated activities of short duration such as interval sprints or circuit training are often recommended [63, 119, 120, 134]. This is based on the presumed lower asthmogenicity of brief exercise, compared with activities of longer duration [133, 135, 141]. Such an assumption needs further substantiation by comparing the asthmogenicity of activities in various combinations of intensity and duration. The trainability of young asthmatics is further evident from their ability to reach top athletic standards, especially in swimming [46].

EFFECTS OF CONDITIONING ON EXERCISE-INDUCED BRONCHOCON-STRICTION. The potential benefit of conditioning in reducing the rate and intensity of EIB is of obvious clinical importance. Studies on this issue are summmarized in Table 1. While some authors found no effect of conditioning on EIB [48, 94, 111, 134, 146, 155], others have reported a decrease in the postexertional fall of peak expiratory flow following a program of circuit training [119], a combined run-swim program [145], or a combination of land activities [64, 70]. An example for the beneficial effect of conditioning is given in Figure 1.

In three of the studies [70, 119, 145] which suggested a decrease in EIB, there was a control group which did not train. This group was not randomly selected and no information is available on differences in the severity of asthma between the experimental and control groups. In contrast, Swann and Hanson [146] randomly assigned 7- to 14-year-old asthmatics to a training group ("intense" calisthenics twice weekly) and a "relaxation" group (relaxation in different body positions, controlled diaphragmatic breathing, and a short game once a week) for three months. Both groups had a significant and similar decrease in the exercise-induced fall of peak-expiratory flow. The authors could not explain why such a mild activity program resulted in reduced EIB. Neither a better compliance to medication nor habituation to the exercise test could be excluded. The small number of participants in the relaxation group ($n = 7$) further detracts from the external validity of the above findings.

An important unresolved issue is the possible interaction between medication and conditioning, or between the clinical severity of the disease and conditioning, and the amelioration of EIB. Thus, the definitive study on the possible effect of conditioning on EIB in asthmatics has yet to be published.

The mechanism for a possible conditioning effect on EIB is not

TABLE 1
*Effects of Conditioning on Exercise-induced Bronchoconstriction*

| Study | N | Experimental Group | | Controls | Conditioning Program | Effect on EIB |
|-------|---|-------|-------|----------|---------------------|---------------|
| | | Age (yr) | Clinical Status | | | |
| Vávra et al. [155] | 6 F<br>9 M | 12–14 | moderate asthma, outpatients | none | 3M, 3/W, gymnastics, ball games | none |
| Fitch et al. [48] | 46 F,M | 9–16 | various, able to swim | healthy, training | 5M, 5/W, swimming | no change in $FEV_{1.0}$; reduction in "disability score" PEF ↓ in all |
| Grilliat et al. [64] | 8 | 11–41 | asthma, competitive athletes | none | 2–17W | none |
| Oseid and Haaland [119] | 34 F<br>52 M | 7–16 | extrinsic asthma with EIB | asthmatics, no training | 3M, 2–3/W, endurance intervals plus intense 14-day camp (3/D) | PEF ↓ in exercise group |
| Leisti et al. [95] | 8 F<br>8 M | 9–13 | asthma diagnosed 4 yr | none | 4M, 2/W, gymnastics, breathing exercise, games | none |
| Schnall et al. [134] | 8 F<br>23 M | 5–16 | ? | none | 10W, 2/W, swim, land, or combination | none |
| Swann et al. [146] | 14 | 8–13 | proven EIB, outpatients | randomly selected asthmatics, "relaxation" program | 3M, 7/W, "intensive" calisthenics | EIB ↓ in both groups |
| Nickerson et al. [111] | 15 | 7–14 | severe asthma, institutionalized | 6-week "control period" but no controls | 6W, 4/W, distance running | episodes of EIB ↓ ; no change in measured EIB |
| Henriksen and Nielsen [70] | 28 | 11 ± 2 | EIB documented, low fitness | asthmatics, no training | 6W, 2/W, games, running, calisthenics | PEF ↓ in exercise group |
| Svenonius et al. [145] | 50 | 8–17 | allergen-mediated asthma | asthmatics, no training | 3–4M, 2/W, calisthenics, running, swimming | EIB ↓ in exercise groups |

$FEV_{1.0}$ = Forced expiratory in the first second; PEF = peak expiratory flow.

FIGURE 1

*Training and exercise-induced bronchoconstriction. Twenty asthmatic children (11 ± 2 years) underwent a 6-week program of calisthenics, team games, and circuit training. A group of 14 asthmatics served as controls. Values are of the lowest peak expiratory flow after a treadmill test. Vertical line denotes 1 SEM.*

SOURCE: Data from Henriksen and Nielsen [70].

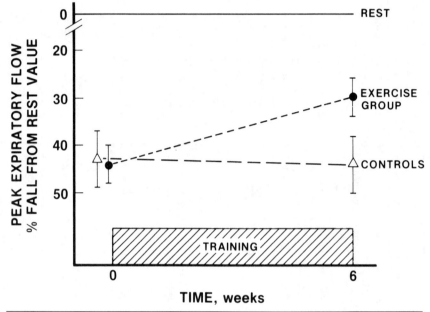

clear. One possiblility is that, with conditioning, submaximal pulmonary ventilation is reduced which causes a lower respiratory heat loss for a given level of exercise [12].

*Cystic Fibrosis*

Cystic fibrosis (CF) is a lethal, hereditary disease which is first manifested in early childhood. It affects exocrine glands in various body systems. Especially affected are the lungs, gastrointestinal tract, sweat glands, and testes. Of particular relevance to exertion is the exceedingly viscous mucus in the respiratory tract which causes airway obstruction and secondary parenchymal damage, infection, and respiratory failure. With the increasing life expectancy of patients with CF more attention is now being paid to quality of life. One issue of interest is the possible incorporation of exercise into their clinical management.

*Trainability of the child with CF.* A number of factors may limit the exercise capability of children with CF. Compared with the healthy child, they respond to exertion with a high respiratory dead space, low alveolar ventilation, airway "hyperreactivity," and a reduced ability to increase their pulmonary diffusion [27, 59, 114, 171]. Those with advanced lung damage respond also with arterial oxygen desaturation [27, 34]. It is pertinent therefore to assess the ability of such children to improve exercise capacity through conditioning.

Orenstein et al. [114] subjected 10- to 30-year-old patients to a three-month jog-walk program (three session per week at 75–80% of peak heart rate). Peak power output and maximal oxygen uptake increased, and submaximal heart rate decreased in the activity group but not in the controls. A similar trainability pattern was reported by Jankowski [85] for 9- to 18-year-old patients who underwent a five-month cycling, prone immersed tethered swimming, weight lifting, and calisthenics program. Prone immersed tethered swimming by itself (at 70–80% of maximal aerobic power) also increased maximal oxygen uptake when carried out for five months [33]. In addition to improvement in maximal aerobic power conditioning was found also to improve the endurance of the respiratory muscles of patients with CF. In the study by Orenstein et al. [114], there was an increase in the time period that the activity group managed to sustain isocapnic hyperpnea (at 65–90% of maximal breathing capacity), as was also found by others [33, 85, 89]. As shown in Figure 2, increased endurance of the respiratory muscles can be achieved either by specific training of these muscles (e.g., breathing against resistance) or by sports which involve the upper body such as swimming or canoeing. While specific training of the respiratory muscles improves their strength and endurance it does not induce any increase in maximal aerobic power of the child [9]. Based on observations as shown in Figure 2, it has been stated [89] that the trainability of the respiratory muscles in children with CF is greater than in healthy ones. It should be realized though that there were only four healthy subjects in this study and they were all adults. Animal studies have shown that chronic exposure to a high respiratory load results in increased oxidative capacity and reduced fatiguability of the ventilatory muscles [88].

Some reports [85, 168, 169] show an increase in certain pulmonary functions at rest. A combined swimming and underwater breathing program (two sessions per week for seven weeks) was accompanied by an 8–10 percent increase in forced vital capacity, forced expiratory volume in the first second, peak expiratory flow, and maximal mid-expiratory flow in 10 patients. While the absence of a control group does not allow one to assume causality between improved functions and training, it is interesting that all functions save the peak expiratory flow reverted to pretraining values 10 weeks after the conclu-

FIGURE 2

*Effect of training on endurance of ventilatory muscles. CF adolescents underwent a 4-week training program that consisted of either specific ventilatory muscle training (n = 4) or swimming and canoeing (n = 7). Four healthy adults served as controls. The criterion for ventilatory muscle endurance was the maximal level of normocapnic ventilation that could be sustained for 15 minutes divided by $FEV_{1.0}$. Vertical line denotes 1 SEM.*
SOURCE: Data from Keens et al. [89]. Reproduced with permission from Bar-or, O. *Pediatric Sports Medicine for the Practitioner.* New York, Springer Verlag, 1983.

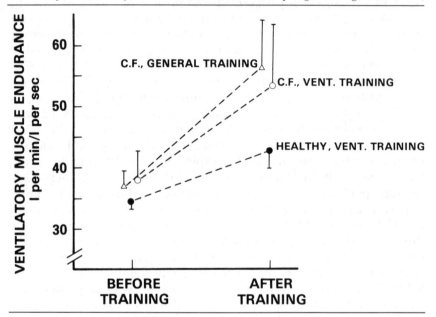

sion of the program [169]. This pattern is shown in Figure 3. Similar results were obtained in another study by the same group in which the program was more intense but shorter (7–8 hours a day for 17 days) [168] and following the 5-month regimen administered by Jankowski [85], but not following the jog-walk intervention by Orenstein et al. [114]. It is not clear why some authors found a training-related improvement in pulmonary functions and others did not. It is possible that, to obtain an increase in pulmonary functions, one must include swimming in the program.

The above studies suggest that children with CF increase their exercise capacity in response to conditioning. Such an increase could be due to improved ventilatory capacity, reduced airway resistance, higher pulmonary diffusion capacity, or adaptation of the skeletal muscles. The actual mechanism is not known. While data are still

FIGURE 3

*Durability of conditioning-induced changes in pulmonary functions of children with cystic fibrosis. Ten 6- to 18-year-old patients participated in a 7-week swimming program, two to three sessions per week. $FEV_{1.0}$ and maximal mid-expiratory flow (MMEF) are compared before the program, at its conclusion, and again 10 weeks later. Vertical line denotes 1 SEM.*
SOURCE: Data from Zach et al. [169]. Reproduced with permission from Bar-Or, O. *Pediatric Sports Medicine for the Practitioner.* New York: Springer Verlag, 1983.

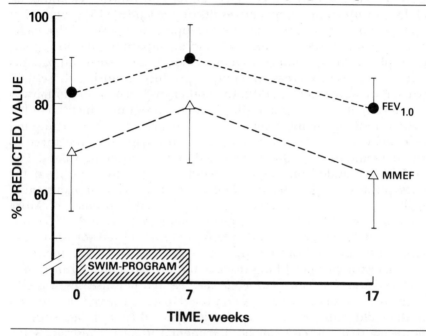

needed on the optimal regimens of aerobic training, practice has shown that interval swimming [85] or jogging [114] are both effective. Some evidence suggests that those patients with low initial fitness levels respond with a higher improvement in maximal aerobic power [114]. However, it is difficult to study such a relationship because those patients with low fitness often suffer from advanced lung damage and cannot be subjected to intense conditioning.

*Clinically beneficial effects of conditioning.* Clearing of mucopurulent secretions from the airways is an important component in the daily management of the child with CF. The traditional regimen combines postural drainage, percussion, chest massage, aerosol inhalation, and vibration by mechanical devices. The main benefit of this routine is the inducing of cough and clearing of the airways. Such a regimen is time-consuming and, to many patients, uncomfortable. It is therefore of clinical interest to find alternative measures of daily pulmonary hygiene which are socially more palatable to the child.

That physical exercise induces cough and mucous clearance was shown in healthy nonsmoking adults [165] and in adults with chronic obstructive lung disease [113]. Mucous clearance in these studies was assessed by serial scans of radioactive aerosol which the subjects inhaled prior to exercise. Two groups [115, 168, 169] have now reported that exertion increases coughing and mucous clearance in children with CF. Preliminary results of one study [115] suggest that cycling can be as effective as chest clapping and postural drainage. During a seven-week swimming program superimposed on regular chest physiotherapy and aerosol inhalation, 6- to 18-year-old patients had a 15 percent increase in sputum production during those days when they were training [169]. In another study, chest physiotherapy was terminated during a 17-day training program which included daily swimming, diving, jogging, and hiking [168]. Even so, coughing frequency and sputum volume increased during the first three to five days and then gradually returned to the pretraining values. The authors concluded that physical activities can reduce the need for chest physiotherapy and aerosol inhalation as a means of maintaining daily pulmonary hygiene. Such a conclusion may be premature. More data are needed on the long-term compliance to, and effects of, exertion in the absence of chest physiotherapy and aerosol inhalation. One must also find out whether daily exercise is feasible for those patients with advanced lung disease and low pulmonary function.

*Potentially deleterious effects of exercise.* As in other diseases, it is ethically difficult to design studies on the damage incurred by exertion to the child with CF. Some epidemiologic and clinical data suggest, however, that exercise can be detrimental to such children. Some patients with CF respond to exercise with arterial $O_2$ desaturation [26, 51]. While there is no proof that such patients suffer any resulting damage, clinical common sense warrants caution. Until proven otherwise, a patient with documented resting or exercise-induced $O_2$ desaturation should not be given highly intense activities. When resting hypoxemia is accompanied by hypercapnia (e.g., arterial $PCO_2$ of 50 mmHg or more), no exertion should be prescribed [85].

It has been reported [90] that, during climatic heat waves, children with CF dehydrate readily and are at an increased risk of heat-related illness. The assumption was that the aberration in the function of the eccrine sweat glands results in excessive loss of salt and, possibly, of fluids. No studies are available which, based on sound epidemiological principles, determine the relative risk for heat-related illness incurred by the child with CF. Orenstein and his group recently compared the response to exercise in the heat (70 min cycling at 50%

maximal aerobic power in 37–38°C dry bulb, 24–29°C wet bulb temperature) of 12- to 31-year-old male and female patients to that of healthy controls. Sweating rate and the increase in heart rate, rectal temperature, plasma renin activity, and serum aldosterone were similar in both groups during a single exposure [116], as was the degree of acclimatization to heat following exposures on eight consecutive days [117]. These data suggest that, under the above conditions, adolescents and young adults with mild CF thermoregulate and acclimatize to heat adequately. Further information is needed on the thermoregulatory response of younger CF patients, and of those with more advanced disease. Data are also needed on the ability of these patients to replenish the fluid losses which they incur during prolonged exposure to exercise in the heat.

## CARDIOVASCULAR DISEASES

### Congenital Heart Diseases
Congenital heart diseases are the most prevalent congenital structural defects. One convenient division is into cyanotic and noncyanotic heart disease. Cyanosis, at rest or during exercise, may occur from a right-to-left shunt as in tetralogy of Fallot. The noncyanotic defects with most relevance to exercise are aortic stenosis, in which the narrow aortic outlet interferes with the outflow from the left ventricle; pulmonary stenosis, in which the right outflow is diminished; coarctation of the aorta, which is a narrowing of the lumen in the thoracic aorta (seldom in the abdominal aorta); and complete heart block, in which there is a dissociation between the atrial rate and the ventricular rate, the latter being abnormally low.

While the maximal aerobic power of many children with congenital heart defects is within normal limits [37], there are others with a distinctly subnormal performance. Such a low aerobic power may be attributable in part to hypoactivity due to overprotection and parental fear of a "heart attack" [20], but it can also result from specific hemodynamic deficits which limit the $O_2$ transport. These should be recognized whenever an intervention program is contemplated for children with a congenital heart defect. Examples are the low stroke volume in aortic stenosis (AS) [35, 148], pulmonary stenosis [74, 108], or tetralogy of Fallot (TF) [36, 106]; low "forward" cardiac output in atrial or ventricular septal defect [17, 75]; high venous admixture and arterial $O_2$ desaturation, as in TF [61, 148]; and low ventricular rate, as in complete congenital heart block (CCHB) [149, 151] (for a review see [12, 13]). The main purpose of surgical correction in congenital heart disease is the improvement of hemodynamic function. Still, one often finds that in spite of anatomical correction of the defect hemodynamic functions and maximal aerobic power remain subnormal following surgery [44, 62, 83, 86, 106, 128]. These persistent deficiencies have been attributed to, among other causes, irreversible damage in the myocardium [72, 86, 87] or in the pulmonary circulation [102, 128].

*Trainability of the child with congenital heart disease.* Is it possible, in spite of the above hemodynamic deficiencies, to train the $O_2$ transport system of the child with congenital heart defect? The limited information available to answer this question is summarized in Table 2 and Figure 4. In the three reported studies [62, 105, 128], children and adolescents with various defects entered a conditioning program 1 to 16 years after corrective surgery. Programs lasted between five and nine weeks and emphasized aerobic activities at intensities of 65 to 80 percent maximal heart rate, or 50 to 70 percent maximal $O_2$ uptake. Only two of the studies included a control group [105, 128]. These were healthy children who trained, but there were no control groups of patients who remained sedentary. In all three studies there was an increase in the peak power output but not in maximal $O_2$ uptake. Submaximal heart rate decreased, and in one study, there was also a decrease in percentage body fat among the boys and an unexplained increase in mechanical efficiency during cycling. The above pattern is in line with conditioning results shown in various studies [15, 39, 54, 132, 167] with healthy prepubertal children, especially in their first decade. It may reflect a better economy of movement, without a concomitant increase in maximal aerobic power. Alternatively, it is possible that maximal $O_2$ uptake does not reflect the "real" maximal aerobic power in such young children. It is not clear, however, why 10- to 17-year-old patients in these three studies responded to aerobic conditioning as do children in their first decade of life. It is possible that some irreversible myocardial or vascular damage prevented these patients from increasing their $O_2$ transport capability but no hemodynamic data are available to substantiate such a notion. More intervention studies are needed which will incorporate such variables as stroke volume, cardiac output, intracardiac and intravascular pressures, and gas content in the circulation. Data are also needed on trainability as related to the severity of the disease, time elapsed after surgical repair, age of the child, the level of habitual activity and preintervention fitness.

*Detrimental effects of exercise in congenital heart disease*

AORTIC STENOSIS. Exertion can trigger one or more of the following in the child with AS: syncope, chest pain, ischemic electrocardiographic changes, and sudden death. As a general rule, the prevalence of these adverse reactions is related to the severity of the left outflow tract obstruction [12, 29, 41, 68, 81, 158]. There are, however, chil-

TABLE 2
*Effects of Conditioning in Congenital Heart Disease*

| Study | Experimental Group | | | | Controls | Conditioning Program | Results |
| | Defects | N | Age (yr) | Time since Surgery (yr) | | | |
|---|---|---|---|---|---|---|---|
| Miller et al. [105] | ASD PS CA VSD | 5 F 7 M | 10–15 | 1–7 | healthy, training | 5W, daily, cycling at 80% HR max | peak power ↑ $\dot{V}O_2$ max no change |
| Goldberg et al. [62] | TF VSD | 13 F 13 M | 7–17 | 3–16 | none | 6W, 3/W, cycling at 50–70% $\dot{V}O_2$ max | peak power ↑ $\dot{V}O_2$max no change $\dot{V}O_2$submax ↓ % fat ↓ in boys |
| Ruttenberg et al. [128] | AS TF TGA AVC | 12 F,M | 7–18 | over 1 | healthy, training | 9W, 3/W, walk-jog at 65–75% HR max | maximal treadmill time ↑ $\dot{V}O_2$ max no change |

AS = aortic stenosis; ASD = atrial septal defect; AVC = atrioventricular canal; CA = coarctation of the aorta; PS = pulmonary stenosis; TF = tetralogy of Fallot; TGA = transposition of great vessels; VSD = ventricular septal defect.

FIGURE 4

*Conditioning in congenital heart disease. Thirteen girls and 13 boys (13.9 ± 3 years) with either tetralogy of Fallot or ventricular septal defect underwent a 6-week cycling program, at 50 to 70 percent of maximal $O_2$ uptake. All subjects had a surgical repair some years prior to testing. Vertical line denotes 1 SD; \*, p < 0.1; \*\*, p < 0.01.*
SOURCE: Data from Goldberg et al. [62].

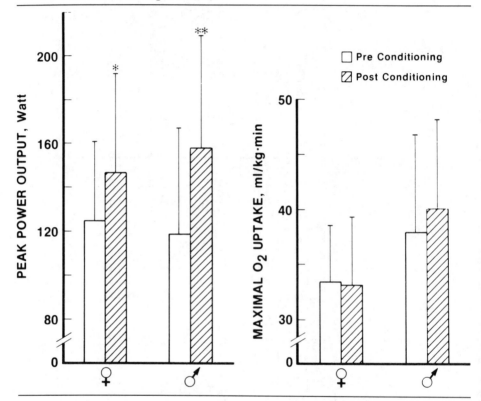

dren who respond to exercise with ST segmental depression [84], or syncope, in the absence of marked left outflow tract obstruction. There is sometimes also a discrepancy between the postsurgical increase in the patency of the left outflow tract, on the one hand, and the persistence of adverse effects of exercise, on the other. This has been documented for exertional ST changes [154].

COARCTATION OF THE AORTA (CA). High systolic arterial blood pressure is often seen in the child with CA at rest and especially during exercise. Pressures as high as 300 mmHg have been documented during intense activities [38, 80, 150]. Coarctectomy often corrects such an exertional hypertensive response. Many patients, however, may still respond to exercise with a high systolic pressure following an anatomically successful operation [80, 150]. The mechanism for such persisting changes is not clear.

Patients with CA may respond to exercise with ischemic ST changes. Segmental ST depression of 1–4 mm was found, for example, in two-thirds of female and one-third of male patients during maximal exertion [82]. This response is of particular importance in the light of the association which has been described [102] between early coronary heart disease and CA. It is yet to be shown whether those patients with exercise-induced ST depression are at a greater risk for coronary heart disease than patients who do not have such a response. The mechanism for ischemic changes in CA is not known.

COMPLETE CONGENITAL HEART BLOCK. While patients with CCHB do not, as a rule, need to restrict their physical activity below the limits imposed by a compromised $O_2$ transport, two abnormal responses to exercise must be recognized: syncope and ventricular dysrhythmia.

Syncope of the Stokes-Adams type may occur during [136] or following [104] exertion. Its prevalence in children with CCHB is not documented.

Exercise-induced ventricular dysrhythmia, ranging from single premature beats to ventricular tachycardia, is a common occurrence in children and adolescents with CCHB. Of patients who exercise, 28 to 75 percent respond with ventricular dysrhythmia [30, 76, 149, 151, 159, 164]. The rate of occurrence does not seem to depend on whether the patient has an isolated heart block or associated lesions, nor on the gender or exercise tolerance of the child [164]. While maximal exertion seems to elicit more dysrhythmia than does submaximal exertion no threshold load was described for this phenomenon.

For fear of exercise-induced detrimental effects physicians all too often prescribe rest to children with congenital heart disease. The need for knowledge of the permissible activities for such patients is a challenge for future research.

### Juvenile Hypertension

Hypertension (HT) among adolescents has emerged as an important pediatric issue [98, 147]. One point of concern to clinicians and patients alike is the possible need for a lifetime drug regimen in a virtually asymptomatic young patient. The use of physical conditioning as a potential alternative means of lowering the blood pressure in juvenile HT is therefore of both clinical and public health importance.

In adults with HT, physical conditioning has been associated with lowering of some 5–25 mmHg in resting systolic pressure and 3–15 mmHg in resting diastolic pressure [152]. This was shown, for example, in a randomized controlled study of middle-aged males with "borderline" HT who underwent a four-month endurance program [91]. The biological and clinical implications of such a decrease in pressures, as well as the long-term carryover, are yet to be established.

Few data are available on the response to conditioning of adolescents with HT. Hagberg and his group have evaluated the effects of endurance running [66, 67] and of weight training [65] on 14- to 18-year-old girls and boys whose resting blood pressure was persistently above the 95th percentile for age and sex. A 6-month, three-sessions-per-week jogging program at 60 to 65 percent of maximal $O_2$ uptake resulted in a reduction of 8 mmHg in systolic pressure and 5 mmHg in diastolic pressure. When reassessed 9 months after cessation of the program, pressures returned to their preconditioning levels [67]. Five of the subjects continued with 5 months of weight training immediately following the jogging program. As shown in Figure 5 their systolic blood pressure remained low but reverted to the preconditioning level 12 months after the cessation of the weight-training program [65]. The main drawback of the above project was a lack of a randomly selected control group. The controls were adolescents who would not join the jogging program. The authors do not give specific data but state that this group had no change in blood pressure throughout the project. In another study [92], the resting blood pressure of 15- to 17-year-old boys with essential HT did not change following a 2-month program of unspecified weight training.

The mechanisms by which conditioning may induce lowering of blood pressure in the adolescent with HT are not clear. The effect seems to be independent of changes in body size, adiposity, or maximal aerobic power [65, 67]. For a review of the possible mechanisms in adults and in animals see Bjorntrop [23] and Tipton [153].

*Permissible activities for adolescents with hypertension.* Adult hypertensives respond to any given exercise load with higher blood pressure than do age-matched normotensives [153] and the rise in blood pressure at a given metabolic level is greater during static exercise than during rhythmic exercise [24, 139]. In adolescents, while systolic pressure reached higher values in those with HT than in normotensives, the increment in pressure from rest to maximal rhythmic exercise was similar in both groups [45, 49]. Although the response to static exercise was evaluated in normotensive and in hypertensive adolescents [49, 131], there are no studies which attempt to equate the metabolic level in static and rhythmic exertion. One cannot conclude, therefore, that static exertion involves more risk than rhythmic ex-

FIGURE 5

*Training in hypertension. Five 15-year-old girls and boys with essential hypertension took part in a 5-month endurance program, followed by 5 months of weight training. They were retested 12 months later. Vertical line denotes 1 SEM.*
SOURCE: Data from Hagberg et al. [65].

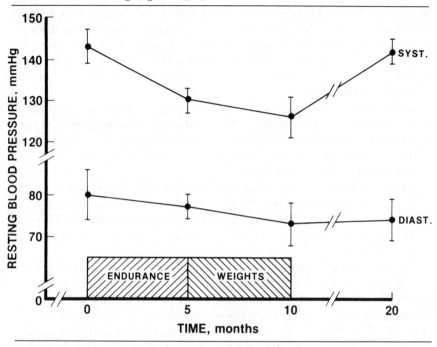

ercise in juvenile HT. Even so, recommendations have been made [147] to curtail the participation of hypertensive adolescents in such activities as wrestling or weight lifting.

Future studies should address such questions as: What are the optimal conditioning regimens for adolescents with HT? Is there any long-range carryover to the lowering of blood pressure by conditioning? Is there any interaction between drug therapy and conditioning in juvenile HT? Are the mechanisms for lowering pressure through conditioning different in adolescence and middle age?

*Coronary Risk and Physical Conditioning*
While coronary artery disease is almost invariably first manifested during adult years, atherosclerosis has been gaining recognition as a pediatric issue [56, 96, 123, 157]. A major question is whether changes in the lifestyle of the child or adolescent can reduce the risk of de-

veloping atherosclerosis in later years. Of specific relevance to this review is the question of whether an increase in physical activity during early life can help prevent coronary heart disease in adulthood.

Unlike studies with adults, criteria for the effectiveness of intervention during childhood cannot be such end points as angina pectoris, myocardial infarction, or sudden death. An alternative approach is to look for the changes that physical conditioning may induce in coronary risk factors. Such an approach assumes that there are risk factors that can be identified in children [19, 54, 93, 99, 162]. It is further assumed that such coronary risk factors "track" into adulthood [96, 110, 123].

Risk factors that might conceivably be modified by increased physical activity are hypertension, obesity, diabetes mellitus, high serum lipids, and low concentration of high-density lipoprotein cholesterol (HDL-C). It is also conceivable that an active lifestyle may reduce the tendency to cigarette smoking.

The effects of exercise on hypertension are discussed in a separate section. Neither obesity nor diabetes mellitus are categorized as cardiovascular diseases. Detailed analysis of the relationship between exertion and obesity or diabetes mellitus is therefore beyond the scope of this review.

Various studies have shown that increased physical activity, with or without a reduction in calorie intake, can induce weight and body fat loss in obese children and adolescents [109, 122, 137]. There are no data however which determine the carryover of the effect into adulthood. In fact, weight loss and fat loss do not seem to be sustained beyond the duration of the intervention program [32, 103, 121]. For a further review see Bar-Or [12].

While exertion is highly relevant to the daily clinical management of the child with diabetes mellitus [12], there are no data to show whether physical conditioning can affect the course of the disease or diminish any of its complications.

*Blood lipids and physical conditioning: Cross-sectional data.* Both cross-sectional [42, 71, 94, 107, 112, 129, 152, 156] and longitudinal [53, 54, 97, 161] studies are available which examine the relationship between serum lipids and physical activity of children and adolescents. Valimaki et al. [156] assessed lipid and lipoprotein profiles in 11- to 13-year-old track and field athletes of both sexes and nonathletes of the same age. Among the females, HDL-C was higher (1.61 vs. 1.29 mmol/L) and total triglycerides were lower (0.68 vs. 1.11 mmol/L) in the athletes. In the males, HDL-C was higher in the athletes (1.67 vs. 1.32 mmol/L). One deficiency in this study is the marked difference in body size between the activity groups. Thorland and Gilliam [152] compared lipid and lipoprotein levels in "active" and "less active" 8.3- to 10.8-year-old Caucasian boys. Activity was assessed by recall questionnaires and by time-and-motion logs. Serum total triglycerides in the active boys were significantly lower (0.59 vs. 0.77 mmol/L) and their ratio of HDL-C to total cholesterol was higher (0.33 vs. 0.29) than in the less active ones. These differences were independent of body adiposity. A similar trend was reported for 14.5-year-old Polish school children who attended either a sport school or regular school [112]. A positive relationship between HDL-C/total cholesterol ratio and activity level was reported for black male adolescents but not for preadolescents [42]. In other studies, neither serum triglycerides [71] nor HDL-C [94] were related to the activity level of adolescent males.

The above data do not tell whether it is the physical activity *per se* or the level of fitness of these children that may explain the differences in the lipid and lipoprotein profiles. An attempt to answer this question was made by Saris [129] who assessed habitual activity (24-hour recording of heart rate), maximal aerobic power, adiposity, and blood lipids in 6- to 10-year-old girls and boys. Those children with high aerobic power had a high HDL-C/total cholesterol ratio, irrespective of their habitual activity. The conclusion from this study is not clear, however, because those children with high aerobic power were also leaner and the effect of adiposity was not partialed out.

*Blood lipids and physical conditioning: Longitudinal data.* Intervention studies of this issue are summarized in Table 3. In none of these was serum triglyceride concentration significantly changed. Total cholesterol decreased in one study [161], in which overweight girls and boys underwent a combined diet (4,200 kJ per day) and exercise regimen. It is impossible to tell whether this reduction was due to the treatment or due to the weight loss of these children. Fourteen 8- to 10-year-old healthy girls underwent a six-week conditioning program at school [53]. The five-per-week activity sessions included calisthenics, rope jumping, various games, and a once per week 12-minute run. Measured one day after the program, HDL-C and HDL-C/total cholesterol were higher than the initial values (0.72 vs. 0.52 mmol/L and 0.19 vs. 0.15). The change in HDL-C/total cholesterol was transitory, disappearing eight days later. Lack of a control group does not permit assumption of a causal relationship between the lipoprotein profile and physical conditioning in these girls. This omission was corrected in two recent studies in which preadolescents [54] and adolescents [97] were randomly assigned to a conditioning or a control group [97]. Activities included walking, running at 80–85

TABLE 3
*Physical Conditioning and Blood Lipids in Children*

| Study | N | Age, yr | Controls | Conditioning Program | Effect | | | | |
| --- | --- | --- | --- | --- | --- | --- | --- | --- | --- |
| | | | | | TG | HDL-C | Total C | $\frac{\text{HDL-C}}{\text{Total C}}$ | % Body Fat |
| Gilliam and Burke [53] | 14 F | 8–10 | none | 6W, 5/W, calisthenics, running, games | — | increase | N.S. | increase | — |
| Widhalm et al. [161] | 7 F 7 M | 11–13 | not randomly selected | 3W "intensive" training; low-calorie diet | N.S. | N.S. | decrease | — | body weight → (subjects obese) |
| Gilliam and Freedson [54] | 11 F,M | 7–9 | randomly selected; regular P.E. HR = 150 | 12W, 4/W, aerobic P.E. HR = 165 | N.S. | — | N.S. | — | N.S. |
| Linder et al. [97] | 29 M | 11–17 | randomly selected; regular summer activities | 8W, 4/W, walk-jog, games, 80% HR max | N.S. | N.S. | N.S. | N.S. | — |

percent of maximal heart rate, soccer, and rugby. In spite of an increase in peak mechanical power, there were no changes in the lipid or the lipoprotein profiles.

The findings of these well-designed studies and other cross-sectional and longitudinal ones leave open the possible usefulness of conditioning as a means for altering the lipid and lipoprotein profiles in nonobese children and adolescents. Intervention programs of a duration longer than a few months are indicated. It is also important to find out whether exercise can potentiate the effect of diet on blood lipids, with or without weight loss.

Although cigarette smoking is a major coronary risk factor, no data are available on the effect of physical conditioning on this habit among adolescents. One survey from Switzerland [21] suggested that adolescents who are active in a sports club smoke less than sedentary adolescents. More studies are needed to ascertain any association between smoking and the level of physical activity.

Other questions still unanswered include: Are there specific groups with high coronary risk (e.g., coarctation of the aorta or familial hypercholesterolemia) that may benefit from conditioning more than the healthy young population? Are there any long-lasting effects of conditioning on coronary risk factors? Is there any threshold physical activity during childhood beyond which beneficial effects may be discerned?

## CHALLENGES FOR FUTURE RESEARCH

While the body of knowledge reviewed in this chapter introduces some responses to conditioning in pediatric cardiorespiratory disease, more research is needed to further understand mechanisms and causality. Such research must be based on strict epidemiologic and design principles, not commonly adhered to hitherto. The following are topics that should be investigated. Their selection reflects the bias of this author, and the list is by no means comprehensive.

- The effects of conditioning on the clinical course of disease. This is particularly important in conditions of a progressive nature such as lung damage in cystic fibrosis, or pulmonary hypertension in ventricular septal defect.
- The interaction between conditioning and other modes of therapy, such as drugs, cardiac surgery, cardiac pacing, chest percussion, or relaxation exercises.
- The positive and negative effects of conditioning on specific pathophysiologic deficits in cardiorespiratory disease.
- The permissible physical activities for children in whom exercise may cause detrimental effects.

- The relevance of physical conditioning during childhood to the prevention of adulthood degenerative diseases such as hypertension or coronary artery disease.
- The beneficial and detrimental effects of conditioning in acquired pediatric cardiorespiratory diseases such as rheumatic valvular disease, cardiomyopathy, dysrhythmias, chronic bronchitis, or bronchiectasis.
- The means for the improvement of compliance in intervention studies.
- The psychosocial impact of conditioning in the child with a real or a presumed cardiovascular or respiratory illness.

REFERENCES

1. Afzelius-Frisk, I., C. Grimby, and N. Linderhold. Physical training in patients with asthma. *Le Poum. Coeur* 33:33–37, 1977.
2. Anderson, S.D. Physiological aspects of exercise-induced bronchoconstriction. Ph.D. thesis, University of London, 1972.
3. Anderson, S.D. Exercise-induced asthma: Current views. *Patient Management* 6:43–55, 1982.
4. Anderson, S.D., P.J. Rozea, R. Dolton, and D.A. Lindsay. Inhaled and oral bronchodilator therapy in exercise-induced asthma. *Aust. N.Z. J. Med.* 5:544–550, 1975.
5. Anderson, S.D., and R.E. Schoeffel. Respiratory heat and water loss during exercise in patients with asthma. *Eur. J. Respir. Dis.* 63:472–480, 1982.
6. Anderson, S.D., R.E. Schoeffel, R. Follet, C.P. Perry, E. Daviskas, and M. Kendall. Sensitivity to heat and water loss at rest and during exercise in asthmatic patients. *Eur. J. Respir. Dis.* 63:459–471, 1982.
7. Anderson, S., J.P. Seale, L. Ferris, R. Schoeffel, and D.A. Lindsay. An evaluation of pharmacotherapy for exercise-induced asthma. *J. Allergy Clin. Immunol.* 64:612–614, 1979.
8. Anderson, S.D., J.P. Seale, P. Rozea, L. Bandles, G. Theobald, and D.A. Lindsay. Inhaled and oral salbutamol in exercise-induced asthma. *Am. Rev. Respir. Dis.* 114:493–500, 1976.
9. Asher, M.I., R.L. Pardy, A.L. Coates, E. Thomas, and P.T. Macklem. The effects of inspiratory muscle training in patients with cystic fibrosis. *Am. Rev. Respir. Dis.* 126:855–859, 1982.
10. Badiei, B., J. Faciane, and R.M. Sly. Effect of theophylline, ephedrine and their combination upon exercise-induced airway obstruction. *Ann. Allergy* 35:32–36, 1975.
11. Bar-Or, O. Climatic conditions and their effect on exercise-induced asthma. In *The Asthmatic Child in Play and Sport.* S. Oseid and A.M. Edwards (eds.). London: Pitman Books 1983, pp. 61–73.
12. Bar-Or, O. *Pediatric Sports Medicine for the Practitioner: From Physiologic Principles to Clinical Application.* New York: Springer Verlag, 1983.
13. Bar-Or, O. Specific pathophysiologic factors which limit the exercise capacity of the sick child. *Med. Sci. Sports Exercise,* in press.
14. Bar-Or, O., I. Neuman, and R. Dotan. Effects of dry and humid climates on exercise-induced asthma in children and preadolescents. *J. Allergy Clin. Immunol.* 60:163–168, 1977.

15. Bar-Or, O., and L.D. Zwiren. Physiological effects of increased frequency of physical education classes and of endurance conditioning on 9- to 10-year-old girls and boys. In *Pediatric Work Physiology*. O. Bar-Or (ed.). Natanya: Wingate Institute, 1973, pp. 183–198.

16. Bar-Yishay, E., I. Gur, O. Inbar, I. Neuman, R.A. Dlin, and S. Godfrey. Differences between swimming and running as stimuli for exercise-induced asthma. *Eur. J. Appl. Physiol.* 48:387–397, 1982.

17. Bay, G., A.M. Abrahamsen, and C. Muller. Left-to-right slant in atrial septal defect at rest and during exercise. *Acta Med. Scand.* 190:205–209, 1971.

18. Ben-Dov, I., E. Bar-Yishay, and S. Godfrey. Refractory period after exercise-induced asthma unexplained by respiratory heat loss. *Am. Rev. Respir. Dis.* 125:530–534, 1982.

19. Berg, K., S.P. Sady, D. Beal, M. Savage, and J. Smith. Developing an elementary school CHD prevention program. *Physician Sportsmed.* 11:99–105, 1983.

20. Bergman, A.B., and S.J. Stamm. The morbidity of cardiac nondisease in school children. *New Engl. J. Med.* 276:1008–1013, 1967.

21. Biener, K. Tobacco use and adolescent attitudes toward sports (in German) *Schweiz. Rundschau. Sportmed.* 65:78–81, 1976.

22. Bierman, C.W., G.G. Shapiro, W.E. Pierson, and C.S. Dorsett. Acute and chronictheophylline therapy in exercise-induced bronchospasm. *Pediatrics* 60:845–849, 1977.

23. Bjorntorp, P. Hypertension and exercise. *Hypertension* 4(Suppl III):56–59, 1982.

24. Blomqvist, C.G., S.F. Lewis, W.F. Taylor, and R.M. Graham. Similarity of the hemodynamic responses to static and dynamic exercise of small muscle groups. *Circ. Res.* 48(Suppl I):187–192, 1981.

25. Bundgaard, A., A. Schmidt, T. Ingemann-Hansen, et al. Exercise-induced asthma after swimming and bicycle exercise. *Eur. J. Respir. Dis.* 63:245–248, 1982.

26. Bundgaard, A., T. Ingemann-Hannsen, A. Schmidt, J. Halkjaer-Kristensen, and I. Bloch. Influence of temperature and relative humidity of inhaled gas on exercise-induced asthma. *Eur. J. Respir. Dis.* 63:239–244, 1982.

27. Cerny, F.J., T.P. Pullano, and G.J.A. Cropp. Cardiorespiratory adaptations to exercise in cystic fibrosis. *Am. Rev. Respir. Dis.* 126:217–220, 1982.

28. Cerrina, J., A. Denjean, G. Alexandre, A. Lockhart, and P. Duroux. Inhibition of exercise-induced asthma by a calcium antagonist, nifedipine. *Am. Rev. Respir. Dis.* 123:156–160, 1981.

29. Chandramouli, B., D.A. Ehmke, and R.M. Lauer. Exercise-induced electrocardiographic changes in children with congenital aortic stenosis. *J. Pediatrics* 87:725–730, 1975.

30. Chawla, K., M. Serratto, J. Cruz, R. Chaquimia, R. Miller, H. Hastrieter, and W.D. Towne. Response to maximal and submaximal exercise testing in patients with congenital heart block. *Circulation* 56(Suppl III):171, 1977 (Abstract).

31. Chen, W.Y., and D.J. Horton. Heat and water loss from the airways and exercise-induced asthma. *Respiration* 34:305–313, 1977.

32. Christakis, G., S. Sajecki, R.W. Hillman, E. Miller, S. Blumenthal, and M. Archer. Effect of a combined nutrition, education and physical fitness program on the weight status of obese high school boys. *Fed. Proc.* 25:15–19, 1966.

33. Clement, M., L.W. Jankowski, and P.H. Beaudry. Prone immersion physical therapy in three children with cystic fibrosis: A pilot study. *Nurs. Res.* 28:325–330, 1979.

34. Cropp, G.J., T.P. Pullano, F.J. Cerny, and I.T. Nathanson. Exercise tolerance and cardiorespiratory adjustments at peak work capacity in cystic fibrosis. *Am. Rev. Respir. Dis.* 126:211–216, 1982.

35. Cueto, L., and J.H. Moller. Haemodynamics of exercise in children with isolated aortic valvular disease. *Br. Heart J.* 35:93–98, 1973.

36. Cumming, G.R. Exercise studies in children after corrective surgery for tetralogy of fallot. In *Frontiers of Activity and Child Health.* H. Lavallée and R.J. Shephard (eds.). Quebec: Pelican, 1977, pp. 371–384.

37. Cumming, G. Maximal exercise capacity of children with heart defects. *Am. J. Cardiol.* 42:613–619, 1978.

38. Cumming, G.R., and G.H. Mir. Exercise haemodynamics of coarctation of the aorta. Acute effects of propranolol. *Br. Heart J.* 32:365–369, 1970.

39. Daniels, J., and N. Oldridge. Changes in oxygen consumption of young boys during growth and running training. *Med. Sci. Sports* 3:161–165, 1971.

40. Deal, E.C. Jr., E.R. McFadden, Jr., R.H. Ingram, Jr., R.H. Strauss, and J.J. Jaeger. Role of respiratory heat exchange in production of exercise-induced asthma. *J. Appl. Physiol. Respirat. Environ. Exercise Physiol.* 46:467–475, 1979.

41. Doyle, E.F., P. Arumugham, E. Lara, M.R. Rutkowski, and B. Kiely. Sudden death in young patients with congenital aortic stenosis. *Pediatrics* 53:481–489, 1974.

42. DuRant, R.H., C.W. Linder, J.W. Harkess, and R.G. Gray. The relationship between physical activity and serum lipids and lipoproteins in black children and adolescents. *J. Adolesc. Health Care* 3:75–81, 1982.

43. Edmunds, A.T., M. Tooley, and S. Godfrey. The refractory period after EIA: Its duration and relation to the severity of exercise. *Am. Rev. Resp. Dis.* 117:247–254, 1978.

44. Epstein, S.E., G.D. Beiser, R.E. Goldstein, D.R. Rosing, D.R. Redwood, and A.G. Morrow. Hemodynamic abnormalities in response to mild and intense exercise following operative correction of an atrial septal defect or tetralogy of fallot. *Circulation* 45:1065–1075, 1973.

45. Falkner, B., and D.T. Lowenthal. Dynamic exercise response in hypertensive adolescents. *Int. J. Ped. Nephrol.* 1:161–165, 1980.

46. Fitch, K.D., and S. Godfrey. Asthma and athletic performance. *J. Am. Med. Assoc.* 236:152–157, 1976.

47. Fitch, K.D., and A.R. Morton. Specificity of exercise in exercise-induced asthma. *Br. Med. J.* 4:577–581, 1971.

48. Fitch, K.D., A.R. Morton, and B.A. Blanksby. Effects of swimming training on children with asthma. *Arch. Dis. Child* 51:190–194, 1976.

49. Fixler, D.E., W.P. Laird, R. Brown, et al. Response of hypertensive adolescents to dynamic and isometric exercise stress. *Pediatrics* 64:579–583, 1979.

50. Francis, P.W.J., I.R.B. Krastins, and H. Levison. Oral and inhaled salbutamol in the prevention of exercise-induced bronchospasm. *Pediatrics* 66:103–108, 1980.

51. Germann, K., D. Orenstein, and J. Horowitz. Changes in oxygenation during exercise in cystic fibrosis. *Med. Sci. Sports Exercise* 12:105, 1980 (Abstract).

52. Geubelle, F., C. Ernould, and M. Jovanovic. Working capacity and physical training in asthmatic children at 1800 m altitude. *Acta Ped. Scand. Suppl* 217:93–98, 1971.

53. Gilliam, T.B., and M.B. Burke. Effects of exercise on serum lipids and lipoproteins in girls, ages 8 to 10 years. *Artery* 4:203–213, 1978.

54. Gilliam, T.B., and P.S. Freedson. Effects of a 12-week school physical fitness program on peak $VO_2$, body composition and blood lipids in 7- to 9-year-old children. *Int. J. Sports Med.* 1:73–78, 1980.

55. Gilliam, T.B., V. Katch, W. Thorland, and A. Weltman. Prevalence of coronary

heart disease risk factors in active children, 7- to 12-years of age. *Med. Sci. Sports* 9:21–25, 1977.

56. Glueck, C.J. Detection of risk factors for coronary artery disease in children: Semmelweis revisited? *Pediatrics* 66:834–837, 1980.
57. Godfrey, S. *Exercise Testing in Children. Applications in Health and Disease.* Philadelphia: W.B. Saunders, 1974.
58. Godfrey, S., and P. König. Inhibition of exercise-induced asthma by different pharmacological pathways. *Thorax* 31:137–143, 1976.
59. Godfrey, S., and M. Mearns. Pulmonary function and response to exercise in cystic fibrosis. *Arch. Dis. Child.* 46:144–151, 1971.
60. Godfrey, S., M. Silverman, and S. Anderson. The use of treadmill for assessing EIA and the effect of varying the severity and duration of exercise. *Pediatrics* 56:893–899, 1975.
61. Gold, W.M., L.F. Mattioli, and A.C. Price. Response to exercise in patients with tetralogy of Fallot with systemic-pulmonary anastomoses. *Pediatrics* 43:781–793, 1969.
62. Goldberg, B., R.R. Fripp, G. Lister, J. Loke, J.A. Nicholas, and N.S. Talner. Effect of physical training on exercise performance of children following surgical repair of congenital heart disease. *Pediatrics* 68:691–699, 1981.
63. Graff-Lonnevig, V., S. Bevegard, B.O. Eriksson, S. Kraepelien, and B. Saltin. Two years' follow-up of asthmatic boys participating in a physical activity programme. *Acta Paed. Scand.* 69:347–352, 1980.
64. Grilliat, J.P., H. Viniaker, M. Vaillandet, and M.G. Ohlsson. Rehabilitation of asthmatic patients to effort (in French). *Rev. Fr. Mal. Resp.* 5:531–440, 1977.
65. Hagberg, J.M., A.A. Ehsani, D. Goldring, A. Hernandez, D.R. Sinacore, and J.O. Holloszy. Effect of weight training on blood pressure and hemodynamics in hypertensive adolescents. *J. Pediatr.* 104:147–151, 1984.
66. Hagberg, J.M., A.A. Ehsani, G.W. Heath, D. Goldring, T. Hernandez, and J.O. Holloszy. Beneficial effects of endurance exercise training in adolescent hypertension. Presented at 29th Annual Meeting of American College of Cardiology, 1980 (Abstract).
67. Hagberg, J.M., D. Goldring, A.A. Ehsani, G.W. Heath, A. Hernandez, K. Schechtman, and J.O. Holloszy. Effect of exercise training on the blood pressure and hemodynamic features of hypertensive adolescents. *Am. J. Cardiol.* 52:763–768, 1983.
68. Halloran, K.H. The telemetered exercise electrocardiograph in congenital aortic stenosis. *Pediatrics* 47:31–39, 1971.
69. Henriksen, J.M., R. Dahl, and G.R. Lundquist. Influence of relative humidity and repeated exercise on exercise-induced bronchoconstriction. *Allergy* 36:463–470, 1981.
70. Henriksen, J.M., and T. Nielsen. Effect of physical training on exercise-induced bronchoconstriction. *Acta Paed. Scand.* 72:31–36, 1983.
71. Hickie, J.B., J. Sutton, P. Russo, J. Ruys, and E.W. Keagen. Serum cholesterol and serum triglyceride levels in Australian adolescent males. *Med. J. Aust.* 1:825–828, 1974.
72. Hirschfeld, S., A.J. Tuboku-Metzger, G. Borkat, J. Ankeney, J. Clayman, and J. Liebman. Comparison of exercise and catheterization results following total surgical correction of tetralogy of Fallot. *J. Thorac. Cardiovasc. Surg.* 75:446–451, 1978.
73. Hirt, M. Physical conditioning in asthma. *Ann. Allergy* 22:229–237, 1964.
74. Howitt, G. Hemodynamic effects of exercise in pulmonary stenosis. *Br. Heart J.* 28:152–160, 1966.

75. Hugenholtz, P.G., and A.S. Nadas. Exercise studies in patients with congenital heart disease. *Pediatrics* 32:769–775, 1963.
76. Ikkos, D., and J.S. Hanson. Response to exercise in congenital complete atrioventricular block. *Circulation* 22:583–590, 1960.
77. Inbar, O., D.X. Alvarez, and H.A. Lyons. Exercise-induced asthma: A comparison between two modes of exercise stress. *Eur. J. Resp. Dis.* 62:160–167, 1981.
78. Inbar, O., R. Dotan, R.A. Dlin, I. Neuman, and O. Bar-Or. Breathing dry or humid air and exercise-induced asthma during swimming. *Eur. J. Appl. Physiol.* 44:43–50, 1980.
79. Itkin, I.H., and M. Nachman. The effect of exercise on the hospitalized asthmatic patient. *J. Allergy* 37:253–263, 1966.
80. James, F.W., and S. Kaplan. Systolic hypertension during submaximal exercise after correction of coarctation of aorta. *Circulation* 49, 50(Suppl II):27–34, 1974.
81. James, F.W., and S. Kaplan. Exercise testing in children. *Primary Cardiol.* 3:34–40, 1977.
82. James, F.W., S. Kaplan, and D.C. Schwartz. Ischemic ST segments during exercise in children after coarctectomy. *Am. J. Cardiol.* 37:145, 1976 (Abstract).
83. James, F.W., S. Kaplan, D.C. Schwartz, T.-Ch. Chou, J.J. Sandker, and V. Naylor. Response to exercise in patients after total surgical correction of tetralogy of fallot. *Circulation* 54:671–679, 1976.
84. James. F.W., D.C. Schwartz, S. Kaplan, and S.P. Spilkin. Exercise electrocardiogram, blood pressure, and working capacity in young patients with valvular or discrete subvalvular aortic stenosis. *Am. J. Cardiol.* 50:769–775, 1982.
85. Jankowski, L.W. Exercise testing and exercise prescription for individuals with cystic fibrosis. In *Testing and Exercise Prescription for Special Cases.* J.S. Skinner (Ed.). Philadelphia: Lea & Febiger, in press.
86. Johnson, A.M. Impaired exercise response and other residua of pulmonary stenosis after valvotomy. *Br. Heart J.* 24:375–388, 1962.
87. Jonsson, B., and S.J.K. Lee. Haemodynamic effects of exercise in isolated pulmonary stenosis before and after surgery. *Br. Heart J.* 30:60–66, 1968.
88. Keens, T.G., V. Chen, P. Patel, P. O'Brien, H. Levison, and C.D. Ianuzzo. Cellular adaptions of the ventilatory muscles to a chronic increased respiratory load. *J. Appl. Physiol.* 44:905–908, 1978.
89. Keens, T.G., I.R.B. Krastins, E.M. Wannamaker, H. Levinson, O.N. Crozier, and C. Bryan. Ventilatory muscle endurance training in normal subjects and patients with cystic fibrosis. *Am. Rev. Resp. Dis.* 116:853–860, 1977.
90. Kessler, W.R., and D.H. Andersen. Heat prostration in fibrocystic disease of the pancreas and other conditions. *Pediatrics* 8:648–656, 1951.
91. Kukkonen, K., R. Rauramaa, E. Vontilainen, and E. Länsimies. Physical training of middle-aged men with borderline hypertension. *Ann. Clin. Res.* 14(Suppl 34):139–145, 1982.
92. Laird, W.P., D.E. Fixler, and C.D. Swanbom. Effect of chronic weight lifting on the blood pressure in hypertensive adolescents. *Prev. Med.* 8:184, 1979 (Abstract).
93. Lauer, R.M., W.E. Conner, P.E. Leaverton, M. Reiter, and R. Clarke. Coronary heart disease risk factors in children. The Muscatine Study. *J. Pediatr.* 86:697–703, 1975.
94. Lee, H.J. Nutritional status of selected teenagers in Kentucky. *Am. J. Clin. Nutr.* 31:1453–1464, 1978.
95. Leisti, S., M.-J. Finnilä, and E. Kiura. Effects of physical training on hormonal responses to exercise in asthmatic children. *Arch. Dis. Child.* 54:524–528, 1979.

96. Linder, C.W., and R.H. DuRant. Exercise, serum lipids, and cardiovascular disease: Risk factors in children. *Ped. Clin. North Am.* 29:1341–1354, 1982.
97. Linder, C.W., R.H. DuRant, and O.M. Mahoney. The effect of physical conditioning on serum lipids and lipoproteins in white male adolescents. *Med. Sci. Sports Exercise* 15:232–236, 1983.
98. Loggie, J.M.H. Epidemiology of childhood hypertension. In *Hypertension in Children and Adolescents*. G. Giovannelli (ed.). New York: Raven, 1981, pp. 9–13.
99. Lundberg, U. Note on Type A behavior and cardiovascular responses to challenge in 3–6-year old children. *J. Psychosom. Res.* 27:39–42, 1983.
100. Malo, J.L., S. Filiatrault, and R.R. Martin. Combined effects of exercise and exposure to outside cold air on lung functions of asthmatics. *Bull. Eur. Physiopathol. Respir.* 16:623–635, 1980.
101. Mangla, P.K., and M.P.S. Menon. Effect of nasal and oral breathing on exercise-induced asthma. *Clin. Allergy* 11:433–439, 1981.
102. Maron, B.J., D.R. Redwood, J.W. Hirshfeld, R.E. Goldstein, A.G. Morrow, and S.E. Epstein. Postoperative assessment of patients with ventricular septal defect and pulmonary hypertension. Response to intense upright exercise. *Circulation* 48:864–874, 1973.
103. Mayer, J. Obesity during childhood. In *Childhood Obesity*. M. Winnick (ed.). New York: Wiley, 1975, pp. 73–80.
104. Michaelson, M., and M.A. Engle. Congenital complete heart block: An international study. The natural history. *Cardiovasc. Clin.* 4:85–101, 1972.
105. Miller, W.W., D.S. Young, C.G. Blomqvist, P.S. Strange, R.L. Johnson, and J.H. Mitchell. Physical training in children with congenital heart disease. In *Frontiers of Activity and Child Health*. H. Lavallée and R.J. Shephard (eds.). Quebec: Pelican, 1977, pp. 363–369.
106. Mocellin, R., C. Bastanier, W. Hofacker, and K. Bühlmeyer. Exercise performance in children and adolescents after surgical repair of tetralogy of Fallot. *Eur. J. Cardiol.* 4:367–374, 1976.
107. Moffat, R.J., and T.B. Gilliam. Serum lipids and lipoproteins as affected by exercise: A review. *Artery* 6:1–19, 1979.
108. Moller, J.H., S. Rao, and R.V. Lucas. Exercise hemodynamics of pulmonary valvular stenosis (study of 64 children). *Circulation* 46:1018–1026, 1972.
109. Moody, D.L., J.H. Wilmore, R.N. Girandola, and J.P. Royce. The effects of a jogging program on the body composition of normal and obese high school girls. *Med. Sci. Sports* 4:210–213, 1972.
110. Morton, W.E., and J.C. Knudsen. Correlates of hypertension in young men. *Prev. Med.* 4:258–267, 1975.
111. Nickerson, B.G., D.B. Bautista, M.A. Namey, W. Richards, and T.G. Keens. Distance running improves fitness in asthmatic children without pulmonary complications or changes in exercise-induced bronchospasm. *Pediatrics* 71:147–152, 1983.
112. Nizankowska-Blaz, T., and T. Ambramowicz. Effects of intensive physical training on serum lipids and lipoproteins. *Acta Paed. Scand.* 72:357–359, 1983.
113. Oldenburg, F.A., M.B. Dolovich, J.M. Montgomery, and H.T. Newhouse. Effects of postural drainage, exercise and cough on mucus clearance in chronic bronchitis. *Am. Rev. Resp. Dis.* 120:739–745, 1979.
114. Orenstein, D.M., B.A. Franklin, C.F. Doershuk, H.K. Hellerstein, K.J. Germann, J.G. Horowitz, and R.C. Stern. Exercise conditioning and cardiopulmonary fitness in cystic fibrosis. The effects of a three-month supervised running program. *Chest* 80:392–398, 1981.

115. Orenstein, D.M., K.G. Henks, and F.J. Cerny. Exercise and cystic fibrosis. *Physician Sportsmed.* 11:57–63, 1983.
116. Orenstein, D.M., K.G. Henke, D.L. Costill, C.F. Doershuk, P.J. Lemon, and R.C. Stern. Exercise and heat stress in cystic fibrosis patients. *Pediatr. Res.* 17:267–269, 1983.
117. Orenstein, D.M., K.G. Henke, and C.G. Green. Heat acclimation in cystic fibrosis. *J. Appl. Physiol. Respir. Environ. Exercise Physiol.* In Press.
118. Oseid, S. Asthma and physical activity. *Scand. J. Soc. Med.* (Suppl) 29:227–234, 1982.
119. Oseid, S., and K. Haaland. Exercise studies on asthmatic children before and after regular physical training. In *Swimming Medicine IV.* B. Eriksson, and B. Furberg (eds.). Baltimore: University Park Press, 1978, pp. 32–41.
120. Oseid, S., M. Kendall, R.B. Larsen, and R. Selbekk. Physical activity programs for children with exercise-induced asthma. In *Swimming Medicine IV.* B. Eriksson, and B. Furberg (eds.). Baltimore: University Park Press, 1978, pp. 42–51.
121. Pařizková, J., and M. Vamberová. Body composition as a criterion of the suitability of reducing regimens in obese children. *Dev. Med. Child Neurol.* 9:202–211, 1967.
122. Pařizková, J., M. Veneckova, and M. Vamberová. A study of changes in some functional indicators following reduction of excessive fat in obese children. *Physiol. Bohemoslov.* 11:351–357, 1962.
123. Pate, R.R., and S.N. Blair. Exercise and the prevention of atherosclerosis: Pediatric implications. In *Atherosclerosis: Its Pediatric Aspects.* W.B. Strong (ed.). New York: Grune and Stratton, 1978, pp. 251–285.
124. Patel, K.R. The effect of calcium antagonist, nifedipine in exercise-induced asthma. *Clin. Allerg.* 5:429–432, 1981.
125. Petersen, K.H., and T.R. McElhenney. Effects of a physical fitness program upon asthmatic boys. *Pediatrics* 35:295–299, 1965.
126. Pierson, W.E. The effect of drugs on exercise-induced asthma. In *The Asthmatic Child in Play and Sport.* S. Oseid and A.M. Edwards (eds.). Bath: Pitman Press, 1983, pp. 187–196.
127. Rachelefsky, G.S., D.P. Tashkin, R.M. Katz, H. Kershnar, and S.C. Siegel. Comparison of aerosolized atropine, isoproterenol, atropine plus isoproterenol, disodium cromoglycate and placebo in the prevention of exercise-induced asthma. *Chest* 73:1017–1019, 1978.
128. Ruttenberg, H.D., T.D. Adams, G.S. Orsmond, R.K. Conlee, and A.G. Fisher. Effects of exercise training on aerobic fitness in children after open heart surgery. *Pediatr. Cardiol.* 4:19–24, 1983.
129. Saris, W.H.M. Aerobic power and daily physical activity in children. With special reference to methods and cardiovascular risk indicators. Doctoral dissertation, Catholic University, Nijmegen, Krips Repro. Meppel., 1982.
130. Schachter, E.N., E. Lach, and M. Lee. The protective effect of cold weather mask on exercise-induced asthma. *Ann. Allergy* 46:12–16, 1981.
131. Schieken, R.M., and D.F. Geller. The cardiovascular effect of isometric exercise in children. *Clin. Res.* 26:741A, 1978 (Abstract).
132. Schmücker, B., and W. Hollmann. The aerobic capacity of trained athletes from 6 to 7 years of age on. *Acta Paed. Belg.* 28(Suppl):92–101, 1974.
133. Schnall, R-P., and L.I. Landau. Protective effect of repeated short sprints in exercise-induced asthma. *Thorax* 35:828–832, 1980.
134. Schnall, R., P. Ford, I. Gillam, and L. Landau. Swimming and dry land exercises in children with asthma. *Aust. Paediatr. J.* 18:23–27, 1982.
135. Schnall, R., L.I. Landau, and P.D. Phelan. The use of short periods of exercise

in the prevention and reversal of exercise-induced asthma. In *The Asthmatic Child in Play and Sport.* S. Oseid and A.M. Edwards (eds.). Bath: Pitman Press, 1983, pp. 107–115.

136. Scrapelli, E.M., and A.M. Rudolph. The hemodynamics of congenital heart block. *Prog. Cardiovasc. Dis.* 6:327–342, 1964.

137. Seltzer, C.C., and J. Mayer. An effective weight control program in a public school system. *Am. J. Public Health* 60:679–689, 1970.

138. Shephard, R.J. Exercise-induced bronchospasm: A review. *Med. Sci. Sports* 9:1–10, 1977.

139. Shepherd, J.T., C.G. Blomqvist, A.R. Lind, J.H. Mitchell, and B. Saltin. Static (isometric) exercise: Retrospection and introspection. *Circ. Res.* 48(Suppl I):1179–1188, 1981.

140. Shturman-Ellstein, R., R.J. Zeballos, J.M. Buckley, and J.F. Souhrada. The beneficial effect of nasal breathing on exercise-induced bronchoconstriction. *Am. Rev. Respir. Dis.* 118:65–73, 1978.

141. Silverman, M., and S.D. Anderson. Standardization of exercise tests in asthmatic children. *Arch. Dis. Child.* 47:882–889, 1972.

142. Sly, R.M. Effect of β-adrenoreceptor stimulants on exercise-induced asthma. *Pediatrics* 56:910–915, 1975.

143. Sly, R.M., and S.R. O'Brien. The effect of oral terbutaline on exercise-induced asthma. *Ann. Allergy* 48:151–155, 1982.

144. Strauss, R.H., E.R. McFadden, Jr., R.H. Ingram, Jr., E. Chandler Deal, Jr., and J.J. Jaeger. Influence of heat and humidity on the airway obstruction induced by exercise in asthma. *J. Clin. Invest.* 61:433–440, 1978.

145. Svenonius, E., R. Kautto, and M. Arborelius, Jr. Improvement after training of children with exercise-induced asthma. *Acta Paed. Scand.* 72:23–30, 1983.

146. Swann, I.L., and C.A. Hanson. Double-blind prospective study of the effect of physical training on childhood asthma. In *The Asthmatic Child in Play and Sport.* S. Oseid and A.M. Edwards (eds.). Bath: Pitman Press, 1983, pp. 318–322.

147. Task Force on Blood Pressure Control in Children. Report of the task force on blood pressure control in children. *Pediatrics* 59:797–820, 1977.

148. Taylor, M.R.H. The response to exercise of children with congenital heart disease. Ph.D. thesis, University of London, 1972.

149. Taylor, M.R.H., and S. Godfrey. Exercise studies in congenital heart block. *Br. Heart J.* 34:930–935, 1972.

150. Taylor, S.H., and K.W. Donald. Circulatory studies at rest and during exercise in coarctation of the aorta before and after operation. *Br. Heart J.* 22:117–139, 1960.

151. Thorén, C., P. Herin, and J. Vávra. Studies of submaximal and maximal exercise in congenital complete heart block. *Acta Paed. Belg.* 28(Suppl):132–143, 1974.

152. Thorland, W.G., and T.B. Gilliam. Comparison of serum lipids between habitually high and low active pre-adolescent males. *Med. Sci. Sports Ex.* 13:316–321, 1981.

153. Tipton, C.M. Exercise, training, and hypertension. In *Exercise Sport Sci. Rev.* 12:245–306, 1984.

154. Tuboku-Metzger, A., S. Hirschfeld, G. Borkat, and J. Liebman. Hemodynamic correlates of exercise testing in children with aortic stenosis. *Circulation* 53, 54(Suppl II):48, 1976 (Abstract).

155. Vávra, J., M. Máček, B. Mrzena, and V. Spicak. Intensive physical training in children with bronchial asthma. *Acta Paed. Scand. Suppl.* 217:90–92, 1971.

156. Välimäki, I., M.L. Hursti, L. Pihlakoski, and J. Viikari. Exercise performance

and serum lipids in relation to physical activity in school children. *Int. J. Sport Med.* 1:132–136, 1980.

157. Voller, R.D., and W.B. Strong. Pediatric aspects of atherosclerosis. *Am. Heart J.* 101:815–836, 1981.

158. Wagner, H.R., W.H. Weidman, R.C. Ellison, and O.S. Miettinen. Indirect assessment of severity in aortic stenosis. *Circulation* 56(Suppl. I):20–23, 1977.

159. Watson, G., D. Freed, and J. Strieder. Cardiac output during exercise in children with idiopathic complete heart block. In *Frontiers of Activity and Child Health.* H. Lavallée and R.J. Shephard (eds.). Quebec: Pelican, 1977, pp. 393–400.

160. Weinstein, R.E., J.A. Anderson, P. Kvale, and L.C. Sweet. Effects of humidification on exercise-induced asthma (EIA). *J. Allergy Clin. Immunol.* 57:250–251, 1976 (Abstract).

161. Widhalm, K., E. Maxa, and H. Zyman. Effect of diet and exercise upon the cholesterol and triglyceride content of plasma lipoproteins in overweight children. *Eur. J. Pediatr.* 127:121–126, 1978.

162. Wilmore, J.H., and McNamara J.J. Prevalence of coronary heart disease risk factors in boys, 8 to 12 years of age. *J. Pediatrics* 84:527–533, 1974.

163. Wilson, B.A., and J.N. Evans. Standardization of work intensity for evaluation of exercise-induced bronchoconstriction. *Eur. J. Appl. Physiol.* 47:289–294, 1981.

164. Winkler, R.B., M.D. Freed, and A.S. Nadas. Exercise-induced ventricular ectopy in children and young adults with complete heart block. *Am. Heart J.* 99:87–92, 1980.

165. Wolff, R.K., M.B. Dolovich, G. Obminski, and M.T. Newhouse. Effects of exercise and eucapnic hyperventilation on bronchial clearance in man. *J. Appl. Physiol. Respirat. Environ. Exercise Physiol.* 43:46–50, 1977.

166. Yeung, R., G.M. Nolan, and H. Levison. Comparison of the effects of inhaled SCH 1000 and fenoterol on exercise-induced bronchospasm in children. *Pediatrics* 66:109–114, 1980.

167. Yoshida, T., I. Ishiko, and I. Muraoka. Effect of endurance training on cardiorespiratory functions of 5-year-old children. *Int. J. Sports Med.* 1:91–94, 1980.

168. Zach, M., B. Oberwaldner, and F. Hausler. Cystic fibrosis; physical exercise vs. chest physiotherapy. *Arch. Dis. Child.* 57:587–589, 1982.

169. Zach, M.S., B. Purrer, and B. Oberwalder. Effect of swimming on forced expiration and sputum clearance in cystic fibrosis. *Lancet* 2:1201–1203, 1981.

170. Zeballos, R.J., R. Shturman-Ellstein, J.F. McNally, Jr., J.E. Hirsch, and J.F. Souhrada. The role of hyperventilation in exercise-induced bronchoconstriction. *Am. Rev. Respir. Dis.* 118:877–884, 1978.

171. Zelkowitz, P.S., and S.T. Giammona. Effects of gravity and exercise on the pulmonary diffusing capacity in children with cystic fibrosis. *J. Pediatr.* 74:393–398, 1969.

# Fluid Shifts During Exercise

LEO C. SENAY, JR., Ph.D.
JAMES M. PIVARNIK, Ph.D.

In humans and other mammals, blood performs specific functions that have been divided into six time-honored categories [84]. Of these, we shall only be indirectly concerned with the conveyance of nutrients and the transport of nonvolatile waste products and hormones. More directly relevant will be those functions which both influence and are influenced by rhythmic exercise. Briefly, these functions are the transport of gases to and from the lungs and tissues, heat transport and regulation of body temperature, and water and electrolyte homeostasis. Of these last three functions, we shall focus upon water and electrolyte dynamics during exercise.

Before we catalog and explore various studies, we wish to introduce a number of background facts, thoughts, and suppositions which we have found useful in attempting to explain various experimental findings.

## BODY WATER COMPARTMENTS

Total body water as a percentage of body weight is said to range from 40 to 70 percent [74, 120]. The main reason for this large percentage variation is neither age nor sex but the fat content of the population upon whom the measurements were done. For our purposes, we will concentrate upon both men and women in the age group of 20–30 years with the understanding that much of what we will discuss can be applied with slight modification to older or younger persons.

The total body water content of men in the third decade is usually taken as 60 percent of total body weight and 50 percent for women. The different percentage for men and women is a simple function of body fat content. Adipose tissue contains little water and since the fat content of an average female ranges between 25 and 30 percent of total body weight, the proportion of lean body mass to total body weight is thus lower in women. The lean body mass for all persons is said to be 73 percent water; thus, if two persons had the same body weight but one had twice as much adipose tissue, his or her total body water as a percentage of body weight would be less than the

335

other. The distribution of total body water is much the same in both men and women [45, 74, 120]. Approximately 50–55 percent of the total body water is contained within the intracellular compartment. Thus the intracellular water of a 70-kg man would be 21–23 kg and that of a 55-kg woman would be 15–16.5 kg (1 kg water is approximately 1 liter). There is a degree of uncertainty in all such calculations. Total body water, as determined with tritium has reasonable precision, but in order to calculate intracellular water extracellular volume must be measured [74, 125]. This volume depends on the size of the chemical species employed in applying the dilution principle to the extracellular compartment. In general, the larger the particle, the smaller the volume measured. Simply put, the volume of distribution for various ions and molecular species in the extracellular compartment differ because of the structure and contents of interstitial space.

For our purposes, we place one-third of the total body water for both men and women in the extracellular compartment. This would amount to approximately 14 kg in a 70-kg man and 10.1 kg in a 55-kg woman.

The extracellular water is also subdivided into plasma water and interstitial water. Approximately 3 kg of the extracellular water is contained within the vascular volume as plasma water in an average male subject, while for the average female, plasma water would be about 2.4 kg. Clearly, both vascular and interstitial water are in intimate contact with each other at the level of the capillary beds of both the systemic and pulmonary circulation.

The arithmetically inclined reader will have noted that the sum of extracellular water and intracellular water does not equal total body water. There are certain volumes not included in our consideration of body fluids in exercise., i.e., cerebrospinal fluid, aqueous humor of the eye, inaccessible bone water, and water contained in dense connective tissue [74, 120]. There is one fluid volume in the body that widely fluctuates depending on whether the individual is pre- or postabsorptive. This variable volume of fluid within the gastrointestinal tract cannot be entirely ignored for it may act as a reservoir during the early stages of dehydration.

At rest, the distribution of body water among and between compartments is a steady state governed by a number of forces and metabolic events. Given adequate water and salt intake, tonicity and volume of total body water appears to be a cooperative function between several hormones and the kidney. The interesting item about this control is that the secretion of arginine vasopressin and aldosterone, the two hormones most responsible for body water content and tonicity, chiefly depends upon events occurring within and to the vascular volume.

Intracellular volume is a balance struck between the activity of the ionic pumps, chiefly $Na^+ - K^+$ adenosine triphosphatase (ATPase), and the diffusion of water into the cells. It should be noted here that this balance can be upset either by changing the osmotic gradient from interstitial fluid to cell or by altering the activity of the ionic pump [120].

The magnitude of the extracellular volume is related to its function of providing the proper environment for cells and tissues. This function requires that a portion of the extracellular volume cycle between lungs and tissues in order to supply oxygen and to remove carbon dioxide. The total circulating volume, of which the red cells are part, is determined by receptors in both heart and kidney [85]. The setting of this volume also assists in determining total extracellular volume. As noted above, the contents of plasma are in intimate contact with interstitial fluid across capillary walls. Starling forces determine the direction of exchange and, in turn, these forces are dependent upon the pumping action of the heart and the distribution of protein between the vascular volume and the interstitial space. Any reduction in plasma volume evokes a hormonal response which acts to return the plasma (and blood) volume to a level at which both adequate venous return and renal arterial pressure are obtained.

## CAPILLARIES AND EXERCISE

The equilibrium of substances across capillary walls is the point of attack during rhythmic exercise. Though deserving of exhaustive treatment, we limit our discussion to those items relevant to the experimental results presented later.

With onset of exercise or shortly thereafter, resistance vessels dilate thus allowing more blood to flow through parallel capillary channels. While tradition has it that this is the main reason for increased blood supply to active muscle, Hudlicka et al. [52] noted that much of the increase in capillary blood flow to an exercising muscle is due to an increase in velocity of flow. Nevertheless, with capillary dilatation more capillary surface area is made available, thus increasing the potential for movement of materials both into and out of the vascular volume. Simultaneously, with the reduction in precapillary resistance, there is a relative increase in postcapillary resistance—probably as a result of decreased venous compliance [97] (i.e., decrease in venous volume and an increase in venous tone). Thus, the stage is set for increased capillary exchange due to increased filtration pressure. If no other forces operated, the exchange would quickly come into a new equilibrium, but during rhythmic exercise this may not occur for some time and depends upon a number of factors varying from intensity of exercise to subject position.

Since mean arterial pressure and postcapillary resistance appear to rise in rhythmic exercise there is most likely an increase in capillary hydrostatic pressure [27, 63]. This in and of itself would be sufficient to increase the exit of fluid across capillary walls, but when coupled with osmotic events within the muscle fibers, the conditions are fulfilled for a cooperative influence on water movement out of the vascular compartment.

In certain exercise studies, the permeability of the capillary walls has also been suspected of changing—usually increasing if protein loss can be used as a measure of permeability [51, 107]. At this stage of our knowledge, if protein loss does accompany exercise the exact mechanism has not been described. The simplest explanation has an increase in capillary pressure distorting the junctions of endothelial cells, thus allowing passage of large molecules through these gaps. Recent findings indicate that protein moves from capillary and post-capillary lumen to interstitial space by vesicular transcytosis [104]. Whether rate of vesicular transport changes during exercise we do not know but we do know that the endothelial cells of skeletal muscle capillaries contain a very large population of vesicles. Hence, if more capillaries dilate with exercise, more vesicles may be made available. Also, we have no knowledge of what changes in capillary and small venule $PCO_2$, pH, lactic acid, osmolarity, $K^+$, adenosine triphosphate (ATP), and adenosine may do to the electrical charges borne by the glycocalyx, a structural and electrical barrier lying between capillary lumen and the endothelial cell proper.

## INTERSTITIAL SPACE

Lying between the muscle cell and the capillary endothelial cells is interstitial space, and across the capillary walls, the two volumes, vascular and interstitial, are in intimate communication [45]. The interstitial volume is usually ignored; that is, all operations that cause materials to move from cell to blood operate as in a vacuum. There has been little or no consideration of the influence of interstitial contents and properties on observations derived from blood samples. Some data imply that the dynamics of the interstitial volume are of importance when considering the influence of rhythmic exercise on body fluids [45].

Certain other properties of interstitial space should also be considered as influencing fluid translocation into or out of the vascular volume. Chief among these is compliance, i.e., the change in volume per unit change in pressure. Much is made of venous compliance and its role in maintaining cardiac output [98], but aside from certain basic measurements [30, 75], little attempt has been made to integrate tissue compliance into our understanding of exercise-induced changes in plasma volume.

## BODY POSITION AND FLUID SHIFTS

In 1979, it was noted that among the reports focused on fluid shifts during exercise "disagreements abound—in situations where one worker finds an increase in a certain parameter, another investigator reports a decrease" [110]. It was further suggested that these differences were probably based on a number of items including sex, age, hydration, training, heat acclimation, mode of exercise, and environmental temperature.

Omitted in this list was an extremely important group of factors related to the preexercise control position and the time spent in this position before the start of exercise. As we shall see, supine and upright preexercise positions are not comparable.

Thompson et al. [118] clearly described alterations in blood volume with change in posture. In general, circulating blood volume was greater in the supine (11%) than in the upright posture. Furthermore, the reduction in blood volume was chiefly due to a reduction in plasma volume (PV).

Later reports by Waterfield [127], Eisenberg [26], and Tan et al. [117] confirmed Thompson's results, i.e., with assumption of the upright posture there was a rapid increase in the hematocrit (Hct) and a decrease when the subject reclined. These results were steadfastly ignored by most, if not all the investigators attempting to catalog body fluid shifts during dynamic exercise. In a series of three papers [20, 46, 47], Horvath and co-workers forcibly brought home the fact that much of what was being contested could be attributed to different control positions of the pre- and postexercising subject. In the first of this series Hagan et al. [46] reported that Hct (and PV) did not become reasonably stable for at least 20 minutes after subjects shifted from standing to supine or vice-versa. Furthermore, in a cool environment (23 ± 2°C and 50% relative humidity, RH) the fluid that was lost or gained was essentially protein free. Calculations of changes in PV based on the formula employed by Dill and Costill [21], indicated that after 35 minutes in the standing position (after 35 minutes supine) plasma volume of seven subjects was reduced an average of 16.2 percent. The explanation given by Hagen et al. [46] was that superimposed upon the basic Starling-Landis hypothesis of capillary fluid exchange were increases (standing) and decreases (supine) in the hydrostatic columns of blood lying below the heart in the venous system. With this report, the stage was set for experiments explaining the interaction of exercise superimposed upon different preexercise postures. The next paper in this series considered alterations in PV during exercise as a function of preexercise posture and elevated environmental temperature [20]. To appreciate these experiments the methodology must be understood. Five males participated in six separate tests consisting of 45 minutes of rest followed by 45 minutes of submaximal exercise on a cycle ergometer. Three of the tests were conducted at 30 percent of the subjects' $\dot{V}O_2$max and three were at 50 percent $\dot{V}O_2$max. Since the body fluid dynamics at different oxygen consumptions did not differ statistically, the results were combined. Three postures were employed: upright, low-sit, and supine. In the upright posture, the subject sat upon a modified cycle ergometer with legs dependant; in the low-sit position, the torso was upright, the legs horizontal; In the supine posture, legs and torso were horizontal. All experiments took place in a chamber maintained at 49.5°C ± 1°C and 31 percent RH. Movement to the selected position was permitted only after the subjects had spent 30 minutes in the supine position. Care was taken to avoid extraneous movement during transfer to the cycle ergometer in all positions. Blood sampling at appropriate intervals showed that the upright, resting subjects lost 17.3 percent of their PV in 45 minutes; the low-sit lost 9 percent; and the supine 2.2 percent in 45 minutes. With exercise, the upright subjects lost only an additional 2.7 percent, the low-sit group lost another 7.1 percent, and the supine subjects lost an additional 11 percent of plasma volume. In all cases, the fluid gained or lost was isotonic with plasma and apparently protein free. The environmental temperature did not appear to greatly influence fluid shifts. Diaz et al. [20] ascribed most of the upright loss to hydrostatic events while the rapid (10 minutes) loss of PV at start of exercise in the low-sit and supine position was mainly assigned to the increase in capillary hydrostatic pressure. As we shall see, such reasoning, while basically correct, is somewhat simplistic.

In the final paper, Hagan et al. [47] showed that depending on whether one selected a supine or upright posture as a control position (and after 60 minutes in that posture) exercising at 30 percent $\dot{V}O_2$max in the upright position could result in either a 10.1 percent reduction in PV (from supine) or a 4 percent increase in plasma volume (from upright). In general, Hagan et al. [47] ascribed preexercise shifts in PV to the hydrostatic pressure established in a particular position. In the upright position, the hydrostatic pressure results in maximum volume loss, and the authors believe that no further change occurs during exercise. What these authors failed to consider is that while the volume loss at rest is due to hydrostatic events lack of further net volume loss with exercise may mean that the level of exercise produces a sufficient osmotic gradient such that the water is retained in the interstitial spaces by osmotic forces, not hydrostatic forces. McMurray [69] recently reported a series of experiments that add support to osmotic retention during exercise. He studied six subjects who, in two separate experiments, swam and cycled at similar relative oxygen consumptions. Again, the experimental design is important. After lying supine for 30 minutes, a blood sample was obtained and the subjects were then moved to either a cycle ergometer or a sem-iprone position immersed in a swimming pool. On the cycle, legs were dependant. After the 35-minute resting period, the subjects cycled or swam at 70 percent $\dot{V}O_2max$. When compared to supine rest, the PV loss was essentially the same in both swimming and cycling subjects. Clearly, the exercise in the pool was not greatly influenced by gravity.

It does seem that static forces determine PV before exercise begins, but once under way, it is the osmotic events that predominate [63]. Consideration of actual measurements support this hypothesis. Pollack and Wood [87] measured pressure within the saphenous vein at the ankle at rest and during exercise in several postures. When standing, this pressure averaged 86.8 mmHg (range 78.5–92.5 mmHg). When the subjects walked upon a treadmill at 1.7, 2.6, or 3.3 mph, venous pressure fell within a few steps to a new stable level of 22, 24, and 24 mmHg, respectively. Clearly, if a subject remained standing (or dangled his legs) for some period of time, the hydrostatic pressure would have become maximum in less than 30 seconds. The increase in tissue volume would then be a function of tissue compliance.

In quantifying loss of plasma volume as a function of time and position, Horvath's group has effectively described this compliance of interstitial space and noted that, in the upright posture, little fluid is lost from the vascular volume after 35 minutes [46]. Now, if the subject begins to walk (or cycle) the venous pressure immediately drops. The former static pressures no longer operate, and thus, if only hydrostatic gradients are involved, fluid must leave the interstitial space; alternatively, one must hypothesize an increase in post arteriolar pressure to match the decrease in venous pressure. The reason that the fluid volume in tissue does not greatly change upon start of exercise after standing for long periods is the establishment of a new force—increased osmotic pressure resulting from the increase in muscle metabolism. Indeed, as discussed later, the changes in osmotic gradients in muscle during long-term exercise coupled with the changing contents of interstitial space and plasma and the muscle pump leads to PV maintenance in the face of those forces now simplistically assumed to maintain a lower PV.

What then is a suitable control position for a given exercise study? How long should the subject be forced to remain in this position? There are no absolute answers for body fluids continually adjust to the state in which the body exists. For example, Hagan et al. [46, 47] showed that 35 minutes after shifting from upright to supine position blood volume assumed reasonably constant values. But in this position, Saltin et al. [101] showed that the final blood volume is not arrived at for some weeks. Therefore, one could argue that the true basic blood volume of humans can only be measured in a gravity-free environment accompanied by minimal exercise. The prudent investigator will recognize that if treatment of control and experimental subject is the same, including position and time spent in this position, then the investigator can make valid comparisons between the two. Arguments about what is and is not a control condition will certainly persist, but any particular combination of position and time may be more a matter of personal choice than of unassailable facts.

## SHORT-TERM EXERCISE

*Cycle*
Although we will be dealing with what is termed "endurance" exercise, further subdivision is needed. Keeping in mind that the definition of endurance relates to resistance to fatigue, one should consider exercises that use large muscle groups for a "reasonable period of time." For purposes of this review, we divide the studies done on body fluids and endurance exercise into four sections: (1) studies in which exercise lasted from 1 to 29 minutes (the subjects could have gone on longer had the experiment warranted); (2) studies in which exercise lasted anywhere from 30 minutes to several hours; (3) studies spanning distances greater than 42.2 km or lasting longer than a day; (4) studies of the body fluid dynamics associated with maximal exercise; that is, exercise performed at an intensity equal to or greater than aerobic capacity. Obviously these exercise bouts could only last a very short time. Within each of these time-related groupings are many other divisions such as type of exercise, intensity, ambient temperature and humidity, sex, training state, and hydration state of the subjects.

One of the first attempts to examine blood volume parameters during exercise in humans was reported by Schneider and Havens in 1915 [105]. They had subjects perform various moderate exercise tasks including riding a stationary cycle for 15 to 20 minutes. This caused a 7 percent increase in hemoglobin (Hb) concentration and an increase in red blood cell concentration as well. If the exercise was repeated, the hemoconcentration returned. They concluded that the splanchnic area was most likely a source of red blood cells during exercise. This has since been shown to be untrue [22, 23, 82] by many investigators. It is now well established that any hemoconcentration occurring during exercise is a result of a decrease in PV. Kaltreider and Meneely [55] compared normal men and heart patients during a 10-minute moderate ergometer ride. They found a decrease in PV at the end of exercise and a return to normal some 25 minutes later. There appeared to be no difference in the response of normals when compared to the heart patients. Uehlengen and Buhlmann [119] compared short-term cycle exercise in five males in either a sitting or supine position. Each subject exercised at a moderate intensity ($\dot{V}O_2$ = 1.2–1.5 L/min) for 5 minutes. Plasma volume decreased 3.6 percent during supine exercise and by 10 percent if the subject was seated. This result lends credence to an increased hydrostatic component during seated as opposed to supine exercise that could force the plasma water into the interstitium. When the supine cycle exercise test was repeated a few years later by another German group [62] the same small PV losses were reported. Ekblom et al. [28] studied the effect of training state on vascular dynamics. They had male subjects ride for 8 minutes at each of three submaximal levels of exercise separated by 10-minute rest periods. The series of experiments was repeated after the subjects had engaged in a 16-week training program of various types of running which increased their aerobic capacities an average of 16 percent. Based on changes in Hct, a linear increase in PV loss was seen as exercise intensity increased. This linearity held for both untrained and trained subjects although the percentage of PV lost after training was greater than before training even though the exercise was actually performed at a lower percentage of aerobic capacity. This study also showed a greater arterial-venous oxygen difference ($A_{O_2} - \dot{V}O_2$) and cardiac output (entirely due to increased stroke volume) during the posttraining experiments.

Convertino et al. [12] had four male subjects ride a cycle ergometer for six minutes at various submaximal exercise intensities both before and after training. Thirty minutes of seated rest preceded the experiments, and blood samples were taken pre and postexercise in the seated position. At similar absolute levels of exercise, the percentage decrease in PV during exercise was less in training subjects. When based on relative levels of $\dot{V}O_2$max, the percentage losses of PV were similar in trained and untrained subjects.

Lundvall et al. [63] were the first to attempt to quantify the vascular volume fluxes during short-term cycle exercise in males. By measuring leg volume, they calculated that 1,100 ml of fluid left the vascular spaces during 6 minutes of heavy exercise. The measured PV loss (from labeled albumin) was 600 ml, so it was concluded that 500 ml of fluid reentered from inactive tissues. They theorized that half of the return was due to an increased arterial osmolality ($+22$ mOsm/kg water). The other half was most likely due to a decreased capillary hydrostatic pressure possibly due to sympathetic vasoconstrictor activity in inactive areas.

Costill et al. [13] studied 10 males during various submaximal exercise intensities for 10 minutes each after the subjects had been subjected to a dehydration of 4 percent of body weight. The loss of PV was a linear function of exercise intensity in both the control and dehydrated subjects. Losses ranged from 4 to 12 percent at cycle loads increasing from 30 to 80 percent of $\dot{V}O_2$max. Since red cell volume decreased after dehydration, changes in Hb concentration were needed to determine PV loss. Changes in Hct alone would underestimate the true PV loss under this condition.

Nadel et al. [77] investigated the effect of ambient temperatures on PV dynamics at two submaximal exercise levels. Three healthy but unacclimatized males cycled for 20 to 25 minutes at 40 and 70 percent $\dot{V}O_2$max in three different temperatures (20, 26, 36°C). It was concluded that the loss of PV was related to the intensity of exercise and independent of the skin temperature which was governed by the environmental temperature.

The interrelationship of changes in PV, osmolality, vasopressin (ADH), and plasma renin activity (PRA) was explored by Convertino et al. [11]. Fifteen healthy men of simliar aerobic capacity exercised for six minutes at each of three submaximal workloads. Along with the usual linear decrease in PV were increases in ADH and PRA.

The effect of the muscle mass involved in cycle exercise was examined by Miles et al. [71]. They studied arm crank versus leg crank exercise with male subjects in a seated position. The men exercised with either arms or legs for seven minutes at each of three submaximal workloads. The amount of oxygen used was the same regardless of the limbs being used. However, since $\dot{V}O_2$max with legs was found to be higher (3.3 L/min) than that of arms (2.3 L/min), the relative levels of exercise were different. The results showed a linear decrease in PV as exercise increased, with the loss being independent of muscle mass used but instead related to the percentage of $\dot{V}O_2$max for the particular exercise being done. The PV losses were also found to be related to the mean arterial pressure developed at each workload.

*Treadmill*

The number of short-term (<30 min) cycle ergometer exercise studies far outweighs similar walking, running, or block-stepping experiments. Blood samples can be obtained with comparative ease with cycle subjects and, coupled with the naive assumption that cycle and treadmill exercise are equivalent, convenience generally won the day.

Dill et al. [22] gave credit to Zuntz and Shunburg as being the first to demonstrate that hemoconcentration occurs in exercise; however, these authors performed the first well-defined quantitative experiments. Ten male subjects rested in bed for 20 minutes. A control blood sample was drawn and the subject arose and immediately started to run at 9.3 km/hr and did so for 20 minutes. At 20 minutes, the subject "jumped on the bed" and a second blood sample was drawn within 1 minute. Hematocrits increased (X ± SD) by 5.7 ± 2.7 percent and plasma protein concentrations ([PP]) increased 10.7 ± 4.6 percent ($n = 9$). This particular workload is equivalent to 10 METS (1 MET equals a $\dot{V}O_2$ of 3.5 ml $O_2$/kg) and, for a 70-kg man, requires approximately 2.4–2.5 L/min of oxygen. A reasonable assumption then would have these subjects exercising at 50–70 percent $\dot{V}O_2$max. Keys and Taylor [56] later calculated that the loss in PV in the Dill et al. [21] experiment was accompanied by an 0.4 percent decrease in total circulating protein (TCP).

In a study of the origin of increased plasma potassium during exercise, Kilburn [57] reported Hct and Hb on 7 control male subjects (22–23 years) and 10 of 29 patients before and during a 6-minute treadmill walk. After a resting arterial blood sample (subject position not stated), the 7 controls walked at 2.5 to 3.5 mph on a treadmill "with sufficient grade to produce oxygen consumptions of 1155–3619 ml/min, average 2152 ml/min." A second blood sample was drawn between the 5th and 6th minute of exercise. For the control subjects, Hct increased 3.7 percent but Hb did not change. Results were similar for the ambulatory patients though consuming, on average, 900 ml less oxygen per minute. As we shall see, not having the subjects work at the same relative work load certainly makes these results difficult to interpret, as does the lack of information about the control position. With a 3.7 percent increase in Hct and a probable PV loss of 2.8 percent, these results are qualitatively similar to those of Dill et al [22]. Data similar to those of Dill et al. [22] were published in 1974 by Ferguson and Guest [31]. They reported two sets of 10-minute experiments and one of 1 hour in length (see below). Control blood samples were drawn from subjects ($n = 29$, mean age 23.5 years) who had been supine for 10 minutes. They arose and immediately walked on a treadmill set at an angle of 10 degrees and a speed of 4.8 km/hr (3 mph) for 10 minutes. A supine postexercise sample was taken within 1 minute of the end of exercise and a final supine sample was taken 1 hour after exercise. Resting Hct values (X ± SEM) were 42.0 ± 0.5; immediately postexercise, 47.5 ± 0.4, and 1 hour postexercise, 42.7 ± 0.4. These subjects suffered a 13.1 percent increase in Hct which would indicate an approximate decrease in PV of some 21–24 percent! Ferguson and Guest [31] also reported that, for a group of 14 subjects, the Hct response to this form of exercise (labeled as strenuous) was not appreciably influenced by conditioning. These experiments resembled those of Dill et al. [22] but probably required a higher oxygen consumption.

With the report of Galbo et al. [39], we were introduced to an apparent dichotomy in results that remains with us. In the experiments of Galbo et al. [39], eight reasonably fit men (average $\dot{V}O_2$max = 55 ml·kg$^{-1}$·min$^{-1}$) sat for 45 minutes, then stood on the treadmill for determinations of $\dot{V}O_2$ and a control blood sample. The subjects then ran for 10 minutes at 50 percent $\dot{V}O_2$max, rested 15 minutes, ran for 10 minutes at 75 percent $\dot{V}O_2$max, rested for 15 minutes, then ended the exercise session with a maximum effort. A postexercise resting sample was taken, but time and position were not given. The preexercise Hct (X ± SEM) was 44.9 ± 1.1 and the Hct values for samples taken during the last 2 minutes of exercise were 45.7 ± 1.1, 47.2 ± 1 and 48.0 ± 1.2, respectively, for the 50 percent, 75 percent, and maximum effort. Clearly PV loss was directly related to the intensity of exercise. But then, Galbo et al. [39] had these same subjects perform repeated 20-minute bouts of exercise at 75 percent $\dot{V}O_2$max separated by 10-minute intervals until exhaustion. These experiments were done on the day following the 10-minute experiments. Similar positions and sampling times were observed. Compared to pre and postexercising Hct values of 44.5 ± 0.8 and 44.1 ± 0.8, the Hcts for three bouts of exercise were 45.6 ± 1, 45.8 ± 0.2, and 44.8 ± 0.8. Clearly, when compared to the 10-minute 75 percent $\dot{V}O_2$max hematocrits, the hemoconcentration was slight, at best. Same subjects, same form of exercise, but the exercise bout was twice as long. Similar results were obtained in another study [40]. Here, Galbo et al. had seven 20–28 year-old men (average $\dot{V}O_2$max 49 ml·kg$^{-1}$min$^{-1}$) run repeated 30-minute bouts of exercise at 60 percent $\dot{V}O_2$max. The initial bout of exercise falls within our present purview while the complete experiment fits our intermediate category. The blood sample taken after 28–30 minutes of the first exercise period gave a Hct similar to the rest (standing) preexercise value. No hemoconcentration was seen.

With one extremely important difference, Wilkerson et al. [134] reported on the influence of 20 minutes of treadmill exercise using 30, 45, 60, 75, and 95 percent of $\dot{V}O_2$max. Here, five men (29 ± 2.2

years) had a control blood sample drawn some 14 minutes after assuming a seated position, having spent the preceding 40 minutes reclining on a bed. The subject then stood quietly by the treadmill for 2 minutes and then stepped onto the treadmill and started to exercise. Additional blood samples were drawn at 9, 14, and 19 minutes of each exercise bout. Compared to the seated values, PV loss averaged 73 ml, 108 ml, and 140 ml at 30, 45, and 60 percent $\dot{V}O_2$. At 75 percent $\dot{V}O_2$max the reduction in PV averaged some 306 ml, while in those three subjects exercising to 20 minutes at 90 percent $\dot{V}O_2$max the loss averaged 363 ml. The authors noted a "break" in their data between 60 and 75 percent $\dot{V}O_2$max where plasma volume precipitously decreased. We would like to point out that the relationship of PV to percentage $\dot{V}O_2$max seen in this treadmill study resembles that seen for persons on a cycle ergometer [115].

The only apparent difference between the experiments of Galbo et al. [39, 40] and of Wilkerson et al. [134] is the position of the subject at control sample time—standing vs. sitting. We do not believe that the differences in the control positions satisfactorily explains the differences noted in loss of plasma volume. It may well be that the position of the sampling arm before and during blood drawing was also different [133].

In a study designed to examine the influence of hydration upon fluid shifts during heat exposure, Sawka et al. [102] reported that PV losses were not significant during the first 20 minutes of exercise. The results were similar for six male and six female subjects while walking at 28–30 percent $\dot{V}O_2$max (49°C, RH = 20%) Control blood samples were drawn after the subjects had been quietly standing for 20 minutes. The eventual outcome of these studies will be addressed below.

As the reader will appreciate, there is a paucity of data as to the influence of short-term walking or running upon body fluid dynamics.

## EXERCISE INTERMEDIATE-TERM

*Cycle*
Many investigations have been carried out involving exercise on a cycle ergometer. This seems to be the instrument of choice when studying long-term stress which may be combined with training and/ or heat acclimation. The ease of drawing blood from the arms during an exercise bout while the arms are stationary is of great importance in any experiment and is a major convenience when taking serial samples during a lengthy work bout on a stationary bike. Also, a cycle

ergometer is less expensive than a treadmill and a good deal more portable.

In 1977, Novosadova [81] examined changes in PV and [PP] following 60 minutes of submaximal exercise at "room temperature". He found only a slight hemoconcentration if the level of exercise was 40 percent of $\dot{V}O_2$max and a 7 percent decrease in PV at 67 percent of $\dot{V}O_2$max. The loss occurred in the first 10 minutes of exercise. Thirty minutes of supine rest preceded exercise, but the position of the first blood sample was unclear. Van Beaumont et al. [124] had subjects sit on an ergometer for 30 minutes before a 30-minute ride at various submaximal intensities (40-70% $\dot{V}O_2$max). Plasma volume decreased anywhere from 8 to 15 percent depending on workload, with most of the loss incurred by 10 minutes. There were no changes in red cell volume (RCV) during the exercise sessions.

McMurray [69] had five trained swimmers ride a stationary cycle for 30 minutes at 70 percent of their maximal heart rate. During the exercise, PV decreased 17 percent when compared to a resting, supine volume. The hemoconcentration occurred within 10 minutes of exercise with no further fluid changes in the final 20 minutes. Plasma protein tended to leave the vascular space during the cycle exercise. Harrison et al. [51] examined a combined exercise/heat stress where subjects exercised on a cycle ergometer at 25 percent of max at 42°C (RH = 63%) on one occasion and at 55 percent of max at 30°C (RH = 62%) on another. In both cases PV loss reached 15 percent by 50 minutes of exercise. However, it was a linear decrease in the low exercise/high temperature setting, while almost all losses occurred by 5 minutes using the high percentage $\dot{V}O_2$max/low temperature protocol. Plasma proteins (PP) were lost in both situations, and they hypothesized that sweat rate differences might have affected the kinetics of PV changes. Hemoglobin concentration was included in the estimate of PV loss since RCV decreased at least 1 percent during the exercise. A somewhat rapid decline in PV with little or no further changes seems to be the central theme of the previous four studies. There apparently is a reestablishment of a new "exercise plasma volume" due to the changes in hydrostatic, osmotic, and oncotic events which occur during rhythmic exercise on cycle ergometers.

Ekblom [27] studied the effects of training programs on PV dynamics during intense submaximal cycle exercise. Seven male subjects rode a cycle ergometer for one hour at 75 percent of aerobic capacity both before and after a 22-week training program. The exercise resulted in a PV losss of 11–13 percent regardless of training state. All losses were seen by 5 minutes of exercise. A net protein flux did not appear to occur in any of the exercise test sessions. Since the resting blood samples were taken after subjects sat for 60 minutes on the cycle ergometer, the exercise PV loss was most surely due to the exercise itself. Melin et al. [70] had well-trained, trained, and untrained men cycle to exhaustion at exercise intensities approximating 80 percent of $\dot{V}O_2$max. Based on Hct measurements, well-trained subjects lost only 4 percent of their PV while the less conditioned men lost 11–12 percent. Changes in PP indicate that protein tended to enter the vascular compartment in the well-trained subjects, but tended to leave the vascular space in the other two groups. The result emphasizes the role of PP in PV maintenance during exercise.

The effect of heat acclimation on PV in exercise was examined by Bonner et al. [6]. Five healthy males were tested before and after a 13-day "hot bath" heat acclimation program which increased resting PV some 6–7 percent. The test sessions consisted of 155 minutes of sitting in a hot room (48°C, RH = 36%) followed by 30 minutes of cycle exercise (50 watts) at the same temperature. The 11–13 percent loss of PV during exercise was not affected by the heat acclimation. Harrison et al. [50] used a similar protocol, having subjects pedal a bike for 45 minutes (75 watts) after sitting in a hot room (45°C, RH = 40%) for 30 minutes. These sessions preceded and followed an 11-day "hot bath" acclimation program in which resting PV increased 16 percent. During the cycle exercise, PV decreased approximately 11 percent before, and 14 percent after acclimation. Plasma protein values indicate that protein was lost from the vascular space after acclimation, possibly accounting for the greater PV decrease in spite of identical workloads.

Saltin [99] reported the effects of dehydration on exercise performance. Oxygen consumption at various submaximal workloads was not changed but the ability to perform maximal work was impaired. He found that after dehydration, lactate levels were decreased, as was the time of maximal exercise. This may indicate a reduced ability to perform anaerobic work. Claremont et al. [8] had seven subjects ride in the heat (39°C, RH = 35%) for 2 hours either with or without an acute diuretic treatment. When the subjects were given the diuretic furosemide (Lasix), their resting PV was isoosmotically decreased 15 percent as compared to control conditions. Plasma volume decreased 3–4 percent more during the exercise. In the hydrated state, a 6–8 percent hemoconcentration occurred by 10 minutes with little change thereafter. Harrison et al. [49] immersed four subjects in hot water for 90 minutes and then had them sit and eventually cycle for 45 minutes in a hot (45°C, RH = 30%) environment. In one case the water immersion caused hypohydration, while in two other situations hydration was maintained by frequent water or saline ingestion by the subjects. The water immersion treatments caused a difference in resting PV while subjects later sat in the heat. However, the PV decreases due to the exercise which followed were 4–6 percent in all cases. Gaebelein and Senay [36] studied four male subjects who performed 60 minutes of cycle exercise in either a hydrated or a hypohydrated state. Although the initial hydration states were associated with plasma osmolality differences of approximately 12 mOsm/kg$^{-1}$, the exercise stress (32°C, RH = 90%) produced similar losses (-8%) of PV in both cases.

The previous investigations have suggested that, regardless of extraneous conditions, PV tends to decrease to some extent during lengthy cycle ergometer exercise. Additionally, the degree of hemoconcentration is frequently related to the dynamics of TCP within the vascular compartment. Several others have attempted to shed additional light on the vascular fluxes which occur during cycle ergometer exercise. DeLanne, Barnes, and Brouha [19] studied changes in concentration of various PP fractions during cycle exercise. They reported an increase in the albumin to globulin (A/G) ratio during 30 minutes of ergometer exercise. They postulated that the small (molecular weight, mw, 69,000) albumin molecules were able to return more quickly to the circulation, most likely via the lymphatic system. The small beta globulin fraction (mw, = 90,000) tended to leave the circulation and not return, while the very large alpha 2 globulin (mw, = 820,000) appeared to increase with the onset of exercise. Only minor variations were found in the medium weight (mw, = 150,000) gamma globulins. Assuming a major role for the lymphatic system in protein return to the vascular volume seems reasonable since the lymph flow increases greatly during exercise via the pumping action of muscles. Olszewski et al. [83] found an 85 percent increase in lymphatic flow in the leg during cycle ergometer exercise. Lymphatic protein concentration tended to decrease while return of protein to the vascular system increased some 52 percent.

Other cycle ergometer exercise studies have dealt with blood flow to various nonactive regions of the body. Aurell et al. [4] used inulin and paraaminohippuric acid to measure changes in glomerular filtration rate (GFR) and renal plasma flow (RPF) during 45 minutes of exercise. As exercise intensity increased, a slight drop in GFR was reported while successive reduction in RPF occurred. Johnson and Rowell [36] measured changes in forearm skin and muscle blood flow during a one hour ride of moderate intensity. They reported a progressive rise in forearm flow while forearm muscle flow decreased. Apparently, flow in the nonactive region was confined to the skin area for thermoregulation. The perfusion of skin capillaries could lead to hemoconcentration due to increased hydrostatic pressure. Edwards et al. [25] expanded on this idea in a cycle experiment in which four subjects had their skin alternately heated and cooled while exercising. They postulated that an initial hemoconcentration would be followed by a further gradual PV reduction if the exercise were done in the heat. No further PV loss would occur if the skin circulation was limited. The results supported their postulate.

Up to this point the cycling experiments reported have all dealt with adult male subjects. While many generalities may be drawn from old to young or male to female, this is not necessarily true in all cases. The most striking age-related contradiction to the literature presented thus far involves a study by Macek et al. [64]. Ten prepubertal boys cycled for one hour at room temperature. Plasma volume increased some 4–5 percent at an exercise intensity equaling 40 percent of $\dot{V}O_2$max and no change was found at 50 percent of $\dot{V}O_2$max. The maintenance of PV was related to an influx of protein into the plasma. The authors were quite taken with these results which contradict most other studies showing hemoconcentration during cycle exercise. Unfortunately, the length of time at rest and control position are not clear in the paper. The authors speculated about a possible relationship of PV maintenance with low plasma lactate levels but this idea was not very convincing, even in their own minds.

A number of investigators have studied women as subjects during cycle ergometer exercise. Considering body size, fatness, and hormonal differences, results found with females might shed some light on the causes behind exercise PV changes. Senay and Fortney [111] examined untrained females performing 40 minutes of cycle exercise in cool (20°C) and hot (45°C) environments. Although the exercise was performed at a relatively low intensity (30% $\dot{V}O_2$max), a large reduction in PV occurred in both the cool (-12.8%) and hot (-17.7%) sessions. This decrease occurred even though PP increased or was maintained. The authors hypothesized that the exaggerated PV reduction might be due to an increased osmotic gradient at a given percentage $\dot{V}O_2$max in women, or perhaps a lesser capillary density which would hinder diffusion of particles from muscle to blood. The same investigators [33] later studied the effects of a training and heat acclimation program on females who performed 45 minutes of submaximal (40%) cycle exercise in the same cool and hot environments as previously reported. At the end of a 4-week training program, aerobic capacity of the women increased 15 percent while resting PV expanded 9 percent. Four weeks of heat acclimation increased PV an additional 7 percent with maintenance of $\dot{V}O_2$max. During the exercise tests, PV decreased more in the hot (-11.3%) then in the cool (-6.3%). On a percentage basis, PV reduction was the same in the two experiments (pre vs. post) but a greater absolute loss occurred after training/acclimation due to the expanded PV.

DeLanne et al. [19] used six men and six women when they studied the previously reported changes in protein fractions during cycle exercise. The sex of the subject had little or no bearing on the results. Gaebelein and Senay [37] repeated their hyper/hypohydration study with five females. They again found that although preexercise hydration state was associated with a difference in resting osmolality, PV dynamics during 60 minutes of ergometer exercise were similar, resulting in a hemoconcentration of approximately 12 percent. The same authors [38] repeated a similar exercise protocol and fluid manipulation with five additional women, but this time the subjects performed the exercise bouts both in mid-follicular and mid-luteal phases of their menstrual cycles. During the follicular phase, preexercise plasma osmolalities depended on subject hydration status, and during exercise the PV decreased 7.5 percent following hyperhydration and 11.6 percent after hypohydration. During the luteal phase, the fluid balance manipulation did not alter resting osmolalities, and PV decreases during exercise were approximately 7.5 percent in all cases. These results seem to indicate that the phase of the menstrual cycle (and possibly hormonal state) plays a role in vascular volume changes in endurance cycle exercise.

*Treadmill, Walking, Running*
Here we have placed experiments with exercise times greater than 30 minutes but which take place within several hours. Much of what has been recorded in such a time frame concerns the influence of long distance running on body fluid dynamics. In short-term exercise (<30 min), individual subjects were seldom highly trained but in the present category (>30 min) most if not all the subjects could be considered highly trained. Additionally, there are variations in ambient temperature, in body positions at which control blood samples were drawn in the preevent timing of the control blood samples, and in subject hydration.

There is almost a decade between the first and the second report on our list. Wells and Horvath [128] set out to study the influence of exercise in the heat (48°C vapor pressure = 11 mm Hg) on various hematologic parameters during three phases of the menstrual cycle. Seven untrained females had a blood sample drawn upon arrival at the laboratory. Following a number of preparatory operations, including a bath, the subjects entered the hot room and reclined upon a cot for 45 minutes. This was followed by 45 minutes of exercise on a treadmill set so as to elicit an oxygen consumption of 50 percent $\dot{V}O_2$max. After exercise, the subject again reclined in the heat for 45 minutes. At the end of the second resting period, a post-exercise sample was taken. The inflence of the exercise upon Hct, Hb, and [PP] was said to be minimal in all three stages of the menstrual cycle.

Considering the sample times and the different ambient temperatures at which the pre and post samples were taken, it is difficult to believe that the authors were studying the effect of exercise.

As noted in the previous section, Sawka et al. [101] examined the influence of hypohydration upon fluid shifts in an environment similar to that employed by Wells and Horvath [128]. The subjects of Sawka et al. [101] walked on a treadmill in the heat for two 30-minute periods separated by a 10-minute rest in the heat. Resting blood samples were taken from 12 subjects (6 males, 6 females) standing in an antechamber, and further blood samples were taken after 30 minutes of exercise in each exercise bout. The first samples have been commented on above and here we shall concentrate on the results for the final sample. During the course of walking on the treadmill at 28–30 percent $\dot{V}O_2max$, the subjects, when euhydrated, increased their PV by 4 percent but decreased their volume by the same amount when hypohydrated some 5 percent of body weight. A reduction in red cell volume during the hypohydration experiments was also observed. In both the euhydrated and the hypohydrated experiments, the [PP] remained relatively constant. The authors felt this was due to an efflux of some 8 g of protein during hypohydration exercise and an influx of some 8–11 g during euhydration exercise. Sawka et al. [102] reasoned that the decrease in TCP was due to a decrease in lymph flow such that influx of protein fell short of efflux because of capillary dilatation and other factors. Judged against Senay's hypothesis [107] this seems reasonable.

Edwards and Harrison [24] reported a series of experiments designed to study the influence of skin temperature upon Hct and Hb concentration during treadmill running. Four male subjects sat in a chair upon a treadmill for 45 minutes, after which a blood sample was drawn. They then stood up for 20 minutes and a second blood sample was obtained. On one day, the subjects then ran at 10 km/hr up a 2 percent slope for 60 minutes or until they refused to continue. On another day, the subjects ran for 90 minutes and, by use of a liquid conditioned coverall, had their skin cooled between the 30th and 60th minute. For a final experiment, all subjects ran for 48 minutes with equal periods of no skin temperature (Ts) manipulations, skin heating, and skin cooling. In all experiments, the very act of standing up from a sitting position caused an average increase in Hct and Hb of 6.2 percent and 5.9 percent, respectively. Neither running nor changes in Ts resulted in any consistent alteration in intravascular volume, though Edwards and Harrison claimed wide subject variability. The sit-stand change in Hct confirms the earlier observation of Senay et al. [115].

The results of Galbo et al. [39, 40] and Edwards and Harrison [24] are in agreement as to fluid shifts during treadmill running at times greater than 10 minutes. Whether Edwards and Harrison assessed blood changes during the first 10 minutes of exercise is not known. Based on these two studies, with equivalent control sampling postures, the initial response to running is a modest early reduction in plasma volume (<10 min). With continued exercise, the PV is restored to near its resting value. This leaves a number of questions.

1. What is the biological variability among and between subjects?
2. What are the body fluid responses during treadmill efforts at graded oxygen consumption? The results of Galbo et al. [39, 40] and Edwards and Harrison [24] are at odds with those of Wilkerson et al. [134], particularly at the higher levels of $\dot{V}O_2$.
3. What influence does training have upon these responses?
4. Have experiments been done to measure protein dynamics?
5. Are there variations due to sex and age?

Partial answers to these questions were reported by Pivarnik et al. [86]. Six endurance-trained and heat-acclimatized males participated in three separate experiments. As a control, the subject sat upon a stool with legs hanging free for 90 minutes. A blood sample was taken at the end of this period. In a room set at 23.8 ± 0.8°C and RH 74.5 ± 8.6 percent the subjects next exercised at one of three levels of oxygen consumption for 1 hour or, in the most severe exercise, until exhausted. Exercise levels were 37, 56, and 74 percent $\dot{V}O_2$max. A postexercise sample was taken within 1 minute after exercise ceased. Total body water losses ranged from 0.74 to 1.27 percent of preexercise body weight. At 37 percent $\dot{V}O_2$max, PV increased 3.29 percent, appeared stable (-0.47%) at 56 percent $\dot{V}O_2$max and decreased slightly at 74 percent $\dot{V}O_2$max. Concomitantly, there were significant increases in TCP at all three levels of exercise. These results resemble those of Galbo et al. [39, 40] and of Edwards and Harrison [24] as well as Wilkerson et al. [134], but only at the two lowest workloads. Pivarnik et al. [86] did not confirm the findings of Wilkerson et al. that PV loss accelerated at exercise levels above 60 percent $\dot{V}O_2$max. The influence of training and heat acclimatization on the results of Pivarnik et al. [86] are not known.

As noted earlier, the report of Ferguson and Guest [31] also contained results on seven subjects who walked at 3 mph (4.8 km/hr) on a treadmill set at an angle of 5° for 1 hour. Again, control blood samples were taken after 10 minutes of supine rest, within 1 minute of the end of exercise (subjects supine) and 1 hour after end of exercise. Control Hct (mean ± SD) was 42.1 ± 1.1, and after exercise, 44.4 ± 1.2. The final postexercise Hct averaged 41.4 ± 0.9. The question arises in this and similar experiments as to what forces the 8–9 percent decrease in PV could be ascribed. Diaz et al. [20] would have us believe that much if not all of the loss is due to hydrostatic events while McMurray [69] suggests that osmotic forces control events during exercise.

The complexity of fluid shifts during 2 hours of running can be appreciated by applying a few simple calculations to the results reported by Costill, Kammer, and Fisher [16]. The report describes the results where four highly trained runners ran for 2 hours at 74 percent $\dot{V}O_2$max on three separate occasions. During one run, no replacement fluids were given, for another run a glucose-electrolyte fluid was ingested, and during an additional run water was given. A prerun control blood sample was taken, but the position of the subjects was not given. Additional blood samples were taken at 10 and 120 minutes. Based on Hct values, the subjects without fluid replacement lost both fluid and protein during the first 10 minutes of exercise but in the next 110 minutes, fluid loss did not greatly increase and TCP increased. In these same subjects, when given the glucose-electrolyte fluid, the Hct showed a 3 percent increase at 10 minutes and a 3.4 percent increase at 120 minutes. The [PP] increased by 11 percent in the first 10 minutes and ended at 16.9 percent. Clearly, protein had been immediately added to the vascular volume and over the course of the experiment more had been added. In the final run, with water replacement, the fluid loss seemed to account for the increase in [PP] both at 10 and 120 minutes. Here we have the same subjects on three different occasions yielding three different results. The fluid regimens had no influence on the 10 minute values. What caused such variations? There are two findings which should be emphasized. Regardless of fluid regimen, the TCP after 120 minutes of running was as great or greater than that recorded at 10 minutes of exercise. The second point is extremely important. When confronted with body weight losses from 4.8–6.2 percent and no fluid replacement, the PV decreased by 100 ml in the final 110 minutes of the no-fluid run. This is an approximate calculation based on an assumed initial blood volume of 6 L. Considering an average body weight loss of 3.5 kg during this time, the stability of the PV could be termed remarkable.

Rocker et al. [94] reported similar results for similar experiments. In their study, 11 well-trained marathoners ran 32 km in about 2 hours. Body weight loss averaged 3.9 percent. Using iodinated albumin, PV was first determined in the supine position before exercise. The postrun PV was calculated from the initial PV and the postrun Hct and Hb. The postrun blood samples revealed no significant change in PV but did contain an increased amount of protein. Unfortunately, the position of the postrun subjects was not stated. The only apparent environmental difference between the Costill et al. no-fluid regimen [16] and the experiments of Rocker et al. [94] was that of ambient temperature—25°C for Costill et al. and 5–15°C for Rocker et al.

To this point, all the upright running studies we have described indicate that once exercise is under way, PV is rather well maintained even in the face of a considerable loss of total body water. The disagreement among these studies seems to be confined to the position the subjects assume for the control blood sample for this does seem to influence the direction (and magnitude?) of PV loss.

We are not finished with our consideration of adult runners, but we believe that having presented a picture which we discuss later on the basis of position, oncotic and hydrostatic pressures, and muscle metabolism, it is the right moment to consider a study whose results were quite different.

Macek et al. [64] reported results of an extensive series of experiments with 10 prepubertal boys as subjects. All experiments took place at an ambient temperature of 24°C. Two treadmill exercises were completed by each subject on separate days: for 1 hour, the boys exercised at either 36 percent or 60 percent of their $\dot{V}O_2$max. Blood samples were obtained at rest and at 10, 20, 40, and 60 minutes of exercise. The rest position was not given. There were no significant changes in Hct values during exercise at 60 percent $\dot{V}O_2$max, but at 36 percent $\dot{V}O_2$max there was a 5 percent increase in PV in all exercise samples when compared with the resting value. There were no changes in the amount of protein within the vascular volume in either the 36 percent or the 60 percent $\dot{V}O_2$max experiments. One would guess from the lack of rest-to-exercise differences in Hct that the control samples were taken in an upright posture. Nevertheless, the absence of net protein movement is striking, as is the apparent ineffectiveness of increased muscle osmotic pressure in drawing plasma water from the intramuscular compartment.

In a series of experiments similar to those of Rocker et al. [94] wherein thermal dehydration was compared to exercise dehydration, Costill and Fink [20] presented data on six subjects who exercised for 2 hours or until they had suffered a 4 percent body weight loss. Five of the subjects ran on the treadmill and one subject performed on a cycle ergometer in order to induce hypohydration. Although it is impossible to separate the cyclist from the treadmill subjects, we feel that his results did not overly influence the reported numbers. All experiments took place at an ambient temperature of 22.2°C, RH 40–45 percent; control and postexercise samples were taken in the supine position and those taken after 10 minutes of exercise and after a 2 percent and 4 percent reduction in body weight were taken in the upright position. We have recalculated the percentage changes in PV based upon the formulas used by Dill and Costill [21] for Costill and Fink [15] used Hb concentrations only for their calculations. We would add that the differences were not great. During the first 10 minutes of exercise the subjects apparently suffered a 12 percent reduction in plasma volume. We say apparent because, unlike the experiments of Edwards and Harrison [24], and Diaz et al. [20] we have no information as to initial postural changes. There was not only a reduction in PV, but there was also an evident loss of protein from the vascular volume. The reason we say this is that there was a 5 percent increase in [PP] which accompanied a 12 percent reduction in PV. Clearly if the TCP had been constant, the increase in [PP] would have been 13.6 percent. Based on an assumed PV of 3,200 ml, the loss of PP amounted to some 16 g. Over the course of the dehydration to 4 percent, the PV which had decreased by 12 percent with the first 10 minutes only decreased an additional 2 percent. Here again we see that in the face of a 2.8-kg reduction in body water, PV remains rather stable. Accompanying the minor changes in PV with dehydration was an increase in the protein content of the vascular volume. Whereas the 12 percent decrease in PV at 10 minutes was accompanied by a 5 percent increase in [PP], at 4 percent dehydration, the 15 percent reduction in PV was now accompanied by a 12 percent increase in [PP]. Thus, in spite of apparent differences in control positions of the subjects, the results for men are reasonably consistent within the exercise period; PV is maintained and protein accumulates within the vascular volume.

Considering the number of persons running standard marathons (42 km) the amount of hard data as to internal body fluid dynamics is miniscule. Hard data must be gathered and disseminated in order to properly educate all persons engaged in endurance exercise. Only then will there be proper attention given to salt and water balance by the average runner.

In hindsight, results reported for marathon runners appear to be an extension of those noted above. In the most thorough study to date, Maron et al. [65, 66], in addition to Hct, Hb, and total protein also determined plasma epinephrine, norepinephrine, cortisol, free fatty acids, glycerol, triglycerides, glucose, lactate, and pyruvate. These workers did baseline studies 10 days before the race and followed changes for three days after the race. We will confine our attention to those indicators of volume alterations during the race day and the postrace days. The average PV decreased 4.7 percent during the race, and the reduction in total body weight averaged 4.3 percent. In addition, Maron et al. [65] found that 27 g of protein were added to the vascular volume. Such an addition undoubtedly assisted in stabilizing the PV during the marathon. The influence of the increase in TCP could be discerned in the postrace observations—particularly on day 2 after the race [66]. Here, the PV has expanded some 19 percent. The authors reason that this was due to salt and water retention, but to do so the subjects would have had to gain an additional 3 kg over their control body weights for Na+ and water are generally equitably distributed in the extracellular compartment. Since body weights were not given, we cannot affirm or deny such an event. However, the intravascular protein mass appears stable and since 1 g of protein is said to "hold" 15 ml of water [103] the protein added to the vascular volume during the marathon could be responsible for an increase in PV of 400 ml during the postrace hydration period. Here again we see small or inconsequential changes in PV during the exercise period in spite of considerable reductions in total body water.

The report of Myrhe et al. [76] injects a Shoenbergian dissonance into our theme. These workers followed four male and two female runners (average age 48 years) during a marathon where the wet bulb globe thermometer index (WBGT) varied from 15.5°C near the start of the race to 24.5°C toward the end. Only three subjects finished, but due to an unfortunate accident (a broken test tube or two) the complete results for the entire race were only available for two male subjects. However, after the subjects sat for 30 to 45 minutes a control blood sample was taken. Other samples were taken at 16 and 34 km and within 2–7 minutes after the finish of the race. Of those who finished, one subject suffered a 3.9 percent loss in body weight and a 5 percent decrease in PV, a second subject lost 3.4 percent body weight and had a 13 percent decrease in PV, and the third subject suffered a weight loss of 6.7 percent and a PV reduction of approximately 27 percent. The first subject also had a 15 percent increase in [PP], and the second subject increased his [PP] some 10 percent. Since all runners arrived at the 16-km sampling point, Myrhe et al. [76] found that in four of the runners the increase in [PP] could be entirely ascribed to the decrease in PV, while in the two remaining runners protein was added to the vascular volume. In discussing these data, Myrhe et al. did not refer to the data of Maron et al. [65, 66] and with these few subjects and samples they indicate that the hypothesis as to protein influx and accumulation during exercise, while viable, is on tenuous grounds. We disagree, though older runners may differ in their body fluid dynamics. The results of Macek et al. [64] and Myrhe et al. [76] await confirmation.

Kolka et al. [61] drew blood samples on three subjects at 4.8-km intervals throughout a marathon. The prerace sample was taken after the subject had been in an upright position for 30 minutes. The postrace sample was taken in the upright position from only one subject (subject II) because the other two subjects could not stand up—a condition common to inexperienced marathoners. In addition, their subject I not only lost water by sweating, but he also had repeated episodes of regurgitation after 30 km. In spite of his problems, subject I finished with a PV some 11 percent larger than when he started and a weight loss of 4.49 kg. Subject II (stand up postrace sample) also had an 11 percent increase in PV with a body weight loss of 3.36 kg. Subject III had a remarkable 21 percent increase in his PV while losing 3.13 kg of weight. No data as to [PP] were collected. Dry bulb temperature averaged 19.4°C with a water vapor presssure of 9.5 Torr (RH = 40%). The least that could be said about the study of Kolka et al. [61] is that PV appeared to be maintained in spite of large losses in total body water (8%).

Wells et al. [129] report quite different results. On a cool day (10.6°–15°C, RH = 67% with a strong wind) blood was drawn within 10 minutes of ending the race. The subjects were seated. The control samples had been drawn one week earlier. It is therefore impossible to comment on specific fluid shifts on the day of the marathon. Based on their control and immediate postrace sample, Wells et al. [129] report a 12.8 percent decrease in PV for six males and a 7.7 percent decrease for four female runners. Body weight could not be obtained after the race, and hence we do not know the degree of whole body water loss. Calculated from presented figures, there appeared to be a small increase in the total TCP in the vascular volume for both male and female subjects. Interestingly, on a percentage basis, the globulins increased slightly more than did albumin. It would appear then that for these subjects retention and addition of protein to the vascular volume did not protect this volume as had happened in previous reports [16, 61, 65, 66]. However, this may be more apparent than real because in order to assess the influence of exercise upon volume there must be a measurement of volume immediately before the start of exercise in the appropriate posture. As Edwards and Harrison pointed out, just changing from sitting to upright posture increases the Hct [24].

Finally, Whiting et al. [131] reported results on some 90 subjects who finished a marathon on a cool (10–12°C, Rh = 74 percent) day. Aside from a remarkable feat of logistics in just obtaining pre and postrace blood samples, the authors managed to include an astonishing range of subjects, i.e., age 20–62 years, height 164–193 cm, weight 50.8–94 kg, and finishing times of 144–307 minutes. No positions were stated for pre and postrace blood sampling. During the race the subjects lost an average 2.09 ± 0.77 kg (mean ± SD) or 2.9 ± 0.8 percent of their body weights. Simultaneously they suffered an average loss in PV of 4.7 percent. This was accompanied by an average 8.2 percent increase in [PP], but the standard deviation of this increase was rather large, ± 12.4, thus indicating that some subjects gained a good deal of protein while others may have lost as much. Whiting et al. [131] do not seem to be aware of the literature on protein movement or chose to be rather selective in what they considered pertinent to discuss. In the end, the data of Whiting et al. support a shift of protein into the vascular volume, thus indirectly supporting the theme that a stable plasma volume probably relfects a stable or increased TCP.

*Block Stepping*

Block stepping is a descendant of the Master's two-step test [61] via the Harvard step test [10]. Such tests have proved valuable in the assessment of individual fitness. Because experiments in most exercise laboratories are limited as to equipment and space, the need to service large numbers of subjects has never arisen. When one is faced with the task of heat acclimating 300,000 to 400,000 men a year, economy and ease of application must be considered. Thus, under the direction of Wyndham, the Human Sciences Laboratory of the Chamber of Mines of South Africa introduced block stepping as the preferred form of exercise during heat acclimation of recruits to the gold mining industry. Numerous internal reports are available from the Chamber of Mines as to the application of block stepping in testing human performance [138].

The first use of block stepping to examine changes in PV was reported by Cullumbine and Koch [18]. They had 13 Ceylonese men step on and off stools 20 inches (50.8 cm) high some 30 times per minute (Harvard step test). The subjects had an average body weight (± SD) of 49.4 ± 18 kg (range 40.5–68.6 kg) and height of 159.2 ± 8.5 cm. Based on these measurements and the fact that stepping on and off a block some 30 cm in height at a rate of 24 times a minute is done at a cost of 1.3–1.4 L/min of oxygen, it would seem reasonable to assume that the subjects of Cullumbine and Koch [18] were exercising at or above 60–70 percent of $\dot{V}O_2$max. In 6 subjects who had but one initial injection of Evans Blue, the 5 minutes of exercise caused a decrease in PV (± SD) of 20.2 ± 7.1 percent. A second test was done on seven different subjects. The only difference between the two tests was that resting PV was determined by an initial injection of Evans Blue in both tests but a second injection of Evans Blue was given postexercise to obtain a second measure of PV. In both experiments the subjects were seated from 90 to 120 minutes before the step test and were again seated after the test. In the second test the PV decreased 16 ± 4.4 percent. Plasma volume took 25–75 minutes to return to preexercise values. Interestingly, Cullumbine and Koch [18] also determined extracellular volume using thiocyanate as the indicator ion. They found an average increase in extracellular fluid volume of almost 2 L during recovery. The source of this fluid was not identified. The average PV (±SD) of these 13 subjects was 2,548 ± 351 ml. Calculations based on height and weight by the formula of Allen et al. [2] gave plasma volumes some 500 ml less.

Senay [106, 107] initially used block stepping to examine the influence of various ambient temperatures upon vascular volumes and constituents before and after heat acclimation. He had trained his subjects [107] for 12 to 14 days before the experiments began. Control and postexercise blood samples were taken from seated subjects. When subjects were kept cool (20°C), hemodilution occurred during block stepping ($\dot{V}O_2 \sim 1$ L $O_2$ min$^{-1}$). In warm environments (40°C or 30°C) hemoconcentration generally occurred. These latter results were reversed after heat acclimation. At the time, Senay believed his results were influenced only by the ambient temperatures and the state of heat acclimation of his subjects. That training should also be considered influential was noted in later studies.

Block stepping was employed by Senay and Kok [112] in examining the body fluid responses of heat-tolerant and heat-intolerant men. Control blood samples were taken with subjects seated, but all other samples were taken while the subjects continued to step. Regardless of whether the subjects were heat tolerant or intolerant, or exercising at 30 or 50 percent $\dot{V}O_2$max, hemodilution occurs in a hot environment. Clearly these were not your average untrained, nonheat-exposed subjects. The heat-tolerant subjects were heat acclimated and, to some degree, were trained ($\dot{V}O_2$max = 49.9 ml·kg$^{-1}$ min$^{-1}$). The heat intolerant subjects had lower $\dot{V}O_2$max (41.1 ml·kg$^{-1}$ min$^{-1}$), and in addition, they could not be acclimated to heat. Though there were basic differences in the amounts of fluid and protein moved into and out of the vascular volume, both groups of men behaved similarly, i.e., hemodilution was accompanied by an influx of protein into the vascular volume. There was the possibility that those responses were due to an elevated ambient temperature (Ta) (33.3°C, RH 90%).

The next study of Senay and Kok [113] had different results. Four untrained men block-stepped and one subject cycled at an energy cost of 35 W. At this time we were still under the impression that rhythmic exercises that required the same energy expenditure were equivalent. Again. control blood samples were obtained from seated subjects while the remaining blood samples were drawn as the subjects continued to exercise. During the first two standard tests (block stepping for 4 hours at 18–22°C) the subjects lost both protein and fluid from their vascular compartments. In a third similar test done after the subjects had trained for some 14 days, these results were reversed; i.e., the subjects added fluid and protein to their vascular volume. These results were again obtained in three sequential cool tests over a period of 20 days. For the last test the men were also heat acclimated, but this added little to the fluid and protein movement in the cool environment. The men also were allowed to drink water ad lib in all the six standard tests, but osmodilution only occurred over the last four tests. Training served to stabilize plasma volume and protein content when these same subjects stepped in the heat (33.8°C, RH 90%). The influence of heat acclimation upon fluid dynamics is discussed later.

From these results, it would appear that training influences the direction of both protein and fluid shifts between the vascular and extravascular compartments. Therefore, in the heat-tolerant–intolerant study of Senay and Kok [112], the direction of fluid and protein flux was probably due to the previous training of the subjects. The magnitude of the fluxes were apparently further influenced by ambient temperature and subject heat acclimation [113, 114].

Later, Senay [109] again combined a hot environment with block stepping, and again the subjects were trained for 2 weeks before the initial heat exposure. In 12 subjects, there was a suggestion of hemodilution and protein influx. One group of 6 subjects continued to train (block stepping) while an equal number were heat acclimated (block stepping). Upon a second 2-hour heat exposure (33.8°C, RH = 90%) significant hemodilution occurred within 10 minutes of the start of exercise in both the trained and acclimated group. The only difference between the two groups was that the acclimated subjects maintained the hemodilution for the entire heat exposure. It should be emphasized that control blood samples were drawn with the subjects seated while all other blood samples were taken as the subjects continued to exercise.

Most recently, Gaebelein and Senay [36] have compared the responses of four men to cycle ergometer and block-stepping exercise. In both forms of exercise, the subjects were both trained and heat exposed during ther week prior to the test heat exposure. Therefore, the subjects may have been partially heat acclimated on the test days. For the block-stepping studies, the subjects participated in two tests, once while hydrated and once while mildly dehydrated (osmolality increased by 3.6%). Control blood samples were taken from seated subjects. The subjects then entered an environmental chamber set at 32.2°C db, 30°C wet bulb (wb) and block stepped for 60 minutes at a rate of 12–15 steps/min to a height of 23 cm. Additional blood samples were taken at 10-minute intervals. During the exercise, Hb and Hct measurements appeared to display significant increases only after 40 minutes of exercise. The increases in both parameters, although significant, indicated a loss of PV of some 5 percent. Interestingly, the body fluid dynamics during block stepping did not appear to be influenced by hydration state.

In their most recent report, Gaebelein and Senay [37] followed a similar protocol in examining the vascular volume changes during cycling and stepping in five female subjects. The hydration state of the subjects did not influence fluid shifts during exercise although the dehydrated women displayed plasma osmolarities 10 mOsm higher than when hydrated. For the hydrated subjects, PV decreased some 9 percent during the 60 minutes of exercise (Hb-Hct). A similar loss occurred in the dehydrated subjects. In both hydrated and dehydrated subjects there was no net gain or loss of PP from the vascular volume during these experiments.

In these two studies of Gaebelein and Senay [36, 37], both male and female subjects suffered a reduction in PV while stepping in a hot environment. Both groups of subjects had been exposed to stepping and heat during the week preceding the test experiments. However, the training was not rigorous, and the subjects may have become only partially heat acclimated. Therefore, it is not surprising that the results for these two groups of subjects resemble those reported by Senay and Kok upon exposure of untrained and unacclimated men to a similar regimen [113].

In summary, whether or not hemodilution occurs during block stepping apparently depends upon the rigor of the exercise, the training state of the subjects, the ambient temperature, and whether or not the subject is heat acclimated.

## LONG-TERM EXERCISE

### Walking, Running, Skiing

We are concerned here with runs or walks over distances ranging from 42.2 km to 500 km. As endurance running grows in popularity such events are becoming more popular as tests of male and female conditioning and courage. Witness the increase in the number of entrants for such events as the Iron Man Triathalon. At the moment, our objective information as to the influence of such long-term exercise upon fluid dynamics is limited. During a standard marathon (42.2 km), the general concern is water intake. Whether the water is given as a pure solution or as a drink lightly laced with electrolytes and glucose seems to be of little practical importance. In longer runs, however, both electrolytes and food are ingested along with water.

McKechnie et al. [68] confined their observations to changes in protein fractions as a result of running 92 km. Their subjects had blood samples drawn immediately after the marathon and again some two weeks later. These latter samples were considered controls. No data concerned with PV, blood volumes, Hct, and so on, were reported. Further complicating the report was that five fewer subjects donated blood two weeks after the marathom. The only notable difference between the immediate and two-week sample was the concentration of albumin. It was significantly higher (0.64 g/dl, P < 0.001) immediately after the race when compared to two weeks after the race. The remaining four fractions measured ($\alpha_1$, $\alpha_2$, $\beta$, $\gamma$globulins) were the same in both blood samples.

Poortmans and Haralambie [89] were also interested in individual protein fractions in serum and urine before and after 11 men (29–81 years) ran 100 km. These investigators reported [PP] and 10 individual protein fractions in blood and urine prior to, immediately after, and 1 day after recovery. Based on Hct and Hb values, PV did not significantly change during the run, nor did the concentration of serum proteins. Again, the position of the subjects when blood samples were taken was not revealed. The prerun sample was taken 2 hours before the run while the postrum sample was drawn within 15 minutes of the finish time. Poortmans and Haralambie [89] confirmed the findings of McKechnie et al. [68] as to a significant increase in albumin concentration (+0.32 g/dl) during the race. The authors believe that the changes in albumin, along with significant increases in other PP fractions, are due to protein influx into the vascular volume during exercise. Clearly, if total protein concentrations did not significantly change and certain individual fractions also increased their concentration, other fractions had to leave the vascular volume. Poortmans and Haralambie also reported evidence of moderate hemolysis.

Noakes and Carter [80] reported fluid and electrolyte determinations for subjects who ran 160 km. All subjects save one lost body weight, but in spite of weight loss, plasma electrolytes were maintained within normal limits. In their most extreme cases, the increase in Hct was approximately 5 percent, and interestingly, though Hct values went up, the Hb concentration went down. In general, the PV appeared to be reasonably well maintained during the run. According to Noakes and Carter's plasma protein values, the stability of PV could not be ascribed to stability (or increase) of PP [79]. In some cases there was little change in [PP], in others there were marked increases, and in several cases [PP] decreased rather substantially. These results could be used to support a variety of positions as to the mechanism of PV regulation during exercise. It would seem reasonable to repeat such a study.

In two papers, Pugh [90,91] recorded increased blood volume in six subjects who "hill walked" 29 miles in about 8–9 hours on two separate occasions. Water was available during these walks and the temperature varied between 6 to 12°C for one walk and between -2 to 2.5°C for the other. The red cell volume was determined by the carbon monoxide technique before and after both walks. Red cell volume remained unchanged while PV increased some 233 ml (7.3%, an average which included both walks). Accompanying the increase in PV was an average increase in TCP of some 17 g. Again, if the Scatchard et al;. [103] value of 15 ml water/g protein could be applied, the protein movement could account for the entire increase in PV of the walkers.

Williams et al. [135] and Milledge et al. [72] have recently extended Pugh's work and report, respectively, on the results of seven and four consecutive days of hill walking. Both studies were carefully planned and executed. the first study [135] was faced with trying to explain a 22 percent increase in PV during the course of exercise. The metabolic bookkeeping indicated that the maximum water retention occurred the fifth day of walking and averaged 650 ml. The cumulative $Na^+$ balance amounted to some 350 mmol on day 5. Since the $[Na^+]$ in plasma remained constant throughout the study, Williams et al. [135] were forced to conclude that the extracellular volume had to expand 2.5 L of which but 650 ml could be accounted for by water retention. Intracellular water was assumed to be the source of the 1.8 L needed to balance the fluid bookkeeping. This decrease in intracellular water was not accompanied by any net loss of $K^+$. Williams et al. may have thus accounted for the $Na^+$ retention, but their suggestions leave them with hypertonic cells—a curious denial of osmotic forces. It would seem somewhat more reasonable to assume that the retained $Na^+$ may not have remained in the extracellular volume as Williams et al. [135] assumed and that the PV expansion could have been based on a protein shift as found by Pugh [89, 90]. No protein determinations were done and we are thus without adequate clues as to how the PV was so greatly expanded during consecutive days of hill walking.

Milledge et al. [72] confirmed the expansion of PV during four consecutive days of hill walking. Body weights were not given, nor was PP determined. Based on $Na^+$ retention, the authors calculated a fluid retention of some 1.84 L, one-half of which they placed in the vascular volume and the other half as edema fluid in the lower limbs. What causes a NaCl solution to be selectively sequestered in the vascular volume and thus increase PV by some 26 percent? Protein data are needed to clarify this point.

One of the reports most often quoted as to the expansion of blood volume during long-term endurance exercise is that of Astrand and

Saltin [3]. Their six subjects suffered an average weight reduction of 5.5 percent, but when PV was determined 1 hour after the race, the volume had increased an average of 410 ml or 11 percent. What most authors fail to point out is that the Hct taken before the 85 km cross country ski race averaged 44.7 percent while the Hct taken immediately after the race averaged 45.9 percent. Thus, during the race, the PV decreased about 5 percent—the gain in volume occurred during the postrace recovery period, when the Hct value fell to 43.1. Refsum et al. [92] essentially confirmed these results when they measured Hb and total serum protein concentrations in 41 men who participated in a 90-km cross-country ski race. The subjects suffered a net body weight loss of 1.93 kg (2.6%). Concomitantly, the Hb values decreased significantly ($P < 0.001$) from a prerace average value of 15.01 g/dl to 14.45 g/dl. This 3.7 percent reduction in Hb could be assumed to be due to 5–6 percent increase in PV. There were no changes in [PP] hence the increase in PV probably was due to a net influx of fluid with a [PP] similar to that already present in the vascular volume.

Neither of the ski reports described the positions of the subjects while blood was drawn, and in the study of Astrand and Saltin [3] we do not know how much time elapsed between the control sample and the start of exercise.

## MAXIMAL EXERCISE

*Cycle*

As stated earlier, vascular volume changes during exercise are basically controlled by changes in hydrostatic and osmotic forces. During maximal ergometer exercise these forces should be pushed to their limit due to the large increase in blood flow and metabolic rate that occurs.

Poortmans [88] studied 28 highly trained (olympic caliber) men during a $\dot{V}O_2$max test at room temperature. He reported that percentage increases in [PP] were greater then percentage increase in Hct and concluded that protein must have entered the vascular spaces during the exercise. However, his interpretation is not valid since he directly compared percentages without calculating the actual PV change that did indeed occur. In reality, the PV decreased 11.1 percent while [PP] increased only 8.6 percent. This indicated a loss of protein from the vascular volume. Further inspection of his reported protein fractions indicated no change in total circulating albumin and gamma globulin, while alpha macroglobulin and beta lipoprotein decreased. Van Beaumont et al. [123] found similar changes with six untrained subjects ($\dot{V}O_2$max $= 38.3$ ml·kg$^{-1}$ min$^{-1}$). They reported a decrease in PV of 15.6 percent and a loss of TCP of some 4 percent immediately following maximal cycle exercise. Van Beaumont [121] later designed an experiment to assess red cell size during maximal exercise. Although the reported results on the constancy of red cells appear dubious due to methodological problems [13], the same decrease of 15–16 percent in PV was found. No protein changes were reported in this experiment.

Wilkerson et al. [132] measured PV change in 10 healthy ($\dot{V}O_2$max = 43.5 ml·kg$^{-1}$ min$^{-1}$) men. Plasma volume decreased 14 percent while [PP] increased a similar amount, indicating no change in TCP. The postexercise samples were taken at least four minutes after the exercise so it is possible that the values immediately following exercise may have been somewhat different. Eight untrained subjects ($\dot{V}O_2$max = 44 ml/kg$^{-1}$) were studied by Senay et al. [115]. A decrease of some 15–18 percent of resting PV was found as well as a decrease in TCP. Greenleaf et al. [44] measured PV shifts after maximal supine as well as seated ergometer exercise in four subjects. They reported the same 16–17 percent decline in PV regardless of exercise position. As has been shown previously, PP decreased as well. The authors also make a case for the idea that PV loss during cycle exercise is directly related to intensity of exercise. Additionally, the decreases seen at 65 percent of maximum seem to hold for any greater intensity of exercise including maximum. This idea appears reasonable, based on the studies reported in the present review. However, deviations may occur depending on hydration state of the subject or ambient temperature.

Supramaximal cycle exercise has also been studied. This is exercise done at an intensity greater than that performed at aerobic capacity. Obviously these sessions can be carried out for only a minimum of time before acute fatigue develops. Green et al. [41] trained four male subjects for three days with supramaximal exercise. The protocol was 1 minute of cycling at 120 percent of $\dot{V}O_2$max followed by 4 minutes rest. This continued for 24 repetitions or until exhaustion. The PV dynamics during the first of these training days resulted in a hemoconcentration of 14 percent. Interestingly, resting PV increased 11.6 percent after the training. Although a decrease in TCP of 4.3 percent was reported during the exercise, changes in resting PP were not reported. Sjogaard and Saltin [116] attempted to detect changes in extra and intracellular water spaces of muscle during supramaximal exercise. Six subjects performed 3-x-3-minute cycle exercises at 120 percent of maximum. A loss in PV of some 20–21 percent was accompanied by a slight decrease in PP. Total muscle water increased in the active vastus lateralis muscle while no change occurred in the triceps. The increase in intracellular muscle water was much less than that in the extracellular space of the muscle even though an osmotic gradient based on lactate should have accounted for a greater intracellular water change. The authors surmised that the filtration of water from the capillary bed into the interstital spaces might be largely under the influence of an increased mean capillary pressure in the muscle. Mohsenin and Gonzalez [73] measured tissue pressure and oncotic pressure during supramaximal exercise. Six healthy men cycled for 3 minutes at 105 percent of peak $\dot{V}O_2$ after 3 minutes of warm up. Interstitial pressure was measured via the wick technique [30]. Plasma volume (-17.2%) as well as TCP (-4.6%) decreased during the exercise. Plasma osmolality increased some 16 mOsm. In support of Sjogaard and Saltin [116], they found that tissue fluid pressure increased in the vastus lateralis muscle but did not change in the triceps. The increase in plasma osmolality as well as in interstitial pressure most likely helped to prevent any further loss of PV at this intense exercise. It would seem reasonable to conclude that this limit occurs at all submaximal workloads but with less disturbance (and less plasma volume loss) of the resting forces governing compartmental fluid volumes.

*Treadmill*
There is no agreement as to the influence of a bout of maximal exercise upon PV. Galbo et al. [39] drew a control blood sample as the subject stood upon the treadmill, then had the subjects run at 74 percent $\dot{V}O_2$max for 2 minutes. The exercise level (load) was then increased every 25 seconds until the subject could no longer continue (4–5 min). The Hct increased to 48 ± 1.2 (n = 8) from 44.9 ± 1.1, approximating a PV loss of some 12 percent. Wilkerson et al. [132] had 10 subjects perform a constant speed incremental slope test. Blood samples were taken from seated subjects 1 minute prior to exercise and 4 minutes after end of exercise. Calculations based on Hb-Hct values indicate that these subjects suffered an average reduction in PV of some 14.4 percent during maximum exercise. There may also have been a slight loss of PP from the vascular compartment. A similar loss in PV was recorded by van Beaumont et al. [124] for 12 men who attained $\dot{V}O_2$max upon a treadmill. Preexercise position was not specified but a postexercise blood sample was taken from the seated subject 2 minutes after end of exercise. The mean loss in PV was 15.7–16 percent. The results of these three studies appear to be at odds with those of Senay et al. [115]. Among the four studies the only obvious difference was the speed of the treadmill. For 17 walking subjects, nine of whom had repeat studies done, Senay et al. [116] increased the treadmill angle 3 percent every 3 minutes until $\dot{V}O_2$max was reached. Though individual subjects may have increased or decreased their PV, there was no significant change in

mean values throughout the entire procedure. Protein content of plasma appeared to be maintained throughout the exercise. Blood samples had been obtained with the subjects seated and then during every 3rd minute upon the treadmill. We believe that sampling from the exercising subject is not the same as sampling from the postexercise subject, regardless of time. Again, the different results may also reflect different protocols.

## TRAINING AND ACCLIMATION

The effect of training and heat acclimation on body fluid responses during endurance exercise has yet to be extensively analyzed in this review. We have already mentioned the fact that for a given body weight, trained individuals tend to be leaner than those who are untrained. Assuming that this means an increased body water/body weight ratio, this volume increase may have important ramifications during exercise. This would be especially true if exercise required both high cardiac output to working muscles and high sweat rates for thermoregulation.

Basic blood constituent values have been reported by several investigators. Kjellberg et al. [60] reported the differences between Hb and blood volume values of trained and normal individuals. Blood volume of untrained, fit, and extremely fit men ranged from 5.2 to 6.6 to 7.4 L, respectively. While Hb concentrations were fairly consistent, contents ranged from 805 g in untrained, 995 g in trained, and 1,130 g in well-trained men. Women followed this same pattern but at lower absolute volumes. Untrained women were reported to have blood volumes of 4.1 L and Hb of 555 g on average, while values of trained women were higher at 5.7 L of blood and 800 g of Hb. Hemoglobin concentrations again were similar among all women but were lower than those of men at any level of fitness.

Oscai et al. [84] reported blood volumes of 14 men before and after a 16-week running program. While aerobic capacities increased some 17 percent, blood volume increased approximately 6 percent (338 ml). All of the increase in vascular volume was contained in the plasma.

Another study differentiating blood volume in men due to training state was done by Brotherhood et al. [8]. Fitting the numbers to a blood volume/body weight scale, athletes were found to have higher blood volumes ($93.1$ ml/kg$^{-1}$) than nonathletes ($74.5$ ml/kg$^{-1}$). Additionally, total Hb content of the athletes was reported to be 20 percent higher than that of sedentary men.

Remes [93] studied the effect of a long-term physical training program on blood volume. A 4 percent increase in red blood cells (RBCs) was found in soldiers who had been involved in a six-month military training program. No changes in PV were found after the training. Although the red cells were determined by a very reliable technique ($^{51}Cr$), there was poor control of actual training time and effort during the six-month period. Additionally, an increase of 16 percent in predicted aerobic capacity was found, although the test used (Astrand-Rhyming) has an accuracy of $\pm 10$ percent at best.

Rocker et al. [95] measured PV and PP in 49 sedentary men and 40 athletes. Plasma volumes were found to be 600 ml greater in the athletes. Total circulating proteins as well as albumin contents were also greater in the trained subjects. To achieve the same hemoconcentration during an exercise bout, the athletes would be able to lose a greater amount of their PV on an absolute basis.

Four men trained on a cycle ergometer two hours per day, at 65 percent peak $\dot{V}O_2$, for eight consecutive days (db = 25°C). Although PP was not measured, resting PV of the subjects increased, on average, 440 ml (12.3%) after training [12].

As has been previously discussed in the section on block stepping, Senay [108] found a greater influx of PP and PV during an exercise bout after subjects were endurance trained and heat acclimatized. In a later experimeent [107] the same results were found during mild exercise in the heat, and he hypothesized the importance of cutaneous blood flow as a vehicle of PP and PV increase in the trained/acclimatized subjects.

Nadel et al. [79] investigated the mechanism of thermal acclimatization to exercise and heat stress. A group of unfit subjects were trained on a cycle ergometer at 80 percent of $\dot{V}O_2$max for 10 days, followed by a combined exercise/heat acclimation procedure in hot and dry or wet environments. It was found that training increased the sweat rate at a given internal temperature, or central sweating drive. If heat acclimation was added to the training, not only was sweat rate enhanced but sweating was initiated at a lower core temperature. Both of these adaptations would be of obvious advantage during an exercise bout in the heat as body temperature could be more effectively maintained at a given exercise intensity and ambient temperature.

Convertino et al. [11] attempted to separate the roles of exercise and thermal stress on the mechanisms of hypervolemia seen during training/heat acclimation programs. Subjects either sat in the heat (42°C, RH 93°) for 2 hours a day for 8 consecutive days or exercised on a cycle ergometer at room temperature (27°C, RH 60%) for the same length of time. Resting PV increased 177 ml in the heat acclimated group and 427 ml in the exercise trained group. From the data reported it appears as though the moderate PV expansion was due to increased ionic content since the increases in body weight during acclimation matched the approximate increase in extracellular volume. This was definitely not the case in the trained subjects whose body weights would have had to increase some 1.8 kg (not just 0.8 kg) by the end of the 8 days of exercise. The hypervolemia was attributed to the 32 g increase in PP seen in the cycle-trained subjects.

The effects of an 11 day exercise/heat acclimation program on PV responses during cycling in the heat were examined by Harrison et al. [50]. The exercise test consisted of a 45-minute ergometer ride at 75 W in an ambient temperature of 45°C (RH 40%). The acclimation period resulted in a PV increase of 12.9 percent accompanied by an increase in PP. Plasma volume decrease during the exercise amounted to 11.2 percent in the pretest and 14.0 percent in the posttest. Although sweat rates appeared to be similar both before and after acclimation, core and skin temperatures were lower in the posttest. Although both exercise tests were conducted at 75 W, it is possible that this constituted a lower relative work intensity due to a mild training effect produced during the 11-day exercise/acclimation period.

## FLUID AND ELECTROLYTE INGESTION

*General Comments*
In all forms of endurance exercise, if carried on long enough, and regardless of environment, fluid and electrolyte balance becomes a problem for the exercising subject. The solution to this problem is based upon three factors: (1) How much fluid is lost by the subject? (2) How much water (or dilute salt solution) is available to the subject? (3) How much fluid will the subject actually drink?

From personal observations on these items, we will show that what has been observed during marathons can be predicted, given normal human performance.

An average subject running a standard marathon on a partly cloudy day where the ambient temperature is 10°–15°C will suffer a gross body weight loss of from 3–4 kg. This weight loss is primarily sweat and its composition is hypotonic to the body. Now if [Na$^+$] in this fluid is assumed to be 50 mEq/L then the subject would have retained 90 mEq/L$^{-1}$ Na$^+$ for each liter of water lost. Therefore, to return extracellular [Na$^+$] to prerace values would require a water intake of approximately 1.9–2.6 L. If sweating subjects are left to their own devices, they will ingest but 25–35 percent of the volume lost as sweat [112]. Voluntarily then, our average subject will ingest 250–350 ml water/kg water loss. That these amounts actually balance the Na$^+$ retention may be pure chance, but seldom does an endurance athlete finish a contest of 2–4 hours without suffering a net weight loss. Water ingestion, though effective in maintaining the ionic concentrations, does not return the volume of total body water to prerace values, and hence the subject suffers a volume deficit. Since PV appears reasonably maintained, the volume deficit must reside elsewhere, and since protein has left the interstitial volume, this must be where the deficit resides. In summary, if the ratio of water loss to water ingestion does not equal 3:1–4:1, body osmolarity and electrolyte concentrations will probably increase.

*Walking, Running*
In reviewing running and walking, whether on a treadmill in a controlled environment or outdoors where heat exchange can be rather variable, the movement of fluid and protein into and out the vascular compartment has been our main concern. It would appear that maintenance of blood volume accompanies long-term exercise in spite of loss of body water. Those studies which list electrolyte and osmotic pressure changes during long-term endurance exercise indicate that the elevation in $[Na^+]$ and osmotic pressure are proportional to net water loss. In the first study to be concerned with such items Rose et al. [97] did not determine net fluid loss but did find a 4.1 percent increase in plasma osmolarity and a 4.3 percent increase in plasma $[Na^+]$. Both of these changes were significant ($P < 0.05$). The increase in plasma $[K^+]$ was some 13 percent ($P < 0.05$) whereas $[Cl^-]$ showed a nonsignificant increase of 1 percent. Both $[Mg^{++}]$ and $[Ca^{++}]$ decreased, with the decrease in $[Mg^{++}]$ being significant.

Maron et al. [65, 66] and Noakes and Carter [80] recorded no significant changes in electrolytes during runs of 42.2 and 160 km, respectively. Refsum et al. [91] also reported no change in $[Na^+]$, $[K^+]$, and $[Cl^-]$ after subjects skied 90 km and confirmed the results of Rose et al. [97] in that $[Ca^{++}]$ and $[Mg^{++}]$ both significantly decreased. Astrand and Saltin [3], however, reported a 4.9 percent increase in $[Na^+]$ after an 85-km ski race. Though $[Na^+]$ increased significantly, $[Cl^-]$ did not change. The different results reported by Refsum et al. [92] and Astrand and Saltin [3] could have been predicted from net losses in body water, i.e., the subjects of Refsum et al. had a net decrease in body weight of 1.93 kg while the subjects of Astrand and Saltin had a net weight loss of 3.9 kg. The results posted by Whiting et al. [131] as to changes in $[Na^+]$ during a marathon agree with the results of Astrand and Saltin [3], though their mean weight losses of 90 subjects was but 2.09 kg. In these subjects, the type of fluid ingested (glucose-electrolyte or water) did not seem to influence changes in $[Na^+]$.

Even in subjects who ran 500 km in 20 days, the prerun plasma

[Na$^+$] and osmolarity did not differ from control values except before the second run day. In order to maintain such balance, Wade et al. [126] found that Na$^+$ was conserved by the kidney up to 20 hours after cessation of the daily run. In this study, hormonal influences upon day-to-day Na$^+$ balance were evident, but in a one-day effort, hormonal influence as to Na$^+$ balance and osmotic pressure are not as prominent.

### Cycle Ergometer

When considering fluid replacement during an endurance exercise bout, one should keep in mind the reason behind the importance of such a practice. During prolonged exercise, particularly in the heat, relatively large amounts of water and salt may be lost from the body due to profuse sweating. If the exercise is of reasonable intensity in addition to being lengthy, glycogen stores may eventually be depleted. Any method of fluid replacement which could incorporate an addition to body electrolye and glucose store would be of obvious benefit to the endurance athlete. For the casual reader, basic information as to human responses to water deprivation can be found in the classic publications of Adolph and Associates [1] and Wolf [136].

Costill and Saltin [7], reported a rather extensive investigation of the factors which affect gastric emptying during rest and exercise. The experimental protocol included ingestion of various concentrations of glucose/electrolyte solution, the temperature of which ranged from 5–35°C. Exercise was performed for 20 minutes on a cycle ergometer at various percentages of $\dot{V}O_2$max (40–90%). It was found that maximal gastric emptying of approximately 380 ml/15 min occurred if replacement fluid tonicity was 214 mOsm/L. Exercise did not retard this process until intensity became greater than 60 percent of $\dot{V}O_2$max. Three subjects performed the exercise for 2 hours, but this had no additional effect on gastric emptying.

Costill et al. [16] reported the effects of water and electrolyte replacement during 2-hour treadmill runs. As pointed out earlier, the results were extremely variable. There was internal consistency in the fact that serum electrolyte values increased if no fluid was given, did not appreciably change if the glucose/salt solution was taken, and decreased if only water was ingested. Differences in control Hct and PP values most likely affected the PV changes during this exercise. There was no report of a possible influence of randomization of experimental conditions so that the differences may be due to the sequence in which the protocol was conducted. Additionally, subject position during blood sampling was not given. There was little hemoconcentration during most (110 min) of exercise regardless of what was or was not drunk. Inspection of PP values indicates an addition of protein to the vascular volume in all cases. This finding is entirely consistent with most previous reports dealing with lengthy running exercise.

Van Beaumont et al. [122] had subjects perform 75 minutes of cycle exercise at 32 percent (30 min) and at 64 percent (45 min) of $\dot{V}O_2$max. Body weight changes during the exercise were continuously monitored and any losses were replaced with water. This fluid replacement prevented any loss in PV by the end of exercise. Based on the near consensus finding of rapid (5–10 min) hemoconcentration during ergometer exercise, body weight maintenance via continual fluid ingestion obviously reversed this trend.

Kirsch et al. [58] studied the effects of fluid replacement during lengthy bicycle exercise. Half of 10 well-trained cyclists drank an electrolyte replacement fluid at various points during a 90-km race. Total volume ingested by each subject was approximately 1.5 percent of body weight. The other five subjects abstained. The fluid replacement group lost only 2.5 percent of their body weight as opposed to a 4.1 percent loss by the nondrinking subjects. The conclusion of the authors that the fluid replacement prevented a PV loss during the race was based on a PV measurement taken 90 minutes postrace. By comparing the reported hematocrits taken prior to and only 10 minutes after the race, PV decreased 7–8 percent regardless of hydration status. Perhaps an additional 80 minutes after the race was required for a sufficient volume of fluid to be absorbed and to return PV to prerace levels.

Costill et al. [14] examined the effect of different fluids drunk during a heat acclimation procedure. Subjects rode a cycle ergometer in the heat until their body weights decreased by 3 percent. They were allowed to drink either water or an electrolyte replacement drink ad lib during the exercise. Regardless of what the subjects drank, resting PV increased approximately 10.5 percent. Since body weights did not increase, an expanded total extracellular volume (due to increased electrolyte content) was not the likely cause of the PV increases. Although [PP] were not reported in this particular study an increase in TCP in the vascular volume following heat acclimation has been shown in many previous investigations. Francis and MacGregor [35] had 10 subjects drink a water or electrolyte replacement drink (hypotonic) during 2 hours of cycle exercise performed at 32°C (RH 45–50%). The amount drunk was equal to the amount lost through sweat, urine, and respiration. Thus body weight did not change. The authors reported no changes in Hct, Hb, or [PP] in either group indicating a maintenance of PV, most likely due to the fluid replacement. This has been shown previously but closer inspection of Hct and Hb reveals a decrease in MCHC of some 8 percent in both groups. Additionally the absolute MCHC values (>39.0) were much higher than even the upper end of the average range seen in healthy men (32.0–36.0). Considering the small or nonexistent serum electrolyte changes, red cell swelling of such magnitude seems inconsistent with the findings presented. Francis [34] reported a similar experiment but added a group of subjects who received no fluid during the exercise. It was again reported that both fluid replacement regimens were associated with PV maintenance and no change in body weights at the end of 2 hours of exercise. However, the group receiving no fluid lost 9 percent of their PV by 1 hour and 17 percent by 2 hours at the termination of exercise. It appears that these results again indicate that water and possibly limited electrolyte replacement during cycle exercise may prevent the normal hemoconcentration that usually occurs. Although Francis computed the PV changes via Hb and Hct, only the Hct were graphically presented. Therefore it was impossible to assess accurately any changes in MCHC among the hydrated subjects. However, a 14.8 percent increase in Hct associated with only a 17.7 percent decrease in PV in the nondrinking subjects suggests red cell swelling. This is unlikely with a 2.4-kg loss in body weight.

The effects of isotonic and hypertonic electrolyte solutions drunk during exercise in the cool and in the heat were explored by Greenleaf and Brock [42]. The authors suggest that hypertonic drinks may aid in PV maintenance during cycle exercise in the heat. However it is difficult to interpret accurately the results since the figures presented seem to differ from the written text. An additional confounding factor may have been the lack of a blood sample taken at the actual beginning of the exercise bouts.

Nadel et al. [78] investigated the effect of hydration state on thermoregulation during exercise. Four men cycled for 30 minutes in the heat (35°C) in either a euhydrated, hypohydrated, or hyperhydrated state. Hypohydration was induced via a diuretic and resulted in a decrease in resting PV of some 17–21 percent. Hyperhydration (due to ingestion of 1.8 L of water prior to exercise) had no real effect on resting PV. Hypohydrated subjects exhibited a decreased skin blood flow during the exercise. This occurred as a physiologic effort to maintain cardiac output to the working muscles at the expense of body cooling. Esophageal temperature rose much quicker in these subjects as they cycled. Hyperhydration had no effect on exercise thermoregulation but did allow for the exercise to be performed at a lower heart rate.

## CONCLUDING THOUGHTS

The transfer of fluid, protein, and ions into and out of the vascular volume must obey the laws of chemistry and physics. Thus, in erecting a general hypothesis which attempts to explain diverse observations, we must be able to explain what happens when subjects assume various resting postures, what happens when they move, and what influence rate and force of movement play.

The tissues which appear to be the recipient of gravity's largess are the dependant legs. Clearly, changes in PV brought about by moving from the supine to the erect (and postures in between) position are a function of the length of the hydrostatic column, the compliance of muscle compartments, the compliance of the extramuscular compartments, the number of patient capillaries, the permeability of capillary walls, the total interstitial pressure, the plasma and interstitial fluid oncotic pressures, and the time spent in position.

If we could answer two elementary questions, we could construct a proper foundation for our hypothesis. The first question is, What is (are) the compliance(s) of skeletal muscle? The second question is, What is (are) the compliance(s) of extramuscular leg tissue?

There is at present no absolute answer to the first question. In describing three muscle compartments, Hargans et al. [48] refer to the anterior compartment of the lower leg as "a marginally compliant compartment." Wells et al. [130] noted that resting intramuscular pressure immediately responded to increases in venous pressure but the response was not a "square wave." During 70 minutes of standing, there was an initial rapid rise in intramuscular hydrostatic pressure followed by a slow increase in pressure of the anterior tibial muscle, reaching 60 cm $H_2O$. Rodbard[96] emphasized that the connective tissue capsules present in and around skeletal muscles separated the interstitial fluid into discrete intra- and extracapsular fluids. Thus, if hydrostatic pressure is suddenly increased, the compliance of the skeletal muscle would seem to be the sum of a number of parallel compartments.

Hargans et al. [48] also noted that an isometric contraction produced intracompartmental pressure from 60 to 95 mmHg. This certainly must be due to the low compliance of the connective tissue surrounding the muscle fibers. Measurements of muscle compliance have been made in various animals [29, 75], but until further information in human subjects has been recorded, the extrapolation of these results to humans is extremely questionable.

The rapidity of attaining equilibrium venous pressures upon standing has been recorded by Pollack and Wood [87]. They noted that it took approximately 22 seconds for pressure within the saphenous vein to reach its maximum steady state value. It would appear then that the response of the pressure within the various muscle compartments would be almost as rapid. Therefore, we suggest that in inactive muscles, there occurs a rapid pressure equilibration upon moving from supine to sitting to upright postures and that the actual volume moved from inside the vascular volume to the interstitial volume of the muscle compartments depends on the compliance of the connective tissue delineating the boundaries of these compartments. We feel that the actual volume transferred is not of any great magnitude.

If this is true, then just where is the fluid sequestered that leaves the vascular compartment? We nominate the interstitial space of the extramuscular compartments in the legs. When the observations on saphenous vein pressures are coupled with those of Wells et al. [130] as to the pressures in subcutaneous tissue and volume expansion of the legs in the upright posture the following appears logical. Upon assuming a resting upright posture, the increase in venous hydrostatic pressure is fairly rapid, as is intracompartmental muscle pressure. The subcutaneous pressure does not so respond. Wells et al. [130] found that even after 100 minutes of standing, the subcutaneous pressure in the calf was 12.5 cm $H_2O$ (9.2 mmHg). Other observations showed that increased venous pressure, while causing a rise in subcutaneous pressure, was considerably damped. Also, the pressures then remained reasonably constant (and low) even though the volume of the limb continued to increase. Therefore, it is reasonable to state that the limbs are minimally a two-compartment system—one having a high compliance and one a low compliance. The limit of expansion of both compartments is set by the surrounding connective tissue— in the case of the extramuscular compartment this is the skin. Thus, the muscle compartments quickly come into pressure and volume equilibrium, while the more compliant extramuscular compartment has a much longer equilibration time and probably accommodates a larger volume of fluid from the vascular compartment. Indeed, Wells et al. [130] found that even after 2.5 hours the leg was still increasing in volume. We wish to suggest that when persons move from supine to upright static posture, the immediate fluid loss is due to fluid movement into both muscle and extramuscular compartments, but it is our feeling that after 3–5 minutes of quiet standing the fluid loss is mainly into extramuscular space. The results of Hagan et al. [46] indirectly support this postulate. When their subjects stood up after spending 35 minutes in the supine position, they ($n = 7$) lost, on average, some 16.2 percent of their plasma volume in 35 minutes of standing. Other similar studies from Horvath's laboratory [20, 47], van Beaumont et al. [124], and Greenleaf et al. [44] have established an apparent upper limit of 20 percent on PV loss in the upright position. What these investigators have seemingly overlooked is that the larger the absolute PV, the larger the absolute volume that is lost during standing. We have noted that the subjects of Hagan et al. [46]

have blood volumes ranging from 74.6 to 106.6 ml/kg of body weight. When we calculated a regression line such that PV was the dependent variable and blood volume (ml/kg) the independent variable we found that $\Delta PV = 18.04 \, (BV) - 957.8, \, r = 0.74 \, (P < 0.05)$. The correlation coefficient was considerably increased when we plotted the absolute PV as the independent variable and the loss of plasma volume as the dependent variable. This relationship was $\Delta \, PV \, (ml) = 0.422 \, (PV) - 954, \, r = 0.86 \, (P < 0.05)$. Basically, what these equations tell us is the more PV you have the more you lose. The subjects probably differed very little in their muscle mass (legs) and the differences in absolute volume lost will probably be found sequestered in the extra muscle compartment of the leg. Why a subject with a larger PV loses more volume upon standing probably reflects the fact that, in order to raise protein osmotic pressure a given amount, both low-volume and high-volume subjects must lose the same amount of fluid from each unit of plasma—hence the larger the volume the larger the absolute loss into a space which can accommodate this volume.

The description of events during quiet standing is based upon hydrostatic pressure, tissue compliance, and to some extent protein osmotic pressure. What then happens when the subjects start to walk, run, cycle, or block step? We shall first consider walking and running. With the first few steps, the hydrostatic pressure at or above the ankle falls some 60–65 mmHg [87]. A similar pressure drop must occur within the muscle compartments. However, the hydrostatic gradient from muscle to capillaries is gradually opposed by a developing osmotic gradient from capillary to muscle [63, 115]. The rapidity with which the latter develops probably depends upon the rate and force of muscle contraction. As we have pointed out elsewhere [106, 107], and has been reiterated by Greenleaf et al. [43] and van Beaumont et al. [124], the point at which fluid leaving and entering a muscle probably balances is when the muscle exercises at 40–60 percent of its maximum oxygen consumption. Below that point fluid will probably leave the muscle; above that point fluid will remain within the muscle because of the increasing osmotic gradient. Because the fluid sequestered within the resting muscle is limited in volume, a slow rate of fluid from the extra-muscle compartment begins to offset the loss to the muscle, which Galbo et al. [39, 40] has also shown. This is where two forms of rhythmic exercise—treadmill and cycle—differ. It is in the fluid return from extramuscle compartments [115]. In the case of treadmill and long-distance running fluid does not remain sequestered in the extramuscle compartment. Over a period of time this fluid seems to be returned. In cycle exercise, there is an occasional hint of fluid return, but the existing results point to a lack of fluid return to the vascular compartment from the extramuscle compartment of the legs. This may be more apparent than real since the appropriate experiments may not have been done.

Running, walking, and cycling are ordinarily done in an upright position, and PV reduction during exercise is determined by both hydrostatic and osmotic gradients. Loss of PV decreases cardiac output and increases blood viscosity. Whether the increase in oxygen-carrying capacity due to hemoconcentration completely offsets both these negative events is questionable. Training, then, rhythmically causes PV retraction and expansion on a daily basis. As training continues, PV expands at a faster rate than does red blood cell mass, with the final result that trained individuals have enlarged blood volumes. Since the increase in blood volume includes a proportionally greater increase in PV, contraction as well as a mild exercise level must be used to detect an increase in PV. These experiments have not been done, though block stepping comes close.

With the drop in venous hydrostatic pressure because of muscle contraction, what of the volume sequestered within the extramuscular compartments? In brief, the exit of this fluid will depend upon the properties of this space and the existing hydrostatic (and oncotic) gradients. In short, one should not expect a rapid return of fluid from the extramuscular compartments.

The events within the muscle compartments during exercise bear further consideration. The results of Lundvall and Melander [63] and of Sjogaard and Saltin [116] indicate that the amount of fluid leaving the vascular volume is a function of exercise intensity (see also Greenleaf et al. [44] for a summary). However, none of these experiments cited have partitioned the fluid loss into that due to hydrostatic events and that due to osmotic events.

Returning to our standing subject, if he or she exercises at levels in excess of 50 percent $\dot{V}Ol_2$max, we would probably detect a further decrease in plasma volume due to the increase in the sums of hydrostatic and muscle osmotic pressures. This Galbo et al. [39] has shown. If our subjects continue to exercise, the muscle compartment will equilibrate, but the slow return of exercise will then lead to a similar unit loss of fluid but in the end, the circulating PV in the trained person is greater than in the untrained. Thus, cardiac output would be better maintained at submaximal workloads. The same results could be obtained if training decreased the compliance of the extramuscular compartments in the legs. Perhaps this also occurs, but appropriate studies have not been done.

If a trained person is exposed to heat, there is a further increase in PV [114], but this additional volume may not be permanent [137]. As we have noted elsewhere, heat-induced increases in PV of trained subjects is not evident after 21 days of continued training and heat exposure [6, 110]. In the interim, two events have occurred which decrease the demand for the heat-induced volume, first, sweat rate has increased and second, the subjects appear to have gained the ability to enlarge their PV when faced with a warm environment [112]. Apparently, this is done by moving both protein and fluid from the extramuscular to the intravascular compartments. Though said with certainty, this area—training and heat exposure—needs more thorough investigation since most of the above claims are suggestive rather than conclusive.

Finally, hypohydration appears to have little influence upon circulating blood volume until subjects have lost 4–5 percent of their total body weight. Information is limited as to the influence of greater amounts of water loss upon PV during endurance exercise. What is available suggests that above a certain level of total body water loss, PV suffers a disproportionate decrease [76]. It is important to recognize that it is only necessary to return water in an amount needed to adjust osmolarity and ion concentrations to maintain adequate hydration during medium length endurance exercise (e.g., a standard marathon). During longer bouts of exercise, maintenance of volume may become a problem that can be alleviated by ingestion of a hypotonic solution of sodium chloride.

## REFERENCES

1. Adolph, E.F., and Associates. *Physiology of Man in the Desert.* New York: Interscience, 1947.
2. Allen, T.H., M.T. Peng, K.P. Chen, T.F. Huang, C. Chang, and H.S. Fang. Prediction of blood volume and adiposity in man from body weight and cube of height. *Metabolism* 5:329–345, 1956.
3. Astrand, P.-O., and B. Saltin. Plasma and red cell volume after prolonged severe exercise. *J. Appl. Physiol.* 19:829–832, 1964.
4. Aurell, M., M. Carlsson, G. Grimby, and B. Hood. Plasma concentration and urinary excretion of certain electrolytes during supine work. *J. Appl. Physiol.* 22:633–638, 1967.
5. Bass, D.E., E.R. Buskirk, P.F. Iampietro, and M. Mager. Comparison of blood volume during physical conditioning, heat acclimation and sedentary living. *J. Appl. Physiol.* 12:186–188, 1958.
6. Bonner, R.M., M.H. Harrison, C.J. Hall, and R.J. Edwards. Effect of heat acclimatization on intravascular responses to acute heat stress in man. *J. Appl. Physiol.* 41:708–713, 1976.
7. Brotherhood, J., B. Brozovic, and L. Pugh. Hematological status of middle- and long-distance runners. *Clin. Sci. Mol. Med.* 48:139–145, 1975.
8. Claremont, A.D., D.L. Costill, W. Fink, and P. van Handel. Heat tolerance following diuretic induced dehydration. *Med. Sci. Sports* 8:239–243, 1976.
9. Cogswell, R.C., C.R. Henderson, and G. Berryman. Some observations of the effects of training on pulse rate, blood pressure and endurance in humans using the step test (Harvard), treadmill and electrodynamic brake bicycle. *Am. J. Physiol.* 146:420–430, 1946.
10. Convertino, V.A., J.E. Greenleaf, and E.M. Bernauer. Role of thermal and

exercise factors in the mechanism of hypervolmia. *J. Appl. Physiol.* 48:657–664, 1980.

11. Convertino, V.A., L.C. Keil, E.M. Bernauer, and J.E. Greenleaf. Plasma volume, osmolality, vasopressin and renin activity during graded exercise in man. *J. Appl. Physiol.* 50:123–128, 1981.

12. Convertino, V.A., L.C. Keil, and J.E. Greenleaf. Plasma volume, renin, and vasopressin responses to graded exercise after training. *J. Appl. Physiol.* 54:508–514, 1983.

13. Costill, D.L., L. Branam, D. Eddy, and W. Fink. Alterations in red cell volume following exercise and dehydration. *J. Appl. Physiol.* 37:912–916, 1974.

14. Costill, D.L., R. Cote, E. Miller, T. Miller, and S. Wynder. Water and electrolyte replacement during repeated days of work in the heat. *Aviat. Space Environ. Med.* 46:795–800, 1975.

15. Costill, D.L., and W.J. Fink. Plasma volume changes following exercise and thermal dehydration. *J. Appl. Physiol.* 37:521–535, 1974.

16. Costill, D.L., W.F. Kammer, and A. Fisher. Fluid ingestion during distance running. *Arch. Environ. Health* 21:520–525, 1970.

17. Costill, D.L., and B. Saltin. Factors limiting gastric emptying during rest and exercise. *J. Appl. Physiol.* 37:679–683, 1974.

18. Cullumbine. H., and A.C. Koch. The changes in plasma and tissue fluid volume following exercise. *J. Exp. Physiol.* 35:39–46, 1949.

19. Delanne, R., J.R. Barnes, and L. Brouha. Changes in concentration of plasma protein fractions during muscular work and recovery. *J. Appl. Physiol.* 13:97–104, 1958.

20. Diaz, F.J., D.R. Bransford, K. Kobayashi, S.M. Horvath, and R.G. McMurray. Plasma volume changes during rest and exercise in different postures in a hot humid environment. *J. Appl. Physiol.* 47:798–803, 1979.

21. Dill, D.B., and D.L. Costill. Calculation of percentage changes in volume of blood, plasma, and red cells in dehydration. *J. Appl. Physiol* 37:247–248, 1974.

22. Dill, D.B., J.H. Talbott, and H.T. Edwards. Studies in muscular activity. VI. Response of several individuals to a fixed task. *J. Physiol. (Lond.)* 69:267–305, 1930.

23. Ebert, R.V., and E.A. Stead. Demonstration that in normal man no reserves of blood are mobilized by exercise, epinephrine and hemorrhage. *Am J. Med. Sci.* 201:655–664, 1941.

24. Edwards, R.J., and M.H. Harrison. Changes in haematocrit and haemoglobin concentration during treadmill running. *J. Physiol. (Lond.)* 334:51P, 1983.

25. Edwards, R.J., M.H. Harrison, L.A. Cochrane, and F.J. Mills. Blood volume and protein responses to skin cooling and warming during cycle exercise. *Eur. J. Appl. Physiol.* 50:195–206, 1983.

26. Eisenberg, S. Effect of posture and position of the venous sampling site on the hematocrit and serum protein concentration. *J. Lab. Clin. Med.* 61:755–760, 1963.

27. Ekblom, B. Effect of physical training on circulation during prolonged severe exercise. *Acta Physiol. Scand.* 78:145–158, 1970.

28. Ekblom, B., and L. Hermansen. Cardiac output in athletes. *J. Appl. Physiol.* 25:619–625, 1968.

29. Eliassen, E., B. Folkow, S.M. Hilton, B. Oberg, and B. Rippe. Pressure-volume characteristics of the interstitial fluid space in the skeletal muscle of the cat. *Acta Physiol. Scand.* 90:583–593, 1974.

30. Fadnes, H.O., R.K. Reed, and K. Aukland. Interstitial fluid pressure in rats measured with a modified wick technique. *Microvasc. Res.* 14:27–36, 1977.

31. Ferguson, E.W., and M.M. Guest. Exercise, physical conditioning, blood coagulation and fibrinolysis. *Thromb. diath. Haem.* 31:63–71, 1974.

32. Fortney, S.M., E.R. Nadel, C.B. Wenger, and J.R. Bove. Effect of acute alterations of blood volume in circulatory performance in humans. *J. Appl. Physiol.* 50:292–298, 1981.

33. Fortney, S.M., and L.C. Senay, Jr. Effect of training and heat acclimation on exercise responses of sedentary females. *J. Appl. Physiol.* 47:978–984, 1979.

34. Francis, K.T. Effect of water and electrolyte replacement during exercise in the heat on biochemical indices of stress and performance. *Aviat. Space Environ. Med.* 50:115–119, 1979.

35. Francis, K.T., and R. MacGregor, III. Effect of exercise in the heat on plasma renin and aldosterone with either water or a potassium-rich electrolyte solution. *Aviat. Space Environ. Med.* 49:461–465, 1978.

36. Gaebelein, C.J., and L.C. Senay, Jr. Influence of exercise type, hydration, and heat on plasma volume shifts in men. *J. Appl. Physiol.* 49:119–123, 1980.

37. Gaebelein, C.J. and L.C. Senay, Jr. Vascular volume changes during cycling and stepping in women at two hydration levels. *Eur. J. Appl. Physiol.* 48:1–10, 1982.

38. Gaebelein, C.J., and L.C. Senay, Jr. Vascular volume dynamics during ergometer exercise at different menstrual phases. *Eur. J. Appl. Physiol.* 50:1–11, 1982.

39. Galbo, H., J.J. Holst, and N.J. Christensen. Glucagon and plasma catecholamine responses to graded and prolonged exercise in man. *J. Appl. Physiol.* 38:70–76, 1975.

40. Galbo, H., J.J. Holst, N.J. Christensen, and J. Hilsted. Glucagon and plasma catecholamines during beta-receptor blockade in exercising man. *J. Appl. Physiol.* 40:855–863, 1976.

41. Green, J.H., J.A. Thomson, M.E. Ball, R.L. Hughson, M.E. Houston, and M.T. Sharratt. Alterations in blood volume following short-term supramaximal exercise. *J. Appl. Physiol.* 56:145–149, 1984.

42. Greenleaf, J.E., and P.J. Brock. $Na^+$ and $Ca^{2+}$ ingestion plasma volume—electrolyte distribution at rest and exercise. *J. Appl. Physiol. 48:838–847, 1980.*

43. Greenleaf, J.E., V.A. Convertino, R.W. Stremel, E.M. Bernauer, W.C. Adams, S.R. Vignau, and P.J. Brock. Plasma $[Na^+]$, $[Ca^{2+}]$, and volume shifts and thermoregulation during exercise in man. *J. Appl. Physiol.* 43:1026–1032, 1977.

44. Greenleaf, J.E., W. van Beaumont, P.J. Brock, J.T. Morse, and G.R. Mangseth. Plasma volume and electrolyte shifts with heavy exercise in sitting and supine positions. *Am. J. Physiol.* 236:R206–R214, 1979.

45. Guyton, A.C., A.E. Taylor, and H.J. Granger. *Circulatory Physiology II. Dynamics and Control of the Body Fluids.* Philadelphia: Saunders, 1975.

46. Hagan, R.D., F.J. Diaz, and S.M. Horvath. Plasma volume changes with movement to supine and standing positions. *J. Appl. Physiol.* 45:414–418, 1978.

47. Hagan, R.D., F.J. Diaz, R.G. McMurray, and S.M. Horvath. Plasma volume changes related to posture and exercise. *Proc. Soc. Exp. Biol. Med.* 165:155–160, 1980.

48. Hargens, A.R., S.J. Mubarak, C.A. Owens, L.P. Garetto, and W.H. Akeson. Interstitial fluid pressure in muscle and compartment syndromes in man. *Microvasc. Res.* 14:1–10, 1977.

49. Harrison, M.H., R.J. Edwards, and P.A. Fennessy. Intravascular volume and tonicity as.factors in the regulation of body temperature. *J. Appl. Physiol.* 44:69–75, 1978.

50. Harrison, M.H., R.J. Edwards, M.J. Graveney, L.A. Cochrane, and J.A. Davies. Blood volume and plasma protein responses to heat acclimation in humans. *J. Appl. Physiol.* 50:597–604, 1981.

51. Harrison, M.H., R.J. Edwards, and D.R. Leitch. Effect of exercise and thermal stress on plasma volume. *J. Appl. Physiol.* 39:925–931, 1975.
52. Hudlicka, O., B.W. Zweifach, and K.R. Tyler. Capillary recruitment and flow velocity in skeletal muscle after contractions. *Microvasc. Res.* 23:201–213, 1982.
53. Iseri, L.T., E.J. Balatony, J.R. Evans, and M.G. Crane. Pathogenesis of congestive heat failure. Effect of posture and exercise on plasma volume and plasma constituents. *Ann. Int. Med.* 55:384–394, 1961.
54. Johnson, J.M., and L.B. Rowell. Forearm skin and muscle vascular responses to prolonged leg exercise in man. *J. Appl. Physiol.* 39:920–924, 1975.
55. Kaltreider, N.L., and G.M. Meneely. The effect of exercise on the volume of the blood. *J. Clin. Invest.* 19:627–634, 1940.
56. Keyes, A., and H. Taylor. The behavior of the plasma colloids in recovery from brief severe work and the question as to the permeability of the capillaries to protein. *J. Biol. Chem.* 109:55–66, 1935.
57. Kilburn, K.H. Muscular origin of elevated plasma potassium during exercise. *J. Appl. Physiol.* 21:675–678, 1966.
58. Kirsch, K., G. Schultze, L. Rocker, V. Bierbaum, and P. Eckert. The effect of exercise and dehydration on plasma volume and central venous pressure. *Zeit. F. Kardiol.* 62:49–58, 1973.
59. Kirsch, K.A., H. von Ameln, and J.H. Wicke. Fluid control mechanisms after exercise dehydration. *Eur. J. Appl. Physiol.* 47:191–196, 1981.
60. Kjellberg, S.R., V. Rudhe, and T.S. Jostrand. Increase of the amount of hemoglobin and blood volume in connection with physical training. *Acta Physiol. Scand.* 19:146–151, 1950.
61. Kolka, M.A., L.A. Stephenson, and J.E. Wilkerson. Erythrocyte indices during a competitive marathon. *J. Appl. Physiol.* 52:168–172, 1982.
62. Konig, E., W. Wildmann, N. Zollner. Veranderungen des plasma volumes durch normale und maximale arbeit im sitzen. *Zeit. Ges. Exp. Med.* 141:350–366, 1966.
63. Lundvall, J., S. Mellander, H. Westling, and T. White. Fluid transfer between blood and tissue during exercise. *Acta Physiol. Scand.* 85:258–269, 1972.
64. Macek, M., J. Vavra, and J. Novosadova. Prolonged exercise in prepubertal boys. II. Changes in plasma volume and in some blood constituents. *Eur. J. Appl. Physiol.* 35:299–303, 1976.
65. Maron, M.B., S.M. Horvath, and J.E. Wilkerson. Acute blood biochemical alterations in response to marathon running. *Eur. J. Appl. Physiol.* 34:173–181, 1975.
66. Maron, M.B., S.M. Horvath, and J.E. Wilkerson. Blood biochemical alterations during recovery from competitive marathon running. *Eur. J. Appl. Physiol.* 36:231–238, 1977.
67. Master, A.M., and E.T. Oppenheimer. A simple exercise tolerance test for circulatory efficiency with standard tables for normal individuals. *Am. J. Med. Sci.* 177:223–243, 1929.
68. McKechnie, J.K., W.P. Leary, and S.J. Joubert. Some electrocardiographic and biochemical changes recorded in marathon runners. *S. Afr. Med. J.* 41:722–725, 1967.
69. McMurray, R.G. Plasma volume changes during submaximal swimming. *Eur. J. Appl. Physiol.* 51:347–356, 1983.
70. Melin, B., J.P. Eclache, G. Geelen, G. Annat, A.M. Allevard, E. Jarsaillon, A. Zebidi, J.J. Legros, and C.G. Harib. Plasma AVP, neurophysin, renin activity, and aldosterone during submaximal exercise performed until exhaustion in trained and untrained men. *Eur. J. Appl. Physiol.* 44:141–151, 1980.

71. Miles, D.S., M.N. Sawka, R.M. Glaser, and J.S. Petrofsky, Plasma volume shifts during progressive arm and leg exercise. *J. Appl. Physiol.* 54:491–495, 1983.
72. Milledge, J.S., E.I. Bryson, D.M. Catley, R. Hesp, N. Luff, B.D. Mintz, M.W.J. Olden, N.N. Payne, M.P. Ward, and W.R. Withey. Sodium balance, fluid homeostasis and the renin-aldosterone system during the prolonged exercise of hill walking. *Clin Sci.* 62:595–604, 1982.
73. Mohsenin, V., and R. Gonzalez. Tissue pressure and plasma oncotic pressure during exercise. *J. Appl. Physiol.* 56:102–108, 1984.
74. Moore, F.D., K.H. Oleson, J.D. McMurrey, H.V. Parker, M.R. Ball, and C.M. Boyden. *The Body Cell Mass and Its Supporting Environment. Body Composition in Health and Disease.* Philadelphia: Saunders, 1963.
75. Moremoto, T., K. Miki, H. Nose, Y. Tanaka, and S. Yamada. Transvascular fluid shift after blood volume modification in relation to compliances of the total vascular bed and interstitial fluid space. *Jpn. J. Physiol.* 31:869–878, 1981.
76. Myhre, L.G., G.H. Hartung, and D.M. Tucker. Plasma volume and blood metabolites in middle-aged runners during a warm weather marathon. *Eur. J. Appl. Physiol.* 48:227–240, 1982.
77. Nadel, E.R., E. Cafarelli, M.F. Roberts, and C.B. Wenger. Circulatory regulation during exercise in different ambient temperatures. *J. Appl. Physiol.* 46:430–437, 1979.
78. Nadel, E.R., S.M. Fortney, and C.B. Wenger. Effect of hydration state on circulatory and thermal regulation. *J. Appl. Physiol.* 47:715–721, 1980.
79. Nadel, E.R., K.B. Pandolf, and J.A.J. Stolwijk. Mechanisms of thermal acclimation to exercise and heat. *J. Appl. Physiol.* 37:515–520, 1974.
80. Noakes, T.D., and J.W. Carter. Biochemical parameters in athletes before and after having run 160 kilometers. *S. Afr. Med. J.* 50:1562–1566, 1976.
81. Novosadova, J. The changes in hematocrit, hemoglobin, plasma volume and proteins during and after different types of exercise. *Eur. J. Appl. Physiol.* 35:223–230, 1977.
82. Nylin, G. The effect of heavy muscular and work on the volume of circulating red corpuscles in man. *Am. J. Physiol.* 149:180–184, 1947.
83. Olszewski, W., A. Engeset, P.M. Jaeger, J. Sokolowski, and L. Theodorsen. Flow and composition of leg lymph in normal men during venous stasis, muscular activity and local hyperthermia. *Acta Physiol. Scand.* 99:149–155, 1977.
84. Oscai, L.B., B.T. Williams, and B.A. Hertig. Effect of exercise on blood volume. *J. Appl. Physiol.* 24:622–624, 1968.
85. Paglia, D.E., and E.P. Cronkite. Blood and lymph. In *Physiological Basis of Medical Practice.* 10th ed. J.R. Brobeck (ed.), Baltimore: Williams and Wilkins, 1979, pp. 4-3–4-9.
86. Pivarnik, J.M., E.M. Leeds, and J.E. Wilkerson. Effect of endurance exercise in metabolic water production and plasma volume. *J. Appl. Physiol.* 56:613–618, 1984.
87. Pollack, A.A., and E.H. Wood. Venous pressure in the saphenous vein at the ankle in man during exercise and changes in posture. *J. Appl. Physiol.* 1:649–662, 1949.
88. Poortmans, J.R. Serum protein determination during short exhaustive physical activity. *J. Appl. Physiol.* 30:190–192, 1971.
89. Poortmans, J.R., and G. Haralambi. Biochemical changes in a 100 km run: Proteins in serum and urine. *Eur. J. Appl. Physiol.* 40:245–254, 1979.
90. Pugh, L.G.C.E. Blood volume changes in outdoor exercise of 8–10 hour duration. *J. Physiol. (Lond.)* 200:345–351, 1969.

91. Pugh, L.G.C.E. Thermal, metabolic, blood and circulatory adjustment in prolonged outdoor exercise. *Br. Med. J.* 2:657–662, 1969.
92. Refsum, H.E., B. Tveit, H.D. Meen, and S.B. Stromme. Serum electrolyte, fluid and acid base balance after prolonged heavy exercise at low environmental temperature. *Scand. J. Clin. Lab. Invest.* 32:117–122, 1973.
93. Remes, K. Effect of long-term physical training on total red cell volume. *Scand. J. Clin. Lab. Invest.* 39:311–319, 1979.
94. Rocker, L., K. Kirsch, J. Wicke, and H. Stoboy. Role of protein in regulation of plasma volume during heat stress and exercise. *Isr. J. Med. Sci.* 12:840–843, 1976.
95. Rocker, L., K.A. Kirsch, and H. Stoboy. Plasma volume, albumin, and globulin concentrations and their intravascular masses. *Eur. J. Appl. Physiol.* 36:57–64, 1976.
96. Rodbard, S. An evaluation of "Interstitial" fluids. *Lymphology* 8:142–148, 1975.
97. Rose, L.I., D.R. Carroll, S.L. Lowe, E.W. Peterson, and K.H. Cooper. Serum electrolyte changes after marathon running. *J. Appl. Physiol.* 29:449–451, 1970.
98. Rowell, L.B. Human cardiovascular adjustment to exercise and thermal stress. *Physiol. Rev.* 54:75–159, 1974.
99. Saltin, B. Aerobic and anaerobic work capacity after dehydration. *J. Appl. Physiol.* 19:1114–1118, 1964.
100. Saltin, B. Circulatory response to submaximal and maximal exercise after thermal dehydration. *J. Appl. Physiol.* 19:1125–1132, 1965.
101. Saltin, B., G. Blomquist, J.H. Mitchell, R.L. Johnson, Jr., K. Wildenthal, and C.B. Chapman. Response to exercise after bed rest and after training. A longitudinal study of adaptive changes in oxygen transport and body composition. *Circulation* 38 (Suppl. VII):1–78, 1968.
102. Sawka, M.N., R.P. Francesconi, N.A. Pimental, and K.B. Pandolf. Hydration and vascular fluid shifts during exercise in the heat. *J. Appl. Physiol.* 56:91–96, 1984.
103. Scatchard, G., A.C. Batchelder, and A. Brown. Chemical, clinical and immunological studies on the products of human plasma fractionation. VI. The osmotic pressure of plasma and of serum albumin. *J. Clin. Invest.* 23:458–464, 1944.
104. Schneeberger, E.E. Proteins and vesicular transport in capillary endothelium. *Fed. Proc.* 42:2419–2424, 1983.
105. Schneider, E.C., and L.C. Havens. Changes in the blood after muscular activity and during training. *Am. J. Physiol.* 36:239–259, 1915.
106. Senay, L.C., Jr. Movement of water, protein and crystalloids between vascular and extra-vascular compartments in heat-exposed men during dehydration and following limited relief of dehydration. *J. Physiol.* 210:617–635, 1970.
107. Senay, L.C., Jr. Changes in plasma volume and protein content during exposures of working men to various temperatures before and after acclimatization to heat: separation of the roles of cutaneous and skeletal muscle circulation. *J. Physiol. (Lond.)* 224:61–81, 1972.
108. Senay, L.C., Jr. Plasma volumes and constituents of heat-exposed men before and after acclimatization. *J. Appl. Physiol.* 38:570–575, 1975.
109. Senay, L.C., Jr. Early response of plasma contents on exposure of working men to heat. *J. Appl. Physiol.* 44:166–170, 1978.
110. Senay, L.C., Jr. Effects of exercise in the heat on body fluid distribution. *Med. Sci. Sports* 11:42–48, 1979.
111. Senay, L.C., Jr., and S. Fortney. Untrained females: effects of submaximal exercise and heat on body fluids. *J. Appl. Physiol.* 39:643–647, 1975.

112. Senay, L.C., and R. Kok. Body fluid response of heat-tolerant and intolerant men to work in a hot wet environment. *J. Appl. Physiol.* 40:55–59, 1976.

113. Senay, L.C., and R. Kok. Effects of training and heat aclimatization on blood plasma contents of exercising men. *J. Appl. Physiol.* 43:591–599, 1977.

114. Senay, L.C., D. Mitchell, and C.H. Wyndham. Acclimatization in a hot, humid environment: body fluid adjustments. *J. Appl. Physiol.* 40:786–796, 1976.

115. Senay, L.C., Jr., G. Rogers, and P. Jooste. Changes in blood plasma during progressive treadmill and cycle exercise. *J. Appl. Physiol.* 49:59–65, 1980.

116. Sjogaard, G., and B. Saltin. Extra- and intracellular water spaces in muscles of man at rest and with dynamic exercise. *Am. J. Physiol.* 243:R271–R280, 1982.

117. Tan, M.H., E.G. Wilmshurst, R.E. Gleason, and J.S. Soeldner. Effect of posture on serum lipids. *New Engl. J. Med.* 289:416–418, 1973.

118. Thompson, W.O., P.K. Thompson, and M.E. Daily. The effect of posture upon the composition and volume of the blood in man. *J. Clin. Invest.* 5:573–604, 1928.

119. Uehlengen, A., and A. Buhlmann. Das erhalten des Blutvolumens wahrend kurzfristiger korperlichen Arbeit. *Cardiologia* 38:357–370, 1961.

120. Valtin, H. *Renal function: Mechanisms Preserving Fluid and Solute Balance in Health,* 2nd ed. Boston: Little, Brown, 1983.

121. van Beaumont, W. Red cell volume with changes in plasma osmolarity during maximal exercise. *J. Appl. Physiol.* 35:47–50, 1973.

122. van Beaumont, W., J.E. Greenleaf, and L. Juhos. Disproportional changes in hematocrit, plasma volume, and proteins during exercise and bed rest. *J. Appl. Physiol.* 33:55–61, 1972.

123. van Beaumont, W., J.C. Strand, J.S. Petrofsky, S.G. Hipskino, and J.E. Greenleaf. Changes in total plasma content of electrolytes and proteins with maximal exercise. *J. Appl. Physiol.* 34:102–106, 1973.

124. van Beaumont, W., S. Underkofler, and S. van Beaumont. Erythrocyte volume, plasma volume, and acid-base changes in exercise and heat dehydration. *J. Appl. Physiol.* 50:1255–1262, 1981.

125. Veall, N., C.J. Edmonds, R. Hesp, and T. Smith. Methods and problems in the measurement of body water and electrolyte pools with radionuclide traces. *Contrib. Nephrol.* 21:10–14, 1980.

126. Wade, C.E., R.H. Dressendorfer, J.C. O'Brien, and J.R. Claybaugh. Renal function, aldosterone, and vasopressin excretion following repeated long distance running. *J. Appl. Physiol.* 50:709–712, 1981.

127. Waterfield, R.L. The effect of posture on the circulating blood volume. *J. Physiol. (Lond.)* 72:100–120, 1931.

128. Wells, C., and S.M. Horvath. Responses to exercise in a hot environment as related to the menstrual cycle. *J. Appl. Physiol.* 36:299–302, 1974.

129. Wells, C.L., J.R. Stern, and L.H. Hecht. Hematological changes following a marathon race in male and female runners. *Eur. J. Appl. Physiol.* 48:41–49, 1982.

130. Wells, H.S., J.B. Youmans, and D.G. Milller, Jr. Tissue pressure (intra-cutaneous, subcutaneous, and intramuscular) as related to venous pressure, capillary filtration and other factors. *J. Clin. Invest.* 17:489–499, 1938.

131. Whiting, P.H., R.J. Maughan, and J.D.B. Miller. Dehydration and serum biochemical changes in marathon runners. *Eur. J. Appl. Physiol.* 52:183–187, 1984.

132. Wilkerson, J.E., D.L. Batterton, and S.M. Horvath. Ammonia production following maximal exercise: treadmill vs. bicycle testing. *Eur. J. Appl. Physiol.* 34:169–172, 1975.

133. Wilkerson, J.E., and M.L. Gaddis. Apparent alterations in plasma volume with arm position changes. *Fed. Proc.* 43:1016, 1984.

134. Wilkerson, J.E., B. Gutin, and S.M. Horvath. Exercise-induced changes in blood, red cell, and plasma volumes in man. *Med. Sci. Sports* 9:155–158, 1977.

135. Williams. E.S., M.P. Ward, J.S. Milledge, W.R. Withery, M.W.J. Older, and M.L. Forsling. Effect of the exercise of seven consecutive days hill-walking on fluid homeostasis. *Clin. Sci.* 56:305–316, 1979.

136. Wolf, A.V. *Thirst: Physiology of the Urge to Drink and Problems of Water Lack.* Springfield, Ill.: Thomas, 1958.

137. Wyndham, C.H., A.J.A. Benade, C.G. Williams, N.B. Strydom, A. Golding, and A.J.A. Heyns. Changes in central circulation and body fluid spaces during acclimatization to heat. *J. Appl. Physiol.* 25:586–593, 1968.

138. Wyndham, C.H., and N.B. Strydom. Acclimatizing men to heat in climatic chambers on mines. *J. S. Afr. Inst. Mining Metall.* 70:60–67, 1969.

# Biomechanics of Running

KEITH R. WILLIAMS, Ph.D.

An understanding of the biomechanical aspects of running is of interest for a number of reasons: (1) knowledge of the movements of body segments may provide information useful to a basic understanding of the mechanisms of the neuromusculoskeletal system; (2) identification of optimal running mechanics may help improve the performance for athletes of all levels; and (3) knowledge of injury mechanisms related to running may aid in the prevention of injuries. Because of the recent running boom more people, often grossly out of shape, are running higher mileages than ever before, and this is leading to increases in the number and types of injuries.

A number of reviews of the biomechanics of running have been available in the past [5, 18, 63, 107, 123, 174, 175], and the present effort is directed toward reevaluating and supplementing the information in them. An attempt has been made to make only statements about biomechanical aspects of running which can be substantiated by the available research. The majority of information available is descriptive, but there are also studies which have examined causative relationships. While there have been studies aimed at determining causative relationships between biomechanical aspects of running and injury or performance, the limited results available make it difficult to identify specific interactions. Readers interested in the correct mechanics of running will be disappointed, since there are few areas where there is unequivocal evidence that one method of running is best.

## FACTORS THAT AFFECT BIOMECHANICAL ANALYSES

Any analysis on the biomechanics of running involves a number of factors that may affect the results obtained. While most investigators take special care to control as many variables as possible, there are still numerous instances where this has not been done.

In reviewing the literature, I attempted to evaluate experimental methods and protocols and to identify those variables which might have a specific influence on the results. Some of the factors that may affect results are:

1. Speed. Differences in speed affect the majority of biomechanical parameters measured during running.

389

2. Sample size. The larger the sample size the more representative the results are likely to be in relation to the general running population.

3. Sex. Most measures of biomechanical parameters during running do not show differences based on sex. Where the sex of subjects is likely to be a factor, specific comments are made.

4. Age. The vast majority of studies have involved young adults, and unless noted this is the age group described.

5. Anatomical and muscular characteristics. Differences in body dimensions, strength, or flexibility could influence a number of biomechanical measures. For some measures, a substantial error could be introduced through inaccuracies of the inertial characteristics of subjects [190].

6. Ability or state of training. The ability or state of training of a runner has a demonstrated effect on certain biomechanical measurements.

7. Experimental conditions and procedures of analysis. The equipment, facilities, protocol, and techniques of analysis may also influence the results. For example, comparisons of treadmill vs. overground running or two-dimensional vs. three-dimensional analyses show some differences specifically related to experimental procedures. Digitizing and data smoothing are other likely sources for errors [135].

8. Fatigue. Fatigue can affect a number of biomechanical parameters.

9. Handicap/pathology. The presence of a handicap or pathology is likely to influence a wide variety of biomechanical factors. While alterations in walking mechanics due to these factors have been studied extensively, few investigations have examined running.

10. Footwear/surfaces. The type of shoes or running surfaces involved can affect a number of biomechanical variables.

## TREADMILL AND OVERGROUND RUNNING

Studies which have examined the mechanical differences between running on a treadmill and overground have yielded conflicting results [54, 63, 68, 82, 138, 185], and at present it is impossible to clearly identify any differences consistently found in the literature. In some studies [54, 185] three or fewer subjects have been used, and the applicability of these results is questionable. Speed of running may be a factor in variations between overground and treadmill running. When significant differences have been reported, they have generally been for speeds greater than 5 m/s [54, 68, 91, 138], with a few exceptions for isolated measures at lower speeds [54, 138]. The majority of comparisons between treadmill and overground running show nonsignificant differences.

In studies where mean speeds of running were lower than 5 m/s, only a few significant differences have been reported. Nelson et al. [138] showed vertical and horizontal velocities of the center of mass (COM) to be less variable and vertical velocity of the COM to be lower on the treadmill compared to overground. While Dal Monte et al. [54] showed a lower stride length (SL) and vertical oscillation of the COM for treadmill running, it should be noted that only three subjects were involved and they were highly trained on the treadmill.

Running on the treadmill at speeds above 5 m/s compared to overground running has shown differences for the following measures: increased SL and decreased stride rate (SR) [138], decreased SL and increased SR [68], no significance (NS) [82]; increased support time [138], NS [68, 82]; decreased nonsupport time [68], NS [82, 138]; less variability and lower vertical velocities of the COM [138].

Only rarely have differences in angular kinematics of the limbs been measured. Frishberg [82] reported that five subjects sprinting at 9.2 m/s showed treadmill measures at foot strike for the angle of the thigh to be significantly more vertical and measures of the lower leg to be significantly less vertical when compared to overground running. Angular displacement of the lower leg was significantly greater on the treadmill vs. overground, and the thigh showed less angular displacement and lower angular velocities on the treadmill. Sykes [185] found greater hip and knee extension at toe off and increased ankle range of motion on the treadmill compared to overground for his single subject running at 6.9 m/s. Schwab et al. [167] found electromyographic activity in lower extremity muscles to be very similar when comparing treadmill to overground running.

While some differences in mechanics have been found between treadmill and overground conditions, less is known about the source of these variations. Winter [199] measured fluctuations in the velocity of a treadmill belt during running and hypothesized that a transfer of energy occurred between the treadmill and the runner during contact. At foot contact the runner would receive energy from the treadmill, and at toe off the runner would impart energy to the belt due to the propulsive forces at the foot. These energy changes could have an effect on kinematics during running and might be a reason for some of the differences noted.

Van Ingen Schenau [188] described in detail the differences in mechanical energy considerations when analyzing treadmill versus overground running. He demonstrated how some mechanical variables are affected by the selection of an external reference frame rather than one moving with the belt. This may also be a reason for the differences between treadmill and overground running noted. He states that if a moving reference is used and the treadmill has a strong enough driving mechanism such that the energy transfer just mentioned is minimized, the only differences between overground and treadmill running should come from differences in air resistance or perceptual processes. Perhaps these suggestions will allow for more definitive knowledge of the differences between overground and treadmill running to be obtained.

## KINEMATICS OF RUNNING

A number of authors have described movements of the segments in the lower extremities during a running cycle. Some of these have cited references documenting the movements described [18, 70, 71, 123], while others have described movement sequences but did not reference their sources [107, 122, 174, 175]. A sequential description of the running motion will not be included here, and interested readers are referred to these sources for information. Specific kinematic parameters associated with various phases of running will be discussed.

### Stride Length and Stride Rate

Stride length and stride rate are among the most studied parameters in running. The terms step, stride, and cycle length are ambiguous. Stride or step length is defined here as the distance from the point of initial contact of one foot to the point of initial contact of the opposite foot, and cycle length represents the distance traveled between successive contact points of the same foot. Stride time (ST) is defined as the time between the instant of contact with one foot and the next instant of contact with the opposite foot, and SR is the inverse of ST.

*Changes with speed.* Though a number of people have investigated the changes which occur in SL and SR as velocity (V) increases, relatively few have examined a range of speeds from a slow jog to sprinting. From studies where the same subjects ran at several speeds [69, 102, 105, 109, 119, 138, 140, 163, 172], or from a variety of studies where subjects ran at only one speed [40, 42–44, 67, 72, 82, 86, 193, 200], it is obvious that there is an increase in SL and SR with increasing V. For speeds up to 7 m/s these increases have been reported as being mostly linear, while at higher speeds there has typically been a smaller increment in SL and a greater increment in SR for a given increase in V (Fig. 1). This would indicate that at high speeds runners increase their speed by increasing SR to a relatively greater extent than SL. Examples of the range of values reported

FIGURE 1

*Variations in stride length and stride rate with running velocity.*

SOURCE: Reprinted with permission from Luhtanen, P. and P.V. Komi, Mechanical factors influencing running speed. In *Biomechanics VI-B*. E. Asmussen and K. Jorgensen, eds. Baltimore: University Park Press, 1978, pp. 23–29.

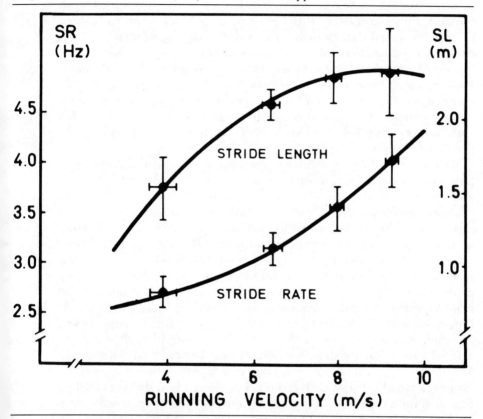

are a mean SL of 0.97 m and SR of 2.59/s for males running on a treadmill at 2.5 m/s [69], and a mean SL of 2.17 m and SR of 4.24/s for males running on a treadmill at 9.2 m/s [82].

The precise interaction of SL and SR at very high speeds has not been investigated in detail, and may not exactly follow the pattern outlined above. Chapman [44] examined changes in SL and SR over a range of high speeds from 6.7 to 9.5 m/s and found greater increases in SL at the higher end of the speed range than was found at lower speeds, with a concurrent drop in SR. These results are opposite to those expected from the results illustrated in Figure 1. Since the study involved only a single world-class female sprinter, it is possible that the results were due to individual adaptations.

Occasionally SL has been further subdivided by measuring the distance moved during the support vs. nonsupport phases of the running stride, termed "support length." It would seem possible that at high speeds range of motion limitations in the involved joints might prevent further increases in support length as running speed is increased. This is consistent with the findings of MacMahon and Green [132] who stated that the distance traveled during one contact was constant for an individual independent of running speed. While Cavagna et al. [33] described similar results for overground speeds above approximately 5 m/s, the same was not true for lower speeds. In contrast, Grillner [90] found that support length increased with increasing speed throughout a speed range from 1.7 to 8.3 m/s for eight subjects running on a treadmill. There is no obvious explanation for these contradictory results.

*Sex and anthropometric influences on stride length.* Conflicting results have been reported when comparing stride parameters between male and female runners. Nelson et al. [137] found that 21 elite women running overground at speeds from 4.8 to 6.7 m/s on average used significantly shorter absolute SLs and faster SRs than a control group of 10 college-level male runners running at the same speeds. When SL was expressed as a percentage of body height (HT) however, the women ran with relative strides significantly greater than the strides of the males (104%). To run with shorter strides at the same speed would require that SR be greater, and the authors suggested that the longer relative strides of the women were an effort to compensate for their shorter stature. If this is true then the difference may be related to size rather than sex. Elliott and Blanksby [69] measured SLs for physical education students and reported that women running on a treadmill at speeds from 2.5 to 5.5 m/s had shorter absolute SLs than men running at the same speeds, but showed no differences in relative SL. It is possible that the differences between these two studies might be caused by the different speeds of running used or the different ability levels of the groups involved.

The assumption that stride length is related to body size is supported in some but not all studies. SL has been reported to be about 75 percent HT and 150 percent leg length (LL) at a speed of 3 m/s [163], 100 percent HT and 196 percent LL at 5.5m/sec [69], and 125 percent HT at 9.2 m/s [82]. Several investigations have shown correlations of 0.6–0.7 between SL and LL or SL and HT for male and female physical education students [69], untrained males [187], and good male runners [40]. In contrast to these results are studies where low correlations were reported for relatively homogeneous groups of good male [42, 193] and female [1] runners, and for a group of elite male runners [40]. In all of these studies the variability in HT and LL among subjects was similar, the speeds of running ranged between 3 and 5.5 m/s, and studies included overground and treadmill running. Specific characteristics from each subject population or methodological factors which might explain the different correlations are not apparent. These varied results emphasize that significant individual variations in the relationship between SL and LL are likely to exist, and caution should be taken in applying predictive equations for optimal SL based on LL and V.

*Stride length and performance.* Dillman [63] reviewed a number of studies in which SLs of trained vs. untrained (or good vs. poor runners) were compared, and reported that, in general, the trained (or good) runners had longer strides at a given speed of running compared to the untrained (or poor) runners. A problem with many of these studies is that the number of subjects in each classification was small. For example, Hoshikawa [102] found a single excellent runner to have longer strides than four average runners and three poor runners. In contrast, Cavanagh et al. [40] compared 14 elite distance runners with 8 good collegiate runners running at 5.0 m/s on a treadmill and reported that on average the good runners had longer absolute and relative SLs than did the elite runners. Kunz and Kauffman [114] found 3 elite sprinters to have longer strides than 16 decathletes during a 100-m sprint. These differences can be explained, however, by the faster speeds of the sprinters and do not necessarily reflect a pattern indicative of superior running form. With the relatively few subjects involved in some studies and the conflicting results found in others, there does not seem to be sufficient data to support a statement that better runners take longer or shorter strides.

*Changes in stride length with training.* Nelson and Gregor [139] followed a group of collegiate distance runners over a period of four years and found that SL at a given speed decreased in 9 of 10 subjects. Since performance times improved during this same time period, it might be considered that they became "better" runners and that a part of their improved performance was due to shortening SL. Of course, over such a long period of time there could be a myriad of other factors involved as well, and it would be impossible to develop a convincing argument that changes in SL were the most important. Girardin and Roy [86] measured SL during a 4,000-m performance run both before and after a six-week nondirected training period. Subjects selected their own steady pace for the runs. While SL might be expected to increase if the runners ran faster after training, it might also change if runners were able to optimize their running mechanics over the training period. Results showed no differences in SL or SR which could not be explained in terms of changes in speed, though allowing the subjects to choose their own speeds and the lack of specific performance objectives in the testing sessions may have affected the results.

*Stride length and uphill or downhill running.* The effects on SL and SR of running either uphill or downhill were investigated by Nelson et al. [138, 140] for 16 male subjects at speeds from 3.4 to 6.4 m/s. Significant results showed a decrease in SL and increase in SR for uphill running with an increase in SL and a decrease in SR for downhill running.

### Support and Nonsupport Times

As running speed increases, the time for a running cycle has been reported to decrease, changing, for example, from 746 ms at 3.4 m/s to 492 ms at 9.2 m/s [165]. From a variety of studies it is evident that both the absolute and relative time spent in support also decrease as running speed increases [8, 12, 44, 72, 82, 119, 138–140, 200]. Typical relative changes range from approximately 68 percent of cycle time at 3.35 m/s [138] to 54 percent at 6.4 m/s [138] and 47 percent at 9.2 m/s [82], though there was substantial individual variability.

Luhtanen and Komi [119] split the support phase into eccentric and concentric phases, which they defined as the time period when the body COM moved either downward (eccentric phase) or upward (concentric phase). They showed that relative times for both phases decreased similarly across a speed range of 3.9–9.3 m/s for overground running, with the eccentric phase occupying approximately 34 percent of support time.

While changes in relative nonsupport times complemented those occurring in relative support time, absolute nonsupport times did not change consistently across the entire range of running speeds. Over the range of speeds from 2.5 to 6.4 m/s some studies have shown increases in nonsupport time with increased running speed for either treadmill or overground running [68, 138]. Other studies, however, have reported only slight differences in nonsupport time as speed increased, with the longest times occurring at intermediate speeds [119, 139, 140].

### Joint and Segment Angles

Many investigators have shown how joint angles vary throughout the running cycle. Figure 2 illustrates angle conventions used here, and data from various sources have been converted to this system. Figure 3 shows diagrams plotting the thigh angle vs. knee angle and the knee angle vs. ankle angle over a running cycle. Angle-angle diagrams have the advantage of showing interrelationships among the changes occurring at adjacent joints. While most authors have used thigh

FIGURE 2

*Angle conventions for the trunk, thigh, knee, and ankle as viewed from the side, and the lower leg, heel, and rearfoot as viewed from the rear.*

## ANGLE CONVENTIONS

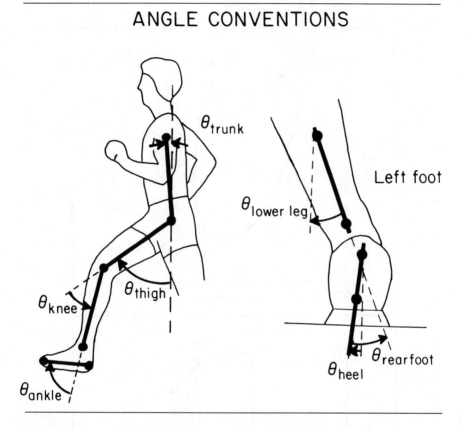

angle, as is done here, some have measured the angle of the hip between the trunk and thigh.

*Thigh angles.* Maximal thigh angles during hip flexion occur prior to foot strike and are more flexed with increasing running speed [40, 61, 67, 70, 72, 172]. Examples of thigh angles at different speeds are 25.7 degrees at 3.5 m/s [70] and 45 degrees at 4.5 m/s [40] for treadmill running and 59 degrees at 8 m/s [61] for overground running. Thigh angles at foot strike do not appear to change appreciably with increased running speed, at least at speeds above 4 m/s [40, 47, 61, 67, 70, 82, 193]. Values typical of those reported are 20.8 at 3.4 m/s [70] and 30 degrees at 5.0 m/s [40] for treadmill running, and 29.6 degrees at 5.5 m/s [67] and 28.9 degrees at 9.2 m/s [82] for treadmill running.

FIGURE 3

*Knee-thigh and knee-ankle angle-angle diagrams for one cycle of running.*
*Values are in degrees and are mean curves for 31 subjects running at 3.6*
*m/s. FS = foot strike; TO = toe-off.*

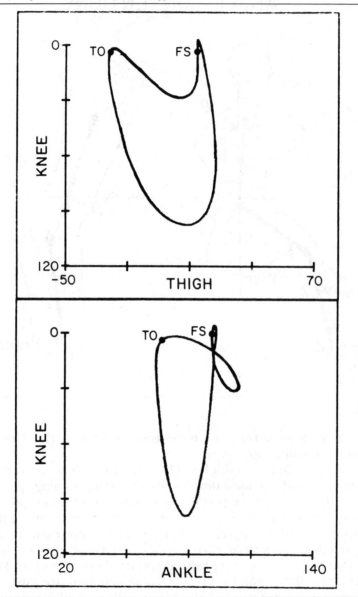

At toe off, thigh angles have been shown to be in the range of −24.0 at 3.57 m/s [193] to −29 to −32 degrees at speeds of 8–9 m/s [61, 82], where a negative number indicates a position of hip extension. The hip has been reported to continue to extend several degrees after toe off [61, 67, 70, 193]. It would appear that anatomical features may limit thigh extension since maximal values are near the limits for passive range of motion [121].

*Knee angles and lower leg positions.* The knee angle at foot strike has generally been reported to be in the range of 21 to 30 degrees [12, 47, 48, 61, 70, 72]. A wide variety of angles have been shown for knee flexion during support, with values ranging from 38 to 50 degrees for speeds from 3.4 to 7.5 m/s [11, 12, 14, 40]. Neither measure has shown a clear trend as running speed increased.

At toe-off the knee is not fully extended, and though evidence is conflicting, the trend is toward greater extension with increasing speed [12, 40, 61, 70]. Examples of values are 27.3 degrees at 2.5 m/s [70], 23.0 degrees at 5.0 m/s [40], and 18 degrees at 8.0 m/s. Slight continued extension has been found following toe-off [70].

During the swing phase maximal knee flexion has been shown to increase with increased running speed, with the advantages of such changes being a decreased moment of inertia of the lower extremity about the hip joint and thus less resistance to hip flexion [40, 61, 90, 193]. Using an electrogoniometer, Grillner [90] found knee flexion angles during swing to increase from 30 degrees at 1 m/s to greater than 120 degrees at 8 m/s, with similar changes found by Sinning [172]. Maximal extension of the knee has been shown to occur prior to contact with the ground and by the time contact is made it has flexed only a few degrees [12, 193].

A great deal of interest has been shown in the position of the lower leg at initial ground contact. It has been hypothesized that leg position may affect the changes in the horizontal velocity of the body which occur during contact. The rear of the foot has been reported to be approximately 22–26 cm horizontally in front of the hip at foot strike, with this distance decreasing slightly with increased running speed [11, 12, 40, 86]. A great deal of variability is typical between subjects [11]. The angle of the lower leg with the vertical at foot strike is approximately 8–11 degrees at lower speeds from 3.4 to 4.5 m/s [12, 200], and nearly vertical at higher speeds [11, 61, 82], with one exception which found the lower leg to be less vertical in sprinting [200]. Data from Bates et al. [11] showed no relationship between leg angle at foot strike and the amount of decrease in horizontal velocity during the contact phase.

*Ankle and foot angles.* There is little data available describing the angles of plantar flexion and dorsiflexion at various phases of the running cycle, and those available have used several different landmarks to define ankle angle. Using the conventions shown in Figure 2, dorsiflexion angles at foot strike have been found in the range 84–101 degrees [40, 48, 193] with no systematic changes with speed apparent from the data available. Plantar flexion angles at toe-off of 75 degrees have been reported for 3.6 m/s [193], and Cavanagh et al. [40] found that elite runners showed smaller plantar flexion angles at toe-off compared to a group of good runners (67 vs. 59 degrees, respectively). While it has been stated that the ankle does not plantar-flex immediately following contact [124], angle-angle diagrams from other studies have shown that it does [73, 185, 193]. Whether the initial contact of the foot is in a rearfoot or midfoot position will have an obvious influence upon whether plantar flexion will occur.

The position of the foot at foot strike is determined by the combined influences of the hip, knee, and ankle positions. Foot position has been measured either from cinematographic data or from the center of pressure paths as determined from force platform data, and runners have been classified as rearfoot, midfoot, or forefoot strikers depending upon the general area of the foot that makes first ground contact. Cavanagh and Lafortune [39] found 12 of 17 runners at 4.5 m/s to be rearfoot strikers as determined from center of pressure data, with the remainder classified as midfoot strikers. For running at a single speed there is a great deal of variability between subjects in initial contact position. For example, at relatively slow speeds the point of contact ranges from 0 percent to as much as 73 percent of shoe length as measured from the heel [34, 193]. Kerr et al. [108] used cinematographic data to classify 753 distance runners and found that approximately 80 percent were rearfoot strikers and the remainder were midfoot strikers. Faster runners tended to be midfoot strikers.

The "angle of gait," or position of the foot relative to the direction of forward movement, for 64 subjects over a speed range from 2.3 to 8.6 m/s had a mean value of 6.1 degrees of abduction [101]. Considerable individual variability among subjects was found, and all subjects did not show the same changes with increasing speed. Abduction increased as speed increased for almost half the subjects.

*Movements of the Trunk and Arms*
Vertical oscillation of the COM has been shown to decrease with increased running speed [31, 105, 119]. For example, Luhtanen and Komi [119] reported oscillations of 10.9, 8.6, 7.0, and 6.7 cm for speeds of 3.9, 6.4, 8.0, and 9.3 m/s, respectively, for six subjects. Ito et al. [105] showed similar results for three subjects over speeds ranging from 1.9 to 6.1 m/s, and in addition they split the vertical move-

ments into up and down phases of the support and nonsupport periods to identify more precisely what caused the changes with speed. Results showed that while the COM vertical displacement decreased markedly during contact, it actually increased slightly during the flight period. Hinrichs [97] compared the vertical movements of the total body with those of the body minus arms to evaluate how the arms affect oscillations of the COM. Within a speed range from 3.8 to 5.4 m/s results showed the COM to have approximately a 0.5-cm greater oscillation when the arms were included than when they were not. The arms slightly reduced the movements of the COM in the anteroposterior and mediolateral directions.

An erect posture has been considered by some to be good running form [107, 174, 175]. However, most of the literature has reported runners to lean slightly forward throughout the cycle. Figure 2 shows the conventions used to define the trunk angle. At foot strike, trunk lean has been shown to be in the range of 4–7 degrees for runners traveling at steady speeds up to 7 m/s [72, 86, 193, 200], and seems to increase slightly with increased running speed. Frishberg [82] reported a mean angle of 11.6 degrees for subjects sprinting at 9.2 m/s. These data were collected when subjects were midway through a 100-m sprint and had achieved steady maximal velocity. In only one study was a posture showing a completely erect trunk angle found [67]. Following contact with the ground the forward lean of the trunk has been reported to increase until midsupport, reaching values in the range of 12–13 degrees for speeds just over 5 m/s [67, 72]. At toe-off the trunk angle is at values similar to those found at foot contact [67, 72].

Trunk rotation and movements of the arms have seldom been reported for running. Using three-dimensional cinematography techniques, Williams [194] investigated changes in wrist position and hip and shoulder rotation for 31 subjects while running overground at 3.6 m/s. There were large differences in the range and patterns of wrist movement and hip (mean 24.3 degrees) and shoulder (mean 26.7 degrees) rotation. Hinrichs [97] reported that the shoulder joint moves through one flexion and one extension phase during a running cycle, whereas the elbow showed two phases of each motion.

*Velocity Changes within the Running Cycle*
*Heel velocity at contact.* It has often been observed that the lower extremity moves backward relative to the hip at the time of foot strike [62], such that the speed of the foot, though still in a forward direction, is less than the speed of the COM of the body. Heel velocity has been reported to be approximately 1.0 to 1.4 m/s immediately before contact with the ground for running speeds in the range of

3.5–4.5 m/s on a treadmill [48] or overground [34, 41]. Mean values for the horizontal component of heel velocity (ranging from 0.9 to 1.3 m/s) are generally found to be slightly higher than means for the vertical component (ranging from 0.55 to 0.75 m/s). Of particular note is the wide variability between subjects in the vertical velocity component (0.16 to 1.2 m/s) reported by Cavanagh [41]. Even at faster running speeds the foot velocity was relatively slow at touchdown as shown by horizontal foot speeds of 0.76 and 1.18 m/s reported for a running speed of 8 m/s [62], and a mean ankle velocity of 1.68 m/s at a running speed of 7.5 m/s [11].

*Velocity changes during the contact period.* Many studies have reported that in constant-speed running there is a decrease in speed of the COM following initial foot contact, followed by an increase in speed during the second half of the support phase. Cavanagh and La-Fortune [39] found a mean decrease in horizontal speed of 0.18 m/s during the braking phase for 17 subjects running at 4.47 m/s, followed by a mean increase 0.27 m/s during the propulsive phase. This would indicate that the speed at toe-off would be greater than that at foot strike, but they hypothesized that effects of air resistance would probably account for the decreases in horizontal speed during flight which would maintain a constant average running speed. Bates et al. [11] reported a great deal of variability between subjects in velocity changes of the COM during support for running at speeds between 7 and 8 m/s in a maximal performance run. Three subjects showed mean decreases in velocity following foot strike of 0.52 m/s, while two runners maintained a nearly constant velocity.

### Angular Momentum
The angular momentum of various body segments during the running cycle has received little attention. Using three-dimensional cinematography, Hinrichs et al. [98] and Hinrichs [97] calculated angular momentum of the body and its segments about vertical (VER), anteroposterior (AP), and mediolateral (ML) axes passing through body's center of mass. Large values for total body angular momentum were reported throughout the running cycle for the AP and ML axes with relatively small values determined about the VER axis (Fig. 4). While the arms contributed very little to total body angular momentum about the AP and ML axes, they were very important, in combination with the head and trunk, in balancing momentum generated by the legs about the VER axis.

### Rearfoot Motion
A number of studies have described rapid movements of the rearfoot during the initial stages of contact with the ground. These movements are complex, involving ankle dorsiflexion, forefoot abduction, and

FIGURE 4
*Vertical component of angular momentum of a typical subject running at 3.6 m/s normalized to body mass (m) and height (l).*
SOURCE: Reprinted with permission from Hinrichs, R.N., P.R. Cavanagh, and K.R. Williams. Upper extremity contributions to angular momentum in running. In *Biomechanics VIII-B.* H. Matsui and K. Kobayashi, eds. Champaign, Ill.: Human Kinetics Publishers, 1983, pp. 641–647.

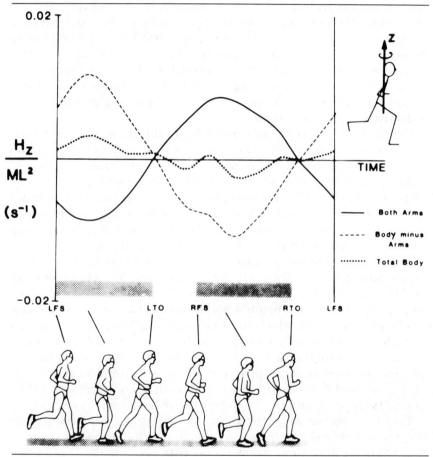

calcaneal eversion; the term "pronation" is typically used to designate the combination of these movements [50]. Clarke et al. [51] have recently reviewed rearfoot motion studies.

A certain amount of pronation is necessary for the foot to assume a flat position on the ground, and is usually thought to be desirable in order to reduce the forces applied to the leg [34, 51]. However, excessive pronation has been hypothesized to alter the stresses in bone, muscle, and ligaments, and has often been suggested as a cause of injuries to the foot, ankle, lower leg, or knee [12, 50, 106, 144, 145, 149, 169, 184]. It should be noted that there is little clear evidence that directly relates excessive pronation to injury [51, 145]. Many runners show a large amount of rearfoot motion without injury symptoms [34]. It is not known exactly what measures of the pronation motion are related to the cause of injury; however, maximal pronation (MP), maximal velocity of pronation (MPV), and duration of pronation (DP) have often been implicated [12, 34, 50, 51]. Though several systems have been used to describe rearfoot movements [50, 145], the rearfoot angle will be defined as shown in Figure 2. A negative value will represent a pronated position and a positive value a supinated position. The pronation movement will be indicated by a decreasing rearfoot angle.

Clarke et al. [51] reported no significant differences in comparing measures of pronation for running on a treadmill and overground at 3.8 m/s. The validity of using markers on the rear of a shoe to indicate the movements of the heel of the foot has been questioned. Nigg et al. [145, 146] cut small windows in the heel of shoes in order to compare shoe vs. heel movements. While there were small systematic shifts in the absolute rearfoot angles recorded, patterns of motion were similar. Several investigations have compared rearfoot measures obtained from cinematography with ground reaction forces or center of pressure patterns, with little success [12, 36, 52]. Hammill et al. [93] have referred to unpublished work where moderate correlations were found between pronation and mediolateral measures of force.

The precision with which rearfoot angle can be measured has not been directly addressed, but is determined by a combination of filmed image size and digitizing accuracy [51]. Because of variations in sample size and methodology, differences between groups in MP as little as 1.2 degrees have been reported as statistically significant [178], and differences as large as 4.0 degrees have been nonsignificant [13].

*Typical rearfoot movement parameters.* At first contact with the ground the foot has been shown to be in a supinated position of 4–12 degrees, and following foot strike pronation occurs very rapidly [12, 34, 50] (Fig. 5). The rapid pronation phase is typically followed by further pronation at a slower rate, and maximal pronation has usually been reported to occur during this slower pronation phase [50, 51]. Time to MP depends on a number of factors and is generally in the range of 60–90 ms. Some runners have not shown the slow pronation phase and as a result have shown much faster times to MP, sometimes less than 35 ms [34, 50].

MP values have been found ranging from −4 to −25 degrees for individual runners in shoes, with mean values typically in the range

FIGURE 5

*Mean rearfoot, lower leg, and heel angles during the initial contact phase for 17 subjects running at 3.8 m/s. FS = foot strike. Toe off occurs after the end of the data presented.*

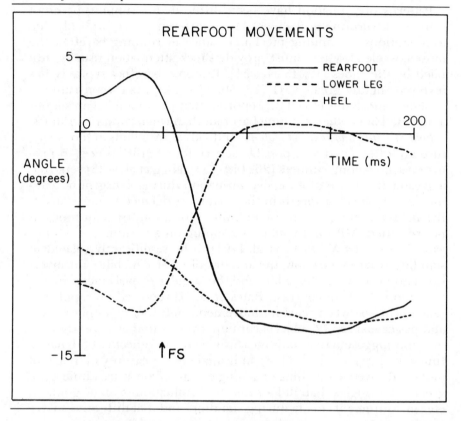

of −8 to −17 degrees [12, 34, 50, 118, 145, 162]. This large variability is due to differences among individuals as well as to the influence of various types of footwear, and may also be influenced by differences in experimental methodology. Clarke et al. [50] reported MPV to average −532 degrees per second (range −206 to −1,005) for 10 subjects running at 3.8 m/s. These values were similar to those reported by Rodgers and LeVeau [162]. Following MP, the foot begins to slowly supinate as the heel lifts off the ground [12, 14, 144, 145].

The effects of running speed on pronation have not been studied extensively, though Bates et al. [12] reported temporal measures as well as MP to be similar for 10 subjects running at 3.35 m/s compared to 3.83–4.47 m/s. From other studies done at various velocities, there is no consistent variation in rearfoot parameters associated with running speed [12, 34, 50, 51, 118, 145, 162]. It may be that changes in the kinematics of the lower extremities with changes in running speed occur to prevent increased pronation.

Patterns of pronation have been different for running barefoot compared to running in shoes. These differences are probably due to alterations in running mechanics since in running barefoot the musculoskeletal system must provide shock attenuation usually supplied by the shoes [12, 13, 48, 51]. Running barefoot typically has involved slightly greater MP [12, 50, 118, 145] than when running in shoes, and Bates et al. [12] reported that pronation began sooner and ended later when running barefoot than when running in shoes.

*Foot structure and rearfoot motion.* Individual variations in foot structure are often cited as a possible source for the differences in pronation seen among runners [26, 149, 184]. Nigg et al. [143] reported a greater incidence of excessive pronation during overground running at self-selected speeds in those runners deemed to have "insufficient" feet, though a precise definition for an insufficient foot was not specified. MP for 13 subjects running on a treadmill at 3.9 m/s was reported by Viitasalo et al. [191] to be significantly related to standing rearfoot position, the amount of passive mobility for inversion and eversion at the ankle, and the angular displacement during pronation [191]. In contrast, Bates et al. [7] reported no significant relationship between rearfoot movements and foot type (pes planus and pes cavus) for 12 subjects running overground at a speed of 4.2 m/s, and suggested that static measures were not reflective of dynamic function. Lippert et al. [118] indicated that measures of rearfoot motion derived from film of a single runner on a treadmill gave greater MP angles than did a subjective evaluation or static goniometer measurements made during standing, and that differences were more systematic than random. The lack of an objective system for defining foot types may be part of the reason for these conflicting results.

*The effect of shoes and orthotics on rearfoot motion.* Runners with symptoms related to excessive pronation often attempt to relieve the problems by either switching to shoes providing more rearfoot control, or by inserting orthotic devices into the shoe. While many runners have apparently been aided by such changes, it is unclear just what changes in rearfoot motion occur or by what mechanisms symptoms are relieved.

Clarke et al. [50] systematically varied midsole hardness, flare of the outsole of the heel, and heel height in running shoes. They reported greater values for MP in softer midsole materials compared to harder ones, and when there was little or no flare compared to substantial flare. Heel height was found to have no effect on pronation parameters in this study, but Stacoff [181] reported increased pronation for one subject as the heel was lifted by inserting heel pads inside the shoes. Bates et al. [9] measured rearfoot movement for four shoe conditions for two subjects running overground at 4.6m/s and reported variations of up to 4.6 degrees in MP.

Studies on the effect of orthotic devices in rearfoot movements have usually not shown the dramatic changes which might be expected. Bates et al. [13] found nonsignificant differences in MP for running with (mean 7.0 degrees) and without (mean 11.0 degrees) orthotic devices for six subjects who regularly used orthotics. Cavanagh et al. [36] also reported large changes in both MP and MPV for four subjects running overground at 5.0 m/s with the insertion of up to three layers of 6-mm thick felt pads in the medial side of running shoes. The thickness of the materials introduced was probably greater than would be found in typical orthotics, and no statistical analysis was done. Nigg et al. [143] used a number of different measurement criteria to conclude that arch supports could have both positive and negative effects on running and jumping movements, implying that negative results were probably due to improper fit of the arch support.

A number of other studies have shown only slight reductions (1–2 degrees) in pronation when comparing runners with and without orthotic devices [118, 162, 178]. Smith et al. [178] reported that a mean difference of 1.2 degrees was significant for eleven subjects running at 3.8 m/s on a treadmill either in shoes or in shoes plus a semirigid orthotic. Rodgers and LeVeau [162] reported no significant differences in MPV when using orthotics. The use of traditional orthotic devices does not appear to cause marked changes in a variety of rearfoot parameters. It may be that the most important measures to evaluate have not been identified, or that subtle differences are sufficient to provide relief from symptoms.

## KINETICS OF RUNNING

### Ground Reaction Forces

During the running cycle, the greatest stress applied to the body undoubtedly occurs during the contact phase. For this reason there has been widespread interest in the ground reaction forces (GRF) exerted on the runner during the contact phase. Ground reaction force-time curves for running have distinct patterns from which a number of measurements can be derived. Researchers have identified as many as 20 measures to analyze GRFs [15], including some derived by applying a Fourier analysis to force-time curves [2]. Only the measures which occur most frequently in the literature are mentioned here. Because there is cycle-to-cycle variability associated with running movements, some investigators have attempted to determine the number of trials necessary to obtain reliable information, or the best methods for averaging trials together [16, 39]. Bates et al. [16] suggested that mean values from eight trials were necessary to obtain stable and reliable data, though their selection of criteria for stability could be subject to debate. Five trial averages have often been used [39, 49, 193].

*Force-time curves.* Figure 6 shows a typical pattern for components of GRFs during running at 3.6 m/s for a rearfoot striker and a midfoot striker [193]. For the vertical ground reaction force (VGRF) curve generated by a rearfoot striker, two distinct peaks of force are typ-

FIGURE 6

*Mean vertical (VGRF), anteroposterior (APGRF), and mediolateral (MLGRF) forces, and center of pressure patterns for one rearfoot striker (solid line) and one midfoot striker (dashed line) running at 3.6 m/s.*

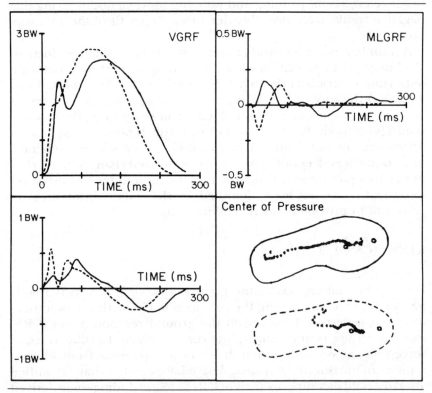

ically seen [16, 39, 48, 49, 142, 151, 163]. The terminology used to describe these peaks has varied among investigators [39, 49, 141, 142, 144], and the conventions suggested by Nigg [141] are used here. The first peak, which occurs very rapidly after initial contact and is influenced primarily by events occurring prior to contact, is referred to as the "impact peak." The second peak, which occurs during mid-support, is referred to as the "active peak," indicating the role the muscles play in its development.

For midfoot or forefoot strikers, the impact peak is typically attenuated or absent [39, 49, 151]. Other factors, such as speed of running or type of footwear, may also affect this peak [141, 142]. McMahon and Greene [132] found that the impact peak disappeared when running on a compliant wooden surface of appropriate stiffness, and DeMoya [58] found triple peaks in VGRF for running in combat boots.

The anteroposterior ground reaction forces (APGRF) also exhibit characteristic shapes, which for running at a constant average speed show retarding impulses during the first half of the contact phase and propulsive impulses during the second half [9, 39]. Rearfoot strikers typically show a single retarding peak, and midfoot strikers biphasic peaks [39], though exceptions to these patterns do occur. Peak APGRFs are generally less than 0.6–0.8 body weight (BW) [39, 163, 164].

Mediolateral forces have the most variability associated with them, and no consistent patterns can be seen. Williams [194] has shown that there is a good correlation ($r = 0.71$) between measures of the average MLGRF impulse and position of the foot relative to the midline of progression during contact with the ground. The great variety in foot placement among individuals may be the reason for the high variability in MLGRF.

*Changes in ground reaction forces with speed.* The greater the speed of running, the greater the magnitudes of the VGRF curves recorded [119, 154, 163, 180, 200]. The magnitude of the VGRF impact peak shows typical mean values ranging from 1.6–2.0 BW at 3.4 m/s to 2.9 BW at 5.4 m/s [163, 180]. At higher speeds runners have the tendency to land more toward the midfoot and the impact peak often disappears. Payne [151], however, found a very large impact peak in excess of 3.5 BW for a sprinter making contact with the rearfoot first while running at 9.5 m/s. The time from initial contact to peak impact force is in the range of 20–30 ms for running in shoes [34, 39, 41, 49]. The magnitude of increases in the active VGRF peak [119, 154, 163, 180, 200] and mean VGRF [105, 120] are less dramatic than those found for the impact peak. Roy [163], for example, found the mean active peak forces from 20 runners to increase only from 2.6 to 2.9 BW for speeds ranging from 3.4 to 5.4 m/s.

Peak APGRFs appear to increase with increased running speed [105, 163], and Roy [164] reported that peak retarding APGRF increased from 0.5 to 0.8 BW and propulsive APGRF increased from 0.3 to 0.5 for speed changes from 3.4 to 5.4 m/s. Roy [163] showed no appreciable changes in MLGRF with increasing speed, with values typically less than 0.3 BW [39, 163].

*Segmental influences on ground reaction forces.* GRFs are determined by the movements of the body, and it is of interest to know to what extent movements of the various segments can influence the GRF. Hinrichs [97] examined indirectly how the arms, legs, and trunk affect VGRF (with the effect referred to as lift) and APGRF (with the effect termed drive) during running by measuring the relative inertial forces of the segments. The arms contributed only 5 percent, the trunk −3 percent (a negative number would indicate that a segment reduced GRFs), and the legs about 98 percent to lift for 21 subjects running at 3.8 m/s. Contributions to drive were more complex, though it was apparent that the arms contributed little.

*Ground reaction forces and footwear.* Shoes help to absorb impact stress during contact with the ground. The literature concerning the effect of footwear on GRFs shows inconsistencies as to the possible differences shoes can make. Differences between various shoe conditions in VGRFs have been found to be both significant [16, 48, 49] and nonsignificant [93] for the active peak, and to be significant [16, 48, 93] and nonsignificant [49] for the impact peak. Differences among the shoes used might have had an effect on significance. Fairly large variations in GRFs among subjects wearing the same type of shoe have been reported. For example, active VGRF peak values between subjects ranged from 2.2 to 3.3 BW in a study by Clarke et al. [49], and from 1.1 to 2.5 BW in a study by Bates et al. [16]. Values in the range of 1.1 BW for the VGRF active peak are extremely low and have not been reported elsewhere, and further evidence that shoes can lower VGRFs to this degree is needed.

Little information is available as to the effect of footwear on APGRFs and MLGRFs. Bates [7, 16] found significant differences in measures of MLGRF impulse between shoes and suggested that these measures are related to pronation.

The influence of orthotic devices in the shoe on GRFs has not been examined widely. Cavanagh et al. [36] showed only minor differences in GRF magnitudes for running with and without orthotic inserts. Hamill et al. [93] reported significant differences in MLGRF impulse due to the insertion of an orthotic device, but no significant differences in VGRF peaks. From the preceding information it is obvious that all subjects in a study should wear the same type of footwear to avoid confounding effects.

*Center of Pressure and Pressure Distribution*

With today's force platforms it is possible to obtain measures of the center of the pressure (CP) distribution during contact with the ground. While this can be somewhat misleading since the CP may be nowhere near the maximal areas of pressure, it provides a general pattern which reflects the changes that occur during contact [19, 39] (Fig. 6). Cavanagh and LaFortune [39] showed distinctly different patterns for rearfoot compared to midfoot strikers, and suggested that this information can be useful in the design of running shoes. Attempts to relate differences in CP patterns to rearfoot motion [52], running economy [193], or the influence of orthotic devices [36] have been unsuccessful, possibly because CP is a global measurement and takes little account of the more subtle changes which might have occurred.

In recent years progress has also been made in the development of procedures to quantify localized pressure distribution under the foot or shoe during running [35, 37, 85, 168]. Vertical forces under areas as small as a square centimeter under the foot or shoe can be recorded at sampling rates in excess of 100 Hz using dedicated microprocessors, with patterns of pressure subsequently displayed graphically in three dimensions or numerically. Distinct areas of high pressure have been reported at various instants in time throughout the contact phase, with the highest pressures measured at the heel, metatarsal heads, and the great toe [37, 85]. Cavanagh and Hennig [37] attached various foam materials to the foot and compared pressure patterns during running on the foam to running barefoot. They reported that peak pressures were reduced when wearing the foam materials, but that the changes in the pressure pattern over time were similar, indicating that midsole material in shoes may not alter pressure distribution under the foot as much as might be thought. Scranton and McMaster [168] found differences in pressure distributions for several subjects which were related to foot structure. More data is needed before definitive statements can be made concerning the effect of foot structure on pressure distribution.

*Other Measures Related to Impact with the Ground*

Ground reaction forces give some idea of the stress the body is subjected to during contact with the ground. There are other measures which can also be used to assess differences in loading or shock absorption. Because of the complexity of the musculoskeletal system, it is very difficult to quantify the forces to which ligaments, muscles, and joints are subjected during various activities. While a number of investigations have measured kinetic factors in walking, very few have done the same in running. Burdett [27] developed a biomechanical model of the ankle joint and predicted forces in the ankle for three subjects during the stance phase of running at 4.5 m/s. Peak joint forces ranged from 9.0 to 13.3 BW with forces in the achilles tendon estimated at 5.3 to 10.0 BW.

Copozzo [29] modeled the movements of the trunk and estimated that axial loads on the lumbar vertebrae increased quickly following foot strike to a level greater than three times the upper body weight. Measuring intraabdominal pressure measurements during running, Grillner et al. [91] reported a phasic variation in intraabdominal pressure where the peak internal pressure coincided with the peak of the vertical ground reaction force. EMG activity in the abdominal muscles was initiated prior to foot strike, and the pressure changes were thought to act as a means of unloading the spine during contact.

Accelerometers have also been used to illustrate differences in shock absorption during contact with the ground during running. Peak accelerations measured by an accelerometer attached to the lower leg have been reported to increase with increased running speed [17, 47] and to vary inconsistently with shoes having different midsole hardnesses and materials [48]. Running barefoot at 3.8 m/s has been found to involve significantly greater peak acceleration values (9.9 g) compared to running in footwear (7.2 g) [48]. The accuracy with which measures of shock absorption can be used to estimate the impact stress applied to the body during contact is not clear. Clarke et al. [48] found poor correlations between VGRF measures, peak shank deceleration during contact as measured by an accelerometer, and the results of impact testing of running shoes on a laboratory impact tester.

*Muscle Moments and Electromyography*
The coordination required to complete a running stride efficiently depends on a complex series of activation of the musculature in the body, particularly in the lower extremity. The forces associated with active muscles, contact with the ground, gravity, and inertial characteristics of the various segments all combine to determine the internal forces and moments within the body. It is difficult to interpret the relationship between estimations of muscle moments and measurements of the electromyographic (EMG) activity of the muscles. Predicted moments about a joint provide information only about net torques. These torques are affected by other anatomical and environmental factors in addition to muscle activity, and as a result EMGs alone do not determine net moments. Examples of muscle activity for the lower extremity are illustrated in Figure 7 for women running

FIGURE 7

*Average integrated EMG (arbitrary units) for lower extremity muscles throughout one running cycle. FS = foot strike; TO = toe-off; VM = vastus medialis; VL = vastus lateralis; RF = rectus femoris; SM = semimembranosus; BF = biceps femoris; ST = semitendinosus; TS = triceps surae; TA = tibialis anterior.*

SOURCE: Adapted from Elliott, B.C., and B.A. Blanksby. The synchronization of muscle activity and body segment movements during a running cycle. *Med. Sci. Sports Exercise* 11:322–327, 1979.

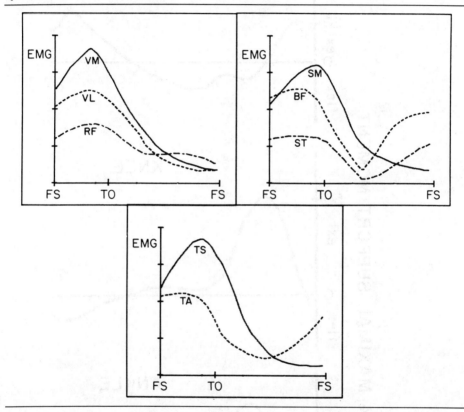

at 3.5 m/s. Net muscle moments about the hip, knee, and ankle are shown in Figure 8 for a slow speed of running.

EMG activity in lower extremity muscles has generally been found to increase with increased running speed [71, 102, 104]. One exception is from Ito et al. [104] who reported average integrated EMGs for four subjects summed from six lower extremity muscles to remain constant for the support phase over a speed range of 3.7–9.3 m/s, but to increase with increasing running speed for the nonsupport

**FIGURE 8**

*Net muscle moments at the hip, knee and ankle during one running cycle at a slow speed. Maximal support moment is the algebraic sum of hip, knee and ankle moments. FS = foot strike, TO = toe off.*

SOURCE: Adapted from Winter, D.A. Moments of force and mechanical power in jogging. *J. Biomech.* 16(1):91–97, 1983.

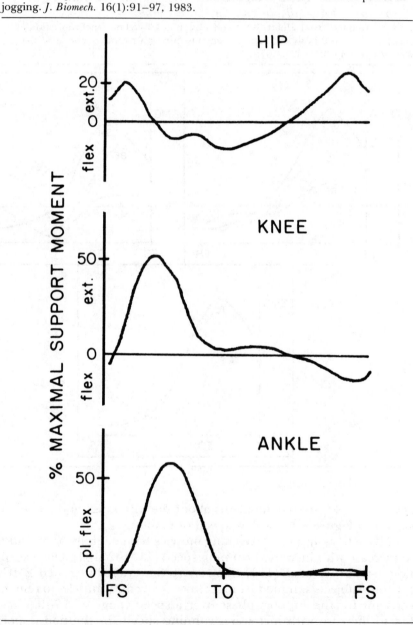

phase. They suggest that the lack of increased EMG activity during support at higher speeds may be related to increased return of elastic energy during the second part of the contact phase. Thus the increased power necessary for faster running speeds could come from elastic energy and increased muscular activation would not be needed. Komi [110] reported muscle activity during the eccentric phase of contact to be much greater in magnitude in all muscles than that found during the concentric phase. These differences were maintained over a speed range of 3–9 m/s, though the magnitude of differences decreased with increasing speed.

*Upper extremity moments and EMG activity.* Hinrichs [97] recently described the EMG activity in relation to moments at the shoulder and elbow for distance running, and found activity in all the upper extremity muscles sampled. At a speed of 5.4 m/s some muscles showed considerable activity, such as 60 pecent of maximal voluntary activity found for the latissimus dorsi. EMG activity in the shoulder and elbow muscles were for the most part well related to changes in net moments about the joints.

*Lower extremity moments and EMG activity*

EMG ACTIVITY AT THE HIP. At foot strike the lower limb segments have been reported to be moving backward relative to the trunk [61, 70, 71, 125] and EMG activity has been found in the hamstrings (H) [70, 71]. An increase in H activity as the support phase continues has been reported as extension of the hip takes place due to concentric (shortening) muscle activity [22, 70, 71]. High activity has also been reported in the rectus femoris (RF) at this time, and by late support the activity in these muscles has diminished [70, 71].

The small amount of activity in the RF during late support and the early part of swing suggests that this muscle did not actively limit hip extension and was not a prime factor in hip flexion. Other unmonitored hip flexors were probably active to cause hip flexion [71]. Another possibility which would explain the minimal hip flexor activity during this time involves transfer of energy. Williams and Cavanagh [196] and Chapman [45] both predicted a large energy transfer across the pelvis at this time. As muscles act eccentrically (lengthening) to slow the forward progression of the lead leg, energy is transfered to the trail leg via forces applied through joints and soft tissue, aiding forward movement. This may reduce the need for concentric muscular activity in the hip flexors. Toward the end of the swing, activity has been reported in H which serve to slow the flexion movement at the hip and subsequently begin the backward rotation of the leg in preparation for foot strike [61, 66, 70, 71]. While Grillner et al. [91] found activity in the rectus abdominus and the oblique muscles to commence prior to foot contact for running at speeds from 4.2 to 5.8 m/s, Capozzo [29] reported no consistent patterns in the same muscles for speeds of 2.9–3.4 m/s. It is possible that different abdominal muscle contributions to respiratory activity at the different speeds involved in these two studies caused these conflicting results.

EMG ACTIVITY AT THE KNEE. At foot strike marked activity has been shown in both the vastus lateralis (VL) and the vastus medialis (VM) in preparation for the rapid loading which subsequently occurs. During early support, the VM, VL, and RF muscles show their greatest activity, contracting during both knee flexion and knee extension. Activity in these muscles diminish toward the end of the support phase [22, 70, 71].

During the early part of swing the knee flexes, and a major part of this flexion is passive and results from the transfer of energy into the lower leg [45] due to the flexor activity occurring at the hip [66, 70, 71]. While some studies have suggested secondary contributions from the H muscles [66, 70, 71], knee extensor activity was also present at this time [71, 103]. Knee extension during the early stages of midswing also appeared to be largely passive, as indicated by a lack of substantial knee extensor activity. The extension of the knee probably resulted from inertial effects as hip flexion was retarded [66, 70, 71]. The quadriceps and H muscles showed increased activity prior to foot strike, most likely in preparation for loading [70, 71, 81].

EMG ACTIVITY AT THE ANKLE. A cocontraction has been reported between the tibialis anterior (TA) and the triceps surae (TS) at foot strike, presumably to establish a stable base of support [70, 71, 81]. TA activity immediately following contact is thought to control movement of the foot to a flat position [70, 71], though some investigators have found no such activity [60, 124]. The absence of TA activity in some studies could be due to different positions of the foot at contact. While a rearfoot striker might need some eccentric TA activity to allow slight plantar flexion immediately following foot strike, midfoot strikers would already be in a flat position and may not need muscular support. High activity has been shown during early support in the TS as eccentric dorsiflexion occurs at the ankle [60, 70, 71, 124]. EMG in these muscles continued to increase into late support as they provided thrust to propel the body into the air [70, 71], though some studies found EMG to cease well before toe-off [22, 124]. Mann and Hagy [124] found TS activity to end before toe-off for running at 2.7 m/s but to remain active through toe-off for a speed of 5.4 m/s, indicating that speed of running may alter TS activity. During swing there was only a small amount of activity in the TA as the foot was put in a dorsiflexed position for contact with the ground [70, 71, 81].

*Lower extremity muscle moments.* The following description of moments acting on the lower extremities during running has been synthesized primarily from studies by Elftman [65] at 8.3 m/s; Elliott and Blanksby [66, 70, 71] at speeds from 2.5 to 5.5 m/s; Winter [198] and Robertson et al. [161] at undesignated slow speeds; Dillman [61] at 8 m/s; and Mann and Sprague [125] at 9.5 m/s. With the exceptions mentioned, these studies were in general agreement on the sequence of moments found at various joints. Because of differences in research protocols in these studies, no attempt is made to quantify the moments and angular velocities of segments during a running cycle.

After foot strike most studies have reported extensor moments at the hip [125, 161, 198], knee [65, 125, 198], and ankle (plantar flexion) [65, 125, 198]. Elftman [65] showed an initial flexor moment at the hip for his single subject, followed by an extensor moment, and Robertson et al. [161] reported an initial dorsiflexor moment at the ankle. In sprinting Mann et al. [125] reported that not all subjects showed the same moment patterns at all joints, and a continuous flexor moment was shown at the knee until midsupport. The authors suggested that this was an attempt to minimize braking action by pulling the body forward and over the point of contact. None of these exceptions to the most common pattern seem to be related to speed.

The hip moment has been reported to change to a flexor moment during midsupport to decelerate the backward rotating thigh [65, 125, 198], while most studies showed that the knee [125, 161, 198] and ankle [65, 125, 198] extensor moments continued throughout foot contact. The peak ankle extensor moment has been reported to occur at approximately 60 percent of stance, and because it occurred later than peak extensor moments found for the hip (20%) and knee (40%), it was thought to be an indicator that the plantar flexor muscles of the ankle provided the principal thrust prior to toe-off [198].

There are some inconsistencies in the data available during the early swing phase. While most studies have shown hip flexor [45, 61, 65, 125, 161, 198] and knee extensor [45, 61, 125, 161, 198] moments during this time, others have found hip extensor and knee flexor moments [70, 71]. No reasons for these differences between studies are apparent. Knee extensor moments would presumably prevent excessively rapid knee flexion.

During late swing, hamstring activity increased and hip extensor and knee flexor moments served to slow the rotation of the thigh and lower leg [61, 65, 70, 71, 125, 198]. While it might be expected that there would be dorsiflexor moments at the ankle during swing to put the foot in position for foot strike, only very small moments have been found. Presumably this was because the low mass of the foot required only small forces to move it [65, 125, 198].

*Mechanical Power*

Although the estimation of mechanical power during running has received great attention over several decades, there has been no consensus as to which analytical methods give the most accurate and meaningful values. Both instantaneous power, where a time varying force at an instant in time is multiplied by the associated time varying velocity, and average power, where instantaneous power is averaged over a running cycle, have been used. This topic has recently received close scrutiny [105, 153, 195–197], and only a brief discussion is included here.

Based on the early work of Fenn [74], Cavagna [31, 32] evaluated the power involved in both running and walking using methods which involved movements of the COM alone, or the COM in conjunction with movements of the limbs. Winter [197] pointed out that measuring power with only movements of the center of mass does not include some contributions from the moving limbs, which he termed "internal" work, and results in underestimations of power. Norman et al. [147] introduced a segmental method which has been used by other investigators [89, 120], but which has since been shown to greatly overestimate power [157, 196, 197].

A segmental method developed by Winter [197] incorporated algorithms which accounted for transfer of energy. This involved both within-segment energy transfer, where energy could be converted between kinetic and potential forms of energy, and between-segment energy transfer, where the energy lost in one segment of the body could be transmitted via forces applied to musculoskeletal structures and result in an increase in energy for another segment. Winter also suggested that the different metabolic costs of positive and negative muscular work could have an effect on the meaning of calculated efficiency ratios, and that perhaps mechanical power values should reflect these effects. Pierrynowski et al. [153] implemented these ideas for walking, and recently Ito et al. [105] used a similar method for running. Shorten [171] further modified Winter's segmental method to account for the influence of elastic strain energy. Williams and Cavanagh [196] developed a model for the estimation of mechanical power during distance running. This model takes into account the influences of energy transfer, differences in positive and negative metabolic energy cost, elastic storage and return of energy, and non-muscular sources of work. While this model provides a means for calculating mechanical power, the authors point out that there are still gaps in existing information and consequently in how exactly to deal with each of the factors mentioned.

*Elastic energy contributions to mechanical power.* The storage and return of elastic energy (ES) has often been cited as a possible major contributor to the power involved in running [31, 32, 74, 87, 120, 171, 196]. During the first half of support energy is stored in the elastic tissues of the musculoskeletal system as eccentric muscular contractions occur. This stored energy is then returned during the last half of the support phase at the same time concentric muscular contractions occur. Power would be generated both by the concentrically contracting muscles and the returned elastic energy. There is some evidence that contributions to power for muscular contractions during this time may also come from potentiation of the muscular contractile mechanism [21]. From investigations using either knee bend [4, 193] or vertical jumping activities [21] there is evidence that performance is enhanced when ES can contribute. Luhtanen and Komi [120] and Ito et al. [105] have used cinematographic data to determine stiffness of the lower extremity during contact with the ground. This data, combined with calculations of mechanical power, was used to estimate the amount of energy stored elastically and the amount of energy subsequently returned. However, due to the assumptions involved in the estimation of elastic contributions, it is impossible to assess the accuracy of values predicted for running.

## BIOMECHANICAL MEASURES AND PERFORMANCE

One of the primary purposes of the biomechanical analysis of running is to identify factors important to performance. The researcher's task is to identify those characteristics that lead to better performance and to provide proof of their importance.

The high degree of variability among individuals in running mechanics makes it difficult to differentiate between subject-specific characteristics and task-specific ones. What is best for one runner may not be good for another, as anthropometric and functional differences may effect optimal movement patterns. There is very little evidence linking biomechanical parameters to optimal performances, and for this reason no attempt is made to identify a list of specific characteristics of better performers. In this section a number of problems inherent in many of the comparative studies available are examined.

As Dillman [63] pointed out, one of the problems involved in comparative studies is that different categories of runners have been used (better, average, poor, skilled, unskilled, trained, untrained, experienced) with little if any objective criteria used for classification. For simplicity these will be refered to by the generic term "performance levels." While several authors have reviewed data concerning differences in performance levels [5, 63, 107, 174, 175], there are many potential problems in the literature upon which the reviews were based, and in some cases the findings were derived from opinions rather than systematic research.

When studies with confounding factors are identified, very few well-structured systematic studies remain. For example, in a number of studies [74, 102, 136, 165, 185], and in others cited by Dillman [63], at least one of the performance level groups was based on data for a single individual. In light of the tremendous variability among subjects in biomechanical measures of running, it is not justifiable to regard conclusions based on a single individual as indicative of "better" runners as a group.

Speed of running can also be a complication. Speed has an effect on many variables, and comparisons among individuals running at different speeds may be misleading. Many studies have presented data for runners running at maximal sprint speeds [11, 37, 59, 74, 116, 136, 180, 192] where there will be differences in many biomechanical variables merely because the better sprinters are running faster. It is difficult if not impossible to sort out which differences are due to variations in speed and which are due to differences in performance abilities. Similar complications appear in studies which allow runners to choose their own speed [86, 103, 165].

Investigators attempting to relate biomechanical measures to performance should control variables that might affect results. If runners are divided into groups, the groups should be clearly defined based on some performance criterion and should involve a sample size that is appropriate for planned statistical analyses and expected measurement errors. The study by Cavanagh et al. [40] serves as an excellent example of such a study. Fourteen elite runners were compared with eight collegiate level runners during treadmill running at a common speed. Ability levels were clearly established based on prior performance, speed was controlled, and the number of subjects was relatively large. If maximal sprinting is of interest, it obviously will be impossible to control speed, and careful consideration should be taken in such analyses when statements of a causative nature are made.

Anthropometric factors influence certain running parameters and may relate to running performance, injuries, or running economy. Lawson and Golding [116] and Dotan et al. [64] found only low correlations between height or leg length and performance times, though Dotan did show a correlation of 0.57 between marathon time and weight divided by height squared. Staheli et al. [182] found no relation between femoral anteversion and running speed for groups of both adults and high school students. Maughan et al. [128] and Campbell [28] found significantly greater strength or power in the lower extremity in sprinters compared to distance runners. Substantial individual variability was found among subjects within each group in both studies.

## BIOMECHANICAL MEASURES AND RUNNING ECONOMY

It has been observed that there is a substantial variation in running economy (submaximal oxygen consumption, or $VO_2$) among subjects running at the same speed [56, 129], and that changes in running economy have been observed with training [23, 53, 129]. It is often implied that these differences in $VO_2$ are linked to the mechanics of running style [23, 42, 56]. Recent reviews by Daniels [56] and Cavanagh and Kram [38] discussed a variety of factors affecting efficiency and running economy. Factors dealing with the biomechanics of running will be discussed here.

One method by which the influence of biomechanical parameters on running economy can be estimated is to measure a large number of parameters and determine which of them relate to differences in $VO_2$. Pollock et al. [155] were able to show differences in submaximal $VO_2$ between groups of elite and good distance runners, but the biomechanical measures obtained on the same subjects by Cavanagh et al. [40] showed only a few relatively minor differences. Williams [193] measured a number of kinematic and kinetic measures on 31 runners, including segmental displacements and velocities, ground reaction forces and center of pressure patterns, mechanical power, and the ability to store and return elastic energy, and examined relationships between these measures and running economy at three speeds. While a number of significant relationships were found for both specific parameters, such as peak GRFs, and global measures, such as mechanical power, a high degree of variability between subjects made it impossible to isolate any as being of primary importance to running economy.

A second method by which biomechanical influences on $VO_2$ can be assessed is to vary one parameter and observe the effect it has on $VO_2$. Variations from the freely chosen SL have been shown to result in an increase in metabolic energy cost [42, 100, 109]. While Hogberg [100] showed that overstriding increased $VO_2$ more than understriding for a single runner, Cavanagh and Williams [42] reported that among their 10 subjects running at 3.8 m/s on a treadmill about half showed greater increases in $VO_2$ when overstriding and half when understriding. Eight subjects ran at or near their optimal SLs, and whether a given subject showed greater increases in $VO_2$ for shorter or longer strides was related to SL relative to LL. Further support for the contention that most runners will optimize SL comes from a study by Van der Walt [187]. In this study a multiple regression analysis was used to show that variations in SL and LL were not important factors in the prediction of $VO_2$ during treadmill running for six untrained subjects at speeds from 2.2 to 3.4 m/s.

Another parameter which is often related to efficiency or running economy is the vertical oscillation of the COM. It is typically hypothesized that the more efficient runner is characterized by a smaller vertical movements of the COM [40, 61, 88, 174]. Gregor and Kirkendall [88] claimed that each of three elite female marathoners showed minimum vertical movements at their race pace, and while Cavangh [40] found lower oscillation in the elite runners when compared to good collegiate runners (7.6 cm compared to 8.0 cm at 5.4 m/s), the results were nonsignificant.

*Effects of Footwear*

Footwear has been shown to effect the energy cost of running. Frederick et al. [78] added weights to running shoes using eight subjects at speeds from 3.8 to 4.9 m/s and reported significant differences in $VO_2$ for added weight as low as 75 g per shoe. $VO_2$ increased by a mean of 1.2 percent for each 100 g per shoe added for running at 3.8 m/s. The effects diminished somewhat at higher speeds up to 4.8 m/s. This increase in $VO_2$ was slightly lower than the 1.9 percent per 100 g found by Catlin and Dressendorfer [30], though differences in midsole material properties may also have affected their results. Another study [83] reported no significant difference in $VO_2$ among footwear conditions for running speeds of 3.0 and 3.7 m/s, even though shoe weight differed by 200 g per shoe. A significant difference was found at 3.3 m/s. Though the variations in $VO_2$ are small with increased weight, they could be important in long runs.

The cushioning properties of running shoes have also been related to running economy [77, 79], though effects are small and depend on the materials involved. Frederick et al. [77] reported that 10 subjects running at 3.8 m/s in shoes with ethyl vinyl acetate (EVA) midsoles showed greater mean $VO_2$s than running in softer, non-EVA shoes. The differences, while statistically significant, were only on the order of 0.5 ml/kg/min.

The effect of the running surface on $VO_2$ seems to be small except under special circumstances. Bonen et al. [20] reported no differences in $VO_2$ for two subjects for running on a treadmill, a cement surface, a Tartan track surface, and a cinder track. Similar results were obtained by Pugh [156] for an all weather track and a cinder surface. McMahon and Greene [132, 133] designed an indoor running track (Harvard) in relation to the stiffness characteristics of the lower extremity of the average runner, and claim that better performances were the result.

### Effects of Air Resistance

The effect of air resistance on the forward progression of a runner is of interest for reasons related to performance, since wind can affect race times, and to experimental methodology, since indoor running studies are usually done on a treadmill. The air resistance encountered by a runner is dependent on running velocity, wind velocity, projected cross-sectional area of the runner, air density, and a drag coefficient [57, 157, 189]. Shanebrook and Jaszczak [170] derived a model for predicting aerodynamic forces on runners and predicted a wide range of values depending on body size.

Pugh [156, 157] reported that the extra oxygen intake associated with running into a wind was proportional to the square of the wind velocity, and the energy cost in overcoming air resistance in track running is 7–8 percent of total metabolic energy costs at middle distance running speeds, and as high as 13–16 percent for sprint running. Davies [57] came to similar conclusions except that the change in energy cost associated with running into a wind was less than the square of the wind velocity for wind speeds higher than 15 m/s, and the energy cost due to air resistance was predicted to be about half of that predicted by Pugh. A tail wind was found to reduce energy costs compared to running with no wind, but the relative effects were much less than those for running into a wind.

Several authors have claimed that running behind another runner should result in a decreased air resistance and a lower energy cost [57, 115, 157]. For a runner traveling 1 m behind another, air resistance was estimated to be decreased by 80 percent [157] causing a reduction in energy cost of approximately 6 percent, saving up to 4 s/400-m lap. Kyle [115] estimated that a spacing of 2 m would result in a 40 percent reduction in air resistance, a 3 percent lower energy cost, and a time reduction of 1.42 s/lap. Hatsell [94] derived a model for energy expenditure of a runner and predicted an optimal strategy for running in the wind on a circular track which is the opposite of what one might expect. Accelerating when the wind is directly in the face and decelerating when the wind is at the back was predicted to reduce energy cost compared to running at a steady pace.

Since an appreciable energy cost is associated with overcoming air resistance, it might be assumed that treadmill running would involve lower energy cost than overground running. Daniels [56] cites a number of studies which give conflicting results and concludes that reduced energy expenditure for treadmill compared to overground running is more likely to be found at higher speeds of running. This would agree well with the effects expected due to increased air resistance in overground but not treadmill running at faster speeds.

*Mechanical Power and Energy Expenditure*

Since mechanical power is a global measure of the movements in running, it seems reasonable to expect that it would be related to energy expenditures. While there are some studies which provide some support for this argument, there is little definitive evidence available. Williams and Cavanagh [196] divided 31 subjects running at the same speed into three groups based on submaximal $VO_2$s and measured mechanical power using a segmental method. While mechanical power measures and $VO_2$ both increased across the low, medium, and high $VO_2$ groups, differences between groups in mechanical power were not statistically significant. The lack of significance may be related to the problems with defining the most appropriate method for calculating power, as mentioned earlier.

Komi et al. [111] compared average mechanical power (at the running speed of onset of blood lactate accumulation) with a number of physiologic measures and reported high correlations between mechanical power and percentage slow twitch fibers and capillary density. Individuals with a greater number of slow twitch fibers and greater capillary density showed less power values compared to others with more fast twitch fibers and lower capillary density. Saito et al. [166] measured mechanical power, derived from movements of the center of mass alone, and energy expenditure in trained vs. untrained runners during a 400-m sprint. Though no differences were found in oxygen consumption or oxygen debt during the run, the trained runners had significantly greater mechanical power than the untrained runners. The authors suggest that these results indicate differences in mechanical efficiency between the groups.

## BIOMECHANICAL MEASURES AND RUNNING INJURIES

Although we can measure segmental movements and ground reaction forces and obtain estimates of muscle, ligament, and bone forces, there is little information available concerning the mechanism of injury to human tissues during running [39, 145]. While some studies have examined the effects of repetitive impact loading in various tissues in animals [150, 160], there is a lack of data delineating the mechanism of stress-related injuries in humans. In the medical fields there is a great volume of literature available concerning the probable cause of injuries and typical treatments, and there is also a body of literature available which relates the structure and function of various joints of the body to possible injury mechanisms. The clinical findings related to injury are not addressed here, and readers are referred to several sources for additional information [24, 25, 46, 106, 113, 117, 126, 149, 152, 176, 184]. Very few systematic investigations have been done which relate structural and functional parameters to injuries, probably due to methodological limitations associated with human subjects research.

*Kinetic and Kinematic Factors*

Investigations into whether the repetitive loading which occurs in long distance running will lead to a greater incidence of osteoarthritis if maintained over a number of years have yielded conflicting results. McDermott and Freyne [131] found degenerative changes were significantly related to genu varum, history of severe injury, and number of years spent in long-distance training. In contrast, Puranen et al. [158] found a reduced frequency of osteoarthritis in former Finnish distance running champions compared to the nonrunning population. Sohn and Micheli [179] surveyed 498 runners and 287 swimmers who were competitive at the collegiate level during the period 1930–1960 and found runners and swimmers to show approximately the same incidence of knee pain. They concluded that there was no positive relationship between running at moderate levels and the development of osteoarthritis in later life, though no nonathletic groups were included for comparison.

Some information is available relating differences in measures of running mechanics to injury. Mann and Sprague [125] estimated muscle moments during sprint running and found a significant correlation ($r = 0.7$) between magnitude of the knee flexor moment at foot strike with a history of hip extensor/knee flexor injury. McDermott et al. [130] were able to demonstrate that runners with anterior compartment pain had a greater mean pressure in the anterior compartment during running than did an asymptomatic control group (66 vs. 100 mmHg). Both Burdett [27] and Nigg et al. [145] cite evidence that estimates of joint and tendon forces during running can exceed the ultimate strengths measured in cadaver studies, illustrating the current inability to specify the limits to which intact tissue can be stressed without injury.

Many implications are made that excessive pronation is related to a number of lower extremity injuries [106, 113, 149, 184], but there is little systematic evidence that this is so. Both Viitasalo and Kvist

[191] and Gehlsen and Seger [84] have found that runners with a history of shin splints exhibited greater pronation during running than did control groups.

*Anthropometric Differences*

Deviation from what might be termed "normal" structure is often cited as a cause for injury [125, 149, 184]. Gross [92] found discrepancies in LL greater than 12 mm in five (14%) of a group of 35 marathoners and concluded that such differences do not prevent runners from undertaking intense training and racing. In contrast, Friberg [80] examined 371 Finnish army members and, based on data for 130 stress fractures, concluded that LL asymmetry may predispose an individual to stress fractures. However, it may be that activities other than running were important to this relationship.

Frederick [76] described the relative changes in loading at the feet for different sized persons. He observed that foot size does not increase in proportion to increases in body weight, and thus heavier runners may be underprotected by running shoes which are designed with an average sized runner in mind. Kreighbaum and Ferrandino [112] assessed the relationship between Morton's toe and stress to the lower extremity. They found no relationship, but reported five measures related to lower extremity anthropometrics, foot dimensions, and weight bearing that were significantly associated with pain.

A common clinical observation is that differences in anatomical structure between men and women might cause differences in loading which would be accentuated in running and other athletic endeavors and might predispose women to injuries [107]. While there are differences in pelvic dimensions between men and women [148], evidence of a greater frequency of knee injuries in women as a result is not substantiated.

## CHANGES IN BIOMECHANICAL MEASURES WITH FATIGUE

Fatigue during running is likely to cause a general loss of coordination and efficiency and lead to a poorer performance. Studies which have evaluated the effects of fatigue have mostly been descriptive, pointing out the changes that occur with fatigue but not identifying how fatigue affects performance or injury. It is likely that changes due to fatigue do not affect all runners in the same manner, and Chapman [43] has pointed out that overall mean values for a group of runners in a fatigued and nonfatigued state may not reflect individual adaptations.

*Distance Running*

Elliott and Blanksby [67] investigated fatigue effects during a 10,000-m run, and some of the problems with studies of fatigue can be identified within this investigation. As the run progressed and the subjects presumably became progressively more fatigued, a number of significant changes were found: a decreased running velocity, reduced SL, more extended lower limb, and slower backward velocity of the foot at foot strike. No significant changes were found in SR, vertical oscillation of the COM, or positions of the trunk, thigh, or leg segments. A confounding factor in these results is the decrease in average velocity from 5.5 to 5.0 m/s from the beginning to the end of the run. Since most biomechanical parameters of running show alterations with velocity, it is impossible to determine whether the changes described were the result of changes in velocity, fatigue, or a combination of both. Certainly it is correct to state that the alterations were the results of fatigue, since the changes in velocity are due to fatigue, but it would be of interest to know to what extent the changes are due to fatigue factors independent of velocity changes. Future studies might include appropriate statistical measures, such as partial correlation or multiple regression analyses, to eliminate the influence of velocity.

In another study by Elliott and Blanksby [72] runners were guided to maintain steady velocities throughout a 3,000-m run, with film taken at 500, 1,300, 2,100, and 2,900 m. Significant differences were reported only between the 2,900-m measures and those from the other three points during the run. At 2,900 m they reported a decreased SL and increased SR, increased support time, and decreased nonsupport time compared to the other measurement times. The lower leg was at a greater angle with the vertical at foot strike, the thigh was less extended at the end of support, and the trunk had a greater forward lean than was found for measurements made earlier during the run.

*Sprinting*

Fatigue effects during sprinting have typically been assessed by filming runners early and again near the end of a 100- or 400-m run. The decrease in velocity with fatigue resulted from decreases in SL and SR [10], though some subjects showed no significant decreases in SL [43, 180]. Differences in temporal variables during support and nonsupport have not been reported to be simple reductions associated with decreased speed [8, 10], and show high individual variability [43]. Increases with fatigue have been reported for support and nonsupport times [10, 43, 180], with some variation in the relative timing of various subphases of support and nonsupport [10].

Extremes of flexion and extension in the lower extremity have been reported to decrease with fatigue [10, 43], though individual differences are evident [43] and studies yield conflicting results [180]. Murase [136] found no changes in vertical oscillations of the COM during the course of a 100-m sprint, and decreased linear velocity of the COM of the lower limb segment during the latter stages of the run. Sprague and Mann [180] found an increased velocity of the foot relative to the ground at foot strike in a fatigued compared to a nonfatigued state, as well as a greater decrease in horizontal velocity during one stride. They also calculated muscle moments in the lower extremity during support and nonsupport, and found that the better sprinters maintained mechanics which were similar to those found in the nonfatigued state to a greater extent than did the poorer sprinters.

## NEURAL FACTORS IN RUNNING

Knowledge of the neuromuscular coordination necessary to produce skilled movements is fundamental to an understanding of the biomechanics of human motion. While many investigations have focused on mechanical aspects of running, few studies have dealt with specific neural influences. There is a wealth of information available from the motor behavior literature concerning general neural activities in human movement, but little is aimed at explaining how neuromuscular integration is important to running performance, economy, or injuries.

James and Brubaker [107] have described the neuromuscular mechanisms during running, and Grillner [55] reviewed factors involved in the control of locomotion in a variety of species. Smith et al. [177], among others, have raised the possibility of the use of spinal generators in the control of locomotion, but no information specific to human running is available. Hatze [95, 96] has emphasized the importance of neural factors when modeling human performance and has presented mathematical models including such considerations.

Dietz et al. [60] examined the contributions of reflex neural input to gastrocnemius activity during the contact phase of running. He concluded that reflex activation of muscle spindles increased EMG above levels otherwise obtained, presumably to aid in control of movement. Frigo et al. [81] studied the relationship between muscle activation and muscle length and reported that maximal excitability came when the muscles were near their optimal length (the length where maximal force could be generated). The method by which they determined optimal length was not clearly specified. Upton and

Radford [186] estimated motorneuron excitability in elite sprinters. They reported that nerve conduction velocities and the total numbers of motor units of elite sprinters were not significantly different from those of a control group, but there was an increased excitability coefficient in the sprinters. Differences in motor coordination between elite sprinters and controls have also been reported, with the elite sprinters performing better on a tapping test [159]. Slater-Hammel [173] questioned whether maximal sprinting speed was limited by neuromuscular mechanisms and reported that subjects were able to achieve higher rates of leg movements when cycling than when running. It was concluded that speed of movement did not limit the maximal speed attained in running.

## BIOMECHANICS OF RUNNING FOR SPECIAL GROUPS

*Children*
There is little information describing the developmental changes which occur in the mechanics of running in children. Fortney [75] cites a number of unpublished theses which examined running style in children. In her own study, Fortney obtained cinematographic and force platform data for 2, 4, and 6, year olds, all running at their maximal speeds. Maximal running speed increased with age and changes were seen in a number of other measures of displacement, velocity, and force magnitude among groups. Of particular note were the very high impact peaks of the vertical ground reaction forces. These averaged 3.4 BW for the 6 year olds and approached 4 BW for the 4 year olds.

Atwater et al. [6] examined the relationship between HT, LL, and speed in 257 children 3 to 6 years of age, and speed was significantly related to HT or LL only in the younger girls. Few sex differences were found. Speed and SL increased with increasing age, with changes greater than would be expected due to increased stature alone; only slight increases in SR were found with increased age. Amano et al. [3] followed a group of 58 4 year olds over a four-year period and reported mean increases of 20 percent in running speed, 17 percent in HT, and 27 percent in SL. SR decreased 3 percent and there was a 10-fold increase in leg power. Matsuo and Fukunaga [127] measured mechanical power from changes in the position of the COM as estimated from ground reaction forces for subjects ranging from 8 to 20 years of age running at several velocities. As expected, maximal running speed increased with increased age, though females showed a plateau or drop in speed after age 14. For all age groups, total external power and power calculated from movements in the horizontal direction increased with increased speed, while power derived from movements in the vertical direction remained constant.

*Amputees*
While a great deal of effort has gone into the analysis of the walking gait for individuals with pathologies or handicaps, relatively little information is available concerning the biomechanics of running for such populations. Miller [134] and Enoka et al. [73] presented data for a number of kinematic and kinetic parameters from below-knee amputees during running. With a few exceptions, amputees were able to adopt running gaits with periods of both support and non-support, and speeds ranged from 2.7 to 8.2 m/s. An average of 54 percent of the amputee running cycle involved contact with the intact leg, with the amputee depending more on stride rate to increase speed than is normally found. Some amputees demonstrated hip and knee movements which were comparable to those for a skilled runner, while others kept the knee on the artificial limb in a straighter position during contact. Knee position also differed for the intact limb in some individuals, with the knee showing a restricted range of motion during swing, presumably to keep the intact foot closer to the ground for a greater feeling of security. Differences were also noted in the ankle kinematics between the intact and the artificial foot. While there were no significant differences in peak GRFs between the intact and artificial leg, or compared to nonamputee runners, there were differences in the pattern of force development [134]. The prosthesis side showed a slower rise to maximum, and generally the impact peak was missing, with an extended unweighting period during takeoff.

## FUTURE DIRECTIONS FOR RESEARCH

The volume of information concerning the biomechanics of running has increased tremendously during the past decade. Technological developments and refined analysis techniques provide the tools for very sophisticated investigations. Despite these advances there is still a lack of information available in certain areas and numerous conflicting results in others.

There is a great need for well-designed investigations of the relationship of biomechanical parameters to performance and injury. These studies, however, also represent the most difficult ones to implement, and unless care is taken in subject selection, experimental procedures, and analysis techniques, results may lack generality. Descriptive data is also needed. Preferably, the existing descriptive data base can be complemented by data resulting from studies which examine causative relationships.

The identification of optimal mechanics for running is a difficult task at best. Because of the high degree of variation in biomechanical parameters found among individuals during running, greater understanding may result from research that is more precisely directed toward the individual. While mean data from a large number of runners can be useful for establishing global trends, applications to an individual will have to be based on parameters specific to the individual. Because the movements of the body cannot be separated from neural and physiologic functions, there is also a need for interdisciplinary research with those in exercise physiology, exercise metabolism, mathematical modeling, and motor behavior.

Athletic coaches are called upon daily to make decisions regarding the influence of running mechanics on performance or injury, but the number of diverse opinions among them as to the characteristics of optimal performance is surpassed only slightly by the number of coaches. Similarly, clinicians have no choice but to come up with preventive and rehabilitative strategies despite not having clear information as to the mechanisms involved in overuse injuries. While much of the data gathered during the past 10 years has been useful to both the coaching and clinical professions, future research should strive to provide information which will lead to an even better understanding of the various mechanisms involved in neuromusculoskeletal functioning during running.

## REFERENCES

1. Adrian, M., and E. Kreighbaum. Mechanics of distance-running during competition. In *Medicine and Sport, Vol. 8: Biomechanics III*. Basel: Karger, 1973, pp. 354–358.
2. Alexander, R.McN., and A.S. Jayes. Fourier analysis of forces exerted in walking and running. *J. Biomech.* 13:383–390, 1980.
3. Amano, Y., S. Mizutani, and T. Hoshikawa. Longitudinal study of running of 58 children over a four-year period. In *Biomechanics VIII-B*, H. Matsui and K. Kobayashi, eds. Champaign, Ill.: Human Kinetics Publishers, 1983, pp. 663–668.
4. Asmussen, E., and F. Bonde-Petersen. Apparent efficiency and storage of elastic energy in human muscles during exercise. *Acta Physiol. Scand.* 92:537–545, 1974.
5. Atwater, A.E. Cinematographic analyses of human movement. *Exercise Sport Sci. Rev.* 1:217–228, 1973.
6. Atwater, A.E., A.M. Morris, J.M. Williams, and J.H. Wilmore. Kinematic aspects of running in 3- to 6-year old boys and girls. *Int. J. Sports. Med.* 4(2):282–283, 1981.
7. Bates, B.T., P.R. Francis, and H. Kinoshita. The interactive effects between foot type and shoe characteristics. *Abstracts from Sixth Annual Conference of American Society of Biomechanics*, Seattle, University of Washington, 1982, p. 78.
8. Bates, B.T., and B.H. Haven. Effects of fatigue on the mechanical characteristics of highly skilled female runners. In *Biomechanics IV*, R.C. Nelson and C.A. Morehouse, eds. Baltimore: University Park Press, 1974, pp. 119–125.

9. Bates, B.T., S.L. James, L.R. Osternig, and J.A. Sawhill. Effects of running shoes on ground reaction forces. In *Biomechanics VII-B*, A. Moreki, K. Fidelus, K. Kedzior, and A. Wit, eds. Baltimore: University Park Press, 1981, pp. 226–233.

10. Bates, B.T., and L.R. Osternig. Fatigue effects in running. *J. Motor Behav.* 9(3):203–207, 1977.

11. Bates, B.T., L.R. Osternig, and B.R. Mason. Variations of velocity within the support phase of running. In *Science in Athletics*, J. Terauds and G. Dales, eds. Del Mar: Academic Publishers, 1979, pp. 51–59.

12. Bates, B.T., L.R. Osternig, and B.R. Mason. Lower extremity function during the support phase of running. In *Biomechanics VI-B*, E. Asmussen and K. Jorgensen, eds. Baltimore: University Park Press, 1978, pp. 30–39.

13. Bates, B.T., L.R. Osternig, B. Mason, and S.L. James. Foot orthotic devices to modify selected aspects of lower extremity mechanics. *Am. J. Sports Med.* 7(6):338–342, 1979.

14. Bates, B.T., L.R. Osternig, B.R. Mason, and S.L. James. Functional variability of the lower extremity during the support phase of running. *Med. Sci. Sports Exercise* 11(4):328–331, 1979.

15. Bates, B.T., L.R. Osternig, J.A. Sawhill, and J. Hamill. Identification of critical variables describing ground reaction forces during running. In *Biomechanics VIII-B*, H. Matsui and K. Kobayshi, eds. Champaign, Ill.: Human Kinetics Publishers, 1983, pp. 635–640.

16. Bates, B.T., L.R. Osternig, J.A. Sawhill, and S.L. James. Assessment of subject variability, subject-shoe interaction, and the evaluation of running shoes using ground reaction force data. *J. Biomech.* 16(3):181–191, 1983.

17. Bhattacharya, A., E.P. McCutcheon, E. Shvartz, and J.E. Greenleaf. Body acceleration distribution and $O_2$ uptake in humans during running and jumping. *J. Appl. Physiol.* 49(5):881–887, 1980.

18. Blanksby, B.A. The biomechanics of running. *Aust. J. Sports Med.* 4(8):34–40, 1972.

19. Boccardi, S., C. Frigo, R. Rodano, G.C. Santambrogio, and A. Pedotti. Analysis of some athletic activities by means of vector diagrams. In *Science in Athletics*, J. Terauds and G. Dales, eds. Del Mar: Academic Publishers, 1979, pp. 183–192.

20. Bonen, A., G.C. Gass, W.A. Kachadorian, and R.E. Johnson. The energy cost of walking and running on different surfaces. *Aust. J. Sports Med.* 6(1):5–11, 1974.

21. Bosco, C., I. Tarkka, and P.V. Komi. Effect of elastic energy and myoelectrical potentiation of triceps surae during stretch-shortening cycle exercises. *Int. J. Sports Med.* 3:137–140, 1982.

22. Brandell, B.R. An analysis of muscle coordination in walking and running gaits. In *Medicine and Sport, Vol. 8: Biomechanics III*. Basel: Karger, 1973, pp. 278–287.

23. Bransford, D.R., and E.T. Howley. Oxygen cost of running in trained and untrained men and women. *Med. Sci. Sports Exercise* 9(1):41–44, 1977.

24. Brinckmann, P., H. Hoefert, and H.Th. Jongen. Sex differences in the skeletal geometry of the human pelvis and hip joint. *J. Biomech.* 14(6):427–430, 1981.

25. Brody, D.M. Running injuries. *Clin. Symp.* 32(4):2–36, 1980.

26. Buchbinder, M.R., N.J. Napora, and E.W. Biggs. The relationship of abnormal pronation to chondromalacia of the patella in distance running. *J. Am. Pod. Assoc.* 69(2):159–162, 1979.

27. Burdett, R.G. Forces predicted at the ankle during running. *Med. Sci. Sports Exercise* 14(4):308–316, 1982.

28. Campbell, D.E. Generation of horsepower at low and high velocity by sprinters and distance runners. *Res. Q.* 50(1):1–8, 1979.

29. Capazzo, A. Force actions in the human trunk during running. *J. Sports Med.* 23:14–22, 1983.
30. Catlin, M.J., and R.H. Dressendorfer. Effect of shoe weight on the energy cost of running. *Med. Sci. Sports Exercise* 11:80, 1979.
31. Cavagna, G.A., L. Komarek, and S. Mazzoleni. The mechanics of sprint running. *J. Physiol. (Lond.)* 217:709–721, 1971.
32. Cavagna, G.A., F.P. Saibene, and R. Margaria. Mechanical work in running. *J. Appl. Physiol.* 19(2):249–256, 1964.
33. Cavagna, G.A., H. Thys, and A. Zamboni. The sources of external work in level walking and running. *J. Physiol. (Lond.)* 262:639–657, 1976.
34. Cavanagh, P.R. The shoe-ground interface in running. In *Symposium on the Foot and Leg in Running Sports*, R.P. Mack, ed. St. Louis: C.V. Mosby, 1982, pp. 30–44.
35. Cavanagh, P.R., and M. Ae. A technique for the display of pressure distribution beneath the foot. *J. Biomech.* 13:69–75, 1980.
36. Cavanagh, P.R., T.C. Clarke, K.R. Williams, and A. Kalenak. An evaluation of the effect of orthotics on force distribution and rearfoot movement during running. Presented at Am. Orthop. Society annual meeting, Lake Placid, 1978.
37. Cavanagh, P.R., E.M. Hennig, R.P. Bunch, and N.H. Macmillan. A new device for the measurement of pressure distribution inside the shoe. In *Biomechanics VIII-B*, H. Matsui and K. Kobayashi, eds. Champaign, Ill.: Human Kinetics Publishers, 1983, pp. 1089–1096.
38. Cavanagh, P.R., and R. Kram. The efficiency of human movement: An overview. *Med. Sci. Sports Exercise* (in press).
39. Cavanagh, P.R., and M.A. LaFortune. Ground reaction forces in distance running. *J. Biomech.* 15(5):397–406, 1980.
40. Cavanagh, P.R., M.L. Pollock, and J. Landa. A biomechanical comparison of elite and good distance runners. In *The Marathon: Physiological, Medical, Epidemiological, and Psychological Studies*, P. Milvy, ed. New York: New York Acad. Sci., 1977, pp. 328–345.
41. Cavanagh, P.R., G.A. Valiant, and K.W. Misevich. Biological aspects of modeling shoe-foot interaction during running. In *Sports Shoes and Playing Surfaces: Biomechanical Properties*, E. Frederick, ed. Champaign, Ill.: Human Kinetics Publishers, 1983, pp. 24–46.
42. Cavanagh, P.R., and K.R. Williams. The effect of stride length variation on oxygen uptake during distance running. *Med. Sci. Sports Exercise* 14(1):30–35, 1982.
43. Chapman, A.E. Hierarchy of changes induced by fatigue in sprinting. *Can. J. Appl. Sport Sci.* 7(2):116–122, 1982.
44. Chapman, A.E., and G.E. Caldwell. Kinetic limitations of maximal sprinting speed. *J. Biomech.* 16(1):79–83, 1983.
45. Chapman, A.E., and G.E. Caldwell. Factors determining changes in lower limb energy during swing in treadmill running. *J. Biomech.* 16(1):69–77, 1983.
46. Clancy, W.G. Runners injuries. Part Two: Evaluation and treatment of specific injuries. *Am. J. Sports Med.* 8(4):287–289, 1980.
47. Clarke, T.E., L.B. Cooper, D.E. Clarke, and C.L. Hamill. The effect of increased running speed upon peak shank deceleration during ground contact. In *Biomechanics IX*. Champaign, Ill.: Human Kinetic Publishers (in press).
48. Clarke, T.C., E.C. Frederick, and L.B. Cooper. Biomechanical measurement of running shoe cushioning properties. In *Biomechanical Aspects of Sports Shoes and Playing Surfaces*, B. Nigg and B. Kerr, eds. Calgary: University of Calgary, 1983, pp. 25–33.
49. Clarke, T.E., E.C. Frederick, and L.B. Cooper. The effects of shoe cushioning upon ground reaction forces in running. *Int. J. Sports Med.* 4:376–381, 1983.

50. Clarke, T.E., E.C. Frederick, and C.L. Hammill. The effects of shoe design parameters on rearfoot control in running. *Med. Sci. Sports Exercise* 15(5):376–381, 1983.

51. Clarke, T.E., E.C. Frederick, and H.F. Hlavac. The study of rearfoot movement in running. Proceedings of the symposium on the biomechanics of sport floors and shoes. In *Sport Shoes and Playing Surfaces: Biomechanical Properties*, E.C. Frederick, ed. Champaign, Ill.: Human Kinetic Publishers, 1983, pp. 166–189.

52. Clarke, T.C., M.L. LaFortune, K.R. Williams, and P.R. Cavanagh. Relationship between center of pressure location and rearfoot movement in distance running. *Med. Sci. Sports Exercise* 12(2):192, 1980.

53. Conley, D.L., G.S. Krahenbuhl, and L.N. Burkett. Training for aerobic capacity and running economy. *Physician Sports Med.* 9(4):107–115, 1981.

54. Dal Monte, A., S. Fucci, and A. Manoni. The treadmill used as a training and a simulator instrument in middle- and long-distance running. In *Medicine and Sport, Vol. 8: Biomechanics III*, Basel: Karger, 1973, pp. 359–363.

55. D'Ambrosia, R., and D. Drez, eds. Prevention and treatment of running injuries. Thorofare, N.J.: Charles B. Slack, 1982.

56. Daniels, J.T. A physiologist's view of running economy. Presented at American College of Sports Medicine Annual Meeting, Montreal, 1983.

57. Davies, C.T.M. Effects of wind assistance and resistance on the forward motion of a runner. *J. Appl. Physiol.* 48(4):702–709, 1980.

58. DeMoya, R.G. A biomechanical comparison of the running shoe and the combat boot. *Military Med.* 147:380–383, 1982.

59. Deshon, D.E., and R.C. Nelson. A cinematographical analysis of sprint running. *Res. Q.* 35(4):451–455, 1964.

60. Dietz, V., D. Schmidtbleicher, and J. Noth. Neuronal mechanisms of human locomotion. *J. Neurophysiol.* 42(5):1212–1222, 1979.

61. Dillman, C.J. A kinetic analysis of the recovery leg during sprint running. In *Selected Topics on Biomechanics*. Proceedings of CIC Symposium on Biomechanics, J.M. Cooper, ed. Chicago: Athletic Institute, 1970, pp. 137–165.

62. Dillman, C.J. Effect of leg segmental movements on foot velocity during the recovery phase of running. In *Biomechanics IV*, R.C. Nelson and C.A. Morehouse, eds. Baltimore: University Park Press, 1974, pp. 98–105.

63. Dillman, C.J. Kinematic analyses of running. *Exercise Sports Sci. Rev.* 3:193–218, 1975.

64. Dotan, R., A. Rotstein, R. Dlin, O. Inbar, H. Kofman, and Y. Kaplansky. Relationships of marathon running to physiological, anthropometric, and training indices. *Eur. J. Appl. Physiol.* 51:281–293, 1983.

65. Elftman, H. The work done by muscles in running. *Am. J. Physiol.* 129:672–684, 1940.

66. Elliott, B.C. The co-ordination of force summation in the lower limb during the recovery phase of treadmill running. *J. Human Move. Stud.* 3:82–87, 1977.

67. Elliott, B.C., and T. Ackland. Biomechanical effects of fatigue on 10,000 meter running technique. *Res. Q. Exercise Sport* 52(2):160–166, 1981.

68. Elliott, B.C., and B.A. Blanksby. A cinematographical analysis of overground and treadmill running by males and females. *Med. Sci. Sports* 8(2):84–87, 1976.

69. Elliott, B.C., and B.A. Blanksby. Optimal stride length considerations for male and female recreational runners. *Br. J. Sports Med.* 13:15–18, 1979.

70. Elliott, B.C., and B.A. Blanksby. A biomechanical analysis of the male jogging action. *J. Human Move. Stud.* 5:42–51, 1979.

71. Elliott, B.C., and B.A. Blanksby. The synchronization of muscle activity and

body segment movements during a running cycle. *Med. Sci. Sports Exercise* 11:322–327, 1979.

72. Elliott, B.C., and A.D. Roberts. A biomechanical evaluation of the role of fatigue in middle-distance running. *Can. J. Appl. Sport Sci.* 5(4):203–207, 1980.

73. Enoka, R.M., D.I. Miller, and E.M. Burgess. Below-knee amputee running gait. *Am. J. phys. Med.* 61(2):66–84, 1982.

74. Fenn, W.O. Work against gravity and work due to velocity changes in running. *Am. J. Physiol.* 93:433–463, 1930.

75. Fortney, V.L. The kinematics and kinetics of the running pattern of two-, four-, and six-year-old children. *Res. Q. Exercise Sport* 54(2):126–135, 1983.

76. Frederick, E.C., and T.E. Clarke. Body size and biomechanical consequences for runners. In *Sports Medicine, Sports Science,* R.C. Cantu and W.J. Gillespie, eds. Lexington, Mass.: Collamore Press, 1984, pp. 47–58.

77. Frederick, E.C., T.C. Clarke, J.L. Hansen, and L.B. Cooper. The effects of shoe cushioning on the oxygen demands of running. In *Biomechanical Aspects of Sports Shoes and Playing Surfaces,* B. Nigg and B. Kerr, eds. Calgary: University of Calgary, 1983, pp. 107–114.

78. Frederick, E.C., J.T. Daniels, and J.W. Hayes. The effect of shoe weight on the aerobic demands of running. In *Proceedings of the World Congress on Sports Medicine, Vienna,* L. Prokop, ed. Vienna, 1983 (in press).

79. Frederick, E.C., E.T. Howley, and S.K. Powers. Lower $O_2$ cost while running in air cushion type shoes. *Med. Sci. Sports Exercise* 12:81–82, 1982.

80. Friberg, O. Leg length asymmetry in stress fractures. *J. Sports Med.* 22:485–488, 1982.

81. Frigo, C., A. Pedotti, and G. Santambrogio. A correlation between muscle and E.C.G. activities during running. In *Science in Athletics,* J. Terauds and G. Dale, eds. Del mar: Academic Publishers, 1979, pp. 61–70.

82. Frishberg, B.A. An analysis of overground and treadmill sprinting. *Med. Sci. Sports Exercise* 15(6):478–485, 1983.

83. Fukuda, H., H. Ohmichi, and M. Miyashita. Effects of shoe weight on oxygen uptake during submaximal running. In *Biomechanical Aspects of Sport Shoes and Playing Surfaces,* B. Nigg and B. Kerr, eds. Calgary: University of Calgary, 1983, pp. 115–119.

84. Gehlsen, G.M., and A. Seger. Selected measures of angular displacement, strength, and flexibility in subjects with and without shin splints. *Res. Q. Exercise Sport* 51(3):478–485, 1980.

85. Gerber, H. A system for measuring dynamic distribution under the human foot. *J. Biomech.* 15(3):225–227, 1982.

86. Girardin, Y., and B.G. Roy. Effects of a nondirective type of training program on the running patterns of male sedentary subjects. In *Biomechanics IV,* R.C. Nelson and C.A. Morehouse, eds. Baltimore: University Park Press, 1984, pp. 119–125.

87. Gollhofer, A., D. Schmidtbleicher, and V. Dietz. Regulation of muscle stiffness in human locomotion. *Int. J. Sports Med.* 5:19–22, 1984.

88. Gregor, R.J., and D. Kirkendall. Performance efficiency of world class female marathon runners. In *Biomechanics VI-B,* E. Asmussen and K. Jorgensen, eds. Baltimore: University Park Press, 1978, pp. 40–45.

89. Grillner, S. Locomotion in vertebrates: Central mechanisms and reflex interaction. *Acta Physiol. Scand.* 86:92–108, 1972.

90. Grillner, S., J. Halbertsma, J. Nilsson, and A. Thorstensson. The adaptation to speed in human locomotion. *Brain Res.* 165:177–182, 1979.

91. Grillner, S., J. Nilsson, and A. Thorstensson. Intra-abdominal pressure changes during natural movements in man. *Acta Physiol. Scand.* 103:275–283, 1978.

92. Gross, R.H. Leg length discrepancy in marathon runners. *Am. J. Sports Med.* 11(3):121–124, 1983.

93. Hammill, J., B.T. Bates, and C.A. White. Evaluation of foot orthotic appliances using ground reaction force data. In *Locomotion II*. Proceedings of the Second Biannual Conference of the Canadian Society for Biomechanics. Kingston, Ontario: Can. Soc. Biomech., 1982, pp. 74–75.

94. Hatsell, C.P. A note on jogging on a windy day. *IEEE Trans. Biomed. Eng.* 22(5):428–429, 1975.

95. Hatze, H. A comprehensive model for human motion simulation and its application to the take-off phase of the long jump. *J. Biomech.* 14(3):135–142, 1981.

96. Hatze, H. Biomechanics of sport: What should the future really hold? *J. Biomech.* 12:237–238, 1979.

97. Hinrichs, R.N. Upper extremity function in running. Ph.D. dissertation, Pennsylvania State University, 1982.

98. Hinrichs, R.N., P.R. Cavanagh, and K.R. Williams. Upper extremity contributions to angular momentum in running. In *Biomechanics VIII-B*, H. Matsui and K. Kobayashi, eds. Champaign, Ill.: Human Kinetics Publishers, 1983, pp. 641–647.

99. Hoffman, K. Stature, leg length, and stride frequency. *Kult. Fiz.* 9, 1964; translated in *Track Technique* 46:1463–1469, 1971.

100. Hogberg, P. How do stride length and stride frequency influence the energy-output during running? *Arbeitsphysiol.* 14:437–441, 1952.

101. Holden, J.P., P.R. Cavanagh, and K.R. Williams. Foot angles during walking and running. In *Biomechanics IX*. Champaign, Ill.: Human Kinetics Publishers (in press).

102. Hoshikawa, T., H. Matsui, and M. Miyashita. Analysis of running pattern in relation to speed. In *Medicine and Sport, Vol. 8: Biomechanics III*. Basel: Karger, 1973, pp. 342–348.

103. Hubbard, A.W. An experimental analysis of running and of certain fundamental differences between trained and untrained runners. *Res. Q.* 10(3):28–38, 1939.

104. Ito, A., T. Fuchimoto, and M. Kaneko. Quantitative analysis of EMG during various speeds of running. In *Biomechanics IX*. Champaign, Ill.: Human Kinetics Publishers (in press).

105. Ito, A., P.V. Komi, B. Sjodin, C. Bosco, and J. Karlsson. Mechanical efficiency of positive work in running at different speeds. *Med. Sci. Sports Exercise* 15(4):299–308, 1983.

106. James, S.L., B.T. Bates, and L.R. Osternig. Injuries to runners. *Am. J. Sports Med.* 6(2):40–50, 1978.

107. James, S.L, and C.E. Brubaker. Biomechanical and neuromuscular aspect of running. *Exercise and Sport Sci. Rev.* 1:189–216.

108. Kerr, B.A., L. Beauchamp, V. Fisher, and R. Neil. Footstrike patterns in distance running. In *Biomechanical Aspects of Sport Shoes and Playing Surfaces*, B. Nigg and B. Kerr, eds. Calgary: University of Calgary, 1983, pp. 135–141.

109. Knuttgen, H.G. Oxygen uptake and pulse rate while running with undetermined and determined stride lengths at different speeds. *Acta Physiol. Scand.* 52:366–371, 1961.

110. Komi, P.V. Biomechanical features of running with special emphasis on load characteristics and mechanical efficiency. In *Biomechanical Aspects of Sport Shoes and Playing Surfaces*, B. Nigg and B. Kerr, eds. Calgary: University of Calgary, 1983, pp. 123–134.

111. Komi, P.V., A. Ito, B. Sjodin, R. Wallenstein, and J. Karlsson. Muscle metabolism, lactate breaking point, and biomechanical features of endurance running. *Int. J. Sports Med.* 2:148–153, 1981.

112. Kreighbaum, E.F., and G.J. Ferrandino. Morton's foot syndrome and its relationship to leg stress in runners. In *Science in Athletics*, J. Terauds and G. Dales, eds. Del Mar: Academic Publishers, 1979, pp. 249–257.

113. Krissoff, W.B., and W.D. Ferris. Runners' injuries. *Physician Sports Med.* 7(12):55–64, 1979.

114. Kunz, H., and D.A. Kaufmann. Biomechanical analysis of sprinting: Decathletes versus champions. *Br. J. Sports Med.* 15(3):177–181, 1981.

115. Kyle, C.R. Reduction of wind resistance and power output of racing cyclists and runners traveling in groups. *Ergonomics* 22(4):387–397, 1979.

116. Lawson, D.L., and L.A. Golding. Physiological parameters limiting performance in middle distance and sprint running. *Aust. J. Sports Med.* 1:18–24, 1979.

117. Leach, R.E., E. DiIorio, and R.A. Harney. Pathological hindfoot conditions in the athlete. *Clin. Orthop.* 177:116–121, 1983.

118. Lippert, F.G., R.M. Harrington, A.S. Woodle, S.G. Newell, and G.L. Scheirman. The measurement of foot and ankle kinematics in a sports medicine clinic. *Abstracts, Sixth Annual Conference of the American Society of Biomechanics.* Seattle: University of Washington, 1982, p. 86.

119. Luhtanen, P., and P.V. Komi. Mechanical factors influencing running speed. In *Biomechanics VI-B*, E. Asmussen and K. Jorgenson, eds. Baltimore: University Park Press, 1978, pp. 23–29.

120. Luhtanen, P., and P.V. Komi. Force-, power-, and elasticity-velocity relationships in walking, running, and jumping. *Eur. J. Appl. Physiol.* 44(3):279–289, 1980.

121. Luttgens, K., and K. Wells. *Kinesiology: Scientific Basis of Human Motion.* Philadelphia: Saunders College Publishing, 1982.

122. Mann, R.A. Biomechanics of walking, running, and sprinting. *Am. J. Sports Med.* 8(5):345–350, 1980.

123. Mann, R.A. Biomechanics of running. *The Foot and Leg in Running Sports*, R.P. Mack, ed. St. Louis: C.V. Mosby, 1982, pp. 1–29.

124. Mann, R.A., and J.L. Hagy. The function of the toes in walking, jogging, and running. *Clin. Orthop.* 142:24–29, 1979.

125. Mann, R., and P. Sprague. A kinetic analysis of the ground leg during sprint running. *Res. Q. Exercise Sport* 51(2):334–348, 1980.

126. Marshall, R.N. Foot mechanics and joggers injuries. *N.Z. Med. J.* 88:288–290, 1978.

127. Matsuo, A., and T. Fukunaga. The effect of age and sex on external mechanical energy in running. In *Biomechanics VIII-B*, H. Matsui and K. Kobayashi, eds. Champaign, Ill.: Human Kinetics Publishers, 1983, pp. 676–680.

128. Maughan, R.J., J.S. Watson, and J. Weir. Relationships between muscle strength and muscle cross-sectional area in male sprinters and endurance runners. *Eur. J. Appl. Physiol.* 50:309–318, 1983.

129. Mayhew, J.L. Oxygen cost and energy expenditure of running in trained runners. *Br. J. Sports Med.* 11(3):116–121, 1977.

130. McDermott, A.G.P., A.E. Marble, R.H. Yabsley, and B. Phillips. Monitoring dynamic anterior compartment pressures during exercise. *Am. J. Sports Med.* 10(2):83–89, 1982.

131. McDermott, M., and P. Freyne. Osteoarthrosis in runners with knee pain. *Br. J. Sports Med.* 17(2):84–97, 1983.

132. McMahon, T.A., and P.R. Greene. The influence of track compliance on running. *J. Biomech.* 12:893–904, 1979.

133. McMahon, T.A., and P.R. Greene. Fast running tracks. *Sci. Am.* 239(6):148–163, 1978.

134. Miller, D.I. Biomechanical considerations in lower extremity amputee running and sports performance. *Aust. J. Sports Med.* 13(3):55–67, 1981.
135. Miller, D.I. Biomechanics of running: What should the future hold? *Can. J. Appl. Sports Sci.* 3:229–236, 1978.
136. Murase, Y., T. Hoshikawa, N. Yasuda, Y. Ikesame, and H. Matsui. Analysis of the changes in progressive speed during 100-meter dash. In *Biomechanics V-B,* P.V. Komi, ed. Baltimore: University Park Press, 1976, pp. 200 –207.
137. Nelson, R.C., C.M. Brooks, and N.L. Pike. Biomechanical comparison of male and female distance runners. In *The Marathon: Physiological, Medical, Epidemiological, and Psychological Studies,* P. Milvy, ed. New York: New York Acad. Sci., 1977, pp. 793–807.
138. Nelson, R.C., C.J. Dillman, P. Lagasse, and P. Bickett. Biomechanics of overground versus treadmill running. *Med. Sci. Sports* 4(4):233–240, 1972.
139. Nelson, R.C., and R.J. Gregor. Biomechanics of distance running: A longitudinal study. *Res. Q.* 47(3):417–428, 1976.
140. Nelson, R.C., and R.G. Osterhoudt. Effects of altered slope and speed on the biomechanics of running. In *Medicine and Sport, Vol. 6: Biomechanics II.* Basel: Karger, 1971, pp. 220–224.
141. Nigg, B.M. External force measurements with sport shoes and playing surfaces. In *Biomechanical Aspects of Sports Shoes and Playing Surfaces,* B. Nigg and B. Kerr, eds. Calgary: University of Calgary, 1983, pp. 11–23.
142. Nigg, B.M., J. Denoth, and P.A. Neukomm. Quantifying the load on the human body: Problems and some possible solutions. In *Biomechanics VII-B,* A. Moreki, K. Fidelus, K. Kedzior, and A. Wit, eds. Baltimore: University Park Press, 1981, pp. 88–99.
143. Nigg, B.M., G. Eberle, D. Frey, S. Luethi, B. Segesser, and B. Weber. Gait analysis and sport-shoe construction. In *Biomechanics VI-A,* E. Asmussen and K. Jorgensen, eds. Baltimore: University Park Press, 1978, pp. 303–309.
144. Nigg, B.M., and S. Luethi. Bewegungsanalysen bein laufschuh. (Movement analysis and running shoes.) *Sportwissenshaft* 3:309–320, 1980.
145. Nigg, B.M., S. Luethi, J. Denoth, and A. Stacoff. Methodological aspects of sport shoe and sport surface analysis. In *Biomechanics VIII-B,* H. Matsui and K. Kobayashi, eds. Champaign, Ill.: Human Kinetic Publishers, 1983, pp. 1041–1052.
146. Nigg, B.M., S. Luethi, B. Segesser, A. Stacoff, H. Guidon, and A. Schneider. Sportschuhkorrekturen. (Sports shoes support inlays.) *Z. Orthop.* 120:34–39, 1982.
147. Norman, R., M. Sharratt, J. Pezzack, and E. Noble. Re-examination of the mechanical efficiency of horizontal treadmill running. In *Biomechanics V-B.* International Series on Biomechanics, P.V. Komi, ed. Baltimore: University Park Press, 1976, pp. 87–93.
148. O'Brien, M., B. Davies, and A. Daggett. Women in sport. In *Science and Sporting Performance: Management or Manipulation,* B. Davies and G. Thomas, eds. Oxford: Clarendon Press, 1982, pp. 52–67.
149. Pagliano, J. Pathological foot types in runners. In *Medicine and Sport, Vol. 12,* E. Jokl, ed. Basel: Karger, 1978, pp. 155–168.
150. Paul, I.L., M.B. Munro, P.J. Abernethy, S.R. Simon, E.L. Radin, and R.M. Rose. Musculo-skeletal shock absorption: Relative contribution of bone and soft tissues at various frequences. *J. Biomech.* 11:237–239, 1978.
151. Payne, A.H. Foot to ground contact forces of elite runners. In *Biomechanics VIII-B,* H. Matsui and K. Kobayashi, eds. Champaign, Ill.: Human Kinetics Publishers, 1983, pp. 746–753.
152. Perry, J. Anatomy and biomechanics of the hindfoot. *Clin. Orthop.* 177:9–15, 1983.

153. Pierrynowski, M.R., D.A. Winter, and R.W. Norman. Transfers of mechanical energy within the total body and mechanical efficiency during treadmill walking. *Ergonomics* 23(2):147–156, 1980.

154. Plamondon, A., and B. Roy. Cinematique et cinetique de la course acceleree. *Can. J. Appl. Sport Sci.* 9(1):42–52, 1984.

155. Pollock, M. Submaximal and maximal working capacity of elite distance runners. In *The Marathon: Physiological, Medical, Epidemiological, and Psychological Studies*, P. Milvy, ed. New York: New York Acad. Sci., 1977, pp. 793–807.

156. Pugh, L.G.C.E. Oxygen intake in track and treadmill running with observations on the effect of air resistance. *J. Physiol. (Lond.)* 207:823–835, 1970.

157. Pugh, L.G.C.E. The influence of wind resistance in running and walking and the mechanical efficiency of work against horizontal or vertical forces. *J. Physiol. (Lond.)* 213:255–276, 1971.

158. Puranen, J., L. Ala-Ketola, P. Peltokallio, and J. Searela. Running and primary osteoarthritis of the hip. *Br. Med. J.* II: 424, 1975.

159. Radford, P.F., and A.R.M. Upton. Trends in speed of alternated movement during development and among elite sprinters. In *Biomechanics V-B*, P.V. Komi, ed. Baltimore: University Park Press, 1976, pp. 188–193.

160. Radin, E.L., R.B. Orr, S.L. Schein, J.L. Kelman, and R.M. Rose. The effects of hard and soft surface walking on sheep knees. *J. Biomech.* 13:196, 1980.

161. Robertson, D.G.E., and J.E. Taunton. Power characteristics of leg muscles during stance phase of running. *Locomotion II*. Proceedings of the Second Biannual Conference of the Canadian Society for Biomechanics. Kingston, Ontario: Can. Soc. of Biomech., 1982, pp. 100–101.

162. Rodgers, M.M., and B.F. LeVeau. Effectiveness of foot orthotic devices used to modify pronation in runners. *Locomotion II*. Proceedings of the Second Biannual Conference of the Canadian Society for Biomechanics. Kingston, Ontario: Can. Soc. of Biomech., 1982, pp. 102–103.

163. Roy, B. Caracteriques biomecaniques de la course d'endurance. *Can. J. Appl. Sport Sci.* 7(2):104–115, 1982.

164. Roy, B. Temporal and dynamic factors of long distance running. In *Biomechanics VII-B*, A. Moreki, K. Fidelus, K. Kodzier, A. Wit, eds. Baltimore: University Park Press, 1981, pp. 226–233.

165. Saito, M., K. Kobayashi, M. Miyashita, and T. Hoshikawa. In *Biomechanics IV*, R.C. Nelson and C.A. Morehouse, eds. Baltimore: University Park press, 1974, pp. 106–111.

166. Saito, M., T. Ohkuwa, Y. Ikegami, and M. Miyamura. Comparisons of sprint running in the trained and untrained runners with respect to chemical and mechanical energy. In *Biomechanics VIII-B*, M. Matsui and K. Kobayashi, eds. Champaign, Ill.: Human Kinetics Publishers, 1983, pp. 963–968.

167. Schwab, G.H., D.R. Moynes, F.W. Jobe, and J. Perry. Lower extremity electromyographic analysis of running gait. *Clin. Orthop.* 176:166–170, 1983.

168. Scranton, P.E., and J.H. McMaster. Momentary distribution of forces under the foot. *J. Biomech.* 9:45–48, 1976.

169. Segesser, B., and B.M. Nigg. Insertionstendiogen am schienbein, achillodynie und uberlastungsfolgen am fuss- Atiologie, biomechanik, therapeutische moglichkeiten. *Orthopade* 9:207–214, 1980.

170. Shanebrook, J.R., and R.D. Jaszczak. Aerodynamic drag analysis of runners. *Med. Sci. Sports* 8(1):43–45, 1976.

171. Shorten, M.R. Mechanical energy changes and elastic energy storage during treadmill running. In *Biomechanics IX*, Champaign, Ill.: Human Kinetics Publishers (in press).

172. Sinning, W.E., and H.L. Forsyth. Lower-limb actions while running at different velocities. *Med. Sci. Sports* 2)1):28–34, 1970.

173. Slater-Hammel, A. Possible neuromuscular mechanisms as limiting factor for rate of leg movement in sprinting. *Res. Q.* 12:745–756, 1941.
174. Slocum, D.B., and W. Bowerman. The biomechanics of running. *Clin. Orthopaed.* 23:39–45, 1962.
175. Slocum, D.B., and S.L. James. Biomechanics of running. *JAMA* 205(11):97–104, 1968.
176. Smart, G.W., J.E. Taunton, and D.B. Clement. Achilles tendon disorders in runners: A review. *Med. Sci. Sports Exercise* 12(4):231–243, 1980.
177. Smith, J.L. Sensorimotor integrations during motor programming. In *Information Processing in Motor Control and Learning*, G. Stelmach, ed. New York: Academic Press, 1978.
178. Smith, L., T. Clarke, and C. Hammill, and F. Santopietro. The effects of soft and semi-rigid orthoses upon rearfoot movement in running. *Med. Sci. Sports Exercise* 15(2):171, 1983.
179. Sohn, R.S., and L.J. Micheli. The effect of running on the pathogenesis of osteoarthritis of the hips and knees. *Med. Sci. Sports Exercise* 16(2):150, 1984.
180. Sprague, P., and R.V. Mann. The effects of muscular fatigue on the kinetics of sprint running. *Res. Q. Exercise Sport* 54(1):60–66, 1983.
181. Stacoff, A., and X. Kaelin. Pronation and sport shoe design. In *Biomechanical Aspects of Sports Shoes and Playing Surfaces*, B. Nigg and B. Kerr, eds. Calgary: University of Calgary, 1983, pp. 143–151.
182. Staheli, L.T., F. Lippert, and P. Denotter. Femoral anteversion and physical performance in adolescent and adult life. *Clin. Orthop.* 129:213–216, 1977.
183. Stoner, L.J., and D. Ben-Sira. Sprinting on the curve. In *Science in Athletics*, J. Torauds and G. Dale, eds. Del Mar: Academic Publishers, 1979, pp. 167–173.
184. Subotnick, S.I. A biomechanical approach to running injuries. In *The Marathon: Physiological, Medical, Epidemiological, and Psychological Studies*, P. Milvy, ed. New York: New York Acad. Sci., 1977, pp. 328–345.
185. Sykes, K. Technique and observation of angular gait patterns in running. *Br. J. Sports Med.* 9(4):181–186, 1975.
186. Upton, A.R.M., and P.F. Radford. Motoneurone excitability in elite sprinters. In *Biomechanics V-A*, P.V. Komi, ed. Baltimore: University Park Press, 1976, pp. 82–87.
187. Van Der Walt, W.H., and C.H. Wyndham. An equation for prediction of energy expenditure of walking and running. *J. Appl. Physiol.* 34(5):559–563, 1973.
188. Van Ingen Schenau, G.J. Some fundamental aspects of the biomechanics of overground versus treadmill locomotion. *Med. Sci. Sports Exercise* 12(4):257–261, 1980.
189. Vaughan, C.L. Simulation of a sprinter, Part I. Development of a model. *Int. J. Bio-med. Computing* 14:65–74, 1983.
190. Vaughan, C.L., J.G. Andrews, and J.G. Hay. Selection of body segment parameters by optimization methods. *J. Biomech. Eng.* 104:38–44, 1982.
191. Viitasalo, J.T., and M. Kvist. Some biomechanical aspects of the foot and ankle in athletes with and without shin splints. *Am. J. Sports Med.* 11(3):125–130, 1983.
192. Volkov, N.I., and V.I. Lapin. Analysis of the velocity curve in sprint running. *Med. Sci. Sports* 11(4):322–337, 1979.
193. Williams, K.R. A biomechanical evaluation of distance running efficiency. Ph.D. dissertation, Pennsylvania State University, 1980.
194. Williams, K.R. Non-sagittal plane movements and forces during distance running. *Abstracts, Sixth Annual Conference of the American Society of Biomechanics.* Seattle: University of Washington, 1982, pp. 24.

195. Williams, K.R. The relationship between mechanical and physiological energy estimates. *Med. Sci. Sports Exercise* (in press).
196. Williams, K.R., and P.R. Cavanagh. A model for the calculation of mechanical power during distance running. *J. Biomech.* 16(2):115–128, 1983.
197. Winter, D.A. A new definition of mechanical work done in human movement. *J. Appl. Physiol.* 46(1):79–83, 1979.
198. Winter, D.A. Moments of force and mechanical power in jogging. *J. Biomech.* 16(1):91–97, 1983.
199. Winter, D.A., B. Arsenault, and S. Wooley. Step-to-step fluctuations in treadmill gait. *Human Locomotion I.* Proceedings of the Biannual Meeting of the Canadian Society of Biomechanics. Ontario: Can. Soc. Biomech., 1980, pp. 28–29.
200. Yoneda, Y., M. Adrian, F. Walker, and D. Dobie. Kinematic and kinetic analysis of sprinting and jogging. In *Science in Athletics*, J. Terauds and G. Dales, eds. Del Mar: Academic Publishers, 1979, pp. 85–91.

# The Mechanical Properties of Human Muscle

ARTHUR E. CHAPMAN, Ph.D.

This review focuses on the mechanical properties of human muscle and is directed toward students of human movement. Initially, mechanical components of muscle are described. These components are conceptual entities and include the contractile component (CC), the series elastic component (SEC), and the parallel elastic component (PEC). They need not be considered as separate anatomical components, and in some respects it is a mistake to do so. The mechanical properties of these components are dealt with separately as are some other properties which have a bearing upon the mechanics. The second section deals with approaches to the modeling of muscular contraction through knowledge of the mechanical behavior of muscle components. The purpose, choice and implementation of a model, and models with different properties are considered. In the third section the motion of components of a muscle model is described under conditions which are found typically in human muscular contraction. The emphasis of this section is that externally measured kinematics and kinetics rarely reflect the behavior of the muscular components. This review concludes with some observations and speculations on the use of muscle in human activities. These observations include a number of studies which would have benefited from a consideration of muscle as a component structure. The speculations are made from the point of view of the directions which may be taken in further research on human muscle.

Students of human muscular contraction may be interested to know that A.V. Hill performed experiments on sprinting in 1927 [78]. In their quest to answer many of the questions raised by this work, Hill and his colleagues performed many classical experiments on isolated amphibian muscles. Since then much work has been performed on subsets of muscle of ever decreasing size. It appears that Hill's original intentions to understand the part played by muscle in human activity have fallen somewhat by the wayside. However, the information resulting from work on muscle at various levels provides us with a substantial basis for a return to the question of how we use our muscles to move around. While it is recognized that human muscular contraction has not been ignored, much of the information on muscle from other fields has been ignored by students of human movement.

443

This review is concerned neither with the effects of training on the mechanical properties of human muscle [7] nor the direct metabolic cost of contraction (see Chapter 2). Similarly, muscular fatigue is not a central theme. However, later sections of this review speculate somewhat on these aspects.

## MECHANICAL BEHAVIOR OF MUSCLE

Much is known about the architecture of muscle, and there have been numerous theories on the nature of the contractile process. The dynamic properties of muscle have been revealed by experiments in vitro. Yet there remains considerable disagreement concerning the fixed or fundamental nature of the mechanical relationships in muscle. Since human intact muscles are difficult to work with, much reliance is placed in this section upon work which has used isolated preparations, single fibers, and further subsets of the muscle.

Over the years the function of human muscle has been variously regarded. Since muscle can either shorten, lengthen, or maintain a constant length when developing tension, a kinematically based definition of its function is inappropriate. The contention throughout this chapter is that the function of muscle is to produce force. This is seen under isometric conditions for stabilization, and under both concentric and eccentric conditions which are equally found in human movement. It would appear reasonable that the role of the contractile tissue is to produce force, and in terms of modeling the muscle, this role has been allocated to the contractile component.

### The Contractile Component (CC)

Considerable theory exists concerning the mechanism by which muscle generates force. Despite the introduction of various theories from time to time, the cross-bridge theory persists. This theory has received much attention from biochemical [90, 171] and mechanical [115, 118] viewpoints and the state of the theory and some criticisms of it have been discussed [103, 119, 139, 140]. Pollack [150] has provided a comprehensive review of much original work and previous reviews of the cross-bridge theory, and his work is mandatory reading for those who aim to understand the nature of muscular contraction. Since the cross-bridge theory is not unambiguously supported by experimental evidence, any use of a CC which is based entirely on this theory must remain theoretical. Whatever the mechanism of force production might prove to be, the phenomenon of contraction appears to exhibit some fundamental properties which are more or less obeyed in many varieties of skeletal muscle.

Since the production of force appears to be the goal of the contractile component, it is pertinent to review those factors which appear to modify the force produced. For example, it is clear that force produced can vary with voluntary activation from zero force to some high level ($F = f$(activation)). Second, experiments on isolated muscle have shown us that the force produced can vary from zero during maximal shortening velocity in an unloaded situation to large forces observed during stretch of an activated muscle ($F = f$(velocity)). Force is also known to vary with the length of the muscle ($F = f$(length)). In addition, the prior history of the state of contraction is known to effect the force developed ($F = f$(history)). The following section considers the effects of these variables on the force produced in skeletal muscle. In considering the CC as an entity, it must be understood that it is a theoretical concept. It is a component representing the behavior of the many force-producing elements, and it cannot be ascribed to any single anatomical site.

*The force velocity (F-V) relationship.* In observing that force produced appeared to be a function of velocity of shortening, Hill [97] equated mechanical and thermal measurements and fitted the following equation to the curve relating force to velocity of shortening of muscle.

$$(P + \text{a})(V + b) = (P_o + \text{a})b \qquad (1)$$

where $P$ = force, $V$ = velocity, $P_o$ = maximal tetanic force, a = a constant with units of force and b = a constant with units of velocity. Other equations have been used to describe the concentric F-V relationship, and as Wilkie [179] pointed out, the choice of any one equation is a matter of convenience. It may be assumed that an equation which relates force to velocity is a mathematical description of the actual mechanical results of contraction. This situation will remain until an equation is derived which is found to take a certain form on the basis of a complete knowledge of the contractile process. However, Huxley [111] developed an equation which was based upon the kinetics of cross-bridge interaction. This would seem to be a more fundamental approach to the nature of the F-V relationship than that based upon measurements of heat. Hill's equation has been successfully applied to the F-V relationship in a wide variety of different muscles from many species [2]. However, among muscles from different animals it varies with the value "a," maximal force at zero velocity ($P_o$) and maximal velocity in an unloaded situation ($V_o$) (see equation 1). Mashima [130] has produced a comprehensive summary of the F-V relationship.

The first significant attempt to assess the applicability of equation 1 to human muscles was made by Hill [98] who examined previous data on elbow flexion [96, 102, 128]. He suggested that equation 1 was applicable to human muscular contraction, as did Dern, Levine, and Blair [65] who increased the range of motion over that used by Hill [98]. Wilkie [179] performed a classical study on the F-V relationship in human elbow flexion. This paper is worthy of study since it points out many of the assumptions and problems inherent in the nature of this work. Wilkie expressed his results in terms of a single equivalent horizontal muscle at the hand and found that Hill's characteristic equation did not fit the points representing instantaneous force and velocity when loads less than approximately 30 percent of the isometric maximum were used. He ascribed this result to the fact that low loads did not allow the hand to reach its greatest possible velocity. When a correction was made for acceleration present during these rapid contractions, the corrected points lay upon a curve which was described adequately by Hill's equation. However, the correction which Wilkie performed seems to have been based upon prior acceptance of suitability of Hill's equation. Yet all subsequent references made to the study performed by Wilkie [179] conclude that he obtained the true F-V relationship for the CC of each subject tested. These results were verified by others who obtained direct readings from transducers of force [43, 145, 146, 188]. In contrast, Tennant [169] obtained a F-V relationship which did not fit Hill's equation when biceps brachii and brachialis contracted under the influence of external tetanic stimulation. The analysis performed by Cavanagh and Grieve [43] was based upon the following analytical process. If the force produced by the CC is transmitted to an external load by a series elastic element, the rate of stretch of the elastic element will depend on the rate of change of force in the CC. Should this force progress from increasing to decreasing, the elastic element will progress from stretching to shortening. At the transition point (where $df/dt = 0$) the velocity of stretch of the elastic element will be zero. Consequently the velocity of the load will equal that of the CC. Therefore values of load velocity and force represent a point on the F-V relationship which is unaffected by stretch of series elastic structures. The performance of many contractions against varying loads yields a number of such points which allow construction of a F-V relationship. The same technique has been used by Baildon and Chapman [16] during forearm rotation, although they found Hill's equation to be a poor fit to the data. In their case, the F-V relationship represented the combined action of a number of muscles which, due to their complex anatomy, may not behave like a single muscle from which Hill's equation was derived. Analysis of this kind is a necessary prerequisite to obtaining the F-V relationship of the CC; otherwise the externally recorded values of velocity do not represent those of the CC. Many devices have been designed to allow measurement of force when external velocity is held constant. Unfortunately, it is force that should be maintained constant in order to obtain CC force and velocity.

The majority of studies on human muscular contraction have used methods of analysis which have not taken into account the elastic structures in series with a contractile tissue. However, many of these have yielded useful information under a variety of experimental conditions and they have demonstrated the areas within which the behaviour of human and isolated muscles is similar. F-V relationships have been produced by others who estimated average rather than instantaneous velocity, and in all cases a large scatter of points was obtained about the fitted F-V relationship [5, 18, 125]. However, these studies indicated that maximal eccentric force produced was up to 30 percent greater than isometric force and that it varied with velocity of lengthening. This has been known for many years [25], and it is certain that Hill's equation is an inadequate fit to the eccentric F-V relationship [123]. Similar results have been produced by other investigators [6, 42, 87, 122].

The flexors of the elbow have been the most widely investigated group of muscles in experiments where an attempt has been made to measure accurately such variables as force and velocity. There appear to have been few attempts to reproduce the type of anlaysis used by either Wilkie [179] or Cavanagh and Grieve [43] in an effort to deduce the F-V relationship of other muscles. Bigland and Lippold [23] obtained a traditional form of the F-V relationship for the plantar flexors of the ankle, although their values of velocity were average rather than instantaneous. While the F-V relationship has not been verified as being universally applicable through all muscle groups within the human body, such evidence as is available does suggest that groups of muscles exhibit some form of F-V relationship which is probably the result of a combination of the separate intrinsic F-V relationships within the group. However, the F-V relationship can never be verified as being absolutely fundamental since many of the conditions under which it is obtained (e.g., stretching a muscle) apparently modify the relationship. The following sections deal with some of these factors.

*The force length (F-L) relationship.* The relationship between maximum muscular force produced isometrically and muscle length has been studied extensively in single fibers, isolated muscle of various species, and in human muscles in vivo. Some work of this nature has been to lend structure and credence to the sliding filament theory of muscular contraction [83, 84]. However, the change in maximal force with a change in length has considerable practical implications for the development of a suitable model of muscle over the full range of muscular contraction.

When a muscle is stimulated under isometric conditions at a variety of lengths, the resulting tension is small at extremes of length and maximal in between these extremes. A characteristic bell-shaped curve exists between tension and length [181]. These phenomena have been investigated by many authors [55] and have been found to apply to single muscle fibers [82–84, 107, 156, 165], whole isolated muscle [2, 13, 19, 22, 25, 51, 73, 79] and muscle in situ [152]. The changes in force obtained here have been explained as being due to the varying numbers of cross-bridges which can become united between the actin and myosin filaments at different lengths of the sarcomere [82, 112, 113]. This is a structural factor affecting the maximal isometric force which can be produced, and Gordon [82] reported that the same force was produced at a given length if the muscle was either set at that length and stimulated, or stimulated and allowed to attain the given length under the resistance of a given load. Similar results were reported for whole isolated sartorious muscle of the frog [2], but they apply only to the part of the F-L relationship below the length at which the muscle is set when the legs of the frogs are pinned out straight. The latter result was shown not to apply at all to the semitendinosis of the frog [33], and Abbott and Aubert [1] demonstrated that the manner in which a given muscle length is attained (shortened or stretched to that length) is a significant determinant of isometric force. Clearly the isometric F-L relationship has a fundamental structural basis which can be modified by events preceding the measurement of the force and length. For example Edman [71] demonstrated a modification of the isometric F-L relationship of single fibers following stretch which enhanced force at relatively long fiber lengths (see section, "History of Events"). Accurate data were produced by Gorden [83, 84] who investigated changes in force when the length of sarcomere of a single muscle fiber of a frog varied between 1.27 $\mu$ and 3.65 $\mu$ ($\mu$ = micrometers). Maximal force was produced over a range of length from 2.05 $\mu$ to 2.2 $\mu$ and if 2.14 $\mu$ (peak force if a bell-shaped curve is fitted to their data) is considered as $L_o$, the total range of length studied was approximately 111 percent of $L_o$ comprising approximately 40 percent of shortening below $L_o$ and 71 percent of lengthening above $L_o$. Other authors [8] varied the range of muscle lengths of whole frog sartorius muscle by approximately 117 percent of $L_o$. Changes in length of this magnitude do not appear to be applicable to human muscle in vivo [134]. The reference length of $L_o$ has been defined variously in the literature. In most cases $L_o$ is that length at which the muscle produces peak isometric forces on the F-V relationship. However, the individual sources of literature should be consulted in order to establish the use of the term $L_o$.

Data from human amputees with cineplastic tunnels through the free end of the muscle shows F-L curves similar to those obtained for isolated whole muscle [155]. However, their results were criticized [179] as being inapplicable to normal human muscle on the grounds that the total variation in length and the forces produced were well below the values obtained for normal human muscle. Yet this work does indicate that a consideration of muscle length is important when examining the forces produced voluntarily by human beings.

When examining the anatomical relationship between the biceps brachii muscle and the elbow joint, the maximal change of the distance between the origin and insertion, between full extension and flexion, is approximately 30 percent of $L_o$ [134]. This is based upon the assumption that $L_o$ is the length of biceps when the elbow joint is set at 90 degrees. If a range of lengths of 30 percent is applied to data from single fibers [84], the maximal change in force over this range would be 10 percent of $P_o$. These proportional values obviously apply to the change in length of the muscle fibers as well as the overall change in length. Wilkie [179] measured the torque produced by the flexor muscles of the elbow over a range of elbow angles between 30 degrees and 120 degrees (zero degrees equals full extension). From this data he calculated the component of force developed parallel to the humerus at each angle of the joint used. Over the range of 40 degrees to 100 degrees he reported a variation force of 13 percent of maximal force. However, examination of his graphs suggests that much greater variations of force were obtained between 30 degrees and 120 degrees, the greatest force being produced at 30 degrees. Pertuzon [145] obtained an increase in force of 50 percent when changing the position of the elbow from 120 degrees to 30 degrees. Again if $L_o$ is considered that length at which the elbow joint is 90 degrees, the change in length accompanying the greatest change in force is approximately 22 percent of $L_o$, and this is below the total possible change in length from full flexion to full extension of the elbow joint. Thus, there appear to be differences among variation of force for a given change in muscle length, depending upon whether the calculations are obtained from either isolated fibers or whole human muscle in vivo. Some of the differences may be accounted for by the consideration that in Wilkie's work a number of different muscles, each having a unique F-L relationship, contributed to the total horizontal flexor force.

Examination of the individual contributions of the separate muscles producing flexion and extension of the elbow indicates that the maximal isometric force of the brachioradialis muscle occurs at 30 degrees of flexion [134]. In addition a total change of force of 80 percent occurs for a change in muscle length of 60 percent of $L_o$, corresponding to a range of the angle of the elbow joint from 180 degrees to 60 degrees [134]. It has also been demonstrated that the maximal isometric flexor moments (the product of force and perpendicular distance between the line of action of the force and the axis of the elbow joint) of individual muscles occur at different angles of the joint [134]. Structural changes of the contractile tissue with varying muscle length, combined with the variation in length of human muscle, is sufficient evidence to necessitate examination of F-L relationships when a model is developed to represent behavior of human muscle over a full range of contraction. Information of this nature is particularly important when a model is required to represent the dynamic behavior of muscles over a full range of muscle lengths.

The fact that contractile force and its rate of development and decay vary with muscle length [176] has considerable implications for the F-V relationship. Since maximal isometric force represents a point of the F-V curve, the F-V relationship must be expected to vary with muscle length. In many of the early experiments in which the F-V relationship was determined, relatively small changes in length of the muscle were produced in the region of the resting length $L_o$ where the value of $P_o$ varies little. Abbott and Wilkie [2] allowed changes in length below $L_o$ to occur during shortening and found that Hill's equation described the F-V relationship of the sartorious muscle of the frog *Rana temporaria* at any given length of the CC. The following equation,

$$(P_L + a)(V_L + b) = ((P_o)_L + a)b \qquad (2)$$

where $L$ = length of CC, which they modified from Hill's equation, implies a family of F-V relationships, each relation being unique to a given length of the CC. In this case the force produced is determined by the values of $P_o$ and $V$ at that length and the values of a and b were shown to be independent of length. The correctness of equation 2 for muscle lengths $L < L_o$ has been verified for the sartorious muscle of *Rana pipiens* [133]. This led to the deduction of a theoretical family of parallel F-V curves and verification of the constancy of a and b as being independent of muscle length. Direct determination of the F-V relationships at different lengths of the CC have been produced using the gracilis anticus muscle of the rat [13]. Once again the approximate parallel orientation of the separate F-V relationships was demonstrated for contractions in the region $L < L_o$, but the shape of the relationship for lengths greater than $L_o$ was considered obscure. Other authors consider that the F-V relationship is unaffected by length changes [33].

The effect of changes in length on the F-V relationship of human muscular tissue has received little attention although the considerable changes in maximal isometric force with joint angle would suggest the presence of variation in force, for a given velocity, through the range of joint motion. With a constant velocity of movement of the hand, force applied parallel to the humerus varies considerably [5]. These results applied equally well to isometric force, and when force was plotted as a function of hand position in the same direction for both isometric and dynamic contractions, the two curves were parallel. The total variation in force was approximately 50 percent of maximal force.

The presence of parallel curves implies changes in maximal intrinsic velocity of shortening $(V_o)$ with changes in muscles length. Such evidence was produced by Edman [68] to the effect that short lengths of $<1.65$ $\mu$ yielded small values of $V_o$, medium lenghts (1.65 $\mu$ to 2.7 $\mu$) yielded constant values of $V_o$, while long lengths of $>2.7$ $\mu$ resulted in a rapid rise in $V_o$. Similar evidence is available on human muscle [16], although Edmans' results suggest little variation in $V_o$ over the range of lengths found in human intact muscle. Thus it appears that a F-V relationship obtained for one joint angle or length of a single equivalent muscle need not necessarily apply to other positions in the range of joint motion.

*Activation of muscle.* In response to a stimulus, the contractile apparatus of a muscle is activated. The profile of activation was originally termed "active state" (AS), (see Hill [101] for discussion) and was considered to be reflected in the force output when the contractile component was neither shortening nor lengthening. Pringle [151] defined AS as "a capacity to shorten and do work, not as a realization of that capacity in mechanical phenomena." These two apparently different definitions of AS both lead to the observations that (1) external recording of force only represents the degree of activity of the contractile mechanism in a steady state isometric contraction; and (2) during dynamic contraction the external force is dependent upon the velocity of movement of the CC which in turn depends partly upon the properties of the SEC, and it cannot represent AS as defined by Hill.

The AS profile (as defined by Hill) has been determined by quick stretch and quick release of muscle at various times during a single twitch [99, 101, 157]. Hill [99] indicated that AS rises rapidly to its maximal value in a single twitch, although others disagree [14, 132]. Hoyle [110] described work which attempted to verify this mechanically deduced AS profile on the basis of measurements of calcium released from the sarcoplasmic reticulum. Since release of calcium did not parallel the AS, the meaning of AS was not made any clearer. The assumption inherent in the mechanical derivation of AS is that it is unaffected by stretches and releases. This has been shown to be untrue during both rapid release [67, 70] and stretch [71] of the muscle fiber. In addition the time course of the AS is a function of sarcomere length [72]. AS is an attractive concept as it represents the driving force of the contractile apparatus. However, the number of factors which apparently affect it have led to its general abandonment in the literature. Even so, some investigators who are concerned with quantifying the driving force of a Hill-type model of muscle continue to favor AS as a concept [105]. Clearly a stimulus leads to mechanical events which yield mechanical output of force, but the traditional concept of AS appears unhelpful in quantifying the response of the contractile apparatus to stimulus [118]. It is not surprising that direct estimates of AS have not been attempted in human muscular contraction. Indirect attempts have been made using the quantified electromyogram as a measure of input to the muscle [50, 85]. As this work was based upon an a priori assumption of the form of the AS, it must be considered to be of questionable validity.

In isolated preparations and in intact muscle in situ, the force produced is known to be related sigmoidally to the rate of stimulation [120, 152], and studies on single motor units in humans have revealed similar results [24, 121, 164]. Henneman [94] and many others have also demonstrated that muscle force is under the influence of the size principle in many types of contraction. This means that small motor units of the slow-twitch variety are recruited first, followed by those of increasing diameter (fast-twitch), and deactivation occurs in the reverse order. Since there is a distribution of size within one type of motor unit, increase of force begins with slow-twitch motor units but continues with simultaneous use of slow- and fast-twitch fibers [95]. Consequently a measure of activation which is based upon numbers of active motor units and their frequencies of firing will exhibit a complex relationship to force produced. Similar complex effects of activation will be seen on F-V relationships.

The release of calcium ions from the sarcoplasmic reticulum is known to be the stimulus for muscular contraction. Attempts by Stein and Wong [163], when using the equations of Julian [117], failed to establish the sigmoidal relationship between activation and the muscle tension. Neither stimulus rate nor calcium release are reasonable variables to measure during human muscular contraction. Yet the following indicates the necessity for estimating activation of the muscle as a measure of input to the musculotendinous system.

When a muscle is activated from rest, it is reasonable to assume the activation does not reach full intensity instantaneously. In fact it has been demonstrated that a more rapid rise in force follows quick release of an active muscle than when muscle is activated from rest [116]. F-V relationships have been obtained for soleus muscle of the rat from isometric and isotonic contractions [142]. Although the results of the isotonic contractions produce a F-V relationship which agrees with Hill's equation, the results of isometric experiments indicate that in the early stages of contraction from rest, low forces are produced with a low velocity of shortening. This result has been attributed to the fact that the muscle takes a finite time to become fully active [142]. This work suggests that a fixed F-V relationship does not apply when the degree of activation is changing rapidly. The same conclusion applies to the effect of a rapid reduction in force (from $P_o$) on the velocity of shortening of individual fibers and bundles of fibers from muscles of frogs and toads [53]. In this case, during the reduction of force, the final steady force is reached well before its associated velocity becomes constant. As the decrement in force is increased, thus increasing the final velocity of shortening, the time taken for the velocity to become constant increases. These results compare well with those which were computed [53] from a model of muscle proposed by Huxley [111]. This work [53] indicates that when force changes rapidly, the contractile process does not respond sufficiently rapidly to allow the F-V relationship to apply instantaneously.

Attempts to monitor activation in human muscular contraction have relied heavily upon recordings of the electromyogram (EMG). As early as 1954 it was demonstrated that a family of F-V relationships may be plotted for different levels of the EMG [23]. This family was thought to coincide at the point of zero force and maximal velocity ($V_o$). However, other work indicates that maximal velocity decreases with a decrease in the number of motor units recruited [147, 148]. This result was achieved by applying a stimulus to the ventral roots of nerves supplying the muscle. It is known that greater forces are obtained in eccentric compared with concentric contraction at a given velocity and level of EMG [23] (see also [50, 124]). Efforts continue in an attempt to reveal the state of activation of the muscle by appropriate treatment of the EMG. Many authors consider that an estimate of this kind will only be coarse [37, 88]. However, Hogan and Mann [106] have produced some recent optimistic work in the development of an optimal multiple-channel myoelectric signal processor. In addition, Hof [104] has described a successful method for EMG to force processing which is based upon known dynamic mechanical properties of muscle. In attempting this work the great problem is that force output is determined by many mechanical variables including muscle velocity, length, and prior history of events. Recorded EMG activity is also influenced by muscle length [89] and muscular fatigue [52]. Indeed the relationship between the time of onset of EMG activity and appearance of external force (electromechanical delay) varies with the conditions of contraction. Since it is shorter when activation begins in the eccentric mode than in concentric contraction [141], there is a temporal factor which confuses the use of EMG as a measure of activation. Consequently, treatment of the EMG must be based upon prior estimates of activation through a model of muscle. However, the dynamic properties of the model are difficult to determine accurately unless activation is known. This circular process will continue unless activation in the model (and therefore treatment of the EMG) is established from some independent physiological recording.

A potentially attractive alternative to EMG as a measure of activation is effort. While the origin of physiological information underlying the perception of effort is controversial [59], consistent repeatable relationships between output force and perceived effort have been reported [27, 59]. Yet the relationship depends upon predominance of fiber type in muscles tested isometrically [17], and it is also different in isometric as opposed to dynamic contraction where peak force is measured [15]. The possible attractiveness of what appears to be this gross measure of activation lies in its potential use in muscle modeling. Should the model be used to help enhance multisegmental performance, it would be necessary to optimize the magnitude and temporal sequence of activation of the system. If this sequence could be translated into effort it may be possible to present the effort required of groups of muscles to the performer. It seems reasonable that individuals could use such information and that the information may be more valuable than a simple profile of kinematics.

*History of events.* It has been known for many years that the properties of the CC are affected by events preceding their measurement, and definitive work in this context has been performed using single muscle fibers [67, 71]. Fibers forced to shorten rapidly produced subsequent isometric forces which were well below those obtained in the absence of shortening. Alternatively isometric force is enhanced following stretch of muscle [1]. Edman indicates that these externally imposed disturbances modify the state of the contractile process by an amount which varies with the magnitude of the disturbance. While the rapid shortening imposed by Edman [67] was far greater than can be observed in human muscle, the imposed stretches (in terms of percentage change in length per second) are applicable to human muscle. It seems clear that the contractile process is enhanced (in magnitude and duration) by stretch [41, 62] by an amount which increases with the amplitude of stretch and the length to which the muscle is stretched [71]. Enhancement following moderate velocities of stretch also depends upon both amplitude and velocity of stretch

[166]. Many complex effects of stretch have been observed in isolated muscle preparations [166]. Fortunately they occur at high velocities which are unlikely to be encountered in normal human muscular contraction. Enhancement is seen in dynamic concentric contraction following stretch such that the F-V relationship is shifted toward increasing forces at any given velocity, but which leaves maximal shortening velocity unaffected [71]. Similar stretch-and-hold contractions of forearm supinators were performed by Thomson [168] who showed that the torque produced at the end of stretch varied with stretch velocity as well as with amplitude of stretch and final forearm position. That these results were somewhat different from those obtained by Edman [71] probably results from the complex nature of forearm supination where it is difficult to establish motion in terms of individual muscle fibers. However, the enhanced effect of stretch in human muscle was shown to persist, although its persistence could not be quantitatively related to the magnitude of the prior stretch.

Muscle output, whether it be force or work done, is clearly affected by enhancement following stretch. Cavagna [39, 40] has discussed the process of enhancement at some length. Work output is known to increase in constant velocity concentric contraction of elbow flexors (and frog muscle) following stretch over work done from a prior isometric development of force [6, 42]. Similar effects have been seen under conditions of inertial loading [46, 48]. Takeoff velocity in vertical jumps is also increased by prior stretch [4, 30]. Yet the actual benefit derived from enhancement of the contractile process tends to be obscured in such activities by other factors. For example, stretch may induce reflex effects which increase subsequent fiber recruitment, and the presence of series elasticity will modify CC velocity which in itself will change force output favorably in some circumstances. Whatever the benefit of stretch, it certainly decays with time and therefore will produce beneficial effects depending upon the nature of loading, which will influence the duration of the concentric contraction.

*Fiber types in muscular contraction.* Dynamic properties of muscle vary with fiber type. Whether the term "active-state" (AS) is appropriate or not, there is little doubt that the time course of activation of the contractile machinery varies between muscles of different species. Hoyle [110] indicated that activation rises faster in the leg muscles of the frog than in a giant fiber from a barnacle. In addition, its rate of decay after a single stimulus is greater in the fast anterior tibial muscle of the rat than in the slower soleus muscle [178]. After the initial rise, activation is thought to be maintained at a maximal value for a period of time. This period has been shown to be less than 3.5 ms in the slow soleus muscle of the cat and less than 2 ms in the fast flexor hallucis longus muscle [36]. Values of the parameters describing the F-V relationship are also determined by the morphological composition of the muscle [54, 117]. Differences in these values begin to appear during differentiation into fast and slow muscles after birth in kittens [56], and after cross innervation performed to change the muscle type from fast to slow and vice versa [35]. It is clear that both fast-twitch and slow-twitch fibers exist in human muscle [34], and Gollnick [81] has reviewed the implications of fiber types for human muscular contraction from mechanical and biochemical viewpoints.

Despite criticisms of the technique of fiber typing from muscle biopsy specimens [109], there appears to be a relationship between an individual's fiber type, muscular performance [29], and athletic event [160]. To attribute a functional causal relationship to such data can be notoriously misleading, but muscle composition can be related to function on theoretical grounds. For example, maximal intrinsic shortening velocity of a muscle will determine to some extent the ultimate steady state achieved in cyclic events such as sprinting. This results from the fact that a F-V relationship which is extended along the velocity axis will allow greater forces to be produced at any given velocity of shortening. Such forces will allow acceleration to continue until the velocity at which no force is produced is reached. This is hypothetical since it has not been proved on strict mechanical grounds.

*The Series Elastic Component (SEC)*
The first attempt to consider the musculotendinous system as contractile and elastic elements in series was made by Hill [97]. This work led to a great deal of investigation on the properties of the SEC of isolated muscle, although the variety of experiments performed with this type of preparation does not appear to have been duplicated in human muscle contracted voluntarily. The successful determination of the properties of the SEC depends upon the type of experiment used to deduce these properties because the SEC does not reside in an anatomically separate unit of the musculotendinous system. Therefore it cannot be removed from the system in order to determine its properties directly. Three types of experiments appear to have been favored in the determination of the properties of the SEC. Jewell and Wilkie [116] used an after-loaded isometric contraction against various loads. This method involves stimulation of the muscle under isometric conditions, and upon achievement of a steady tetanic force, the muscle is released rapidly to shorten against a given load. It should be noted that the F-V relationship of the CC can be obtained by this method. The displacement-time profile in this technique shows

a rapid acceleration just after release followed by a linear phase with slope which indicates the velocity of shortening. This linear phase of shortening against time was extrapolated back to the ordinate (units of displacement) sited at the instant of release on the abscissa (units of time). The magnitude of the intercept on the ordinate was considered as the amount of shortening of the SEC corresponding with the decrement of load from isometric maximum to that lifted. The application of this procedure to results obtained with a variety of loads yielded the relationship between length and tension of the SEC.

An alternative method devised by Hill [100] involved tetanic stimulation under isometric conditions followed by release and subsequent shortening at a fixed, controlled speed. Simultaneous recordings of force allowed the velocity of shortening of the CC to be deduced from the F-V relationship. The difference between CC velocity and external fixed velocity represented the velocity of shortening of the SEC. Integration of this velocity yielded SEC shortening which could be compared with force to give the compliance of the SEC. A third method which was used by Jewell and Wilkie [116] involved computation of the properties of the SEC from the rate of rise of force during an isometric contraction. Since the CC and SEC were considered to be in series, the rate of change of force with respect to time was equal to the rate of change of force with respect to length (instantaneous stiffness of SEC) multiplied by the rate of change of length with respect to time (velocity of the CC). The instantaneous stiffness of the SEC at any value of force could then be obtained if the velocity of shortening of the CC was known, at the same value of force, from the F-V relationship. Each of the three techniques described has been criticized at some time on the grounds that certain assumptions are made concerning behavior of the CC [116].

Results of a variety of experiments have shown that the SEC does not exhibit a fixed elastic modulus when different forces are applied across it [10, 38, 101, 116]. The stiffness of the SEC of a frog sartorius is small at low forces and increases with an increase in force up to approximately half of maximal isometric force [116]. Further increases in force are associated with a constant stiffness of $0.14 \times 10^3$ dynes/cm. This constant stiffness persists when forces greater than isometric maximum are developed by frog gastrocnemius [38]. The statement of some values serves to indicate the magnitude of the stiffness of some mammalian muscles. Wells [77] demonstrated that the SEC of rat tibialis anterior had a stiffness of $4 \times 10^6$ dynes/cm when full isometric force was expressed across it. Such a force would produce extension of the SEC of 5 percent of the resting length of muscle. A stiffness of $0.67 \times 10^6$ dynes/cm was obtained over a range of force of zero to 10 percent of isometric force. In contrast the soleus muscle of the rat showed stiffer propeties than tibialis anterior [77]. Values of stiffness for the SEC of rat gracilis anticus are $0.9 \times 10^6$ dynes/cm and $0.057 \times 10^6$ dynes/cm at 100 percent and 10 percent of maximal isometric force respectively [10]. Extension of the SEC of this muscle under maximal isometric conditions would be 7 percent of the resting length. However, the shape of the relationship between force and length obtained by Bahler [10] was linear from zero force up to about 30 percent of maximal isometric force, whereupon further increases in force produced a continual increase in stiffness of the SEC. Consequently it may be assumed that the stiffness of the SEC varies among muscles of the same and different species.

Considerable attention has been paid to the question of whether the stiffness of the SEC depends only upon the force or whether it also depends upon the degree of activity of the CC. These factors are obviously related for the force applied to the SEC can change with either degrees of activation of the CC or the velocity of shortening of the maximally activated CC. If the SEC partly resides in the sarcomere, it is certain that changes in the state of activity of the sarcomere will affect the stiffness of the SEC. Wilkie [180] assumed that the properties of the SEC were independent of the degree of contractile activity present. While he suggested that part of the SEC resides in some part of the muscle other than the tendon, he concluded that the unknown site could not be intimately connected to the contractile apparatus. This topic was discussed by Hill [101] who stated that the properties of the SEC depended upon the previous history of tension in the CC. Therefore, while Hill [101] and Jewell and Wilkie [116] were in agreement that approximately half of the series stiffness resides in the tendon, their statements on the possible site of the remaining half of the series stiffness conflict. It was suggested by Pringle [151] that part of the series stiffness resides within the A and I bands and Z line of sarcomere. Huxley and Simmons [114] implicate the cross bridges as part of the SEC while Tameyasu and Sugi [167] debate the point. Should Huxley and Simmons [114] be correct then the stiffness of the SEC will vary with the degree of activation and overlap of filaments of the muscle [189]. Others seem to agree with this conclusion [57, 74, 135]. There is indirect evidence that this is the case in human muscular contraction [16].

The possibility that the stiffness of the SEC changes with the previous history of tension in the muscle is an important consideration in the design of experiments used to deduce such stiffness. Should the stiffness depend only upon the force applied, the changes in length of the SEC depend upon an accurate assessment of the shortening of the CC. Therefore accurate estimates of the mechanical properties of the CC are usually required. The experiments performed by Jewell and Wilkie [116] indicate the problems which may be encountered when assumptions are made about the behavior of the CC. These authors determined the stiffness of the SEC by a quick release method and by observing the rise of force during an isometric contraction. It was shown that the latter technique underestimated the stiffness of the SEC at low forces in comparison with the estimate obtained from the former technique, and Hill [101] agreed with this observation. The difference was ascribed to the fact that activation takes time to become fully developed during isometric contraction and that the F-V relationship was therefore inapplicable to the low range of forces. An alternative approach to the problem is to assume constant properties of the SEC during the rise of force in an isometric contraction as a means of obtaining the F-V relationship [142]. An examination of the relationship shown in [142] indicates that in the phase of rising activation, low forces correspond with low velocities of shortening as opposed to the high velocities which are present when the muscle is fully active.

Early investigations of the mechanical properties of the SEC were concerned with changes in the stiffness and the SEC was considered to be undamped [97]. However, the SEC of frog sartorious is considered to be lightly damped by 200–500 dynes/cm/s [185], and a value for damping of 300 dynes/cm/s for the SEC of the rat gracillis anticus has been obtained [10]. A relatively large value of $1.3 \times 10^4$ dynes/cm/s was obtained during an investigation of the tibialis anterior of the rat in situ [177]. Such a value may well have been due to the high viscosity of invading fascia of this type of preparation.

Few of the experiments described have been performed directly on human muscle because of the complications inherent in obtaining constant levels of muscular activation during voluntary contraction. Unfortunately, many experiments have been performed in which the presence of a SEC has been ignored. Consequently, external recordings of force and velocity have been considered to represent the behavior of contractile tissue of muscle. Such criticism does not apply to the study on elbow flexion performed by Wilkie [179] in which the F-V relationship was used, in conjunction with the rate of rise and fall of isometric force, to estimate the stiffness of the SEC. This analytical technique was obviously subject to the errors described previously which were associated with the time taken for activation to become fully developed. It may therefore be concluded that Wilkie underestimated the stiffness of the SEC at low forces. The stiffness was measured at 67 percent of maximal isometric force for the five subjects investigated, and it ranged between 2.8 and 20 Newtons/cm when referred to a single equivalent horizontal muscle at the hand. This is a surprising variation among human beings. Wilkie [179] also demonstrated that the stiffness increased with increasing force, although the data was at variance with that obtained from the frog sartorious [116] in that it did not reach a constant value over a range of forces. In a study performed by Cavanagh and Grieve [43], the F-V relationship was obtained through a range of elbow flexion and was used to deduce the energy stored in the SEC during a single contraction. Their results indicate that considerations of the properties of the SEC are necessary to understand muscular performance because a considerable amount of energy is stored internally before it appears externally as kinetic energy. Similar considerations of the release of energy have been made [42] and Asmussen and Sorensen [6] found that the work performed concentrically after prior eccentric contraction was greater than that performed without prior development of tension. These findings may be interpreted as being due to the storage of potential energy in the SEC by the greater forces applied to it during eccentric contraction. A further point of speculation was made by Komi and Bosco [127] who suggested that different types of muscle fibers, which have different SEC properties, possess different abilities to store and release elastic energy. This was based on the fact that human subjects with greater percentages of fast-twitch fibers were better able to benefit from large muscle stretch in vertical jumping.

The foregoing discussion on isolated muscle suggests that the SEC is lightly damped; that it displays a nonlinear stiffness which varies in magnitude among different muscles; and that its stiffness varies with activation. There is conflicting evidence concerning the anatomical site of part of SEC, and the indirect estimation of its properties appears subject to the type of experiment performed. The mechanical properties of the SEC of human muscle have received little attention, and no information is available on the possible change of stiffness induced by the elevated forces present in human eccentric muscular contraction. Yet a consideration of the presence of the SEC has been shown to be necessary when the external output of work and energy are related to the properties of the contractile tissue.

### The Parallel Elastic Component (PEC)

In most of the experiments on isolated muscle the range of lengths used has been that which does not involve a contribution to force of a PEC. This implies that the PEC can develop considerable forces and this has been shown to be true over large change of length of isolated muscle [181]. The question which remains is the extent to which the PEC is significant in human muscle.

The site of PEC has been thought to be connecting tissue surrounding and invading whole muscle [19] and the sarcolemma in single fibers [165]. The presence of a PEC has been demonstrated in the muscles of human amputees [155]. However, these data have been considered to be inapplicable to normal human muscle, and it has been concluded that the PEC is of no consequence between 40 degrees and 120 degrees of elbow flexion [179]. Experimental evidence suggests that the PEC is an insignificant contributor to force throughout almost the full range of both elbow flexion and forearm supination [44, 49]. Since the PEC is thought not to be damped in any manner [97], the force which it produces may be subtracted from the recorded force to yield the force due to contraction of the muscles. In fact forces produced by the PEC may be indistinguishable from ligamentous and bone on bone forces which are observed in human activities. Consequently, there is little support for the inclusion of a PEC in a model of human muscular contraction within the normal working ranges of the joints.

*Summary of Properties of Human Muscle*
Current evidence of human muscles suggests that the system can be represented by two components, a CC and a SEC in series. The CC is the element which produces force as a function of its degree of activation, its velocity of shortening, its instantaneous length, and the history of events preceding the time when the force is observed. These factors are listed in their suggested order of importance. The SEC behaves as a nonlinear spring-like element which is also lightly damped and has stress-strain characteristics dependent to some extent upon the activation of the muscle. The PEC is thought to be an unimportant factor. These factors and others have been incorporated to some extent in various models of the musculotendinous system which have been produced. Such modeling is considered in the following section.

## MODELS OF MUSCLE

It is difficult to see how this work can be verified in intact human muscular contraction. For example, the mass of the limb segments precludes measurement of the maximal intrinsic velocity of shortening of muscle. Experiments involving externally imposed rapid changes in muscle length are beset by similar problems. Isolated muscles can be given a controlled stimulus (or input), whereas maximal voluntary isometric force in humans is quite variable. Attempts to replicate in humans the experiments which have been performed in isolated muscle are generally doomed to failure. It is suggested that students of human movement are better advised to use the information to construct a model which can be verified as applicable (more or less) to the human condition. This has been done by Hatze

[92]. His work provides a stimulus for other workers either to improve upon the work or to take a completely different approach.

*The Purpose of Modeling*

Modeling of muscle or any other biological tissue serves a number of purposes. It provides a functional summary of what is known about the system and allows the complex interaction of elements to the model to be examined. It aids in estimating optimal ways of performing a task in order to maximize a given output. It allows pretesting of an experimental design which is used to add information on the system. The accuracy of the above depends upon the validity of the model. When prediction of results varies with the actual outcome of experiments the model can be modified subsequently to account for such differences. A model designer and a model user should be one and the same person since any user of the model will probably have data about the intact system which illustrates the suitability of the model. Inadequacies in the model clearly and rapidly force the model user to become a model designer. Modeling of a system can also be used as an educational tool. The result has been to save the lives of many frogs and to enhance greatly the variety of experiments which can be simulated in the laboratory situation.

*The Choice of a Model*

When choosing a suitable model, it is necessary to include only information pertinent to the task in hand. For example, a model with elements which have linear properties has been used in the area of neural control. Having said this, one should be aware that properties which at first sight may not have any particular implications for the task in hand may actually be necessary to include in the model so that mistakes may be avoided. Models of muscle have been based on relationships of conceptual components as first devised by Hill [97] and used by Baildon and Chapman [15] and many others. For this one needs fundamental relationships which describe the behavior of elements of the model and factors needed to describe their operation (for example the F-V relationship varies with activation). Other models can be based on a knowledge of the fundamental process of the contraction (for example the cross-bridge theory) such as that devised by Hatze [92]. This would seem to be the most desirable form of modeling if, and only if all the links in the chain between the contractile process and the external environment are known. A further type of modeling is based on an anatomical representation of the actual structures involved; this requires knowledge of how each structure behaves from the molecular to the gross level. In all cases the model is only as good as the number of facts which are known and the number of assumptions which have to be made.

*Implementation of the Model*

The manner in which a model is implemented depends upon the manner in which it is designed. In some cases it is possible to analyze the model using sets of differential equations which can be solved by Laplace transformation. The problem in this case is to write a Laplace transform for every different condition to which the model might apply or, alternatively, to use a convolution integral on the impulse response of the system. An alternative method is that of iteration in which one starts at a given time with knowledge about how one element is behaving. Then the effect this has on other elements is deduced. This is followed by the effect that these elements have on the original element. Finally time is incremented, and the process begins again. A further method is to solve a set of simultaneous differential equations as one steps through time during the contractile process. A further question of implementation concerns the incorporation of the muscle in the body. The question arises as to whether to use a model which represents an action such as elbow flexion or to incorporate each muscle individually. The former approach was used by Wilkie [179] and Baildon and Chapman [15] and the latter by Pierrynowski [149]. Peres [144] has shown synergy between biceps brachii and brachialis in monkeys which, to some extent justifies the single equivalent muscle concept as used by Bouisset [32].

*Models with Different Properties*

Models have been divided into those with elements exhibiting nonlinear behavior and those with elements displaying linear behavior. This division is somewhat arbitrary since any number of elements displaying linear behavior can be incorporated to produce a nonlinear result. For example, the nonlinear F-V relationship can be linearized by assuming that the contractile component comprises a force generator and a viscous damper. However, if the coefficient of viscosity is allowed to vary with velocity, then the resulting F-V relationship becomes again nonlinear. All models have their shortcomings, and some of these are considered in the following sections.

*A model with elements displaying linear properties.* Models with elements displaying linear behavior have proved very popular due to the relative mathematical ease with which they can be analyzed. Houk [108] modeled the muscle as a parallel combination of force generator and dashpot representing the CC and a Hookean spring as the SEC. He used a Laplace transformation to analyze the suitability of the model during the rise of force in an isometric contraction in response to a step of activation. This type of model gives an exponential rise in force which has a time constant equal to the viscous constant (B) divided by the spring stiffness (K) of the SEC. Since a constant viscosity gives a linear F-V relationship, if B and K are to vary proportionately then the isometric rise will look exponential. Consequently, his results may have been fortuitous. Despite the possible inaccuracy of this model, it does produce an impulse response which can be used in a recursive filter to relate EMG output to force [58, 85]. Houk [108] used this model to determine the output force in relation to an input to the force generator via the nervous system. In a similar vein Green [86] used a parallel combination of a spring and damper as the CC in which the spring and damper were affected by neural input. This model proved useful in the analysis of response of the system to a nervous input in isometric contraction, in the manner of the experiments of Jewell and Wilkie [116], but contractions of a dynamic nature over a large range failed to show usefulness of the model. Fung [77] analyzed the response of cardiac muscle and indicated that the functions of the CC and SEC were to change length and transmit tension respectively. He used Voigt and Maxwell models, and in determining that they were equivalent, he stated that either would serve the purpose of representing the behavior of cardiac muscle. Since skeletal muscle serves a useful purpose when developing force isometrically, consideration of the function of the CC as a changer of length seems somewhat inapplicable to voluntarily activated human muscle. It seems clear that structural and functional differences between cardiac and skeletal muscle require different types of models to account adequately for their behavior. Pertuzon [145] devised a model which comprised many elements displaying linear behavior. He concluded that the model was a valid representation of the behavior of the system under maximal activation, but when activation was known to vary voluntarily the model validity broke down. Since he argued that it was necessary to know the nature of input to the force generator, and since one of the human abilities is to vary activation substantially, his model as it stands leaves something to be desired.

Other workers in the field of neural control have used models of muscle which incorporate the effects of variable nervous innervation. Mannard and Stein [129] deduced that the response of muscle was similar to their model which contained elements displaying linear behavior. Bawa [20] used cat plantaris muscles with springs added in series with the muscle and showed that the muscles response was similar to that of a second-order linear system. While indicating that the response of plantaris muscle fitted such a response, that of soleus did not. The universal applicability of their model is questionable since they showed variation in the rate constants with muscle length, stimulus rate, and stiffness of the external series spring. When calculating the effective muscle stiffness from two elastic components and comparing this with estimates from low-frequency gain, their results were poor, especially for a small added spring and a large muscle specimen [21]. Despite criticisms of this model, Crowe [60] and Van Atteveldt and Crowe [172] used a similar model, but they had to incorporate a nonlinear parallel elastic element to explain their results. Since substantially less parallel elasticity is needed to explain human muscular contraction, this model can hardly be used in the human situation. Chapman and Harrower [51] measured the behavior of rat gastrocnemius muscle in both dynamic and isometric contractions, and they compared the nonlinear F/V relationship and the nonlinear F/L relationship of the SEC with linear representations of these relationships. They concluded that the linear representations were unjustified. While this may be the case for rat gastrocnemius muscle, there may be other muscles for which a linear fit is not a poor approximation. In attempting to examine the concept of resonance in human muscular output Bach, Chapman, and Calvert [9] used a model in which the CC was represented by a force generator and a viscous damper in parallel and the SEC was represented by a linear spring with Hookean behavior. Data for their coefficients of the viscous damper and the series spring were obtained in a manner devised by Cavagna [38]. They used this data in a different situation of voluntarily forced oscillation by the plantar flexors on a force platform to predict and also to measure the frequency of oscillation at which the ratio of force divided by EMG activity was maximized. Prediction and results agreed well in most cases, although with certain subjects the fit was fairly poor. While they justified the use of this model and this approach on the grounds that the predicted optimal frequency was that seen in sprinting, equally good measures of the optimal frequency may well have been obtained with a model comprising nonlinear properties. Since they were able to demonstrate that prediction of results was good when the muscles were fatigued, it is possible that this type of model is justifiable when analyzing the use of human muscles in resonant situations. In a study using a model with nonlinear properties, Baildon and Chapman [16] demonstrated that in a dynamic contraction from rest against an inertia, the predicted torque profile using linear representations of their nonlinear properties was poor. It may be concluded that under certain circumstances a model with linear properties is an acceptable representation of the muscular tendonous system, although it has not been shown that this type of model can successfully account for all the variable forms of human muscular contraction.

*Models with elements demonstrating nonlinear behavior.* In 1938 Hill [97] devised a two-component model comprising a CC and a SEC to represent the phenomena observed in many of his experiments on amphibian muscles. Pringle [151] stated that Hill's model is a conceptual summary rather than an actual representation of components, and this conceptual summary avoids confusion in attempting to identify the motion of all the subsets of the muscle. However, in such a conceptual summary it is necessary to determine many varieties of the functions which have been described in the section on muscle properties. Bahler [11] used data produced by himself and others [10, 12, 13, 180] and deduced a model with two parallel elements to explain results of muscular contractions observed at lengths of less than 120 percent of $L_o$. His force generator behaved in a manner in which force produced was a function of the length and the time after the onset of a given level of stimulation. The second parallel element was viscous-like, and its coefficient depended upon length, velocity, and time after the onset of stimulation. The model was completed by inserting a nonlinear spring in series with the previous parallel combination of two elements. It is uncertain whether further modifications in the model would be necessary to explain behavior at lengths greater than 120 percent of $L_o$ and whether such modifications are necessary for human muscular contraction. A model which was based on that originated by Hill, but with the addition of an activation mechanism regulating the behavior of the CC, was devised by Julian and Moss [118]. In a similar vein Baildon and Chapman [15] used an iterative process to drive a model which incorporated a CC and an SEC which behaved according to a number of the known functions such as the F/V relationship and the F/L relationship of the CC. In the two subjects which these authors used for their experiments, one subject performed very much in accordance with the prediction produced by the model, while the other subject produced results which were less well predicted in the sense that they were extremely variable. This does not necessarily mean that the model is invalid; it is probable that the assumptions concerning the degree to which the poorer subject could activate his muscles consistently were incorrect. However, their predictions on submaximal behavior were quite close to those produced by the individuals who were required to contract with this stated level of submaximal activation (see [64] for a different use of the same type of model). It is clear that any Hill-like model which comprises a CC and a SEC must include all the known relationships between force and other mechanical and temporal variables for it to be successful. The advantage in using this type of model is that many of these relationships can be verified experimentally. While it is true that some effects, such as Edman's force enhancement, are difficult to verify, this type of phenomenological model does not require that the CC and SEC take a particular form on the basis of any anatomical structure. It is felt that the assumptions necessary in the implementation of this model are minimal in comparison with those which use elements displaying linear behavior as a structural representation of the relationships. The latter is difficult to justify.

*Models based on the cross-bridge theory.* A number of models have been developed which are based upon either the structure of filaments in the sarcomere or the cross-bridge theory of how a muscle develops force. Individual muscle fibers have been modeled from a microscopic view by including such factors as elasticity of actin and myosin filaments, elasticity of the sarcolemma and viscous damping due to flow of the sarcoplasm [143]. From this basic model they obtained the mechanical characteristics of a fiber and indicated that information on the basic contractile unit will be applicable to the phenomena associated with motor unit summation. Akazawa [3] devised a model from cross-bridge kinetics and justified it upon the basis that the kinetic constants could be related to constants in Hill's equation. Furthermore, these authors claimed success in explaining the dynamic properties of isometric and isotonic twitches. Cross-bridge kinetics have also been used by Zahalak [187] in an important attempt to relate microscopic mechanisms of contraction to macroscopic behavior of muscle. Recent work by Hatze [92] was based upon a structural model at the level of the sarcomere. He traced the train of events from the action potential to the final output force—a set of relationships which requires many unproven assumptions. He also indicated that the control parameters correspond to the actual neural input. This model was incorporated into a whole body model and used to perform optimization studies on kicking [91] and also the running long jump [92]. Success was claimed for the optimization studies since optimization, which was used to provide kinematics to a performer in kicking, led to a dramatic change in performance after the peformance had become stable due to uncoached practice. The advantage of this type of model is that with a basic model of the sarcomere the behavior of each muscle can be accounted for and scaled appropriately to that muscle. However, some simple experiments are required to estimate values of the parameters which characterize the model. In the conceptual model the optimization process requires experiments to obtain mechanical characteristics of the muscles or groups of muscles involved at each joint which is involved in the task. Considering the number of assumptions which have to be made in this type of work, the question can be raised as to whether much simpler models will do as well.

*A model based upon muscle architecture.* Recently Wottiez [183] and co-workers have developed a model which is based upon the architecture of whole muscle. Using rat plantar flexors, they investigated the effects of fiber length, angle of pennation, and physiological cross-sectional area on such characteristics as twitch time, active and passive tension-length curves, and force-velocity relationships. They began with a simple two-dimensional geometric model, advanced to a three-dimensional model, and completed the work with a prediction of human plantar flexor torque in walking. Using physiological characteristics of individual fibers, they were able to obtain satisfactory predictions of isometric force-length relationships. This work illustrates the relative importance of geometric and physiologic characteristics to outputs of force, work, and power. Further work is needed to incorporate models of single muscles into human joint motion. One important use of such a model is in assessment of the effects of histological composition on muscle output. Unless the architecture of the muscle in question is known, it appears that a knowledge of a muscle's fiber composition is a poor predictor of that muscle's capacity to generate a variety of mechanical outputs [183]. Other attempts at architectural modeling have been made. That of Woittiez [183] appears to be the most recent and comprehensive, and it provides an ample bibliography on other work which need not be replicated in the present review.

## DESCRIPTION OF STATIC AND DYNAMIC CONTRACTION

This section includes a description of motion of the elements of a muscle model and their interaction, the manner in which energy is partitioned, and the generation of power. The point of view taken here is that much of the strategy adopted in achieving a desired muscular output results from the fact that there are at least two identifiable mechanical components in muscle which have different properties. Without consideration of these elements, interpretations of the use of muscles to achieve an output can be misleading. Discussion is related to the observation that there are numerous aims of muscular contraction. The aim of moving a given load as rapidly as possible is obviously different from that of performing work with the least cost to the metabolism. Comparisons are made between this information and that work on human muscular contraction which has purported to derive knowledge about the behavior of muscle on the basis of external recordings.

The model comprises a contractile component (CC) in series with an elastic component (SEC) and, for the sake of simplicity, the behavior of the CC and SEC is described by a F-V relationship and a F-L relationship respectively (see Fig. 1). The concentric part of the F-V relationship is described by Hill's equation fitted to the data of Cavanagh and Grieve [43]. The eccentric part was drawn by hand

FIGURE 1
*A. The relationship between force and velocity of the contractile component (CC) when activated fully (Act = 1) and at one-half of maximal activation (Act = 0.5, dotted line). The relationships labeled τ = are those followed in an isometric contraction when activation of the CC is made to rise exponentially with a time-constant equal to τ (see equation 3). The relationship labeled SEC2 is that followed when the corresponding SEC F-L relationship shown in Figure 1B was used in the model with τ = 0.05 s. The power-velocity relationship is shown by the broken line. B. The force/ extension relationship of the series elastic component (SEC). SEC1 was used for all contractions of the muscle model except for one isometric contraction in which SEC2 was used (see text).*

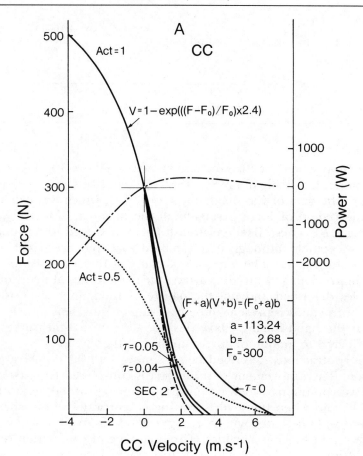

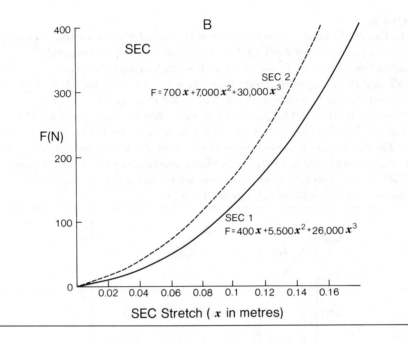

and is represented by the equation shown in Figure 1*A*. The force/ extension relationship of the SEC (SEC1) is described by a polynomial fitted to the data of Cavanagh and Grieve [43] which was extended into the region of force greater than the maximal isometric value (see Fig. 1*B*). These fixed relationships are assumed to be conceptually acceptable although it is admitted that they are based upon empirical evidence. The omission of many of the relationships outlined in previous sections only affects the magnitudes of many of the variables described and not the nature of their interrelationships. The contractions represent those of a single equivalent muscle situated at the hand during elbow flexion. All external measurements are referred to motion or forces applied at the hand.

The contractions described begin simply with an isometric contraction. Then movement of an inertia is considered from two sets of initial conditions; when the load is stationary, at the onset of activation, and when the load is moving eccentrically with respect to the muscle. The latter will be recognized as the typical action of a backswing in striking activities. The final type of contraction represents lifting and lowering a load against gravity in an oscillatory manner at different frequencies. This is typical of the type of motion found in weight training and in the stance phase of running.

*Isometric Contractions (Figs. 1, 2, and 3)*

In this case the muscle begins from rest and contracts with exponential increases in activation at rates described by time constants of 0 s, 0.04 s, and 0.05 s (see Fig. 2) as follows:

$$A = P_o(1 - \exp(t/\tau)) \tag{3}$$

where $A$ = activation in units of force, $P_o$ = isometric maximum (constant at all muscle lengths in this and subsequent types of contraction), $t$ = time in seconds, and $\tau$ = time constant in seconds (time to reach 63% of full activation). For this purpose the force at any velocity is considered to be a linear function of activation, as shown in Figure 1. Although the term isometric is used, it is clear that the contraction does not occur at a constant length of the CC. As the CC shortens and stretches the SEC, the output force is governed by the interaction of the F-V relationship of the CC, the F-L relationship of the SEC, and the modification of the F-V relationship due to rising activation.

FIGURE 2

*Change of force, activation and CC shortening with respect to time during isometric contraction in which the CC was activated at various rates shown by the time constants ($\tau$). Units for activation are those of force (see equation 3). The effect of using a different SEC F-L relationship (SEC2) is also shown ($\tau$ was maintained at 0.05 s in this case). Model results.*

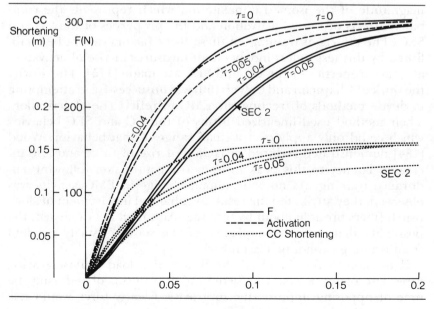

Naturally the force rises more rapidly with an activation time constant of 0 s rather than 0.04 s and 0.05 s (Fig. 2). This is due to the fact that in the former case the maximally activated F-V relationship is instantly obeyed (Fig. 1A). When $\tau = 0.04$ s and 0.05 s a set of submaximal F-V relationshpis are crossed and the final isometric condition is almost achieved before activation reaches its maximum. Figure 1A, which shows how this is done, illustrates the F-V relationships followed throughout the contractions with $\tau = 0.04$ s and 0.05 s in comparison with that which would be followed if activation had become maximal instantaneously ($\tau = 0$). In addition Figure 2 shows how CC shortening (and therefore SEC stretch) changes with time. Whereas changes in rate of force development in an isometric test can reflect changes in an individual's ability to activate a group of muscles, an alternative explanation can be offered.

The two F-V relationships showing different values of $\tau$ (0.04 and 0.05 s) could be obtained from either two individuals, or one individual before and after training, even if rate of activation was unchanged. In other words they could represent two different dynamic capabilities of the CC which would lead to the different rates of rise of force shown in Figure 2. Clearly the CC with the greatest maximal velocity of shortening would produce the best results on the test. In addition, a stiffer SEC (SEC2) will result in a more rapid rise of force despite a constant activation of $\tau = 0.05$ s (see Figs. 1 and 2). Therefore, any isometric test will provide information, in addition to the magnitude of the isometric maximum, which represents the combined effects of rate of activation and the properties of the CC and SEC. The effects of training on these three factors cannot be established by this test unless independent measures of rise of activation and the properties of the CC and SEC are made [175]. This is why the work of Chapman and Calvert [50] was unsuccessful in attempting to devise methods of treating the EMG to reflect rise of activation. Their method used linearized forms of the CC and SEC behavior which could only apply over a small range of that behavior. Wood [184] demonstrated reduced peak rate of rise of force and also increased latency to this peak in isometric contraction following endurance training. As no concomitant change in EMG activity was observed, they attributed the result to enhanced involvement of slow-twitch fibers brought about by training. Although not discussed, the possibility that greater compliance of the series elasticity resulted from training cannot be discounted.

If the contraction involved the lifting of a load against gravity, rapid rise of force would be beneficial as a means of reducing the time of opposing impulse due to gravity. Clearly force would rise most rapidly with $\tau = 0$ s. This illustrates the necessity for producing rapid activation in weight lifting or, alternatively, having a CC with a large $V_o$ or a stiff SEC.

Since the conditions are isometric, no external work is done other than to deform the structure of the force transducer. However, considerable internal work is done as illustrated by the profiles of power delivered by the CC (Fig. 3). Greater peak powers are delivered with the greatest rate of activation (or F-V relationship with a greater $V_o$), but interestingly the peak power is reduced if the SEC stiffness is increased. When SEC stiffness is held constant at SEC1, it can be seen how the greater power profile leads to a greater rate of storage of potential energy in the SEC. Considerations of partitioning of energy in components will be dealt with further in the following sections. However, the profiles of stored energy in the SEC do illustrate that a metabolic cost is incurred in isometric contraction in terms of both increasing the energy stored by power production from the CC and maintaining the stored energy even when the CC has ceased to shorten and deliver mechanical power (force multiplied by velocity). In fact heat measurements substantiate the fact that the initial

FIGURE 3
*Potential energy stored in the SEC as a result of its first derivative, namely power delivered by the CC, in isometric contractions with the time constants (τ) of activation of the CC shown. The result of maintaining τ = 0.05 s and changing the SEC F-L relationship to SEC2 is shown. Model results.*

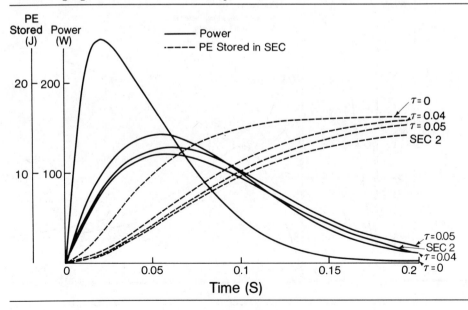

dynamic phase of the CC requires more energy than the final steady
state phase, and that the initial phase is less economical as is the case
with dynamic contraction [80]. Clearly maintenance of stored energy
involves the metabolism in terms of motion at the molecular level.

*Dynamic Contractions Against an Inertia (Figs. 4–7)*
Contractions begin at zero activation and proceed under rising activation with $\tau = 0.05$ s. In one case the purely inertial load (10 kg)
begins with zero velocity ($R$ = rest) and in the other it is traveling
eccentrically at 3 m/s ($S$ = muscle stretch) when activation begins.
Traces $R$ and $S$ have been adjusted in time so that the time of zero
load velocity in each case coincides on the abscissa. This has been
termed zero time.

FIGURE 4
*Force, load displacement, and CC velocity plotted against time during
contraction against an inertial load of 10 kg. At the onset of activation the
load is either at rest (R) or moving in an eccentric direction (S). In both
cases zero velocity of the load occurs at zero time. The horizontal bar on the
vertical line at zero time indicates the magnitude of the isometric maximum
($P_o$). Model results.*

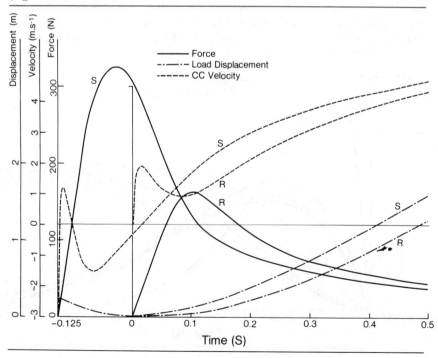

FIGURE 5

*Potential energy stored in the SEC, kinetic energy of the load, and their sum, total energy, plotted against time for the contractions of Figure 4. The asterisks indicate pairs of values of load KE at equal displacements of the load from its position at zero time. Model results.*

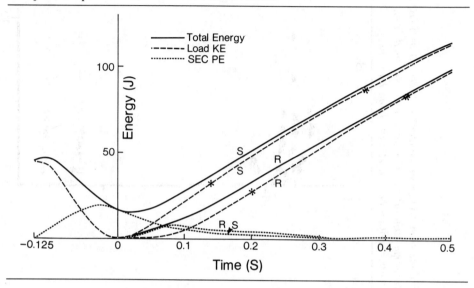

In the case of *S*, activation has been present for 0.125 s when the load reaches zero velocity. By this time activation will have reached 92 percent of its full value (see Fig. 2). Despite the presence of submaximal activation and zero load velocity at this time, the force (*S*) produced is greater than the isometric maximum (Fig. 4). This is due to the fact that the SEC, which has been stretched, is recoiling and allowing the CC to work on the eccentric part of the F-V relationship (see Fig. 4 for CC velocity). Since stretch of an active muscle results in SEC stretch and its consequent modification of CC velocity, it may be said that the arresting of an eccentrically moving load produces conditions at the onset of the concentric phase which approximate that of a prior isometric contraction. As the latter is clearly beneficial [6, 42] but impossible in this type of loading, the prior stretch is the human's way of realizing this benefit. Additional benefits are likely to result from the stretch in terms of an increase in muscle force over that shown. The increase would be due to Edman's "force enhancement" although it is unclear how significant this decaying effect would be in human muscles. Indirect evidence for the presence of force enhancement in human muscular contraction of this kind has been observed [48]. During forearm supination against an inertia, some

FIGURE 6

*The relationship between eccentric work and concentric work done over (A) given concentric times (s) and (B) given concentric angular displacements (Rad) of the load during forearm supination. The data were obtained from one subject using a variety of loads and forearm positions at which concentric motion began. Results from humans.*

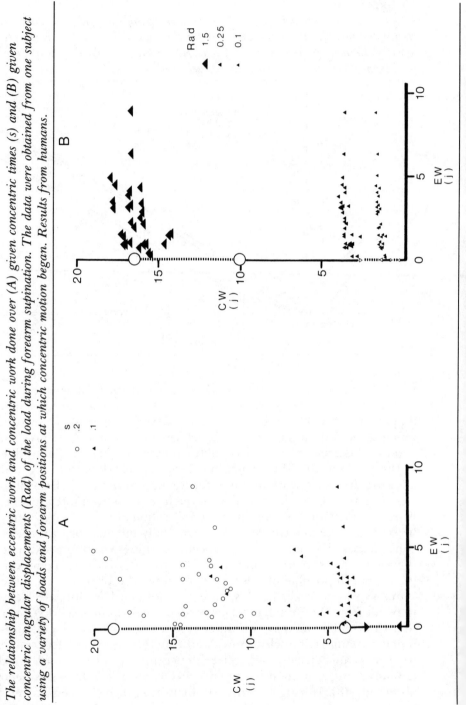

FIGURE 7

*Output power (F × load velocity) and total power (differential of the sum of load KE and SEC PE) plotted against time for contractions R and S shown in Figure 4. Model results.*

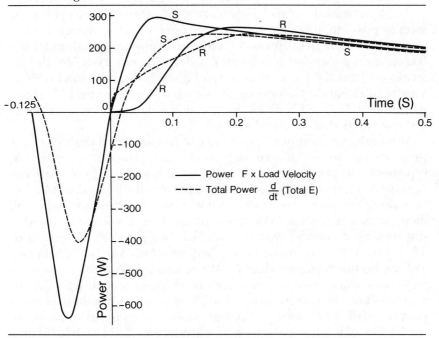

force traces following muscle stretch showed peaks which were greater than the isometric value at that forearm position and which occurred during the concentric phase. This is interpreted as a shift of the F-V relationship along the force axis [71].

The consequence of the difference in force traces R and S is that the mechanical impulse increases very much more rapidly in S than R following zero time. The result is that the load accelerates with a greater magnitude and the velocity rises rapidly leading to large increases in the kinetic energy of the load (Fig. 5). Rapid increases in load velocity require the muscle to shorten more rapidly. Again interaction between the CC and SEC is seen. The muscle force (S in Fig. 4) decreases with increased CC velocity and the SEC recoils further, producing a rapid decrease of potential energy stored in the SEC (Fig. 5). Muscle force in S (Fig. 4) actually falls below that produced in R, and from then on the mechanical impulse accumulated is less in S than in R. Therefore the early large difference in load velocity and KE between S and R decreases very slightly with time

(Fig. 5). Much of the delay in rise of load velocity from rest is due to the fact that the benefits of rising activation are offset by rapid increases in CC velocity due to stretch of the SEC. Force traces R and S are qualitatively the same as those seen in elbow flexion [173].

When the task is to move an inertia with the greatest velocity as soon as possible, it is clear that prior stretch of active muscle is beneficial. If time is not a problem and displacement is a conditioning factor, then somewhat less benefit is derived. For example, the asterisks on load KE traces R and S in Figure 5 show the load KE's at 2 pairs of equal displacements of the load from zero time. It is apparent that load KE's differ by a much smaller amount at equal displacements than at equal times.

Although not seen here, the effect of having variable amounts of prior energy to absorb are as follows. Force trace R in Figure 4, represents no prior stretch. As increasing amounts of eccentric energy are presented to the muscle the trace R will shift in the direction of S along the time axis. Peak force will not only shift left but it will increase in magnitude. Whenever the peak occurs while the load is still moving eccentrically, the force will begin to fall as seen in S. Therefore the force magnitude when zero load velocity is attained will not be much higher than $P_o$. While this will lead to increases in concentric work done (as measured by changes in load KE), the increase will be small in proportion to the eccentric work done in stopping the load. The conclusion is that small amounts of prior eccentric work will lead to substantial increases in concentric work while further increases in eccentric work will not lead to further substantial increases in concentric work. This has been shown to apply in maximally activated human forearm rotation [48] (see Fig. 6). This scenario is based upon the present model which does not include the effect which stretch has on force enhancement. What force enhancement does is to increase the peak force by variable amounts as the magnitude of stretch varies as described above. This effect is relatively small and decays with time [168], but it does not discount the above argument, as Figure 6 shows. It should be noted that in contractions where the velocity is controlled at a constant level, the effects of stretch assume considerably more importance [42] over that predicted by a simple model without history-dependent properties [45].

When the relationship between prior eccentric and subsequent concentric work is observed, it is clear that factors other than prior eccentric work affect concentric work. For example, in Figure 6 a variety of inertias was used. It is clear that more work can be done from rest over a given time using a certain inertia than can be done via eccentric work using another inertia (Fig. 6A). In addition the points in Figure 6 were obtained from different starting angles of the forearm. This represents different muscle lengths at zero load velocity. The effect of the muscle's F-L relationship is not seen in the present model results since no F-L relationship was incorporated. However, this does have an effect on the output. These effects have been summarized in a multiple regression analysis where the dependent variable was either angular velocity of the load or concentric work done over either a given time or a given displacement of concentric motion [49]. The independent variables were moment of inertia, forearm angle at zero load velocity, and either amplitude of stretch or prior eccentric work. The results, which are shown in Table 1, illustrate that the independent variables have more or less effect depending upon the nature of the required output. For example, when attempting to achieve the largest velocity of an inertia over a small displacement, it is beneficial to have as large a muscle stretch as possible. In attempting the same aim over a large displacement, the benefits derived from muscle stretch are reduced. In human muscular contraction, the conditions under which the contraction takes place (load to move, aim of the contraction, amplitude of motion, and time available) determine prior maneuvers which are required to achieve optimal output [26, 46, 173].

A point to stress is that externally recorded motion is not an indication of the motion of the CC. While this will be considered in more detail in the section on oscillatory contraction, it is worth mentioning here in terms of its effect on power output. Figure 7 shows power output in terms of output force multiplied by load velocity along with total power obtained as a differential of total system energy (KE of load plus energy stored in the SEC). The latter is equal to $F$ multiplied by velocity of the CC or muscle power. The difference between the two traces in Figure 7 is the power required to change potential energy in the SEC. In the contraction from rest the early internal stretching of the SEC produces total power which is greater than power output. Therefore, the metabolic cost to the muscle as a power generator is much greater than can be measured by observing external motion of the load to give power output. During the eccentric phase of contraction $S$ the total power requirement is less than power output since energy is supplied to the system by the eccentrically moving load. At zero load velocity the total power produced is negative and represents loss in energy while the output power is zero. In the concentric phase of $S$, output power is greater than total power. This means that measures of concentric output power would yield a cost which is greater than the contractile component has to bear. This is reflected in Figure 5 where the change in total energy during the concentric motion of load is approximately the same in $S$ and $R$ and therefore the cost to the muscle is the same. However, change in KE

TABLE 1
*Coefficients of Regression Variables, All Subjects*

| AV | $B_0$ | SA | MS | $I^{-1/2}$ | $R^2$ | F | $\sigma$ | $\overline{AV}$ | Range | N |
|---|---|---|---|---|---|---|---|---|---|---|
| 0.10 r | 0.33 | −0.11 | 1.20 | 1.08 | 0.82 | 713 | 0.47 | 3.45 | 1.69–7.39 | 467 |
| 0.25 r | 0.61 | −0.19 | 1.09 | 1.81 | 0.86 | 1186 | 0.56 | 5.56 | 3.11–11.41 | 467 |
| 1.50 r | 2.50 | −2.11 | 0.59 | 3.82 | 0.90 | 1129 | 1.08 | 12.05 | 7.05–22.16 | 389 |
| 0.1 s | −5.16 | −0.77 | 4.40 | 3.64 | 0.80 | 621 | 1.74 | 5.30 | 0.70–19.59 | 467 |
| 0.2 s | −3.62 | −1.15 | 2.95 | 5.02 | 0.81 | 559 | 1.56 | 8.51 | 3.30–21.44 | 394 |

| CW | $B_0$ | SA | EW | I | $R^2$ | F | $\sigma$ | $\overline{CW}$ | Range | N |
|---|---|---|---|---|---|---|---|---|---|---|
| 0.10 r | 0.76 | −0.06* | 0.16 | 0.57 | 0.56 | 198 | 0.26 | 1.04 | 0.26–1.98 | 467 |
| 0.25 r | 2.16 | −0.14* | 0.22 | 1.65 | 0.44 | 121 | 0.51 | 2.69 | 1.20–5.29 | 467 |
| 1.50 r | 12.29 | −0.78* | 0.23 | 5.11 | 0.12 | 18 | 1.93 | 13.35 | 8.51–19.27 | 389 |
| 0.1 s | 5.00 | −0.67 | 0.76 | −16.62 | 0.56 | 197 | 1.57 | 2.57 | 0.11–12.70 | 467 |
| 0.2 s | 13.20 | −1.27 | 1.16 | −30.60 | 0.54 | 150 | 2.55 | 7.79 | 1.67–20.39 | 394 |

Coefficients of independent variables which accounted for the variability ($R^2$) of the dependent variables shown in the left-hand column. Dependent variables are angular velocity (AV in radians per second) and concentric work (CW in joules) achieved after 0.1, 0.25, and 1.5 radians (r) and 0.1 and 0.2 seconds (s) of concentric motion. Independent variables are angle at zero velocity (SA in radians), amplitude of muscular stretch (MS in radians), eccentric work (EW in joules), moment of inertia (I in kg m²) and reciprocal of the square root of I ($I^{-1/2}$).
$B_0$ is the value of the dependent variable when all independent variables are set to zero. Also shown are F ratios, the standard errors of estimate ($\sigma$), mean values of the dependent variable ($\overline{AV}$ or $\overline{CW}$), and number of observations (N). Combined data from all subjects and all contractions. All coefficients were significant at $p < 0.01$ except those marked *($p < 0.05$).

of the load is greater in $S$ than $R$ over the same period. Consequently, the efficiency, in terms of change in load energy divided by cost to the muscle, is much greater in $S$ than $R$, the difference being due to stored energy in the SEC in $S$ at the time of zero load velocity. This storage represents a cost to the muscle incurred in the prior eccentric phase, and as shown in Figure 5 the energy change in this phase which is required to store PE in the SEC is substantially greater than the difference in output KE or total energy at any time during the concentric phase. Therefore, it is clear that the overall cost to muscle to do the task is far greater in $S$ than the difference in output KE in the two tasks. Consequently, while the use of prior stretch can be seen to enhance output in terms of achieving a given load KE in the concentric phase, the metabolic cost of this maneuver is substantial. A saving grace is that eccentric tension can be maintained with little ATP breakdown which decreases the relative energy cost of the eccentric phase [61]. However, there are some activities where the stretch-shortening cycle is inevitable and has to be used such as in the stance phase in running. In these cases the presence of an SEC which becomes stretched allows the CC to stretch and shorten with smaller velocities than if the SEC was absent. The CC power (total power) is therefore less as described previously (see Fig. 7), and the metabolic cost involved in CC shortening is less. Overall muscle efficiency in this type of work clearly depends upon the mechanical properties of the muscle's components, but it will also depend upon the rate at which the stretch-shortening cycle is done in relation to the load to be moved [75]. Morgan, Prosky and Warren [136] have illustrated how the presence of a long achilles tendon (which greatly increases compliance of the SEC) allows the CC to undergo small excursions when kangaroos hop, thus reducing the metabolic cost to the animal. It is interesting to speculate on whether one of the qualities of an expert long-distance runner is a compliant SEC in the patellar tendon or in other involved muscle groups.

Average output force and angular velocity of knee extension have been used to determine F-V relationships in vertical jumping with and without a counter movement (prior eccentric phase of knee extensors) [28, 30]. Such a F-V relationship is not a description of the mechanical properties of the CC of the jumping muscle. These authors indicated that the F-V relationship in a jump from a crouch was drastically different from that following a counter movement. In the case of a counter jump force was seen to increase with velocity— a property unknown to the F-V relationship of the CC of skeletal muscle. Reference to Figure 4 will show how the average force in $S$ will always be greater than in $R$, and at any given load displacement the load velocity in $S$ will be somewhat greater than in $R$. Analysis of the present type indicates that the results produced by the above authors could be predicted without modification of the F-V relationship, and that it is the interaction between CC and SEC during and following the eccentric phase which contributed to their results. Again, ascribing changes in the properties of muscles based upon external recordings, average or otherwise, may lead to misinterpretations. Viitasalo [174] examined the effects of training on the relationship between loads carried on the shoulder and takeoff velocity in vertical jumping. This so called F-V relationship was shown to be sensitive to training, although the expression of force and velocity gave no indication of which structures benefited from the training.

*Oscillatory Contractions Against Inertia Plus Gravity (Figs. 8–12)*
This motion can be pictured as holding a mass of 10 kg in the hand and repeatedly activating only the elbow flexors so that the load is moved up and down in an oscillatory fashion. The model was run with a sinusoidal input of activation as shown in Figure 8 and its amplitude and frequency was varied so that a load displacement occurred at 1.0, 2.0, and 2.5 cycles per second (cps) with approximately constant amplitude of 0.1 m as seen in Figure 9.

Figure 8 shows that there is a phasic difference between output force and activation which is dependent upon frequency. Similar results have been obtained during oscillation of the body in a standing posture on a force platform by contraction of plantar flexors [9]. In

FIGURE 8
*Sinusoidal activation of the CC (in units of force) at three frequencies (cycles per second, cps) which resulted in the force required to produce oscillatory motion of a load of 10 kg against gravity. Model results.*

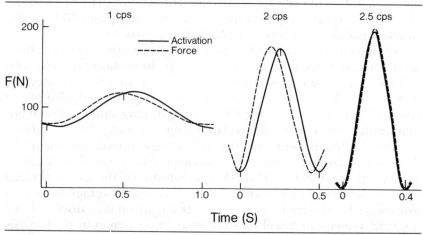

FIGURE 9

*Displacement, velocity, and stretch of the SEC during oscillatory contractions against gravity. Solid and broken lines refer respectively to the kinematics of the CC and the load. SEC stretch is the difference between the solid and broken lines in the displacement traces. Model results.*

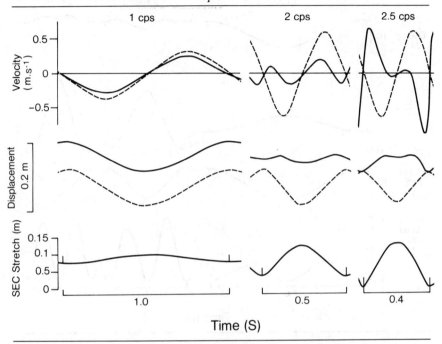

this experiment [9] force amplitude was kept constant, which clearly meant variation of amplitude of motion of the center of mass as frequency was varied. This was achieved by the subjects by varying input to the muscle which was monitored by EMG recording. These authors were able to demonstrate that the ratio of peak force over peak EMG was maximal at a frequency near to the middle of the possible range. This was interpreted as evidence that the human muscular properties are such that there exists a resonant frequency where output force is maximized in relation to input from the nervous system (and presumably metabolic cost to the muscles). An alternative view can be taken with respect to the present model input/output relationships.

In the present work the average activation of the muscle per cycle is the same ($= Mg$ or 98.1 N in force units) at all frequencies, but its duration is 1, 0.5, and 0.4 s at frequencies of 1, 2, and 2.5 cycles per second, respectively. Since amplitude of motion was constant, the

FIGURE 10

*Kinetic and potential energy of the load, potential energy stored in the SEC, and the sum of the three, total energy, during oscillatory contractions against gravity at the frequencies shown. Model results.*

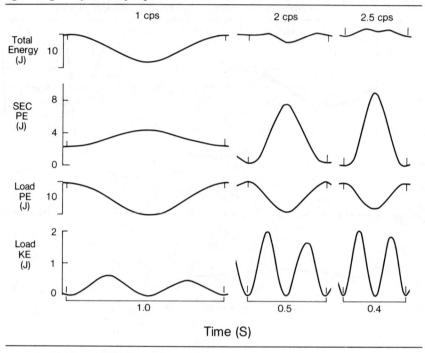

change in load potential energy was the same at all frequencies (Fig. 10). However, fluctuation in load KE and its average value are considerably greater at the two higher frequencies (Fig. 10). Clearly the system gain (in terms of KE of the load over activation) varies with frequency and is greatest at 2.5 cps. With different loads the relationship between gain and frequency will vary. The same can be said for peak output power in relation to average activation (Fig. 11). Fluctuations in total energy (Fig. 10) are much less in the higher frequency oscillations. This is due to the fact that the SEC stores and releases much more PE, the CC undergoes less displacement, and the peak power which it is required to deliver is reduced (Fig. 11). Indeed increased muscular efficiency in small amplitude ankle joint oscillations has been attributed to the interplay between the CC and the SEC [170]. The mechanical results were substantiated on the basis of measures of oxygen consumption and lactate, and oxygen consumption was also used by Bosco [31] who demonstrated increased

FIGURE 11

*Power applied to the load (output power) and total power as the first differential of total energy shown in Figure 10. The latter is equal to force times velocity of the CC. Model results.*

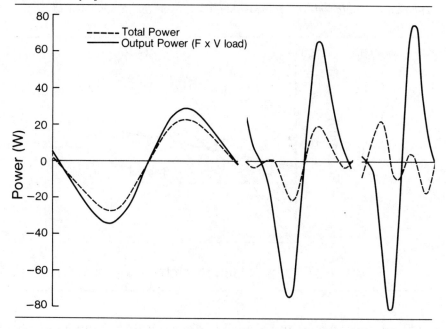

efficiency of concentric work with reduced amplitude (and concomitant increased frequency) of knee motion in jumping.

An alternative view of this type of muscle behavior is to consider the relationship between force applied to the load and load displacement (Fig. 12). Since there is very little hysteresis observed, the muscle can be considered to be acting in a spring-like fashion. This is undoubtedly due to the variable activation, but the effect is to increase the apparent stiffness of the muscle as frequency increases. Observation of the traces of force against CC displacement (broken lines in Fig. 12) reveals that the CC behavior varies with frequency. At 1 cps the CC behaves much like a spring as its displacement trace is very similar to that of the load displacement. However, since the CC amplitude is less than that of the load the apparent CC stiffness is slightly greater than that of the whole muscle. At 2 cps the CC displacement is very small, and when considered in relation to force it has a small hysteresis. This indicates that the CC behaves in a very stiff manner, that some work is lost, and that the overall spring-like behavior is due to the presence of the SEC. At 2.5 cps the CC behaves

FIGURE 12

*The relationship between force and displacement during oscillatory contractions against gravity at the frequencies shown. Solid lines refer to displacement of the load and broken lines refer to CC displacement. Increasing displacement represents lengthening of the muscle. Model results.*

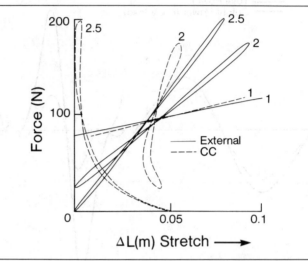

unlike a pure spring, and a small hysteresis is seen. From these observations it is apparent that the muscular system can be regarded as exhibiting pure spring-like behavior only when activation varies, and that consideration of the CC as a pure spring is misleading and depends upon the frequency of an activating input. In fact Nichols and Houk [138] attribute the spring-like behavior to the role which the reflex system plays in modifying activation. Similar arguments have been used to justify the view of the human musculature as spring-like in hopping [186]. Such evidence invalidates the assumption of muscular activity as spring-like when activation is constant [38].

Observations of load and CC displacement show them to be in phase at 1 cps (Fig. 9). At 2 cps the CC displacement occurs at twice the frequency of that of the load, and at 2.5 cps they are approximately out of phase by a half cycle. Traces of CC and load velocities reveal this clearly. This illustrates that measures of eccentric and concentric work which are based upon external measures of displacement are not necessarily a true reflection of the capacity of the contractile tissue to perform eccentric and concentric work. These external measures may provide valuable information of an empirical nature, but they do not yield information on the muscles capacity to do work in relation to its motion. This can only be done by means of the present analytical technique after experiments have been performed to obtain the dynamic characteristics of the components of the muscles. This has implications for the assumptions made when the costs of various types of mechanical work are performed. Recently Williams and Cavanagh [182] demonstrated how vastly variable values of efficiency of running can be obtained depending upon the assumptions made in calculating mechanical energy cost. They devised a coefficient for the relative metabolic efficiency of negative and positive muscular power and applied it on the basis of whether segmental energy was either decreasing or increasing. Data of this kind give no indication of whether the muscular tissue is actually behaving either eccentrically or concentrically. Chapman and Caldwell [47] made statements about the relative concentric and eccentric activity in sprinting on the basis of net moments about joints and joint angular velocity. The present work shows that the muscle CC behavior can be quite different from the story told by external measures. In fact Shorten [161] has demonstrated that the inclusion of an elastic strain energy component in a linked segmental energy model of running resulted in a reduction in the amplitude of the whole body energy curve.

Similar errors exist in work which ascribed concentric and eccentric work to external measurements during a knee-bending exercise at various frequencies on a force platform [76]. In relating the magnitude of the electromyogram to their estimates of the concentric and eccentric work they indicated that muscular efficiency (units not given) varied with frequency. Since they were uncertain about the duration of CC concentric and eccentric behavior, their results do not apply to the efficiency of muscular contraction. Consequently they do not have a measure of muscular efficiency, they merely have measures of the amount of muscle activation when moving up as opposed to moving down.

Many variations in this analysis could have been performed using this model. The F-V relationships, SEC stiffness and time constant of activation could have been varied. The effect of force enhancement, possible changes in SEC stiffness with activation and muscle length, damping of the SEC, and reflex effects of the nervous system could have been included. While it is true that the nervous system of athletic experts can integrate all of this information, its addition to the present work would increase the complexity in the understanding of muscular activity, just as the intuitive appeal of a model is reduced by such maneuvers [85]. The answer to many questions on how to optimize muscle output may lie in effects which have been neglected. The first step is to identify the output to be optimized.

## OBSERVATIONS ON THE USE OF MUSCLE IN HUMAN ACTIVITY

While muscle modeling and experiments to verify the model are interesting exercises, the final aim of the student of human movement in this area must be to use the information to understand and even optimize muscular performance. The main theme of this section is the need for a conceptual model of muscle in relation to human activity. Consequently, it is pertinent to speculate upon the use of human muscles in the performance of many tasks which have similar requirements but which apply to different activities.

The aims of voluntary human muscular contraction vary from skilled movements involving finely controlled small muscles through almost automatic activities such as walking to highly skilled gross movements seen in athletics. Within this spectrum the requirements of the muscles can be quite variable. A wrestler may wish to maximize force in the isometric condition while a baseball pitcher may have maximal release velocity of the ball as his major aim. The list of aims of human muscular contraction is endless. In the final analysis the outcome of our efforts is muscular force, and production of this force represents a cost to the metabolism. In certain activities of short duration the metabolic cost is irrelevant. In other activities, such as distance running, the cost is of primary importance. In some activities the constraints imposed on the use of muscles are anatomical. In others, such as striking activities for accuracy, the constraint is postural. Enhanced muscular work is a prime objective in many activities, while in others the production of mechanical impulse is important. It is quite clear that while the production of force is the role of the muscle, the manner in which force is produced (with respect to time or displacement) is a prime consideration in achieving a physical goal.

In many activities the requirement is to maximize the velocity of a load by means of multisegmental coordinated activity (e.g., throwing a ball or striking with an implement). Consider three segments of the body (the upper arm, the forearm, and hand) linked at the elbow and wrist joints and throwing a ball by motion of the two distal segments in a vertical overhead plane. The upper arm is considered fixed, and the elbow extensors and wrist flexors perform the movement. Either conventional coaching wisdom or casual observation tells us that the proximal (forearm) segment will be moved first, probably in elbow flexion to provide a backswing. Then elbow extension will occur with the wrist fully extended followed somewhat later by wrist flexion which moves the distally located hand relative to the forearm. Elbow extension will begin with a large moment resulting from effects such are seen in force trace $S$ in Figure 4. Such rapid acceleration of elbow extension will require the wrist flexors to produce a large moment since the inertia of hand plus the load will need to be accelerated. Because the wrist flexors are capable of less force than the elbow extensors the wrist remains fully extended using the muscle force plus parallel elasticity and ligamentous forces to provide the total force transmission to the load. This state remains until the velocity of elbow extension has reached a substantial level and the elbow extensor force accelerating the forearm, hand, and load drops as seen in $S$, Figure 4. At some stage the force will drop to a level where the force transmitted by the wrist flexors is less than its isometric value. At this stage the wrist flexors can shorten in accordance with their F-V relationship in order to maximize the load velocity. This in turn results in an equal and opposite load on the elbow extensors which, while tending to reduce forearm velocity, will allow the elbow extensors to maintain a reasonable force and consequent acceleration. This would not occur if the wrist flexion did not take place. When a number of segments are involved, the angular motion of a proximal segment results in opposite angular motion of a distal segment due to the latter's inertia. Consequently, each set of muscles can begin its shortening from a prior stretch induced by the inertia of the distal segment to which the muscles are attached. This clearly enhances output, and it will occur sequentially in time in a proximal to distal direction. I consider this to be what we term timing in skill and, because of relative muscular properties, it will be different among individuals as well as among loads. For example, it has been demonstrated that over 90 percent of all work done in kicking is supplied by the hip flexors, with a small contribution from knee extensors being seen in early swing [159]. Since net moments were calculated, it is not clear whether the above principle was adhered to. Nonetheless it is believed that this principle will apply qualitatively. Such speculation, although based upon knowledge of muscular properties, requires experimental rather than anecdotal verification.

This discussion has centered upon segmental interaction preceding either release of an object or striking with an implement. In the case of striking, the state of muscular contraction at contact will further modify the effect of prior segmental motion. Under certain conditions the object struck will induce a stretch in such muscles as the forearm rotators, flexors, or extensors (in a backhand stroke). Although the exact amplitude of possible stretch has not been investigated, it is likely to be small and of short duration (e.g., half the time a ball is on the racquet). It is possible that the muscles in question will be stretched within the region of their short-range stiffness (SRS) [135, 153]. In this case the whole muscle behaves in a spring-like manner in which little energy is lost in the stretch-shortening cycle. This is undoubtedly beneficial in transmitting the greatest mechanical impulse to the struck object. Furthermore, the amplitude of SRS in an individual's muscle can be coupled with mechanical properties of the racquet to form an interacting mechanical system. Therefore it would seem reasonable that the implement could be matched to the individual to provide optimal output results in striking activities involving maximal effort. This is presently done by the expert performers on the basis of feel, but no scientific approach of this kind seems to have been undertaken.

While the above argument may well apply to the aim of moving a distal segment (ball, shot, or racquet, or foot in kicking), it need not apply in jumping. In this case the distal segment (the foot) moves last of all. In a normal counter movement jump the arms begin upward acceleration when the body is at its lowest point. At this stage the force in the knee extensors will be high according to force trace $S$ in Figure 4. Acceleration of the arms will produce an equal and opposite tendency to accelerate the body downward. Since the CC of the knee extensors will still be in the eccentric mode, it can easily transmit the additional force to the feet which means that the body does not experience the downward acceleration. This will increase the force from which the impulse in the upward phase of the jump begins. Clearly this is beneficial. The upward velocity of the center of mass of the body is related to the sum of angular velocities of all the joints in series between the foot and the center of mass. Clearly the dynamic capabilities of the muscles crossing these joints will interact to maximize this velocity. It has been shown that in vertical and broad jumping, moments about the knee and hip joints peak simultaneously, while peak ankle moment is delayed slightly [158]. This is clearly advantageous since, were any link in this chain to be reduced, the system would tend to collapse at the level of that linkage.

Why can humans raise their center of mass higher (due to greater takeoff velocity) in a running as opposed to a standing jump? In a standing jump there is a limit to the downward velocity which can be achieved in the counter movement before the muscles are put in an extremely mechanically disadvantageous position. In addition, time for activation to rise fully will be limited before upward motion begins. Yet in performing the counter movement by jumping off an elevated platform the eccentric velocity of muscular contraction can be increased, as can time for muscular activation to rise. As a result, greater benefits of prior stretch on ouput variables can be realized more fully [30]. It should be pointed out that there is a limit to the benefit derived from increasing prior stretch, as mentioned in the section on dynamic contraction. In fact Komi [126] demonstrated such a limitation since the height jumped increased with increasing magnitude of drop to the floor up to a limit where further drop heights either did not show benefit or were detrimental. While jumpers cannot carry boxes around off which to jump as in Komi's experiment, they can approximate such effects by arresting a relatively large horizontal motion by eccentric contraction of the jumping muscles. This eccentric action occurs while the body's horizontal motion is reduced so that the subsequently enhanced concentric motion occurs with the body in a suitable position to go upward. The high jump and long jump are examples of this effect.

Weight lifting is similar to vertical jumping in the sense that a mass is moved upward, but the dynamic load in the former is obviously much greater. Observations of this event indicate that motion of the hip, knee, and ankle joints do not occur simultaneously and that ankle plantar flexion is the last motion to occur when hip and knee extension has reached nearly its full range. Obviously mechanically similar activities may be done in a similar fashion, but variations will occur depending upon the nature of the load to move.

Why can we not sprint faster? It is no surprise to say that the human has a limited capacity to accelerate in sprinting. Running at top speed without accelerating means mechanically that a reduction in horizontal momentum while airborne is matched by the net horizontal impulse while on the ground. This impulse is small at high running speeds because the muscles involved are shortening rapidly. Naturally at some stage the muscle velocity is so great no force is produced, and therefore neither is acceleration. One component of increasing running speed would be to train to shift the F-V relationship so that maximal intrinsic shortening velocity is increased (if that is possible).

The concept of resonance has been examined experimentally under unfatigued and fatigued conditions [9]. These authors demonstrated that experimentally determined resonant frequency and frequency of ankle plantar flexion in sprinting both change with the onset of fatigue. While a causal relationship between these two phenomena has not been established, it is suggested that the concept of resonance may hold some clues to the suitability of an athlete for a given activity. The possibility that some athletes may have muscular and anthropometric properties which produce a resonant frequency which is suitable for a given athletic event is attractive and requires further attention. It has been suggested that such a concept may be the basis of a strategy in which the individual moves from a speed optimization to an energy optimization frequency [93].

Distance running presents a different problem to that of sprinting. In this case the aim is to move along at a constant speed with minimal metabolic cost for that speed. The metabolic cost results from the fact that muscles are required to increase and decrease limb energy. It is unclear why this is done at medium stride length and stride frequency and not with very long or short strides with appropriate changes in stride frequency. Possibly the aim is to minimze motion of the CC about zero velocity on the F-V relationship. It is rather superfluous to say that the mechanical properties of muscles hold the key in the end to the running style adopted, but the muscle properties of most importance are yet to be revealed. There are two stages of transduction of energy in this activity. The first is between oxygen supplied to the muscles and the muscular work resulting from this supply. This is not the topic of this review. The second is transduction of muscular work to mechanical work. No investigators have, as yet, documented that the preferred running style is that in which absolute changes in the body's mechanical energy are minimized. This would seem to be a requirement of optimal performance. Yet it may be the case that to do so would involve the muscles in unfavorable mechanical conditions of velocity of shortening and excursions of length. Therefore there would seem to be a trade-off between favorable conditions for maximal muscular efficiency and the mechanics of the task. Whether the experts in distance running have muscular properties which make the best compromise has yet to be revealed.

In performing muscular work to drive machinery, the machine can be designed to take advantage of the dynamic capabilities of human muscle. In bicycling the aim is to move the machine at a given velocity with minimal cost to the metabolism. Assuming that the energy cost is similar at any velocity of shortening, it is clear that there exists a combination of force and velocity at which power output is greatest (see Fig. 1A). It seems obvious that the function of gears is to allow the muscles to work at their most favorable velocity on any gradient of the terrain. In so doing the power output will be greatest. Since the muscles change activation from zero to some value throughout the cycle and we are dealing with angular velocity, it appears that we are trying to maximize some combination of average torque and angular velocity. Indeed Nadeau [173] demonstrated a combination of load and frequency at which power output was maximal on a bicycle ergometer test with maximal effort. The challenge remains to find a method by which bicycling can be performed as a purely eccentric activity. It is in this type of contraction that muscle power is greatest (but unfortunately negative).

## CONCLUSIONS

This review has been concerned with information pertinent to the mechanical properties of human muscle. Since the mechanical properties are numerous and the degree of voluntary control is extensive, it has not been possible to cover all aspects of this area. An attempt has been made to discuss those properties which have a bearing on the outcome of voluntary contraction. Various ways in which these properties are combined in a model form have been considered. The structure of models, their implementation, and the intuitive appeal which they offer has been put forward. Various types of muscular contraction have been modeled with a view to understanding how interaction of model components governs output variables. Speculations have been made concerning some of the questions we might ask about how human muscular contraction allows us to achieve various aims. It is hoped that this work will provide insight into the manner in which muscle components behave, and that these considerations will be born in mind when experiments on human muscular contraction are designed.

I would like to make three final points. The first is that the pronunciation of "eccentric" is with a hard "c" (phonetically "eksentric"). Those individuals who are confused by this inclusion should ignore it. The second point is that the term "isotonic" is frequently misused. It means "constant tension" which is hardly ever found in human muscular contraction, and it certainly is not the converse of "isometric." The third point concerns the term "isokinetic"—Does it have any meaning or is it just a complex way of stating "constant velocity"?

## REFERENCES

1. Abbott, B.C., and X.M. Aubert. The force exerted by active striated muscle during and after change of length. *J. Physiol. Lond.* 117:77–86, 1952.
2. Abbott, B.C., and D.R. Wilkie. The relation between velocity of shortening and the tension-length curve of skeletal muscle. *J. Physiol. Lond.* 120:214–223, 1953.
3. Akazawa, K., M. Yamamoto, K. Fujii, and H. Mashima. A mechanochemical model fo the study of transient contractions of the skeletal muscle. *Jpn. J. Physiol.* 26:9–28, 1976.
4. Asmussen, E., and F. Bonde-Petersen. Storage of elastic energy in skeletal muscles in man. *Acta Physiol. Scand.* 91:35–392, 1974.
5. Asmussen, E., O. Hansen and O. Lammert. The relation between isometric and dynamic muscle strength in man. *Comm. Dan. Nat. Assoc. Infantile Paralysis* No. 20, 1965.
6. Asmussen, E., and N. Sorensen. The wind-up movement in athletics. *Travail Humain* 34:147–156, 1971.
7. Atha, J. Strengthening muscle. *Exercise Sport Sci. Rev.* 9:1–73, 1981.
8. Aubert, X., M.L. Roquet, and J. Van Der Elst. The tension-length diagram of frog's sartorious muscle. *Arch. Intern. Physiol.* 59:239–241, 1951.

9. Bach, T.M., A.E. Chapman, and T.W. Calvert. Mechanical resonance of the human body during voluntary oscillations about the ankle joint. *J. Biomechan.* 16:85–90, 1983.

10. Bahler, A.S. Series elastic component of mammalian skeletal muscle. *Am. J. Physiol.* 213:1560–1564, 1967.

11. Bahler, A.S. Modelling of mammalian skeletal muscle. *IEEE Trans. Bio-Med. Eng.* BME-15:249–256, 1968.

12. Bahler, A.S., and J.T. Fales. Flexible lever system for quantitative measurement of mammalian muscle dynamics. *J. Appl. Physiol.* 21:1421–1426, 1966.

13. Bahler, A.S., J.T. Fales, and K.L. Zierler. The dynamic properties of mammalian skeletal muscles. *J. Gen. Physiol.* 51:369–384, 1968.

14. Bahler, A.S., J.T. Fales, and K.L. Zierler. The active state of mammalian skeletal muscle. *J. Gen. Physiol.* 50:2239–2253, 1967.

15. Baildon, R.W.A., and A.E. Chapman. A new approach to the human muscle model. *J. Biomechan.* 16:803–809, 1983.

16. Baildon, R.W.A., and A.E. Chapman. Mechanical properties of a single equivalent muscle producing forearm supination. *J. Biomechan.* 16:811–819, 1983.

17. Banister, E.W. The perception of effort: an inductive approach. *Eur. J. Appl. Physiol.* 41:141–150, 1979.

18. Bankov, S., and K. Jorgensen. Maximum strength of elbow flexors with pronated and supinated forearm. *Comm. Dan. Nat. Assoc. Infantile Paralysis* No. 29, 1969.

19. Banus, M.G., and A. Zetlin. The relation of isometric tension to length in skeletal muscle. *J. Cell. Comp. Physiol.* 12:403–420, 1938.

20. Bawa, P., A. Mannard, and R.B. Stein. Effects of elastic loads on the contractions of cat muscles. *Biol. Cybernetics* 22:129–137, 1976.

21. Bawa, P, A. Mannard, and R.B. Stein. Predictions and experimental tests of a visco-elastic muscle model using elastic and inertial loads. *Biol. Cybernet.* 22:139–145, 1976.

22. Beck, O. Die gesamte Kraftkurve des tetanisierten Froschgastrocnemius und ihr physiologisch ausgenutzter Anteil. *Pflugers Arch. Ges. Physiol.* 193:495–526, 1922.

23. Bigland, B., and O.C.J. Lippold. Relation between force, velocity and integrated electrical activity in human muscles. *J. Physiol. Lond.* 123:214–224, 1954.

24. Bigland, B., and O.C.J. Lippold. Motor unit activity in the voluntary contraction of human muscles. *J. Physiol. Lond.* 125:322–335, 1954.

25. Blix, M. Dei Lang and Spannung des Muskels. *Skand. Arch. Physiol.* 3:295–318, 1892.

26. Bober, T., E. Jaskolski, and Z. Nowacki. Study on eccentric concentric contraction of the upper extremity muscles. *J. Biomechan.* 13:135–138, 1980.

27. Borg, G. A ratio scaling method for interindividual comparisons. *Sport Inst. Appl. Psychol.* No. 27, 1972.

28. Bosco, C., and P.V. Komi. Potentiation of the mechanical behavior of the human skeletal muscle through prestretching. *Acta Physiol. Scand.* 106:467–472, 1979.

29. Bosco, C., and P.V. Komi. Mechanical characteristics and fiber composition of human leg extensor muscles. *Eur. J. Appl. Physiol.* 41:275–284, 1979.

30. Bosco, C., J.T. Viitasalo, P.V. Komi, and P. Luhtanen. Combined effect of elastic energy and myoelectrical potentiation during stretch-shortening cycle exercise. *Acta Physiol. Scand.* 114:557–565, 1982.

31. Bosco, C., A. Ito, P.V. Komi, P. Luhtanen, P. Rahkila, H. Rusko, and J.T. Viitasalo. Neuromuscular efficiency and mechanical efficiency of human leg extensor muscles during jumping exercises. *Acta Physiol. Scand.* 114:543–550, 1982.

32. Bouisset, S. EMG and muscle force in normal motor activities. In J.E. Desmedt

(ed.), *New developments in EMG and Clinical Neurophysiology*. Vol. 1, pp. 557–583. Basel: S. Karger, 1973.

33. Buchthal, F., and E. Kaiser. The rheology of the cross-striated muscle fibre with particular reference to isotonic contractions. *Dan. Biol. Med.* 21(7), 1951.
34. Buchthal, F., and H. Schmalbruch. Contraction time and fibre types in intact human muscle. *Acta Physiol. Scand.* 79:435–452, 1970.
35. Buller, A.J., C.J. Kean, and K.W. Ranatung. Force-velocity characteristics of cat fast and slow-twitch skeletal muscle following cross-innervation. *J. Physiol. Lond.* 213:66P, 1971.
36. Buller, A.J., and D.M. Lewis. Rate of tension development in isometric tetanic contractions of mammalian fast and slow skeletal fibres. *J. Physiol. Lond.* 176:337–354, 1965.
37. Calvert, T.W., and A.E. Chapman. The relationship between the surface EMG and force-transients in muscle: simulation and experimental studies. *Proc. IEEE* 65:682–689, 1977.
38. Cavagna, G.A. Elastic bounce of the body. *J. Appl. Physiol.* 29:279–282, 1970.
39. Cavagna, G.A. Storage and utilization of elastic energy in skeletal muscle. *Exercise Sports Sci. Rev.* 5:89–129, 1977.
40. Cavagna, G.A. Aspects of efficiency and inefficiency of terrestrial locomotion. In *Biomechanics VIA*, pp. 3–22. Baltimore: University Park Press, 1978.
41. Cavagna, G.A., and G. Citterio. Effect of stretching on the elastic characteristics and the contractile component of frog striated muscle. *J. Physiol. Lond.* 239:1–14, 1974.
42. Cavagna, G.A., B. Dusman, and R. Margaria. Positive work done by a previously stretched muscle. *J. Appl. Physiol.* 24:21–32, 1968.
43. Cavanagh, P.R., and D.W. Grieve. The release and partitioning of mechanical energy during a maximal effort of elbow flexion. *J. Physiol. Lond.* 210:44–45P, 1970.
44. Chapman, A.E. The investigation of mechanical models of muscle based upon direct observations of voluntary dynamic human muscular contraction. Ph.D. thesis, University of London, 1975.
45. Chapman, A.E. Modelling muscle pre-stretch (PS). *Can. J. Appl. Sport Sci.* 4:239, 1979.
46. Chapman, A.E. The effect of "Wind-Up" on forearm rotational velocity. *Can. J. Appl. Sport Sci.* 5:215–219, 1980.
47. Chapman, A.E., and G.E. Caldwell. Factors determining changes in lower limb energy during swing in treadmill running. *J. Biomechan.* 16:69–77, 1983.
48. Chapman, A.E., and G.E. Caldwell. The use of muscle stretch in inertial loading. In *Abstr. IX Int. Congress, Biomechanics*, Waterloo, Ont., Canada, p. 54, 1983.
49. Chapman, A.E., G.E. Caldwell, and S. Selbie. Unpublished data, 1984.
50. Chapman, A.E., and T.W. Calvert. Estimations of active-state from EMG recordings of human muscular contraction. *Electromyogr. Clin. Neurophysiol.* 19:199–222, 1979.
51. Chapman, A.E., and P.T. Harrower. Linear approximations of muscle mechanics in isometric contractions. *Biol. Cybernet.* 27:1–7, 1977.
52. Chapman, A.E., and J.D.G. Troup. Prolonged activity of lumbar erectores spinae. An electromyographic and dydnamometric study of the effect of training. *Ann. Phys. Med.* 10:262–269, 1970.
53. Civan, M.M., and R.J. Podolsky. Contraction kinetics of striated muscle fibres following quick changes in load. *J. Physiol. Lond.* 184:511–534, 1966.
54. Close, R. The relation between intrinsic speed of shortening and duration of the active state of muscle. *J. Physiol. Lond.* 180:542–559, 1965.
55. Close, R.I. Dynamic properties of mammalian skeletal muscles. *Physiol. Rev.* 52:129–197, 1972.

56. Close, R., and J.F.Y. Hoh. Force:velocity properties of kitten muscles. *J. Physiol. Lond.* 192:815–822, 1967.

57. Cnockaert, J.C., E. Pertuzon, F. Goubel, and F. Lestienne. Series elastic component in normal human muscle. *Biomechanics VIA*, pp. 73–78. Baltimore: University Park Press, 1978.

58. Coggshall, J.C., and G.A. Bekey. A stochastic model of skeletal muscle based on motor unit properties. *Mathematical Biosciences* 7:405–419, 1970.

59. Cooper, D.F., G. Grimby, D.A. Jones, and R.H.T. Edwards. Perception of effort in isometric and dynamic contraction. *Eur. J. Appl. Physiol.* 41:173–180, 1979.

60. Crowe, A., H. Van Atteveldt, and H. Groothedde. Simulation studies of contracting skeletal muscles during mechanical stretch. *J. Biomechan.* 13:333–340, 1980.

61. Curtin, N.A., and R.E. Davies. Very high tension with little ATP breakdown by active skeletal muscle. *J. Mechanochem. Cell Motil.* 3:147–154, 1975.

62. Curtin, N.A., and R.C. Woledge. Energy changes and muscular contraction. *Physiol. Rev.* 58:690–761, 1978.

63. Curtin, N.A., and R.C. Woledge. Chemical charge, production of tension and energy following stretch of active muscle of frog. *J. Physiol. Lond.* 197:539–550, 1979.

64. Denoth, J. The dynamic behaviour of a three link model of the human body during impact with the ground. *Abstr. IX Int. Congr. Biomechanics*, Waterloo, Ont., Canada, p. 123, 1983.

65. Dern, R.J., J.M. Levine, and H.A. Blair. Forces exerted at different velocities in human arm movements. *Am. J. Physiol.* 151:415–437, 1947.

66. Duchateau, J., and K. Hainault. Isometric or dynamic training: differential effects on mechanical properties of human muscle. *J. Appl. Physiol. Respirat. Environ. Exercise Physiol.* 56:296–301, 1984.

67. Edman, K.A.P. Mechanical deactivation induced by active shortening of isolated muscle fibres of the frog. *J. Physiol. Lond.* 246:255–275, 1975.

68. Edman, K.A.P. Maximum velocity of shortening in relation to sarcomere length and degree of activation of frog muscle fibres. *J. Physiol. Lond.* 278:9P–10P, 1978.

69. Edman, K.A.P. The velocity of unloaded shortening and its relation to sarcomere length and isometric force in vertebrate muscle fibers. *J. Physiol. Lond.* 291:143–159, 1979.

70. Edman, K.A.P. Depression of mechanical performance by active shortening during twitch and tetanus of vertebrate muscle fibres. *Acta Physiol. Scand.* 109:15–26, 1980.

71. Edman, K.A.P., G. Elzinga, and H.I.M. Noble. Enhancement of mechanical performance by stretch during tetanic contractions of vertebrate skeletal muscle fibres. *J. Physiol. Lond.* 281:139–155, 1978.

72. Edman, K.A.P., and A. Kiessling. The time course of active state in relation to sarcomere length and movement studied in single skeletal muscle fibres of the frog. *Acta Physiol. Scand.* 81:182–196, 1971.

73. Evans, C.L., and A.V. Hill. The relation of length to tension development and heat production on contraction in muscle. *J. Physiol. Lond.* 49:1–16, 1914.

74. Flitney, F.W., and D.G. Hurst. Cross-bridge detachment and sarcomere 'give' during stretch of active frog's muscle. *J. Physiol. Lond.* 276:449–465, 1978.

75. Fukashiro, S., H. Ohmichi, H. Kanehisa, and M. Miyashita. Utilization of stored elastic energy in leg extensors. In *Biomechanics VIIIA*, pp. 258–263. Champaign, Ill.: Human Kinetics Publishers, 1983.

76. Funato, K., H. Ohmichi, and M. Miyashita. Electromyographic analysis on utilization of elastic energy in human leg muscles. *Abstr. IX, Int. Congress Biomechanics*, Waterloo, Ont., Canada, p. 55, 1983.

77. Fung, Y.C. Mathematical representation of the mechanical properties of the heart muscle. *J. Biomechan.* 3:381–404, 1970.
78. Furusawa, K., A.V. Hill, and J.L. Parkinson. The dynamics of sprint running. *Proc. R. Soc.* B102:29–42, 1927.
79. Geffen, L.B. Optimum length for contraction of rat circulated limb muscles. *Arch. Intern. Physiol.* 72:825–834, 1964.
80. Goldspink, G. Energy turnover during contraction of different types of muscle. *Biomechanics VIA*, pp. 27–39. Baltimore: University Park Press, 1978.
81. Gollnick, P.D. Muscle characteristics as a foundation of biomechanics. *Biomechanics VIIIA*, pp. 9–32. Champaign, Ill.: Human Kinetics Publishers, 1983.
82. Gordon, A.M., A.F. Huxley, and F.J. Julian. The length-tension diagram of single vertebrate striated muscle fibres. *J. Physiol. Lond.* 171:28–30P, 1964.
83. Gordon, A.M., A.F. Huxley, and F.J. Julian. Tension development in highly stretched vertebrate muscle fibres. *J. Physiol. Lond.* 184:143–169, 1966.
84. Gordon, A.M., A.F. Huxley, and F.J. Julian. The variation in isometric tension with sarcomere length in vertebrate muscle fibres. *J. Physiol. Lond.* 184:170–192, 1966.
85. Gottlieb, G.L., and G.C. Agarwal. Dynamic relationship between isometric muscle tension and the electromyogram in man. *J. Appl. Physiol.* 30:345–351, 1971.
86. Green, D.G. A note on modelling muscle in physiological regulators. *Med. Biol. Eng.* 1:41–48, 1969.
87. Grieve, D.W., and A.W. Arnott. The production of torque during axial rotation of the trunk. *J. Anat.* 107:147–164, 1970.
88. Grieve, D.W., and P.R. Cavanagh. The validity of quantitative statements about surface electromyograms recorded during locomotion. *Scand. J. Rehab. Med.* Suppl. 3:19–25, 1974.
89. Grieve, D.W., and S.T. Pheasant. Myoelectric activity, posture and isometric torque in man. *EMG. Clin. Neurophysiol.* 16:3–21, 1976.
90. Harrington, W.F. On the origin of the contractile force in skeletal muscle. *Proc. Nat. Acad. Sci. U.S.A.* 76:5066–5070, 1979.
91. Hatze, H. The complete optimization of a human motion. *Math. Biosci.* 28:99–135, 1976.
92. Hatze, H. *Myocybernetic Control Models of Skeletal Muscle*. Pretoria: University of South Africa, 1981.
93. Hatze, H., and J.D. Buys. Energy-optimal control in the mammalian neuromuscular system. *Biol. Cybernet.* 27:9–20, 1977.
94. Henneman, E. Peripheral mechanisms involved in the control of muscle. In: Mountcastle, V.B. (ed.) *Medical Physiology*, pp. 1697–1716; St. Louis: Mosby, 1968.
95. Henneman, E., H.P. Clamann, V.D. Gilles, and R.D. Skinner. Rank order of motoneurons within a pool: law of combination. *J. Neurophysiol.* 373:1338–1349, 1974.
96. Hill, A.V. The maximum work and mechanical efficiency of human muscles and their most economical speed. *J. Physiol. Lond.* 56:19–41, 1922.
97. Hill, A.V. The heat of shortening and the dynamic constants of muscle. *Proc. R. Soc. Lond.* B126:136–195, 1938.
98. Hill, A.V. The dynamic constants of human muscle. *Proc. R. Soc. Lond.* B128:263–274, 1940.
99. Hill, A.V. The abrupt transition from rest to activity in muscles. *Proc. R. Soc. Lond.* B136:399–420, 1949.
100. Hill, A.V. The series elastic component of muscle. *Proc. R. Soc. Lond.* B137:273–280, 1950.
101. Hill, A.V. *First and Last Experiments in Muscle Mechanics*. Cambridge: Cambridge University Press, 1970.

102. Hill, A.V., C.N.H. Long, and H. Lupton. The effect of fatigue on the relation between work and speed in the contraction of human arm muscles. *J. Physiol. Lond.* 58:334–337, 1924.

103. Hill, T.L. Theoretical formalism for the sliding filament model of contraction of striated muscle. *Prog. Biophys. Mol. Biol.* 28:267–340, 1974.

104. Hof, A.L. EMG to force processing. An electrical analogue of the calf muscles for the assessment of their force and work. Ph.D. thesis, Rijksuniversiteit of Groningen, The Netherlands, 1980.

105. Hof, A.L., and J. Van den Berg. Linearity between the weighted sums of the EMG's of the human triceps surae and their total torque. *J. Biomechan.* 10:529–539, 1977.

106. Hogan, N., and R.W. Mann. Myoelectric signal processing: Optimal estimation applied to electromyography—Part 1: Derivation of the optimal myoprocessor. *IEEE Trans. Biomed. Eng.* BME-27:382–410, 1980.

107. Honcke, P. Investigations on the structure of and function of living, isolated, cross striated muscle fibres of mammals. *Acta Physiol. Scand.* 15:(Suppl. 48), 1947.

108. Houk, J.C. *A mathematical model of the stretch reflex in human muscle systems.* M.S. Thesis, M.I.T., Cambridge, Mass., U.S.A., 1963.

109. Houston, M.E. The use of histochemistry in muscle adaptation: a clinical assessment. *Can. J. Appl. Sport Sci.* 3:109–118, 1978.

110. Hoyle, G. How a muscle is turned on and off. *Sci. Am.* 222:84–93, 1970.

111. Huxley, A.F. Muscle structure and theories of contraction. *Prog. Biophys. Biophys. Chem.* 7:257–318, 1957.

112. Huxley, A.F., and R. Niedergerke. Interference microscopy of living muscle fibres. *Nature* 173:971–973, 1954.

113. Huxley, A.F., and L.D. Peachey. The maximum length for contraction in striated muscle. *J. Physiol. Lond.* 146:555–56P, 1959.

114. Huxley, A.F., and R.M. Simmons. Mechanical properties of the cross-bridges of frog striated muscle. *J. Physiol. Lond.* 218:59–60P, 1971.

115. Huxley, A.F., and R.M. Simmons. Mechanical transients and the origin of muscular force. *Cold Spring Harbor Symp. Quant. Biol.* 37:669–680, 1973.

116. Jewell, B.R., and D.R. Wilkie. An analysis of the mechanical components in frog's striated muscle. *J. Physiol. Lond.* 143:515–540, 1958.

117. Julian, F.J. Activation in a skeletal muscle contraction model with a modification for insect fibrillar muscle. *Biophys. J.* 9:547–570, 1969.

118. Julian, F.J., and R.L. Moss. The concept of active-state in striated muscle. *Circ. Res.* 38:54–59, 1976.

119. Julian, F.J., R.L. Moss, and M.R. Sollins. The mechanism for vertebrate striated muscle contraction. *Circ. Res.* 42:2–14, 1978.

120. Julian, F.J., and M.R. Sollins. Regulation of force and speed of shortening in muscle contraction. *Cold Spring Harbour Symp. Quant. Biol.* 37:635–646, 1973.

121. Kanosue, H., M. Yoshida, K. Akazawa, and K. Fujii. The number of active motor units and their firing rates in voluntary contraction of human brachialis muscle. *Jpn. J. Physiol.* 29:427–443, 1979.

122. Karr, O.K. Effective muscle force. Ph.D. thesis, University of Illinois, 1964.

123. Katz, B. The relation between force and speed in muscular contraction. *J. Physiol. Lond.* 96:45–64, 1939.

124. Komi, P.V. Relationship between muscle length, muscle tension, EMG, and velocity of contraction under eccentric and concentric contractions. Paper presented at IVth Int. Congress of Electromyography. Brussels, Sept. 12–15, 1971.

125. Komi, P.V. Measurement of the force-velocity relationship in human muscle under concentric and eccentric contractions. In *Biomechanics III, 3rd Int. Seminar, Rome,* pp. 224–229. Basel: S. Karger, 1973.

126. Komi, P.V. Neuromuscular performance; factors influencing force and speed production. *Scand. J. Sports Sci.* 1:2–15, 1979.

127. Komi, P.V., and C. Bosco. Utilization of elastic energy in jumping and its relation to skeletal muscle fiber composition in man. *Biomechanics VIA*, pp. 79–85. Baltimore: University Park Press, 1978.

128. Lupton, H. The relation between the external work produced and the time occupied in a single muscular contraction in man. *J. Physiol. Lond.* 57:68–75, 1922.

129. Mannard, A., and R.B. Stein. Determination of the frequency response of isometric soleus muscle in the cat using random nerve stimulation. *J. Physiol. Lond.* 229:275–296, 1973.

130. Mashima, H. Force-velocity relation and contractility in striated muscles. *Jpn. J. Physiol.* 34:1–17, 1984.

131. Mashima, H., K. Akazawa, H. Kushima, and K. Fujii. The force-load-velocity relation and the viscous-like force in the frog skeletal muscle. *Jpn. J. Physiol.* 22:103–120, 1972.

132. Mashima, H., K. Akazawa, H. Kushima, and K. Fujii. Graphical analysis and experimental determination of the active state in frog skeletal muscle. *Jpn. J. Physiol.* 23:217–240, 1973.

133. Matsumoto, Y. Validity of the force-velocity relation for muscle contraction in the length region, l<lo. *J. Gen. Physiol.* 50:1125–1137, 1967.

134. Morecki, A., J. Ekiel, K. Fidelus, and K. Nazarczuk. Investigation of the reciprocal participation of muscles in the movements of the upper limbs of man. *Biofizika* 13:306–312, 1968.

135. Morgan, D.L. Separation of active and passive components of short range stiffness of muscle. *Am. J. Physiol.* 232:C45–49, 1977.

136. Morgan, D.L., U. Proske, and D. Warren. Measurements of muscle stiffness and the mechanism of elastic storage of energy in hopping kangaroos. *J. Physiol. Lond.* 282:253–261, 1978.

137. Nadeau, M., J.P. Cuerrier, J. Allard, M. Tardif, and A. Brassard. The muscle power of young active men and women on a bicycle ergometer. *Abstr. IX Int. Congr. Biomechanics.* Waterloo, Ont., Canada, 1983.

138. Nichols, T.R., and J.C. Houk. Reflex compensation for variations in the mechanical properties of a muscle. *Science* 181:182–184, 1973.

139. Noble, M.I.M., and G.H. Pollack. Molecular mechanisms for contraction. *Circ. Res.* 40:333–342, 1977.

140. Noble, M.I.M., and G.H. Pollack. Response to "The mechanism for vertebrate striated muscle contraction." *Circ. Res.* 42:15–16, 1978.

141. Norman, R.W., and P.V. Komi. Electromechanical delay in skeletal muscle under normal movement conditions. *Acta Physiol. Scand.* 106:241–248, 1979.

142. Parmley, W.W., L.A. Yeatman, and E.H. Sonnenblick. Differences between isotonic and isometric force-velocity relations in cardiac and skeletal muscle. *Am. J. Physiol.* 219:546–550, 1970.

143. Pell, K.M., and J.W. Stanfield. Mechanical model of skeletal muscle. *Amer. J. Phys. Med.* 51:23–28, 1972.

144. Peres, G., B. Maton, B. Lanjerit, and C. Phillipe. Electromyographic and mechanical aspects of the coordination between elbow flexors muscles in monkeys. In *Biomechanics VIIIA*, pp. 455–463. Champaign, Ill.: Human Kinetics Publishers, 1983.

145. Pertuzon, E. La contraction musculaire dans le mouvement voluntaire maximal. Ph.D. thesis, University of Lille, 1972.

146. Pertuzon, E., and S. Bouisset. Instantaneous force-velocity relationship in human muscle. *Biomechanics III, 3rd. Int. Seminar, Rome*, pp. 230–234. Basel: Karger, 1973.

147. Petrofsky, J.S., and C.A. Phillips. The influence of recruitment order and fibre composition on the force velocity relationship and fatiguability of skeletal muscles in the cat. *Med. Biol. Eng. Comput.* 18:381–390, 1980.

148. Petrofsky, J.S., and C.A. Phillips. The influence of temperature, initial length and electrical activity on the force-velocity relationship of the medial gastrocnemius muscle of the cat. *J. Biomechan.* 14:297–306, 1981.

149. Pierrynowski, M.R. A physiological model for the solution of individual muscle forces during normal human walking. Ph.D. thesis, Simon Fraser University, 1982.

150. Pollack, G.H. The cross-bridge theory. *Physiol. Rev.* 63:1049–1113, 1983.

151. Pringle, J.W.S. Models of muscle. In models and analogues in biology. *Symp. Soc. Exp. Biol.* 14:41–68, 1960.

152. Rack, P.M.H., and D.R. Westbury. The effect of length and stimulus rate on tension in the isometric cat soleus muscle. *J. Physiol. Lond.* 204:443–460, 1969.

153. Rack, P.M.H., and D.R. Westbury. The short range stiffness of active mammalian muscle and its effect on mechanical properties. *J. Physiol. Lond.* 240:331–350, 1974.

154. Rack, P.M.H., and D.R. Westbury. The stiffness of cat's soleus tendon. *J. Physiol. Lond.* 338:11P, 1983.

155. Ralston, M.J., K.T. Inman, L.A. Strait, and M.D. Shaffrath. Mechanism of human isolated voluntary muscle. *Am. J. Physiol.* 151:612–620, 1947.

156. Ramsey, R.W., and S.F. Street. The isometric length tension diagram of isolated skeletal muscle fibres of the frog. *J. Cell. Comp. Physiol.* 15:11–34, 1940.

157. Ritchie, J.M. The duration of the plateau of full activity in frog muscle. *J. Physiol. Lond.* 124:605–612, 1954.

158. Robertson, D.G.E., and D. Fleming. Summation of forces in standing broad and vertical jumping. *Can. J. Appl. Sport Sci.* 8:207.

159. Robertson. D.G.E., and R.E. Mosher. Work and power of the leg muscles in soccer kicking. *Abstr. IX Congr. Int. Soc. Biomechanics*, p. 104. Waterloo, Ont., Canada, 1983.

160. Saltin, B., J. Hendriksson, E. Nygaard, and P. Anderson. Fiber types and metabolic potentials of skeletal muscles in sedentary men and endurance runners. *Ann. N.Y. Acad. Sci.* 301:3–29, 1977.

161. Shorten, M.R. Mechanical energy changes and elastic energy storage during treadmill running. *Abstr. IX Int. Cong. Biomechanics*, p. 58. Waterloo, Ont., Canada, 1983.

162. Sjogaard, G. Force velocity curve for bicycle work. *Biomechanics VIA*, pp. 93–99. Baltimore: University Park Press, 1978.

163. Stein, R.B., and E.Y.M. Wong. Analysis of models for the activation and contraction of muscles. *J. Theor. Biol.* 46:307–327, 1974.

164. Stephens, J.A., and A. Taylor. Fatigue of maintained voluntary muscle contraction in man. *J. Physiol. Lond.* 220:1–18, 1972.

165. Street, S.F., and R.W. Ramsey. Sarcoledmma: Transmitter of active tension in frog skeletal muscle. *Science* 149:1379–1380, 1965.

166. Sugi, H. Tension changes during and after stretch in frog muscle fibres. *J. Physiol. Lond.* 225:237–253, 1972.

167. Tameyasu, T., and H. Sugi. The origin of the series elastic component in single crayfish muscle fibres. *Experientia* 35:210–211, 1979.

168. Thomson, D.B. The stretch response of human skeletal muscle in situa. M.Sc. thesis, Simon Fraser University, 1983.

169. Tennant, J.A. The dynamic characteristics of human skeletal muscle modeled from surface stimulation. *Report No. NASA CR-1691, Contract No. NGR-05-020-007. Washington, D.C.: NASA, 1971.*

170. Thys, H., G.A. Cavagna, and R. Margaria. The role played by elasticity in an

exercise involving movements of small amplitude. *Pflugers Arch.* 354:281–286, 1975.

171. Tregear, R.T., and S.B. Marston. The cross-bridge theory. *Ann. Rev. Physiol.* 41:723–736, 1979.

172. Van Atteveldt, H., and A. Crowe. Active tension changes in frog skeletal muscle during and after mechanical extension. *J. Biomechan.* 13:323–331, 1980.

173. Van Leemputte, M., A.J. Spaepen, E.J. Willems, and V.V. Stijnen. Influence of pre-stretch on arm flexion. *Biomechanics VIIIA*, pp. 264–270. Champaign, Ill.: Human Kinetics Publishers, 1983.

174. Viitasalo, J.T. Effects of training on force-velocity characteristics. *Abstr. IX Int. Congr. Biomechanics*, p. 126. Waterloo, Ont., Canada, 1983.

175. Viitasalo, J.T., and P.V. Komi. Force-time characteristics and fiber composition in human leg extensor muscles. *Eur. J. Appl. Physiol.* 40:7–15, 1978.

176. Wallinga-de Jonge, W., H.B.K. Boon, K.L. Boon, P.A.M. Griep, and G.C. Lammeree. Force development of fast and slow skeletal muscle at different muscle lengths. *Am. J. Physiol.* 239:C98–C104, 1980.

177. Wells, J.B. Comparison of mechanical properties between slow and fast muscles. *J. Physiol. Lond.* 178:252–269, 1965.

178. Wells, J.B. Relationship between elastic and contractile components in mammalian skeletal muscle. *Nature* 214:198–199, 1967.

179. Wilkie, D.R. The relation between force and velocity in human muscle. *J. Physiol. Lond.* 110:249–280, 1950.

180. Wilkie, D.R. Measurement of the series elastic component at various times during a single muscle twitch. *J. Physiol. Lond.* 134:527–530, 1956.

181. Wilkie, D.R. *Muscle.* London: Edward Arnold, 1968.

182. Williams, K.R., and P.R. Cavanagh. A model for the calculation of mechanical power during distance running. *J. Biomechan.* 16:115–128, 1983.

183. Woittiez, R.D. A quantitative study of muscle architecture a muscle function. Ph.D. thesis, Vrije Universiteit te Amsterdam, 1984.

184. Wood, G.A., F.S. Pyke, P.F. Le Rossignol, and A.R. Munro. Neuromuscular adaptation to training. *Biomechanics VIIIA*, pp. 306–311. Champaign, Ill.: Human Kinetics Publishers, 1983.

185. Woledge, R.C. The thermoelastic effect of change of tension in active muscle. *J. Physiol. Lond.* 155:187–208, 1961.

186. Yamazaki, Y., G. Metarai, and T. Mano. Segmental stretch reflex activity during hopping movements in man. *Biomechanics VIIIA*, pp. 281–288. Champaign, Ill.: Human Kinetics Publishers, 1983.

187. Zahalak, G.I. A distribution-moment approximation for kinetic theories of muscular contraction. *Math. Biosci.* 55:89–114, 1981.

188. Zahalak, G.I., J. Duffy, P.A. Stewart, H.M. Litchman, R.H. Hawley, and P.R. Pasley. Force velocity-EMG data for the skeletal muscle of athletes. *Report No. NSFGK-40010X-32*, Washington, D.C.: National Science Foundation, 20550, 1973.

189. Ford, L.E., A.F. Huxley, and R.M. Simmons. The relation between stiffness and filament overlap in stimulated frog muscle fitness. *J. Physiol. Lond.* 311:219–249, 1981.

# Developmental Aspects of Maximal Aerobic Power in Children

GARY S. KRAHENBUHL, Ed.D, F.A.S.C.M.
JAMES S. SKINNER, Ph.D., F.A.S.C.M.
WENDY M. KOHRT, M.S.

Maximal aerobic power ($\dot{V}O_2$max) is the highest rate of oxygen consumed by the body in a given period of time during exercise involving a significant portion of the muscle mass. It provides a gross measure of the state of the gas transport system and reflects pulmonary, cardiovascular, and muscular components. $\dot{V}O_2$max has been extensively studied because of its role in limiting the capacity to perform aerobic tasks and because it is considered to be the best single index of health-related physical fitness. Studies on adults have demonstrated $\dot{V}O_2$max to be far less malleable than other attributes (e.g., strength). Accordingly, questions about the importance of the childhood years in developing a high $\dot{V}O_2$max have been raised.

Almost no data on $\dot{V}O_2$max are available for the period of early childhood (2–6 years). A few longitudinal and a large number of cross-sectional studies address the years of later childhood (6–12 years), and many studies dealing with the adolescent years have been published. This review examines data collected from subjects ranging from the 4th to the 16th year. Although a large amount of submaximal data has been published (much of which has been directed at predicting $\dot{V}O_2$max from submaximal data), only the literature on maximal data is reviewed. The focus is on normal children, although references to trained athletic samples are provided where appropriate.

## MEASUREMENT OF $\dot{V}O_2$max

The accurate measurement of $\dot{V}O_2$max requires a bout of exercise to exhaustion, something toward which many children are not motivated. A large number of different tests have been employed to create the exercise stress. These tests have featured different modes of activity, widely differing intensities and durations, continuous and intermittent work, and a variety of considerations unique to children. The literature dealing with $\dot{V}O_2$max in children must be viewed in light of the questions and problems which attend its measurement.

503

*Modes of Exercise*

The two most common modes of exercise found in research on children are cycling on the bicycle ergometer and treadmill walking or running. The bicycle has the advantage of being relatively inexpensive and portable, and is easily calibrated. It has the disadvantage of engaging a smaller muscle mass, which may cause local fatigue to terminate exercise before central mechanisms have been fully extended. Bicycle ergometers must be modified for children [64] to such an extent that they are seldom used for subjects under the age of 6 years. Bicycle work is difficult for some children because rhythm must be maintained to ensure the proper workload [8]. It has also been reported that when tested on the bicycle ergometer, children may improve their $\dot{V}O_2$max merely by becoming accustomed to the test [109].

The treadmill has the advantage of engaging a greater muscle mass; this improves the chances for obtaining a $\dot{V}O_2$max value limited by central factors rather than by limb fatigue [112]. It is also suitable without modification for work with very young children. The treadmill has the disadvantage of being expensive and relatively immobile, and is not as easily calibrated.

Step tests have also been used as the mode of exercise in some remote areas [23, 135]. They are clearly the least popular choice and have not been carefully examined.

Several authors [19, 65, 86] have compared the $\dot{V}O_2$max values gathered from the treadmill and the bicycle ergometer. Ikai and Kitagaw [65] reported that treadmill values on children were 8–19 percent higher than those from the bicycle; this difference falls within the range of what has been reported for adults [62]. However, it should be noted that the data for children were drawn from different subjects in separate studies. Boileau and co-workers [19] studied the same question using 21 subjects aged 11–14 who exercised to exhaustion on both the treadmill and the bicycle ergometer. They noted that the two $\dot{V}O_2$max values were highly related ($r = 0.95$ for L/min and $r = 0.84$ for mL/min·kg), but also reported that the values were 7.4–7.9 percent higher on the treadmill. Maček et al. [86] found similar results (7.5–7.9 percent) for 10 prepubertal boys.

*Intensities and Durations*

Many researchers have utilized tests developed for adults without modification. Others have modified these tests to better suit children or have designed tests specifically for children. Some of the more commonly-used tests have been reviewed by Day [43]. The influence of intensity and duration on $\dot{V}O_2$max has been studied by Paterson and Cunningham [102], who compared three continuous, progressively graded treadmill protocols to exhaustion using 8 10–12-year-old boys. The first pace was a walk (90 m/min), the second was a walk-jog (110 m/min), and the third was a running pace (130 m/min). The walking pace resulted in a lower $\dot{V}O_2max$ and a higher coefficient of variation (8% compared to 3% and 5% for the walk-jog and running paces, respectively).

*Intermittent Versus Discontinuous Tests*
Continuous tests generally involve several minutes of warm-up, followed by continuous exercise to exhaustion wherein the workload is stepped up at fixed intervals (normally 1–3 minutes). Intermittent tests involve bouts of work interspersed with periods of rest ranging from 15 minutes to 24 hours. This sequence continues until the subject is unable to finish a workload. Skinner et al. [118] examined the $\dot{V}O_2max$ values achieved by 144 children who performed two continuous tests and one intermittent multistage test. Each load on the intermittent test was followed by 10 minutes of rest. One of the continuous tests was "brief," with the grade increasing 2.5 percent each minute, while the other was "extended" because the grade was increased 2.5 percent every third minute. As no significant differences in $\dot{V}O_2max$ were noted among these protocols, the authors recommended a brief, continuous test to save time.

*Criteria for the Achievement of $\dot{V}O_2max$*
Peak $\dot{V}O_2$ is the highest value achieved by a subject on a work bout to exhaustion. $\dot{V}O_2max$ equals or exceeds peak $\dot{V}O_2$. Although a subject may achieve a peak value, a valid $\dot{V}O_2max$ is not attained unless certain criteria are met. The most common criterion is a leveling or plateau in $\dot{V}O_2$, where an increase in workload is not accompanied by the expected elevation in $\dot{V}O_2$. Other objective indices include a leveling of heart rate several minutes prior to the final workload, a respiratory exchange ratio in excess of 1.0, and high blood lactate levels. Subjective criteria include blanching of the extremities, breathlessness, strong engagement of the auxiliary respiratory muscles, and a reduced ability to maintain the required work [95].

The evidence of a plateau is less common in children than in adults. Data on the significance of this problem are contradictory. Åstrand [8] noted that 50 percent of all children failed to exhibit a plateau, but ventilatory volume, blood lactic acid, and pulse rates were similar in groups who achieved and who failed to achieve a plateau. This suggests that exercise to true exhaustion occurred, even though a plateau was not exhibited. Cunningham et al. [31], on the other hand, exercised 60 10-year-old boys to exhaustion on two treadmill runs. Changes in grade were selected to produce an increase in $\dot{V}O_2$ of 5 mL/min · kg. An increase of 2.1 mL/min · kg or less was considered to represent a plateau. The reliability between the two tests was $r = 0.27$ in subjects who failed to achieve a plateau on either test, $r = 0.60$ for subjects who showed a plateau on one test, and $r = 0.74$ for subjects who exhibited a plateau on both tests. These data suggest that peak $\dot{V}O_2$ and not $\dot{V}O_2$max was actually measured in many of the subjects failing to achieve a plateau.

The presence or absence of a plateau in children was also examined by Cumming and Friesen [28]. Using an intermittent test on the bicycle ergometer, they observed that only 5 of 20 11–15-year-old boys achieved a plateau in both $\dot{V}O_2$ and heart rate; 8 subjects exhibited a plateau only on heart rate and 2 only on $\dot{V}O_2$. The authors concluded that a plateau may not exist for bicycle exercise in many children.

The failure to achieve a plateau may reflect a lack of effort, inappropriate definitions for what constitutes a plateau, or perhaps some other factor. It has been noted that maximal post-exercise lactic acid levels are much lower in children than in adults. After reviewing the results of a number of studies, Cunningham [30] noted that post-exercise lactate levels in children are 6–7 mM in boys and girls aged 7–10 years. Others have noted that this may not reflect a lack of effort as much as a lower muscle phosphofructokinase activity [50].

Shephard [112] has also argued that the use of adult standards for the leveling criterion (i.e., 150 mL/min [128] or 54 mL/min [93]) are inappropriate for children because of their smaller body mass. He recommended a criterion of 2 mL/min · kg for a 5 percent increase in power output.

Despite the problems associated wtih the assurance of $\dot{V}O_2$max by acceptable criteria, the data on intra-individual variation in $\dot{V}O_2$max are encouraging. Cumming [29] reported a mean variation of 4.5 percent for children exercising to exhaustion on 12 different occasions on the bicycle ergometer. Paterson and Cunningham [102] found mean coefficients of variation of 3, 5, and 8 percent for $\dot{V}O_2$max determined by treadmill walk-jogging, running, and walking, respectively. Boileau et al. [19] reported 4.4 and 5.3 percent variation for the treadmill and bicycle, respectively, and Cunningham et al. [31] reported an average mean difference of 2 percent between two $\dot{V}O_2$max tests. Thus, it appears that acceptable data can be gathered, even if the normal criteria are not always satisfied.

*Diurnal and Seasonal Variation*
Experimental studies frequently require testing and retesting at different times of the day and year. Several investigators have studied diurnal and seasonal variation of $\dot{V}O_2$max in children. Cumming et

al. [29] studied 12 children 13–16 years of age. Each child was tested six times in the morning and six times in the afternoon. No differences in $\dot{V}O_2$max were detected. Baggley and Cumming [10] also examined the seasonal variation in $\dot{V}O_2$max and noted significant differences; these may have been due to limitations that weather imposed on the opportunities available to children for spontaneous outdoor activity.

## NORMAL VALUES OF MAXIMAL AEROBIC POWER

$\dot{V}O_2$max in children has been studied longitudinally [ 2, 5, 6, 11, 61, 70, 106, 121] and cross-sectionally [4, 5, 8, 23, 24, 39, 42, 54, 55, 57, 65, 68, 77, 88, 98, 99, 103, 106, 110, 124, 129, 132, 134, 136, 138]. The basic descriptive information from these studies is contained in Tables 1 to 3. An examination of the year-to-year values from the longitudinal studies (Table 1) reveals that $\dot{V}O_2$max expressed in L/min increases with age for all observations. In reviewing the year-to-year, cross-sectional data for untrained males (Table 2), there are only three occasions where a reduction in $\dot{V}O_2$max (L/min) was observed. Nagle et al. [98] noted a 30 ml · min$^{-1}$ drop between a group of 30 boys with a mean age of 14.9 years and a second group of 30 with a mean age of 16.0 years. Yamaji and Miyashita [136] and Yoshizawa [138] noted drops of 210 and 20 mL/min, respectively, for boys of similar age. Although it is intriguing that these exceptions occur at the same age, it should also be noted that the changes are small and could easily be the result of sampling error in these cross-sectional studies.

When the year-to-year values for untrained females (Table 3) are examined in a similar fashion, a high percentage of the observations reflect the expected increase of $\dot{V}O_2$max (L/min) with age. There are, however, many more exceptions to this trend than noted for males. In females, reductions in $\dot{V}O_2$max were observed between the ages of 12 and 17 in six studies [24, 55, 88, 98, 106, 138]. The most striking dropoff in absolute $\dot{V}O_2$max was reported by Yoshizawa [138] in a cross-sectional study of urban Japanese children. $\dot{V}O_2$max dropped from 2.10 L/min at age 14 to 1.49 L/min at age 15. Although $\dot{V}O_2$max increased at ages 16 and 17, it never reached the value exhibited by 14 year olds. With this one exception, reductions in $\dot{V}O_2$max occurred at a later age and were usually less than 50 mL/min; they also could be due to sampling error.

Longitudinal data on $\dot{V}O_2$max expressed relative to body weight (mL/min · kg) show no particular trend (Tables 1–3). These studies span the ages of 8 to 17 years and feature 19 instances where $\dot{V}O_2$max increased and 17 instances where it decreased. The only conclusion

TABLE 1
*Longitudinal Studies of Maximal Aerobic Power in Children*

| Reference | Country | Age | N | Mode* | L/min | mL/min kg |
|-----------|---------|-----|---|-------|-------|-----------|
| *Males* | | | | | | |
| 2,5,6,106 | Norway | 8.4 | 29 | B | 1.44 | 52.7 |
| | | 9.4 | 29 | B | 1.59 | 51.4 |
| | | 10.4 | 31 | B | 2.02 | 60.0 |
| | | 11.4 | 29 | B | 2.07 | 56.9 |
| | | 12.3 | 30 | B | 2.31 | 58.0 |
| | | 13.0 | 29 | B | 2.70 | 61.4 |
| | | 14.0 | 27 | B | 2.82 | 56.6 |
| | | 15.0 | 27 | B | 3.14 | 56.0 |
| 11 | Canada | 8.1 | 51 | T | 1.46 | 56.4 |
| | | 9.1 | 51 | T | 1.72 | 59.5 |
| | | 10.1 | 51 | T | 1.82 | 56.9 |
| | | 11.1 | 51 | T | 1.96 | 56.3 |
| | | 12.0 | 51 | T | 2.18 | 56.6 |
| | | 13.0 | 51 | T | 2.39 | 55.1 |
| | | 14.1 | 51 | T | 2.73 | 54.6 |
| | | 15.0 | 51 | T | 2.94 | 52.6 |
| 61 | Norway | 10.5 | 20 | T | 1.96 | 54.3 |
| | | 11.5 | 20 | T | 2.17 | 54.7 |
| | | 12.5 | 20 | T | 2.52 | 58.1 |
| 70 | Japan (trained) | 9.7 | 7 | T | 1.29 | 47.5 |
| | | 10.7 | 7 | T | 1.42 | 49.8 |
| | | 11.7 | 7 | T | 1.55 | 49.2 |
| | | 12.7 | 7 | T | 1.77 | 47.0 |
| | | 13.7 | 7 | T | 2.54 | 56.9 |
| | | 14.7 | 7 | T | 3.13 | 63.2 |
| | | 15.8 | 5 | T | 3.00 | 55.0 |
| 70 | Japan (un-trained) | 13.2 | 43 | T | 1.91 | 45.0 |
| | | 14.2 | 43 | T | 2.34 | 48.0 |
| | | 15.2 | 43 | T | 2.61 | 49.1 |
| 106 | Germany | 12 | 28 | B | 2.33 | 57.4 |
| | | 13 | 27 | B | 2.50 | 54.1 |
| | | 14 | 26 | B | 2.83 | 52.1 |
| | | 15 | 27 | B | 3.05 | 51.8 |
| | | 16 | 23 | B | 3.00 | 47.1 |
| | | 17 | 26 | B | 3.11 | 47.5 |
| 121 | Czechoslovakia | 10.9 | 114 | T | 1.77 | 48.0 |
| | | 11.9 | 114 | T | 2.05 | 50.7 |
| | | 12.9 | 114 | T | 2.25 | 50.5 |
| *Females* | | | | | | |
| 2,5,6,106 | Norway | 8.2 | 33 | B | 1.25 | 47.4 |
| | | 9.3 | 33 | B | 1.48 | 48.5 |
| | | 10.3 | 34 | B | 1.79 | 52.4 |
| | | 11.2 | 34 | B | 1.88 | 50.1 |
| | | 12.2 | 34 | B | 2.26 | 53.6 |

*B, bicycle; T, treadmill; S, step test.

one can draw from longitudinal data is that $\dot{V}O_2$max expressed relative to body weight is generally stable over time.

Cross-sectional data on males (Table 2) and females (Table 3) suggests a slightly different picture. The year-to-year differences be-

TABLE 2
*Cross-sectional Studies of Maximal Aerobic Power in Untrained Males*

| Reference | Country | Age | N | Mode* | L/min | mL/min kg |
|---|---|---|---|---|---|---|
| 4 | Norway | 10.3 | 14 | B | 1.61 | 49.3 |
| | | 12.4 | 12 | B | 1.89 | 50.4 |
| | | 14.2 | 15 | B | 2.26 | 47.2 |
| | | 16.3 | 13 | B | 3.12 | 49.3 |
| 8 | Sweden | 4–6 | 10 | T | 1.01 | 49.1 |
| | | 7–9 | 12 | T | 1.75 | 56.9 |
| | | 10–11 | 13 | T | 2.04 | 56.1 |
| | | 12–13 | 19 | T | 2.46 | 56.5 |
| | | 14–15 | 10 | T | 3.53 | 59.5 |
| 23 | Malaysia | 13.3 | 8 | S | 1.71 | 45.7 |
| | | 15.5 | 8 | S | 2.06 | 45.1 |
| 39,42 | Great Britain | 7.2 | 8 | B | 1.19 | 48.9 |
| | | 9.0 | 9 | B | 1.38 | 49.2 |
| | | 10.8 | 9 | B | 1.63 | 46.2 |
| | | 12.8 | 12 | B | 2.05 | 49.6 |
| | | 15.1 | 9 | B | 3.06 | 52.7 |
| 54 | Sweden | 11.6 | 8 | B | 1.87 | 42.4 |
| | | 12.6 | 9 | B | 2.33 | 48.9 |
| | | 13.5 | 8 | B | 2.57 | 51.6 |
| | | 15.5 | 8 | B | 3.24 | 52.6 |
| 55 | France | 11 | 21 | B | 1.74 | 49.1 |
| | | 12 | 34 | B | 1.77 | 47.8 |
| | | 13 | 33 | B | 2.10 | 47.8 |
| | | 14 | 28 | B | 2.34 | 43.9 |
| | | 15 | 18 | B | 2.68 | 48.9 |
| | | 16 | 25 | B | 2.69 | 46.1 |
| 57 | Austria | 11.5 | 10 | B | 1.71 | 47.5 |
| | | 12.6 | 15 | B | 2.05 | 46.5 |
| | | 13.5 | 18 | B | 2.24 | 49.0 |
| | | 14.5 | 16 | B | 2.75 | 50.5 |
| 61 | Norway | 10.5 | 20 | B | 1.96 | 54.3 |
| | | 11.5 | 20 | B | 2.17 | 54.7 |
| | | 12.5 | 20 | B | 2.52 | 58.1 |
| 65 | Japan | 8–10 | 19 | B | 1.31 | 50.0 |
| | | 10–11 | 18 | B | 1.50 | 49.1 |
| | | 11–12 | 21 | B | 1.77 | 51.3 |
| | | 12–13 | 14 | B | 1.90 | 44.9 |
| | | 13–14 | 21 | B | 2.13 | 47.5 |
| | | 14–15 | 19 | B | 2.35 | 49.5 |
| | | 15–16 | 13 | B | 2.47 | 48.1 |
| 68 | Netherlands | 13 | 110 | T | 2.54 | 59.3 |
| | | 14 | 64 | T | 2.82 | 58.8 |
| 77 | United States | 10.1 | 5 | B | 1.74 | 49.8 |
| | | 11.4 | 7 | B | 1.97 | 45.8 |
| | | 12.5 | 6 | B | 1.85 | 45.9 |
| | | 13.4 | 8 | B | 2.51 | 48.8 |
| | | 15.2 | 6 | B | 2.76 | 46.7 |
| 88 | Japan | 12 | 18 | T | 1.93 | 46.4 |
| | | 13 | 54 | T | 2.04 | 45.7 |
| | | 14 | 48 | T | 2.28 | 47.1 |
| | | 15 | 47 | T | 2.45 | 45.7 |
| | | 16 | 50 | T | 2.75 | 49.2 |
| 98 | United States | 13.8 | 30 | T | 3.16 | 54.0 |
| | | 14.9 | 30 | T | 3.74 | 56.3 |
| | | 16.0 | 30 | T | 3.71 | 54.0 |

**TABLE 2**
*(continued)*

| Reference | Country | Age | N | Mode* | L/min | mL/min kg |
|---|---|---|---|---|---|---|
| | | 16.9 | 30 | T | 3.87 | 54.7 |
| 99 | Japan | 12–13 | 10 | B | 1.62 | 40.7 |
| | | 14–15 | 10 | B | 2.09 | 42.0 |
| | | 16–17 | 10 | B | 2.41 | 37.7 |
| 124 | Colombia | 6–7.9 | 84 | T | 1.16 | 50.4 |
| | | 8–9.9 | 90 | T | 1.43 | 52.0 |
| | | 10–11.9 | 84 | T | 1.74 | 52.5 |
| | | 12–13.9 | 65 | T | 2.17 | 51.8 |
| | | 14–16.0 | 70 | T | 2.70 | 54.1 |
| 127 | Finland | 12.1 | 19 | B | 2.13 | 51.1 |
| | | 14.6 | 18 | B | 3.11 | 56.0 |
| | | 16.1 | 19 | B | 3.37 | 56.1 |
| 129 | South Africa | 8–9 | 26 | T | 1.56 | 57.7 |
| | | 10–11 | 36 | T | 2.01 | 56.1 |
| | | 12–13 | 38 | T | 2.35 | 59.4 |
| 132 | Canada | 10.0 | 8 | B | 1.59 | 55.4 |
| | | 13.0 | 8 | B | 2.19 | 44.3 |
| | | 16.0 | 8 | B | 2.95 | 48.3 |
| 136 | Japan | 10.2 | 8 | B | 1.10 | 38.6 |
| | | 11.2 | 8 | B | 1.34 | 39.7 |
| | | 12.3 | 10 | B | 1.43 | 39.8 |
| | | 13.4 | 9 | B | 2.05 | 44.5 |
| | | 14.3 | 10 | B | 2.38 | 50.5 |
| | | 15.1 | 8 | B | 2.17 | 47.1 |
| 138 | Japan (urban) | 10 | 5 | B | 1.38 | 45.1 |
| | | 11 | 22 | B | 1.47 | 41.8 |
| | | 12 | 27 | B | 1.99 | 46.3 |
| | | 13 | 15 | B | 2.50 | 49.5 |
| | | 14 | 15 | B | 2.61 | 50.0 |
| | | 15 | 15 | B | 2.70 | 45.9 |
| | | 16 | 15 | B | 2.68 | 44.6 |
| | | 17 | 15 | B | 3.01 | 48.5 |
| 138 | Japan (rural) | 9 | 8 | B | 1.12 | 42.9 |
| | | 10 | 15 | B | 1.30 | 44.2 |
| | | 11 | 21 | B | 1.51 | 46.6 |
| | | 12 | 27 | B | 1.76 | 47.1 |
| | | 13 | 15 | B | 2.24 | 53.6 |
| | | 14 | 15 | B | 2.60 | 53.2 |
| | | 15 | 15 | B | 2.78 | 53.4 |
| | | 16 | 15 | B | 3.08 | 56.2 |
| | | 17 | 15 | B | 3.13 | 52.3 |

*B, bicycle; T, treadmill; S, step test.

tween groups of males go up in 65 instances and down in 38, while differences between groups of females go up in 40 instances and down in 50. These trends suggest that male children slightly increase their $\dot{V}O_2$max relative to body weight with age, while females show a reduction. This observation has been noted in a number of individual reports [4, 8, 54, 55, 65, 88, 99, 106, 127, 136, 138].

The development of $\dot{V}O_2$max may be examined further by plotting

TABLE 3
*Cross-sectional Studies of Maximal Aerobic Power in Untrained Females*

| Reference | Country | Age | N | Mode* | L/min | mL/min kg |
|---|---|---|---|---|---|---|
| 4 | Norway | 10.5 | 18 | B | 1.41 | 41.6 |
| | | 12.2 | 15 | B | 1.66 | 41.9 |
| | | 14.3 | 13 | B | 2.02 | 36.9 |
| | | 16.3 | 9 | B | 2.07 | 38.4 |
| 5 | Norway, central | 8.2 | 22 | B | 1.27 | 49.4 |
| | | 9.3 | 22 | B | 1.49 | 49.9 |
| | | 10.3 | 23 | B | 1.76 | 53.2 |
| | | 11.2 | 23 | B | 1.85 | 51.2 |
| | | 12.2 | 23 | B | 2.29 | 56.1 |
| | Norway, | 8.2 | 11 | B | 1.22 | 43.3 |
| | peripheral | 9.3 | 11 | B | 1.47 | 45.7 |
| | | 10.2 | 11 | B | 1.85 | 50.7 |
| | | 11.2 | 11 | B | 1.94 | 47.7 |
| | | 12.1 | 11 | B | 2.20 | 48.4 |
| 8 | Sweden | 4–6 | 7 | T | 0.88 | 47.9 |
| | | 7–9 | 14 | T | 1.50 | 55.1 |
| | | 10–11 | 13 | T | 1.70 | 52.4 |
| | | 12–13 | 13 | T | 2.31 | 49.8 |
| | | 14–15 | 11 | T | 2.58 | 46.0 |
| 24 | India | 10.5 | 10 | T | 0.86 | 39.8 |
| | | 12.0 | 16 | T | 1.14 | 40.7 |
| | | 14.0 | 15 | T | 1.13 | 33.7 |
| | | 16.0 | 10 | T | 1.43 | 36.7 |
| 39,42 | Great Britain | 6.9 | 7 | B | 0.98 | 43.2 |
| | | 9.2 | 8 | B | 1.16 | 40.0 |
| | | 11.0 | 11 | B | 1.46 | 39.9 |
| | | 13.2 | 11 | B | 1.88 | 40.3 |
| | | 15.3 | 8 | B | 2.11 | 38.9 |
| 55 | France | 11 | 21 | B | 1.47 | 40.0 |
| | | 12 | 35 | B | 1.55 | 40.9 |
| | | 13 | 21 | B | 1.70 | 36.0 |
| | | 14 | 24 | B | 1.66 | 35.7 |
| | | 15 | 15 | B | 1.83 | 36.4 |
| | | 16 | 11 | B | 1.89 | 35.7 |
| 65 | Japan | 8–10 | 20 | B | 1.11 | 43.4 |
| | | 10–11 | 18 | B | 1.22 | 40.8 |
| | | 11–12 | 20 | B | 1.41 | 41.5 |
| | | 13–14 | 19 | B | 1.56 | 35.0 |
| | | 14–15 | 22 | B | 1.71 | 34.9 |
| | | 15–16 | 14 | B | 1.82 | 37.1 |
| 88 | Japan | 12 | 18 | T | 1.68 | 39.6 |
| | | 13 | 57 | T | 1.69 | 37.9 |
| | | 14 | 49 | T | 1.75 | 36.8 |
| | | 15 | 54 | T | 1.72 | 34.1 |
| | | 16 | 43 | T | 1.77 | 34.7 |
| 98 | United States | 14.0 | 30 | T | 2.27 | 41.1 |
| | | 14.9 | 30 | T | 2.30 | 41.2 |
| | | 16.0 | 30 | T | 2.36 | 40.7 |
| | | 17.0 | 30 | T | 2.34 | 40.2 |
| 99 | Japan | 12–13 | 10 | B | 1.44 | 34.9 |
| | | 14–15 | 10 | B | 1.39 | 28.9 |
| | | 16–17 | 6 | B | 1.37 | 26.7 |
| 106 | Norway | 8 | 33 | B | 1.25 | 47.4 |
| | | 9 | 33 | B | 1.48 | 48.5 |

**TABLE 3**
*(continued)*

| Reference | Country | Age | N | Mode* | L/min | mL/min kg |
|-----------|---------|-----|---|-------|-------|-----------|
|  |  | 10 | 34 | B | 1.79 | 52.4 |
|  |  | 11 | 34 | B | 1.88 | 50.1 |
|  |  | 12 | 34 | B | 2.26 | 53.6 |
|  |  | 13 | 33 | B | 2.48 | 51.8 |
|  |  | 14 | 32 | B | 2.35 | 44.7 |
|  |  | 15 | 30 | B | 2.44 | 43.6 |
| 106 | Germany | 12 | 24 | B | 2.19 | 47.9 |
|  |  | 13 | 24 | B | 2.20 | 43.8 |
|  |  | 14 | 22 | B | 2.26 | 41.8 |
|  |  | 15 | 22 | B | 2.18 | 39.1 |
|  |  | 16 | 17 | B | 1.97 | 33.4 |
|  |  | 17 | 19 | B | 2.06 | 35.0 |
| 110 | Czechoslovakia | 11.8 | 294 | B | 1.48 | 37.5 |
|  |  | 14.8 | 322 | B | 1.93 | 37.6 |
| 134 | United States | 7–9 | 20 | B | 1.59 | 53.5 |
|  |  | 10–11 | 20 | B | 1.87 | 50.7 |
|  |  | 12–13 | 22 | B | 2.40 | 48.7 |
| 138 | Japan, urban | 10 | 7 | B | 1.17 | 35.9 |
|  |  | 11 | 18 | B | 1.37 | 37.1 |
|  |  | 12 | 27 | B | 1.56 | 38.7 |
|  |  | 13 | 15 | B | 1.92 | 40.0 |
|  |  | 14 | 15 | B | 2.10 | 41.3 |
|  |  | 15 | 15 | B | 1.49 | 30.8 |
|  |  | 16 | 15 | B | 1.71 | 31.9 |
|  |  | 17 | 15 | B | 1.79 | 32.0 |
| 138 | Japan, rural | 9 | 8 | B | 1.07 | 36.4 |
|  |  | 10 | 13 | B | 1.21 | 38.5 |
|  |  | 11 | 17 | B | 1.22 | 35.4 |
|  |  | 12 | 24 | B | 1.69 | 40.9 |
|  |  | 13 | 15 | B | 1.93 | 42.6 |
|  |  | 14 | 15 | B | 2.04 | 41.9 |
|  |  | 15 | 15 | B | 2.04 | 39.6 |
|  |  | 16 | 15 | B | 1.95 | 39.5 |
|  |  | 17 | 15 | B | 1.87 | 34.3 |

*B, bicycle; T, treadmill; S, step test.

the mean values reported in all studies reviewed. Figure 1 depicts the relationships between absolute $\dot{V}O_2$max and chronological age in untrained children. To correct for variation introduced due to the mode of exercise, all group values from bicycle tests were multiplied by a factor of 1.075, the approximate difference noted earlier between these two modes of exercise. The curves shown represent those selected following a least-squares, goodness-of-fit test of linear, quadratic, and cubic functions. Using the regression lines as a guide, it is clear that male and female children are similar until approximately age 12. At age 14, the difference in $\dot{V}O_2$max (L/min) between untrained males and females is 25 percent. By age 16, the difference exceeds 50 percent. Differences of this magnitude are also noted in

FIGURE 1

*Relationship in children between V̇O₂max (L/min) and chronological age. Data points are mean values representing 5,793 males and 3,508 females [1, 2, 4, 5, 8, 10–12, 14, 15, 19, 20, 23–25, 28, 33, 36, 39, 42, 46, 48, 50, 51, 53–55, 57, 61, 65, 67–70, 73–77, 81, 89, 91, 94, 96, 98, 99, 101, 104, 106–108, 110, 111, 113, 116–119, 121, 122, 124, 126, 127, 131, 132, 134, 136, 139]. Regression lines were selected using a least-squares, goodness-of-fit test. All group data have been "corrected" to treadmill values (bicycle V̇O₂max × 1.075).*

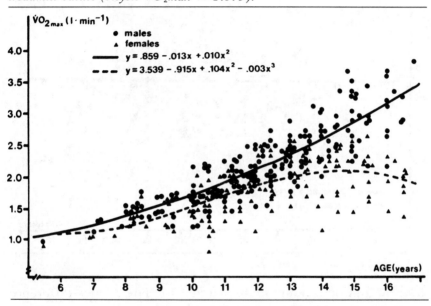

many individual studies [4, 8, 39, 42, 55, 65, 88, 98, 99, 138]. The most common explanations for this phenomenon are (1) the development of greater muscle mass in males and (2) differences between the sexes on time spent performing heavy physical exercise and its social importance.

Figure 2 depicts the relationship between V̇O₂max expressed relative to body weight (mL/min · kg) and age using mean values from the same studies referenced in Figure 1. Again, all group values were corrected by "treadmill" values and least-squares, goodness-of-fit tests were applied in selecting the regression equations. In each case, the linear equation provided the best fit. The regression line for untrained males is almost level (52.8 mL/min · kg at age 6 and increasing to only 53.5 by age 16). The regression line for untrained females slopes downward with age, starting with a value of 52.0 mL/min · kg

FIGURE 2

*Relationship in children between $\dot{V}O_2$max expressed relative to body weight (mL/min · kg) and chronological age (same references as Figure 1). Regression lines were selected using a least-squares, goodness-of-fit test. All group data have been "corrected" to treadmill values (bicycle $\dot{V}O_2$max × 1.075).*

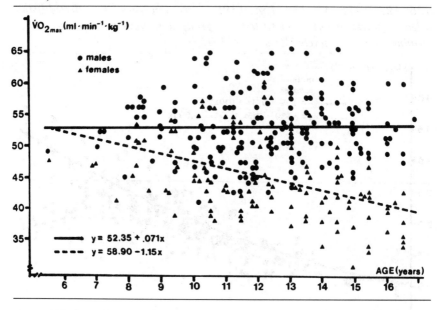

at age 6 and descending to 40.5 at age 16. The relative difference between males and females increases from a negligible 1.5 percent at age 6 to 32 percent at age 16. These same trends have been noted in individual reports [32, 40, 41, 88, 139]. The most common explanation for the discrepancy in mean values for males and females is the greater accumulation of subcutaneous fat in females; this increases the body's mass with tissue that is metabolically less active and which must be transported.

*Trained Children*

A number of investigations have examined $\dot{V}O_2$max in trained males [16–18, 31, 34, 37, 38, 46, 50, 53, 56, 57, 70, 89, 95, 97, 108, 117, 119, 127, 129, 131, 133], trained females [44], and trained males and females [32, 40, 41, 55, 77, 88, 139]. Although the effects of training are examined in a later section, it is of interest to compare the values from trained and untrained subjects. The values for trained groups are higher at all ages, the differences being less in younger children and greater during adolescence. The same trend occurs when comparing the $\dot{V}O_2$max of trained males and females, i.e., the differences are not great in young children but become more pronounced during adolescence. Interestingly, trained males and females are more similar (smaller percentage difference) than are untrained males and females. Using the studies cited above, the relative differences in $\dot{V}O_2$max between trained males and females at 16 years of age are 24 percent for L/min and 18 percent for mL/min · kg, while the relative differences in untrained children are 56 percent and 32 percent, respectively. This discrepancy may support the notion that cultural factors partially explain the plateau and dropoff of absolute (L/min) and the steady decline in relative (mL/min · kg) $\dot{V}O_2$max in untrained females during childhood and adolescence.

## MATURITY-ASSOCIATED VARIATION

As illustrated in Table 4, maximal aerobic power (L/min) in children increases with chronological age. There is no doubt, therefore, that $\dot{V}O_2$max is related to the maturity of the child. At any given chronological age, however, there exists a great deal of variation, not only in $\dot{V}O_2$max, but also in such physical dimensions as height and weight. Many attempts have been made to relate the development of $\dot{V}O_2$max to these structural indices of maturation, as well as to many other growth parameters. The first objective of this section is to identify and discuss the various structural components to which $\dot{V}O_2$max development in children has been related.

Unfortunately, not all of the variation in $\dot{V}O_2$max may be explained by growth in structure. As early as 30 years ago, Asmussen and Heebøll-Nielsen [7] pointed out that both qualitative and quantitative changes occur during growth. Therefore, the latter part of this section focuses on the various functional components of maturation associated with $\dot{V}O_2$max development.

*Structural components*
$\dot{V}O_2$max values in children have been related to many structural parameters for the purpose of standardizing physiologic data. Controversy exists, however, as to exactly what this standard should be. The most commonly used indices have been body weight and height, but there are theoretical arguments for the use of power functions of these variables. Other attempts at standardization have focused on such factors as amount of active tissue, skeletal age, and size of the organs of the oxygen transport system.

*Mass.* Numerous investigations have expressed $\dot{V}O_2$max relative to body mass (mL/min · kg). Åstrand [8, 9] suggested that this parameter gives a good estimate of $\dot{V}O_2$max in nonobese children. Several investigations found very high ($r = 0.80$) correlations between $\dot{V}O_2$max and weight [1, 4, 27, 39, 90, 124], while others reported moderate (0.60 ≤ $r$ < 0.80) correlations [5, 6, 12, 33, 60]. Andersen and Ghesquière [1] found a near linear function between $\dot{V}O_2max$ and age, height, and weight, but multiple regression techniques identified age and weight as the best predictors. In a later study by Andersen et al. [4], body weight and lean body mass were most closely related to $\dot{V}O_2max$ in children 8–17 years of age. They cautioned, however, that these were not the only variables controlling $\dot{V}O_2max$, as a separate analysis on a sample of 8 year olds found much lower correlations than those in the pooled data. A recent investigation by Spurr et al. [124] involving boys of different racial backgrounds showed that 84–89 percent of the variance in $\dot{V}O_2max$ could be explained by body weight.

Few studies have failed to show a significant relationship between $\dot{V}O_2max$ and weight [123, 131]. Šprynarová et al. [123] suggested that the relationship may not have manifested itself in their investigation because of the homogeneity of the subject sample or the impact of some other unidentified factor, but not because the relationship did not exist in the population.

*Lean body mass (LBM).* When $\dot{V}O_2max$ is expressed relative to weight, sex differences become apparent at approximately 11–12 years of age (see Figure 2). It has been suggested that this reflects the increase in adiposity of adolescent girls [4, 6, 9, 26, 67] and that a better unit of reference may be LBM. Regression techniques, however, failed to show much improvement in predictive power when LBM was used in place of total body mass [4–6, 27, 39, 90, 115].

Davies et al. [39] have argued that in an activity where body weight is essentially supported (e.g., bicycle ergometry), $\dot{V}O_2max$ should be related to leg size and composition (i.e., active tissue). They were able to explain more variance in $\dot{V}O_2max$ using leg volume (83%) than with either body weight (72%) or LBM (79%).

Another parameter that has been considered for standardization is cellular mass, which may be determined by measuring total body potassium [27]. However, it does not appear that this index provides any additional advantage over simpler anthropometric measurements in terms of predicting $\dot{V}O_2max$ [18, 27, 48, 131].

*Height.* Many investigators have found the correlation between $\dot{V}O_2max$ and height to be similar to that found between $\dot{V}O_2max$ and weight [1, 5, 6, 27, 33, 39, 90, 131]. In some instances, however, $\dot{V}O_2max$ was not a linear function of height, but rather a power function.

*Power functions of height and mass.* Several authors have discussed theoretical considerations for standardization of physiologic data based on physical dimensions [7, 9, 11, 90, 131]. In each case, length (L) was used as the basic unit of measure to which other measurements were compared. Based on geometric principles, such body areas as the cross-sectional area of a muscle should then be proportional to $L^2$. Volumes of such compartments as the lungs or heart should be proportional to $L^3$. Since $\dot{V}O_2$max is a measure of volume per unit time, it should theoretically be proportional to $L^3/L^1$, or $L^2$ (i.e., $\dot{V}O_2$max $\alpha$ $L^2$).

This line of reasoning may also be used to relate $\dot{V}O_2$max to mass. Using the basic principle that M $\alpha$ $L^3$, arithmetic manipulation shows that $M^{2/3}$ $\alpha$ $L^2$. Since $\dot{V}O_2$max $\alpha$ $L^2$, $\dot{V}O_2$max $\alpha$ $M^{2/3}$ also follows. In effect, this theory suggests that $\dot{V}O_2$max may not be linearly related to weight and height, but rather to weight$^{2/3}$ and height$^2$. A similar theory, which includes an elastic component for biological propor-tions, has been discussed by Bailey et al. [11], who suggested using weight$^{3/4}$ and height$^{2.25}$.

Several studies have focused on various exponential relationships between $\dot{V}O_2$max and height or weight. Andersen and colleagues [1, 4–6] showed that predictive power was not improved by using height$^2$ rather than height. On the other hand, based on longitudinal data comparing increases in height and weight with increases in $\dot{V}O_2$max, Bailey et al. [11] found $\dot{V}O_2$max $\alpha$ height$^{2.46}$. Since this was very close to one of the proposed dimensional theories, they suggested using the relationship $\dot{V}O_2$max $\alpha$ height$^{2.25}$ (analogous to $\dot{V}O_2$max $\alpha$ weight$^{3/4}$) when improvement due to growth must be controlled. McMiken [90] concluded that $\dot{V}O_2$max in children may be predicted using a power function of mass ($\dot{V}O_2$max = 0.076 $M^{0.88}$), except when the children are aerobically trained, in which case a linear function between $\dot{V}O_2$max and mass may be expected. Other investigations demonstrated the following relationships: $\dot{V}O_2$max $\alpha$ height$^{2.2}$ [24], $\dot{V}O_2$max $\alpha$ height$^{1.98}$ [131], and $\dot{V}O_2$max $\alpha$ weight$^{2/3}$ [68]. Åstrand [9] concluded that actual results are not identical to results predicted from body dimension theories and that differences may be due to biological factors that modify muscular function (e.g., hormones).

Another possible explanation for the failure of experimental data to conform to body dimension theories is that many of the investi-gations have used cross-sectional data. Shephard et al. [115] used longitudinal data to reexamine the question of how to optimally stan-dardize $\dot{V}O_2$max in children. They found that $\dot{V}O_2$max correlated well with height, height$^2$, height$^3$, total body mass, and lean body mass, and suggested that more precise exponents are not essential.

*Vital capacity (VC).* Andersen and colleagues [4–6], Åstrand [8], and McMiken [90] looked at the relationship between $\dot{V}O_2$max development and VC growth in children. Åstrand [8] and Andersen et al. [4–6] found linear relationships between these variables, with correlation coefficients ranging from 0.58 to 0.70 in all groups, except in a sample of 8-year-old girls where $r = 0.08$. McMiken [90] tested age, height, mass, LBM, and VC as predictors of $\dot{V}O_2$max. The zero-order correlation coefficient between $\dot{V}O_2$max and VC was 0.87, but VC did not provide much additional power in the multiple regression model than that already attributed to body mass.

*Heart volume (HV)*. Eriksson [48] found that HV increases with age, but that there is actually no change when it is related to height[3]. Shephard et al. [113] and von Döbeln and Eriksson [131] reported significant correlations between $\dot{V}O_2$max and HV. In another report by Eriksson [49], a high correlation between $\dot{V}O_2$max and HV was demonstrated in trained female swimmers. A follow-up study seven years later, however, found no change in HV despite a 29 percent decrease in $\dot{V}O_2$max.

*Skeletal age*. Skeletal age (also referred to as biological age) is most commonly determined by hand-wrist x-ray and is used as an index of maturity in children. In a study involving 11-year-old boys, Bouckaert et al. [20] found skeletal ages ranging from 10 to 14 years. To determine the relationship between $\dot{V}O_2$max and skeletal age, two subgroups were formed: an advanced skeletal group ($\bar{x} = 156$ months) and a retarded skeletal age group ($\bar{x} = 128$ months). They found that both $\dot{V}O_2$max and HV were significantly greater in the advanced group.

Kemper and Verschuur [68] found mean skeletal ages of 12.9, 12.9, 13.8, and 13.8 years for 13-year-old boys and girls and 14-year-old boys and girls, respectively. They determined that $\dot{V}O_2$max increased linearly with skeletal age but that the increase was proportional to increases in height and mass. When $\dot{V}O_2$max was expressed relative to body mass or LBM, a significant inverse relationship with skeletal age was observed. They suggested that this was in accordance with the body dimension theory, which states that $\dot{V}O_2$max increases in proportion to mass$^{2/3}$. Krahenbuhl and Pangrazi [73] also investigated the relationship between $\dot{V}O_2$max (mL/min · kg) and skeletal age in 10-year-old boys, but found a nonsignificant correlation ($r = -0.32$).

*Velocity curves*. Velocity curves have been used to illustrate changes in such parameters as height and $\dot{V}O_2$max during growth. By monitoring the rate of change, the age of growth spurt could be identified.

The Saskatchewan longitudinal growth study [22] monitored 83 boys for nine years (ages 8–16 years) to produce standards for $\dot{V}O_2$max development. Rate of development increased markedly at approximately 12.5 years, presumably corresponding to the takeoff in height velocity. Peak velocity occurred around 14.5 years of age.

A longitudinal study of Japanese boys [70] found that peak height velocity (PHV) and peak weight velocity (PWV) occurred between 13 and 14 years of age. Marked increases in $\dot{V}O_2$max coincided with this growth period, most likely as a result of growth in physical dimensions. The authors suggested that additional increases or decreases in $\dot{V}O_2$max after the growth spurt were due to changes in level of activity. A study from the Netherlands [67] found a similar PHV in boys, but did not relate it to $\dot{V}O_2$max. Rutenfranz et al. [105], in a longitudinal investigation of Norwegian and West German children, found that $\dot{V}O_2$max increased linearly up to the age of PHV, then gradually leveled off. Šprynarová [122] and Ikai and Kitagawa [65] reported similar trends.

*Overview.* It is apparent that many structural parameters have been considered in an attempt to factor out the effects of maturation on $\dot{V}O_2$max. Unfortunately, a "best" index has not yet been identified. Even if the effects of weight, height, and skeletal age are controlled, variation in $\dot{V}O_2$max still exists as chronological age changes. Body weight and height have surfaced repeatedly as good predictors of $\dot{V}O_2$max. There appear to be more question marks as to whether height$^2$, height$^3$, or some other power function should be used. Therefore, weight is probably the best general index for controlling the effects of maturation on $\dot{V}O_2$max in children.

*Functional Components*
The functional parameters that may be associated with maturity-related variance in $\dot{V}O_2$max have not been studied in the same manner as the structural parameters. Rather than using them to standardize $\dot{V}O_2$max in children, functional components have been proposed to be the source of variation not explainable by changes in structure. McMiken [90], for example, suggests that $\dot{V}O_2$max development is definitely related to physical growth but that observed deviations from expected values are due to the modification of biological functions during growth.

Generally speaking, functional changes during growth have not often been directly related to changes in $\dot{V}O_2$max, except in the case of training studies. Therefore, this section focuses on hypothetical variance in $\dot{V}O_2$max based on observed functional changes in children and deals only with function during maximal exercise.

*Cardiovascular function.* It appears that at a given work load, children and adults maintain similar levels of gas exchange, blood gases, and cardiac output (Q). There must be differences in the function of the cardiovascular system, however, since a 5-year-old child has a vital capacity about one-fifth that of an adult and a stroke volume (SV) about one-quarter [58]. Unfortunately, there is a paucity of data documenting the changes in maximal $\dot{Q}$, SV, and oxygen extraction (AVD) that accompany growth. Much of the work in this area has either been carried out at submaximal work loads or has looked at changes due to physical training.

Eriksson [48] compared maximal exercise responses of 11- to 13-year-old boys with typical values from adults. He found that AVD values were comparable to those of adults, while SV and $\dot{Q}$ were significantly lower. When SV was expressed relative to height$^3$, the difference between children and adults was no longer apparent.

Andersen and colleagues [1, 3] compared some cardiovascular parameters in a cross-section of 10 and 14 year olds and reported that the increase in oxygen pulse ($O_2$ pulse) from age 10 to 14 was different for boys and girls [1]. They hypothesized that this was due to an improved AVD in the 14-year-old boys. A later report [3] found that the increase in $O_2$ pulse in girls was linearly related to age; the same relationship was observed in boys up to age 12, after which there was a greater increase in $O_2$ pulse. When $O_2$ pulse was expressed relative to body weight, a linear relationship was established at all ages.

*Ventilatory function.* Maximal minute ventilation ($\dot{V}_E$max) increases with age [8, 24, 58]. Chatterjee et al. [24] found that the increase in $\dot{V}_E$max was proportional to height$^{1.7}$. They also reported that the increase in maximal tidal volume was proportional to height$^{2.9}$. Despite the increase in $\dot{V}_E$max with age, Eriksson [48] found a lower $\dot{V}_E/\dot{V}O_2$ during maximal exercise in 11-year-old boys as compared to adults, suggesting that this was because children have a lower anaerobic capacity. This would limit their ability to work at the supramaximal intensities normally used to determine $\dot{V}O_2$max. Eriksson [48] further showed that the alveolar ventilation ($\dot{V}_A$) at a given $\dot{V}O_2$ ($\dot{V}_A/\dot{V}O_2$) at $\dot{V}O_2$max was similar to values observed in adults, as was the alveolar-arterial oxygen difference ($PAO_2 - PaO_2$).

*Total hemoglobin ($Hb_T$).* Since oxygen is transported by hemoglobin, Åstrand [14] proposed comparing $Hb_T$ to mass and $VO_2$max. Although $Hb_T$ should be proportional to body size, it was found that young boys (<12 years) had only 78 percent of the $Hb_T$ of older boys per kilogram of body weight. $\dot{V}O_2$max and $Hb_T$ were highly correlated ($r = 0.97$) in children and young adults. Von Döbeln [131], on the other hand, reported a nonsignificant correlation between $\dot{V}O_2$max and $Hb_T$ ($r = 0.48$).

Hemoglobin concentration in children is lower than that of the average adult. Eriksson [48] found the average hemoglobin concentration in 11–12-year-old boys to be 12.3 g/dl, while Shephard et al. [113] recorded average concentrations of 14.1 g/dl in girls and boys aged 9–13 years. Average concentrations in adult men and women are 15.8 g/dl and 14.0 g/dl, respectively.

*Blood lactate.* Maximal blood lactate concentrations tend to be lower in children than in adults. Åstrand [8] observed blood lactate concentrations of 6.6 mM in 5-year-old children, compared to 12.1 mM for adults. Davies et al. [42] found concentrations ranging from 6 to 10 mM in children aged 7–15 years. Eriksson and Saltin [54] noted increasing lactate concentrations with advancing age and suggested that low phosphofructokinase activity was one reason [50]. Another explanation was offered by Maček and Vavra [84], who found that children activate their aerobic energy systems earlier and faster than adults and postulated that this makes a high glycolytic capacity unnecessary. Sady [107] also reported quicker $\dot{V}O_2$ and HR responses in children, but the age at which oxygen kinetics "mature" is not yet resolved.

*Overview.* The fact that children differ from adults in some aspects of biological function is not disputed. The effects of these differences on $\dot{V}O_2$max, however, have not been studied in depth. Some possible sources of functional variation have been noted above, but many others (such as enzymatic and hormonal changes) are also likely candidates. The paucity of longitudinal data documenting absolute change, as well as rate of change, in these functional parameters makes it difficult to be more definitive regarding their effect on $\dot{V}O_2$max development.

## TRAINING EFFECTS

### Problems

Just as there are certain problems inherent in testing the maximal aerobic power of children, there are difficulties in studying the effects of training. In the case of adults, one can reasonably assume that any changes that occur are due to the intervention being studied (e.g., training). With children, on the other hand, the simultaneous effects of growth, development, and maturation may mask or actually be greater than those brought about by a particular training program.

Although the need for a control group is evident in any training study, this need is even more important in longitudinal studies on children to account for changes due to growth and maturation. There is always the possibility of preselection when investigators ask for volunteers, when they study athletes or those in sports clubs, or when they request parental permission for a child's participation. Shephard and co-workers [114] also point out that there may be seasonal differences in activity and subsequently in $\dot{V}O_2$max; this variation could make interpretation of training programs difficult, if not impossible. In other words, the investigator should be aware of the seasonal activity patterns of the children being studied and attempt to study the effects of training during relatively stable periods.

Several authors [92, 125, 137] have suggested that preadolescent children tend to have a fairly high level of physical activity. As a result, there should be relatively little variation in their maximal aerobic power. To be effective, therefore, any training program would have to require much more activity than the children might normally get.

Because there are difficulties in obtaining a plateau in $\dot{V}O_2$ in small children [31, 109], the investigator cannot be certain that preadolescent subjects push themselves to their $\dot{V}O_2$max on every test. A good example of this problem can be seen in the study on 6–7-year-old children by Schmücker and Hollmann [109]. After a 10-day familiarization period, the "maximal" $\dot{V}O_2$ of these children rose 8 percent (see Table 4). There were no further increases after four more weeks of unspecified training. Had these children been tested only once before and after training, the results and conclusions of this study would have been quite different.

Most of the training data on children are presented as mean values grouped by age. As discussed later, there are questions about differences in trainability of children before and after puberty. Ideally, therefore, data should be adjusted for differences in maturation (e.g., the adolescent growth spurt). Whether there should also be adjustments for differences in body type is unclear. Although variations in physique are seen before puberty, Dupertuis and Michael [45] found that mesomorphic children were more active and tended to mature sooner than ectomorphs. Unfortunately, they used only extreme somatotypes and no extreme endomorphs were studied.

*Effects of Training*
A general overview of the effects of various training programs on the maximal aerobic power of children can be seen in Table 4. Although there might be some question about the "ideal" units to use for $\dot{V}O_2$max in children, all data herein are reported in milliliters per minute per kilogram of body weight, whether the authors did so or not. One reason is that most, if not all, longitudinal studies carried out over a sufficient period reported significant increases in absolute $\dot{V}O_2$max (L/min). The authors then had to state that this was primarily due to increases in body weight. Because the absolute value is so dependent on body size and because children have such

large differences in body size, it is difficult to evaluate changes due to training alone.

Several authors have questioned whether children are trainable [9, 13, 29, 70, 109, 125, 137]. A study often cited as suggesting that children cannot be trained is that by Cumming et al. [29]. After training for two months beforehand, six boys and six girls aged 13 to 16 years came to a running camp for a week, where they ran long distances each day. Maximal aerobic power was tested twice daily on a bicycle ergometer, and no difference was found over the six days of testing. There are a number of problems with this study which reduce its applicability to the question of trainability. First, all the children had trained before and already exhibited high $\dot{V}O_2$max values (49 and 65 mL/min · kg for girls and boys, respectively), so little improvement should have been expected. This is especially so in the short span of only six days. Because of the specificity of training, the bicycle ergometer probably was not the best testing mode to pick up any changes, had they occurred. With all the running, one wonders why they should be tested twice a day. In fact, it is interesting that $\dot{V}O_2$max did not decrease due to fatigue.

Results in Table 4 show that the maximal aerobic power of children from 8 to 14 years of age can be significantly increased following regular, intensive training. While it is difficult to generalize from this limited number of studies, it appears that endurance exercise was more effective than intermittent programs, even though several studies used intermittent exercise because "it was the type that children seemed to do." In general, physical education programs (or slight additions to them) were not effective for improving maximal aerobic power. On the other hand, there were improvements in running speed and other indices of performance.

As expected, maximal values on the bicycle ergometer were lower than those found on the treadmill. The only exception was the mean value for 10-year-old twins in the study by Weber et al. [132]. In those studies showing significant improvements with training, values on the bicycle ergometer rose from 41–44 to 45–52 mL/min · kg in most studies and from 52–54 to 56–59 mL/min · kg in two studies from Sweden. In the case of the treadmill, there were increases from 45–55 to 50–60 mL/min · kg. Thus, there were increases of 4–5 mL/min · kg with effective training programs, regardless of the mode of testing. This average rise of 8–10 percent is similar to that found in many training studies on adults.

As mentioned earlier, there is a controversy whether training can increase $\dot{V}O_2$max during periods of rapid growth. For example, Ilmarinen and Rutenfranz [66] hypothesized that there would be limited effects of extra training below the age of 12 years and that

TABLE 4
*Effect of Training on Maximal Aerobic Power of Children*

| Reference | Subjects | | | Test Mode | $\dot{V}O_2$ max (mL/min kg) | | Training Program |
| | N | Sex | Age | | Pre | Post | |
|---|---|---|---|---|---|---|---|
| Yoshida et al. [137] | 25 | M+F | 5 | T | 42.1 | 38.9 | 14 mos; 750–1500m: run 5 x/wk |
| | 21 | M+F | 5 | | 43.5 | 41.6 | run 1 x/wk |
| | 11 | M+F | 5 | | 41.6 | 42.8 | control |
| Schmücker and Hollmann [109] | 13 | M+F | 6–7 | B | 41.7 | 44.7 | 10 d habituation; 4 wks training, no difference |
| Brown et al. [21] | 2 | F | 8–9 | T | 36.8 | 48.7* | 12 wks; run 4–5 x 1–2 hr/wk |
| | 2 | F | 10–11 | | 44.6 | 55.6* | |
| | 3 | F | 12–13 | | 46.2 | 56.8* | |
| Lussier and Buskirk [80] | 16 | M+F | 8–12 | T | 55.6 | 59.4* | 12 wks; run 4 x 45 min/wk |
| Bar-Or and Zwiren [15] | 10 | M+F | 8–12 | T | 53.1 | 53.9 | Control |
| | 22 | M | 9–10 | | 50.2 | 49.4 | 9 wks; interval run 2–4 × 40 min/wk |
| | 24 | F | 9–10 | | 44.2 | 46.1 | |
| | 22 | M | 9–10 | | 50.0 | 49.3 | control |
| | 24 | F | 9–10 | | 45.0 | 43.8 | control |
| Vaccaro and Clarke [130] | 15 | M+F | 9–11 | T | 47.3 | 55.4* | 7 mos; swim 4 × 3,000–10,000 yds |
| | | | | | 46.8 | 49.0 | control |
| Stewart and Gutin [125] | 13 | M | 10–12 | T | 49.8 | 49.5 | 8 wks; interval run 4 × 22 min/wk |
| | 11 | | | | 48.4 | 49.2 | control |
| Weber et al. [132] | 4 | M | 10 | B | 55.6 | 66.0* | 10 wks; run 3 × 1 mi; step 3 × 8.5 min; cycle 1 × to exhaustion |
| | 4 | M | 13 | | 43.9 | 48.6* | |
| | 4 | M | 16 | | 48.1 | 56.3* | |
| | 4 | M | 10 | | 55.2 | 58.8 | control twin |
| | 4 | M | 13 | | 44.6 | 49.0 | control twin |
| | 4 | M | 16 | | 48.4 | 49.2 | control twin |

|  |  |  |  |  |  |  |  |
|---|---|---|---|---|---|---|---|
| Ekblom [47] | 6 | M | 11 | B | 53.9 | 59.4* | 6 mos; play and run 2 × 45 min/wk |
|  | 7 | M | 11 |  | 49.9 | 50.2 | control |
| Eriksson et al. [50] | 8 | M | 11–13 | B | 41.8 | 47.4* | 4 mos; run and exercise 3 × 1 hr/wk |
|  | 5 | M | 11–13 |  | 52.6 | 56.0* | 6 wks; cycle ergometer 2 × 20–50 min/wk |
| Eriksson and Koch [53]<br>Massicotte and MacNab [87] | 9 | M | 11–13 | B | 41.0 | 47.8* | 4 mos; run 3 × 1 hr/wk<br>6 wks; cycle 3 × 12 min/wk at: |
|  | 9 | M | 11–13 | B | 46.7 | 51.8* | HR = 170–180 |
|  | 9 | M | 11–13 |  | 47.4 | 48.0 | HR = 150–160 |
|  | 9 | M | 11–13 |  | 46.6 | 48.2 | HR = 130–140 |
|  | 9 | M | 11–13 |  | 45.7 | 44.2 | control |
| Bar-Or et al. [16] | 20 | M | 11–12 | T | 50.5 | (est.) | 2 yrs; track and field 3 x/wk |
|  |  | M | 12–13 |  | 52.6 |  |  |
|  |  | M | 13–14 |  | 61.1* |  |  |
| Daniels and Oldridge [37] | 6 | M | 12 | T | 59.5 | 58.3 | 22 mos; running |
|  | 14 | M | 13 |  | 60.6 | 59.6 | 12 mos; running |
| Šprynarová [121] | 22 | M | 11–13 | T | 49.5 | 51.3 | 3 yrs; testing 1/yr: athletics |
|  | 31 | M | 11–13 |  | 47.6 | 51.1 | basketball |
|  | 38 | M | 11–13 |  | 47.5 | 49.8 | various sports |
|  | 23 | M | 11–13 |  | 47.8 | 50.0 | nonathletes |

*Significant difference.

improved functional capacity would occur mainly between the ages of 12 and 16 years. Eriksson [48], on the other hand, found no apparent advantage in training before or after adolescence.

The question about the trainability of preadolescents was raised when a number of studies showed little or no rise in $\dot{V}O_2$max with training before puberty but substantial increases after puberty [13, 70, 71, 92, 109, 121, 132]. A good example of this is the three-year study of young Czech swimmers by Šprynarová and co-workers [123]. Little difference in $\dot{V}O_2$max was found from the ages of 12 to 14 in these 17 boys and girls, but both showed a marked rise by the age of 15. Similarly, Koch [71] found a 20 percent rise in $\dot{V}O_2$max from age 15 to 16 years in a group of boys "highly motivated for sports and vigorous exercises," with little or no effect during previous years of activity. This implies that younger children are less motivated to train.

Some of the controversy could be due to the inadequacy of the training programs, as discussed previously. Mirwald et al. [92] list several other reasons why this may be so. They are:

1. There is little variation in the physical activity of preadolescent children.

2. Adolescents have a greater range of formalized activities (i.e., there is more opportunity), and these activities are more intense. For example, Flandrois et al. [55] studied young swimmers and found that the 11-year-olds swam only 5 hours per week, while 15–16 year olds swam 10 hours per week.

3. Some children become more active over time because of a genetic predisposition toward certain activities, self-selection, or success. Others do less activity and may drop out, further widening the gap.

One study often cited to support the theory that there is less trainability before puberty is that of Weber et al. [132]. Using identical twins as controls, they trained four twins at each of the following ages: 10, 13, and 16 years. Results suggested that the 10-year-old and 16-year-old twins had much greater improvements in $\dot{V}O_2$max than did the 13 year olds. This was interpreted by the authors and all who cited them to mean that children are less trainable around the age of puberty.

Because the authors reported the maximal aerobic power of the subjects in liters per minute, however, the data were difficult to evaluate without reference to body size. Dividing the mean $\dot{V}O_2$max (L/min) by the mean weights of the subjects produced some extremely high values (Table 4). Thus, it appeared that the 10-year-old twins had values of 1.58 L/min (55–56 mL/min · kg) on the bicycle ergometer before training. As mentioned earlier, these values were higher than those found on the treadmill in other studies cited. The 10-

week training program consisted of (1) running one mile at top speed three times a week, (2) stepping for 8.5 minutes at a heart rate of 162 beats per minute three times a week, and (3) cycling intermittently to exhaustion once a week. After this program, the trained 10-year-old twins increased their mean $\dot{V}O_2$max to 1.96 L/min or 66 mL/min · kg on a bicycle ergometer. Given the high values before training and the near world-class level after only 10 weeks in such a program, it is difficult to accept either the results or the conclusions of this study.

Kobayashi et al. [70] studied seven young boys who trained by running 1–1.5 hours per day, 4–5 times per week from the age of 9 to 14 years. After statistical smoothing of the data, the largest increase in $\dot{V}O_2$max seem to occur during the adolescent growth spurt, as measured by the time of peak height velocity (PHV). At ages more than one year before the onset of PHV, there was little effect of training on these boys, while about one year prior to PHV and thereafter, the increase in $\dot{V}O_2$max was greater than that normally due to age and growth. In this regard, Daniels and Oldridge [37] found no change in $\dot{V}O_2$max (mL/min · kg) during the 12 months of most rapid growth but admitted that their subjects already had very high values (59–60 mL/min · kg) and that little improvement should be expected.

Using a similar approach, Rutenfranz et al. [105] examined the longitudinal results of annual tests of representative samples of 56 boys and 56 girls in Norway and West Germany. $\dot{V}O_2$max (L/min) increased linearly with biological age up to the age of PHV and then plateaued; this increase was almost entirely due to increased body size. Relative to body weight, Norwegian girls showed a slight rise and German girls no difference in $\dot{V}O_2$max up to PHV. Both samples had reductions after PHV. With the boys, Norwegians showed no difference in $\dot{V}O_2$max (mL/min · kg) from PHV − 5 years to PHV + 2 years, while Germans had no difference up to PHV and a drop thereafter. The reductions after PHV were thought to be related to the onset of a more sedentary lifestyle, especially among the girls. Since these children were not engaged in a formalized training study, no inference can be drawn about their trainability. However, the data do suggest that there is little difference in $\dot{V}O_2$max (mL/min · kg) among representative samples of children during the years before adolescence.

Mirwald et al. [92] looked at 14 active and 14 inactive boys with complete data from a group of 205 seven year olds followed until the age of 17 years. While there were no differences in height at any time or in $\dot{V}O_2$max between the two groups before the onset of the adolescent growth spurt, the active boys had larger gains in $\dot{V}O_2$max before, during, and after PHV. In other words, the change was larger and lasted longer in the active boys. The mean peak $\dot{V}O_2$max velocity (i.e., the time of the most pronounced change) occurred after the mean PHV in both active and inactive boys; this supports the conclusions from the study of Kobayashi et al. [70]. Mirwald et al. [92] concluded that activity during the preadolescent period had no significant effect on $\dot{V}O_2$max and that adolescence is the critical period for increasing maximal aerobic power.

Eriksson and Saltin [54] showed that muscles of children had lower absolute levels but approximately the same relative levels of adenosine triphosphate (ATP) as that found in adults. In other words, they had less muscle, but the muscle ATP concentration was similar. Glycogen and CP concentrations tend to be lower in muscles of children. Maximal attainable levels of lactic acid are considerably less in children. In a review article, Cunningham [30] stated that maximal values of blood lactate ranged from 6–7 mM at age seven to 10–12 mM at age 15 in both boys and girls. Corresponding values for men are around 17–18 mM [52]. Thus, it appears that the anaerobic capacity of children is considerably lower and increases after adolescence. Bar-Or [13] suggests that it is this improvement in anaerobic capacity with training that allows children to work closer to their $\dot{V}O_2$max and accounts for much of the improved performance seen, even though the $\dot{V}O_2$max is not changed. He also implies that $\dot{V}O_2$max may not be a valid or sensitive indicator of maximal aerobic power in prepubescent children but does not suggest an alternative measure.

Although studies on rats suggest that lactate production is related to the level of circulating testosterone [78], this has not been confirmed in humans. Mirwald et al. [92] also suggest that higher testosterone secretion increases strength and the maximal production of lactic acid, as well as increasing the amount of erythrocytes and hemoglobin in the blood. Accordingly, all of these factors should magnify the effects of training on $\dot{V}O_2$max after adolescence.

Children already have high levels of such oxidative enzymes as succinate dehydrogenase, but training has been shown to increase the oxidative capacity of both fast- and slow-twitch muscle fibers, along with an 8 percent rise in $\dot{V}O_2$max [51]. As well, Oseid and Hermansen [100] showed that the substrate utilization of 13-year-old boys was the same as that of adult men during prolonged exercise, i.e., they had the same metabolic responses to exercise.

### Overview

From this review, no definitive statement can be made about the optimal age of training (i.e., before, during, or after puberty). It does appear, however, that the maximal aerobic power of children can be significantly increased in response to a vigorous, intensive training program and that this response is not different from that seen with adults.

## RELATIONSHIP OF $\dot{V}O_2$max TO PERFORMANCE

The relationship in children between $\dot{V}O_2$max and endurance performance has been studied by a number of investigators [36–38, 40, 57, 59, 60, 73, 79, 81, 89, 97, 101, 117, 127]. At a given age, the relationship between $\dot{V}O_2$max (L/min) and endurance performance is not strong. The relationship between $\dot{V}O_2$max relative to body weight (mL/min · kg) and endurance performance is generally moderate to high. However, when children are followed longitudinally, their running performance improves, while their $\dot{V}O_2$max (mL/min · kg) does not [37, 38]. Increases in absolute $\dot{V}O_2$max that occur with age have been associated with the improvement in running performance [97], but this is probably not a cause-and-effect phenomenon. Rather, it has been shown that the oxygen requirement (mL/min · kg) of a fixed running pace decreases with age. Therefore, older children are more economical than younger children [8, 37, 38] and reqire a smaller percentage of their $\dot{V}O_2$max to sustain a given pace.

It has been suggested that the young child is less economical due to the higher stride frequency necessitated by shorter limbs [9]. Davies [40] believes that the frequency of leg movement in children is not optimally matched to the force required to produce the most economic conversion of aerobically produced energy to mechanical work.

Using 16 young boys aged 11–15, Sjödin [117] examined the relationship of $\dot{V}O_2$max, running economy (the oxygen requirement of a set submaximal pace), and the running velocity at which the onset of blood lactate accumulation ($V_{OBLA}$) occurs with performance (pace). The relationship between $\dot{V}O_2$max and performance ranged from $r = 0.35$ for 100 m to $r = 0.77$ for 4.2 km. The relationship between $V_{OBLA}$ and performance exceeded that for $\dot{V}O_2$max in every instance but one. Sjödin concluded that a subject with a low aerobic power might compensate with a higher running economy; this might place his $V_{OBLA}$ at about the same pace as a runner with a higher $\dot{V}O_2$max but poorer economy.

It is probably safe to conclude that $\dot{V}O_2$max is not as strongly related to performance in children as it is in adults. Investigators have noted that other factors contribute significantly to the prediction of distance-running capabilities or can remove the association between $\dot{V}O_2$max and performance. Cureton et al. [36] and Gutin et al. [60] noted that when percentage fat was partialled out, the relationship between $\dot{V}O_2$max (mL/min · kg) and performance became nonsignificant. Krahenbuhl and Pangrazi [73] and Cureton et al. [36] also noted the importance of sprint speed. Among normal children, it has been shown that better runners run at a greater proportion of their maximal running speed and thereby experience greater postrun blood lactate levels [73]. This may mean that better runners push themselves harder. Komi et al. [72], however, reported the relationship between $V_{OBLA}$ and the percentage of slow-twitch (type I) fibers in adults to be $r = 0.78$. Thus, rather than giving better efforts, normal children who are good runners may possess muscle metabolic profiles that feature a larger percentage of fast-twitch fibers. This would explain why children who are better distance runners are also faster sprinters, but while performing at the same percentage $\dot{V}O_2$max and higher percentage maximal sprint speeds, they have higher post-exercise blood lactate levels [73].

## MOST APPROPRIATE UNIT OF MEASUREMENT

The use of L/min as the unit of expression for $\dot{V}O_2$max in studying children is clearly not supported. As noted in an earlier section, both height and weight have been shown to relate highly with $\dot{V}O_2$max and serve to control for the effects of growth. Although theoretical arguments abound, the best expression appears to be the old standard, mL/min · kg.

The use of $\dot{V}O_2$max as an index of cardiorespiratory capacity has been reviewed elsewhere [35, 120, 128], with the universal conclusion that $\dot{V}O_2$max should be expressed relative to LBM (mL/min · kgLBM). The rationale for this conclusion is that the resultant value is not contaminated by body fatness, which adds to the body's weight but is metabolically less active and thus causes an underestimation of true cardiorespiratory capacity. Although this is fine in theory, an accurate expression of $\dot{V}O_2$ relative to LBM requires an accurate estimation of body fat and LBM. The equations for estimating these components rely on assumptions for density that clearly do not apply to children [63]. The error thereby introduced is unlikely to be systematic across the ages of childhood and adolescence. Therefore, when used to indicate cardiorespiratory capacity, the practice of expressing $\dot{V}O_2$max relative to LBM has been generally accepted in theory, but not widely practiced.

## CONCLUSIONS

In normal children, $\dot{V}O_2$max (L/min) increases roughly proportional to body size. In males, $\dot{V}O_2$max (mL/min · kg) remains stable throughout childhood and adolescence, while in females, it decreases throughout childhood and adolescence. Trained subjects of either sex exhibit higher $\dot{V}O_2$max values than do untrained subjects. The percentage difference between sexes is smaller in trained than in untrained children.

Although various opinions have been expressed, no optimal age for training has been identified. It appears that children do respond to vigorous, intensive training programs with an average increase of 8–10 percent in $\dot{V}O_2$max (mL/min · kg).

Many structural and functional parameters have been suggested to standardize $\dot{V}O_2$max across the chronological ages of childhood. No strong, data-based arguments have been offered which work more efficiently in practice than body weight, although this approach also has limitations (especially with females).

The relationship between $\dot{V}O_2$max and endurance performance is not as strong in children as in adults. This may be due to less reliable performances by children or related to a variety of physiologic differences between children and adults. It is clear that improvement in distance running performance accompanies maturation without any improvement in $\dot{V}O_2$max corrected for body weight.

REFERENCES

1. Andersen, K.L., and J. Ghesquière. Sex differences in maximal oxygen uptake, heart rate and oxygen pulse at 10 and 14 years in Norwegian children. *Human Biol.* 44:413–432, 1972.
2. Andersen, K.L., J. Rutenfranz, and V. Seliger. The rate of growth in maximal aerobic power of children in Norway. In *Medicine and Sport: Pediatric Work Physiology,* J. Borms and M. Hebbelinck, eds. Basel: Karger, 1978, pp. 52–55.
3. Andersen, K.L., V. Seliger, J. Rutenfranz, and I. Berndt. Physical performance capacity of children in Norway: Heart rate and oxygen pulse in submaximal and maximal exercises: Population parameters in a rural community. *Eur. J. Appl. Physiol.* 33:197–206, 1974.
4. Andersen, K.L., V. Seliger, J. Rutenfranz, and R. Mocellin. Physical performance capacity of children in Norway: Population parameters in a rural inland community with regard to maximal aerobic power. *Eur. J. Appl. Physiol.* 33:177–195, 1974.
5. Andersen, K.L., V. Seliger, J. Rutenfranz, and T. Nesset. Physical performance capacity of children in Norway: The influence of social isolation on the rate of growth in body-size and composition and on the achievement in lung function and maximal aerobic power of children in a rural community. *Eur. J. Appl. Physiol.* 45:155–166, 1980.
6. Andersen, K.L., V. Seliger, J. Rutenfranz, and J. Skrobak-Kaczynski. Physical performance capacity of children in Norway: The rate of growth in maximal aerobic power and the influence of improved physical education of children in a rural community: Population parameters in a rural community. *Eur. J. Appl. Physiol.* 35:49–58, 1976.
7. Asmussen, E., and K. Heebøll-Nielsen. A dimensional analysis of physical performance and growth in boys. *J. Appl. Physiol.* 7:593–603, 1955.
8. Åstrand, P.-O. *Experimental studies of physical working capacity in relation to sex and age.* Copenhagen: Ejnar Munksgaard, 1952.

9. Åstrand, P.-O. The child in sport and physical activity: physiology. In *Child in Sport and Physical Activity*, J.B. Albinson and G.M. Andrew, eds. Baltimore: University Park Press, 1976, pp. 19–33.

10. Baggley, G., and G.R. Cumming. Serial measurements of working aerobic capacity of Winnipeg school children during a year. In *Environmental Effects on Work Performance*, G.R. Cumming, D. Snidal, and A.W. Taylor, eds. Edmonton: Canad. Ass. Sports Sci., 1972, pp. 173–186.

11. Bailey, D.A., W.D. Ross, R.L. Mirwald, and C. Weese. Size dissociation of maximal aerobic power during growth in boys. In *Medicine and Sport: Pediatric Work Physiology*, J. Borms and M. Hebbelinck, eds. Basel: Karger, 1978, pp. 140–151.

12. Bale, P. Pre- and post-adolescents physiological response to exercise. Br. J. Sports Med. 15:246–249, 1981.

13. Bar-Or, O. *Pediatric Sports Medicine for the Practitioner.* New York: Springer-Verlag, 1983.

14. Bar-Or, O., J.S. Skinner, V. Bergsteinová, C. Shearburn, D. Royer, W. Bell, J. Haas, and E.R. Buskirk. Maximal aerobic capacity of 6- to 15-year-old girls and boys with subnormal intelligence quotients. *Acta Paediat. Scand. Suppl.* 217:108–113, 1971.

15. Bar-Or, O., and L.D. Zwiren. Physiological effects of increased frequency of physical education classes and of endurance conditioning on 4- to 10-year-old girls and boys. In *Pediatric Work Physiology*, O. Bar-Or, ed. Natanya: Wingate Institute, 1973, pp. 183–198.

16. Bar-Or, O., L.D. Zwiren, and H. Ruskin. Anthropometric and developmental measurements of 11- to 12-year-old boys, as predictors of performance 2 years later. *Acta Paediat. Belgica Suppl.* 28:214–220, 1974.

17. Berg, K. Body composition and nutrition of adolescent boys training for bicycle racing. *Nutr. Metab.* 14:172–180, 1972.

18. Berg, K., and J. Bjure. Preliminary results of long-term physical training of adolescent boys with respect to body composition, maximal oxygen uptake, and lung volume. *Acta Paediat. Belgica Suppl.* 28:183–190, 1974.

19. Boileau, R.A., V.H. Heyward, and B.H. Massey. Maximal aerobic capacity on the treadmill and bicycle ergometer of boys 11–14 years of age. *J. Sports Med.* 17:153–162, 1977.

20. Bouckaert, J., P. Van Uytvanck, and J. Vrijens. Anthropometrical data, muscle-strength, physiological and selected motor ability factors of 11 year old boys. *Acta Paediat. Belgica Suppl.* 28:60–67, 1974.

21. Brown, C.H., J. Harrower, and M. Deeter. The effects of cross-country running on pre-adolescent girls. *Med. Sci. Sports* 4:1–5, 1972.

22. Cameron, N., R.L. Mirwald, and D.A. Bailey. Standards for the assessment of normal absolute maximal aerobic power. In *Kinanthropometry II*, M. Ostyn, G. Beunen, and J. Simons, eds. Baltimore: University Park Press, 1980, pp. 349–359.

23. Chan, O.-L., M.T. Duncan, J.W. Sundsten, T. Thinakaran, M.N.B.C. Noh, and V. Klissouras. The maximum aerobic power of the Temiars. *Med. Sci. Sports Exercise* 8:235–238, 1976.

24. Chatterjee, S., P.K. Banerjee, P. Chatterjee, and S.R. Maitra. Aerobic capacity of young girls. *Indian J. Med. Res.* 69:327–333, 1979.

25. Chausow, S.A., W.F. Riner, and R.A. Boileau. Metabolic and cardiovascular responses of children during prolonged physical activity. *Res. Q. Exercise Sport* 55:1–7, 1984.

26. Cumming, G.R. Current levels of fitness. *Can. Med. Assoc. J.* 96:868–877, 1967.

27. Cumming, G.R. Maximal oxygen uptake and total body potassium in children. In *Application of Science and Medicine to Sport*, A.W. Taylor, ed. Springfield, Ill.: Thomas, 1975, pp. 54–63.

28. Cumming, G.R., and W. Friesen. Bicycle ergometer measurement of maximal oxygen uptake in children. *Can. J. Physiol. Pharmacol.* 45:937–946, 1967.
29. Cumming, G.R., A. Goodwin, G. Baggley, and J. Antel. Repeated measurements of aerobic capacity during a week of intensive training at a youth track camp. *Can. J. Physiol. Pharmacol.* 45:805–811, 1967.
30. Cunningham, D.A. Physical working capacity of children and adolescents. In. *Encyclopedia of Physical Education, Fitness, and Sports: Training, Environment, Nutrition, and Fitness,* G.A. Stull, ed. Salt Lake City: Brighton, 1980, pp. 481–494.
31. Cunningham, D.A. Reliability and reproducibility of maximal oxygen uptake measurement in children. *Med. Sci. Sports Exercise* 9:104–108, 1977.
32. Cunningham, D.A., and R.B. Eynon. The working capacity of young competitive swimmers, 10–16 years of age. *Med. Sci. Sports Exercise* 5:227–231, 1973.
33. Cunningham, D.A., J.J. Stapleton, I.C. MacDonald, and D.H. Paterson. Daily energy expenditure of young boys as related to maximal aerobic power. *Can. J. Appl. Sport Sci.* 6:207–211, 1981.
34. Cunningham, D.A., P. Telford, and G.T. Swart. The cardiopulmonary capacities of young hockey players: age 10. *Med. Sci. Sports Exercise* 8:23–25, 1976.
35. Cureton, K.J. Distance running tests in children. *J. Health Phys. Educ. Rec. Dance* 53(7):64–66, 1982.
36. Cureton, K.J., R.A. Boileau, T.G. Lohman, and J.E. Misner. Determinants of distance running performance in children: analysis of a path model. *Res. Q. Exercise Sport* 48:270–279, 1977.
37. Daniels, J. and N. Oldridge. Changes in oxygen consumption of young boys during growth and running training. *Med. Sci. Sports Exercise* 3:161–165, 1971.
38. Daniels, J., N. Oldridge, F. Nagle, and B. White. Differences and changes in $\dot{V}O_2$ among young runners 10 to 18 years of age. *Med. Sci. Sports Exercise* 10:200–203, 1978.
39. Davies, C.T.M. Body composition and maximal exercise performance in children. *Human Biol.* 44:195–214, 1972.
40. Davies, C.T.M. Metabolic cost of exercise and physical performance in children with some observations on external loading. *Eur. J. Appl. Physiol.* 45:95–102, 1980.
41. Davies, C.T.M. Thermal responses to exercise in children. *Ergonomics* 24:55–61, 1981.
42. Davies, C.T.M., C. Barnes, and S. Godfrey. Body composition and maximal exercise performance in children. *Human Biol.* 44:195–214, 1972.
43. Day, L. The testing, prediction and significance of maximal aerobic power in children. *Aust. J. Sport Sci.* 1:18–22, 1981.
44. Drinkwater, B.L., and S.M. Horvath. Responses of young female track athletes to exercise. *Med. Sci. Sports Exercise* 3:55–62, 1971.
45. Dupertuis, C., and N. Michael. Comparison of growth in height and weight between ectomorphic and mesomorphic boys. *Child Dev.* 24:203–214, 1953.
46. Ekblom, B. Effect of physical training in adolescent boys. *J. Appl. Physiol.* 27:350–355, 1969.
47. Ekblom, B. Physical training in normal boys in adolescence. *Acta Paediat. Scand. Suppl.* 217:60–62, 1971.
48. Eriksson, B.O. Physical training, oxygen supply and muscle metabolism in 11–13 year old boys. *Acta Physiol. Scand. Suppl.* 384:1–48, 1972.
49. Eriksson, B.O. The child in sport and physical activity: medical aspects. In *Child in Sport and Physical Activity,* J.G. Albinson and G.M. Andrew, eds. Baltimore: University Park Press, 1976, pp. 43–66.
50. Eriksson, B.O., P.D. Gollnick, and B. Saltin. Muscle metabolism and enzyme activities after training in boys 11–13 years old. *Acta Physiol. Scand.* 87:485–497, 1973.

51. Eriksson, B.O., P.D. Gollnick, and B. Saltin. The effect of physical training on muscle enzyme activities and fiber composition in 11-year-old boys. *Acta Paediat. Belgica Suppl.*, 28:245–252, 1974.

52. Eriksson, B., J. Karlsson, and B. Saltin. Muscle metabolites during exercise in pubertal boys. *Acta Paediat. Scand. Suppl.* 217:154–157, 1971.

53. Eriksson, B.O., and G. Koch. Effect of physical training on hemodynamic response during submaximal and maximal exercise in 11–13 year old boys. *Acta Physiol. Scand.* 87:27–39, 1973.

54. Eriksson, B.O., and B. Saltin. Muscle metabolism during exercise in boys aged 11 to 16 years compared to adults. *Acta Paediat. Belgica* Suppl., 28:113–120, 1974.

55. Flandrois, R., M. Grandmontagne, M. Mayet, R. Favier, and J. Frutoso. La consommation maximale d'oxygène chez le jeune français, sa variation avec l'âge, le sexe et l'entraînement. *J. Physiol. Paris* 78:186–194, 1982.

56. Gaisl, G. and J. Buchberger. Determination of the aerobic and anaerobic thresholds of 10–11-year-old boys using blood-gas analysis. In *Children and Exercise IX*, K. Berg and B.O. Eriksson, eds. Baltimore: University Park Press, 1980, pp. 93–98.

57. Gaisl, G., and J. Buchberger. The significance of stress acidosis in judging the physical working capacity of boys aged 11 to 15. In: *Frontiers of Activity and Child Health*, H. Lavallée and R.J. Shephard, eds. Quebec: Pelican, 1977, pp. 161–168.

58. Godfrey, S. The growth and development of the cardiopulmonary responses to exercise. In *Scientific Foundations of Paediatrics*, J.A. Davies and J. Dobbing, eds. Philadelphia: W.B. Saunders, 1974, pp. 271–280.

59. Gutin, B., R.K. Fogle, and K. Stewart. Relationship among submaximal heart rate, aerobic power, and running performance in children. *Res. Q. Exercise Sport* 43:536–539, 1976.

60. Gutin, B., A. Trinidad, C. Norton, E. Giles, A. Giles, and K. Stewart. Morphological and physiological factors related to endurance performance of 11- to 12-year-old girls. *Res. Q. Exercise Sport* 49:44–52, 1978.

61. Hermansen, L., and S. Oseid. Direct and indirect estimation of oxygen uptake in pre-pubertal boys. *Acta Paediat. Scand. Suppl.* 217:18–23, 1971.

62. Hermansen, L., and B. Saltin. Oxygen uptake during maximal treadmill and bicycle exercise. *J. Appl. Physiol.* 26:31–37, 1969.

63. Horswill, C.A., T.G. Lohman, M.H. Slaughter, and R.A. Boileau. Body fatness estimates in children and the influence of water and bone mineral content. *Med. Sci. Sports Exercise* 16:134–135, 1984.

64. Howell, M.L., and R.B.J. MacNab. *The Physical Work Capacity of Canadian Children Aged 7 to 17*. Toronto, Ont.: Canadian Association for Health, Physical Education, and Recreation, 1968, pp. 125–135.

65. Ikai, M., and K. Kitagawa. Maximal oxygen uptake in Japanese related to sex and age. *Med. Sci. Sports Exercise* 4:127–131, 1972.

66. Ilmarinen, J., and J. Rutenfranz. Longitudinal studies of the changes in habitual physical activity of schoolchildren and working adolescents. In *Children and Exercise IX*, K. Berg and B.O. Eriksson, eds. Baltimore: University Park Press, 1980, pp. 149–159.

67. Kemper, H.C.G., H.J.P. Dekker, M.J. Ootjers, B. Post, J. Snel, P.G. Splinter, L. Storm-van Essen, and R. Verschuur. Growth and health of teenagers in the Netherlands: Survey of multidisciplinary longitudinal studies and comparisons to recent results of a Dutch study. *Int. J. Sports Med.* 4:202–214, 1983.

68. Kemper, H.C.G., and R. Verschuur. Maximal aerobic power in 13- and 14-year-old teenagers in relation to biological age. *Int. J. Sports Med.* 2:97–100, 1981.

69. Klissouras, V. Hereditability and adaptive variation. *J. Appl. Physiol.* 31:338–344, 1971.
70. Kobayashi, K., K. Kitamura, M. Miura, H. Sodeyama, Y. Murase, M. Miyashita, and H. Matsui. Aerobic power as related to body-growth and training in Japanese boys: a longitudinal study. *J. Appl. Physiol.* 44:666–672, 1978.
71. Koch, G. Aerobic power, lung dimensions, ventilatory capacity, and muscle blood flow in 12–16-year-old boys with high physical activity. In *Children and Exercise IX*, K. Berg and B.O. Eriksson, eds. Baltimore: University Park Press, 1980, pp. 64–68.
72. Komi, P.V., A. Ito, B. Sjödin, R. Wallensten, and J. Karlsson. Muscle metabolism, lactate breaking point, and biomechanical features of endurance running. *Int. J. Sports Med.* 2:148–153, 1981.
73. Krahenbuhl, G.S., and R.P. Pangrazi. Characteristics associated wtih running performance in young boys. *Med. Sci. Sports Exercise* 15:486–490, 1983.
74. Krahenbuhl, G.S., R.P. Pangrazi, L.N. Burkett, M.J. Schneider, and G. Petersen. Field estimation of $\dot{V}O_2$max in children eight years of age. *Med. Sci. Sports Exercise* 9:37–40, 1977.
75. Krahenbuhl, G.S., R. P. Pangrazi, and E.A. Chomokos. Aerobic responses of young boys to submaximal running. *Res. Q. Exercise Sport* 50:413–421, 1979.
76. Krahenbuhl, G.S., R.P. Pangrazi, G.W. Petersen, L.N. Burkett, and M.J. Schneider. Field testing cardiorespiratory fitness in primary school children. *Med. Sci. Sports Exercise* 10:208–213, 1978.
77. Kramer, J.D. and P.R. Lurie. Maximal oxygen consumption. *Am. J. Dis. Child.* 108:283–297, 1964.
78. Krotkiewski, M., J. Kral, and J. Karlsson. Effects of castration and testosterone substitution on body composition and muscle metabolism in rats. *Acta Physiol. Scand.* 109:233–237, 1980.
79. Larivière, G., H. Lavallée, and R.J. Shephard. Correlations between field tests of performance and laboratory measures of fitness. *Acta Paediat. Belgica Suppl.* 28:19–28, 1974.
80. Lussier, L., and E.R. Buskirk. Effects of an endurance training program on assessment of work capacity in prepubertal children. *Ann. N.Y. Acad. Sci.* 301:734–741, 1977.
81. MacDougall, J.D., P.D. Roche, O. Bar-Or, and J.R. Moroz. Maximal aerobic capacity of Canadian school children: Prediction based on age-related oxygen cost of running. *Int. J. Sports Med.* 4:194–198, 1983.
82. Maček, M., V. Seliger and J. Vavra. Physical fitness of the Czechoslovak population between the ages of 12 and 55 years. Oxygen consumption and pulse oxygen. *Physiol. Bohemoslov.* 28:75–82, 1979.
83. Maček, M. and J. Vavra. Cardiopulmonary and metabolic changes during exercise in children 6–14 years old. *J. Appl. Physiol.* 30:200–204, 1971.
84. Maček, M. and J. Vavra. Oxygen uptake and heart rate with transition from rest to maximal exercise in prepubertal boys. In *Children and Exercise IX*, K. Berg and B.O. Eriksson, eds. Baltimore: University Park Press, 1980, pp. 64–68.
85. Maček, M., and J. Vavra. Prolonged exercise in 14-year-old girls. *Int. J. Sports Med.* 2:228–230, 1981.
86. Maček, M., J. Vavra, and J. Novosadová. Prolonged exercise in prepubertal boys. *Eur. J. Appl. Physiol.* 35:291–298, 1976.
87. Massicotte, D.R., and R.B.J. MacNab. Cardiorespiratory adaptations to training at specified intensities in children. *Med. Sci. Sports Exercise* 6:242–246, 1974.
88. Matsui, H., M. Miyashita, M. Miura, K. Kobayashi, T. Hoshikawa, and S. Kamei. Maximal oxygen uptake and its relation to body weight of Japanese adolescents. *Med. Sci. Sports Exercise* 4:29–32, 1972.

89. Mayers, N., and B. Gutin. Physiological characteristics of elite prepubertal cross-country runners. *Med. Sci. Sports Exercise* 11:172–176, 1979.

90. McMiken, D.F. Maximal aerobic power and physical dimensions of children. *Ann. Human Biol.* 3:141–147, 1976.

91. Metz, K.F., and J.F. Alexander. Estimation of maximal oxygen intake from submaximal work parameters. *Res. Q. Sport Exercise* 42:187–193, 1971.

92. Mirwald, R.L., and D.A. Bailey. Longitudinal comparison of aerobic power in active and inactive boys aged 7.0 to 17.0 years. *Ann. Human Biol.* 8:405–414, 1981.

93. Mitchell, J.H., B.J. Sproule, and C.B. Chapman. The physiological meaning of the maximum oxygen intake test. *J. Clin. Invest.* 37:538–547, 1958.

94. Miyamura, M., H. Kuroda, K. Hirata, and Y. Honda. Evaluation of the step test scores based on the measurement of maximal aerobic power. *J. Sports Med.* 15:316–322, 1975.

95. Mocellin, R., H. Lindemann, J. Rutenfranz, and W. Sbresny. Determination of $W_{170}$ and maximal oxygen uptake in children by different methods. *Acta Paediat. Scand. Suppl.* 217:13–17, 1971.

96. Morse, M., F.W. Schultz, and D.E. Cassels. Relation of age to physiological responses of the older boy (10–17 years) to exercise. *J. Appl. Physiol.* 1:683–709, 1949.

97. Murase, Y., K. Kobayashi, S. Kamei, and H. Matsui. Longitudinal study of aerobic power in superior junior athletes. *Med. Sci. Sports Exercise* 13:180–184, 1981.

98. Nagle, F.J., J. Hagberg, and S. Kamei. Maximal $O_2$ uptake of boys and girls—ages 14–17. *Eur. J. Appl. Physiol.* 36:75–80, 1977.

99. Nakagawa, A., and T. Ishiko. Assessment of aerobic capacity with special reference to sex and age of junior and senior highschool students in Japan. *Jpn. J. Physiol.* 20:118–129, 1970.

100. Oseid, S., and L. Hermansen. Hormonal and metabolic changes during and after prolonged muscular work in prepubertal boys. *Acta Paediat. Scand. Suppl.* 217:147–153, 1971.

101. Palgi, Y., B. Gutin, J. Young, and D. Alejandro. Physiologic and anthropometric factors underlying endurance performance in children. *Int. J. Sports Med.* 5:67–73, 1984.

102. Paterson, D.H., and D.A. Cunningham. Maximal oxygen uptake in children: comparison of treadmill protocols at varied speeds. *Can. J. Appl. Sport. Sci.* 3:188, 1978.

103. Robinson, S. Experimental studies of physical fitness in relation to age. *Arbeitsphysiologie* 10:251–323, 1938.

104. Rodahl, K., P.-O. Åstrand, N.C. Birkhead, T. Hettinger, B. Issekutz, D.M. Jones, and R. Weaver. Physical work capacity. *Arch. Environ. Health* 2:499–510, 1961.

105. Rutenfranz, J., K.L. Andersen, V. Seliger, J. Ilmarinen, F. Klimmer, H. Kylian, M. Rutenfranz, and M. Ruppel. Maximal aerobic power affected by maturation and body growth during childhood and adolescence. *Eur. J. Pediat.* 139:106–112, 1982.

106. Rutenfranz, J., K.L. Andersen, V. Seliger, F. Klimmer, I. Berndt, and M. Ruppel. Maximal aerobic power and body composition during the puberty growth period: Similarities and differences between children in two European countries. *Eur. J. Pediat.* 136:123–133, 1981.

107. Sady, S.P. Transient oxygen uptake and heart rate response at the onset of relative endurance exercise in prepubertal boys and adult men. *Int. J. Sports Med.* 2:240–244, 1981.

108. Sady, S.P., W.H. Thompson, K. Berg, and M. Savage. Physiological character-istics of high-ability prepubescent wrestlers. *Med. Sci. Sports Exercise* 16:72–76, 1984.
109. Schmücker, B., and W. Hollmann. The aerobic capacity of trained athletes from 6 to 7 years of age on. *Acta Paediat. Belgica Suppl.* 28:92–101, 1974.
110. Seliger, V., V. Cermak, P. Handzo, J. Horak, Z. Jirka, M. Maček, M. Pribil, J. Rous, O. Skranc, J. Ulbrich, and J. Urbanek. Physical fitness of the Czechoslovak 12- and 15-year-old population. *Acta Paediat. Scand. Supple.* 217:37–41, 1971.
111. Seliger, V., Z. Trefny, S. Bartunkova, and M. Pauer. The habitual activity and physical fitness of 12 year old boys. *Acta Paediat. Belgica Suppl.* 28:54–59, 1974.
112. Shephard, R.J. The working capacity of schoolchildren. In *Frontiers of Fitness*, R.J. Shephard, ed. Springfield, Ill: Thomas, 1971, pp. 319–344.
113. Shephard, R.J., C. Allen, O. Bar-Or, C.T.M. Davies, S. Degre, R. Hedman, K. Ishii, M. Kaneko, J.R. La Cour, P.E. di Prampero, and V. Seliger. The working capacity of Toronto schoolchildren. *Can. Med. Assoc. J.* 100:560–566, 1969.
114. Shephard, R.J., H. Lavallée, J. Jequier, R. LaBarre, M. Volle, and M. Rajic. Season of birth and variations in stature, body mass and performance. *Human Biol.* 51:299–316, 1979.
115. Shephard, R.J., H. Lavallée, R. LaBarre, J.-C. Jéquier, M. Volle, and M. Rajic. The basis of data standardization in prepubescent children. In *Kinanthropometry II*, M. Ostyn, G. Beunen, and J. Simons, eds. Baltimore: University Park Press, 1980, pp. 360–370.
116. Sills, I.N., and F.J. Cerny. Responses to continuous and intermittent exercise in healthy and insulin-dependent diabetic children. *Med. Sci. Sports Exercise* 15:450–454, 1983.
117. Sjödin, B. The relationships among running economy, aerobic power, muscle power, and onset of blood lactate accumulation in young boys (11–15 years). In *Exercise and Sport Biology*, P.V. Komi, ed. Champaign, Ill.: Human Kinetics, 1982, pp. 57–60.
118. Skinner, J.S., O. Bar-Or, V. Bergsteinová, C.W. Bell, D. Royer, and E.R. Buskirk. Comparison of continuous and intermittent tests for determining maximal ox-ygen intake in children. *Acta Paediat. Scand. Suppl.* 217:24–28, 1971.
119. Sobolová, V., V. Seliger, D. Grussová, J. Machovcová, and V. Zelenka. The influence of age and sports training in swimming on physical fitness. *Acta Paediat. Scand. Suppl.* 217:63–67, 1971.
120. Sparling. P.B. Physiological determinants of distance running performance. *Physician Sportsmed.* 12:68–76, 1984.
121. Šprynarová, S. Development of the relationship between aerobic capacity and the circulatory and respiratory reaction to moderate activity in boys 11–13 years old. *Physiol. Bohemoslov.* 15:253–264, 1966.
122. Šprynarová, S. Longitudinal study of the influence of different physical activity programs on functional capacity of the boys from 11 to 18 years. *Acta Paediat. Belgica Suppl.* 28:204–213, 1974.
123. Šprynarová, S., J. Pařizková and I. Jurinová. Development of the functional capacity and body composition of boy and girl swimmers aged 12–15 years. In *Medicine and Sport: Pediatric Work Physiology*, J. Borms and M. Hebbelinck, eds. Basel: Karger, 1978, pp. 32–38.
124. Spurr, G.B., J.C. Reina, M. Barac-Nieto, and M.G. Maksud. Maximal oxygen consumption of nutritionally normal white, mestizo and black Colombian boys 6–16 years of age. *Human Biol.* 54:553–574, 1982.
125. Stewart, K., and B. Gutin. Effects of physical training on cardiorespiratory fitness in children. *Res. Q. Exercise Sport* 47:110–120, 1976.

126. Sundberg, S. Maximal oxygen uptake in relation to age in blind and normal boys and girls. *Acta Paediat. Scand.* 71:603–608, 1982.
127. Sundberg, S., and R. Elovainio. Cardiorespiratory function in competitive endurance runners aged 12–16 years compared with ordinary boys. *Acta Paediat. Scand.* 71:987–992, 1982.
128. Taylor, H.L., E. Buskirk, and A. Henschel. Maximal oxygen intake as an objective measure of cardio-respiratory performance. *J. Appl. Physiol.* 8:73–80, 1955.
129. Thiart, B.F., and C.T. Wessels. The maximal oxygen intake of physically active boys 8–13 years of age. *Acta Paediat. Belgica Suppl.* 28:48–53, 1974.
130. Vaccaro, P., and D.H. Clarke. Cardiorespiratory alterations in 9 to 11 year old children following a season of competitive swimming. *Med. Sci. Sports Exercise* 10:204–207, 1978.
131. von Döbeln, W., and B.O. Eriksson. Physical training, maximal oxygen uptake and dimensions of the oxygen transporting and metabolizing organs in boys 11–13 yrs. of age. *Acta Paediat. Scand.* 61:653–660, 1972.
132. Weber, G., W. Kartodihardjo, and V. Klissouras. Growth and physical training with reference to heredity. *J. Appl. Physiol.* 40:211–215, 1976.
133. Wells, C.L., E.W. Scrutton, L.D. Archibald, W.P. Cooke, and J.W. De La Mothe. Physical work capacity and maximal oxygen uptake of teenage athletes. *Med. Sci. Sports Exercise* 5:232–238, 1973.
134. Wilmore, J.H., and P.O. Sigerseth. Physical work capacity of young girls, 7–13 years of age. *J. Appl. Physiol.* 22:923–928, 1967.
135. Wyndham, C.H., and A.J. Heyns. 1969. Determinants of oxygen consumption and maximum oxygen intake of Bantu and Caucasian males. *Int. Z. Angew. Physiol.* 27:51–75.
136. Yamaji, K., and M. Miyashita. Oxygen transport system during exhaustive exercise in Japanese boys. *Eur. J. Appl. Physiol.* 36:93–99, 1977.
137. Yoshida, T., I. Ishiko, and I. Muraoka. Effect of endurance training on cardiorespiratory functions of 5-year-old children. *Int. J. Sports Med.* 1:91–94, 1980.
138. Yoshizawa, S. A comparative study of aerobic work capacity in urban and rural adolescents. *J. Human Ergol.* 1:45–65, 1972.
139. Zauner, C.W., and N.Y. Benson. Physiological alterations in young swimmers during three years of intensive training. *J. Sports Med.* 21:179–185, 1981.

# Sport Subcultures

PETER DONNELLY, Ph.D.

We can easily now conceive of a time when there will be only one culture and one civilization on the entire surface of the earth. I don't believe this will happen, because there are contradictory tendencies always at work—on the one hand towards homogenization and on the other towards new distinctions. The more a civilization becomes homogenized, the more internal lines of separation become apparent; and what is gained on one level is immediately lost on another. This is a personal feeling, in that I have no clear proof of the operation of this dialect. But I don't see how mankind can really live without some internal diversity
—C. Lévi-Strauss

Williams [199] has suggested that "culture" is one of the most complex words in the English language. Despite the fact that a great deal of research on subcultures has tended to treat the concept as nonproblematic, there is no reason to suspect that the term "subculture" is any less complex. This review has three basic concerns with regard to the concept of subculture and its applictaion to the study of sport. The first is a review of research dealing with sport subcultures. The second is an examination of theoretical problems and perspectives in the study of subcultures. And the third is a consideration of methodological problems and perspectives together with suggestions for the development of future research in the field of sport subcultures.

## SPORT SUBCULTURES

The significance of research on sport subcultures was first noted by Loy and Kenyon [117], and subsequently by Arnold who recognized that:

To develop a sociology of subcultures we need case studies to provide the data needed for generalizing to a middle-range theory of subcultures. I considered examining regional, ethnic, occupational, or SES (class) subcultures, but each of these presented various methodological or theoretical problems, and I finally decided to look at sport and hobby subcultures. As I began to do so I came to realize that their importance goes beyond merely

539

providing convenient cases for a sociology of subcultures, and that they have a sociological importance in and of themselves ([9], p. 1).

Their importance, Arnold notes, lies in the decline of social classes and the increasing importance of leisure activities which "have come to replace work as the prime *raison-d'être* for millions of Americans" ([9], p. 2). However, it seems far more apparent that leisure activities continue to reflect social classes rather than superseding social class, and that the comment is more a reflection of American sociology and ideology than an accurate picture of the state of affairs. But it is also clear that leisure subcultures and subculture membership has become a significant characteristic of (Western) society since the 1950s, and it seems likely that the study of subcultures may make a far more significant contribution to the sociological enterprise than simply in the development of middle-range theory.

In this review of studies of sport subcultures it should be noted that a number of works that purport to be subcultural have been excluded. This is because they tend to expand the notion of subcultures beyond the parameters that are established in the subsequent discussion of definitions. As such, they tend to confuse the concept and to render it useless as a unit of analysis. These include a number of works that refer to a sport or athletic subculture in general terms. For example, Phillips and Schafer refer to the athletic subculture [153] Snyder and Spreitzer discuss the subculture of sport [177], and Petrie examines the athletic group as an emerging deviant subculture [152]. Similarly, Schafer has contrasted the subculture of sport with the counterculture [170]. These various types are perhaps better thought of as a more general culture of sport forming one of the parent cultures to a large number of specific sport subcultures.

Also excluded are a large number of studies that have considered adolescence as a subculture, and (American) high school athletes as a subculture. Age is considered as an ascribed characteristic and, while it is possible to make certain generalizations and identify certain cultural characteristics that are typical of a specific age group, it is far more fruitful to consider youth or adolescent culture as a parent culture within which it is possible to identify a number of subcultures. With regard to high school athletes, it is apparent that researchers have tended to concentrate upon a very few major sports (usually football) and generalize to all high school athletes from the norms and values of the elite groups. There has been no apparent attempt to determine if the culture of track and field athletes, swimmers, and gymnasts are similar to each other or to the culture of football, basketball, and soccer players in the high school setting. Until this work has been done, it is far better to think of the participants in various sports as relatively distinct subcultural groupings, clearly sharing many characteristics (and even personnel where the sports are played in different seasons), but also possessing a number of unique characteristics that are more common to the specific sport beyond the high school setting than to other sports in that setting.

In attempting to characterize sport subcultures it is probably most useful to classify them, in the manner of Loy et al. [118] as occupational, avocational, and deviant subcultures. Avocational subcultures include all of the sport and leisure subcultures but interface with occupational subcultures at the professional and elite amateur level and with deviant subcultures in areas such as gambling and hustling. As with most typologies there are difficulties of classification here that should be noted. For example, the same sport may appear in all three categories. Soccer is noted as an occupational subculture in a study of the professional game, as an avocational subculture in studies of ethnic soccer clubs, and as a deviant subculture in studies of soccer hooliganism. The location of the studies in a particular category has been made on the basis of their primary emphasis—occupational, avocational, or deviant.

Another issue concerns the emphases given here in comparison to previous reviews of sport subculture studies. For example, many of the studies of ice hockey, because of their emphasis on player violence, have been considered as studies of deviance. They are included here under the heading of occupational subcultures because violence is considered to be normative behavior among professional and elite amateur ice hockey players. Similarly, the subculture of rugby players has frequently been considered as a deviant subculture because of the nongame ritual and drunken behavior of the players. The studies of rugby players are included here under the heading of avocational subcultures again because of the normative nature of the players' behavior, because of the public reaction to that behavior, and because of the contrasting recreational and sportsmanlike behavior of the players during a game. The location of specific sports and studies in particular sections is further justified in the appropriate section.

A final introductory note ought to be made concerning the source of the studies included in this review. In addition to research conducted by social scientists, much useful work may be found in the large body of journalistic and biographical writing on sport, some of which provides excellent insights into the lifestyle and subculture of athletes in a variety of sports. While a number of these sources are examined, perhaps most revealing for the purposes of this review is the comparison of topics (subcultures) selected for research by the sociologists with the work available from other sources. Journalists are frequently assigned or commissioned to write pieces on specific subjects, and such subjects are most often selected with economic and topical concerns in mind. Biographies are usually written by those athletes who have achieved some fame or notoriety in order to warrant a publishing contract. In contrast, sociologists are presumably more free to select their topics of interest, and while a certain amount of chance is involved and sociologists must not be expected to risk their lives as participants in hustling or high-risk sports on a regular basis, the topics that they do select for research are quite revealing in terms of the nature of subcultures. The source of the studies reviewed in the following sections, whether athlete, journalist, or sociologist, is noted for the purposes of such comparisons.

*Occupational Subcultures*
Occupational subcultures in sport include all the various professional roles in sport (e.g., coaches, professional athletes in various sports); in addition to the elite amateur athletes who are frequently amateur only in name (the actual term has even been dropped from the Olympic Charter where athletes are now referred to as "professional" and "nonprofessional") and who frequently find that training and competition represent a full-time occupation; and the athletes who engage in other fully rationalized forms of sport (e.g., many youth, high school, and varsity sports). Where what Webb [197] has termed "professionalized" attitudes to sport are apparent, occupational or preoccupational subcultures in sport are considered to exist.

Ingham [99] has examined the origin of occupational subcultures in sport, tracing their beginnings to the increasing rationalization of sport since the nineteenth century. He suggested that "sport's increased quest for economic efficiency through the use of the merger and increased role specialization reflects Weber's conviction that the pursuit of profit inevitably entails rationalization" (p. 356). Paid specialists, with part-time and eventually full-time positions as athletes, were an inevitable result of the increasing commercialization, professionalization, and bureaucratization of sport. Ingham went on to trace the process of becoming a professional athlete—a shift that is characterized as "from recreation to occupation." It is interesting to note, however, that many young people never begin their involvement in major sports in a recreational manner. More and more are gaining their first experience with a sport in an organized league, coached by an individual who frequently holds 'professionalized' attitudes regarding the conduct of the particular sport. Ingham's study provides a valuable overview of the "work world of sport," and provides an essential historical and theoretical background that is missing in most of the studies of occupational subcultures in sport.

Apart from the athletes in their specific sports, the one general occupational role providing the basis for a subculture in sport is that of the coach. With the growing body of research literature on various aspects of coaching, and the expanding number of courses, degree courses, and certification programs, coaches from various sports and from various countries are beginning to form a significant occupational subculture. Coakley [31] has noted that "the pressure and conflict associated with the role of coach is likely to lead coaches to withdraw from extensive relationships with others" (p. 209) and to employ the subculture as a mutual support system. But the subculture of coaches also typifies the manner in which subcultures are able to ensure conformity. Several studies have noted the generally conservative nature of coaches [127, 168], and the way in which coaches are able to control career access and mobility [128]. The major studies of the subculture have been primarily concerned with American university coaches [127, 168], and they provide significant models for subcultural research because they recognize both "the structural and subcultural conditions that heavily influence coaching behavior" ([31] p. 211), and the fact that subcultures cannot be studied in isolation. In these cases, the relationship of the coach to the remainder of the academic community is considered to be particularly significant.

While the subculture of coaches lends itself fairly readily to participant observation (the most common method of studying subcultures), particularly by sport sociologists employed in physical education departments who occasionally double as coaches, it is far more difficult to become a participant observer in the other occupational subcultures in sport—those of professional and elite amateur athletes. This difficulty is reflected in the available work on the occupational subcultures of athletes which, with a few notable exceptions, largely comprises the work of journalists and athletes.

With regard to the major professional sports in the United States, there are no subcultural studies of professional basketball by sociologists, only one that is to some extent concerned with professional football, and three that have been concerned with professional baseball. In order to gain subcultural insights into professional basketball, it is necessary to consult books such as David Halberstam's, *The Breaks of the Game* [84], or a variety of player biographies (e.g., *Foul*, the biography of Connie Hawkins [205]). Similarly with professional football, apart from one paper by Brower entitled, "Culture Clash: The Inappropriateness of the Black Subculture in the White World of Professional Football" [19], one is obliged to consult Plimpton [155] and a variety of works (often critical) by ex-players [111, 136, 147, 172].

This should not, however, always be considered as "second best" to actual data provided by sociologists. As Tomlinson [192] has noted:

> Our insight into social phenomena can also be enhanced by social actors who develop into social observers of their own (often former) spheres of activity. In this category we can place the previously unreflecting, or coercively constrained social actor who breaks through and "tells it like it really is." The "pro football" establishment in America has been exposed as a big problem in itself by savage contributions to radical critique and the genre of the "sports" novel (p. 23).

With regard to the "sports" novel, Tomlinson particularly mentions Gent's *North Dallas Forty* [70]. Additional note of the significance of novels as a source of data is made subsequently. Tomlinson goes on to consider the insights and contributions to the "sociological imagination" [138] made by writers of the new journalistic school (e.g., Hunter Thompson, Gay Talese, Tom Wolfe), many of whom have written extensively on sport-related themes.

Just as writers such as Parrish and Meggysey exposed the seamier side of professional football in a radical critique, Bouton provided a humorous exposé of the seamier side of the life of professional baseball players in books such as *Ball Four* [17]. This is supplemented by the more serious critique contained in Curt Flood's biography [65], and by the work of insightful baseball journalists such as Angell and Kahn [5, 105]. In work of a more sociological nature, Gmelch [73] has studied the use of magic and superstition among professional baseball players, while both Andreano and Haerle [4, 83] have provided career analyses of the players in the major leagues. Charnofsky [24] has compared the self-image and public image of professional baseball players, and also compared the occupational subculture of boxers with that of baseball players [25].

In the other major sports one is again frequently obliged to employ the accounts of athletes and journalists. For example, Davies' account of a season spent with an English professional soccer team provides an excellent study of groupculture from which certain generalizations to the overall subculture of professional soccer players are also warranted [43]. Wind and McPhee provide certain insights into the world of professional tennis [135, 204], and Plimpton spent time as a participant observer on the professional golf tour [156]. Only Theberge's examination of the careers of women professional golfers provides an example of a sociologist in the role of 'complete observer' and interviewer in this group of sports [189].

It is interesting to compare the previous works with those subcultures of sport occupations in which sociologists have taken a clear interest, at least as observers if not as participants. The latter group include such sports as ice hockey, boxing, professional wrestling, horse racing, stock car racing, bodybuilding, and the youth leagues in baseball and ice hockey. While the former group may be characterized as mainstream, the latter are typically marginal, deviant, or the subject of social criticism. As such, they become far more attractive to sociologists who, because of the nature and development of their particular discipline, are able to gain more kudos from responding to the same "moral panics" [36] regarding social problems as the general public than from studying the normal, mundane or everyday matters that most people take for granted. This tendency is both reflected in, and assisted by, the large body of subcultural theory associated with deviance in comparison to that in the area of occupational subcultures.

Faulkner's studies of professional hockey players [61, 62] have shown that the violence and rough play that appear to many to be a deviant aspect of hockey (and of sport in general) are actually quite normative within the context of the occupational subculture. The players are constrained to fight as an aspect of "identity work" in which they are expected to "make respect." Other aspects of the career of professional hockey players, particularly those associated with career mobility, have been examined by Faulkner [63] and Smith and Diamond [176]. The studies of the occupational subculture of professional (and elite amateur) boxers have also been primarily career and mobility studies [25, 68, 86, 198], while, in contrast, the studies of professional wrestling have tapped a deep-seated fascination with the dramatic aspects of this sham sport and also emphasize the "identity work" necessary to become a successful member of the subculture [91, 167, 181, 183]. The study by Birrell and Turowetz [14] also provides a fascinating comparison of female (intercollegiate) gymnasts with male professional wrestlers in terms of the problems of identity work and the display of character. The two are contrasted in terms of the wrestler's need to create heat in order to engage an audience emotionally and the gymnast's need to display coolness in order to impress the judges.

Klein's examination of contradictions in the subculture of bodybuilders represents an interesting and topical account of a growing sport and an introduciton to a forthcoming series of studies on the topic [109]. Pillsbury's [154] account of stockcar racing in the southeastern United States could be supplemented by numerous journalistic, novelistic, and biographical works on the sport. But Scott's [171] study of horse racing and the related occupational subcultures of jockeys, trainers, and grooms represents one of the more complete accounts of occupational subcultures in sport. The study also indicates the type of information that is available to the sociologist who, for-tuitously, finds that he or she has complete access to all aspects of a particular social setting and is completely accepted as a participant in that setting. Only the novels of Dick Francis provide comparative background information on the subcultures associated with the sport of horse racing. Accounts of other occupational subcultures in sport may be found in journalistic and biographical sources, one of the more significant of which is the work on bullfighting [37, 89]. But there is clearly a great deal of work to be done by sport sociologists in this area.

The little league subcultures of ice hockey and baseball have been included here as examples of "pre-occupational" subcultures. Smith [175], Vaz [194], and Vaz and Thomas [195] have all traced the origins of sanctioned violence and professional attitudes toward win-ning to the Canadian minor hockey programs and to the culture of young hockey players. Similarly, the culture of little league baseball has also been examined as a social problem [20, 46, 164] in which the recreational aspects of children's sport has been sacrificed in favor of the development of winning attitudes, but in neither case has there been any significant move toward resolving the problem.

What is most characteristic of all the studies of occupational sub-cultures in sport (and a number of the studies of avocational sub-cultures) is that they open up the back regions, the nonpublic aspects of the subcultures. These back regions exist in all occupational sub-cultures and include the various accommodations that are made in order to get the job done, the special language, knowledge, and understandings that serve to distinguish the in-group from the out-group, and the various forms of norm-breaking behavior that is hid-den from the general public. Even occupations as apparently mun-dane as sales clerks may develop a special language (argot) in order to converse with other clerks. They may:

> describe their customers as "J.L." (just looking), "T.O." (to be turned over to an ace salesman), "shank" (cheap skate) or "pa-looka" (someone on a buying spree). A "palooka" becomes a "wrap-up" if he buys the first item shown without haggling, and he gets "horned" (overcharged) when he purchases a "skig" or an "L.Y." (last year's goods). All these terms can be used openly in front of an innocent and unsuspecting "proposition" (cus-tomer) ([190], p. 221).

All three types of sport subcultures—the occupational, the avoca-tional, and the deviant—have been particularly productive in the development and use of argot, much of which has slipped into everyday usage (e.g., "behind the eight ball," "strike out," "knockout," "time out," "crestfallen," "stymied," and "bluff"). The accommodations and adaptations that exist in the back regions [74] are frequently more efficient ways of making such work guidelines as policy and procedures manuals functional (hence, the effectiveness of the "work to rule" as an aspect of job action), while the norm-breaking behavior is often a way of humanizing an alienating work situation. One example of this has been described as "leisure taking" at work in a study of the occupational subculture of shipbuilding workers [21], but many of the incidents of shop-floor sabotage may also result from similar needs.

The back regions of sport subcultures may actually contradict the aspects that are exposed to the public. Loy et al. [118], describing Charnofsky's [24] study of major league baseball players, noted that:

> baseball players have traditionally accepted public criticism, signed autographs by the thousands, avoided fraternization off the field with opponents who are friends, and presented images as "All-American" males in order to sell tickets and thereby earn their salary. Yet these beliefs, attitudes, and behaviors may be violated in the "back" or private region of the locker or hotel room, where players often comment that that the adult fan is naive, uninformed, and fickle (p. 193).

The contradiction is also apparent in what has been termed the organizational charter [194] of occupational subcultures in sport, which has been defined as "a more or less formal statement or rhetoric of (their) objectives and ideals" (p. 223). As Ingham [99] has suggested:

> The sport organization is faced with the problem of justifying itself and its mission to the larger community. At the same time, it has to handle the pratical reality of producing a winning team with which the community can identify (p. 361).

While the conflict is apparent in professional team sports when, for example, the quest for profits results in the reloctaion of a franchise without regard for community support and loyalty, it is perhaps most evident in youth sports. Vaz contrasts the "front regions," represented by the organizational charter in minor hockey (although the Little League Baseball Charter is comparable), emphasizing a great many developmental qualities available to the participants (e.g., healthy exercise, character, sportsmanship, teamwork, maturity, self-confidence, etc.), with the back region in which teams are gradually "molded into a tough fighting unit prepared for violence whose primary objective is to win hockey games" ([194], p. 228).

When the back regions of occupational subcultures in sport are revealed, by journalistic, biographical or sociological sources, it is most likely that change in structural and cultural terms will occur. Structural change would include such things as the current attack on drug (ab)use by athletes in professional team sports in North America, and the outlawing of contact for Canadian minor hockey players below 12 years of age. Cultural change is more subtle, and results from the incorporation—the loss of exclusivity and distinctiveness—that occurs as subcultural norms become public knowledge and become barely distinguishable from the parent and dominant culture. For example, once the public became used to the idea that the drinking and carousing of professional athletes revealed by individuals such as Jim Bouton and Joe Namath was not really any different from the behavior of most healthy young men, the subcultures of professional team sport athletes became incorporated into the mainstream. While such subcultures do, in large part, represent the parent culture of sport, it is also highly likely that the re-creation of distinctive occupational subcultures is also under way. The use of drugs such as cocaine may have been part of a move in this direction; an attempt to align the lifestyle of professional athletes with that of others in the entertainment industry and the jet-set. It is also likely that, apart from access problems, the greater sociological emphasis on the marginal or deviant occupational subcultures in sport is also a result of the lack of subcultural distinctiveness of the major sports.

*Avocational Subcultures*
Avocational subcultures in sport include all the recreational sport and leisure subcultures. It is interesting to note that many of the comments made concerning occupational subcultures in sport may also apply to the avocational and the deviant subcultures, and particularly those comments concerning the type of subculture selected for research by sociologists. Again, marginality, deviance, and social concern seem to have been major criteria for selection. While no studies have been found concerning the subculture of softball, or the subculture of jogging/running (although a number of journalistic works are available in this area), there are a great many studies of rugby and a variety of other sports that may be considered as high risk or countercultural. Sociologists have apparently again been attracted to the more distinctive subcultures rather than those that are close to the mainstream. In addition, the avocational subcultures are far more readily accessible to the various aspects of participant observation, and sociologists have frequently been able to translate their own interest in a particular activity into a research project.

However, even when the sports are so well known as to not present a distinctive subculture, the approach taken in the few studies available tends to be quite distinctive, and to seek out relatively inaccessible subcultural aspects of the sports. For example, the two major studies of avocational basketball (both, incidentally, written by journalists) concentrate specifically on urban playground basketball, mainly in and around New York City, and as played primarily by black males residing in the inner city neighborhoods [12, 188]. It is in this setting that characteristics of style and status and technique may differ markedly from the mainstream aspects of the game. While remaining part of the more general subculture of basketball, the inner city game is distinctive enough to represent a special case but also highlights other aspects of the more general subculture (e.g., the difficulty experienced by players in adapting from the freewheeling city game to the often more regimented college game). Cochran [32] has also selected a specific approach to the subculture of basketball by examining the folk aspects of the game.

Similarly, although Kane and Murray [106] discussed the subculture of soccer in rather general terms, the more specific emphasis has been on the aspects of North American ethnicity reflected in the game. For example, Pooley [160] found that membership in ethnic soccer clubs in Milwaukee had the effect of retarding assimilation into American society, whereas several Canadian studies (e.g., McKay [132]) have shown precisely the opposite effect with ethnically based but integrated teams actually promoting assimilation. It seems likely that these studies may have located different moments in the assimilation process—a process that becomes apparent in the light of La Flamme's study of West Indian cricket clubs in Buffalo, New York [112]. La Flamme suggested that, for the first generation of immigrants, membership in ethnic sport clubs "is adaptive in that it eases culture shock through association with that which is familiar" (p. 50). Subsequent generations are more assimilated, and while the clubs may remain in existence, they may, through necessity or for the purposes of improving levels of competition, begin to recruit players from outside the original ethnic group. But the North American ethnic studies must again be seen as a special case of a much larger and international soccer subculture. Morris [141] offered some interesting insights into the scope and complexity of this particular subculture, although his account is based on a rather tenuous sociobiological thesis.

For three additional mainstream sports, the specifically subcultural literature is extremely scarce. In tennis, there is only Hyman's [98] microanalysis of the norms, status systems, and types of player at a single set of public tennis courts in the United States. Swimming is one of the most popular recreational activities, but Hendry [90] has concentrated on the competitive aspects of the sport for British youngsters. And for golf, one is obliged to consult a large body of journalistic and biographical literature, some social histories, and amusing and insightful accounts of hackers at play by Michael Green [79] and Herbert Warren Wind [203].

Green also leads into the next group of sports with his account of the trials and tribulations of amateurs in the sport of sailing [78], a sport which also has a large body of (not specifically sociological) literature. This group of sports may be thought of as nonmainstream but quite popular with fairly large numbers of participants, and providing relatively distinct subcultures that have attracted some sociological attention. On a par with the sport of sailing is skiing which has been examined briefly in subcultural terms by Boroff [16], who emphasized the norms, status systems, and types of skiers, by Knight [110], who takes both a psychological and a subcultural approach, and by Jarka [104], who specifically examined the language of skiers. As noted previously, language (argot) is a significant aspect of the cultural forms of subcultures and is used to emphasize the distinctiveness of the subculture, and to determine an individual's status [47]. Jarka shows how the language of American skiers recapitulates the development and spread of the sport with various aspects of Scandinavian, Austro-German, and French terminology being mixed with more modern and even countercultural American forms of language (see also Loy et al. [118]).

Other sports forming relatively distinctive subcultures in this category include karate and judo, figure skating, cycle racing, pigeon racing, and birding. Both Jacobs [102] and Fritschner [67] emphasize membership in karate clubs (and, as a consequence, membership in the karate subculture) as an alternative status system in the lives of the participants, a status system in which the divisions are clearly distinguishable by belt color and in which hard work is actually rewarded by an elevation in status. Fritschner attempted to ground this in the parent culture of working class males, but this admirable and relatively rare attempt to go beyond the simple description and interpretation of a subculture itself tends to founder because of the rather simplistic and stereotypic parallels that are drawn. These studies may be compared with Goodger and Goodger's [75] general overview of the subculture of judo. Mott's [142] study of pigeon racing, and the study by Frisch-Gauthier and Louchet with which it is compared [66], also locate the sport in the parent working class culture and specifically in the occupational subculture of miners in both England and France. In these cases, the specific links between an occupational and an avocational subculture are examined, as is the historical development of the sport and its subculture. Starosta's [178] study of the social characteristics of figure skaters represents a pre-subcultural study; and in all these cases there is an attempt to go beyond the interactionist type of micro analysis that has been so characteristic of subcultural research.

There is rather more research available on the subculture of cycling and cycle racing, particularly in terms of the social and economic history of the subculture [2, 10, 129]. Aronson [10] in particular is concerned with the early development of the subculture in the United States and with the influence of the bicycle on social change. Nicholson's [145] journalistic account of the Tour de France bicycle race provides an excellent look inside the culture of European (professional) racers, while Albert [1] has examined the way in which knowledge about and the manner of using equipment functions in precisely the same way as language in many subcultures, i.e., as a means of 'gatekeeping' and of determining status within the subculture. Just as language is a significant cultural form in subcultures, so equipment and tools become an important characteristic in many sport and occupational subcultures.

With the rapid growth in popularity of birding (a competitive form of bird watching), partly in association with the expanding environmentalist movement, an interesting and quite distinctive subculture is also developing. Donnelly has examined the activity from a subcultural perspective [55] in terms of, and in comparison to, climbing and the manner in which each of the sports functions in a competitive manner while having no formal means for the verification of competitive achievements. But perhaps the best descriptive account of the subculture of birders has been presented in a humorous book written by the British comedian, Bill Oddie. His *Little Black Bird Book* [146] compares favorably with many of the descriptive sociological accounts of subcultures and contains much relevant material on the meanings and ways of birders.

Finally, in this group of avocational subcultures, note should be made of Manning and Campbell's study of pinball [123], and of an interesting set of studies of dance halls, dance studios, and social dancing. While the activity of dancing cannot precisely be considered as a sport or game, it must be considered as a leisure activity around which there exists both the avocational subculture of dancers and the occupational subculture of dance teachers. The activity came under sociological scrutiny quite early with studies by Moore [140] and Cressey [40] of dance halls in the early 1930s. Cottle examined the place of social dancing in relation to parent cultures based on race and social class [38], and Blum has looked at social (disco) dancing in relation to youth culture [15]. Two additional studies made note of the sexual connotations of dancing in quite different ways. Lopata and Noel [116] considered the controls that exist to prevent the development of relationships between teachers and students at dance studios, while, conversely, Riege [165] conducted a specific occupational comparison between the subcultures of dance teachers and call girls. Far more research is both possible and desirable with respect to dance subcultures, a task that would be aided enormously by the large body of (nonsociological) literature on dance.

While some of the sports (as opposed to dance) in the previous group may be thought of as minor or unusual, particularly in the North American context, they cannot be thought of as in any way oppositional. That is, although the activity and its appropriate set of norms may be distant enough from the mainstream to form a quite distinct subculture, the values of the activity are completely in accord with the mainstream values of the parent sport culture. These include a general ends (rather than means) orientation in which the specific outcome of an event becomes rather more important than the way in which that outcome is achieved, and in which the long-term benefits, rather than the immediate gratification and enjoyment of sport, are emphasized. Specific values include competition, success, fitness, and a set of character traits described by Edwards [59] as the "dominant American sports creed," but which have their counterparts in a number of countries.

The final group of avocational sport subcultures to be considered here provides some of the best work on sport subcultures and may be thought of as oppositional or countercultural. That is, both the values and norms of these sports tend to be distinct from both those of the mainstream or dominant culture and from the parent sport culture, and often distinct enough to appear to be oppositional. The term "oppositional" should not be thought of here as implying any direct type of conflict, but rather indicates that the values and norms of the sport represent an alternative to the mainstream or that they may be thought of as semideviant:

> When a certain behavior is regarded in society as having favorable effects on that society, certain norms are likely to arise which label that behavior as legitimate. Conversely, when a certain behavior is conceived in society as having adverse effects on that society, certain norms are likely to label that behavior as illegitimate, or deviant. It may happen, however, that behavior which by the above criterion should be regarded as deviant, is legitimized by its connection with *other* attitudes and behavior which are regarded as having salutary effects on society, and which consequently fall into a different, legitimate normative domain. When this happens, it is likely that the behavior will not be deviant, but rather semi-deviant ([60], pp. 357–358).

Thus, semideviance is conceived to be quite distinct from the subsequent category of deviant subcultures, and as characteristic of the type of activities that are included in this last group of avocational sport subcultures, namely, hang gliding, sky diving, surfing, climbing/mountaineering, rugby, and motorcycling.

I have argued elsewhere [48] that high-risk adventure sport could well be conceived of as semideviant. The activities are valued because they manifest qualities apparent in mainstream sports and others such as courage and exploration. But, they are often criticized for the apparent needless risk of life, and for the frequently rowdy and countercultural (e.g., surfers during the 1960s) behavior of the participants [193]. The sports are also puzzling to many because the risks are taken with no (or few) material rewards and no audience; thus, the motivation cannot be attributed to either the desire for fame or wealth.

Hang gliding represents a remarkable case study, because the ontogeny of hang gliding tends to recapitulate the phylogeny of high-risk sport subcultures, and probably many other sport subcultures, in a remarkably short period of time. In fact, because of a large number of accidents and a potential threat from and loss of control to a number of federal agencies in the United States, hang gliding developed from its origin to relative maturity in approximately 15 years, achieving a stage of development that is still being resisted by much older sports such as mountaineering. McDougall's [130] study of the subculture of hang gliders has identified three specific stages in the development of a sport subculture—"informal affiliations," "incipient institutions," and "advanced institutional development"— stages that are encapsulated in the hang gliding subculture. Once the last stage is completely in place, the sport may be thought of as completely incorporated with values that conform completely to mainstream values.

The research on the subculture of sky divers [6, 8, 9] tends to be more descriptive, with Arnold particularly emphasizing status systems, norms, and cultural characteristics. Such work is supplemented by De Mott's [44] rather supercilious look at a sky diving world championships, and by several psychological works [108]. In all these cases, as with climbing, there is a tendency to question motives—"Why do you want to jump out of an airplane?" "Why do you want to climb Mount Everest?" However, only De Mott begins to explore the public image, and the interrelationships between sky diver and public that are implied by the question of motive.

In contrast, the research on the surfing subculture (in California, Australia, and New Zealand, but, interestingly, not in Hawaii) has provided some of the better theoretical work on sport subcultures. The principal investigators in this area have been Irwin (California) and Pearson (Australia and New Zealand), both of whom have recognized the importance of examining the history and development of the subculture. Interestingly, the two have also felt constrained in their subsequent work [101, 151] to compare and contrast the subculture of surfers with another subculture—Irwin with hippies, and Pearson with surf life savers. But in these and other works [100, 148–150], the investigators have not gone further to note other cultural and structural relationships that are reflected in the subculture. Other work of interest with regard to surfing includes Wolfe's [206] examination of the groupculture of a Californian gang of surfers, and Devall's [45] comparison of surfers and climbers.

Mitchell's [139] recent study of climbers in California also tends to be limited to subcultural description, but other work on climbers has provided insights in several areas. For example, Csikszentmihalyi [41, 42] and Donnelly [48] have used climbing to begin to ask some difficult questions about the apparent rationality of high-risk sports in which there are almost no material rewards. These activities fall into the category of what Geertz [69] (after Bentham) has called, "deep play"—"play in which the stakes are so high that it is, from (Bentham's) utilitarian standpoint, irrational for men to engage in it at all" (p. 432). As Csikszentmihalyi [42] has suggested, "if one thinks in terms of economic utility and the support of existing cultural values, deep play is useless, if not subversive" (p. 75). Thus, participation in such high-risk sports may, in one sense, be seen as a form of opposition or resistance, and some recent work has begun to develop this approach [56].

Another approach concerns the back regions of high-risk sports. Donnelly's series of articles [50–53] on the myths propagated by climbers and Vanreusel and Renson's comparison of climbers with spelunkers and scuba divers [193] attempt to compare the informal charter of these sports with its particular emphasis on safety, character building and comradeship, with the reality in which real risks are frequently taken, and character and friendships are by no means an automatic consequence of participation. The studies explore a number of reasons for this apparent contradiction. In addition, some of the work on climbers [48, 54] is beginning to explore the relationships between the subculture and the social and cultural settings in which it exists.

Rugby reflects opposition in a different sense. Long a pillar of the British sports establishment, rugby clung to the last vestiges of amateur ideals long after the majority of sports had developed professional attitudes. Thus, in Britain, rugby reflected a conservative resistance to change, a characteristic that was also apparent in the attitudes toward and treatment of women in the subculture [173].

However, as the sport began to develop professional attitudes during the 1960s [58], it also began to reappear and spread in North America replete with all its old ideals of amateurism and sportsmanship. As a means-oriented activity, in which the actual conduct and enjoyment of the game is rather more important than the outcome, and in which visiting opponents become guests of the home team at postgame celebrations, rugby is clearly oppositional to the ends-oriented dominant sport culture in North America where one's opponents are frequently treated as the enemy. The cultural characteristics of the sport in North America have been examined by Thomson [191] and Young [208] who provide interesting descriptions of the drunken and rowdy aspects of the subculture, and by Young and Donnelly [209] who presented an initial examination of the oppositional aspects of the sport.

It is presumed rowdiness of motorcyclists, together with the high risks of the activity, that lend an oppositional character to the sport. Even where it is clearly not warranted, the public perception of motorcyclists is colored by the association with Hell's Angels and easy riders. Perhaps more than any of the subcultures discussed so far, the relation between motorcycling and social class has been examined in detail. Although Alt [3] denies that motorcycling is a specifically working class activity, Arnold[8] is able to note that "among the several hundred people who enter the cross-country motorcycle races each weekend in the California desert, skilled blue collar workers are over-represented" (p. 145), and Martin and Berry [125] and Willis [200] each emphasize the relationships between motorcycling and aspects of the parent working class culture. Quicker [163] Sagnier [169] and Gutkind [82] all provide more descriptive analyses of the subculture of motorcyclists.

The easier access to avocational sport subcultures has resulted in a larger body of work than that in either occupational or deviant sport subcultures and, consequently, a larger body of theoretical work. But the vast majority of the research is descriptive, and often superficially descriptive, capturing little of the richness and complexity of human behavior and interaction. In addition, the theoretical work has largely been concerned with the processes of subculture formation, and has tended to consider specific subcultures as if they were isolated from all other aspects of society. And even where relationships have been considered, they have tended to be with a single subculture or with a single parent culture.

Even obvious relationships such as those between the various high-risk sport subcultures have not been explored in any detail. Arnold [8], Devall [45], and Donnelly [48] have all noted a transfer of membership between these subcultures, and Donnelly [48] and Vanreusel and Renson [193] have noted certain cultural similarities in terms of behavior and attitudes toward risk, but there is an obvious need to develop this area. Also, it is apparent that the effect of a parent culture on sport subcultures has not been explored in any detail. It is clearly no accident that attitudes toward risk and death such as expectations of composure and a strong sense of fatalism should be so evident in Willis's [200] working class motorcyclists, Donnelly's [48] climbers after the sport had democratized to the working class, and in occupational subcultures involving risk such as Cherry's [26] iron-workers in the construction industry. There is also, among the motorcyclists and climbers, a glorification of risk and a sense of accidental death as a "fitting end." These attitudes almost certainly have their origins in both youth culture and male working class culture, and they suggest a number of avenues for more extensive research and theoretical work.

*Deviant Subcultures*
Deviant sport and leisure subcultures, particularly those that involve a deviant career and in which one's actions must be, of necessity, hidden, present enormous difficulties for sociologists in terms of access. In most cases, unless the researcher possesses the requisite skills or is fortunate enough to discover a willing informant, the studies are based on straightforward observation. As a consequence of these difficulties, there are not many studies of deviant subcultures in sport, and those that exist are based upon two principle themes—gambling and hooliganism.

Subcultural studies of gambling fall into three main types: those concerned with hustling; those concerned with gambling in general, and with compulsive forms of gambling; and those concerned with other activities in which gambling frequently occurs.

While it is evident that hustling may occur in a large number of games and sports, including such respectable activities as golf, tennis, and chess, the requisite secrecy and the skills involved have limited studies of hustling to pool, bowling, and cards and dice. Mahigel and Stone [122] have written about hustling in general terms, noting the careers and career contingencies of hustlers, and have also concentrated specifically on hustling in card games [121] where they examine the specific mechanical and interactional skills of a hustler. Although Mahigel and Stone suggest the existence of a network (subculture) of hustlers, this network becomes more evident in Prus and Sharper's [162] far more extensive study of card and dice hustlers.

Steele's [179] study of part-time bowling hustlers emphasized the role of subcultures as alternative status systems for their participants. He noted that the success experienced in bowling, in comparison to the lack of success experienced in the outside world, is worth even more than the money to the hustlers in this activity. But, by far the best work on hustling, and on subcultures in general, is Polsky's set of studies [157–159] on pool hustlers. Not only does Polsky provide the type of insight and description that is evident in many of the better studies of sport subcultures, but he also locates the subculture that is centered on pool playing and poolrooms both historically (in terms of the rise and fall of the game of pool) and in relation to the parent culture of bachelors—"the single heterosexual culture in western civilization" ([182] p. 9). These studies should have, but unfortunately have not provided a model for most subsequent studies of sport subcultures.

Livingston [115] and Lesieur [113] have conducted extensive studies of compulsive gambling, a condition that is generally thought of as psychological but is presented here in primarily sociological, and subcultural, terms. Both authors also consider the efficacy of Gamblers Anonymous and related agencies such as Gamanon in attempting to combat compulsive gambling. Other studies of gambling are not essentially concerned with deviance, but the potential for forms of deviance is always present. They are also primarily concerned with those who bet on horse races at the track—e.g., Herman [93], McKeown [134], and a part of Scott's [171] more general study of the track—and to some extent at betting shops [144]. The spread of off-track betting in the United States has not yet led to a comparable study of the sociology of legalized bookmaking and betting in North America. The range from leisure betting to career betting is represented in these studies, and the studies provide a fascinating view of the various types that form this particular subculture.

The final group of studies of gambling concern activities that are illegal (deviant) primarily because gambling occurs, although, in the case of cockfighting, the concern with cruelty to animals is perhaps more significant. Bryant [22] has provided an analysis of the remaining aspects of the cockfighting subculture in the United States. The sport, along with dogfighting, is remarkable for the tenacity with which it has resisted over 100 years of attempts to eradicate it. Henslin's [92] study of crapshooters is basically a study of the leisure aspects of an occupational subculture (cabdrivers), but it also provides insights into the various magical attempts to influence the run of the dice among craps players in general—a series of rituals that could well be compared to those practiced by other gamblers and by athletes in general. Finally, there are a number of studies of card players [39], and specifically poker players. Lukacs [120] has provided an overview of the history and culture of the game, Martinez and LaFranchi [126] concentrate on types of players and reasons for playing the game, Zurcher [210] focuses on the weekly friendly poker game, and McKenzie [133] looks at the game as an aspect of campus life and as an element in social reproduction or socialization. While such card playing is not essentially deviant, the potential for deviance exists in gambling groups.

Membership in subcultures involves what Steele and Zurcher [180] have referred to as "ephemeral roles." That is, an individual who is a skier and a nurse should not be thought of as a skier when he or she is skiing and a nurse when he or she is nursing (both are a part of the individual's identity), but active membership in either subculture tends to be ephemeral, with skiing having somewhat more of that quality because it is not the individual's full-time occupation. There may even be a seasonal distinction, as McElroy [131] has noted in the case of rugby, with the nurse playing rugby in the summer, skiing in the winter, and nursing all year long. Such ephemerality will also depend to a great extent upon one's commitment to a subculture, and upon one's level of membership [49].

Perhaps one of the most ephemeral roles in sport is that of the so-called soccer hooligan, a member of a subculture that is usually only in active existence in and around game time during the professional soccer season in Britain and other European countries. Because of the moral panics [36] that have been associated with and have probably amplified the definition of soccer hooliganism as a social problem, there have been a large number of sociological studies of this phenomenon, a number of which have taken a subcultural perspective. Among these are Taylor's [186, 187] studies, which locate the phenomenon both historically and culturally in the British working class, and the study by Marsh et al. [124], which adopts a far more limited interactionist approach. Other studies in this area have focused on specific cultural characteristics [103], or have provided summaries of the research on hooliganism [23]. In general terms, the best work on hooliganism is that which goes beyond the enclosed world of the subculture and attempts to describe the phenomenon in structural terms with respect to the class, age, and gender parent cultures of the hooligans.

Despite earlier comments regarding the greater emphasis of sociologists on the marginal, deviant, and problematic aspects of society, and the evidence of that emphasis in the studies of occupational and avocational subcultures in sport, there are remarkably few (with the exception of soccer hooliganism) studies of deviant subcultures in sport. It seems likely that this lack results less from a paucity of such subcultures than from access difficulties, and from a general disinclination to view sport (when it is viewed seriously at all) in other than positive terms. Hoberman [94] has suggested that social critics and academics tend to suspend their critical faculties when it comes to sport, because sport is seen as a part of the other world and not the real world. When combined with the difficulty of access to deviant sport subcultures, this begins to account for the lack of studies. But the deviant sport subcultures tend to be the most distinct of the sport subcultures, removed from both the norms and values of the parent sport culture and highlighting many aspects of the parent culture by their opposition, and have provided some of the better studies of sport subcultures.

Several issues have been raised in this review of sport subculture research, namely, issues of definition, of the relationships among subcultures and subcultures and other cultural groupings, and of methodology. These issues are addressed in the following sections, and suggestions are also made for the conduct of future research.

## THEORETICAL PROBLEMS AND PERSPECTIVES

Because the term "subculture" has slipped into everyday use its exact meaning has not been considered to be problematic. There is, however, something intuitively wrong with a word that has been used to refer everything from a single sport team to the entire black population of the United States, or from a religious cult to the Canadian working class. Such lack of precision renders the term virtually useless as a unit of sociological analysis. As an additional consequence, attempts to develop subculture theory have also been hampered by a lack of adequate definition of the concept. This section addresses the problems of definition, and various attempts to develop frameworks, models, and theories of subcultures.

*The Matter of Definition*
The major problems associated with the definition of subcultures have been reviewed by Donnelly [48] and by Fine and Kleinman [64]. These problems fall into two specific types: (1) researchers and theorists have not been able to agree exactly which types of groups may be considered as subcultures; and (2) they have been unable to determine the characteristics of subcultures. Gordon [76] first defined subculture as "a subdivision of a national culture, composed of a combination of factorable social situations such as class status, ethnic background, regional and rural or urban residence, and religious affiliation, but *forming in their combination a functioning unity which has an integrated impact on the participating individual*" (p. 40, original emphasis). Many investigators have taken this rather global definition and applied it to the group of their choice. Others have created definitions, and even theories, to meet their own specific needs with-

out regard to broader application. There has even been some confusion as to whether the "sub" in subculture refers to smaller units
of larger cultural groupings or, because of the large amount of work
that has been conducted with deviant subcultures, whether it refers
to something that is less than or inferior to the dominant culture.
While the former is generally accepted, this distinction serves to high-
light the confusion that has reigned in this area of research. The
following, adapted from an earlier article on these issues [49], is an
attempt to resolve the definitional problems.

*Ascribed and Achieved Subcultures*
The major deterrent to developing a useful definition of subculture
derives from Gordon's [76] addition of ascribed characteristics to the
earlier and related concept of behavior system [95] that had been
used to refer to groups based on achieved characteristics. Although
there are major difficulties in attempting to formulate a definition
that incorporates groups based on both achieved and ascribed characteristics, when the two are considered separately the problems of
definition and analysis become relatively straightforward.

Ascribed subcultures are based primarily upon social categories to
which people belong because of particulars of birthplace, birthright,
age, or other forms of sociological typing. They include social classes,
ethnic and racial groups, age groups, regional and urban/rural groups,
and major political and religious groups. The difficulty in considering
such groupings as subcultures lies in their lack of specificity. For
example, the fact that an individual belongs to a certain age group,
whether it be adolescence, middle age, or elderly, does not necessarily
mean that he or she shares any common cultural characteristics or
lifestyle with others of the same age group. The situation becomes
even more confusing when it is considered that all individuals simultaneously belong to at least four ascribed subcultures. Even in
Gordon's [77] refinement of "ethclass," where an attempt is made to
resolve some of the confusion by specifying both ethnicity and social
class (e.g., middle class Italian-American), other factors such as age
and region are excluded. Because of the overlap between the various
subcultural categories, and the difficulty of determining boundaries,
specific lifestyles, and cultural characteristics, there are enormous
problems of analysis with all the ascribed subcultures. And yet, there
are clearly certain global characteristics that are recognizable for all
these categories, and that have to be recognized in any form of cultural analysis. Thus, it is more useful to think of these groups as
cultures than as subcultures (e.g., working class culture, youth cul-
ture, black culture); cultures that exist within a dominant culture,

and which are themselves divided into various (overlapping) subcultures.

Subcultures then are based on achieved characteristics, and are groups to which people tend consciously to attain membership. While not referring specifically to achieved subcultures, Loy et al. [118] have noted that three major types of subculture are the occupational, the avocational (based on sport and leisure interests), and the deviant (based on criminal, delinquent, nonconformist, esoteric, or exotic beliefs and behaviors). Such achieved subcultures tend to be quite distinct with boundaries that are relatively easily determined and cultural characteristics that are readily apparent. They are characterized by the fact that members generally seek membership, and learn the meanings and ways [151] of a particular subculture.

However, the theoretical distinction developed here between ascribed cultures and achieved subcultures is not complete because the possibility of achieving membership is an ascribed culture does exist. The processes of geographic and social mobility, marriage, and religious and ideological conversion may all be seen as means of achieving membership in ascribed cultures. But the two categories are, in general terms, distinct, and all subsequent discussion of subcultures precludes ascribed characteristics as a basis for subculture formation.

*Characteristics of Subcultures*
Having prescribed the types of groups that should be considered as subcultures, the task of determining the characteristics of subcultures now becomes relatively straightforward. Donnelly [48] has defined subcultures with respect to their characteristics as follows:

A subculture is 1) an identifiable group within a culture or across cultures, 2) composed of smaller groups and individuals, 3) whose members are similar in values, norms, beliefs, dress, attitudes, language, etc., that are somewhat different from the cultures in which they exist, 4) and which dominate their life style and allocation of resources. 5) Subcultures are formed around activities that have scope and potential, 6) and are actively created and maintained by their members as long as they meet the needs of their members, by 7) face-to-face interaction and other forms of communication (pp. 44–45).

A more extensive discussion of each of these characteristics may be found in Donnelly [49].

This definitional excursion was necessary (1) because of the general confusion in use of the term "subculture"; and (2) because much of the work on sport subcultures is actually about groupcultures—subunits of subcultures (e.g., a specific baseball team is a subunit of the subculture of baseball) from which certain extrapolations may be made to the larger subcultures, but which are far from identical; and (3) because of the much more nebulous ascribed 'cultures' such as 'youth/adolescent culture' and ethnic cultures. Subcultures, as conceived here, must be distinctive and identifiably different from their parent cultures, but share much in common with those cultures. Thus, both hippies and delinquents are a part of youth culture, but are distinctively different and must be analyzed separately. Similarly, dspite Phillips and Schafer's contention [153] that there is a general sport subculture, surfers, football players, and pool hustlers are all members of distinctively different groups, each with their own specific cultural characteristics. Therefore, as noted previously, it is possible to make the case that there is an overriding sport culture in which there are a vast number of sport subcultures that share certain general cultural characteristics with the sport culture, and with youth culture, class cultures, and a variety of ethnic and national cultures. While the study of subcultures may, in the long run, shed light on the formation of ascribed cultures, the two should not be confused at this stage of development.

*Frameworks, Models, and Theories*
Although the vast majority of theoretical work on subcultures has been concerned with youth and delinquent subcultures, much of that work is valuable as a basis for the analysis of sport subcultures. In addition, there are two distinct schools of theoretical literature, the American and the British, the latter of which was built upon the former and has to a great extent superseded it. The American work was largely completed during the 1950s and 1960s and is examined first. The subsequent British work began during the 1970s.

*American subculture theory.* Subculture theory is designed to answer a number of questions. These include "how subcultures are created, why they persist, how individuals come to be members, and what impact they have on the individual and on society" ([118] p. 182). To these may be added such questions as: How significant is the part played by subcultures in the processes of cultural production? How are subcultures related to the parent (ascribed) cultures, and to the dominant culture? But, it should be noted, the study of subcultures ought not to be seen as an end in itself but as a part of the larger attempt to understand the dialectical relationship between human agency (ranging from individual acts to cultural forms) and social structure.

The two major themes that emerge from American subculture theory may be termed "environmental response" and "differential interaction." The first views the emergence of subcultures as a problem-solving response by individuals with similar difficulties or concerns. The second considers the emergence of subcultures to be the result of the proximity of similar individuals or individuals with similar concerns, and the inevitable interaction of these individuals. A third approach, and by far the most significant, combines the two themes: "The crucial condition for the emergence of new cultural forms is the existence, *in effective interaction with one another, of a number of actors with similar problems of adjustment*" ([33], p. 59, original emphasis). Cohen developed this combination into the first "general theory of subcultures" which proceeded from the premise that all human action was an attempt to solve problems produced by both the actor's frame of reference and the situations that he or she confronts. If the problems cannot be solved by means acceptable to the actor's own group, he or she is likely to search for a new group with a more amenable frame of reference. Cohen [33] noted that "one of the fascinating aspects of the social process is the continual realignment of groups, the migration of individuals from one group to another in the unconscious quest for a social milieu favorable to the resolution of their problems of adjustment" (p. 59).

Cohen's theory describes the conditions in which subcultures emerge, referring to both interaction and response processes, and describes how individuals may tentatively seek each other out in order to create a new subculture. In applying the theory to the study of delinquent subcultures, Cohen suggested that working class youth aspire to the middle class models with which they are continually presented but are denied the means to achieve. They resolve this situation by interacting with other working class adolescents with similar problems of adjustment to form a delinquent subculture in conflict with middle class values. This application of Cohen's theory has been widely criticized [107, 137, 174, 184]. "However, the critics have not taken similar exception to the more general theory of subcultures, of which the explanation of delinquency is a special application" ([34], p. 108).

Cohen's work formed the basis of much of the subsequent theoretical work on subcultures (e.g., Irwin [100] and Arnold [7]), and specifically of Pearson's theory of subcultural emergence which was developed with reference to the subculture of surfers. Loy et al. [118] have summarized Pearson's model as follows:

First, a group of individuals with an interest in X (e.g., X = surfing, skiing, hang gliding, etc.) find themselves in a common social situation or structural position that facilitates differential interaction whereby those not involved in X are excluded (e.g., these individuals may have joined a club or be engaging in a sport in the same milieu). As a result, shared attitudes, beliefs and behaviors unique to individuals and to the group become salient, while facets of the dominant culture are selectively (consciously or unconsciously) eliminated. Thus, individual and group beliefs, attitudes and behavior are solidified and a new reference group or subculture emerges. The more this cycle is repeated, the greater the likelihood that channels of communication will be expanded beyond the original group, thereby attracting new recruits to the subculture, although perhaps not to the original group because of geographical or ideological differences. That is, even if individuals do not formally join the original group, they become part of the subculture if they adhere to some of the attitudes, beliefs, norms, and values as communicated to them (pp. 182–183).

Although Pearson's background and research was Australasian, and his primary work in subcultures concerned the surfing and drug subcultures in Australia and New Zealand, his theoretical work was very much in the American tradition.

Fine and Kleinman [64] have provided one of the more recent statements on American subculture theory, and have firmly grounded such work in the symbolic interactionist approach to the study of society. Arguing for a reconceptualization and rejuvenation of the concept, they summarize their position as follows:

It is argued that for the subculture construct to be of maximal usefulness it needs to be linked to processes of interaction. Subculture is reconceptualized in terms of cultural spread occurring through an interlocking group network characterized by multiple group membership, weak ties, structural roles conducive to information spread between groups, and media diffusion. Identification with the referent group serves to motivate the potential member to adopt the artifacts, behaviors, norms, and values characteristic of the subculture (p. 1).

However, although this model captures much of the flavor of American work on subcultures and much of the work on sport subcultures, it is essentially limited to a single paradigm approach. The British work on subcultures has made theoretical advances in precisely the manner suggested by Ritzer [166]—by combining paradigms in order to develop a greater level of understanding.

*British Subculture Theory.* As with its American counterpart, British subculture theory has been primarily concerned with youth and delinquent subcultures. This is particularly reflected in Britain in the attempt to explain the emergence and meaning of such groups as teddy boys, mods, rockers, skinheads, hippies, and punks. British subculture theory represents an attempt to pick up precisely where American theoretical developments stalled in the mid-1960s. As the concept of subculture slipped into the purview of the interactionists in the United States, British theorists and researchers began to test the work of Cohen [33] and others such as Cloward and Ohlin [30] in the British context. That is, they began to examine youth subcultures in terms of their location in the British class structure and to explore their meaning in that sociostructural context.

The American approach was found to be wanting because it was grounded in the ideology of the American dream. The new approach was less committed to a consensual view of society and one of the first studies on youth subcultures by Downes proposed that, rather than experiencing status frustration or discontent, working class boys neither accepted or rejected the values of the (middle class) educational system but simply dissociated themselves from it [57]. This theoretical work was developed by Murdock [143] and Brake [18], but concurrent with their analyses Clarke was beginning to question the whole utility of the concept of subculture [29] and clearly stimulated a number of researchers to specify the parameters of the concept far more precisely; and Young [207] was showing how a merging of labeling theory from the interactionist perspective and anomie theory could be employed to explain the emergence of deviant subcultures.

But, by far the most sophisticated theoretical work at this time, when the subject was receiving a great deal of attention from such groups as the National Deviancy Conference and the Centre for Contemporary Cultural Studies, was being produced by Cohen [35] and Hall and Jefferson [85]. Their approach involved a far more complex view of the problem-solving nature of subcultures, an approach that incorporated both specific family socialization and the more general parent culture. "What we would argue . . . is that the young inherit a cultural orientation from their parents towards a 'problematic' common to the class as a whole, which is likely to weight, shape and signify the meanings they then attach to different areas of their social life" ([28], p. 29). The meaning of the cultural forms in a specific youth subculture could be teased out in the following manner:

> the original mod style could be interpreted as an attempt to realise, but in an *imaginary relation* the conditions of existence of the socially mobile white collar worker. While their *argot* and

ritual forms stressed many of the traditional values of their parent culture, their dress and music reflected the hedonistic image of the affluent consumer ([35], p. 23).

It is this combination of cultural forms, and the meanings attached to them, that led Clarke et al. [28] to suggest that, "it is at the intersection between the located parent culture and the mediating institutions of the dominant culture that youth subcultures arise" (p. 53). But perhaps the most significant contribution of this work is the recognition that the subcultural solution adopted collectively by many youth to the problems and contradictions resulting from their structural location in British society should not be thought of as a realistic way of dealing with the problems. Rather, the solution involves what Cohen [35] has termed a "magical resolution" that often tends to reproduce the problem(s) that it is intended to solve:

when post-war sub-cultures address the problematics of their class experience, they often do so in ways that reproduce the gaps and discrepancies between real negotiations and symbolically displaced "resolutions." They "solve," but in an imaginary way, problems which at the concrete material level remain unresolved ([28], pp. 47–48).

Willis's excellent book on working class schoolboys and the British educational system [202] shows precisely this process.

Thus, the theoretical work on youth subcultures in Britain has extended understanding of the phenomenon in several ways. While accepting the manner of subculture formation addressed by Cohen [33] and Pearson [151], by combining paradigms associated with microsocial and macrosocial concerns they also address the reasons for the occurrence of subcultures, their meaning in the specific cultural context in which they exist, and their relationship to both parent and dominant cultures. This work is significant for the study of sport and leisure subcultures not only because of the theoretical contributions, and the multimethod approach that is possible when paradigms are linked, but also because of the emphasis on the significance of leisure and style as bases for subculture formation. "By treating leisure and style, and what they signify, as core aspects of subcultural analysis, youthful deviance is viewed as being meaningful to the actors involved: leisure styles can provide partial solutions to the shared problems of working-class adolescents" ([185], p. 368). As noted previously, even the aspect of resistance that is seen by researchers such as Hall and Jefferson [85] and Hebdige [88] as characteristic of many youth subcultures, may be incorporated in the analysis of sport and leisure subcultures.

## METHODOLOGICAL PROBLEMS AND PERSPECTIVES

The body of work on sport subcultures reviewed here initially appears quite extensive; however, in actual fact it barely touches the enormous range and variety of sport subcultures and rarely goes beyond a rather superficial descriptive level. Thus it is necessary to compare the work of sociologists to that of journalists and biographers and to ask which is the more sociological. Frequently the answer must be that the description and insights provided by the latter are equal to, and sometimes richer than those provided by the sociologists, and that in neither case (with very few exceptions) is the work truly sociological. This section is devoted to examining how the sociological study of sport subcultures might be made more sociological by considering methodological issues and their inevitable link with theoretical issues.

While a common definition, as noted previously, is imperative to the continuation of useful research in the area of sport subcultures, it is also important to overcome certain methodological limitations. These limitations concern what might be termed the myth of objectivity, and what Willis [201] has called "the hegemonizing tendency of technique" (p. 94).

With regard to the former, although sociology has tended to borrow a philosophy of science from the natural sciences, which tend to presume an objective methodology, in sociology both the researcher and the focus of research are subjects; thus, sociology must be thought of as a subjective, or at least reflexive, science. As Giddens [72] has noted:

> 1) We *cannot* approach society, or 'social facts', as we do objects or events in the natural world, because societies only exist in so far as they are created and re-created in our own actions as human beings. . . .
> 2) . . . Atoms cannot get to know what scientists say about them, or change their behaviour in the light of that knowledge. Human beings can do so. Thus the relation between sociology and its 'subject-matter' is necessarily different from that involved in the natural sciences (pp. 13–15).

The links between cultural anthropology, naturalist sociology, and the interactionist perspective that have dominated research in subcultures have resulted in the primacy of ethnographic research. Participant observation and unstructured interviews have been the basic tools of students of subcultures, and Loy and Segrave have identified several forms of participant observation, giving examples of sports studies employing each type [119]. But, just as some natural scientists are now beginning to recognize the element of subjectivity present in the type of research questions that are asked, "there is now a tendency among field-workers to recognize and reveal, rather than deny and conceal, the part that personal interests, preferences and experiences play in the formulation of field-work plans" ([71], p. 33). Despite the emphasis on objectivity, and the numerous warnings in methodological texts about "going native" and disturbing or disrupting the normal life of the group under study, the group is composed of subjects who act and respond in a subjective manner and cannot be treated as objects.

Willis [201] has suggested that "We are still in need of a method which respects evidence, seeks corroboration and minimizes distortion, *but which is without rationalist natural-science-like pretence*" (p. 91, original emphasis), and has gone a long way toward developing that method. The method embraces rigorous objective methods where they are warranted (i.e., where it is necessary to obtain social facts such as demographic data and records of the type and frequency of certain behaviors), but indicates the necessity of reflexive, qualitative methods in order to answer such questions as: "Why are these things happening? Why has the subject behaved in this way? Why do certain areas remain obscure to the researcher? What differences in orientation lie behind the failure to communicate?" ([201], p. 92).

It is precisely in this use of multiple and appropriate methods that "the hegemonizing tendency of technique" (i.e., the tendency for one technique to be considered more important than others, or for the method itself to be considered more important than the theory) is avoided. In one study Willis [200] used the following group of methods: participant observation, observation, just being around, group discussions, recorded discussions, informal interview, and the use of existing surveys.

Thus, it is apparent that, in subcultural research, all available sources of data should be employed in order to gain as complete an account as possible and the deepest level of understanding of the subculture. The results obtained by previous researchers, both quantitative and qualitative, should be taken into account in addition to the researcher's own survey and participant observation data. Every contact that the researcher makes with the subculture or a member of the subculture becomes a data gathering session. It is impossible to ignore those occasions when one was not formally planning to take field notes, and therefore 'just being around' and informal conversations are as important as more formal participant observation sessions. In addition, the researcher should go beyond these traditional forms of data to see what members of the subculture write about themselves for other members (every sport and many leisure subcultures publish at least one newsletter or magazine) on for the general public in biographies, introductory or how-to books, and general books and magazine articles; and what is written about the subculture by journalists and freelance writers.

Nor should the researcher be constrained by nonfiction since many other forms of writing and artistic work are frequently available and offer points of view that are often unique and frequently enlightening. Barich's meditative *Laughing in the Hills* provides an excellent source for anyone interested in the subculture of horse racing, Hurne's *Yellow Jersey* offers surprising insights into the lives of professional racing cyclists, and Walsh's *Cheat* is a minor thriller that reveals a great deal about the world of competitive angling [13, 97, 196]. The list of novels devoted to sport is now extensive, and many of the authors have engaged in extensive research that is often invaluable to the subcultural researcher. To this should be added poetry, songs (both of which may supplement the narrative folklore of the subculture), painting and sculpture, cartoons, and films (ranging from the surfing and skiing films to those such as *Bang the Drum Slowly* (baseball) that capture important aspects of life in a subculture). But the greatest key to access and interpretation in subcultures is knowledge of the argot, a subfield of subcultural research that has a large body of literature [11, 96, 104]. None of the subtleties of written and spoken data are available to the researcher without knowledge of the particular terminology and usage employed in a specific subculture.

And none of the research achieves sociological/theoretical significance if the subculture is described without history and without reference to the social structures in which it exists. Substantial or thick description is extremely important, particularly if the researcher allows the subjects to speak for themselves, and is open to the richness, the complexity, and even the contradictions involved in human interaction in a subcultural setting. The two principal approaches to the study of subcultures have emphasized this descriptive element. The career model is concerned with describing the life cycle of members of subcultures from initiation to retirement, and this model has recently been reviewed by Prus [161]. The more general interactionist approach is concerned with the way in which social actors make sense of their world, taking the actors' meanings and definition of the situation as the basis for social analysis. The approaches are related in that careers are often described in interactionist terms.

But in sociological terms these approaches only form one side of the volutarist/determinist equation because they assume that individuals are free to act in any manner of their own choosing. The other side of the equation suggests that human behavior is totally constrained by structural and economic inequalities, a view favored by a number of neo-Marxist writers. Giddens [72] has asserted that "no social processes are governed by unalterable laws (and) as human beings, we are not condemned to be swept along by forces that have the inevitability of laws of nature" (p. 26), but also denies the voluntarist approach of complete freedom of choice. The result is the recognition of a "dialectical relationship between socially structured possibilities and human agency" ([81], p. 51). Gruneau [81] has begun to explore this dialectic with respect to play, games and sports noting that these are specifically social practices, forms of cultural production made by and through human agency, but within a set of historically specific social limitations. This dialectical approach has enormous sociological significance both for the manner in which subcultures are studied and for the contribution to the study of human behavior to be made through the study of sport subcultures.

## CONCLUSIONS

Subcultural researchers must both describe a particular subculture, and also situate that subculture within social structure and in terms of its relationship to other cultural groupings. How is a particular subculture related to other subcultures, to the parent sport culture, to other parent cultures such as class, gender, age, race/ethnicity, and region, and to the dominant national and international cultures? The social history of the subculture must also be reviewed in order to examine the changing relationships involving such social processes as democratization and incorporation. The result of this work should be a sociology of subcultures that not only shows how sports and other leisure practices are socially constructed and defined activities, meaningful only to the extent that meaning is attached to them by the participants, but also how "subcultures, with their various 'establishment' and 'countercultural' emphases, have been constitutively inserted into the struggles, the forms of compliance and opposition, social reproduction and transformation, associated with changing patterns of social development" ([80], p. 10).

Some of the work on sport subcultures shows a trend in this direction. For example, the studies of rugby conducted by Dunning and Sheard [58], and the studies of pool hustling by Polsky [158], each recognize the importance of history and social structure. Studies of youth subcultures by Hebdige [88] and Willis [200] provide valuable models for future research. But there are vast amounts of work to be done in this area. Not only have the majority of sport subcultures not been examined, or only superficially studied, but also the work on the large number of hobby and leisure subcultures has not even begun. Apart from one study of stamp collecting [27], the collecting, modeling, and breeding (e.g., show dogs, orchids) subcultures, the radio hams, the gardeners, and the train spotters all await the sociologist's attention and share many features in common with many of the sport subcultures. The cultural studies approach to sport and leisure has been slow in starting for many of the reasons that have plagued the study of sport in general [87], but future studies of sport subcultures should make a significant contribution to this body of work.

## REFERENCES

1. Albert, E. Equipment as a feature of social control in the sport of bicycle racing. In *Sport and the Sociological Imagination*, N. Theberge and P. Donnelly, eds. Fort Worth: Texas Christian University Press, 1984.
2. Alderson, F. *Bicycling: A History*. Newton Abbot: David and Charles, 1972.
3. Alt, J. Popular culture and mass consumption: The motorcycle as cultural commodity. *J. Pop. Culture* 15:129–141, 1982.
4. Andreano, R. The affluent baseball player. *Transaction* 2:10–13, 1965.
5. Angell, R. *The Summer Game*. New York: Viking, 1972.
6. Aran, G. Parachuting. *Am. J. Sociol.* 80:144–152, 1974.
7. Arnold, D.O. A process model of subcultures. In *Subcultures*, D.O. Arnold, ed. Berkeley: The Glendessary Press, 1970.
8. Arnold, D.O. A sociologist looks at sport parachuting. In: *Sport Sociology: Contemporary Themes*, A. Yiannakis, T.D. McIntyre, M.J. Melnick, and D.P. Hart, eds. Dubuque: Kengall/Hunt, 1976.
9. Arnold, D. The social organization of sky diving: A study in vertical mobility. Paper presented at the Pacific Sociological Association Annual Meeting, Portland, Ore., April 1972.
10. Aronson, S.H. The sociology of the bicycle. *Soc. Forces* 30:305–312, 1952.
11. Artiomov, R.N. Socio-linguistic research in sociology of sport. *Int. Rev. Sport Sociol.* 13:95–107, 1978.
12. Axthelm, P. *The City Game*. New York: Harper and Row, 1970.
13. Barich, B. *Laughing in the Hills*. Harmondsworth: Penguin, 1981.
14. Birrell, S., and A. Turowetz. Character work-up and display: Collegiate gymnastics and professional wrestling. *Urban Life* 8:219–246, 1979.
15. Blum, L.H. The discotheque and the phenomenon of alone-togetherness: A study of the young person's response to the frug and comparable current dances. *Adolescence* 1:351–366, 1966/67.
16. Boroff, D. A view of skiers as a subculture. In *Sport, Culture, and Society*, J.W. Loy and G.S. Kenyon, eds. New York: Macmillan, 1969.
17. Bouton, J. *Ball Four*. New York: Dell, 1970.
18. Brake, M. Cultural revolution or alternative delinquency. In *Contemporary Social Problems in Britain*, R. Bailey and J. Young, eds. London: Saxon House, 1973.
19. Brower, J.J. Culture clash: The inappropriateness of the black subculture in the white world of professional football. Paper presented at the Pacific Sociological Association Annual Meeting, Scottsdale, Ariz., May 1973.
20. Brower, J.J. Little League baseballism: Adult dominance in a "child's game." Paper presented at the Pacific Sociological Association Annual Meeting, Victoria, B.C., May 1975.
21. Brown, R., P. Brannen, J. Cousins, and M. Samphier. Leisure in work: The 'occupational culture' of shipbuilding workers. In *Leisure and Society in Britain*, M.A. Smith, S. Parker, and C.S. Smith, eds. London: Allen Lane, 1973.

22. Bryant, C.D. Feathers, spurs, and blood: Cockfighting as a deviant leisure activity. Paper presented at the Southern Sociological Society Annual Meeting, May 1971.

23. Carroll, R. Football hooliganism in England. *Int. Rev. Sport Sociol.* 15:77–92, 1980.

24. Charnofsky, H. The major league professional player: Self conception versus the popular image. *Int. Rev. Sport Sociol.* 3:39–56, 1968.

25. Charnofsky, H. The occupational culture of the ball player and the boxer: A comparison. Paper presented at the Pacific Sociological Association Annual Meeting, Anaheim, Calif., April 1970.

26. Cherry, M. *On High Steel: The Education of an Ironworker.* New York: Quadrangle, 1974.

27. Christ, E.C. The Adult Stamp Collector. Ph.D. dissertation. University of Missouri, 1958.

28. Clarke, J., S. Hall, T. Jefferson, and B. Roberts. Subcultures, cultures and class: A theoretical overview. In *Resistance Through Rituals: Youth Subcultures in Post-War Britain,* S. Hall and T. Jefferson, eds. London: Hutchinson, 1976.

29. Clarke, M. On the concept of subculture. *Br. J. Sociol.* 25:428–441, 1974.

30. Cloward, R., and L. Ohlin. *Delinquency and Opportunity: A Theory of Delinquent Gangs.* Chicago: Free Press, 1960.

31. Coakley, J.J. *Sport in Society: Issues and Controversies* (2nd ed.). St. Louis: C.V. Mosby, 1982.

32. Cochran, R. Folk elements in a non-folk game: The example of basketball. *J. Pop. Culture* 10:398–403, 1976.

33. Cohen, A.K. *Delinquent Boys.* New York: Free Press, 1955.

34. Cohen, A.K. *Deviance and Control.* Englewood Cliffs, N.J.: Prentice-Hall, 1966.

35. Cohen, P. Sub-cultural conflict and working class community. *Working Papers in Cultural Studies, No. 2.* Birmingham: CCCS, University of Birmingham, 1972.

36. Cohen, S. *Folk Devils and Moral Panics: The Creation of the Mods and Rockers.* St. Albans: Paladin, 1973.

37. Collins, L., and D. Lapierre. *Or I'll Dress You In Mourning.* New York: Signet, 1968.

38. Cottle, T.J. Social class and social dancing. *Sociol. Q.* 7:179–196, 1966.

39. Crespi, I. The social significance of card playing as a leisure time activity. *Am. Sociol. Rev.* 21:717–721, 1956.

40. Cressey, P.G. *The Taxi-Dance Hall.* Chicago: University of Chicago Press, 1932.

41. Csikszentmihalyi, M. The Americanization of rock climbing. *The University of Chicago Magazine* 61:21–26, 1969.

42. Csikszentmihalyi, M. *Beyond Boredom and Anxiety.* San Francisco: Jossey-Bass, 1975.

43. Davies, H. *The Glory Game.* London: Sphere, 1973.

44. De Mott, B. *You Don't Say: Studies of Modern American Inhibitions.* New York: Harcourt, Brace and World, 1966.

45. Devall, B. The development of leisure social worlds. Paper presented at the American Sociological Association Annual Meeting, New York, August 1973.

46. Devereux, E.C. Backyard versus Little League baseball: The impoverishment of children's games. In *Social Problems in Athletics,* D. Landers, ed. Urbana: University of Illinois Press, 1976.

47. Donnelly, P. On determining another's skill. Paper presented at the Canadian Sociology and Anthropology Association Annual Meeting, London, Ontario, May 1978.

48. Donnelly, P. The Subculture and Public Image of Climbers. Ph.D. dissertation. University of Massachusetts, 1980.
49. Donnelly, P. Toward a definition of sport subcultures. In: *Sport in the Sociocultural Process* (3d ed.), M. Hart and S. Birrell, eds. Dubuque: Wm. C. Brown, 1981.
50. Donnelly, P. Four fallacies. I: Climbing is not really dangerous. *Mountain* 80:38–40, 1981.
51. Donnelly, P. Four fallacies. II: Climbing is non-competitive. *Mountain* 81:28–31, 1981.
52. Donnelly, P. Four fallacies. III: Climbing is character building. *Mountain* 82:20–23, 1981.
53. Donnelly, P. Four fallacies. IV: Climbing leads people to form close friendships. *Mountain* 83:45–49, 1982.
54. Donnelly, P. Social climbing: A case study of the changing class structure of rock climbing and mountaineering in Britain. In *Studies in the Sociology of Sport,* A.O. Dunleavy, A.W. Miracle, and C.R. Rees, eds. Fort Worth: Texas Christian University Press, 1982.
55. Donnelly, P. On verification: A comparison of climbers and birders. In: *Career Patterns and Career Contingencies in Sport,* A.G. Ingham and E.F. Broom, eds. Vancouver: University of British Columbia, 1982.
56. Donnelly, P. Resistance through sports: Sport and cultural hegemony. In *Sports et Sociétés Contemporaines.* Paris: Société Francaise de Sociologie du Sport, 1984, pp. 397–406.
57. Downes, D. *The Delinquent Solution.* London: Routledge and Kegan Paul, 1966.
58. Dunning, E., and K. Sheard. *Barbarians, Gentlemen and Players: A Sociological Study of the Development of Rugby Football.* New York: New York University Press, 1979.
59. Edwards, H. *Sociology of Sport.* Homewood: Dorsey Press, 1973.
60. Etzioni-Halevy, E. Some patterns of semi-deviance on the Israeli social scene. *Soc. Prob.* 22:356–367, 1975.
61. Faulkner, R. Coming of age in organizations: A comparative study of career contingencies and adult socialization. *Sociol. Work Occup.* 1:131–173, 1974.
62. Faulkner, R. Making violence by doing work: Selves, situations, and the world of professional hockey. *Sociol. Work Occup.* 1:288–312, 1974.
63. Faulkner, R. Coming of age in organizations: A comparative study of the career contingencies of musicians and hockey players. In *Sport and Social Order,* D.W. Ball and J.W. Loy, eds. Reading: Addison-Wesley, 1975.
64. Fine, G.A., and S. Kleinman. Rethinking subculture: An interactionist analysis. *Am. J. Sociol.* 85:1–20, 1979.
65. Flood, C. *The Way It Is.* New York: Trident, 1971.
66. Frisch-Gauthier, J., and P. Louchet. *La Colombophilie Chez les Mineurs du Nord.* Paris: C.N.R.S., 1961.
67. Fritschner, L. Karate: The making and maintenance of an underdog class. Paper presented at the American Sociological Association Annual Meeting, Chicago, Illinois, September 1977.
68. Furst, R.T. Boxing stereotypes versus the cultures of the professional boxer: A sociological decision. *Sport Sociol. Bull.* 3:13–39, 1974.
69. Geertz, C. *The Interpretation of Culture.* New York: Basic Books, 1973.
70. Gent, P. *North Dallas Forty.* New York: Signet, 1973.
71. Georges, R.A., and M.O. Jones. *People Studying People: The Human Element in Field Work.* Berkeley: University of California Press, 1980.
72. Giddens, A. *Sociology: A Brief but Critical Introduction.* London: Macmillan, 1982.

73. Gmelch, G. Magic in professional baseball. In *Games, Sport and Power*, C.P. Stone, ed. New Brunswick: Transaction Books, 1972.

74. Goffman, E. *The Presentation of Self in Everyday Life*. Garden City: Anchor, 1959.

75. Goodger, B.C., and J.M. Goodger. Judo in the light of theory and sociological research. *Int. Rev. Sport Sociol.* 12:5–34, 1977.

76. Gordon, M.M. The concept of subculture and its application. *Soc. Forces* 26:40–42, 1947.

77. Gordon, M.M. The subsociety and the subculture. In: *Assimilation in American Life*, M.M. Gordon, ed. New York: Oxford University Press, 1964.

78. Green, M. *The Art of Coarse Sailing*. London: Arrow, 1968.

79. Green, M. *The Art of Coarse Golf*. London: Arrow, 1971.

80. Gruneau, R. Review of 'Surfing Subcultures of Australia and New Zealand'. *ICSS Bulletin* 21:8–10, 1981.

81. Gruneau, R. *Class, Sports, and Social Development*. Amherst: University of Massachusetts Press, 1983.

82. Gutkind, L. *Bike Fever*. New York: Avon, 1973.

83. Haerle, R. Career patterns and career contingencies of professional baseball players: An occupational analysis. In *Sport and Social Order*, D.W. Ball and J.W. Loy, eds. Reading: Addison-Wesley, 1975.

84. Halberstam, D. *The Breaks of the Game*. New York: Ballantine, 1981.

85. Hall, S., and T. Jefferson. *Resistance Through Rituals: Youth Subcultures in Post-War Britain*. London: Hutchinson, 1976.

86. Hare, N. A study of the black fighter. *Black Scholar* 3:2–9, 1971.

87. Hargreaves, J. Theorising sport: An introduction. In: *Sport, Culture and Ideology*, J. Hargreaves, ed. London: Routledge and Kegan Paul, 1982.

88. Hebdige, D. *Subculture: The Meaning of Style*. London: Methuen, 1979.

89. Hemingway, E. *Death in the Afternoon*. Harmondsworth: Penguin, 1966.

90. Hendry, L.B. Don't put your daughter in the water, Mrs. Worthington: A sociological examination of the subculture of competitive swimming. *Br. J. Phys. Educ.* 2:17–19, 1971.

91. Henricks, T. Professional wrestling as moral order. *Sociol. Inquiry* 44:177–188, 1974.

92. Henslin, J.M. Craps and magic. *Am. J. Sociol.* 73:316–330, 1967.

93. Herman, R.D. Gambling as work: A sociological study of the race track. In *Sociology for Pleasure*, M. Truzzi, ed. Englewood Cliffs, N.J.: Prentice-Hall, 1974.

94. Hoberman, J. Examining our growing sports culture. *Harvard Independent* October 26-November 1, 1978.

95. Hollingshead, A.B. Behavior systems as a field for research. In *Subcultures*, D.O. Arnold, ed. Berkeley: The Glendessary Press, 1970.

96. Huddle, F.P. Baseball jargon. *Am. Speech* 18:103–111, 1943.

97. Hurne, R. *The Yellow Jersey*. New York: Simon and Schuster, 1973.

98. Hyman, H. A sociological analysis of a tennis court. *World Tennis* February:60–61, 1971.

99. Ingham, A. Occupational subcultures in the work world of sport. In *Sport and Social Order*, D.W. Ball and J.W. Loy, eds. Reading: Addison-Wesley, 1975.

100. Irwin, J. Surfers: A Study of the Growth of a Deviant Subculture, M.A. thesis. Berkeley: University of California, 1965.

101. Irwin, J. *Scenes*. Beverly Hills: Sage, 1977.

102. Jacobs, G. Urban samurai: The karate dojo. In *The Participant Observer: Encounters with Social Reality*, G. Jacobs, ed. New York: George Braziller, 1970.

103. Jacobson, S. Chelsea rule—OK. *New Society* 31(27 March):780–783, 1975.

104. Jarka, H. The language of skiers. *Am. Speech* 38:202–208, 1963.

105. Kahn, R. *The Boys of Summer*. New York: Signet, 1971.

106. Kane, J.E., and C. Murray. Suggestions for the sociological study of sport. In:

*Readings in Physical Education,* J.E. Kane, ed. London: Physical Education Association, 1966.

107. Kituse, J.I., and D.C. Dietrick. 'Delinquent Boys': A critique. *Am. Sociol. Rev.* 24:208–215, 1959.

108. Klausner, S.D. Sport parachuting. In *Motivations in Play, Games and Sports,* R. Slovenko and J.A. Knight, eds. Springfield, Ill.: Charles C. Thomas, 1967.

109. Klein, A. Pumping irony: Contradiction in the world of bodybuilding. Paper presented at the North American Society for the Sociology of Sport Annual Meeting, Toronto, Ontario, November 1982.

110. Knight, J.A. Motivation in skiing. *Western J. Surgery, Obstetrics, Gynecology* 69:395–398, 1961.

111. Kramer, J. *Farewell to Football.* New York: Bantam, 1969.

112. LaFlamme, A.G. The role of sport in the development of ethnicity: A case study. *Sport Sociol. Bull.* 6:47–51, 1977.

113. Lesieur, H.R. *The Chase: Career of the Compulsive Gambler.* New York: Anchor, 1977.

114. Levi-Strauss, C. *Myth and Meaning: Five Talks for Radio.* Toronto: University of Toronto Press, 1978.

115. Livingston, J. *Compulsive Gamblers: Observations on Action and Abstinence.* New York: Harper Torchbooks, 1974.

116. Lopata, H.Z., and J.R. Noel. The dance studio: Style without sex. In *Games, Sport and Power,* G.P. Stone, ed. New Brunswick: Transaction Books, 1972.

117. Loy, J.W., and G.S. Kenyon. *Sport, Culture, and Society.* New York: Macmillan, 1969.

118. Loy, J.W., B.D. McPherson, and G.S. Kenyon. *Sport and Social Systems.* Reading: Addison-Wesley, 1978.

119. Loy, J.W., and J.O. Segrave. Research methodology in the sociology of sport. In *Exercise and Sport Science Reviews* (vol. 2), J.H. Wilmore, ed. New York: Academic Press, 1974.

120. Lukacs, J. Poker and American life. *Horizon* 8:56–62, 1963.

121. Mahigel, E.L., and G.P. Stone. Making vs. playing games of cards. In *Games, Sport and Power,* G.P. Stone, ed. New Brunswick: Transaction Books, 1972.

122. Mahigel, E.L., and G.P. Stone. Hustling as a career. In: *Social Problems in Athletics,* D.M. Landers, ed. Urbana: University of Illinois Press, 1976.

123. Manning, P.K., and B. Campbell. Pinball as a game, fad and synecdoche. *Youth Society* 4:333–358, 1973.

124. Marsh, P., E. Rosser, and R. Harré. *The Rules of Disorder.* London: Routledge and Kegan Paul, 1980.

125. Martin, T., and K. Berry. Competitive sport in post-industrial society: The case of the motocross racer. *J. Pop. Culture* 8:107–120, 1974.

126. Martinez, T.M., and R. LaFranchi. Why people play poker. In *Games, Sport and Power,* G.P. Stone, ed. New Brunswick, Transaction Books, 1972.

127. Massengale, J. Coaching as an occupational subculture. *Phi Delta Kappan* 56:140–142, 1974.

128. Massengale, J. The prestigious football coaching staff: Career mobility. In *Career Patterns and Career Contingencies in Sport,* A.G. Ingham and E.F. Broom, eds. Vancouver: University of British Columbia, 1982.

129. Maynard, D.N. The divergent evolution of competitive cycling in the United States and Europe: A materialist perspective. Paper presented at the Association for the Anthropological Study of Play Annual Meeting, London, Ontario, April 1982.

130. McDougall, A.A. The Subculture of Hang Gliders: Social Organization of a High Risk Sport. M.A. thesis. University of Western Ontario, 1979.

131. McElroy, D. Socialization and the seasonal subculture. Paper presented at the

Third International Symposium on the Sociology of Sport, Waterloo, Ont., August 1971.

132. McKay, J. Sport and Ethnicity: Acculturation, Structural Assimilation, and Voluntary Association Involvement among Italian Immigrants in Metropolitan Toronto. M.Sc. thesis. University of Waterloo, 1975.

133. McKenzie, D. Poker and pop: Collegiate gambling groups. In *The Participant Observer: Encounters with Social Reality*, G. Jacobs, ed. New York: George Braziller, 1970.

134. McKeown, B. Horseplayers: Some key elements in identity-construction. Paper presented at the North American Society for the Sociology of Sport Annual Meeting, Toronto, November 1982.

135. McPhee, J. *Levels of the Game*. New York: Bantam, 1969.

136. Meggysey, D. *Out of Their League*. New York: Paperback Library, 1971.

137. Miller, W.B. Lower class culture as a generating milieu of gang delinquency. *J. Soc. Issues* 14:5–19, 1958.

138. Mills, C.W. *The Sociological Imagination*. Harmondsworth, Penguin, 1970.

139. Mitchell, R.G. *Mountain Experience: The Psychology and Sociology of Adventure*. Chicago: University of Chicago Press, 1983.

140. Moore, E.H. Public dance halls in a small city. *Sociol. Soc. Res.* 14:256–263, 1930.

141. Morris, D. *The Soccer Tribe*. London: Jonathan Cape, 1981.

142. Mott, J. Miners, weavers and pigeon racing. In *Leisure and Society in Britain*, M. Smith, S. Parker, and C. Smith, eds. London: Allen Lane, 1973.

143. Murdock, G. Culture and classlessness: The making and unmaking of a contemporary myth. Cited in: *Resistance Through Rituals: Youth Subcultures in Post-War Britain*, S. Hall and T. Jefferson, eds. London: Hutchinson, 1976.

144. Newman, O. The sociology of the betting shop. *Br. J. Sociol.* 19:17–33, 1968.

145. Nicholson, G. *The Great Bike Race*. London: Magnum, 1978.

146. Oddie, B. *Bill Oddie's Little Black Bird Book*. London: Eyre Methuen, 1980.

147. Parrish, B. *They Call it a Game*. New York: Dial Press, 1971.

148. Pearson, K. The symbol of the revolution: A surfboard. Paper presented at the Sociological Association of Australia and New Zealand Conference, Armidale, NSW, 1974.

149. Pearson, K. Subcultures and leisure. Paper presented at the Sociology section of the ANZAAS Conference, Canberra, Australia, January 1975.

150. Pearson, K. Subcultures, drug use and physical activity. Paper presented at the International Congress of Physical Activity Sciences, Quebec City, Quebec, July 1976.

151. Pearson, K. *Surfing Subcultures of Australia and New Zealand*. St. Lucia: University of Queensland Press, 1979.

152. Petrie, B. The athletic group as an emerging deviant subculture. In: *Social Problems in Athletes*, D.M. Landers, ed. Urbana: University of Illinois Press, 1976.

153. Phillips, J., and W. Schafer. Subcultures in sport: A conceptual and methodological approach. In *Sport Sociology: Contemporary Themes*, A. Yiannakis, T.D. McIntyre, M.J. Melnick, and D.P. Hart, eds. Dubuque: Kendall/Hunt, 1976.

154. Pillsbury, R. Carolina thunder: A geography of Southern stock car racing. Paper presented at the Association of American Geographers Annual Meeting, Atlanta, Georgia, April 1973.

155. Plimpton, G. *Paper Lion*. New York: Harper, 1965.

156. Plimpton, G. *The Bogey Man*. New York: Harper, 1968.

157. Polsky, N. The hustler. *Soc. Probl.* 12:3–15, 1964.

158. Polsky, N. *Hustlers, Beats and Others*. New York: Anchor, 1969.

159. Polsky, N. Of pool playing and poolrooms. In *Games, Sport and Power*, G.P. Stone, ed. New Brunswick: Transaction Books, 1972.

160. Pooley, J.C. Ethnic soccer clubs in Milwaukee: A study in assimilation. In: *Sport*

*in the Sociocultural Process,* M. Hart and S. Birrell, eds. Dubuque: Wm. C. Brown, 1981.

161. Prus, R. Career contingencies: Examining patterns of involvement. In *Sport and the Sociological Imagination,* N. Theberge and P. Donnelly, eds. Fort Worth: Texas Christian University Press, 1984.

162. Prus, R., and C.R.D. Sharper. *Road Hustler.* Toronto: Heath, 1977.

163. Quicker, J.C. A typological account of motorcycling. Paper presented at the Pacific Sociological Association Annual Meeting, Portland, Ore., April 1972.

164. Ralbovsky, M. *Destiny's Darlings.* New York: Hawthorn Books, 1974.

165. Riege, M.G. The call girl and the dance teacher: A comparative analysis. In *Sociology for Pleasure,* M. Truzzi, ed. Englewood Cliffs, N.J.: Prentice-Hall, 1974.

166. Ritzer, G. *Sociology: A Multiple Paradigm Science.* Boston: Allyn and Bacon, 1975.

167. Rosenberg, M., and A. Turowetz. The wrestler and the physician: Identity work-up and organizational arrangements. In *Sport and Social Order,* D.W. Ball and J.W. Loy, eds. Reading: Addison-Wesley, 1975.

168. Sage, G. An occupational analysis of the college coach. In *Sport and Social Order,* D.W. Ball and J.W. Loy, eds. Reading: Addison-Wesley, 1975.

169. Sagnier, T. *Bike!* New York: Avon, 1973.

170. Schafer, W. Sport and youth counterculture: Contrasting socialization themes. In *Social Problems in Athletics,* D.M. Landers, ed. Urbana: University of Illinois Press, 1976.

171. Scott, M. *The Racing Game.* Chicago: Aldine, 1968.

172. Shaw, G. *Meat on the Hoof.* New York: Dell, 1973.

173. Sheard, K., and E. Dunning. The rugby football club as a type of male preserve: some sociological notes. *Int. Rev. Sport Sociol.* 8:5–24, 1973.

174. Short, J.F., and F.L. Strodtbeck. *Group Process and Gang Delinquency.* Chicago: University of Chicago Press, 1965.

175. Smith, M.D. The legitimation of violence: Hockey players' perceptions of their reference groups' sanctions for assault. *Can. Rev. Sociol. Anthropol.* 12:72–80, 1975.

176. Smith, M., and F. Diamond. Career mobility in professional hockey. In: *Canadian Sport: Sociological Perspectives,* R. Gruneau and J. Albinson, eds. Don Mills: Addison-Wesley, 1976.

177. Snyder, E.E., and E.A. Spreitzer. *Social Aspects of Sport* (2nd ed.). Englewood Cliffs, N.J.: Prentice-Hall, 1983.

178. Starosta, W. Social characteristics of figure skaters. *Int. Rev. Sport Sociol.* 2:165–178, 1967.

179. Steele, P.D. The bowling hustler: A study of deviance in sport. In: *Social Problems in Athletics,* D.M. Landers, ed. Urbana: University of Illinois Press, 1976.

180. Steele, P., and L. Zurcher. Leisure sports as ephemeral roles. *Pacific Sociol. Rev.* 16:345–356, 1973.

181. Stone, G.P. Wrestling: The great American passion play. In: *Sport: Readings from a Sociological Perspective,* E. Dunning, ed. Toronto: University of Toronto Press, 1972.

182. Stone, G.P. *Games, Sport and Power.* New Brunswick: Transaction Books, 1972.

183. Stone, G.P., and R.A. Oldenberg. Wrestling. In *Motivations in Play, Games and Sports,* R. Slovenko and J. Knight, eds. Springfield, Ill.: Charles C. Thomas, 1967.

184. Sykes, G., and D. Matza. Techniques of neutralization: A theory of delinquency. *Am. Sociol. Rev.* 22:664–670, 1957.

185. Tanner, J. New directions for subcultural theory: An analysis of British working-class youth culture. *Youth and Society* 9:343–372, 1978.

186. Taylor, I. Football mad: A speculative sociology of soccer hooliganism. In *The Sociology of Sport,* E. Dunning, ed. London: Frank Cass, 1971.

187. Taylor, I. Soccer consciousness and soccer hooliganism. In *Images of Deviance,* S. Cohen, ed. Harmondsworth: Penguin, 1971.
188. Telander, R. *Heaven is a Playground.* New York: Tempo Books, 1976.
189. Theberge, N. An occupational analysis of women's professional golf. Ph.D. dissertation. University of Massachusetts, 1977.
190. Thomson, D.S. *Language.* New York: Time-Life Books, 1975.
191. Thomson, R. Sport and deviance: A subcultural analysis. Ph.D. dissertation. University of Alberta, 1977.
192. Tomlinson, A. The sociological imagination, the new journalism, and sport. In *Sport and the Sociological Imagination,* N. Theberge and P. Donnelly, eds. Fort Worth: Texas Christian University Press, 1984.
193. Vanreusel, B., and R. Renson. The social stigma of high risk sport subcultures. In *Studies in the Sociology of Sport,* A.O. Dunleavy, A.W. Miracle, and C.R. Rees, eds. Fort Worth: Texas Christian University Press, 1982.
194. Vaz, E. The culture of young hockey players: Some initial observations. In: *Training: A Scientific Basis,* E. Taylor, ed. Springfield: Charles C. Thomas, 1972.
195. Vaz, E., and D. Thomas. What price victory: An analysis of minor hockey players' attitudes towards winning. *Int. Rev. Sport Sociol.* 9:33–53, 1974.
196. Walsh, B. *Cheat.* London: Robert Hale, 1981.
197. Webb, H. Professionalization of attitudes toward play among adolescents. In *Sociology of Sport,* G.S. Kenyon, ed. Chicago: The Athletic Institute, 1969.
198. Weinberg, S., and H. Arond. The occupational culture of the boxer. *Am. J. Sociol.* 57:460–469, 1952.
199. Williams, R. *Keywords: A Vocabulary of Culture and Society.* London: Flamingo, 1983.
200. Willis, P. *Profane Culture.* London: Routledge and Kegan Paul, 1978.
201. Willis, P. Notes on method. In *Culture, Media, Language,* S. Hall, D. Hobson, A. Lowe, and P. Willis, eds. London: Hutchinson, 1980.
202. Willis, P. *Learning to Labor: How Working Class Kids Get Working Class Jobs.* New York: Columbia University Press, 1981.
203. Wind, H.W. The lure of golf. In *Sport and Society: An Anthology,* J.T. Talamini and C.H. Page, eds. Boston: Little, Brown, 1973.
204. Wind, H.W. The sporting scene: The ever more complex world of tournament tennis. *New Yorker* October 11:93–125, 1976.
205. Wolf, D. *Foul!* New York: Holt, Rinehart and Winston, 1972.
206. Wolfe, T. *The Pump House Gang.* New York: Bantam, 1969.
207. Young, J. New directions in sub-cultural theory. In *Approaches to Sociology: An Introduction to Major Trends in British Sociology,* J. Rex, ed. London: Routledge and Kegan Paul, 1974.
208. Young, K.M. The Subculture of Rugby Players: A Form of Resistance and Incorporation. M.A. thesis. McMaster University, 1983.
209. Young, K.M., and P. Donnelly. The subculture of rugby players, public image and disaffiliation. Paper presented at the North American Society for the Sociology of Sport Annual Meeting, Toronto, November, 1982.
210. Zurcher, L.A. The 'friendly' poker game: A study of an ephemeral role. *Soc. Forces* 49:173–186, 1970.

# Index